FASHION MARKETING

FASHION MARKETING

an anthology of viewpoints and perspectives

Gordon Wills and David Midgley

Cranfield School of Management

in association with
Martin Christopher and Roy Hayhurst

LONDON · GEORGE ALLEN & UNWIN LTD
Ruskin House   Museum Street

ISBN 0 04 380017 3

Printed in Great Britain
in 10 point Times New Roman type
by William Clowes & Sons Limited
London, Colchester and Beccles

Preface

This volume of collected viewpoints and reflections on the fashion process is intended for all whose work is subject to the vagaries of fashion, or who are simply fascinated by it. Although much of the evidence and many of the views are related to textiles and particularly to clothing, there is a growing awareness amongst businessmen that fashion is an increasingly present phenomenon outside of its traditional fields.

The fickleness of fashion has apparently led very few to attempt any detailed analyses let alone projections of trends in the short, medium or long term. We have conducted a four-year search in the literature from Europe and North America and found a strictly limited number of significant contributions. We have found that one of the few elements common to them all is that they occur in the most unlikely places—and have often become very inaccessible indeed to all but the most persistent librarian.

It was this inaccessibility in particular, as well as the usefulness of having all the important contributions easily to hand, which led us to prepare this volume. It has been a prelude to a considerable volume of research activity in a number of textile markets which has been undertaken by the editors since 1968, first at Bradford Management Centre but more recently at Cranfield School of Management. Both marketing and management science academic staff have been involved in studies of short term demand forecasting for various sectors. The Social Science Research Council has also made the editors a grant to further the work in the field of men's outerwear—the industry is based in Leeds. The outcome of that study, when completed by David Midgley, along with Martin Christopher's work in the carpet industry, will also be published by George Allen and Unwin.

As Ada Heather Bigg pointed out in 1893 (see Chapter 2), fashion changes bring problems to manufacturing industry. At Bradford, which of course lay in the heart of textile country, our recognition of the problems caused by fashion processes derived from contact with management in the textile industries during educational programmes and previous research studies into organizational structures.* The forecasting of fashion duration and change is of major managerial concern. In this context, we have defined fashion as a 'current mode of consumption behaviour'. It is clear that changes in fashion have varied consequences. We have postulated that three major classes exist whose time scale will vary from product to product. The three classes are as follows:

(1) *Short Term Variations.* Short term variations are seldom indicative of underlying change. They are normally oscillations about a cycle of trend and

---

* S. Saddik conducted an extensive study of marketing in three sectors of the textile industries. See particularly his 'Manufacturer Toleration of Channels of Distribution', in G. Wills (ed.), *Exploration in Marketing Thought* (Crosby Lockwood, 1971); and, with G. Wills, 'Product Strategy and Management in British Textile Industries', *Journal of Management Studies* (February, 1971), see chapter 31.

have managerial implications for such relatively immediate problems as production scheduling and stockholding policies.

(2) *Cyclical Variations.* Cyclical variations are repetitions of certain features over time about an underlying trend. Here, the management implications are for such decisions as determining investment in production capacity.

(3) *Long Term Trends.* Long term trends are underlying fundamental and continuous changes in the pattern of demand. The managerial implications are of a corporate nature, such as decisions for product strategy, including possible diversification.

Those factors which have been reported as significantly affecting the level and patterns of demand in textile industries, and therefore contributing to the determination of current modes of consumption behaviour, are as follows:

   (i) The state of technology, including materials and processes.
  (ii) The economic environment of the age as it distributes incomes and determines their aggregate proportions and stability.
 (iii) The social structure and climate of the age—political, institutional, economic, religious and educational factors interact to product norms of behaviour, patterns of consumption and patterns of diffusion.
 (iv) The creative ability of designers.
  (v) The marketing infrastructure.
 (vi) The entrepreneurial skills which managers apply.
(vii) The communications media available.

Clearly, few of these factors can ever be considered in isolation. The role of communication media, for example, is closely interrelated with the diffusion process and the marketing infrastructure.

It will be seen from the chapters in this volume that we are a long way from the development of a satisfactory explanation of the fashion process in general. The greatest hope for a clearer pattern of understanding probably lies in the field of 'diffusion theory', where Roy Hayhurst has reviewed the existing spread of knowledge. But that will only perhaps explain the *mechanisms* of diffusion. We must look to the sociologists, psychologists and anthropologists for the true behavioural understanding we ultimately need.

Fashion marketing is, however, not a synonym for new product introduction. It looks at less than the totality of new product introduction problems. It concentrates on the aesthetic and cultural appeal of styling and design. It considers how fashions can both mould and interpret the spirit of the times.

*   *   *

We wish to express our gratitude to our secretarial helpers on this volume—Anne Collinson and Heather McCallum. In particular, we also wish to thank Mrs Beth Tupper and her library colleagues for their literature searches, together with those numerous libraries which, via the Inter-Library Loan Service, have given us access to the almost inaccessible.

Gordon Wills

Contents

Introduction

WHAT DO WE KNOW ABOUT FASHION DYNAMICS?
by Gordon Wills and Martin Christopher

Many of the world famous names in women's fashion have gone into print at various times, to attempt to describe the quintessence of their role in the creation of fashions and styles. Without exception, none has got beyond the level of generalization that for design to be seen to be good it must mirror the spirit of the age. Beaton[1] elegantly suggests: 'fashion is the symbol which describes the subtle and often hidden forces which shape our society—political, economic, psychological . . . the search for the absolute by man who is only able to create the ephemeral.' Beaton[1] also makes the important observation that change, the *sine qua non* of fashion, undermines progress towards aesthetic perfection which can emerge, he suggests, only after long tradition for the same style of garment, viz. church vestments, uniforms, riding habits.

Dior[2] demonstrates less apparent understanding of the factors than Beaton: 'Women have instinctively understood that I dream of making them not only more beautiful but happier.' Yves St Laurent, speaking at a recent conference in Switzerland expressed the opinion 'the couturier does not create fashion, he interprets it.'

Laver[3, 4] is the most prolific descriptive writer on women's costume. He was until recently Keeper of Prints at the Victoria and Albert Museum on which his studies are largely based. He sums up that 'fashion forces seem to be the sum at any given moment of human knowledge and aspirations, the extension on the mental and spiritual plane of evolution', and again 'the mirror of our soul'. He observes a close but lagged inter-relation between clothing, furniture and architecture, a phenomenon somewhat complicated by the different length of purchase cycles, and contents himself with a series of descriptive generalizations, e.g. fashion change is a function of the rate of fashion adoption, female clothing rotates in its degree of exposure of one erotic zone after another.

Robinson[5] points out that fashion and style are not about function but about embellishment and aesthetics. It is this which provides the connecting link between all fashion and style industries. The stimuli for a style or fashion can only derive from comparisons with what is being superseded either immediately or within living memory of the relevant segments of demand.

None of this helps the Marketing Executive greatly in the field of operational planning. It is too empathetic; it lacks, even defies, analysis. Most crucially, a concept of fashion and a rigorous, analytical approach is needed.

The Need for a Concept of Fashion

Paul Nystrom[6] has said that fashion is a fact of social psychology, it is a fact of social emulation and aesthetic imitation. The dynamics that influence fashion adoption and the rate of adoption have yet to be satisfactorily isolated. For a phenomenon that is referred to so frequently, 'fashion' is seldom analysed rigorously. Fashion can be studied from several viewpoints, mainly behavioural, such as psychological, sociological and anthropological; it may also be studied quantitatively; essentially, however, the study must be multi-disciplinary. The adoption of a fashion is almost certainly the result of a complex interaction between many factors. Fashion can be viewed as the end result of an interplay between technology, the political climate, the economic climate, the social climate, the creative ability of designers, the marketing infrastructure, managerial skills, communication levels and cultural features.

No integrated attempt to quantify the factors determining patterns of either style or fashion trends has been traced. A limited number of quantification studies have been undertaken of specific factors, however, and some descriptive studies of structures in relevant sectors of the textile trade have been prepared.

The classic attempt to quantify demand patterns was made by Kroeber and Richardson[7] and extended by Carman[8]. The former examined style as expressed by six dimensions of women's formal dress from 1605–1934. (The dimensions were the vertical and horizontal measures from fashion plates of skirt, waist and *décolletage*.) They concluded that the fundamental proportions of silhouettes changed very slowly, reaching extremes on an average cycle of approximately one century. Oscillations, or fashions, within the main style trend, however, expressed in terms of the annual variations from a five-year moving average and the standard deviation of each year's data, were greatest at the peaks and troughs.

Kroeber and Richardson tentatively suggested that, given the prevailing utilitarian concepts of clothing, the fluctuations to and fro about a norm were to be anticipated, and the high oscillations at extremes could be explained. The 100-year cycle, however, should possibly be attributed to social and political movements which occurred during the period at the turn of the eighteenth, nineteenth and twentieth centuries. They were unable to suggest why social forces should influence any *particular* dimension, however.

Carman extended this same analysis from 1936–63 to examine two hypotheses. Young[9] had suggested that there was a stable cyclical pattern in women's dress design, of a little over 100 years which took dress shape from bell/full skirt—back fullness/bustle—tubular/sheath. To this hypothesis, Carman added his own that there was a secondary, sub-cycle of 30–50 years, attributable to designers, sellers, media, customers, and the diffusion and adoption processes linking these institutional groups. He was able to derive a mathematical model which fitted significantly for both hypotheses throughout most of the original Kroeber and Richardson data, but it broke down after 1935. He lists social instability and cultural phenomena related to female emancipation, e.g. the development of the car and leisure/sports wear, the development of nylon hose, women out at work, growth in leisure time, the life span increases leading to a longer cycle before a style can repeat itself.

He observes, in particular, that there is no longer one fashion on the go at any point in time. There will be many, and because of the development of media and improved education there has been an accelerated rate of diffusion.

12

Overall, the oscillations of demand are now of much higher frequency and lower amplitude.

Beside these major attempts to quantify style trends, all other quantification studies are dwarfed. An area which has been susceptible, however, is the process of diffusion and adoption of fashions. Nystrom produced the classic statement of the concept that fashions were set in the higher social groups, who could afford to indulge in the pursuit of 'staying in fashion'. He suggested that fashions 'trickled down' from Paris *haute couture* to New York, then to the outlying States, and finally throughout the social strata. He is partially supported in this view by Carman and Robinson. This trickle down theory had never been quantified objectively, although it was perfectly possible in many instances to observe it in action.

Fallers[10] has suggested that rather than a direct trickle down of styles and fashion, the individual is lifted up in the wake of rising incomes, hence, although an absolute advance is achieved by the individual in adopting what had become socially acceptable, it may very well not constitute a differential advance. He suggests that status-symbolism is the real motivation behind successful diffusion and therefore adoption. He is supported in this view by Barber and Lobel[11] and was preceded by Veblen[12]. Fallers suggests an investigation examining the role of consumption patterns in an individual's life aspirations, and a psychometric study of the differential perceptions of symbols and tastes. This leads automatically to consideration of, for example, Whyte[13] and Riesman[14] on reference groups, Ferber[15] on household behaviour, and Maslow[16] and Katona[17] on aspiration.

In the past two distinct types of approach have been used to determine the factors affecting purchase of specific items. Ferber summarizes these from the point of view of household expenditures:

'One approach has attempted to explain static differences in product purchase of different households in terms of household characteristics, largely to the exclusion of prices and other market variables; while the other approach has attempted to explain temporal differences in aggregate sales in terms of market variables, largely to the exclusion of household characteristics (though aggregate income does appear in such functions).

Paralleling the consumption function, the first approach has been characterized by the search for so called Engel curves—relationships between specific expenditure and income level, holding other relevant variables constant. The second general approach has utilized sales data and related information from industry sources. This approach has necessarily had to be aggregative in nature and, for this reason, has generally focused on the derivation of time-series relationships; it is exemplified by the search for demand curves, to ascertain how sales fluctuate in response to changes in price, holding other relevant factors constant.'

Neither of these two approaches is likely to yield usable results in the case of fashion adoption. They are not far-reaching enough to include all the relevant variables involved in the diffusion of fashion. An example of some of the major factors involved in skirt purchase would be:

Physiological:	Do I need it for warmth etc.
Economic:	Can I afford it.
Sociological:	Reference group influences.
Psychological:	Ego-involvement.
Cultural:	Men do not wear skirts.
Institutional:	Only certain points-of-sales.

For each individual it is likely that these factors will be arranged in different hierarchies. This point parallels with Maslow's hierarchy of needs. Maslow speaking of needs in general found major needs to be arranged in this order: physiological needs, safety needs, the need for love and affection, the need for self-actualization, the need to know and understand, and aesthetic needs. The identification of the relevant factors can only come from careful ex-post examination of individuals' explanations of how and why they adopted a fashion.

The principal work on the diffusion of innovation amongst consumers is that of Rogers[18] who shows that the communication of ideas between individuals and any resultant adoption of those ideas is a complex mechanism. Rogers defined five stages for every individual in an adoption process, these are:

1. Awareness: the individual becomes cognisant of the innovation but lacks information about it.
2. Interest: the individual is stimulated to seek information about the innovation.
3. Evaluation: the individual considers whether it would make sense to try the innovation.
4. Trial: the individual tries the innovation on a small scale to improve his estimate of its utility.
5. Adoption: the individual decides to make full and regular use of the innovation.

Adoption can be seen therefore as the last phase of a complicated learning process. Further it is a process which differs markedly from person to person. Some people, for example, will adopt innovations before others, and for every fashion item there are apt to be leaders and early adopters.

Rogers saw the distribution of adopters as being roughly normal (see Fig. 1) and this is suggested by empirical studies.

Rogers has tried to characterize the five adopter groups in terms of ideational values. The dominant value of innovators is *venturesomeness*; they like to try new ideas, even at some risk, and are cosmopolitan in orientation. The dominant value of early adopters is *respect*; they enjoy a position in the community as opinion leaders and adopt new ideas early but with discretion. The dominant value of the early majority is *deliberateness*; these people like to adopt new ideas before the average member of the social system although they rarely are leaders. The dominant value of the late majority is *scepticism*; they do not adopt an innovation until the weight of majority opinion seems to legitimize its utility. Finally, the dominant value of the laggards is *tradition*; they are suspicious of any changes, mix with other tradition-bound people, and adopt the innovation only because it has now taken on a measure of tradition itself.

In their study of community buying and other activities Katz and Lazersfeld[19] presented what they termed a 'two-step' flow of influence. In each community, group or sphere there are certain 'influentials' who maintain close contact with the media. The remainder of the community are usually less in contact with the media but are nevertheless influenced personally, largely through informal contact with the 'influentials'.

Katz[20] further postulated that 'in addition to serving as networks of communication, inter-personal relations are also sources of pressure to conform to the group's way of thinking and acting, as well as sources of social support.' The workings of group pressure are clearly evident in the homogeneity of opinion and action observed among individuals in situations of unclarity

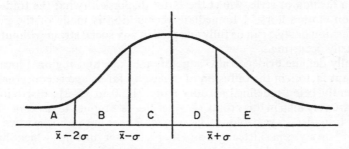

FIG. 1. Adopter classification.

Key: A = Innovators $2\frac{1}{2}\%$ D = Late majority 34%
      B = Early adopters $13\frac{1}{2}\%$ E = Laggards   16%
      C = Early majority 34 %

or uncertainty. Festinger[21] identified two major sources of pressures for uniformity:

(1) Social reality: an opinion, a belief, an attitude is 'correct', 'valid', and 'proper' to the extent that it is anchored in a group of people with similar beliefs, opinions and attitudes.

(2) Group location: pressures toward uniformity among members of a group may arise because such uniformity is desirable or necessary in order for the group to move toward some goal.

In its total effect personal influence seems to be of greater importance in the evaluation stage of the adoption process. Furthermore, it seems to be more important in its effects on later adopters rather than the earlier adopters and in 'risky' situations than in 'safe' situations.

King[22] has published the only substantial quantification of the diffusion of innovation in relation to textiles, which builds on Rogers' thorough analysis of over 1,000 diffusion studies at Michigan State University. From Rogers' analyses, King was quite convinced that different groups would act as innovators in the face of different styles and fashions even within a similar product category. He postulated that the structured social environment necessary for a conventional 'trickle down' diffusion no longer exists. Furthermore, however, mass media offer instant awareness of new fashions to all social strata. Finally, fashion merchandizers seek to differentiate fashions each season as a deliberate strategy. He does not deny that the design and production of fashion goods has a sequence which can be charted, but this is not unique. Empirically, King sought to isolate influential women in a major US community in terms of advising others on millinery selection. His analysis of purchasing behaviour showed them to be in no way significantly more prone to be fashion leaders. Furthermore, the study showed that interaction leading to adoption came from *within* the social group rather than from emulation. Hence, King suggests a 'trickle across' theory. Innovators represent discrete market segments within social strata. The role of the influential and the innovative must accordingly be separated. The former gives the seal of social acceptability, i.e. confirms or rejects a fashion or style, whilst the latter displays it (what the trade terms a 'common clothes horse'). Immediate recognition is made of the possibility that a fashion or style can be fully adopted in any social strata without osmosis necessarily occurring.

Equally definite evidence also suggests that age and regional location are important factors in the diffusion of styles. So far as age is concerned, youth is currently being redefined socially from 21–30 to 15–21; discretionary incomes are very high in this group. (Kayser Bondor report 40 per cent of hosiery sales is to under-25-year-olds.) The *Sunday Times* has published two opinion polls[23, 24] on styles in skirt length and men's trouser turn-ups which show quite clearly that youth and the south lead in adoption of the new styles concerned. This *Sunday Times* survey of skirt length also indicates the extent to which the mini-skirt failed to become universally adopted, although high fashion. A similar study by Jack and Schiffer[25] stresses that the majority will prescribe a parameter control—a role similar to that already described for the influentials by King. Class, Holland[26] suggests, has been replaced by age as a major barrier to fashion adoption. Not only can the young afford to dress well, but they are catered for by what is on offer.

In many fields of fashion adoption we are essentially interested in the case in which the behaviour of one individual may affect that of another and thus it may be legitimate to view the reaction of one individual as a stimulus affecting the behaviour of others. Landahl[27] has built a model demonstrating the effect of such imitation although it suffers from limiting assumptions and generalizations and approaches the problem from a neuro-biophysical angle. Nevertheless it is a field well worth studying further and the information available on stimulus-response mechanisms is fairly well documented.

The concept of intervening variables, which 'provide the psychological framework within which environmental stimuli are interpreted',[28] brings the idea of motivation into the stimulus-response concept. Generally, intervening variables are lumped together in a 'black-box' model (see page 17) with no attempt being made to explain the interactions between them.

If full use is to be made of this concept in a study of fashion dynamics then two things are required:

(a) identification of the relevant variables;
(b) exact determination of the part they play in the fashion adoption process.

In other words it is necessary that we move away from the 'black-box' to a formulation of definite relationships.

Intervening Variables

```
                    ┌─────────────────────┐
                    │  Motives            │
                    │  Beliefs            │
                    │  Assumptions        │
                    │                     │
                    │  Prejudices         │
                    │  Attitudes          │
STIMULUS  ────────▶ │  Aspirations        │ ────────▶ RESPONSE
                    │  Feelings           │
                    │  Emotions           │
                    │  Expectations       │
                    │  Social values      │
                    │  etc.               │
                    └─────────────────────┘
```

Stochastic Approaches

The way in which a fashion spreads may well be modelled by using a stochastic (probabilistic) analogue. For example the probability that a person will come into contact with a fashion can often be estimated; following this, the probability that the person would actually adopt the fashion would be required. Together they make up a simple stochastic process. Obviously much more than this requires to be known about the motivations behind fashion adoption before any model could be built, but the value of such a stochastic analogue would be great.

For our purpose here two stochastic approaches have been studied. The first is an approach which could be utilized in a predictive study of fashion changes; the second may form the basis for predicting the spread of an existing fashion. The techniques involved in these analyses are, respectively, Markov chain processes and Epidemic Theory.

The idea underlying a Markov process model is that the state of a system at time t_1 depends *only* on its state in time t_0. A Markov process is '... a stochastic process such that knowing the outcome of the *last* experiment we can neglect any other information about the past in predicting the future.'[29] The distinguishing aspect of a Markov process is the assumption that the system's 'memory' has a duration of only *one* period.

Applied to fashion dynamics Markov processes could be used predictively by making the aspect of fashion under study equivalent to a 'state', and calculating an individual's probabilities of transition from one fashion 'state' to another. The analogy is best demonstrated by an example:

Let $A =$ long skirt length
Let $B =$ medium skirt length
Let $C =$ short skirt length

2

Then for a group of individuals the following hypothetical matrix of transition probabilities could well exist at time t_0

		Skirt length in t_1		
		A	B	C
Skirt length in t_0	A	0·8	0·2	0
	B	0	0·8	0·2
	C	0	0·1	0·9

This represents the likelihood of the various members of the group switching from one style to another. For example, there is an 80 per cent probability that a person wearing a long skirt length in t_0 will keep that length in period t_1. Similarly there is a 20 per cent chance that she will wear a medium short length in period t_1 and no chance that she will wear a short skirt length. On the other hand a person wearing a short skirt length now (t_0) has only a 10 per cent probability of switching to a medium skirt length in period (t_1).

Now let us say that the proportions of the groups wearing A, B, and C, in period t_0 were as follows:

$$A = 25 \text{ per cent}$$
$$B = 40 \text{ per cent}$$
$$C = 35 \text{ per cent}$$

Then by carrying out the following matrix multiplication:

$$(0·25, 0·4, 0·35) \begin{bmatrix} 0·8 & 0·2 & 0 \\ 0 & 0·8 & 0·2 \\ 0 & 0·1 & 0·9 \end{bmatrix}$$

we can find the percentage memberships of the groups in period t_1, these are:

$$A = 20 \text{ per cent}$$
$$B = 40 \text{ per cent}$$
$$C = 40 \text{ per cent}$$

If we make the assumption that the probabilities of transition will hold constant we can go on to predict group membership in period t_2, e.g.:

$$(0·2, 0·4, 0·4) \begin{bmatrix} 0·8 & 0·2 & 0 \\ 0 & 0·8 & 0·2 \\ 0 & 0·1 & 0·9 \end{bmatrix}$$

that is
$$A = 16 \text{ per cent}$$
$$B = 40 \text{ per cent}$$
$$C = 44 \text{ per cent}$$

If this assumption of a constant probability of transition is valid then we can continue the process. Markov chains are such that they finally achieve what is called a 'steady-state' or a limiting situation where further multiplication of the matrix by the row vector yields the same row vector. In this instance the steady state is:

$$A = 0 \text{ per cent}$$
$$B = 33 \cdot 33 \text{ per cent}$$
$$C = 66 \cdot 66 \text{ per cent}$$

Obviously this example has over-generalized and simplified what is likely to be a complex model. It also makes the dubious assumption that the transition probabilities are constant for all time periods. It assumes in addition that these probabilities can be determined.

As far as this last point is concerned there is likely to be little problem involved in determining transition probabilities of a rough and ready nature. For example a group of 20-year-olds (or any age-group) could be asked: 'Which of the three skirt lengths do you wear now and which do you think you will be wearing in six months?' This could, hypothetically yield the following results:

	Now	6 months time		
		A	B	C
A	50	40	10	0
B	80	0	64	16
C	70	0	8	62

which yields the following probabilities:

	A	B	C			A	B	C
A	40/50	10/50	0/50	=	A	0·8	0·2	0
B	0/80	64/80	16/80		B	0	0·8	0·2
C	0/70	8/70	62/70		C	0	0·1	0·9

The following transition matrix is constructed from *Sunday Times* data for the age group 21–24 (reported September 29, 1968).

	A	B	C
A	0·2	0·7	0·1
B	0	0·9	0·1
C	0	0·2	0·8

This idea is still at a very rudimentary level but could possibly prove a useful starting point for further research.

It has been suggested that there may be certain useful parallels to be drawn between the way in which an epidemic spreads and the way in which a fashion may spread. Further, there may also be an analogy between the cyclical nature of epidemics and the fashion cycle. Essentially the usefulness of epidemic theory will depend upon the validity of the analogy between the diffusion of fashion and epidemics; but first it would be useful to outline the nature of mathematical epidemic theory.

Two approaches to epidemic theory may be identified: the deterministic, and the probabilistic or stochastic. The deterministic approach holds fairly well for large populations which are homogeneous, a situation not often found. Stochastic models introduce probabilities of contact, infection etc. and are thus likely to offer greater realism. For example a determinate model would assume that the actual *number* of new cases of infection in a short time period is proportional to the numbers of both susceptibles and infectives, as well as to the length of the time period; stochastic models assume that the *probability* of *one new case* occurring in a given time period is similarly proportional to the numbers of susceptibles and infectives and the length of the period. A 'susceptible' in fashion dynamics may be taken to be the same as a 'susceptible' in medical terms and likewise an 'infective'.

Bailey[30] has outlined the limitations of deterministic analysis:

'When dealing with large numbers of susceptibles and infectives we should expect the effect of statistical fluctuations on large-scale phenomena to be much reduced. In such circumstances a deterministic model, for which we assume that, for given numbers of susceptibles and infectives and for given attack—and removal—rates, certain definite numbers of new cases will occur in any specified time. Although when the numbers of susceptibles and infectives are not both large it is unwise to press deterministic analysis very far.'

The deterministic approach enables predictions of the numbers of infectives to be made using fairly easy maths. More important though, and this applies to stochastic methods as well, the *rate* of infection can be estimated.

One idea of central importance to epidemic theory which could well be applicable to fashion dynamics is that of a *threshold*. The theory of the threshold states that the introduction of infectious cases into a community of susceptibles would not give rise to an epidemic outbreak if the density of susceptibles were below a certain critical value. If, on the other hand, the critical value were exceeded then there would be an epidemic of a magnitude sufficient to reduce the density of susceptibles as far below the threshold as it was originally above. Landau and Landahl,[31] examine the threshold concept at the *individual* level when they study the imitative behaviour of society. In other words they view imitations as a stimulus-response mechanism only operating when the threshold is crossed.

Epidemic models tend to lack sensitivity in the early stages of an epidemic and this may lessen their utility in a study of fashion dynamics where one is very much concerned with behaviour at the innovative pre-threshold stage. Again epidemic theory is of no use in predicting the arrival of new fashions—although it can perhaps help predict the rate at which an established fashion will change. A curve describing the rate of infection could well appear as in Fig. 2.

We may specify a threshold (TT) below which an innovation will not achieve sufficient 'exposure' to enable its adoption to reach epidemic proportions. If this threshold level is not reached the adoption of the innovation may well fall off as shown in Fig 3. Tentative enquiries in the wool textile industry have suggested that the progress of products in the industry may well correspond to one or other of these two models. A typical distribution of product lines in terms of quantities sold is likely to be bi-modal; in other words the firm has either a lot of lines that sell well and a few that sell badly or vice versa. An

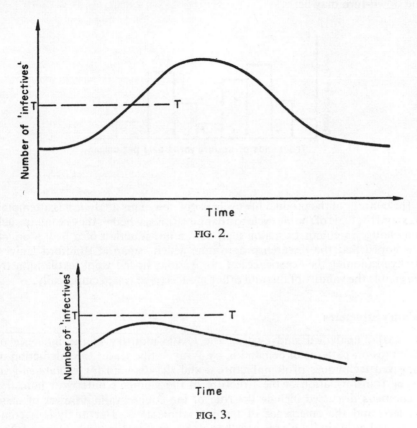

FIG. 2.

FIG. 3.

example from the carpet industry is given in Fig. 4. Perfectly the distribution that marketing managers would like to achieve would be one heavily skewed towards the top end. Such a situation would indicate that his firm's products had satisfactorily passed their thresholds. On the other hand a distribution skewed towards the low end would illustrate a situation where the firm's products were failing to achieve a threshold level thus ensuring their 'take-off' in terms of total sales.

The marketing manager's concern is therefore with identifying exactly where his product is on an epidemic curve. Knowing the approximate size of the threshold would give a real target for promotion, theoretically once this level is reached the adoption of the product would proceed largely under its own steam. Equally important is the need to know how far off the down-turn is.

21

Particularly in those industries where fashion is volatile and where decisions on production and stocks have to be taken many months in advance of sales, such as wool textiles, it can be crucial to be sure that the down-turn will not occur whilst the firm is heavily committed. We would contend therefore that the study of the fashion/epidemic analogue in relation to individual products could well provide some rough indicators of where these two stages of threshold and down-turn may lie.

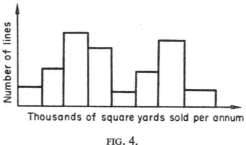

FIG. 4.

The concept of the product life cycle is not new. This analysis has attempted to extend the logic of the life cycle to all innovations, whether they be minor such as a change in colour or major such as the introduction of a new product. It is hoped that the research programme which began at Bradford University by examining the experiences of innovations in the wool textile industry will enable the validity of this and other models to be tested empirically.

Industry Structures

The major analytical study within the textile industry of the influence of structures on patterns of demand is by Wray.[32] She traces the interaction of improved techniques of manufacturers and the demand for *couture-en-gros* on the transformation of the structure of the women's outerwear industry. Phenomena discussed include the role of the countervailing power of mass retailers, and the emergence of fashion wholesalers. Her analysis is complemented by Svennilson's research based theory of textile market therapeutics in Sweden[33]—the attempt by manufacturers to regulate markets in order to generate economies of production via the promotion of branding and/or chain multiples for increased volume off-take, and the widening price differences between standard and speciality goods.

Garland[34] suggests also that a particular combination of styles and technology in the 1920s gave an especial impetus to the growth of mass demand—she singles out the chemise dress and the rise of separates as popular styles. Wray is at great pains to emphasize the importance she feels the war time 'Utility' scheme, with its concomitant freezing of fashions and styles, had on the technology and structure of the outerwear industry. For the first time, manufacturers could see already a period of relatively stable demand and they were prepared to put in mass production machinery on a scale uncontemplated before. After World War II Wray suggests, they had perforce to seek a satisfactory utilization for the equipment.

In the course of her discussion on this point Wray makes clear the basis of this current proposal: that without effective understanding of the processes which give rise to styles and fashions, manufacturers must offer excessive product variation to reduce risk whilst at the same time reducing hopes of economies of large-scale production.

Whilst Wray and Svennilson base their comments on substantial research investigation, a number of 'insiders' have described the existing structures as they operate. The most comprehensive is Amies.[35] He shows the importance of the new wholesaler phenomenon and the department store/multiple chain such as Marks & Spencer, who purchase either models or 'toiles' from *haute couture*. He also demonstrates the role of wholesalers in producing mass fashions without reference to *haute couture*, of which he and Quant are the prominent exponents. His, and Wray's descriptions are endorsed by Halliday[36], and by Thomas[37] in a detailed descriptive analysis of the clothing industry in Leeds, which included men's outerwear.

Amies further points out that the dominant position of Paris in much of the setting of styles and fashions comes from industrial inertia resulting particularly from the infrastructure for the fashion industry which exists there, and, of course, the human skills.

References

1. C. Beaton, *The Glass of Fashion* (Weidenfeld and Nicolson, 1954).
2. C. Dior, *Dior: the Autobiography* (Weidenfeld and Nicolson, 1957).
3. J. Laver, *Taste and Fashion* (Harrap, 1937). (*See* Chapter 22.)
4. D. E. Robinson, 'Fashion Theory and Product Design,' *Harv. Bus. Rev.* vol. 36, (November/December 1958) (*See* Chapter 27.)
5. J. Laver, *Style in Costume* (Oxford University Press, 1949).
6. P. Nystrom, *Economics of Fashion* (Ronald Press, 1928). (*See* Chapter 10.)
7. A. L. Kroeber and J. Richardson, 'Three Centuries of Women's Dress Fashions: a Quantitative Analysis', *Anthropological Records*, vol. 5, (University of California, Berkeley, 1940). (*See* Chapter 3.)
8. J. Carman, 'The Fate of Fashion Cycles in our Modern Society', *Am. Market. Ass. Proceedings* (1966). (*See* Chapter 5.)
9. A. B. Young, *Recurring Cycles of Fashions*; *1760–1937* (Harper & Bros., 1937). (*See* Chapter 4.)
10. L. A. Fallers, 'A Note on the Trickle Effect', *Public Opinion Quarterly* (Autumn 1954). (*See* Chapter 11.)
11. B. Barber and L. S. Lobel, 'Fashion in Women's Clothes and the American Social System', *Social Forces*, vol. 31, pp. 124–131. (*See* Chapter 20.)
12. T. Veblen, *Theory of the leisure class* (New York, Modern Library, 1934).
13. W. H. Whyte, 'The Web of Word of Mouth', *Fortune* (November 1954).
14. D. Reisman, *Lonely Crowd* (Yale U.P., 1950).
15. R. A. Ferber, 'Research on Household Behaviour', *Am. Econ. Rev.* (March 1962).
16. A. H. Maslow, *Motivation and Personality* (Harper 1954).
17. G. Katona, *Psychological Analysis of Economic Behaviour* (McGraw-Hill, 1951).
18. E. Rogers, *Diffusion of Innovations* (Free Press, 1962).
19. Katz and Lazerfeld, *Personal Influence* (Free Press, 1955).
20. Katz, *Public Opinion Quarterly* (Spring 1967).
21. L. Festinger, *Psychological Review*, vol. 57 (1950).
22. C. King, 'A Rebuttal of the Trickle Down Effect', *Am. Market. Ass. Proceedings* (1966). (*See* Chapter 12.)

23. 'Battle of the Hemline', *Sunday Times* (28 May 1967).
24. 'Low Down on the Turn-Ups', *Sunday Times* (4 June 1967).
25. N. K. Jack and B. Schiffer, 'The Limits of Fashion Control', *Am. Soc. Rev.* vol. 13 (1948) pp. 730–738. (*See* Chapter 7.)
26. M. Holland, 'Fashion and Class', *20th Century* (Spring 1965).
27. Landahl, 'Note on the Neurobiophysical Interpretation of Imitative Behaviour', *Bull. Math. Biophys.*, vol. 15 (1953).
28. R. W. Pratt, in G. Schwarz (ed.), *Science in Marketing* (Wiley, 1965), p. 107.
29. J. G. Kemeny and J. L. Snell, *Finite Markov Chains* (Van Nostrand, 1960).
30. N. T. J. Bailey, *Mathematical Theory of Epidemics* (New York, 1957).
31. Landau and Landahl, *Bull. Math. Biophys.* vols. 12 and 15.
32. M. Wray, *The Women's Outerwear Industry* (Duckworth, 1957).
33. I. Svennilson, 'Monopoly and Competition, and their Regulation' (Stockholm School of Economics, 1954).
34. M. Garland, *Fashion* (Penguin, 1962).
35. H. Amies, 'What Makes Fashion?', *J. R. Soc. Arts.*, vol. 112 (June 1964). (*See* Chapter 19).
36. L. Halliday, *The Fashion Makers* (Hodder and Stoughton, 1966).
37. C. Thomas, 'A History of the Leeds Clothing Industry', *Yorkshire Bull. Soc. Econ. Res.* Occasional Paper No. 1 (1955).

Chapter 1

THE STYLING AND TRANSMISSION OF FASHIONS HISTORICALLY CONSIDERED
Winckelmann, Hamilton and Wedgwood in the
'Greek Revival'*
by Dwight E. Robinson

Fashion *is infinitely superior to* merit *in many respects; and it is plain from a thousand instances that if you have a favourite child you wish the public to fondle and take notice of you have only to make choice of proper sponsors.*

Josiah Wedgwood[1]

In a review of a recent play by T. S. Eliot, the critic sums up the action as 'a tragedy of non-communication between parent and child.' We may be sure the reviewer did not intend to raise a doubt in the reader's mind as to whether the father or son in question had difficulty in getting to a telephone, finding a telegraph office or deciphering one another's handwriting. The level of communication he must have had in mind lies deep in the human dependency on expressive symbols. These primary factors of human experience—primary in the sense that nothing stands between them and the raw sensations and impulses—are made up of words, gestures, and images which are, in turn, invariably organized in systems or complexes. These we call by such names as aims, standards and ideals or, more generally, attitudes.[2]

Social thinkers frequently fail to recognize that these symbolic systems or attitudes are part and parcel of any process of human communication or relationship. They miss (perhaps because it is the closest thing to impossible to conceive of human feelings and responses in the abstract, operating, that is to say, independently of symbols) the obvious truth that there can be no communication without a prior agreement as to just what is worth communicating about. This is recognized in everyday parlance when we say that two people 'have nothing in common'. What we mean is that they have no basis for communication. People must, at the least, share some area of concern or direction of interest before the transmission of messages can take on meaning.[3]

Of enormous consequence in social behaviour, albeit largely misunderstood

---

* From the *Journal of Economic History*, No. 4. (December 1960).

because of their subtle and even deceptive nature, are those systems of express-ive symbols we know as styles. I am thinking, of course, of style not so much in the sense of a characteristic way of doing things on the part of an individual person but rather as a general attitude toward design shared by a group of people. Styles in this social context can be properly defined as modes of communication or relationship. It is not straining analogy too far to say that they form a kind of language.

Nothing is more characteristic of our culture than the impulsion it has dis-played over many centuries toward unceasing reformulation of its styles and the tastes connected with them. Every generation or two Western man (to speak of no other) has been driven toward drastic revisions of his aesthetic criteria. For this dynamic process, this pervasive transformation of style, I have been able to find no better word in English usage—embarrassing as some of its connotations may be—than fashion.[4]

In order to illustrate and examine at first hand the historical workings and effects of the fashion process, I have chosen to make a kind of case study of the relationship of three of the central figures (with their ideas) who took part in one of the most far-reaching stylistic upheavals in European history, the so-called Greek Revival. This mighty reorientation in tastes, whose beginnings first made themselves felt around 1750, is almost unique in the interest it holds for the economic historian, since, along with the Gothic Revival and nature worship as other great branches of Romanticism, it was almost exactly syn-chronous with what we call the Industrial Revolution. The steam engine and Hellenism transformed English life at almost exactly the same time.

I hope that my review will be of value to economic historians as a demon-stration that it is not only possible but profitable to study objectively that *deus ex machina* of the text books, changing tastes. And I mean as well to advance the view that economic development has been far more basically and peculiarly dependent on these changes than is commonly supposed. In view of my space limitations, however, I must in the main rest content to let the case speak for itself.

By common consent of the art historians, the first and foremost publicly recognized voice proclaiming the supremacy of Greek art of the classical fifth century B.C. belonged to the German scholar-aesthete, Johann Joachim Winckelmann. Stated in its manifesto-like opening sentence, 'Good taste . . . first arose under the Greek sky,' the thesis of Winckelmann's extraordinary volume of 1755, *Thoughts Concerning the Imitation of Greek Works in Painting and Sculpture*,[5] set forces in motion which were to dominate the European art world for over half a century. Its repercussions are with us still.[6]

Winckelmann was born in Stendal, Brandenburg, in 1717, the year that also saw the birth of Horace Walpole, whose name is invariably linked with the origins of the Gothic Revival. It is well-nigh inconceivable in the present day and age that before the appearance of Winckelmann's *Gedanken* in 1755, it was the unchallenged opinion of connoisseurs that the Romans had been the supreme artists of antiquity. For that matter, many *cognoscenti*, such as G. B. Piranesi, found Winckelmann's views unconvincing right up to the latter's death in 1768. But the triumph of Winckelmann's doctrine was merely a question of time. He had novelty as well as historical consistency on his side, and once the great Goethe, 32 years his junior, became his ardent disciple, the victory of the memory of Periclean Greece over Augustan Rome was assured.[7]

The thought-process whereby Winckelmann arrived at his well-nigh idolatrous Hellenism can, at least at the level of conscious ideas, be simply explained. In the German academies of his day, he had imbibed from their new breed of classical scholars, men of the stamp of C. T. Damm, J. M. Gesner, and J. F. Christ, the presurgent doctrine of the supremacy of Greek philosophy and literature. Surely, decided Winckelmann, if their thought was the model of the ancient world, it was only historical logic that the ancient Greeks must have exercised a matching leadership in art.

So persuaded, he gained access to the antiquary treasures and the rich historical lore of the princes of the Catholic Church by becoming a convert to Catholicism and Secretary to Cardinal Passionei in Rome. From this vantage point, there was no limit to his fertility in inventing devices, flimsily based on mythology, literary references and his own intuitions, whereby to attribute extant marbles to the hands of Phidias, Praxiteles and Myron. Unfortunately, as later scholarship has demonstrated, no single statue apotheosized by Winckelmann was of authentic, classically Greek provenance. All, like the Apollo Belvedere, to which he composed worshipful panegyrics, were, at the earliest, late Hellenistic and most were of the Roman Empire. Yet his pioneer attempt to put artistic criticism on a systematic, chronologically relevant basis has earned him in the eyes of archaeologists a position in the annals of their discipline matching Adam Smith's in economics. Meanwhile, in his espousal of Graecomania, he did more than any other man to set in motion one of the greatest art crazes the Western world has ever seen.

His sermons on the ennobling effects of the masterpieces of his own choosing on the human spirit gave license to the acquisitive everywhere to run all over Europe inspecting, digging up or bidding on limestone relics. At first, of course, all this frenzied interest in the marbles themselves (forged or genuine) only affected some several hundred British plutocrats, German princelings or the like. Yet in the emerging mass market of the day for derivative or simulated embodiments of the 'new-old' taste, Winckelmann's impact is best suggested by the following observation taken from a relatively recent book by a world-famous authority on porcelain. In lamenting the decline of the great days of of the Dresden and Meissen porcelain manufactories, Robert Schmidt, formerly Director of the Schloss museum, Berlin, writes:[8]

'The great scholar and champion of antiquity, J. J. Winckelmann, was one of the first to assail rococo . . . and he broke his stick on our present subject. "Porcelain," said he, "is nearly always made into idiotic puppets." . . . Winckelmann's "beauty" had become a gospel as well as an aesthetic, and men like Robert Adam, Sir William Hamilton, Flaxman and Wedgwood were full of an "admiration" for antique severity, not different in quality from the romantic awe for the sublimity of waterfalls. All of which ended the naughty adventures of "the smiling shepherdesses," and put in their place . . . "a nobler nymphhood".'

Thus, Winckelmann rendered ridiculous and obsolete the Rococo style which for two generations had reigned over the decorative arts of Europe.

Our connecting link between the philosopher-initiator of the Greek Revival and its commercial-industrial exploitation is one of those men whose claims to fame have rather ironically been overshadowed by the greater dramatic interest of the lives of those with whom they were most closely associated. He was a scion of one of the greatest ducal families of Scotland, just out of the direct line; he was the indulgent husband of his second wife, Emma, the woman who became the inspiration and solace of England's greatest naval hero; and, finally and most to the point for our purposes, he provided Josiah Wedgwood with his principal guidance in the treacherous currents of style.

Sir William Hamilton was a career diplomat. Born in 1730, he spent the most active years of his life (1764–1800) as his Brittanic Majesty's minister at the Court of Naples. There he found little enough of an official nature to occupy his energies before Admiral Nelson sailed into the Bay of Naples in 1793. But there was a good deal of practical Scottish enterprise in Sir William. He early undertook pioneering work of lasting significance in volcanology:[9]

'He laboured harder on the slopes of Vesuvius than an exceptionally diligent craftsman would labour in a factory—had Naples possessed any. Within four years he ascended the famous mountain twenty-two times. More than one of these ascents was made at the risk of his life. He made, and caused to be made, innumerable drawings of all the phenomena that he observed . . . and formed too a complete collection of volcanic products. . . . When he had studied Vesuvius under every possible aspect, he went to Etna.'

Soon, however, a new and even more memorable hobby capitivated him: antiquarianism. At first he bought up collections of antique specimens which had formerly been assembled by Italian *dilettanti* principally from the funerary remains of the Etruscans. A little later on, he began to find that the nearby buried cities of Herculaneum and Pompeii provided even more fascinating opportunities for his digging propensities than had his two volcanoes and he went at them with corresponding zeal. The outcome, once again, was a collection of specimens and publication of illustrated descriptions. The latter first took form in his still well-known, three volume work, *Antiquités Etrusques, Etc.*, issued in 1766 and 1767. Actually, the lavish illustrations were mainly of classical Greek vases. In company with everyone else at the time, however, Sir William, by virtue of the fact that the relics had been found in Tuscany, believed them to be Etruscan. It would be many years before it was realized that the Etruscans (for funerary purposes) had imported the urns from Athens. It is noteworthy that even while[10]

'the volumes were still incomplete, Mr Hamilton (sic) circulated proof plates of the work with great liberality. Some of the proofs were lent to our famous English potter, Josiah Wedgwood, and gave a strong impulse to his taste and artistic zeal. But they excited an eager longing for access to the vases themselves, as the only satisfactory models.'

Amusingly enough, the name of the celebrated Wedgwood factory, 'New Etruria,' was taken directly from Hamilton's archaeological misnomer. But nobody minded and before too very long all concerned found the late Hellenistic and Roman urns turning up in such places as Hadrian's villa much better suited to Winckelmannian dictates.

Hamilton's first collection, considered to be 'far more remarkable than any, of its kind, which had come to England', was consigned to the Trustees of the British Museum in 1772. In return, Parliament made a grant to Hamilton of £8,400, a sum probably representing a modest estimate of the costs he had incurred. As before, his commercial friend Wedgwood was hot on the trail. A few years later, the potter[11]

'told a Committee of the House of Commons that, within two years, he had himself brought into England, by his imitations of the Hamilton vases in his manufactory at Etruria, about three times the sum which the collection had cost . . . the country.'

In the last analysis, however, Hamilton's greatest service in the cause of propagating the aesthetic gospel of Winckelmann or, as he styled it, the 'refined' taste, was his hospitality liberally conferred upon his countrymen travelling in the pursuit of culture. Indeed, for most noble or plutocratic Englishmen taking the Grand Tour Naples became a main stop second only to Rome itself. There the elegantly gracious British envoy was always more than ready to show his visitors his artistic treasures (never forgetting Emma herself, she whose classic features inspired him to dub her 'a living antique'), to take them on inspection trips to Pompeii and Herculaneum, and to discourse upon the superiority of the 'Grecian' style. The effects on English residential décor wrought by his returning converts can be readily imagined. If such purveyors of domestic embellishments as Matthew Boulton (Boulton worried about things other than steam engines), the brothers Adam and Wedgwood had employed Hamilton as their chief marketing director he could hardly have done so successful a job. In his amateur capacity, he served as the eighteenth-century forerunner of today's interior decorator, advertising manager, and tourist agent rolled into one.

Whatever students of ceramics may think of Josiah Wedgwood's influence upon pottery from an aesthetic standpoint, none begrudge him the claim to fame inscribed on his epitaph that it was he 'who converted a rude and inconsiderable manufactory into an elegant Art and an important part of National Commerce.'[12] 'All other English potters,' as William Burton has said, 'worked on the principles he had laid down.'[13] Fortunately, Wedgwood's contributions to the progress of ceramic chemistry, marketing techniques, manufacturing technology, and science have already been capably reviewed by historians, permitting us to pass on to the question of his relationship to the style currents flooding the markets he so assiduously sought.[14]

If there is any doubt in the historian's mind about the primary ingredient of Wedgwood's profitable alchemy, there was none in his. So open-eyed was the great potter about the springs of his own commercial success that I could complete the exegesis of this paper by a series of quotations of his own words.

His most general and best-known prescription is set forth in his Catalogue of 1787:[15]

'The progress of the arts, at all times and in every country, depends chiefly upon the encouragement they receive from those who by their rank and affluence are

29

legislators in taste, and who are alone capable of bestowing rewards upon the labours of industry, and the exertions of genius. It is their influence that forms the character of every age; they can turn the currents of human pursuits at their pleasure. . . .'

This encomium to the legislators of taste, be it remembered, was delivered by no servile lackey of the rich and highly placed: Wedgwood was an ardent and open defender of all liberal causes, the American and French Revolutions included.

Few businessmen have left a more informative or engaging account of their operations than Wedgwood has provided in his letters, many of them to his partner Bentley.

On 3 September 1768, he writes of a certain line of classically fashioned vases that 'they must be 18d or 2/- more each, & the black (say Etruscan) vases sent the 27th ult., those charged 9/- must be 10/6, and those 7/6 be 9/-, never mind their being thought dear, do not keep them open in the rooms, show them only to People of Fashion.'[16] A few years later, in January 1770, he indulges, very charmingly, in some light, well-earned exultation.[17]

'Be so good to let us know what is going forward in the Great World. How many Lords and Dukes visit your rooms, praise your beauties, thin your shelves, & fill your purses; and if you will take the trouble to acquaint us with the daily ravages in your stores, we will endeavor to replenish them.'

Wedgwood owed his introduction to the luminaries of connoisseurdom in the first instance to the local Staffordshire nobleman, Earl Gower, on whose family's hereditary soil generations of Wedgwoods had toiled as craftsmen. From his early years he was in constant attendance at the latter's seat of Trentham Hall, often to deliver wares, but as frequently to discuss with his lordship the news of London or to avail himself of the resources of the latter's curio collection and library. What such tutelage meant to the young potter can scarcely be overemphasized. Later, the earl never lost an opportunity to refer his friends and correspondents, a number of whom were royal visitors from abroad, to Wedgwood's show rooms. But perhaps the main service he did him was to introduce him to Lord Cathcart, later Ambassador to the Court of Russia (where he successfully urged upon the Empress Catherine that she patronize Wedgwood ware), who in turn is believed to have performed for Wedgwood the introduction which led to lifelong friendship with Sir William Hamilton.

Students have as yet failed to answer satisfactorily how Wedgwood secured the funds or credit to pay for his expensive mechanical installations and technical experiments as well as to finance his lavish marketing and promotional activities.[18] The answer now seems ready to hand. From the titled top to the middle-class bottom of his world of fashion the appetitite for porcellaneous wares can only be described as voracious. We must not forget that it had been only since 1733 that a Dresden alchemist under the prodding of that most flamboyant of all porcelain collectors, Augustus the Strong of Saxony, had found the secret ingredient, never before known outside of the Far East, of true porcelain. But the mere lust for bric-à-brac, while it might do much to account for Wedgwood's initial success in the local and even domestic markets, does not provide an explanation for Wedgwood's later and greater success in invading the great metropolitan markets of the Western world and in building up for England a hitherto undreamed of export trade.

For this, his master marketing achievement, we must, I think, give the main credit to the missionary efforts of Winckelmann and Hamilton. Had Wedgwood spent tens of thousands of pounds, he could never have succeeded in promoting the wares of lowly Staffordshire at the expense of the prestigious ateliers of the continent such as Meissen, Nymphenburg, Sevres or Limoges one whit so decisively as the pedantic German who so scornfully denigrated the Rococo designs of his native land. Inevitably, Dresden as a porcelain centre found itself entrammelled by its own inimitable tradition. But where Wedgwood would have found it utterly impracticable to have assembled or trained in England a staff of highly skilled modellers and free-hand craftsmen capable of working in the sophisticated manner demanded by the Rococo taste, his homespun Staffordshire workmen were as well if not better fitted to the mechanical reproduction of antique designs, especially when the workbenches of New Etruria were fortified by the technical devices which English ingenuity under the prodding of his practical genius could provide. The only other step he needed to take was to put the British sculptor, John Flaxman, in charge of a studio of modellers in Italy and his supply of tasteful ornaments was assured.

In the last analysis, it was Wedgwood's scrupulous observance of Hamilton's dicta, above all the latter's insistence on that 'subdued harmony of colour' which he deemed to be 'one of the strong objective truths of antique art', that gave Wedgwood a decisive advantage over his competitors. By winning the approval of, and identifying his name with, the well-connected nobleman who was known through polite society as the epitome of connoisseurship, Wedgwood won for his wares that most valuable of marketing attributes, *authority*. Most purchasers of fashion goods are notoriously insecure in their own judgements. By the purchase of Wedgwood's wares, his customers could assure themselves that their worst choices would still lie within the charmed circle of impeccable taste.

Winckelmann through his elaboration, and Hamilton through his propagation, of the master stylistic code of their era furnished the irreducible and indispensable means of one of the most significantly consequential modes of social relationship, stylistic preference. Together they formulated the policy and devised the strategy for the cultural direction of their time, leaving to Wedgwood and his imitators the job of working out the manufacturing methods and marketing tactics needed to execute their orders. This is the connection between the little lesson I have drawn from the late eighteenth century and the topic of this session. It is the clear and distinct function of tastemakers (to employ a term given currency by Russell Lynes) to arrive at, and even to enforce that body of agreement through which stylistic communication becomes operative. Only they can perform this function and their performance is as autonomous as any other form of social leadership. The styling or the creation of fashions, then, is antecedent to their transmission.

The tastes to which Wedgwood the producer catered were in no sense subject to his control and changed entirely independently of any intentions he may have entertained. Indeed, the producer in this case seems merely to have given implementation to the qualitative specifications of consumers in much the same way as the Morse code, for one example, only carries the system of meanings which make purposeful interchange between the sender and receiver of telegraphic messages possible.

Nor viewed in historical perspective does there seem to be the slightest reason to regard the activities of Winckelmann and Hamilton (including the effects they ultimately exerted on economic development) in any way exceptional. In Western culture, tastemakers have always existed and for many centuries they have shown themselves to be as restless and ingenious as industrial entrepreneurs themselves. I hope I will not strain too far the patience of some of my listeners by suggesting that Louis XIV, that Archfiend of the Utilitarian demonology, may be regarded in part as a more powerful and affluent Hamilton, served by his own Winckelmanns. I am thinking not merely of the obvious effects on industry of his self-glorifying programme of chateau-building (a programme which not only set in motion the architectural reconstruction of palatial Europe but, in the process, called forth new products and new techniques) but also of the somewhat more subtle implications for the long-range transformation of consumer standards involved in his oft-rehearsed 'standardization' of the French nobility. That Louis used fashion as an engine of power is a point tellingly made by the remark a courtier addressed to the King upon the former's return from exile: 'Sire, to be long out of your sight is to become ridiculous.'

The style transformation we have discussed left few phases of life untouched. In the closing decades of the eighteenth century, I have been reminded,[19] the middle classes first became confirmed users of soap. What more predictable consequence could have flowed from the retrospective adulation of the body-revering Greeks? And then there was Beau Brummel himself, whose enormous influence on men's clothing down to the present defies a just estimate, but whose style of dress was really nothing more than a transliteration of Winckelmann's 'noble simplicity'. In fact, when the Beau issued forth from his lengthy toilette the effect he created bore strong points of correspondence with a Wedgwood urn.

Nor is the present day without its dependency on taste-makers as a reading of the reminiscences of a Cecil Beaton will make abundantly clear. Of course, it is legitimate to argue that the massive agglutinations of manufacturing and marketing power we have all become so worried about along with the vast, disoriented segments of the buying public on which they batten are strategically poised to muddy and obstruct the socially determined channels of style communication. But to discover that a man has hardening of the arteries or other stoppages is not to deny that his heart remains central to his circulation. From my own reading of the history of style, I cannot doubt that the organ of taste innovation is congenitally and inalienably on the consumer side. Psychology confirms it. Tastes, notoriously subject to the emotions, exhibit much of the tenacity of prejudice in general. It follows that their shift can only be brought about through a process of conversion and this is a private affair in which personal associations figure far more than commericial advertisements.

Nor does it seem to me at all doubtful that the very character of fashion changes—chancey and exogenous as these must be from the economist's viewpoint—most materially influence and alter the structure, the techniques and even the location of industry.

It is no discredit to Wedgwood's entrepreneurial talents nor to his yeoman service to British economic development to question seriously whether but for the tide of the Greek revival—he took it at the flood, Lord knows—he and Staffordshire with him would ever have been led on as they were to fortune. There is a sense, whose full implications we can only faintly perceive, in which Wedgwood and 'the potteries' of his native county were merely *there*, inert as raw materials before a use is discovered for them. And this falls not far short of saying that every contribution the great entrepreneur and his competitors made to economic development waited upon the nod of high fashion.

References

1. Eliza Meteyard, *The Life of Josiah Wedgwood* (London: Hurst and Blackett, 1866), vol. II, p. 378. Letter to Bentley, 19 July, 1779.
2. For masterly analysis of symbolic behaviour, the writings of the late Edward Sapir may be consulted. *See* especially his essay in David G. Mandelbaum (ed.) *Culture, Language, and Personality, Selected Essays* (University of California Press, 1958).
3. The late Vladmir G. Simkhovitch presented an extremely profound and original examination of the dependency of social and historical thought upon changing cultural attitudes in a series of essays, 'Approaches to History I–VI,' which appeared in *The Political Science Quarterly*, vols 44, No. 4 (1929), 45, No. 4 (1930), 47, No. 3 (1932), 48, No. 1 (1933), 49, No. 1 (1934) and 51, No. 1 (1936).
4. For an attempt to account for the nature and timing of alternations in style and taste *see* the present writer's 'Fashion Theory and Product Design,' *Harvard Business Review*, vol. 36, No. 6 (Nov.–Dec. 1958), pp. 126–38.
5. Johann Joachim Winckelmann, *Gedanken über die Nachahmung der Griechischen Werke in der Mahlerey und Bildauerkunst* (Sämtliche Werke. Hrsg. von Joseph Eiselein. Donauoschigen: Verlag deutscher Classiker, 1825–1829), Part I, p. 7. Cited by Henry Caraway Hatfield, *Winckelmann and His German Critics, 1755–1781* (New York, King's Crown Press, 1943), p. 6.
6. For biographic and background information on Winckelmann, *see* Hatfield, *Winckelmann and His German Critics, 1755–1781* and Humphry Trevelyan, *The Popular Background to Goethe's Hellenism* (London, New York and Toronto: Longman's, Green and Co., 1934).
7. Simultaneous, parallel invention shows up in art history just as it does in the physical sciences. The most significant claim rivalling Winckelmann's to independent 'discovery' of the Greeks is that of James 'Athenian' Stuart (1713–1788). Stuart, interested primarily in architecture, braved the risks of exploring Turk-ruled Greece in the years 1751–1754. In 1762, he published his *Antiquities of Athens*.
8. W. A. Thorpe (trans. and ed.) *Porcelain, As an Art and a Mirror of Fashion* (London, Harrap, 1932), p. 212.
9. Edward Edwards, *Lives and Founders of the British Museum* (London, Trubner and Company, 1870), Part I, p. 350.
10. Ibid., p. 352.
11. Ibid., p. 353.
12. Meteyard, *Life*, vol. II, p. 611.
13. As quoted by John Meredith Graham II and Hensleigh Cecil Wedgwood in *Wedgwood* (The Brooklyn Museum, New York, 1948), p. 43.
14. *See*, among others, J. Thomas, 'The Pottery Industry and the Industrial Revolution', *Economic History* (A supplement of the *Economic Journal*) 3, No. 12 (Feb. 1937), pp. 339–414.

Most fortunately, a deeply researched article on Wedgwood which, in my opinion, both complements and tends to reinforce the approach pursued in the present paper, has recently been published. It is M. McKendrick's 'Joshiah Wedgwood: An Eighteenth-Century Entrepreneur in Salesmanship and Marketing Techniques', *The Economic History Review* Second Series, 12, No. 3, (April 1960), pp. 408–33. Professor McKendrick's main concern relative to my present exposition is with Wedgwood's methods of exploiting the prestige affects of fashionable patrons rather than with the morphology of tastes. His article came to my attention only after my own had nearly reached its present form and I made no changes, even of excision, because of it. Our independent arrival at mutually supporting positions seems to me to lend a good deal to the plausibility of our findings concerning consumer initiative.

15. Cited by Graham and Wedgwood, *Wedgwood*, p. 82.
16. Meteyard, *Life*, VII, p. 69. Invoice to Cox, 3 September, 1768.
17. Ibid., p. 175. Letter to Bentley, January 1770.
18. I am indebted to Professor Arthur H. Cole for bringing this pertinent consideration to my attention.
19. Professor Morris L. Morris, University of Washington. Soap consumption for domestic use in England rose from 292 million to 643 million pounds between 1787–88 and 1819–21. *See* G. Talbot Griffith, *Population in the Age of Malthus* (Cambridge University Press, 1926), p. 258.

Chapter 2

THE EVILS OF 'FASHION'*
by Ada Heather Bigg

But seest thou not what a deformed thief this Fashion is?

There are few of us who cannot sympathize with that father of a family who wrote once to the Editor of a ladies' paper, begging him to announce that the fashionable bonnet *this* year would be one of *last* year's done up!

The tale may be apocryphal, but it indicates very completely the cost, the tyranny, and the uselessness of fashion. That fashion serves no useful end is indeed the confirmed opinion of a large number of thinking men and women. Called upon to define fashion, they will instantly show that what they understand by the term is a series of frequently recurring changes undetermined by utility. By this they do not mean to affirm that no change of fashion is ever *accompanied* by utility. They merely allege that it is not because a given new departure in dress or what not is *better* that people combine to bring it about, and there is therefore never any guarantee that there will not be a quick recurrence to the state of things upon which the new departure is an improvement.

It is this circumstance which puts a clear line of demarcation between the changes which go to make up Progress and those which constitute Fashion. There is no danger in a progressive country that stage coaches and horses should ever be substituted for railways and steam. But in a fashionable nation changes as retrogressive as these constantly take place.†

It is this too which gives such precariousness to fashion-regulated industries.

To the producer a new fashion means a change in the wants of the consumers for whom he caters, and it is clear that he will lose or gain just in proportion as he is able to forestall approximately or adapt himself adequately to the changed demand.

But to be able to forecast the demands of the public is only possible if fashion can be reduced to law.

I should be loth to dogmatize, but I fancy the closest study of the history of fashion in the past would fail to evolve any such general laws as would guide the producer to profitable production. There is no average time, for instance, during which a fashion maintains its ascendency. In mediaeval days, some fashion might last 100 years, while another introduced contemporaneously flourished only thirty. The practice of patching, which began in the reign of

---

* From *Nineteenth Century*, Vol. 3, No. 3 (1893).
† Witness the odious farthingale revived for the third time as the crinoline.

Elizabeth, lasted right on into the Hanoverian reigns, reaching its climax, however, under Charles the First, when a young woman in a portrait of that day is shown with a coach and four on her brow, a round spot on her chin, a star on each cheek, and a crescent beneath the left eye. Pointed shoes, when they came in under the Valois kings, remained in one century.

Even when we turn to the origin of fashion we are not much helped.

The Psychological Basis of Fashion

For the purpose of this paper it is scarcely necessary to trace with Herbert Spencer the genesis of fashion from the trophy to the badge and from the badge to the distinctive costume.

But his theory of fashion we may partially accept, and, if it does not sound too presumptuous to say so, slightly amend.

All fashion, he points out, is intrinsically imitative, the imitation springing from two widely divergent motives: (a) reverence for one imitated, or (b) desire to assert equality with him. The tendency to please rulers by avoiding any appearance of superiority to them is exemplified over and over again in the annals of courts. The modification of costume adopted by a monarch to hide some defect—a scar on his neck, or an ill-shaped leg—will be adopted by all his courtiers, and will spread downwards.* Tolerance of this kind of imitation helped, says Spencer, to bring about the other kind by which it has been ultimately superseded.[1]

For nowadays there is very little fashion which is due to reverential imitation. And even if there were, this would scarcely guide producers in determining the character of these products.

It might be easy to divine that if a member of the Royal Family suffering from a sprain limped slightly for some weeks, fatuous fools would at once simulate this limp, and that a shoemaker offering shoes to his customers with one heel higher than the other would reap the reward of his ingenuity.

But no producer, however far-seeing, could forecast the illness or accident which would lead to one member of a royal family limping, or another having to have his head shaved, or a third getting engaged to a high-shouldered bride.

Reverential imitation, then, though an important factor in the past, may be put aside as affecting fashion, and what we have to consider is competitive imitation, and later on a factor of which Spencer takes no account, competitive differentiation.

Competitive Imitation

Competitive imitation, says Spencer, begins quite as early as the reverential.

'Everywhere and always the tendency of the inferior to assert himself has been in antagonism with the restraints imposed on him; and a prevalent way of asserting himself has been to adopt costumes and appliances like those of his superior.'

* Full-bottomed wigs were introduced for the purpose of concealing the higher shoulder of a French Dauphin, and short hair on an occasion when Francis the First had to crop his head closely to allow of a wound being dressed.

Competitive imitation, then, is imitation with a view to establishing in the eyes of the world that relation to those above one which one desires to claim. Those who are quite in the fashion are supposed to be people who from their wealth or position have early opportunities of seeing and adopting the modifications of dress and taste displayed by those highest up in the scale of rank and means.

Hence, the more rapidly they take on a new fashion, the more likely they are to be classed amongst the wealthy and the 'smart'.

Were we looking at the moral aspects of the matter, we should say this was all silly, disgusting, and hateful, but, as it is the industrial aspects which claim our attention, adjectives can be spared.

The style of dress worn by the wealthy and notable will be quickly adopted by all other classes, and the problem for the producer is to discover what determines the adoption in the first place by this comparatively small class of the given style.

Desire for Differentiation

There is no doubt that the tendency on the part of inferiors to assimilate themselves to their superiors is always in conflict with a tendency on the part of superiors to differentiate themselves from inferiors.*

They cannot do this through the medium of sumptuary laws, they cannot by pains and penalties prevent other people imitating them, but they can abandon a style when the imitation has spread very far downwards. This they do perpetually; hence that apparent demand for change as change which is always being deplored.

Thus the desire for novelty is no aesthetic one, springing out of an appreciation of contrast—a perpetual seeking after the ideally beautiful—it is simply due to a wish to assert oneself.

To follow fashion is to claim equality, but to be amongst those who initiate it is to assert absolute supremacy.

The cards from which are woven the materials for the court dress of a leader of fashion will be destroyed directly one dress length has been made. The Parisian model bonnet will be delivered to her before it has entered into commerce and has been copied in any milliner's work-room.† Her desire, and

---

* When servants take to fringes, ladies put theirs back, and now, when every chimney-sweep is a gentleman, every chairwoman a lady, those who formerly figured under such titles prefer to be called men and women. Up to about the seventeenth century it was possible to tell everyone's position in society by his or her clothes, or even by their colours.

> 'Oh, Bell my wiffe, why dost thou floute?
> Now is nowe, and then was then;
> Seeke now all the world throughout,
> Thou ken'st not clownes from gentlemen;
> They are cladde in black, greene, yellowe, or graye,
> Soe far above their owne degree.'
> (Song, 'Take thy Old Cloake about thee.)

Permission, however, was accorded to people to dress in a manner above their station if they wore garments given them by their superiors; cf. Montel (*Histore des divers Etats*, vii. 7).

† The leading dressmakers of modern times will invariably be those who can ensure their clients enjoying, for at least a month or so, a virtual monopoly of some style or fabric. Drapers, too, have to study this desire on the part of customers for things not likely to become

that of her fellows, to wear something which the masses have not yet appropriated becomes then a prominent factor in producing the vagaries of fashion. And the only approach to anything like law in the matter will be this: *Changes dictated by a desire for differentiating oneself from the commonalty will be welcome just in proportion as they are extremely violent, and present innumerable difficulties to speedy imitation.*

It is the operation of this law which calls forth those leaps to extremes which have ever provoked the scorn of the satirist. Aesthetic influences, as concurrently determining factors, are not wholly absent, but they operate more to keep a fashion from going out than to bring a new one in. In fact, two conflicting tendencies are ever at work. On the one hand, in proportion as a fashion spreads downwards it tends to go out. On the other hand, in proportion as it satisfies the desire for beauty, and is appropriate to the needs of the wearer, it tends to persist. In the unequal conflict between them, it is generally the first tendency which carries the day.

People imagine that aestheticism influences more than it does, because they see the whole civilized world ultimately displaying some style of beautiful dress first worn by a French actress. It has caught the popular taste by reason of its beauty, they suppose. As a matter of fact, people hasten to adopt the particular style because the French stage is one of the recognized channels by which new fashions are launched. No personal taste on the part of the actress may have gone to the assumption by her of this or that gown, and none need be exercised by the general public following in her wake. Their power of selection is strictly limited in deciding in favour of one rather than another of the toilettes exhibited by her, and, did all happen to be barbarous, extravagant, and disfiguring, one or other of them would still pass into the current fashions of the moment.

Fashion not due to Imitation

Some manifestations of fashion are not due to imitation at all, but to simultaneous *initiation*. Just as people without any conscious imitation of each other will, in going over a field (if haste be their only object), naturally take an almost identical line across it, till in process of time their steps wear out a footpath, so people on occasion will adopt some uniform fashion because they are affected in some uniform way.

Thus, the introduction of a given style of gown will inevitably lead to a general modification of other details of costume and surroundings.

Falke, in his *Deutsche Trachten und Modenwelt*, mentions that during the period of long wigs, the tulip, stiff and majestic, was the fashionable flower. When skirts are voluminous, full, and made bell-shaped by means of whalebone and hoops, people will naturally tend to give themselves balance, as it were, by making their heads as large as possible, and increasing the size of their

hackneyed. 'I have been shown German printed calicoes,' said a witness before the Commission on Depression of Trade, 'which have been sold in England by a large home-trade Manchester firm, simply because the ground-work was a slightly different shade of tobacco colour than the ground or padded work of Manchester printers. The shopkeepers *would have* the German stuff *because it was smaller in supply, and could not be obtained from British competitors.*'

sleeves. When long dresses are worn, fancy and elaborate petticoats will be displayed. The inadequacy of the Directory and Empire dresses as regards warmth would necessarily lead to mantillas and scarves; and similarly, when a particular colour craze manifests itself in people's selection of wall papers, the dominant tints in carpets and hangings will tend to be in harmonious relation.

Here at least we should seem to be in touch with phenomena of fashion capable of being predicted. The element of uncertainty, however, is even here not to be got rid of. For instance, experience may have shown us that as sleeves become shorter gloves become longer, and we may assume that a manufacturer who, noting the tendency towards short sleeves, prepared betimes for the production of long gloves would be acting wisely. But lace mittens might conceivably meet the requirements of the case quite as well as lengthened gloves, and another manufacturer who successfully put lace mittens on the market might drive long gloves out of the field.

Then again, take the fashion for stained boards. Before the event who could tell whether this would result in an increased or diminished demand for carpets?

As a matter of fact it has resulted in a lessened production of English carpets and a great demand for Turkey and other foreign carpets, which, to meet the increased demands, are now made in much changed qualities and have 'admittedly lost much of the beauty of colouring and excellence of make which were formerly such general characteristics of Oriental carpets.'

On the whole, fashion may be described as the element of uncertainty run wild, and it is in this light we must view it when considering its effect upon production.

Fashion's progress is marked by sudden transfers of prosperity from one class or locality to another class or locality, and the question is, 'Are such transfers advantageous to the country at large?'

There are plenty of people who will answer with an unhesitating 'yes'. They will say that if such transfers come with sufficient frequency, they tend to diffuse periods of exceptional prosperity over widely separated portions of the industrial field, so that in the course of every few years each group of workers engaged in the production of things which fashion affects will in turn have enjoyed some of this prosperity.

In this way industries will be given an opportunity of expanding to the point where they can avail themselves to the utmost of improved machinery, increased division of labour, and all that economy of manufacture consequent upon some utilization of waste not till then profitable.

Then, when the wave of fashion recedes, the industry can devote itself to staple production, or will have secured a hold upon foreign markets; while, of those who have been benefited by the times of exceptionally active trade, many will manage to permanently retain the benefit by the judicious use they have made of higher wages and profits. In this manner most men will get that opportunity which is supposed to come to everyone once in his life.

But there is a reverse side to the medal in the fact that every increase of prosperity secured to a class or locality by change of fashion involves a corresponding loss to some other class or locality. The hard times induced by waning fashion may deprive people not only of all the advantages they have gleaned from the exceptionally good times, but of all those which steady trade had previously bestowed upon them.

Now, as far as the working classes are concerned, it may be taken as an axiom that to descend in the scale of comfort does infinitely more harm than to ascend does good, and that the intensity of the struggle to secure work when work is scarce carries wages far lower down than the keenness of competition to obtain hands when hands are few carries wages up.

How Labour Loses

A few instances taken indiscriminately from the commercial history of our own and other countries will make this abundantly clear. In 1852 fashion in France substituted for cheap thread lace a sort of flowered gimp lace of silk and wool.

Wages went up from 5d a day, the normal earnings of the lace-workers, to 3s 4d. The time of prosperity, however, was fleeting, and, fashion veering round, the wages of the women dropped suddenly to 10d and 1s 3d a day for highly skilled workers, and in 1862, according to Reybaud, to about 4d a day for the ordinary worker. (Mark, that was 4d against the 5d which had been earned in the days of steady trade.[2]) In 1865 and 1868 a great impetus was given to the Venetian glass industry by the increasing demand for beads, particularly in London.

'A great extension of the manufacture took place, the demand for labour considerably exceeded its usual supply, and wages rose so high that all who could do so abandoned their habitual occupation for bead-making. A period of wonderful prosperity was followed by one of corresponding depression. The demand for Venetian beads ceased, and a large number of persons were thrown out of work. Shoemakers, tailors, carpenters, all who had been attracted to the bead manufacture by fancy wages, would have been glad to return to their former employment, but in many cases they found their places filled by new-comers.'

The trade societies did their best to relieve the distress, but there were still in August 1869 as many as 500 persons out of work in consequence of the crisis in the bead trade.[3]

Similarly in 1880, when fashion showed a predilection for Brussels and Alençon lace and a distaste for Valenciennes, the peasant girls of Flanders who made this last kind of lace were reduced to miserably insufficient earnings, and endured the greatest privations.[4]

The revived fashion for edelweiss lace was responsible, according to Mr Mallet, President of the Nottingham Chamber of Commerce, for much of the depression which overtook the Nottingham lace trade a little while back. Similar lace, it is true, had been manufactured in Nottingham forty or fifty years previously, but it had gone so completely out of fashion that not a piece had been made for twenty-five or more years, and the needlewomen who used to make this lace had had to find some other employment.[5]

In 1832 a crisis occurred in the English glove trade, which was ascribed partly to the admission of foreign gloves, but chiefly to the fashion for cotton 'Berlin' gloves.

'Many of the distressed operatives, who had been earning from 20s to 30s a week, were reduced to stone-breaking and road-mending—men at 8d a day, women at 4d—while some of those deprived of their customary means of livelihood went on the rates.'

Again, fashion in 1862 ruined the sewed muslin trade in the North of Ireland. It was stated at the time in a memorial presented to the Queen, that in 1856 there had been employed in this delicate and beautiful branch of industry no fewer than 200,000 women in Ireland and 25,000 in Scotland, the wages of those employed in embroidery alone amounting to £480,300 annually. In 1861 the sum total paid to labour employed in the various details of the manufacture had gone down to £200,000, as against £700,000 so paid in 1856.

A North of England cloth manufacturer,* questioned lately about the effects of fashion on the producing classes, wrote as follows:

'I will speak of experiences of my own. One I give is typical of what goes on in the fashion industries. Within half a mile of this place is a large mill, whose proprietor, an ingenious but entirely ignorant man, had successfully imitated with silk, waste, or mohair, or something else, a sealskin. Now, as this article is very expensive, large numbers of foolish people, unable to purchase the real thing but very anxious to follow the fashion and be thought well of, purchased these goods in such quantities that this man got together a considerable fortune in a few years. *He also got together a large number of workers from other industries*, which, though steadier, did not yield quite as much wage. There was no secret in the production, hence other manufacturers entered into competition and prices were run down. This would not matter; but the public, no longer satisfied with the imitation seal, won't have it at any price, the consequence being that the works are closed, and the *workmen's cottages stand empty.*'

Difficulty of Taking Up even Allied Employment

It is all very well to talk glibly of the ultimate adaptation of labour to altered conditions of demand, but the adaptation is imperfect, even when fashion refrains from deserting an industry altogether, and only singles out a special branch for its capricious favour. It is undoubtedly easier for a maker of Valenciennes lace to take to the making of Brussels lace than it would be for a housemaid or a nail and chain maker. The kid-glove machinists could turn more easily to the Astrakhan branch of the glove trade than the maker of lace mitts to gloving. Costume hands can go in for mantle work with less effort than could the artificial florists.

But though this sort of adaptation is easier it is *not easy*. The process of adaptation—i.e. taking up the work which is most in demand and most like one's own—requires time; and time is just what fashion does not grant. The adaptation painfully and laboriously effected, away it flits, leaving behind the stern necessity for a fresh adaptation.

When one realizes all the physical and mental suffering involved in being out

* Mr George Thompson, of Woodhouse Mills, Huddersfield.

of work, one can understand why Ben Tillett and Tom Mann are found urging the recognition of some kind of communal responsibility, making provision for those who are dislodged from their ordinary occupations by changes of fashion. To do away with the tyranny of fashion would, however, be the more desirable consummation.

Dead Season and Overtime

Irregularity of work—that is to say, periods of exhausting and excessive toil alternating with periods of demoralizing and profitless idleness—must also be laid to the account of fashion's variations.

Said Mr Jonathan Peate, giving evidence before the Labour Commission:

'The fickleness of taste and the perpetual occurrence of new demands which cannot be foreseen have made it impossible to distribute the work more easily. The demand for certain classes of goods at fixed periods has ceased altogether. It is now only safe to manufacture to order. To create a stock of goods is most foolhardy.'

Fashion Makes Commodities Dearer

But it may be urged that the displacement of labour which so invariably accompanies sudden changes of fashion must not be held to justify us in condemning fashion, since inventions which no sensible person would wish to check are attended in their first stages by precisely the same phenomenon.

Inventions, however, increase the sum total of production, fashion does not. It simply changes the proportion in which the constituents of the sum total of production stand to each other. Inventions cheapen, fashion makes things dearer.

True, as Roscher points out, the vast demand which fashion brings into play is favourable to enterprise on a large scale and to all the economy in production which the factory system entails. But, on the other hand, fashion and its caprices have to be reckoned with, and the whole advantage of economy in production may be swallowed up by the vicissitudes which attend the getting off of the finished products.

All the probable loss incidental on an adverse change of fashion has to be allowed for (not only by the producer, but by the distributor) *in the price of the product*. If goods are heavy—that is to say, do not commend themselves to the buyers of large firms—manufacturers are put to the greatest straits to minimize their loss.

'Sudden changes of fashion (writes a partner in the great Saltaire alpaca manufacture) are, as you may imagine, a source of annoyance to all manufacturers, and, in cases where the raw material already provided, or the goods already made do not in any way meet the new requirements, or the machinery already in hand is not adapted to the new fashions, then there is an almost inevitable loss.'

Asked further how big firms strove to avert such loss, he answered:

'We have not, as you may surmise, quite the same remedy as have the large retail houses with their winter and summer sales. When change of fashion has thrown on our hands a lot of raw material we, in some cases, sell it in that state, if we can see our way to do so without great loss; in other cases we work up the material mixed with other wools, or substitute another kind of warp, or alter the make of the cloth or the style of finish, so as to approximate as near as possible to the exigencies of the moment. In other words, we do the best we can in each individual case.'

But sometimes no best is possible. When the Princess May's engagement to the Duke of Clarence was first announced, manufacturers at once set to work to introduce May blossom into all their season materials. Large quantities of mousselines de laine and brocades were brought out, with a pattern of white May running over them. The sad death of the Prince gave an ill-omened character to such goods, and it taxed all the resources of the dealers to dispose of them.

Difficulty of Minimizing Loss

Now in cases of this kind, where the value of goods is partially destroyed without the goods themselves suffering the least change of form, attempts are often made to foist them on the provinces. In Paris there are houses which buy up everything as it begins to go out of fashion, and then send it into the provinces and to foreign parts.[6] But, as I was assured by a courteous representative of Messrs Debenham's firm, this mode of minimizing loss is less effectual than it was. Fashion papers, to say nothing of detailed journalistic descriptions of the toilettes of fashionable personages, keep provincials wide awake. Australia, it is true, takes after-season goods (their midwinter being the time of our midsummer), but she will accept nothing that has not gone off well here. If the price of goods did not on the whole cover these inevitable losses occasioned by fashion, it would cease to be profitable to manufacture.

In the same way the retailer, in fixing his price, has to cover the contingency of having to sell off his unsold stocks at those winter and summer sales which of late years have become such a feature in retail transactions.* The first loss is the least loss is the experience of firms like Debenham's, Marshall and Snelgrove's, etc., and they will not pay rent for unsaleable articles, but clear off things at any sacrifice.

The Pattern System

The immense development of the pattern-publishing system, rendering it easy for the public to successfully assimilate new fashion in about the space of six months, is another cause which makes for instability. Butterick's patterns circulate hugely in America, England, and the Colonies, this firm having 175 agencies, mostly amongst drapers, and an organ with a monthly circulation of 500,000. At first the policy of the firm was simply to follow fashion, but now it is endeavouring to lead fashion, and it is barely possible that within certain limits it will realize this ambition. When it does, however, fashion will tend to become more stable again, the differentiating impulse being forced then to find its satisfaction in excellence of quality rather than in any originality of style.

* The sales are ceasing to answer their purpose of carrying off surplus stocks in proportion as the circumstances of modern industry make it more vital for the merchant to get rid of them. Purchasers prefer to pay more for goods, or buy inferior qualities and be in the fashion.

Fashion's Reversioners

Many people try to show that if the operation of fashion enhances for one set of purchasers the prices of all goods subject to fluctuations through fashion, it at the same time lowers the price of these goods at a subsequent period for another class of purchasers. Goods are bought at sales at prices out of all proportion to their original cost, so those who buy them must gain.

This, however, is a very debatable point. Every woman's experience tells her that dresses and stuffs are bought on these occasions simply because they are cheap, and not because the purchaser really needs them. Now, it was a wise saying of our grandmothers, that 'however little you may pay for a thing, if you don't want it, it is always dear'.

Again, though poor relations and needy hangers-on may obtain the reversion of garments of a cut and quality far superior to those which their own means would purchase, we must set against this gain the loss which they in their turn suffer when they too have to discard what fashion no longer allows even them to wear. So true is it that 'the fashion wears out more apparel than the man'.

Unless we are prepared to say that every change in the distribution of wealth, no matter how brought about, is admirable, we must concede that the cheapening of goods through their going out of fashion is no more an advantage to the country than is the cheapening of works of art during a time of commercial depression. Some individuals gain what other individuals lose, but the nation is not benefited. Indeed, if the depression be continued long enough to check artistic effort it loses.

Does Fashion Stimulate and Elevate Production?

Not content with denying that fashion means *loss* to the community, there are individuals who will boldly declare that it means gain.

Milliners, dressmakers, tailors, haberdashers, florists, hairdressers, etc.— retail firms generally dealing in fashion-regulated commodities—unite in saying that fashion is the very life of trade. They will tell you that the power to produce is more than production, and that it is this power which fashion fosters. They will add that through fashion are evolved various qualities economically valuable to the community—versatility, ingenuity, skill, resource, taste, and I know not what beside.* There is a measure of truth in this, but the necessity of evolving these qualities in this one way is not so apparent.

As Mrs Bryant (B.Sc.) pointed out when the subject was recently under discussion:

'Any advantages of this kind secured by change of fashion or *variation of style in time* could be secured in much greater degree and with better artistic effect in consumption by more *variety of style in space*, each woman trying to wear that which suited her best. If a more serious attempt at genuine effect in dress were made by us all, dress would be much more closely adapted to individual variation of physique, and this would create at all times a great demand on the inventive powers of those engaged in the manufacture of dress.'

*Against this we must balance the absolute waste involved in the demonetization, so to speak, of skill acquired by long-continued exercise in a given direction. A tailor lamented to me that hardly had he left off spoiling material and learnt how to cut out a lady's long jacket bodice than these bodices ceased to be fashionable and his new skill became useless.

44

Apart from any realization of Mrs Bryant's ideal, however, I am of opinion that the ordinary and natural changes caused by seasonal fluctuations, national catastrophes, new inventions, and general progress, would suffice to develop and utilize all the versatility and alertness necessary for staple production on the best lines.*

I incline to the belief that fashion does not so much develop these qualities in the nation at large as it does in a limited number of individuals.

Professor Marshall's ideal manufacturer, we know (if he makes goods not to meet special orders but for the general market), must combine in his one person all the qualities needful for an organizer of labour—a natural leader of men—with all those other qualities which are essential to a merchant, to a caterer for the public. Thanks to the ceaseless changes of fashion, a tendency is exhibiting itself to separate more and more these functions, and to evolve a class of men who are not necessarily capable of organizing labour at all, but who, as Professor Marshall puts it, have a power of forecasting the broad movements of production and consumption.

To such men, fashion is fruitful in opportunities. Like all experts, however, they justify their existence by artificially multiplying the occasions for their services, and, not content with successfully feeling the pulse of popular caprice, they set themselves to make it beat as they themselves determine. They no longer forecast, they to a certain extent create fashion. Bitter are the complaints brought by manufacturers against these men.

'Their existence depends upon fomenting discontent in the minds of the purchaser', says one manufacturer. He himself will leave to the competitive manufacturer the 'pandering to the cupidity of merchants and tailors'.

This class of experts, who begin by being buyers and end by being powers, do for fashions what Reuter's Telegraph Agency does for news. All the fabrics and designs of pre-eminent manufacturers and *artistes en modes* got ready for the coming season are communicated to other manufacturers, who proceed to reproduce them in cheaper form for a lower stratum of consumer.

Growing Instability of Fashion

The existence of the class already alluded to is one of the circumstances which must tend to make fashion ever less and less stable.[7]

But another cause tending to increase the changes of fashion is the immense cheapening of all products consumed by the masses. As Roscher points out, fashion was still relatively stable in the Middle Ages because articles of wearing apparel were proportionately dearer than they are today. Joinville wore a garment bequeathed to him by his father and mother; and in Persia shawls are frequently inherited through many generations.

Fashion, indeed, never gets the same hold upon luxuries of a very costly kind. Take Cashmere shawls, for instance, where one of the finer sorts will employ the labour of three men for a whole year. Look again at carpets. Really good reproductions from the best Oriental sources, viz. original rugs and carpets, most of them centuries old, are subject to few fluctuations in demand. For the same reason, sealskin jackets change their shape less frequently than cloth.

* Sateen was brought out during a period of national depression, and much lessened the general distress at Preston.

Fashion nowadays affects those things most which by reason of their price are within the reach of the largest numbers. In this connection the influence of the *sewing machine* must not be overlooked. This has increased immeasurably the instability of fashion. Before cheap stuffs were not worth making up, but, the labour of sewing having been lessened, cheap fabrics are in constant demand.

Summary

There is nothing elevated or laudable in the psychological basis of fashion which can compensate for the evils accompanying its progress. Fashion is just the outcome of an ignoble desire to flaunt (real or simulated) superiority in the eyes of the world. Fashionable people are even more anxious nowadays to be *unlike* those they consider beneath them than to be like those they consider above them. The more modern civilization enables the imitating many to quickly assimilate the garb and customs of the differentiating few, the more frequent must the changes of fashion be, till at length the very extent of the evil calls forth a remedy.

It is possible this remedy may be on the lines of Mrs Bryant's suggestion. Or it may be a national, if not an international, garb will be evolved, which will get stereotyped like the coat, trousers, and high hat of the nineteenth-century man. It must be remembered that until the fourteenth century men were even more the slaves of fashion than women, and many a Claudio would lie 'ten nights awake carving the fashion of a new doublet'.[8]

But whether reforms are possible or not, the first step towards reform is a clear vision of things as they are. It is impossible to maintain that aesthetics have much to do with fashion. It is impossible likewise to cheat ourselves into believing that incessantly changing fashions are good for trade. So far as the working classes are concerned, the displacement of labour induced by waning fashion does them more harm than increased employment due to developing fashion does good. As to manufacturers, they are hampered in their operations, production becoming more speculative every day. As to consumers, they have to pay higher prices for all products subject to fashion's influence, while the diversion of their time and thought to trivial matters of dress is also an economic loss to the community. The only gainers are a limited class of experts and dealers. All the economically valuable qualities said to be developed by the necessity fashion imposes of 'keeping on the alert' can be developed by the ordinary and inevitable crisis through which staple production passes, and could be better secured by a greater variety in dress at any given time.

References

1. *Ceremonial Institutions*, Chap. 11, p. 207.
2. Cf. *Le Travail des Femmes* (Leroy Beaulieu).
3. *Report on the Condition of Industrial Classes*, 1871, lxviii.
4. Cf. *Revue des Deux Mondes*, vol. 42, 1880.
5. Cf. *Report of the Commission on Depression in Trade and Industry*.
6. *Principles of Political Economy* (Roscher), vol. 2, 188.
7. Cf. Quicherat, *Histoire du Costume*.
8. Cf. Miss Hill, *History of British Costume*.

Chapter 3

THREE CENTURIES OF
WOMEN'S DRESS FASHIONS
A Quantitative Analysis*
by Jane Richardson and A. L. Kroeber

This study was the first pioneering attempt at quantification of the fashion process. The work of many later authors builds upon its historical examination of basic stylistic trends.

The Problem

This study is an attempt to define stylistic changes in an objective and quantitative manner.[1] That dress fashions were chosen for investigation, rather than works of pure or industrial art, is due to the greater ease of obtaining material which is not only fairly abundant but strictly comparable from decade to decade and even from century to century. This desideratum enforces that the range of material be narrow: one cannot compare landscapes with genres, atmospheric treatments with portraits. Also the material must not be too utilitarian: chairs in one period may be primarily objects of a certain degree of state, in another they may deliberately consider comfort or serve for lounging. Women's evening or formal dress has fulfilled a fairly constant function for several centuries. At the same time it is about as free from utilitarian motivation as dress can well be. Furthermore, for well over a century it has been designed and published in fashion plates, which have often been preserved where most of the costumes themselves have long since perished or become inaccessibly scattered. In short, formal dress, as a topic for investigation, possesses the advantages of representing an art which while not of the highest order is relatively free and self-sufficient; relatively little limited or warped by considerations of external utility; specific and uniform enough to be comparable from one period to another; of a nature which precludes complete repetitive crystallization and stand-still; and on which, with reasonable industry of search, there can be accumulated fairly adequate information over a long span of time.

It is for these reasons that this type of costume has been chosen for study, rather than because of any special importance or interest which it may possess in

* From *Anthropological Records*, Vol. 5, No. 2 (1940). Originally published by the University of California Press; reprinted by permission of The Regents of the University of California.

itself. In other words, it provides a convenient and promising set of data for a study of the problem of how stylistic or aesthetic changes prove to take place when they are examined quantitatively instead of through subjective intuition or feeling. It cannot of course be asserted that the change behaviour of women's evening dress would follow the same patterns as style changes in painting or music or even in some other type of dress. But any findings will presumably have some significance for the wider problem of how aesthetic styles change in general; to which in turn we must have some answer before we can hope to inquire fruitfully why they change.

The investigation had its beginning in a brief article by Kroeber in 1919.[2] The techniques of examination there developed, which will be explained in a moment, are now applied to a much larger body of material. The assembling of this new material was the first contribution of Richardson. Whereas the earlier article covered the seventy-six years from 1844 to 1919, the present study carries on to 1936 as well as back to 1787, continuously except for two years (1822, 1833) for which no data were encountered. This doubles the span for continuous data. Back of 1787, contemporary portraits and pictures had largely to be substituted for pre-wear fashion plates, and they run fewer; but a fair set of specimens was assembled back to 1605. Our total time range is thus three hundred and thirty-two years—longer, we believe, than in the overwhelming majority of statistical studies in economics. To be sure, the seriation is badly broken before 1787. The decade 1631–40 yielded twenty-one available illustrations, the double decade 1691–1710 none at all; 1711–20, twenty, but 1721–30 only three. Our pre-1787 findings are therefore far less significant and reliable than those since 1787. Our more detailed analysis is accordingly based wholly on the last one hundred and fifty years. But the findings made there, projected backward, and supported by the intermittent materials over the preceding one hundred and eighty-two years, allow some tentative conclusions for the whole span of three hundred and thirty-two years.

To the figures computed and plotted year by year, we have added a five-year moving average, which of course smoothes out the mere annual variations and gives a much more vivid picture of the trend of fashion at any one time. On the other hand, the deviation or fluctuation of each year's style from the average for five years is also much more clearly brought out by this new device. This annual fluctuation is obviously a measure of the stability of the style.

Another type of variability is that within the year. How different are the several dresses of one year from one another, as expressed by their 'sigma' or standard deviation from their mean? The sigmas as compared over a period of years express the changes in variability.

In short, we have worked out quantities which express the extremes of certain features of women's dress style; the times of these extremes and the intervals between them; the rapidity and consistency of the trends of change; and the degree of homogeneity or stability of the style both in a given year and over longer spans.

The Measures

The traits or features of dresses dealt with number six. These comprise three vertical and three horizontal diameters: of the skirt or dress as a whole, of the constricted middle or waist, and of the *décolletage* or cut-out at the neck. We are really examining the dimensions of the silhouette of the whole dress. There are many other features of probably equal significance, and of which fashion is perhaps even more conscious: trains, sleeves, girdles, flounces, yokes, and so on. All these however come and go. They are never permanent, but sooner or later disappear completely for a time. This means that only short-range comparisons can be instituted for them. The skirt and waist diameters, however, and in full dress the *décolletage*, cannot be escaped, as long as the fundamental style of women's wear remains at all. It is this permanence of the six silhouette dimensions that has led to our confining attention to them.

All measurements were made on fashion plates or other pictures with calipers and ruler in millimeters. To render them comparable, they had to be reduced to a common standard. For this the 'total length of figure' was chosen and recorded as measurement No. 1. The six dimensions were then converted into percentage proportions of this. It is these percentages that are presented and dealt with throughout. It seems useless to publish the raw or absolute measures; but they have been preserved. Actually, the basic measurement No. 1 is not the whole length of figure, but the length up to the middle of the mouth. The top of the head does not answer, because of varying increments of coiffure and headdress.

All six of the dimensions are maximum diameters. They are as follows:

> No. 2, length of skirt or dress.
> No. 3, length of waist.
> No. 4, length (or depth) of *décolletage*.
> No. 5, width of skirt.
> No. 7, width or thickness of waist.
> No. 8, width of *décolletage*.

Originally another measure was made: No. 6, maximum width of skirt if this width occurred above the hem. This was soon dropped as too irregular in occurrence, and it is mentioned only to account for the gap in the numbering; though stylistically, as in recent years, this diameter may be of importance.

In detail, the measurements were executed as follows:

No. 1, or base: Total length of figure from the centre of the mouth to the tip of the forward toe.

No. 2: Distance from the mouth to the bottom of the centre front of the skirt.

No. 3: Distance from the mouth to the minimum diameter across the waist. The girdle, or the lower edge of the corsage part of the dress, may coincide with this or lie above or below this diameter. The girdle and edge have been disregarded because neither is a permanent feature.

No. 4: Depth or length of the *décolletage*, measured from the mouth to the middle of the upper corsage edge in front.

No. 5: Diameter of the skirt at its hem or base.

No. 7: Minimum diameter in the region of the waist. See comment under No. 3.

No. 8: Width of the *décolletage* across the shoulders.

Full-face or nearly full-face figures were used so far as possible. If the cases available were few, profiles and near-profiles were included. A side view eliminates *décolletage* breadth, and, if the forearm is held horizontally as is frequent in some periods, one or both waist measures may also be lost. Otherwise, profiles, and especially semiprofiles, seem mostly to yield in fashion plates results not very different from full-face views.

In the seasons covered by monthly fashion journals, the winter months are of course the ones in question for full dress. So far as possible, illustrations were sought in the January to March issues. If these did not suffice, the April to June numbers of the journal were examined, or preferably the December and November issues of the preceding calendar year. For instance, January–March of 1850 plus November–December of 1849 have been counted as 1850.

An absolute requirement was that each particular figure be dated in a specific year. Reconstructed 'typical' fashions, even if for a given year, such as abound in most histories of costume, were of course of no use. Moreover, no approximate datings were included. The only exception occurs in the case of a few Van Dyck and Watteau portraits, whose dates are known to fall within periods of several years. As the pre-1787 data have been used only in ten-year blocks, these approximations would not matter unless the period lapped over from one block into another. Such overlaps have not been used statistically, except that a group of ten Watteaus dated 1710–16 has been included in the 1711–20 average.

The old Kroeber measurements for 1844–1919 were limited to ten figures for each year. Generally some of these ten failed to show one or more of the six diameters. Richardson sought as many examples as possible, so that there would not be less than ten cases for each measurement. This was not a hard task for the last decade and a half. Back of 1844, however, ten ladies per year became a rarity; ten full-face views hardly ever occurred. Therefore it was necessary to get perhaps six dimensions from one figure, content oneself with two from the next, and hope that in the end none of the dimensions would be wholly unrepresented for the year. Nevertheless, there were richer years: 1799 yielded twelve illustrations; 1809, fifteen; 1841, twenty-six.

Sources

To fill out the years from 1920 to 1936, *Vogue* and *Harper's Bazaar* were consulted, and, for 1920, *Costume Royal*. Each of these American magazines devotes a great deal of space to the creations of Paris designers. If, however, there were not sufficient of these Paris models in a given year, the gap was filled by unsigned American style plates.

Before 1844, it was necessary to go from one broken set to another, to the few books of copious dated illustrations (Price: *Dame Fashion*; Saschel and Boehn), and to the engravings, drawings, and portraits by fashionable painters of fashionable women. In these different sources it was possible to find many plates from the *Petit Courrier des Dames*, previously used by Kroeber for 1844–68, and other elegant lithographs issued in monthly or quarterly series such as *Wiener Moden*, the *Galerie des Modes*, and the Ankerman engravings for the *Ladies' National Magazine*, of London.

Seasonal fashion plates are scarce, however, before the French Revolution, not only on account of their age, but also because they were not published to a great extent. Hence we became increasingly dependent on painters and engravers, such as Winterhalter, Debucourt, Reynolds, Moreau le Jeune, Chodowiecki, Boucher, Nattier, Fragonard, Hogarth, Watteau, Terborch, Codde, Velasquez, Van Dyck, and minor painters of the Dutch and French schools.

The idealized lithographed fashion plates from 1789 on, whether published in Paris, Karlsbad, or Vienna, are strikingly uniform. There are changes in face and pose only with the advent of the wood-cut and the zinc-engraved ink drawing and photograph of recent years. The earlier painters are less subject to conventionalization than the lithographers. Faces and attitudes are individualized, waists are thicker, and the excellent likenesses are often far closer to the photograph of today than to the draftsman's or lithographer's formalized delineations. The change from lithograph or drawing to photograph is comparable to the reversed change from painting to lithograph. Thus we may say of our span of three hundred and thirty-two years, that the data are rather conventionalized for the hundred years 1789–1889, but are tempered with realism before and after.

Match of Old and New Data

Although the measurements are easily taken, the question may arise as to comparability of the Kroeber data for 1844–1919, and those of Richardson for the remaining years. In none of the six measures as tabulated or graphed, is there any large offset between 1843 and 1844, and only one (No. 5) between 1919 and 1920. However, to see if there were any personal equation of measurement, 1844–46 and 1919 were measured on new data by Richardson, and a comparison with the Kroeber measures is herewith appended (table 1).

TABLE 1 *Comparability of Observers**

Dimen.	1844		1845		1846		1919	
	K	R	K	R	K	R	K	R
2	97·9[10]	98·2[23]	97·5[10]	97·3[11]	98·2[9]	98·0[10]	84·2[10]	89·4[18]
3	28·9[10]	28·8[17]	27·9[10]	26·9[10]	28·4[9]	28·8[9]	24·1[10]	25·0[18]
4	14·6[10]	14·3[23]	14·1[9]	13·1[10]	13·1[8]	12·0[10]	14·2[9]	14·9[18]
5	57·0[7]	58·2[14]	59·4[6]	58·1[7]	57·3[4]	62·8[7]	33·2[10]	12·5[18]
7	8·2[10]	9·7[13]	8·4[4]	9·8[10]	8·3[7]	8·8[9]	13·2[9]	13·9[18]
8	20·3[10]	19·2[20]	19·7[8]	19·2[9]	18·7[6]	19·3[8]	12·9[8]	10·2[18]

* Superior figures to the right are the number of pictures measured from which the percentage averages here given are derived.

The two sets of data for 1844–46 seem similar enough. In only one case, dimension 5 for 1846, is the difference of the two sets of averaged measures more than 1·5.

The 1919 comparisons, however, show a startling difference of 20·7 in dimension 5: 33·2 against 12·5. Here Kroeber's data were taken solely from the March number of *Vogue*.[3] Four of these dresses had trains, six did not. His percentages run (* denoting train): 33; 22; 13† or *33; 10; 19 or *67; 16 or *60; 19 or *64; 17; 17; 9. He used the higher train widths for his average of 33·2. The Richardson series for 1919 was taken from *Vogue* of December 1918, and from *Costume Royal* for April and June, 1919. All eighteen of these illustrations have no trains and they average 12·5. The Kroeber average for the ten widths minus trains is 17·5. This is much nearer the Richardson value of 12·5, and it fits well between Kroeber 1918, 20·3, and Richardson 1920, 16·7.

The other larger discrepancies for 1919 are in skirt length: Kroeber 84·2, Richardson 89·4; and in *décolletage* width: Kroeber 12·9, Richardson 10·2. These we cannot explain, unless it be that since 1919 falls in a period of high individual variability, as shown by the standard deviations, any two samples of ten and eighteen plates, respectively, might well differ as much. The period adjacent to 1844–46 is one of much less fashion variability, hence the two sets of measurements coincide more closely.

On the whole, it seems that the sets of measurements of the two observers are sufficiently alike to be treated as parts of one series.

Another problem concerns the difference between the signed French and the anonymous American designs, as shown in any one magazine, and also what difference might exist between the magazines themselves. Table 2 shows such variations.

TABLE 2 *Comparability of Sources*

Dimen.	1919 *Vogue* ord. models (Dec. 1918)	1919 *Costume Royal* ord. mod. (Apr. June)	1919 *Costume Royal* French models (Apr. June)	1920 *Vogue* ord. models (Feb. May)	1920 *Costume Royal* ord. mod. (Apr. June)	1920 *Costume Royal* French models* (Apr. June)
2	89·7	91·0	87·7	83·3	83·0	79·7
3	24·9	26·0	25·1	26·4	26·1	27·4
4	17·5	13·2	14·0	16·4	15·3	13·7
5	12·6	10·0	14·9	15·2	17·6	15·7
7	13·8	13·0	14·8	14·5	14·9	14·6
8	11·1	9·0	10·5	12·2	12·5	13·0

* Includes one French model from *Vogue*.

On only one case does a range as great as 4·3 occur: No. 4, 1919, 17·5 and 13·2. This is about one and a half times the standard deviation for the period 1916–22: 3·6, 0·8, 2·1, 2·0, 2·5, 3·7, 4·6, mean 2·8. There is a suggestion that the French models of 1919 are closer to the ordinary ones of 1920: compare dimensions 2, 7. This may reflect the fact that the French models used in 1919 and 1920 are late spring models, and are already pointing the way to fashions of the following winter.

Our conclusion is that any difference between the Kroeber and Richardson measurements, and between models of different magazines, or dresses of French

† The smaller number given for the trained dress is the width of the skirt exclusive of the train. These measures are from the manuscript data.

and American design, seems to be less, on the whole, than the fashion changes from year to year. This also holds as regards the change in illustrations from drawings to photographs of living models in the second decade of the present century, on which Kroeber has previously given some sample data.[4]

Measurement Data

The data obtained from the several thousand measurements made by the two authors, respectively twenty years ago and more recently, will now be given in the form of means for each dimension or proportion in each year studied.

For instance, for 1806, eleven fashion plates or illustrations were found which showed length of skirt without impairment. These, in terms of the total length of figure as defined, ran to 95·0, 97·5, 98·5, 97·3, 98·0, 97·1, 97·4, 98·5, 99·5, 97·5, 98·4 per cent. (In other words, the first plate measured showed a 'length of figure' [from mouth down] of 119 mm., a length to bottom of skirt of 113 mm.; the second is 95·0 per cent of the first. The second plate happened also to have the figure length 119 mm.; but the skirt length 116, giving 97·5 per cent, and so on.) The mean of these eleven percentages is 97·7, which is therefore the value assigned to dimension No. 2 for 1806. Two of the eleven plates did not show the full width of skirt; the nine that did, yielded 25·2, 46·3, 13·0, 57·0, 35·6, 50·4, 48·5, 35·1, 35·2 per cent, whose mean, 38·4, is the dimension No. 5 value for 1806. The individual raw and percentaged measurements, as here cited in illustration, are being preserved, and the latter have of course been used in calculation of the standard deviations or variability coefficients presented and discussed on page 81; but they are not printed on account of cost. Their means for each dimension each year replace them.

These means, on which all our other quantitative expressions rest, are given in tables 3 and 4. The first of these two tables covers the period from 1787 to 1936, in which almost every consecutive year is represented and for most years the data are reasonably sufficient. (See figs. 1–2, pp. 59–60.) The second table covers the preceding one hundred and eighty-two years from 1605 to 1786, where the data are both discontinuous and fewer. In both these tables, the small superior figures at the right indicate the number of cases measured.

Next follow combinations of these year-by-year means into the averages for longer blocks of years. Table 5 covers the whole three hundred and thirty-two years in ten-year periods. (See figs. 3, 4, 5.) This seemed a better interval than five-year averagings on account of the irregularity of the data before 1787. It should be noted that these values, and all other averages of the year-by-year means, are unweighted for number of cases. For instance, for the decade 1641–50, only four dated illustrations were found: three for 1641 and one for 1647. In dimension 5, skirt width, the three for 1641 averaged 72·2, the one for 1647 was 78·0. The mean of these two values is 75·1, which is the one that will be found in table 5 for this decade; whereas the weighted average would be 73·7.

Table 6 gives the five-year means for the fuller period 1787–1926. Table 7 combines these by pairs into ten-year means. It is, however, not a mere replica of the last part of table 5, because the absolute dates are different: where table 5 treats the years 1881–90 as a unit, table 7 lumps 1877–86.

TABLE 3 *Ratio of Dress Diameters to Height of Figure: Year-by-year Means, 1787–1936*

Year	2 L.Sk.	3 L.Wai.	4 L.Dec.	5 W.Sk.	7 W.Wai.	8 W.Dec.
1787	98·7^3	27·4^3	7·2^3	56·3^4	11·2^1	7·9^1
1788	96·1^4	20·8^4	8·9^2	51·1^2	16·5^1	
1789	96·9^7	23·2^6	10·3^7	55·1^5	14·9^4	10·7^3
1790	98·6^8	25·8^6	7·9^7	51·0^7	9·9^5	7·6^1
1791	98·3^4	25·4^4	11·9^4	53·2^3	9·0^4	8·5^3
1792	98·5^1	25·4^2	9·8^1	58·4^2	9·3^2	
1793	98·1^3	23·7^4	5·3^3	52·1^3	10·6^4	
1794	100·0^2	18·8^2	9·9^2	43·3^2	14·4^2	9·7^2
1795	96·9^8	20·1^7	12·9^7	52·6^6	12·3^5	7·0^2
1796	98·2^5	20·6^4	10·2^4	43·8^3	18·0^1	
1797	99·4^3	20·7^2	13·3^2	49·3^3	14·9^2	8·0^1
1798	98·6^8	19·9^9	11·5^8	44·4^{10}	10·5^9	10·3^8
1799	97·7^{12}	19·4^{13}	11·6^{12}	42·7^7	11·2^{10}	9·5^{10}
1800	98·1^{11}	18·1^{11}	10·5^{11}	42·9^{11}	12·0^8	11·9^6
1801	96·4^7	17·9^6	15·5^4	42·2^6	16·0^2	11·9^2
1802	100·0^2	19·4^2	16·3^1	59·6^1	11·3^2	14·9^1
1803	97·7^{12}	19·0^{12}	12·6^{10}	38·5^8	12·8^8	13·0^8
1804	95·1^{10}	19·4^{10}	12·3^8	44·7^9	13·5^5	14·3^4
1805	97·3^{12}	18·3^{11}	14·4^{10}	35·0^7	14·8^5	14·3^6
1806	97·7^{11}	17·9^{11}	12·5^9	38·5^9	14·3^6	12·8^5
1807	96·5^{18}	18·3^{18}	11·0^{15}	37·8^{15}	15·2^8	14·7^6
1808	95·6^{10}	18·9^7	11·8^9	32·6^7	14·1^3	13·8^5
1809	95·8^{15}	17·4^{15}	11·7^{14}	24·8^{13}	15·1^{13}	13·7^{13}
1810	95·6^7	21·0^6	13·5^7	24·2^7	12·9^5	12·3^4
1811	94·4^8	21·7^7	13·3^6	27·2^8	13·5^7	15·0^5
1812	92·7^4	20·9^4	13·0^3	29·4^4	13·4^2	17·0^2
1813	88·0^3	19·2^3	11·1^3	28·9^3	14·4^3	19·8^3
1814	94·2^4	19·8^4	13·2^3	31·3^4	12·8^4	17·2^3
1815	92·9^5	17·3^5	11·9^4	45·8^5	13·6^3	15·2^5
1816	91·6^3	17·2^3	12·0^3	39·8^3	12·0^2	16·6^2
1817	94·7^2	20·1^2	16·5^2	42·9^2	13·5^1	9·6^2
1818	93·9^3	20·6^3	11·3^2	38·6^3	11·3^2	16·4^2
1819	90·1^1	15·5^1	13·2^1	41·1^1	10·1^1	16·3^1
1820	92·2^3	21·4^3	13·2^2	37·0^3	10·0^3	17·2^2
1821	96·4^3	21·7^3	10·1^2	42·7^3	11·2^2	17·8^3
1822						
1823	96·9^3	24·4^3	12·1^2	46·3^3	10·3^8	18·3^2
1824	92·5^2	21·5^2	13·8^2	38·1^2	12·4^2	18·1^2
1825	95·5^1	25·4^1	10·9^1	48·6^1	10·1^1	22·5^1
1826	95·0^2	25·2^2	10·8^2	48·5^2	10·4^2	17·0^2
1827	92·8^6	28·4^5	12·2^5	53·2^6	11·2^6	23·2^3
1828	90·4^{10}	26·7^{10}	12·2^8	49·6^{10}	10·0^6	21·3^9
1829	93·9^3	26·7^3	12·2^1	55·6^3	11·3^3	21·4^2
1830	93·7^9	27·9^9	12·2^4	48·7^8	12·1^8	24·7^2
1831	94·8^4	23·7^4	12·1^3	44·2^4	13·5^3	21·2^1
1832	90·8	26·4	12·9	54·4	11·0	23·8
1833						
1834	89·4^4	27·0^4	14·0^3	64·3^3	9·8^4	23·9^3

TABLE 3 (*continued*)

Year	2 L.Sk.	3 L.Wai.	4 L.Dec.	5 W.Sk.	7 W.Wai.	8 W.Dec.
1835	$92{\cdot}9^9$	$28{\cdot}0^9$	$12{\cdot}7^7$	$67{\cdot}0^9$	$9{\cdot}4^9$	$17{\cdot}0^7$
1836	$95{\cdot}9^{14}$	$26{\cdot}9^{13}$	$12{\cdot}9^{14}$	$70{\cdot}0^{12}$	$9{\cdot}4^9$	$17{\cdot}9^{10}$
1837	$95{\cdot}7^{11}$	$27{\cdot}3^{10}$	$13{\cdot}4^9$	$62{\cdot}3^8$	$9{\cdot}1^8$	$19{\cdot}1^6$
1838	$97{\cdot}0^{10}$	$28{\cdot}9^{10}$	$14{\cdot}0^8$	$70{\cdot}9^8$	$9{\cdot}1^5$	$19{\cdot}9^6$
1839	$97{\cdot}1^{14}$	$28{\cdot}7^{13}$	$14{\cdot}8^{13}$	$63{\cdot}6^{13}$	$9{\cdot}5^{10}$	$20{\cdot}7^{10}$
1840	$97{\cdot}0^{22}$	$28{\cdot}4^{21}$	$14{\cdot}3^{20}$	$63{\cdot}9^{15}$	$9{\cdot}0^{20}$	$20{\cdot}6^{18}$
1841	$96{\cdot}9^{26}$	$29{\cdot}1^{23}$	$14{\cdot}8^{26}$	$64{\cdot}6^{17}$	$8{\cdot}8^{17}$	$19{\cdot}3^{19}$
1842	$96{\cdot}9^{17}$	$29{\cdot}2^{13}$	$14{\cdot}5^{16}$	$60{\cdot}0^{14}$	$9{\cdot}1^9$	$18{\cdot}0^8$
1843	$97{\cdot}3^{24}$	$29{\cdot}0^{21}$	$14{\cdot}4^{22}$	$60{\cdot}1^{16}$	$9{\cdot}1^{16}$	$20{\cdot}7^{19}$
1844	$98{\cdot}2^{10}$	$28{\cdot}8^{10}$	$14{\cdot}4^{10}$	$58{\cdot}2^7$	$9{\cdot}0^{10}$	$19{\cdot}2^{10}$
1845	$97{\cdot}5^{10}$	$27{\cdot}9^{10}$	$14{\cdot}1^9$	$59{\cdot}4^6$	$8{\cdot}4^4$	$19{\cdot}8^8$
1846	$98{\cdot}3^9$	$28{\cdot}4^9$	$13{\cdot}1^8$	$57{\cdot}3^4$	$8{\cdot}3^7$	$18{\cdot}7^6$
1847	$98{\cdot}4^{10}$	$28{\cdot}9^9$	$14{\cdot}8^9$	$64{\cdot}8^4$	$8{\cdot}8^6$	$19{\cdot}6^8$
1848	$98{\cdot}0^{10}$	$27{\cdot}8^{10}$	$13{\cdot}4^{10}$	$59{\cdot}6^5$	$8{\cdot}5^8$	$20{\cdot}0^{10}$
1849	$97{\cdot}9^{10}$	$28{\cdot}7^{10}$	$13{\cdot}3^9$	$62{\cdot}7^6$	$8{\cdot}4^8$	$20{\cdot}0^9$
1850	$97{\cdot}8^{10}$	$28{\cdot}6^{10}$	$12{\cdot}7^{10}$	$64{\cdot}2^6$	$8{\cdot}3^8$	$20{\cdot}7^{10}$
1851	$98{\cdot}7^{10}$	$29{\cdot}4^{10}$	$13{\cdot}9^{10}$	$61{\cdot}3^7$	$8{\cdot}4^9$	$21{\cdot}2^8$
1852	$97{\cdot}6^{10}$	$27{\cdot}0^{10}$	$14{\cdot}1^9$	$70{\cdot}3^6$	$8{\cdot}3^{10}$	$21{\cdot}4^9$
1853	$98{\cdot}1^{10}$	$27{\cdot}7^{10}$	$12{\cdot}8^{10}$	$70{\cdot}2^6$	$7{\cdot}8^8$	$21{\cdot}2^9$
1854	$97{\cdot}9^{10}$	$27{\cdot}0^{10}$	$14{\cdot}1^{10}$	$79{\cdot}3^7$	$8{\cdot}4^9$	$20{\cdot}6^8$
1855	$98{\cdot}2^{10}$	$27{\cdot}9^{10}$	$13{\cdot}3^{10}$	$83{\cdot}0^4$	$9{\cdot}0^8$	$21{\cdot}0^{10}$
1856	$98{\cdot}3^9$	$27{\cdot}7^9$	$13{\cdot}4^7$	$89{\cdot}2^4$	$8{\cdot}6^5$	$19{\cdot}1^9$
1857	$98{\cdot}4^{10}$	$26{\cdot}7^{10}$	$13{\cdot}9^{10}$	$86{\cdot}2^5$	$8{\cdot}0^5$	$19{\cdot}6^{10}$
1858	$99{\cdot}6^{10}$	$26{\cdot}8^{10}$	$15{\cdot}2^{10}$	$100{\cdot}3^6$	$7{\cdot}9^7$	$18{\cdot}8^{10}$
1859	$100{\cdot}0^{10}$	$25{\cdot}3^9$	$14{\cdot}4^{10}$	$115{\cdot}6^9$	$7{\cdot}8^3$	$18{\cdot}3^8$
1860	$99{\cdot}8^{10}$	$24{\cdot}8^{10}$	$12{\cdot}3^{10}$	$107{\cdot}1^7$	$7{\cdot}6^5$	$18{\cdot}1^9$
1861	$100{\cdot}0^{10}$	$24{\cdot}9^{10}$	$12{\cdot}3^{10}$	$104{\cdot}3^9$	$8{\cdot}0^4$	$17{\cdot}8^{10}$
1862	$99{\cdot}6^{10}$	$24{\cdot}1^{10}$	$13{\cdot}2^{10}$	$96{\cdot}1^9$	$7{\cdot}6^8$	$17{\cdot}9^9$
1863	$98{\cdot}7^{10}$	$24{\cdot}9^7$	$13{\cdot}1^9$	$101{\cdot}6^9$	$9{\cdot}0^8$	$17{\cdot}1^9$
1864	$99{\cdot}5^{10}$	$23{\cdot}9^7$	$13{\cdot}5^9$	$100{\cdot}1^1$	$8{\cdot}5^5$	$18{\cdot}1^9$
1865	$99{\cdot}8^{10}$	$22{\cdot}8^9$	$12{\cdot}7^9$	$108{\cdot}6^1$	$8{\cdot}6^7$	$17{\cdot}5^8$
1866	$99{\cdot}8^9$	$22{\cdot}4^9$	$12{\cdot}8^{10}$	$99{\cdot}8^2$	$8{\cdot}2^9$	$18{\cdot}0^9$
1867	$97{\cdot}9^{10}$	$21{\cdot}2^{10}$	$11{\cdot}7^9$	$98{\cdot}7^9$	$8{\cdot}1^9$	$16{\cdot}7^9$
1868	$98{\cdot}8^{10}$	$22{\cdot}0^9$	$12{\cdot}7^7$	$88{\cdot}4^{10}$	$9{\cdot}0^8$	$16{\cdot}1^8$
1869	$100{\cdot}0^{10}$	$21{\cdot}8^{10}$	$13{\cdot}6^9$	$85{\cdot}5^8$	$9{\cdot}0^4$	$16{\cdot}0^7$
1870	$99{\cdot}1^9$	$22{\cdot}2^9$	$12{\cdot}0^8$	$88{\cdot}0^6$	$9{\cdot}2^4$	$18{\cdot}5^6$
1871	$99{\cdot}3^{10}$	$22{\cdot}0^9$	$13{\cdot}0^6$	$74{\cdot}9^8$	$9{\cdot}0^3$	$16{\cdot}4^5$
1872	$99{\cdot}3^{10}$	$22{\cdot}9^{10}$	$15{\cdot}0^6$	$77{\cdot}6^8$	$11{\cdot}0^3$	$16{\cdot}7^2$
1873	$99{\cdot}2^{10}$	$24{\cdot}5^{10}$	$13{\cdot}8^5$	$84{\cdot}8^{10}$	$10{\cdot}1^6$	$18{\cdot}3^3$
1874	$99{\cdot}2^9$	$22{\cdot}2^{10}$	$14{\cdot}1^7$	$84{\cdot}5^6$	$9{\cdot}5^3$	$15{\cdot}0^4$
1875	$100{\cdot}0^{10}$	$22{\cdot}3^9$	$14{\cdot}1^7$	$79{\cdot}0^7$	$10{\cdot}4^5$	$17{\cdot}0^5$
1876	$99{\cdot}2^{10}$	$23{\cdot}6^{10}$	$13{\cdot}4^7$	$84{\cdot}8^8$	$9{\cdot}5^4$	$13{\cdot}5^2$
1877	$98{\cdot}7^{10}$	$23{\cdot}8^{10}$	$13{\cdot}5^6$	$76{\cdot}4^{10}$	$8{\cdot}7^6$	$13{\cdot}7^6$
1878	$99{\cdot}0^{10}$	$24{\cdot}8^{10}$	$14{\cdot}5^6$	$70{\cdot}9^8$	$8{\cdot}9^6$	$14{\cdot}6^8$
1879	$98{\cdot}7^{10}$	$26{\cdot}1^{10}$	$13{\cdot}3^6$	$62{\cdot}0^5$	$8{\cdot}8^8$	$15{\cdot}0^8$
1880	$98{\cdot}8^{10}$	$27{\cdot}6^{10}$	$15{\cdot}4^6$	$68{\cdot}8^6$	$8{\cdot}8^8$	$14{\cdot}1^8$
1881	$97{\cdot}7^{10}$	$27{\cdot}6^{10}$	$14{\cdot}2^7$	$52{\cdot}3^7$	$8{\cdot}5^9$	$14{\cdot}7^6$
1882	$96{\cdot}6^{10}$	$26{\cdot}0^{10}$	$12{\cdot}8^8$	$56{\cdot}0^8$	$7{\cdot}8^7$	$15{\cdot}3^7$
1883	$96{\cdot}9^{10}$	$26{\cdot}0^{10}$	$12{\cdot}8^9$	$54{\cdot}7^7$	$8{\cdot}6^8$	$17{\cdot}3^7$
1884	$96{\cdot}4^{10}$	$26{\cdot}2^{10}$	$13{\cdot}1^9$	$52{\cdot}2^9$	$8{\cdot}2^6$	$14{\cdot}5^5$

TABLE 3 (*continued*)

Year	2 L.Sk.	3 L.Wai.	4 L.Dec.	5 W.Sk.	7 W.Wai.	8 W.Dec.
1885	97·0[10]	27·4[10]	14·0[7]	56·0[6]	8·7[8]	15·2[5]
1886	95·8[9]	27·3[10]	14·9[9]	56·6[9]	8·9[10]	14·8[8]
1887	95·6[10]	27·2[10]	12·9[8]	50·9[9]	8·3[8]	14·2[8]
1888	95·7[10]	27·6[10]	14·1[9]	57·8[8]	8·3[10]	13·1[9]
1889	96·7[10]	27·7[10]	13·7[10]	51·5[9]	9·6[8]	13·2[9]
1890	97·3[10]	28·2[10]	14·1[8]	50·2[10]	8·5[10]	13·5[8]
1891	97·3[10]	28·3[10]	14·4[9]	53·7[9]	9·2[10]	12·6[5]
1892	97·4[10]	28·8[10]	13·4[7]	51·1[10]	9·2[10]	14·3[9]
1893	98·8[10]	27·0[10]	13·6[8]	55·0[10]	9·3[9]	13·3[8]
1894	98·2[10]	28·8[10]	14·0[9]	55·5[10]	9·2[10]	14·0[9]
1895	98·7[10]	27·4[10]	14·0[9]	60·7[9]	8·6[7]	15·0[7]
1896	99·2[10]	27·9[10]	14·3[10]	68·3[8]	9·6[7]	15·2[9]
1897	99·9[10]	28·9[10]	14·4[10]	60·0[10]	8·6[9]	15·8[10]
1898	99·8[10]	29·5[10]	14·7[10]	53·0[10]	8·1[8]	11·9[9]
1899	100·0[10]	29·7[10]	14·6[9]	65·3[10]	9·3[9]	12·5[10]
1900	99·3[10]	30·5[10]	15·1[10]	52·5[10]	8·7[10]	13·4[9]
1901	99·7[10]	30·5[10]	12·5[10]	64·8[10]	9·4[10]	13·3[10]
1902	100·0[10]	30·1[10]	13·1[9]	58·9[10]	9·9[8]	11·1[6]
1903	100·0[10]	32·6[9]	15·2[9]	50·4[10]	9·6[8]	13·0[7]
1904	100·0[10]	32·3[10]	14·0[9]	56·5[10]	9·9[8]	14·8[7]
1905	100·0[10]	30·3[10]	14·6[10]	53·7[10]	9·2[9]	15·3[8]
1906	99·6[10]	28·8[10]	16·2[5]	56·0[10]	9·5[8]	11·2[5]
1907	99·6[10]	28·0[10]	13·3[9]	51·2[10]	9·7[6]	12·3[7]
1908	99·3[10]	25·4[9]	11·7[9]	49·0[10]	10·9[8]	12·9[8]
1909	99·7[10]	24·3[10]	14·6[7]	38·4[10]	12·8[9]	12·1[10]
1910	99·2[10]	25·2[10]	13·3[8]	32·9[9]	11·7[9]	13·0[9]
1911	98·7[10]	26·1[10]	14·2[6]	23·2[10]	12·0[9]	12·2[6]
1912	98·3[10]	24·3[10]	13·4[9]	27·4[10]	13·2[9]	11·5[7]
1913	92·6[9]	25·5[10]	15·4[7]	33·7[7]	13·6[9]	13·3[10]
1914	91·8[9]	25·3[10]	14·4[7]	29·1[7]	13·9[10]	15·2[4]
1915	91·1[10]	24·4[9]	16·2[6]	46·1[10]	13·7[9]	11·2[5]
1916	84·3[10]	25·0[9]	16·4[9]	49·1[10]	12·6[9]	12·3[6]
1917	88·1[10]	24·3[8]	14·8[9]	55·7[4]	13·0[9]	11·4[7]
1918	85·3[10]	24·2[10]	13·7[9]	20·3[8]	13·4[10]	10·6[8]
1919	84·2[10]	24·1[10]	14·2[9]	33·2[10]	13·2[9]	12·9[8]
1920	82·2[17]	26·5[17]	15·0[17]	16·8[17]	14·7[17]	12·9[17]
1921	83·1[21]	27·9[21]	13·4[21]	26·0[21]	15·2[21]	14·7[21]
1922	86·0[14]	33·3[14]	14·3[14]	26·4[14]	16·5[14]	13·1[14]
1923	90·7[10]	30·9[10]	13·3[10]	22·4[10]	15·4[10]	14·8[10]
1924	85·6[13]	38·0[13]	13·0[13]	21·3[13]	15·9[13]	13·3[13]
1925	77·0[10]	35·5[10]	12·6[10]	22·0[10]	15·6[10]	12·6[10]
1926	72·2[11]	31·9[11]	15·8[11]	16·5[11]	14·2[11]	12·3[11]
1927	69·7[11]	37·9[11]	13·0[11]	18·0[11]	13·8[11]	11·2[11]
1928	70·0[10]	36·2[10]	15·0[10]	21·2[10]	14·7[10]	12·1[10]
1929	71·2[20]	32·5[20]	13·0[20]	26·0[20]	13·4[20]	11·1[10]
1930	89·0[20]	28·1[20]	14·6[20]	25·9[20]	16·5[20]	11·7[20]
1931	95·1[13]	26·8[12]	14·9[12]	26·0[12]	13·0[12]	12·8[12]
1932	97·3[10]	24·4[10]	11·4[10]	25·8[10]	11·0[10]	10·3[10]
1933	98·3[10]	25·0[10]	11·2[10]	25·9[10]	13·1[10]	13·2[10]
1934	99·3[10]	25·0[10]	9·3[10]	26·2[10]	13·7[10]	11·8[10]
1935	98·2[17]	25·2[16]	11·1[19]	38·7[16]	9·9[12]	11·4[12]
1936	98·8[25]	25·3[23]	11·8[22]	33·8[21]	10·7[17]	9·8[16]

TABLE 4 *Year-by-year Means, 1605–1786*

Year	2	3	4	5	7	8
1605	100·0	23·5	7·0	76·4		
1610	97·1[2]	19·4[2]	3·6[2]	68·1	11·6[2]	5·8[2]
1613	95·9	22·5	8·5	78·9	14·1	8·5
1617	100.0	21·7	2·8		13·0	5·7
1622–27	100·0[2]	25·2[2]	3·7[2]		13·6	7·9
1625		26·5	16·3		16·3	
1628	96·4	28·6	2·4	53·5	14·3	4·8
1629	97·4[4]	25·9[2]	7·6[4]	41·7[3]	11·3	6·7[3]
1630	100·0	25·9	2·8		11·1	5·5
1631	100·0[2]	23·7[2]	4·8[2]	54·5[2]		6·3[2]
1633	99·2[3]	24·3[3]	13·2[3]	49·6[2]	14·8	16·3[3]
1634	97·8[3]	22·6[3]	6·7[3]	50·4[3]		7·6[3]
1635	100·0[4]	24·1[4]	9·7[4]	52·6		13·0[4]
1636	100·0[2]	21·2[2]	13·1	35·6		16·2
1638	100·0	24·1	11·1	63·0		14·8
1639	100·0[3]	23·5[3]	14·1[3]	52·2[3]		15·5[3]
1640	99·0[3]	23·9[4]	14·2	46·4[4]		14·2[2]
1641	100·0[3]	26·1[2]	10·1[3]	72·2[3]	15·8	13·7[3]
1647	100·0	27·1	3·1	78·0		9·3
1656–57	100·0	36·6	10·0	87·5	17·5	
1658	100·0	27·4	6·8	82·2	11·7	10·9
1659	100·0	29·2	9·0	126·2	16·2	22·2
1660	100·0[2]	29·7[2]	12·2[2]	88·9[2]		18·8[2]
1666	100·0	32·2	11·3	58·0		
1667	98·4		6·9	45·0		
1668	100·0	30·2	15·1	75·5		22·6
1678	97·5	33·3	15·4	33·4	10·2	
1679	97·6[2]	23·3	11·6	40·0[2]		
1680	96·2	31·5	14·8	40·8	9·3	16·7
1683	97·3[2]	29·1[2]	12·3	30·1[2]	12·4[2]	
1685	100·0		13·1	63·7	11·9	
1686	99·2	29·1		48·7		
1710–16	99·4[9]	24·9[7]	13·7[5]	52·6[5]	13·6[4]	13·6[3]
1711	96·5	29·0	15·3	73·8	11·9	14·5
1714	97·5[2]	25·3[2]	10·0	25·5	10·0	10·0
1715	100·0[2]	26·7[2]		46·4[2]	17·4	13·0
1716–18	98·7[2]	25·7[2]	12·1	58·3[2]	10·7	
1717	96·4	21·4	14·3	50·0		
1719	100·0			46·5		
1720	100·0[2]	29·4	15·0[2]	97·0	14·7	14·7
1721	89·6			62·3		
1726	100·0	26·6	18·3			15·0
1728	100·0		10·5	57·9		
1731	92·8[2]		12·9	61·3[2]		
1734	98·0[3]	26·1[3]	15·3[2]	76·4	12·5[2]	13·2
1735	96·2[2]	28·8[3]	13·5[2]	66·6	12·8	13·8
1738	96·4[4]	27·9[5]	16·4[5]	54·2[4]	16·7	10·9[3]

TABLE 4 (*continued*)

Year	2	3	4	5	7	8
1739	97·0	28·2	13·4		13·4	23·9
1740	99·0	28·6	14·3	64·3	13·4	11·6
1742	93·8²	25·6²	7·7	134·5	10·8	
1743		27·5	13·3		14·2	10·0
1744	100·0	24·3	14·2	70·0	11·4	
1744–45	96·4		12·5	91·0		7·1
1749	95·6	28·6	14·2	102·9	12·9	20·0
1750	97·2²	25·2	15·4²	101·0		18·7
1751	96·5	30·1	15·1	100·7	12·3	21·2
1752	98·5²	26·2²	14·4²	44·9	14·3	12·3
1753	93·5²	26·9²	10·9	31·8²	10·0	
1755	95·2²	30·3³	16·7	59·0³	13·0	8·8
1757	91·4	27·5	14·7	58·4		14·3
1758	97·2	31·2	12·2	39·7		
1759	98·0	30·2	17·4	80·3	14·5	13·0
1761	89·5	25·0	16·8	65·1	14·5	12·2
1762–64	92·3	25·0	15·6²	72·3	12·7²	11·5
1765	94·5³	27·3³	13·1³	65·9	12·3²	10·9³
1766	97·6		14·9	35·6		
1767	95·5		11·5	48·4		
1769	95·5	31·4²	15·2²	59·0		9·6
1770	98·4	22·1	11·6	34·8		8·8
1771	98·5	30·8	19·2	40·0		
1772	95·0	28·9	16·5	101·0	16·5	
1773	91·8⁷	24·8⁶	11·8⁶	46·4⁷	13·6	9·8²
1775	96·5⁵	26·3²	13·8⁵	57·6⁴	12·9	6·8
1776	95·9³	27·9³	16·0³	72·5²	10·3²	12·4²
1777	95·4⁵	26·8⁴	12·8⁵	77·0³	10·7³	9·9⁴
1778	92·4²	33·5²	18·4²	55·3²	10·9	8·7
1779	92·3²	30·8²	16·5²	41·6²		
1780	90·3³	26·6³	15·5³	57·9³	8·6	8·3²
1781	92·2²	23·9	16·4	57·5		10·5
1784	93·3⁴	24·4⁴	11·0³	50·0²	9·2	11·0²
1786	97·4	23·7	8·8	36·8		

Next comes the 'trend' or moving average, in table 8. Here the value for any given dimension for 1840 is the average of the values for 1838, 1839, 1840, 1841, 1842 as found in table 3; for 1841, of 1839, 1840, 1841, 1842, 1843. In this way, the 'exceptionalness' of any single year is minimized by its being merged with the years on either side, and a smoother curve results. For instance, from 1846 to 1855 skirt length was to all intents and purposes at a stand-still. The individual year 1852 comes out, in the measurements that happened to be made, somewhat lower than any other in that decade: 97·6 as against nine others ranging from 97·8 to 98·7. It is doubtful whether a fluctuation so small as this is either significant or reliable. The moving average, which stays at 98·0, 98·1, 98·2 for the decade, probably gives a truer picture of the events. On account of its much greater steadiness, its variations are also much more readily grasped,

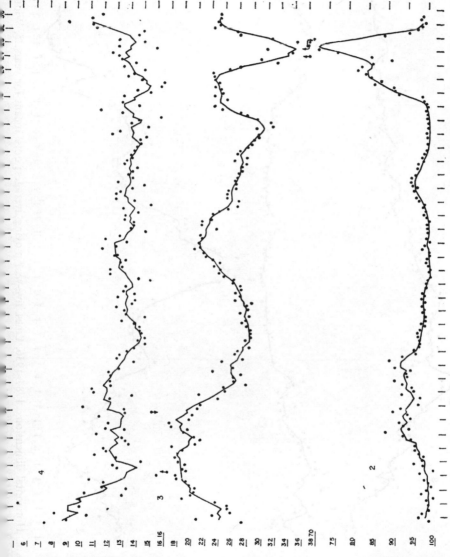

FIG. 1. Vertical dimensions, 1787–1936. Lines, five-year moving averages; dots, means for years. 2, Length of skirt; 3, of waist; 4 of *décolletage.*

59

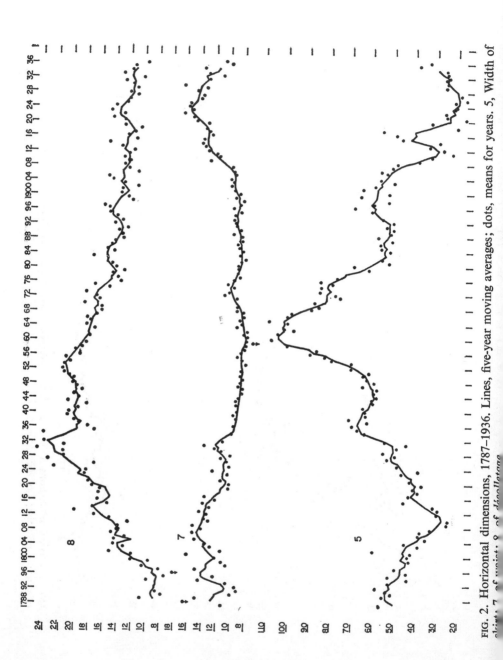

FIG. 2. Horizontal dimensions, 1787–1936. Lines, five-year moving averages; dots, means for years. 5, Width of skirt 7 of waist 8 of décolletage

TABLE 5 *Ten-year Averages, 1605–1936**

Period	2	3	4	5	7	8
1605–10	$98 \cdot 6^3$	$21 \cdot 5^3$	$5 \cdot 3^3$	$72 \cdot 3^2$	$11 \cdot 6^2$	$5 \cdot 8^2$
1611–20	$98 \cdot 0^2$	$22 \cdot 1^2$	$5 \cdot 7^2$	$78 \cdot 9^1$	$13 \cdot 6^2$	$7 \cdot 1^2$
1621–30	$98 \cdot 5^8$	$26 \cdot 4^7$	$6 \cdot 6^9$	$47 \cdot 6^4$	$13 \cdot 3^5$	$6 \cdot 2^6$
1631–40	$99 \cdot 5^{21}$	$23 \cdot 4^{22}$	$10 \cdot 9^{18}$	$50 \cdot 5^{17}$	$14 \cdot 8^1$	$13 \cdot 0^{19}$
1641–50	$100 \cdot 0^4$	$26 \cdot 6^3$	$6 \cdot 6^4$	$75 \cdot 1^4$	$15 \cdot 8^1$	$11 \cdot 5^4$
1651–60	$100 \cdot 0^5$	$30 \cdot 7^5$	$9 \cdot 5^5$	$96 \cdot 2^5$	$14 \cdot 0^2$	$17 \cdot 4^5$
1661–70	$99 \cdot 5^3$	$31 \cdot 2^2$	$11 \cdot 1^3$	$59 \cdot 5^3$		$22 \cdot 6^1$
1671–80	$97 \cdot 1^4$	$29 \cdot 4^3$	$13 \cdot 9^3$	$38 \cdot 1^4$	$9 \cdot 8^2$	$16 \cdot 7^1$
1681–90	$98 \cdot 8^4$	$29 \cdot 2^3$	$12 \cdot 7^2$	$47 \cdot 5^4$	$12 \cdot 2^3$	
1691–1700						
1701–10						
1711–20	$98 \cdot 6^{20}$	$26 \cdot 1^{16}$	$13 \cdot 4^{11}$	$56 \cdot 3^{15}$	$13 \cdot 1^9$	$13 \cdot 2^7$
1721–30	$96 \cdot 5^3$	$26 \cdot 6^1$	$14 \cdot 4^2$	$60 \cdot 1^2$		$15 \cdot 0^1$
1731–40	$96 \cdot 6^{14}$	$27 \cdot 9^{13}$	$14 \cdot 3^{12}$	$60 \cdot 7^9$	$13 \cdot 8^6$	$14 \cdot 7^7$
1741–50	$96 \cdot 6^7$	$26 \cdot 2^6$	$12 \cdot 9^7$	$99 \cdot 9^5$	$12 \cdot 3^4$	$14 \cdot 0^4$
1751–60	$95 \cdot 8^{10}$	$28 \cdot 9^{11}$	$14 \cdot 5^8$	$60 \cdot 2^{10}$	$12 \cdot 8^5$	$13 \cdot 9^5$
1761–70	$94 \cdot 8^9$	$26 \cdot 3^8$	$14 \cdot 1^{11}$	$54 \cdot 4^7$	$13 \cdot 2^5$	$10 \cdot 6^7$
1771–80	$94 \cdot 2^{29}$	$28 \cdot 5^{24}$	$15 \cdot 6^{28}$	$50 \cdot 9^{26}$	$11 \cdot 9^{10}$	$9 \cdot 3^{12}$
1781–90	$96 \cdot 2^{29}$	$24 \cdot 2^{25}$	$10 \cdot 1^{24}$	$51 \cdot 1^{21}$	$12 \cdot 3^{12}$	$9 \cdot 5^8$
1791–1800	$98 \cdot 4^{57}$	$21 \cdot 2^{58}$	$10 \cdot 7^{54}$	$48 \cdot 3^{49}$	$12 \cdot 2^{47}$	$9 \cdot 3^{32}$
1801–10	$96 \cdot 8^{104}$	$18 \cdot 8^{98}$	$13 \cdot 2^{97}$	$37 \cdot 8^{82}$	$14 \cdot 0^{57}$	$13 \cdot 6^{54}$
1811–20	$92 \cdot 5^{36}$	$19 \cdot 4^{35}$	$12 \cdot 9^{29}$	$36 \cdot 2^{36}$	$12 \cdot 5^{28}$	$16 \cdot 0^{27}$
1821–30	$94 \cdot 1^{39}$	$25 \cdot 3^{38}$	$11 \cdot 8^{27}$	$47 \cdot 9^{38}$	$11 \cdot 0^{31}$	$20 \cdot 5^{26}$
1831–40	$94 \cdot 5^{91}$	$27 \cdot 3^{86}$	$13 \cdot 5^{80}$	$62 \cdot 3^{75}$	$10 \cdot 0^{70}$	$20 \cdot 5^{63}$
1841–50	$97 \cdot 7^{136}$	$28 \cdot 6^{125}$	$14 \cdot 0^{130}$	$61 \cdot 1^{87}$	$8 \cdot 7^{92}$	$19 \cdot 6^{107}$
1851–60	$98 \cdot 7^{99}$	$27 \cdot 0^{98}$	$13 \cdot 7^{96}$	$86 \cdot 3^{61}$	$8 \cdot 2^{70}$	$19 \cdot 9^{90}$
1861–70	$99 \cdot 3^{98}$	$23 \cdot 0^{90}$	$12 \cdot 8^{85}$	$97 \cdot 1^{86}$	$8 \cdot 5^{62}$	$17 \cdot 4^{82}$
1871–80	$99 \cdot 1^{99}$	$24 \cdot 0^{98}$	$14 \cdot 0^{62}$	$76 \cdot 4^{75}$	$9 \cdot 5^{52}$	$15 \cdot 4^{52}$
1881–90	$96 \cdot 6^{96}$	$27 \cdot 1^{100}$	$13 \cdot 7^{84}$	$53 \cdot 8^{83}$	$8 \cdot 5^{83}$	$14 \cdot 6^{72}$
1891–1900	$98 \cdot 9^{100}$	$28 \cdot 7^{100}$	$14 \cdot 3^{91}$	$57 \cdot 5^{96}$	$9 \cdot 0^{89}$	$13 \cdot 8^{85}$
1901–10	$99 \cdot 7^{100}$	$28 \cdot 8^{98}$	$13 \cdot 9^{85}$	$51 \cdot 2^{99}$	$10 \cdot 3^{84}$	$12 \cdot 9^{74}$
1911–20	$89 \cdot 7^{103}$	$25 \cdot 0^{103}$	$14 \cdot 8^{88}$	$33 \cdot 5^{104}$	$13 \cdot 3^{100}$	$12 \cdot 4^{77}$
1921–30	$79 \cdot 5^{140}$	$33 \cdot 2^{104}$	$13 \cdot 8^{140}$	$22 \cdot 6^{140}$	$15 \cdot 1^{140}$	$12 \cdot 7^{140}$
1931–36	$97 \cdot 8^{85}$	$25 \cdot 3^{81}$	$11 \cdot 6^{83}$	$29 \cdot 4^{79}$	$11 \cdot 9^{71}$	$11 \cdot 6^{70}$

* To 1780, all the percentaged means within a decade have been averaged, irrespective of the year means in table 4. From 1781, the values are averaged from the year means for each decade as given in tables 4 and 3.

when they do become appreciable. Take for example the moving average of waist length for 1923–32, which runs, slightly rounded from table 8: 33, 34, 35, 36, 35, 34, 33, 30, 28, 26, as against the year-by-year values of 30, 38, 36, 32, 38, 36, 33, 28, 27, 24 of table 3. The smoothed or idealized moving-average series brings out 1926 as the peak of the curve. In the actual figures this is, however, low year for the series of six from 1924 to 1929, and the peak is left double and indeterminate between 1924 and 1927. We assume that there are statistical techniques expressing the probability and improbability of 1926 really being a year of temporary recession near the climax of the curve or on the

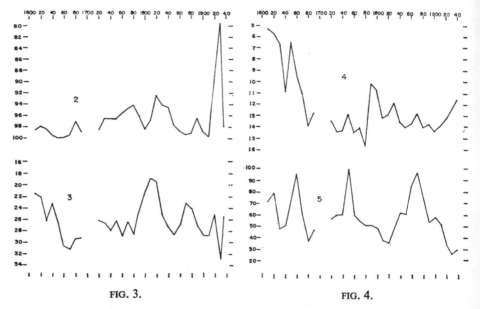

FIG. 3.

FIG. 4.

FIG. 3. Skirt length and waist length, dimensions 2 and 3, by ten-year means, 1605–1936.

FIG. 4. *Décolletage* depth and skirt width, dimensions 4 and 5, by ten-year means, 1605–1936.

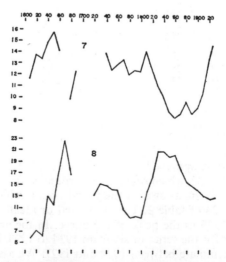

FIG. 5. Waist width and *décolletage* width, dimensions 7 and 8, by ten-year means, 1605–1936.

TABLE 6 *Five-year Averages, 1788–1936*

Period	2	3	4	5	7	8
1788–91	97·7	*24·5	†9·2	53·3	12·3	8·7
1792–96	*98·3	21·7	9·6	50·0	12·9	8·4
1797–1801	98·0	19·2	12·5	44·3	12·9	10·3
1802–06	97·6	†18·8	*13·6	43·3	13·3	13·9
1807–11	95·6	19·5	12·3	†29·3	*14·1	13·9
1812–16	†91·9	18·9	12·2	35·0	13·2	17·2
1817–21	93·5	19·9	12·9	40·5	11·2	15·5
1822–26	95·0	24·1	†11·9	45·4	10·8	19·0
1827–31	93·1	26·7	12·2	50·3	11·6	*22·4
1832–36	92·3	27·1	13·1	63·9	9·9	20·7
1837–41	96·7	28·5	14·3	65·1	9·1	19·9
1842–46	97·6	*28·7	14·1	59·0	8·8	19·3
1847–51	98·2	*28·7	13·6	62·5	8·5	20·3
1852–56	98·0	27·5	13·5	78·4	8·4	20·7
1857–61	*99·6	25·7	13·6	*102·7	†7·9	18·5
1862–66	99·5	23·6	13·4	101·2	8·4	17·7
1867–71	99·0	†21·8	12·6	87·1	8·9	16·7
1872–76	99·4	23·1	14·1	82·1	10·1	16·1
1877–81	98·6	26·0	14·2	66·1	8·7	14·4
1882–86	†96·5	26·6	13·5	55·1	8·4	15·4
1887–91	†96·5	27·8	13·8	52·8	8·8	13·3
1892–96	98·5	28·0	13·9	58·1	9·2	14·4
1897–1901	99·7	29·9	14·3	59·1	8·8	13·4
1902–06	*99·9	*30·8	*14·6	55·1	9·6	13·1
1907–11	99·3	25·8	13·4	38·9	11·4	12·5
1912–16	91·6	†24·9	15·2	37·1	13·4	12·7
1917–21	84·6	25·4	14·2	30·4	13·9	12·5
1922–26	82·3	*33·9	13·8	†21·7	*15·5	13·2
1927–31	†79·0	32·3	14·1	23·4	14·3	11·8
1932–36	98·4	25·0	†11·0	30·1	11·8	†11·3

* High points.   † Low points.

TABLE 7 *Ten-year Averages, 1788–1936, by Decades Ending in 6*

Period	2	3	4	5	7	8
1788–96	98·3	23·1	9·4	51·7	12·6	8·5
1797–1806	97·8	19·0	13·1	43·8	13·1	12·1
1807–16	93·7	19·2	12·3	32·2	13·7	15·5
1817–26	94·1	21·8	12·4	42·6	11·0	17·0
1827–36	92·7	26·9	12·6	56·3	10·9	21·6
1837–46	97·2	28·6	14·2	62·0	8·9	19·6
1847–56	98·1	28·1	13·6	70·5	8·5	20·5
1857–66	99·5	24·7	13·3	102·0	8·1	18·1
1867–76	99·2	22·5	13·4	84·6	9·5	16·4
1877–86	97·6	26·3	13·9	60·6	8·6	14·9
1887–96	97·5	27·9	13·9	55·5	9·0	13·8
1897–1906	99·8	30·3	14·4	57·1	9·2	13·2
1907–16	95·5	25·4	14·3	38·0	12·4	12·6
1917–26	83·4	29·7	14·0	26·1	14·7	12·9
1927–36	88·7	28·6	12·5	26·8	13·0	11·5

TABLE 8 *Five-year Moving Average of Dress Diameters, 1788–1934*

Year	2 L.Sk.	3 L.Wai.	4 L.Dec.	5 W.Sk.	7 W.Wai.	8 W.Dec.
1788	97·5	24·2	†8·6	50·1	12·5	
1789	97·7	24·5	9·2	53·3	12·3	8·7
1790	97·7	24·1	9·8	53·8	11·9	8·9
1791	98·1	*24·7	9·0	*54·0	10·7	8·9
1792	*98·7	23·8	9·0	51·6	10·6	8·6
1793	98·4	22·7	10·0	51·9	11·1	8·4
1794	98·3	21·7	9·6	50·0	12·9	8·4
1795	98·5	20·8	10·3	48·2	14·0	†8·2
1796	98·6	20·0	11·6	46·7	14·0	8·8
1797	98·2	20·1	11·9	46·6	13·4	8·7
1798	98·4	19·7	11·4	44·6	13·3	9·9
1799	98·0	19·2	12·5	44·3	12·9	10·3
1800	98·2	18·9	13·1	46·4	12·2	11·7
1801	98·0	18·8	13·3	45·2	12·7	12·2
1802	97·5	18·8	13·4	45·6	13·1	13·2
1803	97·3	18·8	*14·2	44·9	13·7	13·7
1804	97·6	18·8	13·6	43·3	13·3	13·8
1805	96·9	18·6	12·6	38·9	14·1	11·8
1806	96·4	18·6	12·4	37·7	14·4	14·0
1807	96·6	18·2	12·3	33·7	*14·7	13·9
1808	96·2	18·7	12·1	31·6	14·3	13·5
1809	95·6	19·5	12·3	29·3	14·1	13·9
1810	95·8	20·0	12·7	27·6	13·8	14·4
1811	93·3	20·0	12·5	†26·9	13·8	15·6
1812	93·0	20·5	12·8	28·2	13·4	16·3
1813	92·4	19·8	12·5	32·5	13·5	16·8
1814	†91·9	18·9	12·2	35·0	13·2	17·2
1815	92·3	18·7	12·9	37·7	13·3	15·7
1816	93·5	19·0	13·0	39·7	12·6	15·0
1817	92·6	†18·1	13·0	41·6	12·1	14·8
1818	92·5	19·0	13·2	39·9	11·4	15·2
1819	93·5	19·9	12·9	40·5	11·2	15·5
1820	93·2	19·8	12·0	39·9	10·7	16·9
1821	93·9	20·8	12·2	41·8	10·4	17·4
1822	94·5	22·3	12·3	41·0	11·0	17·9
1823	95·3	23·3	†11·7	43·9	11·0	19·2
1824	95·0	24·1	11·9	45·4	10·8	19·0
1825	94·5	25·0	12·0	46·9	10·9	19·8
1826	93·2	25·4	12·0	47·6	10·8	20·4
1827	93·5	26·5	†11·7	51·1	10·6	21·1
1828	93·2	27·0	11·9	51·1	11·0	21·5
1829	93·1	26·7	12·2	50·3	11·6	22·4
1830	92·7	26·3	12·3	50·5	11·6	22·5
1831	93·3	26·2	12·4	50·7	12·0	22·8
1832	92·2	26·3	12·8	54·9	11·6	*23·4
1833	92·0	26·2	12·9	57·5	10·9	21·5
1834	92·3	27·1	13·1	63·9	9·9	20·7
1835	93·5	27·3	13·3	65·9	9·4	19·5
1836	94·2	27·6	13·4	66·9	9·4	19·6

* High points   † Low points.

TABLE 8 (*continued*)

Year	2 L.Sk.	3 L.Wai.	4 L.Dec.	5 W.Sk.	7 W.Wai.	8 W.Dec.
1837	95·7	28·0	13·6	66·8	9·3	18·9
1838	96·5	28·0	13·9	66·1	9·2	19·6
1839	96·7	28·5	14·3	65·1	9·1	19·9
1840	97·0	*28·9	14·5	64·6	9·1	19·7
1841	97·0	*28·9	*14·6	62·4	9·1	19·9
1842	97·3	*28·9	14·5	61·4	9·0	19·6
1843	97·4	28·8	14·4	60·5	8·9	19·4
1844	97·6	28·7	14·1	59·0	8·8	19·3
1845	97·9	28·6	14·2	60·0	8·7	19·6
1846	98·1	28·4	14·0	59·9	8·6	19·5
1847	98·0	28·3	13·7	60·8	8·5	19·6
1848	98·1	28·5	13·5	61·7	8·5	19·8
1849	98·2	28·7	13·6	62·5	8·5	20·3
1850	98·0	28·3	13·5	63·6	8·4	20·7
1851	98·0	28·3	13·4	65·7	8·2	20·9
1852	98·0	27·9	13·5	69·1	8·3	21·0
1853	98·1	27·8	13·6	72·8	8·4	21·1
1854	98·0	27·5	13·5	78·4	8·4	20·7
1855	98·2	27·4	13·5	81·6	8·4	20·3
1856	98·5	27·2	14·0	87·6	8·4	19·8
1857	98·9	26·9	14·0	94·9	8·3	19·4
1858	99·2	26·3	13·8	99·7	8·0	18·8
1859	99·6	25·7	13·6	102·7	7·9	18·5
1860	*99·8	25·2	13·5	104·7	†7·8	18·2
1861	99·6	24·8	13·1	*104·9	8·0	17·8
1862	99·5	24·5	12·9	101·8	8·1	17·8
1863	99·5	24·1	13·0	102·1	8·3	17·7
1864	99·5	23·6	13·1	101·2	8·4	17·7
1865	99·1	23·0	12·8	101·8	8·5	17·5
1866	99·2	22·5	12·7	99·1	8·5	17·3
1867	99·4	22·4	12·7	96·2	8·6	16·9
1868	99·1	21·9	†12·6	92·1	8·7	17·1
1869	99·0	†21·8	†12·6	87·1	8·9	16·7
1870	99·3	22·2	13·3	82·9	9·4	16·7
1871	99·4	22·7	13·5	82·2	9·7	17·2
1872	99·2	22·8	13·6	82·0	9·8	17·0
1873	99·4	22·8	14·0	80·2	10·0	16·7
1874	99·4	23·1	14·1	82·1	10·1	16·1
1875	99·3	23·3	13·8	81·9	9·6	15·5
1876	99·2	23·3	13·9	79·1	9·4	14·8
1877	99·1	24·1	13·8	74·6	9·3	14·8
1878	98·9	25·2	14·0	72·6	8·9	14·2
1879	98·6	26·0	14·2	66·1	8·7	14·4
1880	98·2	26·4	14·0	62·0	8·6	14·7
1881	97·7	26·7	13·7	58·8	8·5	15·3
1882	97·3	26·7	13·7	56·8	8·4	15·2
1883	96·9	26·6	13·4	54·2	8·4	15·4
1884	96·5	26·6	13·5	55·1	8·4	15·4
1885	96·3	26·8	13·5	54·1	8·5	15·2

* High points.   † Low points.

5

TABLE 8 (*continued*)

Year	2 L.Sk.	3 L.Wai.	4 L.Dec.	5 W.Sk.	7 W.Wai.	8 W.Dec.
1886	†96·1	27·1	13·8	55·7	8·5	14·3
1887	96·2	27·4	13·9	55·6	8·8	14·1
1888	96·2	27·6	13·9	53·4	8·7	13·8
1889	96·5	27·8	13·8	52·8	8·8	13·3
1890	96·9	28·1	13·9	52·9	9·0	13·3
1891	97·5	28·0	13·8	52·3	9·2	13·4
1892	97·8	28·2	13·9	53·1	9·1	13·5
1893	98·1	28·1	13·9	55·2	9·1	13·8
1894	98·5	28·0	13·9	58·1	9·2	14·6
1895	99·0	28·0	14·1	59·9	9·1	14·7
1896	99·2	28·5	14·3	59·5	8·8	14·4
1897	99·5	28·7	14·4	61·5	8·8	14·1
1898	99·6	29·3	14·6	59·8	8·9	13·8
1899	99·7	29·8	14·3	59·1	8·8	13·4
1900	99·8	30·1	14·0	58·9	9·1	12·4
1901	99·8	30·7	14·1	58·4	9·4	12·7
1902	99·8	*31·2	14·0	56·6	9·5	13·1
1903	*99·9	*31·2	13·9	56·9	9·6	13·5
1904	*99·9	30·8	14·6	55·1	9·6	13·1
1905	99·8	30·4	14·7	53·5	9·6	13·3
1906	99·7	29·0	14·0	53·3	9·8	13·3
1907	99·6	27·4	14·1	49·7	10·4	12·8
1908	99·5	26·3	13·8	45·5	10·9	12·3
1909	99·3	25·8	13·4	38·9	11·4	12·5
1910	99·0	25·1	13·4	34·2	12·1	12·3
1911	97·7	25·1	14·2	31·1	12·7	12·4
1912	96·1	25·3	14·1	29·3	12·9	13·0
1913	94·5	25·1	14·7	31·9	13·3	12·7
1914	91·6	24·9	15·2	37·1	13·4	12·7
1915	89·6	24·9	*15·4	43·1	13·4	12·7
1916	88·1	24·6	15·1	40·5	13·3	12·1
1917	86·6	†24·4	15·1	41·3	13·2	11·7
1918	84·8	24·8	14·8	35·4	13·4	12·0
1919	84·6	25·4	·14·2	30·8	13·9	12·5
1920	84·2	27·2	14·1	24·5	14·6	12·8
1921	85·2	28·5	14·0	25·0	15·0	13·7
1922	85·5	31·3	13·8	22·6	15·5	13·8
1923	84·5	33·1	13·3	23·6	*15·7	13·7
1924	82·3	34·9	13·8	21·7	15·5	13·2
1925	79·0	34·8	13·5	20·0	15·0	12·8
1926	74·9	*35·9	13·9	†19·8	14·8	12·3
1927	†72·0	34·8	13·9	20·7	14·3	11·9
1928	74·4	33·3	14·3	21·5	14·5	11·7
1929	79·0	32·3	14·1	23·4	14·3	11·8
1930	84·5	29·6	13·8	25·0	13·7	11·6
1931	90·2	27·4	13·0	25·9	13·4	11·8
1932	95·8	25·9	12·3	26·0	13·5	12·0
1933	97·6	25·3	11·6	28·5	12·1	11·9
1934	98·4	25·0	†11·0	30·1	11·7	†11·3

* High points. † Low points.

contrary of its low value being merely a by-product of the unrepresentativeness of the small number of pictures measured. But these techniques are cumbersome, and the issues involved are small. Whether the waist line over a period of one hundred and fifty years reached its lowest position (highest percentage) precisely in 1926 or perhaps rather in either 1924 or 1927, can be of no great moment. The essential truth seems sufficiently expressed, and certainly much more vividly, by the moving average.

For this reason we have graphed the moving averages in figures 1 and 2 (pp. 59–60). These should be considered our basic diagrams. We have shown in these diagrams also the actual values for each year, from table 3; but these values have been indicated by disparate points or dots, whereas the moving-average values are connected by a continuous line.

Earlier than 1787, the data are too scattered for a satisfactory moving average, and it has not been attempted. Its place is partially taken by the means of means in ten-year blocks in the first part of table 5.

Descriptive History of the Proportions of Dress

Each dimension of dress appears to have a more or less independent history. At least it can be considered independently. It seems advisable to treat the histories of the six diameters in two ways: first, descriptively, herewith; and again quantitatively, in the following section on Periodicity.

The problem of the relations of the several dimensions to each other, as they integrate into a whole style of dress, or the structural skeleton of a style, will be touched on in still another section, p. 79, on Interrelations of Dimensions; and again in the interpretation attempted on p. 81 on Variability and Stability.

Width of Skirt

The series begins with a fairly wide skirt, exemplified by the smooth, padded cone-shaped skirt of the Spanish fashions of the late sixteenth century, or the squarer Queen Elizabeth dress. However, the year 1605 lies in the midst of a gradual tendency toward narrowing. The farthingale (vertugarde, crinoline), which is very wide about 1570,[5] is completely out by 1625–30,[6] when skirts attain a relative minimum of width. Increasing diameters then follow until about 1660. This is reflected in the court styles painted by Rubens under Marie de Medici, by Callot, and in Van Dyck's regal portraits. Holland's wealthy bourgeois women in black satin with white lace, painted by Codde, Rembrandt, and Terborch, are also typical of the scene. The Spanish Hapsburg portraits of Velasquez illustrate a court dress of extraordinary uniformity and enormous width.

After 1660, a fine series of fashion plates by Bonnard shows a narrowing skirt. As early as 1665 the farthingale is ousted from general wear, but not at court.[7] For a while there is in France, as elsewhere, considerable discrepancy between court regulations and the freer flowing currents of general fashion, but in the end it is court dress that has to yield to the pressure of the narrowing trend. In the latter part of the reign of Louis XIV, beginning about 1680, the farthingale starts a long slow recovery. In Watteau, then Hogarth, and later in the magnificent Versailles galaxy including Boucher and Nattier, we see a gradual approach to the maximum of skirt width reached about 1750. The Paris gowns that find their way to the American colonies corroborate, though with less luxury, the fashions seen in the portraits of Mme de Pompadour.

After 1750 or so, the trend of the eighteenth century, though still hampered by court regulations, is a steady narrowing. A jog in the decade 1771–80

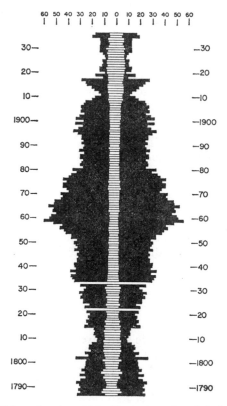

FIG. 6. Skirt width and waist width, dimensions 5 and 6, showing generally inverse relation, 1787–1936.

coincides with Marie Antoinette's reintroduction in 1774 of the wide flat farthingale, exquisitely depicted in the engravings of Moreau-le-Jeune. In general, though, what is lost in width is made up in the train. The works of Chodowiecki, Reynolds, Romney, and Gainsborough, and the fine engravings of France and England of the later eighteenth century recall the general picture. By the time of the French Revolution the farthingale is discarded, and a mere pillow at the back gives the necessary fullness. One would have said that the imitation of classic dress during and after the Directoire was a novel idea, symbolizing, perhaps, the beginning of a new and 'natural' life. Instead we see that the clinging skirts are merely the culmination of a drift that had its inception fifty years before. The years up to 1800–08 derive fullness from the trains

68

that are occasionally found. Eighteen hundred and ten to eighteen hundred and eleven is at the bottom of the curve, with a trainless, short skirt.

Then the trend turns slowly to rise. Its peak in 1859–61 (figs. 2, 4, 6) was the result of the adoption of the farthingale again, now called crinoline. Afterward a gradual narrowing set in, destined to attain its limit of possibility in the middle twenties of our century. Since then, skirts seem to be gradually widening. A return, several decades hence, to a crinoline wider than the wearer might be difficult in this day of automobiles, but the effect could be achieved with a train.

With peaks of fullness at about 1570, 1660, 1750, 1860, and of narrowness around 1625, 1680, 1810, and 1925, the full period is therefore about a hundred years. Oscillations within these huge curves now seem somewhat dwarfed. Many of them are due to the temporary introduction of the train, which seems to have little effect on the general drift.

Length of Skirt

This dimension is also analysed in terms of cycles, each being the time within which the hem leaves and returns to the ground. The periods of maximum length are the double decade 1641–60, 1794, 1860, and 1902–05, with a near-approach in 1934–36. These suggest a diminishing wave length. This curve has several special features, too. The 1860 and 1905 maxima are separated by a recession that remains rather small, and they may have to be counted together. A similar doubleness occurs in the minima. It is difficult to decide whether 1813 or 1833 represents the true extreme of skirt brevity in the early nineteenth century. Moreover, the eighteenth-century minimum falls around 1780, only a decade and a half before the century's maximum under the Directoire of 1794. Similarly, the recent minimum of 1927 is preceded by a near-minimum only eight years earlier. At this time skirts nearly reach their upper limit of possibility, and probably our less definable limits of decency. Glib explanations of the acting forces range through such things as war-time emergency, relaxing of sex morals, driving of motor-cars, a passing tendency toward non-femininity to emphasize equality with men. But even a superficial consideration of the whole trend, of dress-function and other aspects of the silhouette, reveals the inadequacy of these phrases. The violent increase in variability within the years themselves in the late nineteen-twenties will be recalled, the result of the conflict between the knee-length dress and the long 'robe de style'. Since then the styles have been more homogeneous.

These peculiarities of the periodic curve for the skirt length and its variability will also be discussed more fully in the statistical sections, pages 71, 78, and 81.

Position of the Waist

Since the beginning of the intensive year-by-year record in 1787, there have been crests of short-waistedness in 1807, 1869, 1917, and 1936 or still to be reached; and intervening maxima of low waists in 1842, 1903, and 1926. The period thus shortens as time goes on. This tendency holds also if the more intermittent pre-1787 data are included.

However, the extreme minima and maxima are fewer. The curve begins around 1605–10 with a very high waist, but sinks with the advent of the corseted V-waist. Its rise again to the apex in 1807 is slow except at the very end. This gives a period of about two hundred years. The pendulum then swings back. A slow drift toward long-waistedness sets in. Our previously established swings prove but oscillations in a greater cycle. One hundred and nineteen years after 1807, in 1926, the lowest point is reached. The tide has probably now turned into the second half or upswing. One would have said that the long waists of 1926 were another cultural abnormality following the war: they prove to be the normal trough of a tremendous curve. Moreover, one recalls with interest the similarly long-waisted, girdled frocks of 1450–1550, pictured for example in the early Gobelins and in the court of Maximilian I.

Diameter of the Waist

Inasmuch as it is impossible to perceive the trend in this dimension from the 1844–1919 data alone, Kroeber's former estimates prove to relate chiefly to minor irregularities.

In 1605 a sturdy corset[8] achieves the tiny waist that for some time has been de rigueur on every formal occasion. One may call to mind some of the portraits of Queen Elizabeth. This corset goes out gradually in the next few decades. Voluminous sleeves make it hard to get waist diameters for the seventeenth century. Our few measurements are supported by an impression gained from the Van Dyck and Dutch portraits that waists are amply wide up to 1660 or so. The sharp drop soon after is the result of the reintroduction in 1670[9] of the corset. After 1680 the trend changes. The considerable width for most of the eighteenth century is surprising, because one has the feeling that waists are quite slender. Though court dress is undoubtedly more exacting in this respect, the effect of slimness is achieved without real constriction partly by the slenderizing V of the corsage, and partly by juxtaposition to full skirts. A minimal extreme seems only to have been reached just before the fall of the French monarchy, after which diameters increase. A loose sash tied in the back is typical of the Revolution itself. With 'Greek' dress as a pattern during and after the Directoire, the waist is wide. Following to a certain extent anatomical exigencies, though this we well know is not always so, waists increase in diameter as they shorten. The widest are those of Empire dresses, directly under the breasts.

There now starts a very gradual constriction. At the turn of the trend during the eighteen-fifties and sixties, the diameter approximates Queen Elizabeth's famous edict (fig. 6). The breathing spell of 1872–75 is negligible. Not until the opening of the twentieth century does the enlarging of the waist show itself in earnest. The maximum comes in 1923, just one hundred and sixteen years from the previous peak.

Décolletage

It is difficult at first to see major significant movements in this endlessly fluctuating line. The longer span of three centuries reveals a more significant form of the curve. The ruffed high neck of the Spanish sixteenth-century mode persists briefly in France. French *décolletage* is mostly low during the seventeenth and eighteenth centuries, under the particular influence of court dress. The fichued throat of the French Revolution is the apex of height, then a new decline ensues. For 1844–1919, 'the most striking event in the history of *décolletage* depth is its increase in recent years.'[10] This reaches its maximum around 1915. A reverse culminates in the rather high necks of 1934–35. The evidence is not wholly satisfactory, however, on which to base a periodicity.

Width of Décolletage

It is indeed true that 'this trait appears to have a very long periodicity.'[11] The high ruffed necks of 1605 open the series at one limit of possibility. Wide lace collars lead to a more open *décolletage*, and the outer limit of possibility, a point several inches down the arm, is reached about 1670. A gradual narrowing ends in the close kerchief of the Revolution. It should be noticed that the width of *décolletage* of eighteenth-century dress and even court dress is not great. It is depth that is emphasized, so the general effect is that of a deep square. A rapid widening in the early nineteenth century brings a peak around 1832. Since then for a hundred years the trend has been toward less exposure of the shoulders.

Periodicity

It seems worth inquiring in how far there may be any more or less constant duration to the swings of the fashion pendulum just described; whether there is any period of years within or near which such swings tend to accomplish themselves. There is, of course, no necessary reason why even in one feature or dimension the time for change from one extreme to the opposite and back again should be constant over several centuries, nor why the rate of change should be the same in separate features within a given century. At the same time there might be a cause or causes tending to operate toward uniformity; and in so far as there might be, the first step toward its recognition would be determination of the degree of uniformity which exists, and of the time value expressing the uniformity.

On the whole, the style changes are so long in their range, and so progressive, that there is no great difficulty, as soon as data are sufficiently ample, in determining recurrent maxima and minima. We call a full wave length the time interval from one crest to the next, or from trough to trough. For instance, skirts were clearly at minimum width in 1811 and again in 1926; at their fullest, not far from 1749 and about 1860. This gives wave lengths of 115 and 111 years respectively; or half wave lengths—one-way swings—of 62, 49, and 66 years. For waist width, correspondingly alternating maxima and minima fall at about 1780, 1807, 1860, 1923,* giving wave lengths of 72 and 116 years, and one-way swings of 27, 45, 71 years.

Actually the situation is often less simple, because of minor crests and troughs. Say a dimension of 20, the lowest in a century, changes gradually over fifty years to a value of 40, which is the highest reached in a century or so. If about halfway up the climb there is a recession which in five or six years carries the value from say 31 back to 28, after which the upward march is resumed, this recession is obviously a minor fluctuation. It is no doubt stylistically and historically significant, but less so than the longer and larger swing from 20

* The moving-average figures are used.

to 40 on which it is superimposed. Suppose, however, that in twenty years the value of 35 has been reached, that the recession lasts ten years and carries down to 25, and that in the following twenty years the value mounts again and reaches 40. What have we then? Still a secondary fluctuation, although an accentuated one? Or three swings of 20, 10, 20 years duration and 15, 10, 15 points amplitude? Obviously, if the answer is to be not wholly subjective or arbitrary, it has to be rendered, so far as possible, in terms of all known values for the trait in question; also in comparison with the trend of durations of undeniable swings; and in some degree with reference to high and low values and durations in other traits. At that, there are likely to remain some cases difficult to adjudge, and others dubious because of insufficient data; but enough may emerge clear-cut to justify the inquiry.

Skirt Length (Dimension 2)

The first half of the seventeenth century is a time of full-length skirts. From 1605 to 1640, half of the dress pictures measured have a length of 100; for only one of the years on which there are data does the average fall below 96. From 1641 to 1660 full length is even more unanimous: all of nine specimens available are full 100 per cent. We can take the midpoint of this double decade, namely 1650–51, as the moment of climax of length.

Thereafter there is slow shortening. From 1661 to 1690, three years show 100; six years, values of 96 to 99. Then there is a twenty years' gap in data. From 1711 to 1730 the length is still about the same as before the gap.

From 1731, however, shortening increases progressively to about 1780: successive decades average 96·6, 96·6, 95·8, 94·8, 94·2. The peak is evidently comprised in 1778–81: 92·4, 92·3, 90·3, 92·2.

Now follows a rapid lengthening, expressed in higher percentages. The 1784 value is up (skirt longer), 1787 reaches nearly 99, 1790–93* are all over 98, Directoire styles of 1794 touch 100. The moving-average crests are 1792, 98·7, and 1796, 98·6.

This full length is only momentarily held, in contrast with the long persistence around 100 the century before. The years 1795–1803 oscillate between 97 and 100. Length decreases progressively from 97·6 in 1804 to 91·9 in 1814.† It is, however, not certain that 1814 is the true crest of the wave, because a second peak of shortness comes at 1833 with 92.0‡ Between lies a swell of partial lengthening of the hem. This whole double decade 1814–33 is something of a unit: it has shorter skirts than any period in the preceding two centuries.

At any rate, skirts lengthen progressively after 1833. By 1836 the moving average has reached 94; by 1841, 97; 1846, 98; 1858, 99; 1860, 99·8. The first individual year to show full 100 per cent length for every dress examined is 1859; thereafter three more such years occur sporadically until 1875; then no others until 1899. Between 1875 and 1899 there is a minor shortening, reaching 96·1 in the moving average for 1886 and 95·5 actual mean in 1887. This temporary recession is steady from year to year, both up and down, but is modest. The real maximum of length comes in 1903–04, with 99·9 in the moving

* From here on, moving-average maxima and minima are used.
† The lowest individual year is 1813, with 87·9.
‡ No data for 1833; minimum year is 1834, 89·3.

average, and the four successive years 1902 to 1905 showing actual averages of 100.

Since 1905, no year has shown a full 100. For about a quinquennium, the shortening was timid and barely perceptible. But by 1911, the moving average has fallen below 98; by 1914, below 92; by 1919, below 85. This, the year in which Kroeber's first study terminated, seemed the limit. However, by 1925 the moving average fell below 80, and in 1927 dipped to the minimum of 72 (year figure 69·7).

Once this corner was turned, the lengthening was rapid: 1929, 79; 1930, 84; 1931, 90; 1934, 98.

If now we summarize, these are the maxima and minima:

TABLE 9 *Dates of Maximum and Minimum Skirt Length**

Years	Maximum	Minimum
c. 1650	100	
1780		90
1792–96	99	
1814		92
1823	95	
1833		92
1860	100	
1886		96
1903–04	100	
1927		72
? 1934	98	

* Moving-average values after 1788.

It will be seen that two extremes have been double peaked: the short skirt of 1814 and 1833, the long one of 1860 and 1903–04. Passing over the recessions within these as minor, we have: *1650, †1780, *1794, †1833, *1903, †1927. The resulting wave lengths, crest to crest and trough to trough, are 144 (1794 minus 1650), 53, 109, and 94 years. The average of these four is 100 years—the empirically found value of the skirt-length cycle in modern European history.

TABLE 10 *Summary of Periodicity in Skirt Length*

1650	Max.		
1780		Min.	
1794	Max.		Max.–Max.: 144 years
1833		Min.	Min.–Min. : 53 years
1903	Max.		Max.–Max.: 109 years
1927		Min.	Min.–Min. : 94 years

Average of four waves: 100 years

Skirt Width (Dimension 5)

Skirt width shows three cycles in three centuries: four peaks of slimness, three of fullness.

TABLE 11 *Dates of Maximum and Minimum Skirt Width*

Years	Maximum	Minimum
1629		42
1651–60	96 (1659, 126)	
1678–80		39
1749–51	101	
1811		27
1861	105 (1859, 116)	
1926		20

These convert as follows:

TABLE 12 *Summary of Periodicity in Skirt Width*

Year	Extremes		Intervals, years
1629		Narrow	
1655±	Full		
1679±		Narrow	50
1750±	Full		95
1811		Narrow	132
1861	Full		111
1926		Narrow	115

The average is a fraction over 100 years.

The histories of costume give 1570 as the maximum of farthingale expansion. This date lies about eighty-five years before the 1655 peak of fullness. The inclusion of this earlier wave length would reduce the average from 101·3 to 98 years. So far as the periodicity of this skirt width has changed during the last three and a half centuries, it seems to have slowed.

Waist Length (Dimension 3)

From here on, we are concerned with smaller measures—waist and shoulders—and our values, which are percentages of the body height, run lower. For our first dimension, length of waist, the periodicity is also somewhat less.

It must be remembered that this measure refers to the vertical height of the narrowest part of the middle of the silhouette figure. The belt, or demarcation of blouse and skirt, may fall lower, especially in front, but has been disregarded because it is not always present.

The minimum position found (lowest percentage, highest position on the body) is 18, or less than a fifth of the body height;* the maximum, 36, or over a third. These are moving-average values; the actual means for particular years are somewhat more extreme: 17 for 1809 and 1815–16, 38 in 1927. The several minima—or high-waist peaks—fall between 18 and 25; the maxima of low-waistedness between 29 and 36.

---

* As body height has been calculated from the mouth, the place of the waist line at its highest would be a full fifth down from the real body height at its highest position (lowest percentages); probably two-fifths when lowest on the body (highest percentages).

These are the indicated crests:

TABLE 13 *Periodicity in Waist Length*

	High waist	Low waist	Intervals, years Min.–Min.	Intervals, years Max.–Max.
1605–10	21			
1661–70		31		
1711–20	26		108	
1751–60		29		90
1817	18		101	
1842		29		86
1869	22		52	
1902/03		31		60
1917	24		48	
1926		36		24
Average			77	65

The average of 77 and 65 gives 71 years as the mean duration of a complete wave.

The decrease of wave length is steady and notable.

Waist Width (Dimension 7)

Waist width or diameter fluctuates between about 8 and 16 per cent of figure height, in fashion plates. The duration of its swings—contrary to that of waist position—does not appear to be shortening. Early data are unusually few, on account of arm interference and art conventions. (See table 14.)

TABLE 14 *Periodicity in Waist Width*

Decades	Extremes (10-yr. av.)	Extreme value of year	Extreme year	Approx. max.	Approx. min.	Interval	
1641–50	15·8		c. 1645	16			
1671–80	9·8		c. 1675		10		
1731–40	13·8		c. 1735	14		90	
1771–80	11·9	1780: 8·6	c. 1780		9		105
1801–10	14·0	1807: 14·7	1807	15		72	
1851–60	8·2	1860: 7·8	1860		8		80
1921–30	15·1	1923: 15·7	1923	16		116	
Average						93	93

The mean full wave length is 93 years, with rather low variability from 72 to 116.

Décolletage (Dimension 4)

For the first thirty years of our record there was no *décolletage* in the modern sense. For the next thirty, it alternates with mere neck opening. Thereafter, we can properly speak of breast exposure as standard in court or formal dress. However, there is a long period from about 1670 to 1780 in which shifts of

75

trend are difficult to define, although depth of cutout grows gradually greater. Around 1784 there is a swift change: *décolletage* as such almost disappears, and stays out for a decade. 1794–96 bring it back, and a maximum is reached in 1803, with a moving-average percentage of 14. Twenty years later, around 1823–27, there is a minimum just below 12. By 1834, the figure is back above 13*; and for a century, to 1931 inclusive, the moving average (and very few actual year values) does not fall below 12·5. During this century, the moving average several times goes above 14, with minor peaks in 1841, 1874, 1879, 1898, 1905, and a final and highest one in 1915 at 15·4. The intervening dips in the curve—*décolletage* shortenings—are, however, so slight that they cannot fairly be construed as basic waves. They are only oscillations in a slowly deepening trend, which climaxes around 1915. From this 1915 climax the raising of the *décolletage* (smaller values) is gradual, with even a recession to more than 14 as late as 1928. With 1932, however, the break comes: the *décolletage* is transferred to the back, the neck-line rises sharply in front. A seeming minimum is reached within three years: 1934, 11.

It is clear that after *décolletage* once was accepted (or reaccepted) as a feature of formal dress, in the early seventeenth century, it tended to remain established with only minor fluctuations, except for three sharp but temporary crises. The first of these was in 1784–94, when *décolletage* proper simply went out. The second was a longer period, marked in 1806–13, and even more so in 1820–28, with peak about 1823, when *décolletage* remained in force, but partially sacrificed depth in order to obtain an effect of breadth. The third was the recent years, when the breast was covered to expose the back.

The situation as regards this proportion, and the factors at work in its changes, are therefore of a somewhat different order from those concerned in the proportions so far considered. It must be remembered also that the dimensions of skirt and waist length and breadth express the outline of the dress or figure as a whole, but *décolletage* really refers to a feature internal to the figure. As regards dress, in the literal sense, it is negative instead of positive.

TABLE 15 *Periodicity in Décolletage*

Period	Value	Year	Approx. max.	Approx. min.	Intervals	
1605–10	5·4					
1631–40	10·8	1635±	11			
1641–50	6·6	1645±		7		
1771–80	15·2	1778	18		143	
1788	8·6	1788		9		143
1803	14·2	1803	14		25	
1823, 1827	11·7	1825±		12		37
1841	14·6	1841	15		38	
1868–69	12·6	1869		13		44
1915	15·4	1915	15		74	
1934	11·0	1934		11		65
Average					70	72

* In view of the tendency toward inverse relation between depth and width of *décolletage*, discussed on pp. 67–79, it should however be noted that the minima and maxima of the two dimensions do not coincide in time. Depth, minimum in 1823–27; width, maximum in 1832.

If we consolidate the second and third waves with the fourth, as there is possible warrant for doing because their extremes are less accentuated, we have left two crest-to-crest waves of 143 and 137 years respectively, and two trough-to-trough ones of 143 and 144—a mean of 142, instead of 71 as in the table.

These mean wave lengths do not signify too much. What we can also see is two long spans, 1645–1778 and 1788–1915, in which *décolletage* gradually deepens to a maximum; punctuated by several brief reversals, c. 1635–45, 1778–88, 1803–23, 1841–69, 1915–34. This gives for the periods of deepening of *décolletage* an average of 140 years, for those of raising, 18 years. In other words, the wave profile is markedly skew. The cutout creeps slowly downward, then jumps back up rapidly.

Décolletage Width (Dimension 8)

Décolletage proper does not exist in our series, for width any more than depth, before 1630. After that date, it gets established rather more rapidly, however, and reaches a peak, with nearly full shoulder exposure or percentage value of about 21, around 1659–68. Our data are blank between 1680 and 1710. After that, the value declines gradually through the eighteenth century, at any rate during its second half; the trend in the first half is not quite clear. The minimum width is reached with a value of 8 in 1795, a few years after the sudden minimum of *décolletage* depth in 1788. From here there is a climb of nearly forty years to above 23 in 1832. Thereafter the record is one of slow narrowing to the present. The last year of the moving average, 1934, is lower, with 11·3, than any year since 1800, 11·6. The last actual year, 1936, shows 9·8. The long swing toward narrowing of neck-opening may thus be not yet completed.

There are several temporary recessions in the century of drift: 1847–53, 1878–83, 1890–95, 1900–03, 1917–22. But these add only one to two points, each time, while the century-long decrease drift is from 23 to 11; so they clearly are superficial oscillations. As with depth, there is a tendency toward slow creep —in this instance toward narrowing; broken by definitely briefer and sharper-curve reversals.

TABLE 16 *Periodicity in Décolletage Width*

Years	Value	Intervals	
1659–68	21·2		
1795	8·3		
1832	23·4	168	
1936	11·3		141+

It is evident that the wave profiles are again skew. But *décolletage* width mounts rapidly to its maximum and then shrinks gradually, whereas *décolletage* depth is reduced suddenly and then increases again for a long time. This inverse relation is reflected in the ratio of the two dimensions, as shown in table 18. The ratio (4/8) sinks rapidly for 30 years to 1827–31, then climbs slowly for 85 years to 1912–16.

Comparison

If now we bring our six sets of periodicity findings together, we have the following:

TABLE 17 *Comparison of Six Periodicities*

Dimensions	Mean wave lengths, years
No. 2 Skirt length	100
No. 5 Skirt width	100
No. 3 Waist length	71
No. 7 Waist width	93
No. 4 *Décolletage* length	71
No. 8 *Décolletage* width	154
Mean of six	98

We are not wholly clear how much weight should be attached to this clustering of the wave lengths of change in our six dress dimensions around a value approximating a century. The question is in how far the significance lies in the intrinsic fact of a century-value, or, on the other hand, in the nearly synchronous clustering of peaks in certain periods, which might be due to a common cause. This problem is discussed further on p. 81.

One thing, however, is certain—whether or not the six mean wave lengths do or do not bear relation to one another—namely, that women's dress fashions change slowly, as regards the fundamental proportions of the silhouette or contour. On the average, any one proportion is a half-century swinging from its extreme of length or fullness to extreme of brevity or narrowness, and another half-century swinging back. This is more than would usually be supposed, in view of the civilized world's general assumption that women's dress fashions are in their nature not only unstable but capriciously and rapidly unstable.

Oscillations

It also seems worth while to try to estimate the average duration of minor fluctuations or transient oscillations over and above the major swings or trends so far considered. This would require first of all the reliable determination of the long-time trends. The deviations from this of the actual averages for each of a series of years would then give the periods for which the actual style, with respect to any one trait, remained above or below its underlying trend.

As regards statistical execution, however, the matter is not so simple. On account of the small number of measures, no mean for a particular year is very reliable; and its probable error would have to be taken into account. Moreover, the basic trend can be differently expressed; for instance by three-, five-, nine-, or fifteen-year moving averages; or by more elaborate methods. A moving average from its very nature produces certain apparent fluctuations in the actual annual means, even when the latter are proceeding in a regular curve in rounding a peak. Suppose for instance successive annual values run 69, 70, 71, 72, 73, 75, 78, 82, 87, 82, 78, 75, 73, 72, 71, 70, 69. As the sharper rise begins, the moving average climbs ahead of the actual values; at the peak it is considerably lower; then falls more slowly so that it is higher for a while. In other words, in the rounding of such a corner, we get three departures of the two lines from each other: that is, of the year-by-year graph and the moving-average graph; though each is a perfectly symmetrical curve. In short, three apparent fluctuations are due merely to the mathematical properties of the technique used.

Since the fewness and variability of the primary measurements thus appear to render an elaborate treatment hardly worth while, we shall proceed to see cursorily what the surface results are.

Dimension 3 shows 38 full oscillations of annual means from the five-year moving average in the one hundred and forty-seven years from 1788 to 1934; that is, 38 periods when the actual value moves from above the moving average to below it and back above again (see tables 3, 8). This gives an apparent mean of 3·87 years, $\sigma = 4·11$.*

Dimensions 4, 5, 7, 8 show 40, 38, 38, 41 oscillations in the same one hundred and forty-seven years; the mean for these dimensions is 3·77 years.

Dimension 2 cannot be directly compared with these, because the measured values often reach 100, but cannot pass it: a dress as worn may surpass the distance to the ground, but in the fashion plate, as soon as the toe becomes invisible, the measurement has to be read: skirt length = 100. The range of variation is therefore small when dresses are near the limit of length, and the number of oscillations would rise to 55 and the mean duration fall to 2·5 years. If we count only fluctuations passing from below 99·5 to above 100·5 of the moving average, or vice versa,† the number of oscillations is 40, and their average duration 3·68 years.

The average length of oscillation, between 3·5 and 4 years, is not far from the average duration generally assumed for the business cycle. This is probably a coincidence. The value will scarcely be very significant until there are more individual measurements available for each year and until more technical statistical consideration is given the moving-average 'trend' which forms one of the two variables whose relation expresses the oscillations.

The *size* of deviation of the actual average for each year from the moving-average trend is, however, almost certainly significant for stability of style, as discussed below on page 81.

Interrelations of Dimensions

We have computed about half the relations between dimensions, and present them herewith in summary. (Table 18.) The variations come out very much like those for diameters considered alone. This is due largely to the fact that the six separate dimensions mostly show significant maxima or minima in the decades around 1810 and 1920, so that these tend to be repeated, sometimes with accentuation, in the ratios. Also, skirt length varies so little, proportionately to the other dimensions, that any ratio into which it enters becomes

* For one-way fluctuations (intervals between crossings of the two lines), $M = 1·95$, $\sigma = 2·13$.

† That is, the year-to-year line not only crosses the moving average, but crosses it with a motion of at least 1·0.

TABLE 18 *Interrelations of Certain Dimensions, by Five-year Periods, 1788–1936*

Period	5/2	7/3	4/8	4/3	7/5	8/5	7/8
1788–91	54·6	50·2	105·7	37·6	23·1	16·3	141·4
1792–96	50·9	59·4	114.3	44·2	25·8	16·8	*153·6
1797–1801	45·2	67·2	*121·4	65·1	29·1	23·3	125·2
1802–06	44·4	70·7	97·8	*72·3	30·7	32·1	96·4
1807–11	†30·6	*72·3	88·5	63·1	*48·1	47·4	101·4
1812–16	38·1	69·8	70·9	64·6	37·7	*49·1	76·7
1817–21	43·3	56·3	83·2	64·8	27·7	38·3	72·3
1822–26	47·8	44·8	62·6	49·4	23·8	43·9	56·8
1827–31	54·0	43·4	†54·5	†45·7	23·1	44·5	51·8
1832–36	69·3	36·5	63·3	48·3	15·5	32·4	47·8
1837–41	67·3	31·9	71·9	50·2	14·0	30·6	45·7
1842–46	60·5	30·7	73·1	49·1	14·9	33·7	45·6
1847–51	63·6	†29·6	67·0	47·4	13·6	32·5	41·9
1852–56	80·0	30·5	65·2	49·1	10·7	26·4	†40·6
1857–61	*103·1	31·5	73·5	52·9	†7·9	18·0	43·8
1862–66	101·7	35·6	74·0	55·5	8·3	†17·5	47·5
1867–71	88·0	40·8	75·5	57·8	10·2	19·2	52·9
1872–76	82·6	*43·7	87·6	*61·0	12·3	19·6	62·7
1877–81	67·0	33·5	98·6	54·6	13·2	21·8	60·4
1882–86	57·1	31·6	87·7	50·8	15·2	27·9	54·5
1887–91	54·7	31·7	103·8	49·6	16·7	25·2	66·2
1892–96	59·0	32·9	96·5	49·6	15·8	24·8	63·9
1897–1901	59·3	†29·5	106·7	48·0	14·9	22·7	65·7
1902–06	55·2	31·2	111·5	†47·4	17·4	23·8	73·3
1907–11	39·2	44·2	107·2	51·9	29·3	32·1	91·2
1912–16	40·5	53·8	*119·7	*61·0	36·1	34·2	105·5
1917–21	35·9	*54·7	113·6	55·9	45·7	41·1	111·2
1922–26	†26·4	45·7	104·5	40·7	*71·4	*60·8	117·4
1927–31	29·6	44·3	119·5	43·7	61·1	50·4	*121·2
1932–36	30·6	47·2	97·3	44·0	39·2	37·5	104·4

largely a function of the other measure. On the other hand, waist length, which shows five crests instead of the usual three since 1800, produces five crests in those ratios into which it enters. (Table 19.)

TABLE 19 *Periodicity of Dimension Interrelations*

Horizontal and Vertical Ratio of Same Part of Dress:

5/2: Minima, 1807–11, 1922–26 (interval, 115 years)
7/3: Maxima, 1807–11, 1872–76 (interval, 65 years)
Maxima, 1872–76, 1917–21 (interval, 45 years)
Minima, 1847–51, 1897–01 (interval, 50 years)
4/8: Maxima, 1797–01, 1912–16 (interval, 115 years)

Vertical Diameters *inter se*:
4/3: Max., 1802–06, 1872–76 (70 years)
Max., 1872–76, 1912–16 (40 years)
Min., 1827–31, 1902–06 (75 years)

Horizontal Diameters *inter se*:
7/5: Max., 1807–11, 1922–26 (115 years)
8/5: Max., 1812–16, 1922–26 (110 years)
7/8: Max., 1792–96, 1927–31 (135 years)

Variability and Stability of Style

The question of when, under what circumstances, and why traits of fashion are relatively stable and unstable is approached by us in two ways.

One is a year-by-year comparison of the standard deviations of the means for each trait; that is, the variability *inter se* of the actual measurements which go into the annual average. This is probably the most satisfactory expression of stability and instability.

The second method is to compare each annual average with the 'trend' or moving average for the same year. If the latter is held constant at 100, how many per cent above or below 100 is the actual average for the year? Thus for skirt width, the moving average for 1801 is 45·2, the yearly mean 42·1, or 6·9 per cent less. For 1802, on the other hand, the moving average has gone up only to 45·6, but the year's mean is 59·6, or 31 per cent higher. For 1803 the deviation is 10·3 per cent under. Obviously this is a period in which the style for skirt width was highly variable from year to year, even though the trend is pretty consistently in one direction for two decades. By contrast, the years 1854–58, which also show a strong one-way trend in this dimension, run 101·1, 101·7, 101·8, 90·8, 100·3; and 1839–43, with the trend change mild, show 97·8, 99·1, 103·5, 98·2, 99·8. It is plain that the year-to-year fluctuation was much more marked in 1801–03 than in 1839–43 or 1854–58. In other words the fashion, with respect to this trait at least, was much less stable in its trend in the earlier period than in the two later.

The objection which can be made against this second measure is that it expresses the relation of an actual year average to a short moving average to which it contributes; also that the moving average, our base, possesses properties, in relation to the actual sequence of events, which vary according to the nature of the sequence of events. It behaves somewhat differently when it is steadily progressing in one direction and when it is turning a corner; and again, in different parts of its curve around the turn. It is for this reason that the series of simple percentaged standard deviations, or variability coefficients, is probably sounder. However, these coefficients directly express only the variability or instability within one year: how much the several fashion plates for 1801 differ from one another, for example; instability over several years must be inferred by comparison. The annual deviations from the moving average express variability within a span of years directly. We therefore use this measure also. On the whole, the two measures give results fairly in agreement. Those by the method of deviation from the trend will be presented first.

Year-to-Year Variability (Percentage Deviations of Annual Mean from Moving Average)

The percentages by which each annual mean deviates from the five-year moving average for the same year—the basic data for this section—are given in table 20. More convenient are tables 21 and 22, which express the same values averaged for five- and ten-year periods respectively. We have thought it unnecessary to diagram these results separately; in substance they are shown in figures 1 and 2 (pp. 59, 60), where the line represents the moving average, and dots the annual means.

TABLE 20 *Percentage Deviations of Actual Year Means from Trend, 1788–1934*

Year	2	3	4	5	7	8
1788	1·4	14·0	3·5	2·0	32·0	
1789	0·8	5·3	12·0	3·4	21·1	23·0
1790	0·9	7·1	19·4	5·2	16·8	14·6
1791	0·2	2·8	32·2	1·5	15·9	4·5
1792	0·2	6·7	8·9	13·2	12·3	
1793	0·3	4·4	47·0	0·4	4·5	
1794	1·7	13·4	3·1	13·4	11·6	15·5
1795	1·6	3·4	25·2	9·1	12·1	14·6
1796	0·4	3·0	12·1	6·2	28·6	
1797	1·2	3·0	11·8	5·8	11·2	8·0
1798	0·2	1·0	0·9	0·4	21·1	4·0
1799	0·3	1·0	7·2	3·6	13·2	7·8
1800	0·1	4·2	19·8	7·5	1·6	1·7
1801	1·6	4·8	16·5	6·6	26·0	2·5
1802	2·6	3·2	21·6	30·7	13·7	12·9
1803	0·4	1·1	11·3	12·5	6·6	5·1
1804	2·6	3·2	9·6	3·2	1·5	2·9
1805	0·4	1·6	14·3	10·0	5·0	21·2
1806	1·3	3·8	0·8	2·1	0·7	8·6
1807	0·1	0·5	10·6	12·2	3·4	5·8
1808	0·6	1·1	2·5	3·2	1·4	2·2
1809	0·2	10·8	4·9	15·4	6·4	1·4
1810	0·8	5·0	6·3	12·3	6·5	14·6
1811	1·2	8·5	6·4	1·1	2·2	3·8
1812	0·3	2·0	1·6	4·3	0·0	4·3
1813	4·8	3·0	11·2	11·1	6·7	17·9
1814	2·5	4·8	8·2	10·6	3·0	0·0
1815	0·7	7·5	7·8	21·5	2·3	3·2
1816	2·0	9·5	7·7	0·3	4·8	10·7
1817	2·3	11·0	26·9	3·1	11·6	35·1
1818	1·5	8·4	14·4	3·3	0·9	7·9
1819	3·6	22·1	2·3	1·5	9·8	5·2
1820	1·1	8·1	10·0	7·3	6·5	1·8
1821	2·7	4·3	17·2	2·2	7·7	2·3
1822						
1823	1·7	4·7	3·4	5·5	6·4	4·7
1824	2·6	10·8	16·0	16·1	14·8	4·7
1825	1·1	1·6	9·2	3·6	7·3	13·6
1826	1·9	0·8	10·0	1·9	3·7	16·7
1827	0·7	7·2	4·3	4·7	5·7	10·0
1828	3·0	1·1	2·5	2·9	9·1	0·9
1829	0·6	0·0	0·0	10·5	2·6	4·5
1830	1·1	6·1	0·8	3·6	4·3	9·8
1831	1·6	9·5	2·4	12·8	12·5	7·0
1832	1·5	0·4	0·8	2·8	5·2	1·7
1833						
1834	3·1	0·4	6·9	0·6	1·0	15·6
1835	0·6	2·6	4·5	1·7	0·0	12·8
1836	1·8	2·5	3·7	4·6	0·0	8·7

TABLE 20 (*continued*)

Year	2	3	4	5	7	8
1837	0·0	2·5	1·5	6·7	2·2	1·1
1838	0·5	3·2	0·7	7·3	1·1	1·5
1839	0·4	0·7	3·5	2·3	4·4	4·0
1840	0·0	1·7	1·4	1·1	1·1	4·6
1841	0·1	0·7	1·4	3·5	3·3	3·0
1842	0·4	1·0	0·0	2·3	1·1	8·2
1843	0·1	0·7	0·0	0·7	2·2	6·7
1844	0·6	0·3	2·1	1·4	2·3	0·5
1845	0·4	2·4	0·7	1·0	3·4	1·0
1846	0·2	0·0	6·4	4·3	3·5	4·1
1847	0·4	2·1	8·0	6·6	3·5	0·0
1848	0·1	2·5	0·7	3·4	0·0	1·0
1849	0·3	0·0	2·2	0·3	1·2	1·5
1850	0·2	1·1	5·9	0·9	1·2	0·0
1851	0·7	3·9	3·7	6·7	2·4	1·4
1852	0·4	3·2	4·4	1·7	0·0	1·9
1853	0·0	0·4	5·9	3·6	7·1	0·5
1854	0·1	1·8	4·4	1·1	0·0	0·5
1855	0·0	1·8	1·5	1·7	7·1	3·4
1856	0·2	1·8	4·3	1·8	2·4	3·5
1857	0·5	0·7	0·7	9·2	3·6	1·0
1858	0·4	1·9	10·1	0·6	1·2	0·0
1859	0·4	1·6	5·9	12·6	1·3	1·1
1860	0·0	1·6	8·9	2·3	2·6	0·5
1861	0·4	0·4	6·1	0·6	0·0	0·0
1862	0·1	1·6	2·3	5·6	6·2	0·6
1863	0·8	3·3	0·8	0·5	8·4	3·4
1864	0·0	1·3	3·1	1·1	1·2	2·3
1865	0·7	0·9	0·8	6·7	1·2	0·0
1866	0·6	0·4	0·8	0·7	3·5	4·0
1867	1·5	3·6	7·9	2·6	5·8	1·2
1868	0·3	0·5	0·8	4·0	3·4	5·8
1869	1·0	0·0	9·5	1·8	1·1	4·2
1870	0·2	0·0	9·8	6·2	2·1	10·8
1871	0·1	3·1	3·7	8·9	7·2	4·6
1872	0·1	0·4	10·3	5·4	12·2	0·6
1873	0·2	7·5	1·4	5·7	1·0	9·6
1874	0·2	3·9	0·0	2·9	5·9	6·8
1875	0·7	4·3	2·2	3·5	8·3	9·7
1876	0·0	1·3	3·6	7·2	1·1	8·8
1877	0·4	1·2	2·2	2·4	6·5	7·4
1878	0·1	1·6	3·6	2·3	0·0	2·8
1879	0·1	0·4	6·3	6·2	1·1	4·2
1880	0·6	4·5	10·0	11·0	2·3	4·1
1881	0·0	3·4	3·6	11·1	0·0	3·9
1882	0·7	2·6	6·6	1·4	7·1	0·7
1883	0·0	2·3	4·5	0·9	2·4	12·3
1884	0·1	1·5	3·0	5·3	2·4	6·5
1885	0·7	2·2	3·7	3·5	2·4	0·0

TABLE 20 (*continued*)

Year	2	3	4	5	7	8
1886	0·3	0·7	8·0	3·5	4·7	3·5
1887	0·6	0·7	7·2	6·8	5·7	0·7
1888	0·5	0·0	1·4	8·2	4·6	5·1
1889	0·2	0·4	0·7	2·5	9·1	0·8
1890	0·4	0·4	1·4	5·1	5·6	1·5
1891	0·2	1·1	4·3	2·7	0·0	6·0
1892	0·4	2·1	3·6	3·8	1·1	5·9
1893	0·7	3·9	2·2	0·4	2·2	3·6
1894	0·3	2·9	0·7	4·5	0·0	4·1
1895	0·3	2·1	0·7	1·3	5·5	2·0
1896	0·0	2·1	0·0	14·8	9·1	5·6
1897	0·4	0·7	0·0	2·4	2·3	12·1
1898	0·2	0·7	0·7	11·4	9·0	13·8
1899	0·3	0·3	2·1	10·5	5·7	6·7
1900	0·5	1·3	7·9	10·9	4·4	8·1
1901	0·1	0·7	11·3	11·0	0·0	4·7
1902	0·2	3·5	6·4	4·1	4·2	15·3
1903	0·1	4·5	9·4	11·4	0·0	3·7
1904	0·1	4·9	4·1	2·5	3·1	13·0
1905	0·2	0·3	0·7	0·4	4·2	15·0
1906	0·1	0·7	15·7	5·1	3·1	15·8
1907	0·0	2·2	5·7	3·0	6·7	3·9
1908	0·2	3·4	15·2	7·7	0·0	4·9
1909	0·4	5·8	9·0	1·3	12·3	3·2
1910	0·2	0·4	0·7	3·8	3·3	5·7
1911	1·0	4·0	0·0	25·4	5·5	1·6
1912	2·3	4·0	5·0	6·5	2·3	11·5
1913	2·0	1·6	4·8	5·6	2·3	4·7
1914	0·2	1·6	5·3	21·6	3·7	19·7
1915	1·7	2·0	5·2	7·0	2·2	11·8
1916	4·3	1·6	8·6	21·2	5·3	1·7
1917	1·7	0·4	2·0	39·7	1·5	2·6
1918	0·6	2·4	7·4	42·7	0·0	11·7
1919	0·5	5·1	0·0	7·8	5·0	3·2
1920	2·4	2·6	6·4	31·4	0·7	0·8
1921	2·5	2·1	4·3	4·0	1·3	7·3
1922	0·6	6·4	3·6	16·8	6·5	5·1
1923	7·3	6·6	0·0	5·1	1·9	8·0
1924	4·0	12·1	5·8	1·8	2·6	0·8
1925	2·5	2·0	6·7	10·0	4·0	1·6
1926	3·6	11·1	13·7	16·7	4·1	0·0
1927	3·2	8·9	6·5	13·0	3·5	5·9
1928	5·9	8·7	4·9	1·4	1·4	3·4
1929	9·9	0·6	7·8	11·1	6·3	5·9
1930	5·3	5·1	5·8	3·6	20·4	0·9
1931	5·4	2·2	14·6	0·4	3·0	8·5
1932	1·6	5·8	7·3	0·8	18·5	14·2
1933	0·7	1·2	3·4	9·1	8·3	10·9
1934	0·9	0·0	15·5	13·0	17·1	4·4

First of all, it is clear that the proportionate amount of deviation varies among the six dimensions dealt with. On the whole, the large diameters have low variabilities. Thus, skirt length, the absolutely largest dimension, has 5·9 as its highest five-year-mean percentage deviation (table 21), while 19 out of

TABLE 21 *Five-year Averages of Annual Deviations from Trend, 1788–1934*

Period	2	3	4	5	7	8
1788–91	0·8	7·3	16·8	3·0	21·5	14·0
1792–96	0·8	6·2	19·3	8·5	13·8	15·0
1797–1801	0·7	2·8	11·2	4·8	14·6	4·8
1802–06	1·5	2·6	11·5	11·7	5·5	10·1
1807–11	0·6	5·2	6·1	8·8	4·0	5·5
1812–16	2·1	5·4	7·3	9·6	3·4	7·2
1817–21	2·2	10·8	14·2	3·5	7·3	10·5
1822–26	1·8	4·5	9·6	6·8	8·1	9·9
1827–31	1·4	4·8	2·0	6·9	6·8	6·4
1832–36	1·8	1·5	4·0	2·4	1·6	9·7
1837–41	0·2	1·8	1·7	4·2	2·4	2·8
1842–46	0·3	0·9	1·8	1·9	2·5	4·1
1847–51	0·3	1·9	4·1	3·6	1·7	0·8
1852–56	0·1	1·8	4·1	2·0	3·3	2·0
1857–61	0·3	1·2	6·3	5·1	1·7	0·5
1862–66	0·4	1·5	1·6	2·9	4·1	2·1
1867–71	0·6	1·4	6·3	4·7	3·9	5·3
1872–76	0·2	3·5	3·5	4·9	5·7	7·1
1877–81	0·2	2·2	5·1	6·6	2·0	4·5
1882–86	0·4	1·9	5·2	2·9	3·8	4·6
1887–91	0·4	0·5	3·0	5·1	5·0	2·8
1892–96	0·3	2·6	1·4	5·0	3·6	4·2
1897–1901	0·3	0·7	4·4	9·2	4·3	9·1
1902–06	0·1	2·8	7·3	4·7	2·9	12·6
1907–11	0·4	3·2	6·1	8·2	5·6	3·9
1912–16	2·1	2·2	5·8	12·4	3·2	9·9
1917–21	1·5	2·5	4·0	25·1	1·7	5·1
1922–26	3·6	7·6	6·0	10·1	3·8	3·1
1927–31	5·9	5·1	7·9	5·9	6·9	4·9
1932–34	1·1	2·3	8·7	7·6	14·6	9·8

30 values are under 1·0. Waist length rises to a maximum of 10·8, and only thrice falls below 1·0. *Décolletage* depth, on the other hand, rises as high as 19·3, and never goes below 1·4. The transverse diameters, which of course average lower than the longitudinal, run about like *décolletage* depth.

Next, it is clear that while 1835–1910 is a time of small deviations or high year-to-year stability for all six traits, these traits vary considerably among themselves as to whether their greatest instability falls in the period before or after the long quiet span, and whether early or late in 1788–1835. Thus, skirt length and width (Nos. 2 and 5) attain their greatest variability in post-World War years; the waist and *décolletage* dimensions vary most before 1821—in fact, all except waist length (No. 3), before 1803. These dozen early years 1788–1799, in the moving-average record, are only fairly conspicuous for number of maxima or minima attained, in spite of their high deviations. 1802–16 show more wave crests, but the year-to-year variability averages lower in four of the six dimensions (tables 20, 21, 22).

TABLE 22 *Ten-year Averages of Annual Deviations from Trend, 1788–1934*

Period	2	3	4	5	7	8
1788–96	0·8	6·8	18·1	5·8	17·6	14·5
1797–1806	1·1	2·7	11·4	8·3	10·1	7·5
1807–16	1·4	5·3	6·7	9·2	3·7	6·4
1817–26	2·0	7·7	11·9	5·2	7·7	10·2
1827–36	1·6	3·2	3·0	4·7	4·2	8·1
1837–46	0·3	1·4	1·8	3·1	2·5	3·5
1847–56	0·2	1·9	4·1	2·8	2·5	1·4
1857–66	0·4	1·4	4·0	4·0	2·9	1·3
1867–76	0·4	2·5	4·9	4·8	4·8	6·2
1877–86	0·3	2·1	5·2	4·8	2·9	4·6
1887–96	0·4	1·6	2·2	5·1	4·3	3·5
1897–1906	0·2	1·8	5·9	7·0	3·6	10·9
1907–16	1·3	2·7	6·0	10·3	4·4	6·9
1917–26	2·6	5·1	5·0	17·7	2·8	4·1
1927–34	3·5	3·7	8·3	6·8	10·8	7·4

Figure 7 shows graphically all deviations of the year from the trend, above a certain magnitude. This magnitude has been chosen so that the number of large deviations represented would be about the same for each of the six dimensions. Convenient values are 3 per cent for No. 2, skirt length; 6 per cent for No. 3, waist length; and 12 per cent for the others. These are designated in the figure as 'fluctuation units'. For instance, for trait No. 4, *décolletage* depth, the year-from-trend percentage deviations beginning in 1788 (table 20) are 3·5, 12·0, 19·4, 32·2, 8·9, 47·0. In terms of 12-per-cent units, these equal 0, 1, 1, 2, 0, 3; and they are entered by as many crosses on the vertical line denoting dimension No. 4 in the figure.

The number of crosses in this figure is approximately the same for the six traits. Thus:

	Number of fluc-tuation units	Number of years in which these occur
Dimension 2	16	13
Dimension 3	28	23
Dimension 4	24	19
Dimension 5	29	22
Dimension 7	21	18
Dimension 8	23	22

That there is a relation between large year-to-year fluctuations and wave crests or troughs is clear from figure 7, as compared with figures 3–6, 8–11. It is also clear that the relation is by no means simple or complete. Sometimes the fluctuations pile up in the years surrounding a peak; thus, dimension 2, 1926–27.* In other cases, the fluctuations are most extreme some years before or after: dimension 3, 1807; 4, 1804; 5, 1926; 7, 1811, 1923. Several times the fluctuations cluster continuously between a near-by crest and trough:

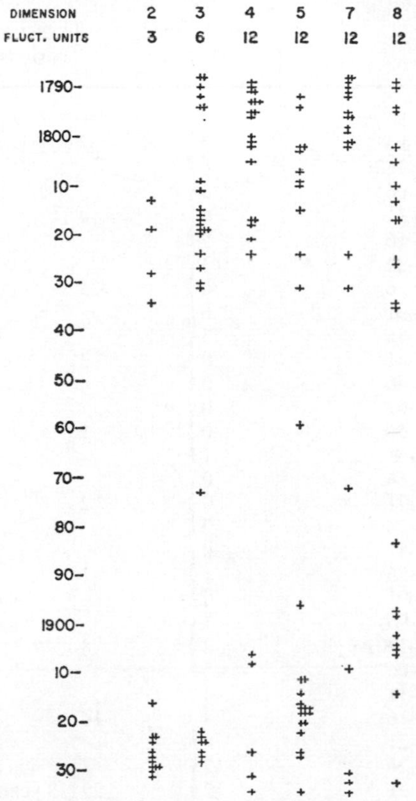

DIMENSION	2	3	4	5	7	8
FLUCT. UNITS	3	6	12	12	12	12

FIG. 7. Frequency of deviations from five-year moving-average trend, by fluctuation units per year, 1788–1934

dimension 4, 1788–1803; 5, 1912–26; 8, 1795–1832. On the other hand, there are crests without any accompanying marked annual fluctuations: dimension 3, 1860, 1903; 4, 1892, 1902/03; 7, 1852; and smaller clusters of fluctuations remote from any peak: dimension 7, 1824–31; 8, 1897–1903.

Essentially, each larger fluctuation represents a one-year reversal of the current five-year trend. Periods of many accentuated fluctuations therefore are periods in which style is as it were two-minded or under strain; even though it may be moving rapidly in a certain direction, the movement is meeting with resistance. Periods of only minor fluctuation, on the contrary, may be construed as times in which style is progressing harmoniously and whole-mindedly,

* This is probably at least in part a function of the moving average rounding a sharp crest.

whether the change be rapid or slow. It is clear that 1840–1900 was such a period of harmony, although it attained maxima in fullness of skirt and slenderness of waist and near-maxima in length of skirt and both long and high waistedness. Table 23 summarizes these differences by both five- and fifteen-year intervals.

TABLE 23 *Frequency of Fluctuation Units, 1788–1934* (as per fig. 7)

	In 5-year periods	In 15-year periods
1788–91	14 ⎫	
1792–96	17 ⎬	37 (14 years)*
1797–1801	6 ⎭	
1802–06	8 ⎫	
1807–11	6 ⎬	19
1812–16	5 ⎭	
1817–21	13 ⎫	
1822–26	6 ⎬	25
1827–31	6 ⎭	
1832–36	3 ⎫	
1837–41	0 ⎬	3
1842–46	0 ⎭	
1847–51	0 ⎫	
1852–56	0 ⎬	1
1857–61	1 ⎭	
1862–66	0 ⎫	
1867–71	0 ⎬	2
1872–76	2 ⎭	
1877–81	0 ⎫	
1882–86	1 ⎬	1
1887–91	0 ⎭	
1892–96	1 ⎫	
1897–1901	2 ⎬	8
1902–06	5 ⎭	
1907–11	4 ⎫	
1912–16	4 ⎬	16
1917–21	8 ⎭	
1922–26	12 ⎫	
1927–31	12 ⎬	29 (13 years)†
1932–34	5 ⎭	

* At rate of 40 in 15 years.   † At rate of 33 in 15 years.

It will be seen that the pre-1836 period of unsettlement is really double. The fluctuations are most marked and most numerous before 1800, then diminish, to resume again after 1815 and straggle along until about 1835. In historical terms, the Revolution-Directoire epoch was highly unstable, the Empire fairly settled, the twenty years after Moscow and Waterloo unsettled again. By 1830 quiet was impending, and 1848 was well within a long calm.

Unsettlement began again, in one feature, about 1900; became acute in another in 1911; in still others about 1920, 1923, 1930. By 1933 it had definitely diminished, except possibly in one feature: waist width. It is evident that the beginning of the era is pre-World War, its peak post-War. Only in one trait, skirt diameter, do the greatest fluctuations occur during the War itself. The specific cause of this exception seems to be a sharp reversal about 1915 in a narrowing trend which had come to a preliminary peak in 1912, but did not reach its extreme until 1926. This extreme was reached and passed with much less wobbling.

If we compare the two eras of frequent annual reversals, it is apparent that the earlier, 1788–1837, is more accentuated and may prove to have been longer; at any rate if the quieting down since 1932 continues after 1936. Fluctuations in all waist and *décolletage* dimensions are definitely more marked during the earlier unsettled era; in skirt proportions, during the later. This difference is of interest because the Napoleonic period also attained sharp climaxes in shortness and narrowness of skirt; but rather peacefully, so to speak, as compared with the 1926–27 climaxes. It would seem as if 1811–14 manipulated the skirt so far as it could without basically questioning its nature, whereas 1926–27 was calling its very existence into question; temporarily trying to rupture the basic pattern of skirt, so to speak. The earlier era was somewhat similarly, though on the whole less acutely, disturbed about waist and *décolletage* proportions. In brief, its revolutionizing attempts concerned the bust; the recent ones, the legs.

In connection with the somewhat greater frequency of early fluctuations, a statistical caution must be noted. Before 1834, the average number of observations per year is well under ten; since 1920, above ten. The annual means are therefore less well founded for the early era. Where observations number only five, three, two, or one for a year, fluctuations from the trend may be due to smallness of the random sample used; in other words, they may be apparent rather than real.

However, the long nineteenth-century or Victorian calm of small fluctuations is clearly beyond possibility of doubt.

Variability Within the Year

This is the standard deviation or sigma of the individual measures around their mean for year. For uniformity among the six dimensions, these sigmas are expressed in percentages of their means; that is, they have been converted into Coefficients of Variability, $V = 100\ \sigma/M$.

The full list of V's is given in table 24; their five- and ten-year averages in tables 25 and 26.

TABLE 24 *Percentage Sigmas of Annual Means, 1787–1936* $(V = 100\ \sigma/M)$

Year	2	3	4	5	7	8
1787	1·0	3·4	18·3	14·3		
1788	3·3	2·3	38·2	11·9		
1789	3·3	7·4	34·7	10·6	25·9	56·0
1790	0·9	16·7	65·7	10·6	16·8	
1791	0·7	5·8	11·2	7·1	8·3	23·3
1792		1·8			3·8	
1793	0·3	6·2	59·2	4·1	16·3	
1794	0·0	6·4	7·1	10·2	14·6	21·1

TABLE 24 (*continued*)

Year	2	3	4	5	7	8
1795	3·3	7·6	24·6	15·8	6·9	10·7
1796	0·5	8·7	44·7	3·8		
1797	0·9	3·6	0·0	16·2	1·7	
1798	0·8	5·2	12·9	7·2	11·1	22·2
1799	1·1	8·1	21·0	14·5	15·3	26·3
1800	0·7	12·4	22·1	14·4	16·1	12·9
1801	1·4	11·8	9·5	29·2	9·4	5·9
1802	0·0	6·7			3·5	
1803	1·3	11·1	17·5	39·1	7·6	16·6
1804	3·6	9·3	36·6	27·9	5·9	18·6
1805	1·1	8·0	8·3	24·7	12·7	12·3
1806	1·1	7·4	18·5	33·6	11·4	21·6
1807	1·9	10·0	18·0	28·8	10·6	10·8
1808	2·0	11·2	11·8	41·7	10·4	28·9
1809	2·5	11·9	16·5	38·0	10·7	19·3
1810	3·1	12·6	13·0	37·6	11·7	18·2
1811	4·0	14·9	11·3	41·1	6·6	12·6
1812	1·7	13·1	7·0	49·6	11·9	12·0
1813	9·0	18·6	17·7	42·2	9·5	16·7
1814	5·5	8·5	4·2	14·3	8·6	15·8
1815	2·9	9·6	7·4	33·9	9·7	17·6
1816	2·8	9·4	31·7	17·1	4·1	12·5
1817	2·4	5·0	30·3	14·1		19·8
1818	0·5	24·7	1·8	9·0	4·9	6·1
1819						
1820	5·7	7·5	1·9	4·6	5·8	2·3
1821	2·3	7·9	6·9	3·8	4·0	10·0
1822						
1823	1·7	7·2	1·4	1·9	4·4	2·7
1824	6·5	12·6	18·1	33·0	8·9	2·2
1825						
1826	2·1	23·7	0·0	6·2	3·5	12·6
1827	3·9	9·9	9·5	7·4	17·1	5·2
1828	2·9	7·0	8·0	2·8	8·1	10·1
1829	2·5	7·9		11·6	6·7	5·4
1830	2·3	8·2	10·4	6·2	14·9	2·0
1831	2·5	13·9	3·4	9·6	7·1	
1832	1·2	4·5	2·2	12·6	5·5	5·0
1833						
1834	4·5	4·2	13·8	6·8	5·7	12·0
1835	1·4	5·7	19·7	12·0	1·1	37·2
1836	1·7	7·5	14·2	4·6	4·1	12·5
1837	1·4	6·9	16·2	16·1	8·5	22·2
1838	0·9	5·8	12·7	5·5	7·6	12·5
1839	0·5	4·4	12·4	11·2	15·8	6·5
1840	2·0	6·5	14·2	10·3	16·7	15·4
1841	0·7	4·1	11·2	8·5	8·4	15·9
1842	2·9	5·8	12·4	13·6	16·8	21·4
1843	1·4	5·1	12·4	9·0	8·8	10·7
1844	1·2	4·2	11·1	6·2	6·8	5·8

TABLE 24 (*continued*)

Year	2	3	4	5	7	8
1845	0·5	3·7	9·1	4·7	5·8	4·2
1846	1·1	3·5	8·6	1·6	5·7	5·0
1847	0·8	5·8	10·4	1·7	4·2	6·9
1848	0·0	4·5	10·6	3·9	5·9	7·6
1849	1·0	2·2	8·7	6·7	8·2	6·5
1850	0·4	4·2	8·0	5·7	8·1	6·1
1851	0·9	3·8	10·9	8·5	6·0	5·2
1852	1·3	3·7	9·6	7·4	5·5	10·4
1853	0·7	2·8	10·1	5·4	5·6	11·9
1854	0·3	2·9	9·3	12·7	8·2	7·6
1855	1·0	5·9	9·0	9·6	7·9	8·0
1856	1·3	6·1	15·1	3·5	5·7	5·8
1857	0·8	6·5	13·9	3·7	14·8	13·7
1858	0·8	2·6	15·5	7·2	8·1	7·4
1859	0·0	3·2	14·9	4·1	10·1	19·2
1860	0·6	5·9	2·7	2·7	6·4	7·6
1861	0·0	4·2	11·5	7·0	12·5	4·2
1862	0·8	6·3	14·6	6·2	11·4	7·6
1863	1·4	1·4	7·6	4·7	0·0	9·9
1864	1·0	4·7	3·7	3·9	7·4	9·6
1865	0·4	5·0	12·7	4·7	5·8	8·6
1866	0·6	4·9	13·3	1·5	9·5	7·8
1867	1·5	4·6	15·9	7·2	7·9	12·0
1868	1·5	6·8	8·1	15·1	12·5	12·9
1869	0·0	2·8	10·4	10·7	0·0	9·4
1870	1·3	6·3	10·9	16·3	17·2	17·0
1871	0·9	7·7	12·5	21·8	0·0	17·5
1872	1·1	8·7	16·1	12·6	7·5	7·4
1873	1·3	5·8	9·6	9·5	8·2	22·1
1874	1·0	3·9	4·5	12·4	5·3	14·1
1875	0·0	7·3	8·0	10·2	4·7	3·7
1876	1·2	7·9	10·4	8·9	11·8	25·9
1877	1·0	4·2	8·3	13·5	10·8	16·1
1878	1·6	5·9	11·8	15·1	6·5	17·8
1879	1·1	3·6	10·0	13·0	4·9	9·4
1880	1·1	3·3	8·9	25·1	4·1	7·4
1881	1·7	4·9	10·3	30·9	5·9	8·5
1882	2·4	3·8	11·1	39·4	4·7	12·9
1883	0·9	6·4	7·1	34·3	6·1	8·1
1884	1·8	4·5	6·8	25·9	9·9	7·1
1885	1·9	5·3	8·5	33·5	9·6	13·4
1886	1·4	7·5	12·0	27·0	16·5	21·1
1887	1·7	4·3	7·4	23·6	9·1	9·9
1888	1·0	5·9	12·3	32·4	12·0	14·1
1889	2·0	5·6	8·1	26·7	13·8	17·1
1890	1·1	5·2	9·6	21·6	7·9	13·8
1891	1·2	6·9	10·4	27·2	7·0	8·7
1892	0·9	6·4	11·8	22·2	7·7	20·8
1893	1·2	7·8	15·2	27·5	14·2	16·3
1894	1·0	6·9	7·5	15·3	8·2	13·5

TABLE 24 (*continued*)

Year	2	3	4	5	7	8
1895	1·2	8·5	10·6	15·6	8·5	19·2
1896	1·2	5·4	12·5	7·1	13·5	12·7
1897	0·3	3·3	15·6	9·2	5·8	15·4
1898	0·6	4·8	24·7	9·0	10·1	20·7
1899	0·0	3·7	8·1	11·0	12·7	12·5
1900	0·8	5·0	12·8	8·2	7·3	14·2
1901	0·6	7·1	14·0	6·0	9·4	31·8
1902	0·0	9·1	15·5	14·2	7·9	22·3
1903	0·0	8·3	14·0	18·5	7·1	22·9
1904	0·0	5·0	17·8	10·3	6·8	14·3
1905	0·0	3·0	9·3	7·7	3·6	12·4
1906	0·9	8·3	13·7	5·0	10·5	20·6
1907	0·8	6·2	13·2	20·2	16·5	17·2
1908	1·0	6·2	23·1	11·3	13·8	19·2
1909	0·6	7·4	25·1	15·7	13·5	14·9
1910	1·8	6·8	17·9	24·7	7·8	13·0
1911	1·1	4·3	15·9	24·4	7·8	12·0
1912	2·1	8·4	8·7	19·4	9·3	9·3
1913	4·4	7·3	20·5	37·1	15·0	16·2
1914	2·2	6·1	18·8	46·0	14·5	11·8
1915	3·4	13·1	12·0	51·5	10·8	10·4
1916	4·3	8·0	21·7	27·3	12·4	21·8
1917	5·3	5·7	5·3	36·0	19·1	10·7
1918	1·9	7·6	14·9	40·8	7·6	11·5
1919	6·6	10·6	13·9	64·5	8·6	12·5
1920	3·8	6·2	16·4	44·3	9·3	17·4
1921	5·1	14·8	27·5	35·8	13·5	26·6
1922	3·8	10·7	31·9	54·5	10·2	12·6
1923	3·0	17·6	30·6	52·6	6·9	21·5
1924	4·6	13·3	19·7	44·7	11·4	9·6
1925	3·3	19·8	28·0	30·4	11·3	15·9
1926	3·1	19·2	18·5	17·6	8·3	15·5
1927	1·9	13·2	17·3	19·0	13·8	15·0
1928	5·4	7·7	18·3	52·3	11·3	8·0
1929	4·4	10·8	12·7	23·0	24·2	23·1
1930	6·4	12·1	10·4	19·2	31·0	10·1
1931	3·8	11·3	21·7	19·7	17·4	28·5
1932	2·6	12·4	22·3	29·6	17·3	24·2
1933	3·0	8·8	28·6	27·3	26·2	21·9
1934	1·4	8·1	44·7	23·8	16·4	35·3
1935	2·1	14·1	33·8	29·2	23·5	29·1
1936	2·1	10·0	32·8	39·3	17·3	36·6

It is at once evident that the variability is markedly different among the six dimensions. Dress length, dimension 2, again shows much the lowest variability, and waist length next least. The four other dimensions run about alike; though the two *décolletage* measures show a strong preponderance of V's between 10 and 20. The little subjoined table (no. 27, based on table 25) shows the distribution of size of five-year averaged V's.

TABLE 25 *Five-year Averages of Percentage Sigmas, 1787–1936* (V = 100 σ/M)

Period	2	3	4	5	7	8
1787–91	1·8	7·1	33·6	10·9	10·2	19·8
1792–96	0·8	5·8	27·1	6·8	8·3	15·9
1797–1801	1·0	8·2	13·1	16·3	10·7	13·5
1802–06	1·4	8·5	16·2	25·1	8·2	13·8
1807–11	2·7	12·1	14·1	37·4	10·0	18·0
1812–16	4·4	11·8	13·6	31·4	8·8	14·9
1817–21	2·2	9·0	8·2	6·3	3·0	9·6
1822–26	2·6	10·5	4·9	10·3	4·2	4·4
1827–31	2·8	9·4	6·3	7·5	10·8	4·5
1832–36	2·2	5·5	12·5	9·0	4·1	16·7
1837–41	1·1	5·5	13·3	10·3	11·4	14·5
1842–46	1·4	4·5	10·7	7·0	8·8	9·4
1847–51	0·6	4·1	9·7	5·3	6·5	6·5
1852–56	0·9	4·3	10·6	7·7	6·6	8·7
1857–61	0·4	4·5	11·7	4·9	10·4	10·4
1862–66	0·8	4·5	10·4	4·2	6·8	8·7
1867–71	1·0	5·6	11·6	14·2	7·3	13·8
1872–76	0·9	6·7	9·7	10·7	7·5	14·6
1877–81	1·3	4·4	9·9	19·5	6·4	11·8
1882–86	1·7	5·5	9·1	32·0	9·4	12·5
1887–91	1·4	5·6	9·6	26·3	10·0	12·6
1892–96	1·1	7·0	11·5	17·5	10·4	16·5
1897–1901	0·5	4·8	15·0	8·7	9·1	18·9
1902–06	0·2	6·7	14·1	11·1	7·2	18·5
1907–11	1·3	6·2	19·0	19·3	11·9	15·3
1912–16	3·5	8·6	16·3	36·3	12·4	13·9
1917–21	4·5	9·0	15·6	44·3	11·6	15·7
1922–26	3·6	16·1	25·7	40·0	9·6	15·0
1927–31	4·4	11·0	16·1	26·6	19·5	16·9
1932–36	2·2	10·7	32·4	29·8	20·1	29·4

TABLE 26 *Ten-year Averages of Percentage Sigmas, 1787–1936* (V = 100 σ/M)

Period	2	3	4	5	7	8
1787–96	1·3	7·0	*30·4	8·9	9·3	‡17·9
1797–1806	1·2	8·4	14·7	20·7	9·5	13·7
1807–16	‡3·6	‡12·0	13·9	‡34·4	9·4	16·5
1817–26	2·4	10·0	6·6	8·3	3·6	6·0
1827–36	2·5	7·5	9·4	8·3	7·5	10·6
1837–46	1·3	5·0	12·0	8·7	‡10·1	12·0
1847–56	0·8	4·2	10·2	6·5	6·5	7·6
1857–66	0·6	4·5	11·1	4·6	8·6	9·6
1867–76	0·9	6·2	10·7	12·5	7·4	14·2
1877–86	1·5	5·0	9·5	25·8	7·9	12·2
1887–96	1·1	6·3	10·6	21·9	10·2	14·6
1897–1906	0·3	5·8	14·6	9·9	8·2	18·7
1907–16	2·5	7·4	17·7	27·8	12·2	14·6
1917–26	*4·1	*12·6	20·7	*42·2	10·7	15·4
1927–36	3·3	10·9	‡24·3	28·2	‡19·8	*23·2

* Highest value in column.
‡ Second highest (other than in adjacent ennia).

TABLE 27 *Distribution of Size of Variability Coefficients (Five-year Averages) Among the Six Measures*

Variability coefficients	2	3	4	5	7	8
1·9 or less	19	—	—	—	—	—
2·0–4·9	11	7	1	2	3	2
5·0–9·9	—	17	7	8	14	5
10·0–19·9	—	6	18	10	12	22
20·0–50·0	—	—	4	10	1	1

It can be concluded from this that dress length, and next to it waist length, can be varied least from the ideal norm of a given moment if a dress is to be within fashion. With respect to *décolletage* and all transverse dimensions, the style is much less strict, and much more variability is exercised, within the year and within a five-year period. What our aesthetic taste assumes as primary in the style norm, and inhibits too great departures therefrom, is the length of the dress as a whole; next, the position of the waist constriction. Skirt fullness, waist diameter, and length and breadth of *décolletage* are allowed much more individual variation from dress to dress.*

The first thing that is evident from tables 25 and 26 is that there are once more an early period of high variability, a middle one of low, and a recent one that is high again. A table could be constructed that would be similar to table 23. Instead, in table 28 we give the maxima of V in five-year means.

Much the same appears from the stars and double daggers in the ten-year table 26.

As before, high variability tends to be associated with extreme of dimension, but not consistently so. The reason for the inconsistency is in this case clear, and will be the next point discussed.

It occurred to us to plot together the dimension means and their variability coefficients on scales calculated to bring out such similarity of course as they might or might not possess. Five-year averages were used to plot skirt and waist, ten-year for *décolletage*. Figures 8 to 10 show the results.

It is clear that in four cases out of six, and mainly in a fifth, there is a definite and surprising relation between *large* dimension and *low* variability; conversely, when the dimension shrinks, the variability goes up. This is very conspicuous for both skirt and both *décolletage* diameters (Nos. 2, 5, 4, 8; figs. 8, 10). It holds also fairly well for waist length (No. 3; fig. 9), except before 1821 and after 1921, when it reverses.† Waist width (No. 7; fig. 9) must be read

---

* These different behaviours of the six dimensions are perhaps partly a function of their absolute size: No. 2 is of course by far the largest measurement, and Nos. 4, 7, and 8 the smallest. With the small dimensions, the probability of error of caliper measurement is greater, presumably tending to increase the variability. However, the differences are not wholly a function of size, because skirt width (No. 5) consistently runs larger than waist length (No. 3), yet has a variability like that of the small dimensions. At least a considerable part of the variability difference between the dimensions therefore represents stylistic quality.

† In No. 3 of Fig. 9, V above 10 and M below 20 or above 32 have been indicated by extra blackness of line, to emphasize that before 1821 and after 1921 the variability reacts to extreme means in opposite manner.

TABLE 28 *Maxima of Five-year Averages of Coefficients of Variability*

Period	2	3	4	5	7	8
1787–91			34			40
1792–96						
1797–1801					11	
1802–06						
1807–11		12		37		
1812–16	4					
1817–21						
1822–26						
1827–31					11	
1832–36						
1837–41					11	
1842–46						
1847–51						
1852–56						
1857–61						
1862–66						
1867–71						
1872–76						
1877–81						
1882–86						
1887–91						
1892–96						
1897–1901						
1902–06						
1907–11						
1912–16						
1917–21	5			44		
1922–26		16				
1927–31						
1932–36			32		20	29

reversed (low variability accompanying low mean values) throughout, to achieve the best fit.

Now what is the meaning of this relation of dimension magnitude and variability? Evidently that when fashion brings a given trait to a certain magnitude, the style is harmonious and well-knit on that point, and individual productions, or designs, are in close concord. Conversely, when this magnitude is departed from the style is under strain as regards that feature, and efforts are made simultaneously to recede from the magnitude attained and to advance beyond it. In other words, from the angle of underlying pattern of style, there seems to be an optimum magnitude or proportion for each feature, when variability is low, and the style is concurred in because it is felt to be satisfying.

There appears no reason why this explanation should not be applicable to the minority of cases in which low variability accompanies low mean values. That is to say, in most of our traits the basic style is felt as satisfying, and remains stable, when the silhouette dimension is ample; but in other traits, when it is small or medium.

On this interpretation we can construct a basic or ideal pattern of Occidental women's evening or formal dress during the past 150 years. It has a long skirt, ample at the bottom; an expanse of bare breast and shoulders, as deep and wide as possible, although for mechanical reasons only one diameter can well be at maximum at the same time; as slender a waist as possible; and a middle or natural waist-line position, between 22 and 30 by our scale; when the waist line gets beyond these limits, and crowds either the breasts or the hips, the basic pattern is violated, resistance and extravagance are developed, and the variability rises.

To put it differently, a confining corset may be uncomfortable to the wearer, but it is felt as aesthetically satisfying by Europeans of the last century and a

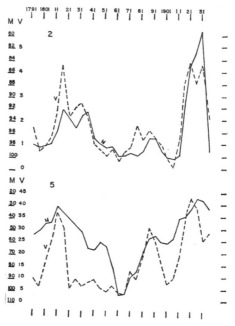

FIG. 8. Relation of variability (V) and amplitude of dimension (M) in skirt length (2) and width (5), 1787–1936.

half, even if it constricts unnaturally, provided it comes at or near the natural waist. Skirts on the other hand cannot be too full or too long, and breast and shoulder exposure too ample in evening dresses, to satisfy the ideal of the style.

However, we have not only this basic pattern or ideal style, which is aesthetic with a tingeing of the erotic, but also a concept of temporary mode or fashion as such, which demands change, and, when it has exhausted the possibilities of material, colour, and accessories, goes on to alter the fundamental proportions, in other words the basic aesthetic pattern. With such alteration there comes strain, simultaneous pulling forward and back; violent jumps in opposite directions within one or two or three years, and heightened statistical variability.

The several proportions are successfully attacked and distorted by fashion at somewhat different times, and hence the picture is complicated. Nevertheless, there emerge periods of a generation or so when fashion is particularly active in its attempts to break up or pervert the basic pattern. Such are the decades 1785 to 1835, and 1910 to the present. Between them, there lies a longer period of essential agreement and stability and low variability, in which fashion accepted, or fulfilled, the pattern while modifying it in superficial detail.

We have too few data to compute variabilities before 1787. This is unfortunate because most of the eighteenth century evidently resembled the middle and late nineteenth in holding fairly close to what we have determined as the

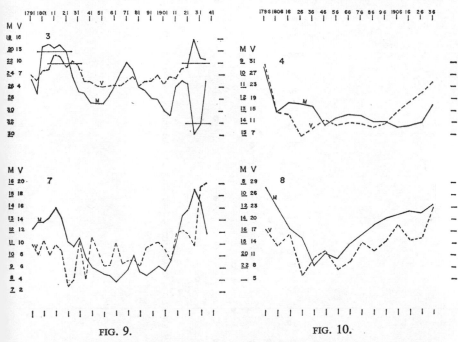

FIG. 9.   FIG. 10.

FIG. 9. Relation of variability (V) and amplitude of dimension (M) in waist length (3) and width (7), 1787–1936.

FIG. 10. Relation of variability (V) and amplitude of dimension (M) in *décolletage* depth (4) and width (8), 1787–1936.

basic pattern: the skirt full and rather long, at least not markedly short; the waist, if not narrow, at least accentuated, and in median position; *décolletage* considerable. If our hypothesis holds, the bulk of the eighteenth century should accordingly prove to be a period of low variability, on assembly of sufficient data.*

* It would also be desirable to try to define the basic pattern of dress by inclusion of more features than the six so far dealt with. The treatment of the arms, bust, and hips, in the basic pattern, have not been considered at all. There are important traits here: sleeves; prominence and position of the bust; proportion of the hips to shoulders, bust, and base of skirt—compare for instance the Grecian bend and bustle fashions with the recent one of hips larger than base of the skirt. But the difficulties are considerable in dealing with these features over longer ranges of times: some disappear and reappear, others require profile views for full measurement. Nevertheless something could no doubt be ascertained by further analysis.

97

7

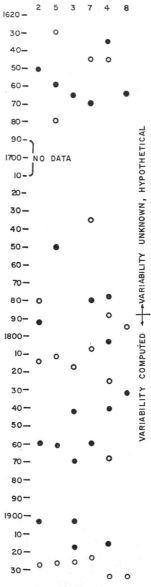

FIG. 11. Clustering of extremes as related to variability. Solid circles: Maxima in dimensions 2, 5, 4, 8; minima in 7; moderate crests in 3; associated with low variabilities and conformity to pattern since 1787 (no earlier data available on variability). Hollow circles: Minima in dimensions 2, 5, 4, 8; maxima in 7; extreme crests in 3; associated with high variabilities and pattern strain since 1787 (no earlier data available on variability).

However, we can make the trial assumption that the specific associations of variabilities with crests which we have found to hold since 1787 also held before that date, and see how the results plot out. That is to say, while we have no reliably computable variabilities for most of the seventeenth and eighteenth centuries, we do have fair approximations to the points in time at which the maxima and minima of dimensions fall; and by plotting the maxima and minima for the whole three-hundred-odd years, we may hope to discover whether the pre-1787 period shows a tendency toward clustering of crests comparable to that after 1787. The result of the experiment is shown in figure 11. Solid circles show those dimension crests, whether maxima or minima, which since 1787 have been associated with low variabilities and pattern stability; hollow circles, crests with the opposite association.

The diagram makes it evident that there was a clustering of crests between 1630 and 1680. Seven of the ten crests in this period fall between 1645 and 1665.

However, the ten crests are nearly evenly divided between those hypothetically associated with high and with low variability, and the two kinds are interdistributed scatteringly. While we may accordingly infer that the mid-seventeenth century was a period of attainment of style dimension extremes, and rapid alternation between extremes in at least some features, there is nothing to prove that the particular post-1787 associations of one of a pair of extremes with heightened variability already held in the seventeenth century.

Now follow nearly a hundred years, from 1680 to 1777, with but two peaks, in dimensions 5 and 7. Even on allowance for their being no data for 1690–1710, there remains a three-quarter-century span with but these two crests. Under such pervading stability, variability may be presumed to have been low.

The next forty years, 1778 to 1817, show eleven crests. Four of these are of the type determined as of low variability, seven of high. Moreover, the low-variability ones fall mostly within the first half of the period (mean date 1788), the high in the latter half (mean date 1802).

The following eighty-odd years, to 1900, possess nine crests, seven of them of low-variability type. The period seems to consist of two spans. First, some two decades, 1825–42, of quieting down from the preceding turbulence. Then a long calm, only slightly ruffled by four low-variability crests (and one high) in the 1860–69 decade, and none at all for three decades after. This Victorian era was certainly placid in fashion.

From 1900 to date, there are ten crests, the four earliest of low variability, the last six of high. Or we might say that 1903–17 was a time in which variability was increasing but only low-variability maxima were reached; it was a final phase of the preceding stable period: strain was already manifest but reaffirmations of the dying pattern were being made. The period 1923–34, by contrast, shows in every feature examined a crest which is in extreme opposition to what prevailed during the long Victorian calm and is in each instance accompanied by very high variability. Table 29 summarizes this.

It is clear from this table as well as figure 11 that there occur in European women's dress alternating longer periods in which a basic pattern of style is rather stably adhered to, relatively few extremes of proportion or dimension are sought, and those all in a direction accompanied by only low variability

TABLE 29 *Extremes of Dimension and Variability by Period*

Period (rounded)	Years	Low var.	High var.	Total	Per decade
			Dimension extremes		
1630–1680	50	(6)	(4)	10	2·0
1681–1777	97	(1)	(1)	2	0·2
1778–1817	40	4	7	11*	2·7
1818–1902	105	7	2	9	0·9
1903–1934	32	4	6	10	3·1

* The variability type of three crests before 1787 is not known.

from year to year and dress to dress; and shorter periods in which basic pattern is disrupted or transformed, extremes of proportion are numerous, and high variability prevails.

This differentiation of periods is positive in all respects for the era since 1787. It holds as regards stability of basic pattern and infrequency of extremes for the hundred and eighty years preceding. Whether it also holds for the association of variability with those extremes which conflict with enduring stable patterns, we have not the evidence to prove or disprove; but at least there is nothing in the imperfect pre-1787 picture to argue against such variability association.

Causality of Change

We are now in position better to weigh the several possible causes of changes in variability.

The primary factor would seem to be adherence to or departure from an ideal though unconscious pattern for formal clothing of women. The consistent conformity of variability to certain magnitudes of proportion—mostly a conformity of low variabilities to high magnitudes—leaves little room for any other conclusion.

A second possible explanation, that high variability is a function of extremes of proportion, falls as such. It is true for a full waist and a narrow or short skirt, untrue for slender waist or full or long skirt. The explanation holds only so far as it is subsumed in that of the basic pattern.

A third possible explanation, that generic or nonstylistic factors unsettle fashion at certain times, is not eliminated, but is pushed into the background of further investigation. After all, such a cause would be an ultimate, not an immediate one. It may well be that unsettled times make for unsettled styles. Revolution, Napoleonic and World wars, struggles over the rights of man, Communism and Fascism, the motor and jazz, may contribute to fashions trying to stretch and disrupt its fundamental stylistic pattern. But while such an influence is easily conjectured, it is difficult to prove. In any event, there seems no clear reason for the specific fashion extremes which such a set of causes might be thought to produce. Social and political unsettlement as such might produce stylistic unsettlement and variability as such; but there is nothing to show that it would *per se* produce thick waists, ultra-high or low ones, short and tight skirts. If there is a connection here, it seems that it must be through alteration of the basic semi-unconscious pattern, through an urge to unsettle or disrupt this; and that when increased fashion variability occurs, it is as a direct function of pattern stress, and only indirectly, and less certainly, of socio-political instability. In short, generic historic causes tending toward social and cultural instability may produce instability in dress styles also; but their effect on style is expressed in stress upon the existent long-range basic pattern of dress, and the changes effected have meaning only in terms of the pattern.

Concretely, it would be absurd to say that the Napoleonic wars, or the complex set of historic forces underlying them, specifically produced high-waisted dresses, and the World War low-waisted ones. They both probably did produce an unsettlement of style, which, however, resulted in extremity of high and low waistedness respectively.*

Herewith arises another question: whether the crests and troughs of waves of fashion, its periodicities discussed on p. 79, are perhaps also to be sought not in anything inherent in fashion, but rather in more general historic causes. In favour of such a view is the heavier clustering of trait extremes in Revolutionary-Napoleonic, World-War, and immediately subsequent decades. But again there are crests also in the intervening period. What is specifically characteristic of the agitated periods is not so much extremes of dimension or proportion, as extremes of high variability; and these in turn correlate with certain minima and maxima of proportion, but not with their opposites. The significant fact remains that high variability is not associated with *any* dimensional crest, but always† with only one of a pair of opposing extremes. This throws us back on the basic pattern as something that must be recognized.

Now, one can indeed accept this basic pattern, but accept it as something intrinsically tending to remain more or less static over a long period, or the whole of a civilization; and then attribute the more marked variations from it to broader historic disturbing causes, rather than to anything stylistically inherent and tending from within toward swings away from and back toward the pattern. On this view the century-long cycle which we have found to hold for most of our fashion traits would not be a property of style *per se*, but a by-product of the fact that Europe happened to be generically disturbed in the decades around 1800 and 1920.

Conclusions

Our first finding is that the basic dimensions of modern European feminine dress alternate with fair regularity between maxima and minima which in most cases average about fifty years apart, so that the full-wave length of their periodicity is around a century.

---

* The Empire mode was consciously Greek or Neo-Classic. It professed to take over from antiquity a full and rather high waist and a falling instead of flaring skirt. It obviously did not take over from antiquity its own short skirt and wide *décolletage*, nor its ultra-high waist, nor a tight, undraped skirt, nor short puff-sleeves. In brief, Empire dress style fell in with the catchwords of its day, and in consonance with the social currents and political currents of its time, which aimed toward the Classic, accepted just as much of Classic dress style as suited its own trends, and for the rest followed these trends while calmly ignoring or violating all the remaining features of its supposed model.

† Excepting dimension 3, waist length, where low variability is associated with medium magnitude.

101

By comparison, annual changes, and even those of moderately long periods of moderate length, generally are markedly less in degree or amplitude. This conclusion applies to the major proportions of the total silhouette. Super-structural features have not been examined quantitatively, but appear to develop and pass away completely in briefer cycles. The present study is concerned with the variations in persistent features.

There appear accordingly to be two components in dress fashions. One is mode in the proper sense: that factor which makes this year's clothes different from last year's or from those of five years ago. The other is a much more stable and slowly changing factor, which each year's mode takes for granted and builds upon. It cannot be pretended that these two factors are definably distinguishable throughout. Behaviouristically, however, they can mostly be separated by the length and regularity of the changes due to the more under-lying component.

It is evident that the basic features of style as distinct from more rapidly fluctuating mode, being taken for granted at any given moment, are largely unconscious in the sense that they are felt as axiomatic and derivations are made from them, but they are not tampered with, except again unconsciously.

This in turn seems to imply that the role of particular individuals in moulding basic dress style is slight. The influence of creative or important individuals is probably largely exerted on the accessories of transient mode. How great it is there, has never been objectively examined, and would be difficult to investigate. Historians of fashion may be partly right or mainly fictitious in the influence they assign to Marie Antoinette, Recamier, Eugénie, and the various Princes of Wales. The reverse is much more likely, that individuals conform to the style which they find in existence, operate in minor ways within its configuration, and at times of coincidence receive false credit for 'causing' one or more of its features.

The long swings of proportion which we have determined seem comparable to what economists call secular trends, which also carry oscillations or lesser cyclic movements on their surface. No one attributes either these larger economic trends or the fluctuations to individual initiative. It is of course conceivable that economic determinants are social in their nature and stylistic ones individual. In fact this is often assumed. However, such an assumption is naïve in the sense of being critically untested. It is rather more likely that what holds in one domain of human culture holds also in another. At any rate, the burden of proof must rest on the contrary view. And this burden has certainly doubled since we have shown that dress-style changes behave historically somewhat like economic ones; in the stateliness of their march, or trend, for instance, and in their superimposed cycles or oscillations.

The evidence to date shows that when a proportion has swung one way to its extreme and gone halfway the other, it may oscillate for a decade or two part way back to the first extreme, but normally it resumes its swing toward the opposite. But this is a behaviouristic finding, and *a priori* may just as well be due to cultural as to personal causes. So far as individuals are concerned, the total situation seems overwhelmingly to indicate that their actions are determined by the style far more than they can determine it.

No generic significance can be claimed for the value of a century found for the average periodicity or wave length of dress proportions. It is only a mean, though it is rather closely adhered to in three of our six features. Obviously, other features, or styles other than modern European ones, may possess quite different periodicities. In fact, there is no reason why style in general, or even dress style, should necessarily swing rhythmically back and forth. Our findings apply only to the material analysed.

Definitely significant is the fact that there are periods of high and of low variability of style. These come out much alike whether it is a matter of variations of yearly averages from the five-year moving mean, or of variations of individual dresses from the year's mean. Within the last century and a half, 1787–1835 (especially before 1820) and 1920–36 are periods of high variability. The intervening seventy-five or more years show low variability. The available measures scarcely allow of variability computations for most of the eighteenth century, but the general pattern apparently underwent no very marked alterations in that century until after 1775.

The two high-variability periods also contain more crests or extremes of proportion than the intervening seventy-five years or than the stable bulk of the eighteenth century. There is therefore a relation between extremes and variability.

However, this relation is one-sided. For four of the six proportions examined, variability rises as the proportion or diameter shrinks, becomes low as this reaches ampleness. For a fifth proportion, waist width, the relation is the opposite. For the sixth, variability becomes acute when the measure is either very high or very low.

High variability thus is more completely limited to certain periods than are extremes of the proportions or diameters themselves. Those of the diameter extremes which are accompanied by low variability fall in some cases into the long stable interval.

The best explanation that we are able to suggest for these phenomena is that of a basic pattern of women's dress style, toward which European culture of recent centuries has been tending as an ideal. This pattern comprises amplitude in most dimensions, scantness or medium value in others. As these proportions are achieved, there are equilibrium, relative stability, and low variability. The pattern may be said to be saturated. At other times, most or all of the proportions are at the opposite extreme, which may be construed as one of strain, and variability rises high. This basic or ideal pattern, for Europe of the last two or three centuries, requires a skirt that is both full and long, a waist that is abnormally constructed but in nearly proper anatomical position, and *décolletage* that is ample both vertically and horizontally.

The periods of computed high variability and therefore of 'strain' or perversion of pattern coincide fairly closely with the Revolutionary-Napoleonic and World War-post-War eras. Generic cultural or historic influences can therefore probably be assumed to affect dress-style changes. Sociocultural stress and unsettlement seem to produce fashion strain and instability. However, they exert their influence upon an existing stylistic pattern, which they dislocate or invert. Without reference to this pattern, their effect would not be understood.

While we have no reliable variability measures before 1787, it is clear that in

103

the decades surrounding 1650–60 there was an accumulation of proportion extremes similar to those of 1787–1835 and 1910–36. The mid-seventeenth century may thus have been a third period of pattern strain, rapid change, and variability.

The explanation propounded is not that revolution, war, and sociocultural unsettlement in themselves produce scant skirts and thick and high or low waists, but that they disrupt the established dress style and tend to its over-throw or inversion. The directions taken in this process depend on the style pattern: they are subversive or centrifugal to it. By contrast, in 'normal' periods dress is relatively stable in basic proportions and features: its variations tend to be slight and transient—fluctuations of mode rather than changes of style. In another civilization, with a different basic pattern of dress style, generic sociocultural unsettlement might also produce unsettlement of dress style but with quite different specific expressions—slender waists and flaring skirts, for instance, or the introduction or abolition of *décolletage*.

It is conceivable that the method pursued in this study may be of utility as a generic measure of sociocultural unsettlement. Also, it provides an objective description of one of the basic patterns characteristic of a given civilization for several centuries, and may serve as a precedent for the more exact definition of other stylistic patterns in the same or other civilizations.

It also seems possible that the correlation with general conditions explains the near-regularity in the periodicities of dress. If these largely express pattern disturbances due to disturbances more general in the culture, there is no need to fall back on assumptions of an unknown factor inherent in dress itself and making for rhythmic change.

We have deliberately avoided explanation of our phenomena in terms of psychological factors such as imitation, emulation, or competition, which are a stock explanation: the leaders want to surpass the mass, so they keep going one step farther, until a physical limit is reached, when they turn about and head the procession back. We do not deny that such psychological motiva-tions may be operative. We do believe that as explanations they are con-jectural, and scientifically useless, because, to date at least, they depend on factors which are unmeasurable and undefinable. On the contrary, we think we have shown that through behaviouristic and inductive procedures operating wholly within the sociocultural level, functional correlations can be established for such supposedly refractory cultural manifestations as style and fashion changes.

References

1. For their kindness and generosity in offering their collections of original fashion plates as source material for this survey, the authors wish to express their appreciation to the Department of Decorative Art, and the late Mr Robert P. Utter, of the University of California; to Mr John Howell, Mrs Morton Gibbons, and the S. & G. Gump Company, of San Francisco; and to Mrs August Ericson, of Berkeley. Assistance in the preparation of these materials was furnished by the personnel of Works Projects Administration Official Project No. 665-08-3-30, Unit A-15.
2. 'On the Principle of Order in Civilization as Exemplified by Changes of Fashion', *Amer. Anthr.* vol. 21, pp. 235–263. Cited hereafter as Kroeber.
3. Kroeber, p. 244.

4. Kroeber, p. 244.
5. M. Köhler and E. von Sichart, *A History of Costume* (New York: G. Howard Watt 1933), p. 237. Cited hereafter as Köhler.
6. Köhler, p. 314.
7. Köhler, p. 288.
8. Köhler, p. 320: invented (by the Spanish) in the first half of the sixteenth century.
9. Köhler, p. 320.
10. Kroeber, p. 257.
11. Kroeber, p. 256.

Chapter 4

RECURRING CYCLES OF FASHION*
by Agnes Brook Young

This extract presents an analysis of similar historical period to that described in Chapter 3. The author identifies a shorter cycle as a more valuable analytical tool.

Fashion has its Laws

I shall deal with the fashions of women's dress during the past two centuries. The central feature of the discussion is a continuous annual series of illustrations of the most fully typical costumes worn during the 178 years from 1760 through 1937. Practically all the reading matter in the book is a discussion of these pictures. This is not at all a history of recent costume, nor is it a compiled catalogue of the changes in fashion in modern times. It is a discussion of the apparently inescapable evidence showing that, when the typical annual fashions are arranged chronologically in unbroken series over a long term of years, their changes appear to follow rather definite laws of modification and development within an almost unchanging pattern of evolution.

If it is really true that the changes of fashion in women's dress follow well-defined rules, there must be some good explanation to account for the fact that these rules were not discovered long ago. The explanation needs to cover much more than our prolonged tardiness in discovering the rules or the laws which govern the changes in fashion; it needs to show convincingly the possibility that such laws can exist. During all our modern period, and even in ancient times, the literatures of many nations have expressed the general belief of mankind that the fashions of women's dress are fickle, disorderly, capricious, and utterly unpredictable. The evidence here presented seems to show that these almost universally accepted beliefs are not valid. And so we need to consider just how the illustrations of dresses reproduced in this book differ as evidence from those scores of previous volumes.

The illustrations in this book, showing the dresses worn year by year over a century and three quarters, have been most carefully selected as representing the most fully typical dresses of each year. This sort of selection has not been attempted in previous studies, which have instead mainly shown dresses that were striking examples of those worn in selected periods, or costumes of notable people, or modes chosen to exemplify some particular feature of the fashions of a period. Probably it is true that most of the illustrations in the published histories of fashion really represent exceptional styles of their years than typical

* From Agnes Brook Young, *Recurring Cycles of Fashion 1760–1937* (Harper & Row, 1937).

ones. And it may well be that the almost universally accepted beliefs in the lawlessness of fashion have tended to influence students toward selecting exceptional costumes as subjects of discussions.

Perhaps the distinction may be made clearer if we consider the analogy of the studies that economists make of the movements of stock prices. Here is a field of activity in which change is going on constantly, and in which the numbers of individual changes are almost limitless. Every day the prices of great numbers of individual securities advance, while those of numerous others decline, and still others remain unchanged. Nevertheless, there is in reality a general average change over long periods, first in one direction and then in the other. And these general tendencies produce the long advances which stock traders call bull markets, and the declines which they term bear markets. Economists call them market cycles.

The individual declines are numerous even while general prices are advancing in bull markets. And there are many advances throughout the periods of generally decreasing prices in bear markets. But the long term trends cannot be judged or studied by noting these exceptions. We have in this country detailed records of millions of changes in security prices extending back over more than one hundred years, but it is only during the past forty years or so that students of such matters have learned how to use the average price changes of selected typical stocks to measure the central tendencies of the long term changes. By studying these typical movements instead of the individual ones they have indentified the cycles, and almost all economic knowledge of these matters has been developed in recent years since these new methods were employed.

This study of typical fashions in women's dress, arranged in unbroken annual sequence for 178 years, reaches conclusions which may well be stated here at the outset in brief outline. These conclusions are that in modern times the changes in prevailing fashions in women's dress have moved through a series of recurring cycles lasting for about a third of a century each; that during each cycle the annual fashion changes have been variations and modifications from one central type fashion; and finally that there have been in all only three of these central types of fashion, which have succeeded one another in unchanging sequence over the past two centuries.

The evidence in support of these conclusions is inherent in the illustrations themselves, which are presented in chronological order in Chapters IV through VIII [not reproduced here]. And all the reading matter in these and the other chapters is an appeal to the evidence. There are no tables of figures, and not many diagrams have been used. Yet in reality this book is the report of an extended statistical study. At its inception it had the limited objective of trying to find out what changes had actually taken place in this country in recent years in the prevailing fashions in women's dress. It slowly developed into a long statistical research, as the writer became convinced that typical fashions really do exist, and that an adequate study of fashion changes is dependent on the possibility of identifying and comparing these typical fashions, year by year, and over long series of years.

The concept of the existence of typical fashions in women's dress in a given year is implicit in the very nature of fashion itself. Many women can tell at a glance which ones among the other women they meet at a social gathering are wearing this year's dresses. They can tell it as surely as the automobile dealer can recognize at a glance this year's Buick and last year's model, without needing to examine the serial numbers. The reason why the woman who is keenly interested in fashion, and well informed about it, can immediately recognize this year's fashions is that there is always a typical annual fashion, as well as numerous modifications of it and many variants from it.

The controlling factor in changes in women's dress is that all women desire to wear each year dresses which are sufficiently different from those of last year so as to be unmistakably recognizable by the initiated as being of the latest mode, and yet at the same time neither identical with those of other women, nor so different from them as to be undesirably conspicuous. This governing principle in fashion has long been recognized, and more than a century ago the English critic, Hazlitt, made the penetrating observation that the two things which fashion abhors most are vulgarity and singularity. He also wrote that fashion was gentility fleeing from vulgarity.

Fashion in dress is a process of continuous slow change of typical annual modes, accompanied each year by innumerable slight variations from the dominant type. The changes must be continuous, for otherwise the fashion would promptly cease to be fashionable. It must be sufficiently rapid to outmode previous fashions every year, but it must be sufficiently slow to prevent the leaders from outdistancing their followers. It follows from these inexorable conditions, which control the evolution of fashions in women's dress, that the annual change which outmodes annually the styles of the year before must be a slight but significant alteration in the central type of generally accepted costume, from which the numberless modifications are restricted variations. If we can surely identify these most truly typical styles year by year over a long period of time, we shall have the material for studying and comparing them, and for tracing and even measuring their changes. That is what this book undertakes to do.

The continuous process of change which we call fashion is not handicapped by any compulsion to make progress. In a real sense, fashion is evolution without destination. The world generally considers that progress in material things consists in changes that make them more useful, or better looking, or less expensive. In the long run fashion never attains these objectives. Its ideal is slow continuous change, unhampered by the restrictions of either aesthetics or practicality.

This piece of research began to assume its present form when the writer first realized that it would not be possible for annual fashion changes regularly to outmode existing styles unless practically all the fashionable dresses of each year possessed in common certain rather definite characteristics. It is because they do possess in common those particular characteristics that they belong to the mode of that year, and not to that of some other year. And it is the alteration of those essential style characteristics by the annual fashion change which outmodes them and replaces them by a new set of characteristics which constitute the style of the next year.

We may well restate this for emphasis. We know that fashion outmodes previous styles each year, so there must be a continuous change under way. We know this continuous change must be relatively slow because only the initiated can recognize the differences from one year to the next. Finally, if fashion in dress is a slow continuous change, outmoding each year that which had general acceptance, and substituting for it something slightly different, then there must of necessity always exist a typical expression of fashion, or a typical style, on which the changes are operating. If there were numerous types, no one change could outmode them all, and if there were numerous annual changes, there could be no accepted fashion. The conclusion must be that the process of fashion is a process of slow continuous change of typical costumes. Fashion always tolerates, encourages, and even requires each year numerous variations from the central type. But the typical fashion exists and it is on it that the annual changes that are essentially significant and controlling take place.

It is because the dresses that are in fashion in a given year do possess in common certain features which might be technically termed their differentiating fashion characteristics that it becomes possible to identify a typical fashion for each year. These typical dresses, illustrated in later chapters, are the ones selected from the available costumes of each year as most fully combining in themselves the differentiating fashion characteristics of their years. In the following chapter there is a description of the method by which these selections of the annual typicals were made. The methods were the product of much experimenting and careful testing, and though they now appear relatively simple, it is believed that they are reliable and produce adequately accurate results.

The final outcome of this part of the undertaking was the assembling of the continuous annual series of illustrations of the typical yearly fashions prevailing in women's daytime dresses from 1760 to the present time. These illustrations should show, and it is believed that they do faithfully show, what really happened during that long span of years in the prevailing trends and dominant currents of fashion change. In this series the illustrations for the first thirty years or so are less surely typical of the fashions which prevailed in those years than are the illustrations for the later periods, when the material available for selection is much more ample in volume, and so affords better evidence to tell us what the fashions and their changes actually were.

After considerable experimenting, it was decided to make up the series wholly from street and daytime dresses, and to exclude evening gowns. The reason for this was partly that only a small proportion of the feminine population ever wears evening gowns, and partly because evening dresses always tend to be extreme in their rendering of the current modes, and often feature fashion trends which are shortlived. The daytime dresses from which the selections of the annual typicals were made may be described as being the kinds of dresses which women wore in each year for daytime calls and for shopping.

As this long series of illustrations was being worked over and having its gaps filled in, and being improved as new material became available in collections of fashion prints and in the stacks and files of libraries here and abroad, it gradually became apparent that change in women's dress has not only been going on constantly during the past 178 years, but also that the changes have moved in a series of well-defined cycles, each of which has lasted for something more than thirty years.

In some ways the fact that fashions move in cycles is not a novel idea.

Everyone who has given even the slightest attention to the history of modern dress knows that at about the time of our Civil War, and for a good many years before that, hoop skirts were in fashion and constituted the most dominant feature of women's dress. Again, the older people among us can remember that after the Civil War and for a long period extending perhaps to about the turn of the century, women commonly wore dresses with skirts which were extended backwards by the use of bustles, or by some substitute arrangement having the same effect.

Finally, we all realize that since about the beginning of this century prevailing dress fashions have excluded both hoops and bustles and have dictated that dresses should be more nearly form-fitting. Here we have then in modern times three periods of not greatly unequal duration in which prevailing fashions were dominated by the forms and contours of the skirts. In their aggregate those three periods cover something more than one hundred years. This book considers that each one of these three periods may properly be termed a fashion cycle, because each is clearly a well-defined entity possessing in its own right an individuality that entitles it to such a designation.

We are all accustomed to discussions of fashion which emphasize its lawlessness, its fickle character, its changeability, and the impossibility of predicting what it will do next. Nevertheless, it is clear that such characterizations are valid only in most restricted degrees, for we may always be safely confident that there are many changes that fashion will not make. It will not dictate that hoop skirts shall be worn in one year, skirts with bustles in the following year, and form-fitting skirts in the third year. In point of fact, it never in modern times has made any sudden changes. Fashion changes continuously, but always slowly, and as we shall see, its changes during the past two centuries have been in a series of well-defined cycles that have followed one another in regular and unchanging order.

In these three simple distinctions or classifications, which do not need to be substantiated by any extended historical research, we have a hint of the possible existence of cycles in fashion changes. It was in part this very hint which led to the conclusion that there has been under way ever since 1760 a succession of well-defined style cycles and that the distinguishing characteristic by which these cycles have been marked has been the shape of the skirts.

In the long process of selecting the illustrations of the most truly typical fashions for each of the 178 years, the procedure was adopted of arranging the tracings or photostats of the fashion plates on long rows of card tables, and then comparing, assorting, discarding and substituting in accord with the statistical evidence that was being compiled concerning them. When the series of typical skirts was nearing final form, it became evident to anyone who would walk to and fro along the tables on which the pictures were arranged in chronological order, year after year, and decade after decade, that minor fashion changes had taken place every year in the long period of over a century and three quarters, but that major changes in the types of dresses approved by fashion had occurred only every three or four decades.

For example, the hoop skirt was not a fashion of short, sporadic occurrences, but the dominating factor in the typically accepted fashions of every year from about 1830 to 1870. Clearly that span of almost four decades was a hoop-skirt period in women's fashions, and all the numerous changes and variations in other features or details of accepted costumes are subordinate facts compared with this major and dominating one. It may be noted in passing that this is referred to as a hoop-skirt period in a popular use of that term, rather than in a technically accurate one, for many of the dresses of that time did not, in fact, have hoops.

Continued analysis and inspection, based on this observation of the characteristics of the hoop-skirt period, showed that a classification based on the types of skirts would be equally valid for the entire period from 1760 to date. During the first four decades of that long span of years the typical fashions were those of dresses having bustles, or at least extended backward much as they would have been if actually supported behind by bustles. American women of our Revolutionary War period wore gowns of that sort. There followed a period of several decades when dresses were generally tubular in form, much as are those to which we are accustomed today. Next came the hoop-skirt period, then the dresses with bustles or back-fullness, which were worn up to and even beyond the time of the War with Spain, and finally this present period of tubular skirts.

The conclusion which was borne in upon one who walked back and forth in front of the tables on which were arranged the pictures showing the typical fashions for the 178 years was that the only really major fashion changes were those in the types of skirts. This was clear in spite of the fact that change of some sort was continuous, and constantly bringing about such alterations as that of sleeves from long and tight to short and full, or neck lines from deep v-shaped to high, or repeated shifts in the waist line. Moreover, during this entire span of years there had been only three of these skirt types.

Each type, when definitely established, had maintained its dominance for three or four decades, and then had given way to one of the other two types. If these general inferences can be fully supported by the evidence, they lead to the conclusions that the determining factor in major fashion types is the general form of the skirt, and that the period of years during which one definite type of skirt characterizes the accepted fashions of dress may properly be termed fashion cycle.

The three types of skirts are illustrated in the drawing on page 113 showing figures in solid line and the three types of skirts in dotted outline. The first figure stands squarely in the centre of a large bell, which is wide at the base; the second stands at the front of a skirt with all the fullness at the back; and the third stands in a cylinder, which has almost the same width at top and bottom.

The classification of fashions on the basis of the skirt is not new. It was primarily to skirt structure that Grand-Carteret referred when he wrote: 'The two conceptions of fashion; the one is built out from the woman's body by all sorts of contrivances; the other more or less follows its lines.' Outside of these two principles, he points out, there can only be half-measures.

Clearly his division is both valid and important, but it would be more so if he had noted that fashions of one type persist for long periods of years, and that the supporting framework which forms the basis of one of his classifications is of two distinct sorts. Though his figure-conforming group yields to no logical subdivision, the built-out class may readily be divided into skirts which are

112

held away from the figure all the way around, after the manner of the hoop, and those which protrude only in back. As each of these styles completely dominated fashion for approximately a third of the last century, there seems good reason to regard them both as major fashions.

If we could have the 178 pictures of typical fashions reproduced on as many cards, which we could hold in our hands like playing cards, we would find that they could easily be sorted into the three groups. The principle which would govern the sorting would be the relation of the mass of the skirt to the figure beneath. When the sorting was finished and the resulting three piles examined, they would be seen to contain dresses like those which appear in silhouette on pages 115, 116 and 117.

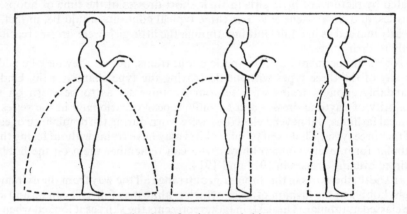

FIG. 1. The three fundamental skirt contours.

The first of these illustrations on page 115 represents dresses in which the figure stands at the front of the skirt with the bulk in the back. This sort of contour has been referred to as the bustle type, but since for the student of costume the term 'bustle' has a special and restricted connotation, it may be wiser to call this the back-fullness type. It will then include any dress having this characteristic structure, whether the dress has an actual bustle beneath or is made to protrude simply by its own bulk, for obviously dresses having this shape belong to this group, no matter how they are made.

The little silhouettes show, in fact, that the back-fullness effect was achieved in a number of ways, though the details of dressmaking devices of cutting and draping appear more clearly in the year-by-year series, in Chapters IV and VII [not reproduced here]. They show a good deal of variety in the size of this back-fullness, which was sometimes enormous and protruded like a shelf from the waist, as in 1790, 1875 and 1885, and sometimes small and rather lower down, as in 1880. Now and again the dresses were somewhat short, as that of 1780, and at other times they developed trains, as in 1875 and 1895. The differences between the little figures are, in fact, considerable, but it is interesting to observe that the back-fullness effect which is common to them all loses nothing thereby. On the contrary, it seems to emerge all the more clearly as a fundamental structural principle.

113

The next group of illustrations represents the tubular type and appears on page 116. There are more illustrations on this page because their slimness makes it possible, not because there were more variants of this type of skirt. They comprise Grand-Carteret's group of dresses, which follow more or less the natural lines of the figure without an attempt to create an artificial form. Many of these dresses we can remember from our own experience.

The chief difference between dresses in this group is in the length of the skirts, which range all the way from the extremely short skirts, which were in fashion between 1925 and 1930, to those which touch the floor. Great as this difference is, however, it does no damage to the characteristic appearance of the type. This is true of short skirts in the other two types as well, and might be illustrated by pictures of little girls in their short dresses at the time of hoops, of bustles, and the present day. The three typical contours would be, in fact, as clearly marked as in adult clothing, though the little girls wear dresses reaching only to their knees.

A similar comment might be made about trains, in that they may be added to any of the three types without destroying the type characteristic. Understandably enough, trains were seldom so universal as to be worn on the majority of daytime dresses and so only appear occasionally in the series of typical fashions, but nevertheless they were worn during the dominance of each of the three types. That even tubular skirts may have trains without losing their tubular form, every woman knows who can remember them on the hobble-skirted evening dresses in 1913 and 1914.

In width, the skirts in this tubular group range all the way from the extremely tight hobble to the fashion of 1825, which is almost as full as it can be and still be classed as tubular. This last, in fact, represents the skirt as it looked when on the verge of discarding altogether the tubular form and taking on the bell-shaped contour, which is illustrated on page 117.

This third page of silhouettes represents skirts which form a wide circle at the bottom and taper upward to the waist. This cannot correctly be called the hoop-skirt type, because actual hoops were worn only for a part of the long period during which this type was popular, nor can we name it after the crinoline for the same reason. Long ago such skirts were occasionally referred to as beehive skirts, because they were similar in outline to the plaited straw hives of a former day. The simile is a good one, but the name is perhaps too unfamiliar for modern use, and for this reason it might be well to substitute the less descriptive term 'bell-shaped'. The dresses on this page are also similar that little need be said about them beyond noting that there are slight differences in length and width and location of waist line.

The illustrations on these three pages with their accompanying dates show that though each type dominated fashion for long periods, not one of them retained an absolutely static form. Examination of the yearly typicals brought out the further interesting fact that the variants which each type produces were great enough to keep fashion constantly changing. In fact, during the whole 178 years women were under the constant necessity of renewing their wardrobes in order not to be out of fashion, exactly as they are today, and the change was so fast for those who could afford the pace that clothes had continually to be discarded long before they were worn out. In this way the variants within the

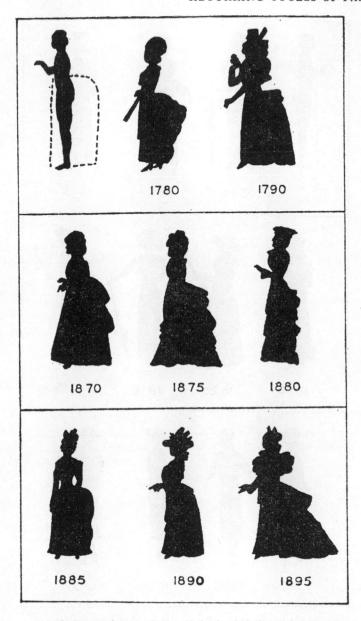

1780 1790

1870 1875 1880

1885 1890 1895

FIG. 2. Recurring examples of the back-fullness contour.

types fed the endless craving for novelty and provided for the perpetual change
which has been recognized since ancient times as an outstanding characteristic
of fashion. It is no contradiction, but a generalization which fits all three types,
to say that though fashion retained given structural characteristics for long

115

FIG. 3. Recurring examples of the tubular contour.

stretches, fashion never stood still. A type might then be defined as a given structural characteristic including numerous variants.

The evidence which was furnished by the bringing together of the year-by-year fashions which were the actual prevailing typical dresses of women in

116

FIG. 4. Recurring examples of the bell-shaped contour.

Europe and America for the past 178 years might be summarized by saying that during this long period feminine dress was of three main types and may be classified into three basic groups. The classification is guided by the skirt, and in reality by the contour and mass of the skirt in its relation to the figure beneath.

117

Each of the three types, back-fullness, tubular and bell, lasted for long periods of time, during which its characteristic structure completely dominated fashion. During these periods of dominance a regular and steady change occurred annually—and almost it might be said, seasonally—but in such a way as to preserve the dominant form of the type, the change taking place, as it were, within the boundaries of the dominant silhouette. Fashion in modern times has consistently followed this pattern of evolutionary change based on the contour of the skirt.

The conclusion that fashion has followed a regular course conflicts with ancient and firmly held beliefs in the lawlessness of style. Probably it is true that the literatures of all modern nations contain somewhat bitter and cynical expressions of the general conviction that it is futile to apply the rules of reason to the vagaries of women's dress. Modern civilization has accepted as axiomatic the proposition that women's fashions could not be judged or compared or even discussed in any common-sense terms and so the attempt to do so ought not to be made. We know that it is not merely a modern attitude, for we find it as clearly expressed in the literature of classic antiquity in the Roman dictum that differences in taste must not even be discussed, *de gustibus non disputandum est.*

Despite this record of age-old conviction this book maintains that, during the past two hundred years at least, changes in women's fashions have conformed to the almost rigid rules outlined in this chapter, and that the changes have moved in cycles which have, so far, been more nearly uniform in length and more closely constant in character than any of the cycle series in business and industry that have been charted by the economists.

If this is true, it is clear that changes in women's styles are not arbitrarily created by a little set of fashion dictators in Paris. Each season the Paris designers present a number of variations on the mode, which become fashionable only if women all over the world approve them, and disappear rapidly into oblivion if they do not. There seems to be no doubt that the Paris designers are themselves swayed by and subject to the great cycle trends, and that their pre-eminence in their field depends on their ability to follow Chandler's recipe for leadership, 'Look to see where the people are going and lead them where they drive you.'

The fact that women's fashions appear to be in their major characteristics a series of steadily evolving variations of only three principal types, which have so far succeeded one another in an unvarying sequence, has much significance. The existence of typical styles carries the implication that fashion changes can be accurately recorded, studied and measured. The presence of a pattern in the change insures that fashion changes can profitably be charted and in some important respects can even be predicted.

Three Cycles per Century

Each of the cycles which are characterized by the shapes and contours of the skirts appears to last about a third of a century, and since there are only three of them, each basic fashion reappears at intervals of a hundred years. If we had a full series of small photographs, each representing the most nearly typical

118

dress of a single year, and if we should arrange them in chronological order on a series of tables, we should see that this is true. Such a year-by-year arrangement of the illustrations of annual fashions from 1760 through 1937 is to be found further on in this book [not reproduced here], and there the fact of style reappearances after the lapse of a century may be verified.

The first back-fullness cycle lasted from 1760 through 1795, or 36 years, when it gave way to a tubular cycle which persisted from 1796 through 1829, or 34 years. That was followed by the bell, or so-called hoop-skirt, cycle, which continued from 1830 through 1867, or a period of 38 years. Thus, the three cycles brought us through our Civil War period, to a time just a little more than one hundred years from the beginning of our first back-fullness cycle in 1760. Then, in 1868 a new back-fullness cycle started, and we recall it as a period when bustles were in use. It lasted through 1899, or for 32 years, and was followed by the tubular cycle which has lasted up to the present time. The earlier tubular cycle began in 1796, or 104 years before this one.

The approximate regularity in the duration of the fashion cycles is truly impressive. In the century and three-quarters under review the cycles have been as follows:

> Back-fullness, 1760 through 1795, or 36 years
> Tubular, 1796 through 1829, or 34 years
> Bell, 1830 through 1867, or 38 years
> Back-fullness, 1868 through 1899, or 32 years
> Tubular, 1900 through 1937, or 38 years so far.

One cannot but be hesitant in attempting to interpret such an astonishing set of dates and data. Here are carefully selected illustrations of typical fashions, year by year, for 178 years. They are so continuously changing that each typical fashion differs visibly from those that precede and those that follow it. This never-ending change is perhaps the most important single fact about the modern dress of women. And yet the illustrations, the dates, and the figures for the duration of cycles seem to indicate that the ceaseless changes are in reality confined within a framework of almost iron-bound rigidity.

The relatively uniform duration of the cycles, and the definiteness with which they may be identified by using the classifications here adopted, do not mean that there are no zones of doubt at the end of one cycle and the beginning of the next. The fact is that each transition does present its doubtful cases. When one of the dominant cycle types is drawing toward its close, and is about to make way for its successor, it begins slowly to lose its characteristic appearance and to assume some of the features of the type which is soon to succeed it. In this way the transitions are made gradually. There is no sharp break, and no exact point at which it is possible to say that all dresses before this are unquestionably of one type, and all coming after it are unquestionably of the succeeding type. Rather, the two types gradually merge in the course of the transition, with the old one reluctantly fading away, and the new one progressively becoming dominant.

These transitions are so gradual and smooth that people living through them are seldom aware that anything out of the ordinary is happening. During the transition years, fashion unfolds as steadily, as tranquilly, and even as slowly as at other times, but there is an essential difference in the nature of the change. During the continued dominance of a given cycle type the annual, or normal, change never interferes with the characteristic form and contour of the skirt. The changes are continuous, but they take place within the confines of the established typical silhouette. During transition years, on the other hand, it is the silhouette of the skirt form which succumbs to fundamental change and becomes rapidly modified into the different, succeeding type.

The progress of the typical fashions during the long series of years for which the records have here been compiled may in part be likened to an automobile journey beginning at Baltimore and going westward over the old National Pike. The first part of the journey is over the coastal plains and rolling country east of the mountains. After a while the mountains themselves are reached, and the character of the scenery, the farm lands and all the natural surroundings is changed. The differences are real and unmistakable, and yet it would be quite impossible to drive a stake at some point beside the road to mark the place where the mountains begin. So it is similarly clear that one dress cycle differs in its fundamental characteristics from the one that preceded it, and even so it is not easy to designate the exact point at which the former one terminated and the succeeding one began.

We may follow somewhat further the figure of the automobile trip and note that just beyond Wheeling the mountains have been left behind and the level country of the Middle West has been entered, and once more it would be difficult to mark the exact location of the transition point. Now if the journey could be continued all the way to the Pacific with repetitions of the three kinds of country—the rolling hills of the seaboard strip, the mountains, and the flat lands of the Middle West—in that order, and if the number of miles through each kind of country were about the same as in each of the other two, we should have a fairly good comparison with the progress of the fashions.

We shall have an even better comparison, if we let our imaginations run a little more freely and think of the automobile trip as running in the other direction eastward from some city located about where Columbus is. First comes a long stretch of Middle West relatively level country. Its changes are gradual, its whole character is one of moderation, and we may liken it to the tubular cycle in the fashions. The scenery changes all the time and no mile is just like the one just completed, and in this also it is like the fashions, which are in continuous evolution with no year duplicating the preceding one, or any earlier one.

Now we reach the mountains without being able to state the exact point at which they begin, and this stretch of highway and country side we may liken to the cycle of the bell-shaped skirts. This is a portion of the trip in which the changes are wide in scope and of large dimensions, and as we get into the highest altitudes the visible extremes of peak and valley are so great that it is quite possible to think of them as having counterparts in the fashion cycle in the enormous hoop skirts and their flamboyant ornamentation of the Civil War period.

Next we emerge from the mountains without being quite able to state at exactly what point we leave them behind, and we enter the rolling country of the coastal strip. This country we may liken to the back-fullness cycle. It has not the level restraint of the Middle West, which we compared to the tubular fashion cycle, nor the extremes of the mountains, which we have just thought of as being like the bell-skirt cycle, but it has the characteristics that are in a way like crosses or compromises between those of the other two, but which are nevertheless so different that they constitute an entity in themselves. Now, if this journey eastward were not stopped by the ocean, but could instead continue indefinitely, it would be like the procession of the fashion cycles.

It would consist of equal stretches of the Middle West, the mountains, and the rolling hills of the seaboard slope, always repeating in that order, changing continuously mile by mile, always with indistinctly marked boundaries, but invariably exhibiting nevertheless perfectly recognizable characteristics, except for the brief transition places. So the fashion cycles follow one another with the annual changes continuously under way, but without disturbing the unchanging order of the cycle from tubular, to bell, to back-fullness. At least, they have not changed yet in the century and three-quarters for which we have these records, although this cannot be treated as demonstrating that they never can change.

It has not been found possible to follow the year-by-year typical fashions prior to 1760, but there is fairly convincing evidence that if we could do so, we should have one more of the cycles appearing in its expected place and sequence. There is reasonably good evidence that a cycle of bell-skirted fashions existed from about 1720 or 1725 to 1760. The modes of the period survive in the paintings of Watteau, Boucher, LeClerc and Fragonard, and they are strikingly similar to the hoop-skirt fashions prevailing here and abroad in the years before and during our Civil War.

If we add this cycle to our previous record, we can lengthen our sequence of recurring cycles to cover more than two centuries, as follows:

> Bell, 1725 through 1759
> Back-fullness, 1760 through 1795
> Tubular, 1796 through 1829
> Bell, 1830 through 1867
> Back-fullness, 1868 through 1899
> Tubular, 1900 through 1937 so far.

The regularity of the recurrences is impressively shown by the fact that the second bell cycle appeared 105 years after the first one, the second back-fullness cycle 108 years later than the earlier one, and the second tubular cycle 104 years after its predecessor of the same type. The six cycles of fashion have covered a little more than two centuries of time, and now one wonders whether or not this present tubular cycle is really about to complete its allotted span, and to be followed by another bell cycle.

The three cycles and the recurrence of each appear strikingly in the famous exhibition of costumes in the Victoria and Albert Museum in South Kensington. There one may see the actual dresses in display cases arranged chronologically down a long gallery. It is one of the few exhibits of its kind anywhere in the world which are sufficiently extensive to afford a perspective of fashion over any considerable period. The actual costumes are by no means truly typical of the prevailing fashions of their years, but nevertheless they make the evolution of fashion and the dominance of recurring types admirably vivid. Where the original dresses may thus be seen, rather than pictures and fashion plates representing them, it becomes evident that the great bell skirts of the middle eighteenth century period were almost literally duplicated by the hoop skirts of our Civil War time; that the back-fullness dresses worn in the period following our Revolutionary War were again in fashion a century later; and, finally, that the reason why the present fashions are so often referred to as the Regency fashions is because of their marked similarity to those that prevailed in the time of George IV, who was regent of England from 1811 to 1830.

Whether or not the sequence of the recurring types that has remained unchanged in the past will be maintained in the future, no one can tell. We are even now at a time when the tubular cycle should shortly, according to precedent, be replaced by another type. If the old order is maintained, we should in time have bell skirts once more.

If there is in reality a fixed order in the cycles, that phenomenon may be susceptible of a more logical explanation than would at first thought be apparent. In the first place, there are only three basic types of skirts. There is the tubular skirt, which is relatively form-fitting, and there are skirts held away from the body on some sort of supporting framework, or its equivalent. These necessarily fall into two classes, and only two—the bell skirt, which may be large or moderate in circumference, and the back-fullness skirt. Much research has failed to devise any other lasting type. A front-fullness skirt is impracticable, and side-fullness styles of the pannier mode have been repeatedly introduced as variants in back-fullness and even in bell cycles, but they have never survived long enough to establish themselves in cycles of their own. Probably it is really true that there are only three distinctively fundamental types of skirts and that there cannot be any more. If so, the reason for the unchanging order of their reappearance in the dress cycles becomes a relatively simple matter to explain.

This reason is to be found in that curious trait of human nature which leads us to look back at almost all relatively recent styles as rather amusingly distasteful. We think of Model T Fords as being funny, and of ten-year-old radios as looking grotesque, and of rocking chairs as fit only to be relegated to attics. This dislike of recent former fashions usually extends back in the case of dress to include all the fashions that we can individually remember. We should not seriously think of reviving any of them, and so they are always subject to a kind of taboo. Moreover, the older women among us who are still of an age to participate actively in fashion retain just as acutely disagreeable impressions of the fashions of their girlhood days and the fashions they remember their mothers wearing as the younger women do of the fashions that prevailed ten or fifteen years ago.

At present, the older women among us retain memories of the back-fullness fashions of their girlhood days, and so the present fashion taboos cover all the earlier forms of the tubular skirts of this cycle, and the back-fullness styles of the previous cycle as well. If we are to change soon to a new cycle, it can only be to a bell cycle, for the other alternative is barred. Probably it is fair to say that at any given time there are two types of fashions that women in general consider ugly and ridiculous. One group consists of the earlier variants of the current cycle, and the other comprises the fashions of the previous cycle. Thus the

122

general antipathy toward remembered fashions explains the unchanging order of sequence in the recurrence of fashion cycles; there are only two choices for a new cycle, and the one of these which is remembered is taboo.

The current popular aversion to the back-fullness type is well known to designers of stage costumes, and constitutes one of their present-day problems. The revival on the stage of dresses of this sort is almost sure to be greeted by the audience as constituting a comic effect, and that reaction can be avoided only by designing the dresses with skilled care and calculated moderation. On the other hand, the same audiences are almost equally ready to regard the hoop-skirts of the bell type as being quaint and charming. Moreover, this dislike for remembered fashions seems to be very old, for writers on fashion in the past have often commented on it. Apparently, remembered fashions cannot successfully be revived, even when only a few people remember them and so, as long as there are only three fundamental fashion types, and each cycle can endure for only about a third of a century, the new cycle that comes in must always be a reappearance of the second one back, or the cycle that came into vogue about a century earlier.

The recurring cycles of fashion may be likened to the tunes of the barrel organ that Alfred Noyes wrote about. The organ is so constituted that it plays only three tunes, and it must repeat these three over and over again. They are long tunes, as the fashion cycles are long, and they are made up of many bars and phrases. They are so long, in fact, that by the time the organ grinder has wound out one of them he is so far down the street that the people about him have heard only the latter part of the preceding tune. When the last of the three tunes is played, the organ is able to produce nothing new, and the first tune begins to repeat itself. The poet supplied us with the simile when he wrote: 'And as the music changes, the song runs round again'. But now the barrel organ is out of earshot of those who heard it before, and to the new group of listeners the recurrence of the first tune, like the recurrence of the unremembered fashion cycle, has all the charm of novelty.

X   If it is true that the unchanging sequences of these recurring cycles of fashion really represent the working out of a procedure that is so orderly that it almost amounts to a law of the evolution of fashion, then it must also be true that the changes from year to year are not the products of chance and caprice to anything like the extent and degree that discussions of these matters have usually assumed. Apparently, fashion is by no means ruled by a comparatively small group of designers in Paris and elsewhere, who are commonly regarded as being the arbiters of style. Rather, it must be that the arbiters, unknown to themselves, are in actuality ruled and restricted within somewhat narrow limits by the unsuspected working of a fundamental principle of change. When, as not infrequently happens, they make the mistake of producing fashions which the world refuses to accept, it may well be because they have tried to depart too sharply from the acceptable phase of the cycle prevailing at the time, or even to encroach on one of the other cycles.

X   In summary, the thesis of this book is that women's dress fashions comprise three fundamental types which depend on the form and contour of the skirt. These may be designated as the back-fullness type, the tubular type, and the bell-shaped type. These three types may be termed major cycle types, since

123

they dominate fashion for extended periods of time, and in regularly recurring sequences. Each one dominates in turn, excluding the other two, over periods of approximately a third of a century, and for the past two hundred years they have done so in the order of back-fullness type, bell-shaped type and tubular type.

It might be argued that a complete cycle of fashion in women's apparel should probably be considered to include the full century or more that has now twice elapsed before the fashions began to be repeated in nearly true duplication of those that prevailed a hundred years earlier.

It has, however, seemed wiser, and certainly more convenient, to consider that a fashion cycle consists of the period of thirty-five years or so during which fashions are dominated by one fundamental skirt type, from which the year-to-year changes are variants, never repeating themselves, but never so far departing from the fundamental type as to alter its nature or to threaten its dominance. These long periods are themselves individual entities in the history of modern fashion, and each is worthy of being separately designated as a fashion cycle.

Probably there are practical implications of the principles that have been discussed which are quite worthy of careful consideration by all who are actively engaged in designing or merchandising women's apparel. If it is true that dress designers have in reality long been ruled and restricted by the workings of unsuspected principles of change, then it would seem to be clearly to their advantage if they could be consciously guided by these principles.

The first step in such guidance would be to study and understand the nature of the current cycle. This would involve a study of its duration so far, and of the phases through which it has passed. It would include a detailed knowledge of the year-by-year typicals which have appeared in it so far. The study would be concentrated on those changes that have taken place in the forms and contours of the skirts which have been accorded acceptance from year to year.

The more immediately useful guidance is to be derived from the annual typical fashions that have made up the current cycle since its inception. As it is a fundamental principle that the changes in the typicals are always continuous and always slow, the designer may rest assured that a sudden change will prove to be an erroneous one. This knowledge will not tell him what modifications he ought to introduce, but it will warn him that there are many and perhaps tempting changes which ought not to be introduced yet. This is not positive forecasting, but it is an important kind of negative forecasting. It is this sort of guidance which should enable the designer to capitalize the clarity of his hindsight, for, as Byron wrote, 'the best of prophets of the future is the past'.

Chapter 5

THE FATE OF FASHION CYCLES
IN OUR MODERN SOCIETY*

by James M. Carman

Modern theories of the diffusion of innovation in our society seem to refute the notions of fashion cycles and a trickle-down theory of fashion adoption. Is this because the cyclical and trickle-down theories were always inadequate, because the adoption process of our society has changed, or because new vehicles for the diffusion of innovations are superimposed on the older ones? This paper attempts to answer this question by examining the regularities to some characteristics of fashion in women's dresses over the past 176 years and to relate deviations from the regular cyclical pattern with changes in our social institutions.

The purpose of this paper is to examine the regularity, or lack of regularity, which exists in some characteristics of fashion in women's dresses over a very long period of time, and to speculate on what the findings might indicate about adoption and diffusion of fashion in our modern and affluent society.

While changes in women's fashions are generally considered to be irregular, mysterious, and unpredictable, anthropologists, by the late 1930s had identified long-run time trends which indeed do appear to contain at least some degree of statistical regularity.[1] Their debates at that time sound not unlike the debates of economists of that day over the determinism of the 'business cycle'.

While I have always considered time series analysis of data which are produced by large numbers of interacting human behavioural decisions to be essentially anti-intellectual in nature, one is hard put to find a casual model which will explain how low women's necklines will go next year—particularly in California. Further, the time series analysis about to be presented is intended only to describe some of the regularities in fashion cycles that have occurred. Previous studies of fashion cycles have made no attempt to fit curves to the data.

As an initial hypothesis, the analysis employs a theory of fashion cycles in women's dresses formulated in 1937 by Agnes Young.[2] Mrs Young hypothesized that there is a stable cyclical pattern in the design of women's dresses.

* From *Science, Technology and Society Proceedings* (American Marketing Association, 1966).

Each cycle, which lasts a little over one hundred years, contains three phases: a bell or full-skirt phase, a back-fullness or bustle phase, and a tubular or sheath phase. The phases are not distinct, but evolve gradually from one phase to the next. While this theory centres on the shape of the skirt, many of the measurable characteristics of the dress are interrelated, at least partially, to the three phases.

Historically, a bell phase began in about 1725. Early bell-phase dresses have high Empire waists. As the phase progresses, the waist becomes longer, or lower, but the skirt remains full. Eventually, the fullness in the skirt becomes concentrated in the back to such an extent that a bustle form evolves. Mrs Young identifies 1760 as the beginning of this back-fullness phase. Throughout the back-fullness phase the severity of the bustle decreases and, as it does, the waistline moves higher. In the course of time, the bustle disappears, as Mrs Young says it did in 1796, and the tubular phase begins. Waistlines during a tubular phase are a bit unpredictable. However, there is a natural evolution to skirt fullness from the tubular phase. Thus, Mrs Young identifies the second bell phase as beginning in 1830. The cycle which began in 1725 lasted 104 years. According to Mrs Young, the second bell phase evolved into the second back-fullness phase in 1868 and into the second tubular phase in 1900.

This analysis suggests that the waistline moves up and down (or, in our terminology, becomes longer or shorter) with the cycle. Likewise, the width of the waist varies as a function of the skirt cycle, being smaller in the bell and back-fullness phases and wider in the tubular phase. With a wide waist, designers have more freedom to raise and lower the minimum waistline, and this accounts for the irregularity in waist lengths during tubular phases.

Now, in addition to the Young hypothesis, we tested another hypothesis of our own. This hypothesis is that oscillating around the Young cycle is another, shorter cycle with a period of 30 to 50 years, instead of 110 years, the approximate period of Young's cycles. These shorter cyclical effects have, historically, some degree of regularity and are generated by the interaction of a variety of social institutions such as designers, sellers, media, consumers, and the adoption and diffusion processes which link them.

The Data

The data for this study include three characteristics of women's evening dresses. Evening attire includes cocktail, dinner, and formal dresses.

The time period studied is 1786 through 1965. All statistics used in the analysis are five-year moving averages. Thus, we lose two years on each end so that the actual number of observations is 176 years. The moving averages were used to remove some of the small, year-to-year, irregular variations which exist in addition to cyclical and trend variations.

The data for 1786 through 1936 are secondary, obtained from a study published by A. L. Kroeber and Jane Richardson Hanks in 1940.[3] The data since 1936 were collected specifically for this study by following exactly the Kroeber-Hanks procedure. The source of the data since 1920 is exclusively *Vogue* and *Harpers Bazaar* magazines. Both of these magazines were quality fashion magazines before 1900, but were only two of a number of available and reliable French, English, and American fashion periodicals used by Professor Kroeber

126

for the period from 1844 to 1919. Prior to 1844, any available source, either in this country or in Europe, was used as a source of data. Actually, Professor Kroeber's data go all the way back to 1605. However, before 1788 there were no fashion periodicals of any kind, and the data were quite crude.

The data contain statistics on six characteristics of evening dress: skirt width and length; waist width and length; *décolletage* width and length. Here we will concern ourselves with only the three of these which are most clearly related to the Young hypothesis. Skirt lengths stayed at floor level for the first 125 years of the period and, therefore, do not provide enough data for study. The neck-line data, while an interesting study in their own right, seem to vary independently from skirt variations. The statistics on all the three remaining series are the percentages of the total height of appropriate female figures as measured from the centre of the mouth to the tip of the forward toe. The figures were found by measuring illustrations of full-view models in the high-fashion periodicals with a ruler graduated in millimetres. The magazines used in each year were January, February, March, and November and December of the previous year. Prior to 1920, each average is based on at least ten figures. In more recent years, about twenty figures were used in the calculation of each yearly average. Values for the three dimensions were measured as follows:

Skirt width: diameter of the skirt at its hem or base
Waist width: minimum diameter in the region of the waist
Waist length: distance from the mouth to the minimum diameter across the waist.

The Model

The technique of analysis was to construct mathematical time-series models based on the two hypothesized cyclical patterns: Young cycles and the institutional interaction cycles. Since the models all involve cyclical behaviour, the functional forms had to be of a type which would generate cyclical patterns, i.e. either difference equations or sinusoidal functions. Because of the lack of any serious theory of the factors which cause fashion cycles, and because of the relatively long length of cycles, the latter functional form was chosen as being adequate to identify any periodicity which may exist. The sinusoidal functions were then transformed into linear form and best fit curves were calculated using standard least squares techniques. A period of 147 years, 1788 to 1934, was used to estimate the parameters of each function. Because the models used to estimate the time-series curves for each of the three dimensions are different from one another, each will be described separately.

Skirt Width Because the Young hypothesis is concerned primarily with the shape of the skirt and because the waist dimensions are, to some extent, dependent on the shape of the skirt, skirt width became the chief dimension for testing the two hypotheses. The overall series of skirt width shows a great amount of variability even after filtering out irregular movements by use of the five-year moving averages. However, major movements in the series are not inconsistent with the Young hypothesis. The width of the skirt should decrease continuously from the extreme width of the first bell phase through the back-fullness phase until the extreme of the first tubular phase is reached (1811). The width should then increase from the tubular phase into the second bell phase (1830) and continue to increase until a maximum is reached (1861). Skirt width should then decrease into the second back-fullness phase (1868) and on into the second tubular phase (1900). The minimum of the second tubular phase occurs in 1926.

The first task in building a model for skirt width, then, was to fit a periodic function to this small segment of the Young cycle. The equation used is of the form:

$$S = a\cos\frac{2\pi}{P}(t - t_0) + C \tag{1}$$

where: S is skirt width as a percentage of height
a is the amplitude of the Young cycle
P is the period of the Young cycle
C is the mean
t_0 is a point where the angle equals zero.

After fitting this function, a runs test was used to test the null hypothesis that the deviations about the cycle were random.[4] In every case in this research, this null hypothesis was rejected with an alpha risk of less than five per cent.

Since this null hypothesis was rejected, the institutional interaction cycle was added to the Young cycle:

$$S = a\cos\frac{2\pi}{P}(t - t_0) + a'\cos\frac{2\pi}{P'}(t - t'_0) + C \tag{2}$$

where a', P', and t'_0 have the same meaning as in (1) except that they represent the institutional cycle rather than the Young cycle. The problem of estimating the parameter of this equation is that the unknowns P, t_0, P', and t'_0 all appear in the argument of the cosine. This problem can be partially overcome by using a transformation suggested by Brown.[5] Through use of a trigonometric identity,

$$\cos(t - t_0) = \sin t \sin t_0 + \cos t \cos t_0$$

we can expand (2) into:

$$S = A\sin\frac{2\pi}{P}t + B\cos\frac{2\pi}{P}t + A'\sin\frac{2\pi}{P'}t + B'\cos\frac{2\pi}{P'}t + C$$

where

$$A = a\sin\frac{2\pi}{P}t_0 \qquad\qquad B' = a'\cos\frac{2\pi}{P'}t'_0$$

$$A' = a'\sin\frac{2\pi}{P'}t'_0 \qquad\qquad a = \sqrt{A^2 + B^2}$$

$$B = a\cos\frac{2\pi}{P}t_0 \qquad\qquad t_0 = \frac{P}{2\pi}\arctan\frac{B}{A}$$

P and P' still remain in the cosine argument. These were estimated by essentially a two-stage, least squares technique. First, (1) was iterated with a number of

128

values of P until R^2 was a maximum. Second, this value was substituted into (3) and this equation was iterated to find the value of P' which maximized R^2. Simplifying back to normal form, the model can be written as:

$$S = a\cos\frac{2\pi}{P}(t - t_0) + a'\cos\frac{2\pi}{P'}(t - t'_0) + C. \tag{4}$$

Waist Length The length of the waist is the dimension of the three which is least subject to the Young cycle. However, inspection of the data showed that throughout the entire 176-year period there has been a constant trend toward lowering the waistline. Therefore, the waist length model has three components: the linear trend, the institutional cycle, and the dependency on skirt width. This model can be written, in additive fashion, as:

$$L = b(t - t'_0) + a'\cos\frac{2\pi}{P'}(t - t'_0) + dS_t + eS_{t-1} + fS_{t-2} + C \tag{5}$$

where the variables have the same meaning as above only with references to the length of the waist. P' and t'_0 were estimated by the same technique used for skirt width.

Waist Width The data for the width of the waist exhibit a long cycle which is almost the exact inverse of the width of the skirt. This phenomenon could be expected. Full skirt designs accentuate small waistlines and tubular skirts are usually accompanied by loose waistlines. Thus, the Young cycle in waist width can be represented by making the width of the waist a function of the width of the skirt. Again, an institutional cycle is hypothesized. In addition, a dependency of waist width on waist length was tested. This model, which has three components, can be written as follows:

$$W = a'\cos\frac{2\pi}{P'}(t - t'_0) + bS_t + dL_t + C. \tag{6}$$

Again, the notation is the same except that P' and t'_0 are not necessarily the same values as those in the previous model.

Results

Skirt Width Following the two-step iteration procedure described above, the prediction equation which maximized the variance explained for the years 1788 through 1934 was:

$$S = 59{\cdot}57 + 25{\cdot}34\cos\frac{2\pi}{111}(t - 1754) + 9{\cdot}29\cos\frac{2\pi}{38}(t - 1828) \tag{7}$$

$$R^2 = 0{\cdot}847 \qquad\qquad \sigma u = 6{\cdot}69$$

Both regression coefficients are significant with very little alpha risk. Thus, for the width of the skirt, the Young cycle has a period of 111 years and the institutional cycle has a period of 38 years. In Figure 1 are plotted the actual and predicted values for the period 1788 through 1963. Note that for the years since 1936, the actual changes are far different from those predicted. The Young cycle seems to have disappeared and the cyclical movement that remains has a period of less than 38 years.

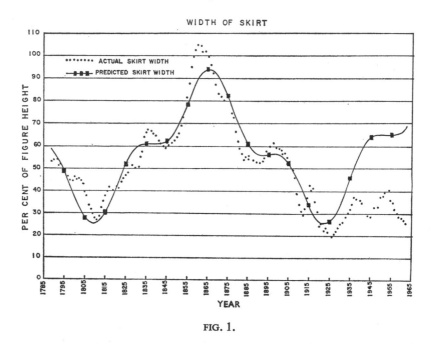

FIG. 1.

Waist Length Again following a stepwise procedure, the additive function which explained the greatest proportion of the variance in the length of the waist for the years 1790 through 1934 was:

$$L = 21 \cdot 42 + 0 \cdot 0621(t - 1814) - 1 \cdot 91 \cos\frac{2\pi}{48}(t - 1814) + 0 \cdot 147 S_t - 0 \cdot 128 S_{t-2}$$

$$R^2 = 0 \cdot 557 \qquad\qquad \sigma u = 2 \cdot 63$$

(8)

Again, the regression coefficients are significant with alpha risk of less than one per cent. The length of the waist is the characteristic, of the three studied, which is least subject to the Young cycle, and, of the three factors in this function, the dependency on the width of the skirt is the least important. Likewise, we have been able to explain less of the total variance for the length of the waist than for the other two. The period of the institutional cycle is 48 years, as compared to 38 for skirt width and 31 for waist width. In Figure 2 are plotted the actual and predicted values for 1790 through 1963. For the years 1920 through 1926, waists were lower than predicted because of the extreme tubular fashions of the day. Since 1929, waists have been somewhat higher than predicted, indicating the trend term may not be appropriate. The most interesting thing about this series is that in the last thirty years, the data exhibit much more stability than previously.

130

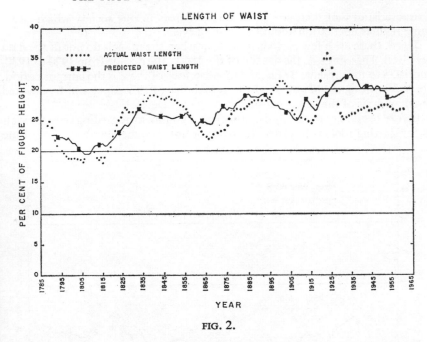

LENGTH OF WAIST

FIG. 2.

Waist Width The prediction equation which explained the greatest proportion of the variance in the width of the waist for the years 1788 through 1934 was:

$$W = 19.785 - 0.0903S_t - 0.1595L_t + 0.817 \cos \frac{2\pi}{31}(t - 1819) \qquad (9)$$

$$R^2 = 0.773 \qquad\qquad \sigma u = 1.07$$

Again, the regression coefficients are significant with very small alpha risk. The width of the waist is highly dependent on the width of the skirt ($\beta = -0.837$) and, to a lesser degree, is dependent on the length of the waist ($\beta = -0.281$). Waist width picks up the Young cycle from the skirt width term. The Young cycle is quite evident in Figure 3, where both the actual and predicted values are plotted for 1788 through 1963. Unlike the other two series, the waist width prediction equation seems to be as efficient in the more recent period as it was previously. Obviously, this is caused by the more nearly 'technological' dependence of waist width on both skirt width and waist length.

Interpretation of the Findings

The key points in the results may be summarized as follows. First, throughout most of the period of 176 years, the Young hypothesis, as unsatisfying as it is, stands up very well.

Second, the data fit the models quite well. The proportion of variance explained is fairly high; the waist dimensions do follow the regular pattern of changes in skirt width; and each of the three dimensions is subject to the hypothesized institutional cycles. In addition, it is clear concerning all three

131

characteristics that there are institutional forces in our society which cause some regular fluctuation about the Young cycle.

Third, there are a few periods in history when the models do not fit the data very well. These include the decade of the 1860s, the decade from 1920 to 1930, and 1935 to the present. By far, the most serious of these is the current period, i.e. 1935 through 1965. Most of the remainder of this paper will be devoted to an analysis of this latter period.

Before beginning the analysis, however, a comment regarding these models as forecasting tools is in order. It is important to remember that at no time

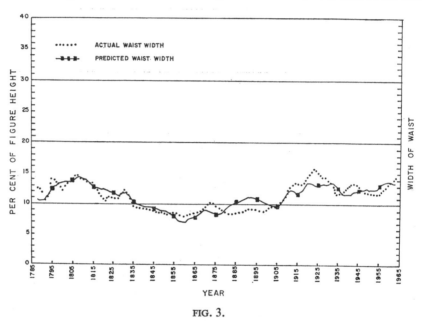

FIG. 3.

has it been suggested that these models are of any value as a forecasting tool. First, as we will argue later, there is no assurance that the cultural and institutional forces influencing fashion from 1788 to 1930 are in existence today. Second, the models probably do not do an accurate enough job of forecasting to be of much help to the dress designer or manufacturer. Third, the use of five-year moving averages mask many of the actual year-to-year fluctuations in the data. Fourth, the many varied characteristics of a dress leave much to be determined beyond the three dimensions studied here. For example, in the second quarter of the nineteenth century, the emphasis in women's fashion was on sleeve design. The emphasis in this paper is not on forecasting, but rather on what a study of these long-term trends may reveal about the process of fashion adoption and diffusion in our society today.

The data show clearly some periods of extreme disturbance and, more recently, a period of extreme stability. It should be useful at this point to advance and discuss some hypotheses as to the causes of these deviations from the established long-term patterns.

132

The first hypothesis was suggested by Kroeber and Hanks, as well as other students of fashion having an anthropological bent. The hypothesis is that instability in fashion accompanies general instability in the society. Thus, instability in fashion has been reported in the period in or immediately following the Napoleonic Wars, the Civil War, the Spanish-American War, and both World Wars. While this hypothesis may have some merit, it is also possible to identify periods of social instability that were not accompanied by fashion instability. Also, it is difficult to explain the period of 1950 to the present with this hypothesis.

Concentrating now on modern times, the second hypothesis, also suggested in the anthropological literature, has to do with a number of cultural phenomena, all at least vaguely related to the emancipation of women. Remember that a Young tubular phase began about 1900. While no record has been found that the suffragettes actively campaigned to change women's dress styles, by 1914 skirts were higher than they had ever been before. About this time, too, women became very interested in the problems of entering, riding in, and even driving an automobile. In a tubular phase, the only thing required to solve this problem was to shorten skirt lengths. Superimposed on those two important changes was World War I, followed by the 'roaring twenties'. By the mid-twenties, evening dresses had shorter skirts and wider waists than ever before in history. While this 'madness' had passed and fashion had returned to the Young cycle by the end of the twenties, it is clear that the emancipation of women, the development of the automobile and nylon hosiery, and the drastic shift from floor-length skirts, have made permanent changes in our culture which, one could argue, are significant enough to have spelled the end of the Young cycle. This is an important conclusion to note, for without it, this emancipation hypothesis will not explain the deviations since 1935.

The third hypothesis concerning changes in Young cycles will be briefly stated without comment. Each phase of a Young cycle lasts about one generation. As life spans increase, the period of the Young cycles will increase because women will not want to go through much more than one complete Young cycle in a lifetime. Thus, today we are still in the Young tubular phase which started in 1900, and soon this phase will evolve into a bell phase.

Application to Diffusion Theory

So much for hypotheses which deal with variations from Young cycles. The relevant finding in the empirical analysis for students of diffusion theory today is that not only has the Young cycle seemed to stop and remain constant since 1935, but also the social institution interaction cycle effect has diminished significantly since that time. This effect can be seen in Figures 1 and 2 and also may have been operating somewhat earlier than the 1935 dates used to designate the beginning of the change in the long-run pattern. Actually, the effect is as much one of decreasing the period, i.e. increasing the frequency of the institutional interaction cycles, as it is one of decreasing amplitude. Particularly in waist length, Figure 2, there seems to be a decrease in the amplitude of the cycles.

An inspection of the pictures from which the data were constructed immediately suggests that frequency has increased and that the decrease in amplitude stems from two causes. First, since the data are five-year moving averages, an increase in frequency of the cycle will result in a decrease in the amplitude of the moving averages.

Second, in recent decades we have had an increasing number of different styles available on the market at any given time. In the earlier period, an evening dress was a standard, full-length gown. Now, however, there are many types of evening dresses. First, knee-length cocktail dresses became appropriate for some occasions and full-length formals appropriate for others. Then, cocktail dresses became more acceptable for occasions where previously only full-length dresses were worn. Finally, we have had a return of the full-length 'hostess' skirt. Today, evening dresses would include all three styles. Thus, since the late 1930s, the data should be treated as at least three time-series rather than one. The result is an over-aggregation which causes fluctuations in individual styles to be cancelled out by fluctuations in others and a resulting decrease in the amplitude of the aggregate.

What has caused this diversity of popular styles? What has caused the increase in the rate at which fashions change, and what is the cause of these fashion cycles in the first place?

It was suggested earlier that institutional cycles are generated by the inter-action of designers, manufacturers, sellers, communication media, consumers, and the adoption and diffusion process which links them. Historically, the adoption and diffusion process has been based on a 'trickle-down' model of fashion adoption which places emphasis on the vertical flow of adoption from higher to lower socio-economic classes. Nystrom actually talks of geographic and vertical flow processes—geographically from Paris to New York to Chicago to St Louis to Des Moines, etc., and vertically from upper class to lower class.[6] Nystrom acknowledges that his 'trickle-down' theory was strongly influenced by Veblen.

Charles King has directly challenged the 'trickle-down' theory. His research suggests that the spread of fashion within cultural classes is much more important today than is vertical flow. He has stated that 'the historical evidence quoted by the early theorists strongly indicates the vertical flow process may have been functional in earlier periods in different types of class structures' but is no longer functional today.[7] Because the empirical evidence presented here suggests that the cycles produced by the adoption process did undergo a change about 1935, it would be of value to review the changes that have taken place in each of the relevant social institutions since that time.

First, there are the designers who originate the dress designs. With the exception of a few periods in history when France was plagued with wars, Paris has been, and is, the fashion design centre of the world. Has there been a change in the Paris design industry which would cause a change in long-term fashion cycles? The answer is affirmative, and the time of the change is con-sistent with the findings in our analysis. The change is in to whom the designers sell.

In 1928, Nystrom reports that there were 80,000 dressmaking establishments in Paris which derived the largest portion of their volume from individual customers in Paris or other parts of France. English women, in dollar volume of sales, came next to the French themselves. Professional buyers from the United States probably ranked third in volume of purchases.[8] However, professional buyers were only permitted to the third showing of a season's new designs—the first was for the press and the second for individual buyers. By 1957, thirty per cent of the Paris volume was accounted for by professional buyers and these buyers received much better treatment by the designers. Note, however, that this change was in response to the demand of manufacturers and big retailers, and was not a change initiated by the designers.

Why has the demand of manufacturers and sellers become more important than the demand of individual customers? Mass-produced clothing and large-scale retailers who emphasized fashion goods both got their start midway in the nineteenth century. While these industries have advanced technologically, certainly the garment industry and retailers have not been famous for their achievements in automation.

Similar, although somewhat more dramatic, findings are observable from an investigation of other variables. For instance, fashion monthlies available in Paris and London in 1850 were clearly as elegant as *Vogue* at its best. In addition, the role of important persons in setting fashion, which is to some measure generated by press coverage, has not diminished much over the years. Marie Antoinette is believed by some to be the last member of royalty to be a fashion leader. However, Nystrom reports that the popular, but unfashionable, Lafayette set American fashions for women and men back five years as a result of a visit in 1823; that a Hungarian patriot established a new fashion in men's hats as the result of a visit in 1851; and that Prince Albert did the same with his long frock coat in 1860.[9] In our day, who can deny the impact on American fashion of Jacqueline Kennedy?

It is true that the 'popular press' does cover fashion and is much bigger and more important than it was in 1850; and it is true that radio, motion pictures, and television are all new media which can, and probably have, speeded up fashion cycles since the 1920s and 30s. However, the media would not speed up the cycles if the bulk of consumers were not fashion purchasers. In short, the point is that the roots of the changes in fashion design, manufacturing, selling, and communication, all rest in changes in the consumer sector of our society. These changes are in response to the desire on the part of the large majority of consumers to innovate and to be fashionable in their styles of life.

What has caused the mass consumer market to become fashion conscious? The answer is fairly obvious. Higher levels of educational attainment have given more persons an appreciation for 'the finer and more genteel' artifacts of life. More education and the rather massive attack on unequal income distribution have greatly affected the purchasing power of the mass of American women. Eras of fashion interest have opened up in every period of rising general prosperity in history. In no period has there been the purchasing power available today. Increased leisure time also has the effect of increasing interest in fashion. Persons who work long hours have little opportunity to think of fashion, to shop for fashionable things, or to wear their fashionable clothing.

With all of these changes in the consumer sector accompanied by the changes in media and the responses of designers, manufacturers, and sellers, it is to be expected that fashion cycles become more frequent and styles more numerous. As consumers search for new ways to be fashionable, sellers try to provide these ways, and the media diffuse their ideas.

Finally, a word about diffusion processes. With increasing education and income, the relative size of cultural classes in our society is bound to change, and mobility from class to class is bound to remain relatively easy. Further, if the lower middle class has an interest in fashion merchandise, economics dictate that manufacturers and sellers will provide lower-priced imitations of high-fashion designers.

However, it does not follow from any of the findings of this research or from any of the implications just suggested that the vertical flow of social contagion through which new fashions are adopted is any less important today than it ever was. It does suggest that horizontal flows have increased in importance; it does show that flow processes are operating at a faster rate than ever before in history and that geographic flow processes are not as important as they once were. But, emulation of one cultural group by another is still a big element in our society, and research designed to study diffusion processes must not overlook this fact. The message these time series seem to be giving is that processes of adoption and diffusion in our society today are more complicated than at any time in history.

References

1. A L Kroeber and Jane Richardson Hanks, 'Three Centuries of Women's Dress Fashions: A Quantitative Analysis', *Anthropological Records*, vol. 5 (1940), (Berkeley: University of California) and Agnes Brooks Young, *Recurring Cycles of Fashions 1760–1937* (New York and London, Harper and Bros., 1937).
2. Young, loc. cit.
3. Kroeber and Hanks, loc. cit.
4. Sidney Siegel, *Nonparametric Statistics for the Behavioral Sciences* (New York, McGraw-Hill Book Co., 1956), p. 140.
5. Robert Brown, *Smoothing, Forecasting and Prediction of Discrete Time Series* (N. J., Prentice-Hall, Inc., 1962), p. 76.
6. Paul H. Nystrom, *Economics of Fashion* (New York, Ronald Press, 1928). (*See* Chapter 10.)
7. Charles King, 'Fashion Adaptation: A Rebuttal of the Trickle Down Theory', in Stephan A. Greyser (ed.), *Toward Scientific Marketing* (Proceedings of the Winter Conference of the American Marketing Association, 1963), p. 111. (*See* Chapter 12.)
8. Nystrom, op. cit., p. 200.
9. Op cit., pp. 84–85.

Chapter 6

FASHION, SUMPTUARY LAWS, AND BUSINESS*
by Herman Freudenberger

A remarkable instance of the interaction of business, society, and government unfolds in this study of the origins and effects of seventeenth- and eighteenth-century restricts on luxury.

During the 150 years from 1650 to 1800 many European governments tried to regulate in some way the dress of their people. England was a conspicuous exception in that it had had no formal clothing ordinances on the law books since 1604.[1] Even there, however, the dead were forced to follow a fashion: they had to go to their graves in woollen shrouds made in England.

Such interference in the private lives of the people was nothing new. Sumptuary legislation and clothing ordinances had been fairly common since the Middle Ages. Condemned by the Church as the vice of avarice, sumptuousness in dress was also considered a social evil if indulged in by the wrong people. Thus, in 1327, under Edward III of England, a law was enacted to control 'the outrageous and excessive apparel of divers people against their estate and degree'.[2] In the sixteenth century, the moralistic and social motivations for such laws were intensified through the Reformation and as the result of the increasing mobility of the European people. Money, the great equalizer, came into the hands of more people and they frequently used it to give outward expression to their social ambitions. The power of money unquestionably posed a threat to the established privilege, whether rural and landed or urban and corporate. The exclusive use of fine cloth and other luxuries was one way in which traditional elites wanted to retain a visible position of eminence.

Sumptuary laws had still other justifications. Fear of the foreign—for fashion in many places came from abroad—and fear of change itself contributed to the enactment of sumptuary legislation.[3] Even reasons of population can be given, as in the case of Lucca, where the tradition of expensive dowries threatened to reduce the city's population; fathers became hard pressed to outfit their daughters so as to make them eligible for a good match. The municipality therefore ordered a limitation on the number of expensive dresses per individual; but in practice the ordinance was unenforceable.† Moral and

* From *Business History Review* (1963).
† I am indebted to Dr Florence Edler de Roover for this information.

social considerations were still involved in the clothing ordinances of the seventeenth and eighteenth centuries. But the problems of business and economic life as a whole had now become more pressing. This was the era when the means of achieving economic development were being hotly debated. Moreover, it was the period during which fashion in dress began to assume increasing importance.

What is fashion? It is 'a lady... of the strangest unconstant Constitution... who changes in the twinkle of an eye', so an eighteenth-century gentleman wrote disapprovingly. Introduced to society by her elder brother Taste, she had become the object of the adoration of the crowd.[4] A desire for 'tasteful' uniqueness may be the origin of a fashion; but its eventual result is emulation of the many. The fashion leader striving for uniqueness, as well as the imitator, attempting through dress to associate vicariously with the persons of prestige, will have to be willing to pay higher prices than normally. Fashion, thus, is unquestionably a luxury and since the seventeenth century has displayed itself chiefly in female attire. As a luxury it may have made part of the major contribution to modern capitalism that Werner Sombart maintained. The production of luxuries, he asserted, in many important cases made the employment of capitalistic organizational techniques necessary and may have been a stimulus toward their development.[5] It also symbolizes Thorstein Veblen's conspicuous consumption, a disease of urbanized society. Fashions, in Veblen's terms, hardly made a beneficial contribution to the lives of the people. It wasted substance that might have been better employed.

Whether a positive or negative influence on the welfare of people, fashion represents outward proof of the affluence of society. This was also true in the seventeenth and eighteenth centuries when fashions as well as affluence were less widespread than today. As far as business was concerned, the frequent obsolescence of fashionable wearing apparel provided it with new opportunities and new risks. The short and unpredictable dominance of one type of dress, fashion properly speaking, introduced a great uncertainty in the market. This allowed the businessman who guessed right windfall profits and could entail great loss for the one who made the wrong decision.

Even before the seventeenth century there had been changes in the style of dress. They had, however, been relatively slow and a particular type of attire lasted for decades and, at times, for centuries. These long cycles might be called *Tracht* or costume cycles, for lack of a better term, to differentiate them from the short periods of fashion, which operated within the longer cycles.

During the Middle Ages there were few changes in dress and consequently the *Tracht* cycles are the only ones to be considered. Furthermore, these changes were mainly in male attire and were, as one might expect, determined by military considerations. In the fourteenth century, for example, the introduction of plate armour instead of chain-mail necessitated a change in clothing.[6] More than a century later, a new cycle of male dress was inaugurated by the clothing worn by victorious Swiss mercenaries. This was followed in the sixteenth century by the emulation of the dress of another victorious soldiery, the Spanish. Fame in war brought imitation in peace. These long cycles, it may be noted, involved only minimally the dress of women, who had not yet become very 'clothes conscious'.[7] About 1630 this situation changed; fashion in the apparel of women became an important factor in European society.[8]

What accounts for this phenomenon? Urbanization and the attendant rise of the bourgeoisie seem to have been major causes. The medieval castle gave little opportunity for individual display; its society was too isolated and its life too primitive. Moreover, town life was more gregarious and more socially mobile. A person's pedigree was not as important as before and his position at a given time carried greater weight. Outward display was therefore a method by which he could give overt expression of his wealth. He used the same method, too, in social competition with the nobleman, whose social standing in the medieval context was still superior to that of a merchant or other commoner.[9] As his desire for outward show of wealth increased, the wealthy burgher may have wanted, in Veblen's terms, to show his position by having his wife wear clothes that emphasized the leisure to which her husband's wealth had assigned her.[10] Fashion and luxury may, on the other hand, have gotten their main impetus from the competition between the mistress or prostitute and the wife for the affection of the man, using, among other things, the method of fashionable dress to provide the stronger attraction. This at least, is Sombart's thesis.[11] In either case, it was the city that was the scene of fashion. This said, it must also be noted that the royal courts were the places of the greatest ostentation and that the courtiers vied with each other in display. The desire for distinctiveness was here the more important consideration. Queen Elizabeth I of England forbade emulation of her style of dress and at her death left 6,000 fine garments behind.[12] Uniqueness but also variety were satisfied by such large accumulations of wearing apparel. Apparently, a certain amount of boredom at court was relieved by frequent changes in dress. Thus, the Russian Czarina Anna, living in the first half of the eighteenth century, required that her courtiers appear in a different suit each time they were in her presence.[13]

On the other hand, at some eighteenth-century courts instead of uniqueness it was homogeneity in dress that was sought. Court uniforms were prescribed in the Russia of Catherine the Great, in Bavaria, in Sweden, and in the Hapsburg monarchy under Maria Theresa. In most cases regardless of the prevailing trend, their purpose was to distinguish the courtiers and other aristocrats from the ambitious bourgeoisie. For, despite the many complaints of eighteenth-century writers that the lowest classes aped their betters in matters of dress, the competition was essentially between the nobles, on the one hand, and the merchants, financiers, and other middle-class persons on the other hand. The newly wealthy and socially ambitious were especially anxious to look like aristocrats, a process that the impoverishing aristocrats wanted to prevent through sumptuary legislation.[14] The staid burghers of Swiss and German city-states, like those of Rembrandt's Holland, retained the conservative black costume of Spain. Similarly, during our period the clergy kept to simple dress for everyday purposes. Before the Reformation, however, they had been as clothes conscious as any dandy at court.[15]

Although the upper classes wanted to parade their distinctiveness through fashionable dress, their fashion many times was deliberately patterned on that of their supposed inferiors. For example, during the seventeenth century the loose fitting jacket of the peasant became popular. Or, to give another example, in eighteenth-century England men considered it fashionable to 'look like Stage-Coachmen, Jockeys, and Pick-Pockets', as *Gentleman's Magazine* scornfully reported in 1739.[16] And, who were the most successful in setting the fashion? The people of the theatre, certainly not a group in the highest repute.[17] Moreover, prostitutes and mistresses were commonly among the most fashionable and were even the initiators of fashion.[18] Under such conditions it is evident that excess in clothing could hardly be curbed by deliberately allowing only prostitutes and rascals to wear certain styles of clothes.[19] Even so, the French King Henry III tried this psychological manoeuvre in the late sixteenth century as did the Duc de Sully, the great minister of his successor Henry IV.[20]

Sully's clothing ordinances as well as his actions in general were intended to strengthen France. He saw an outflow of money, principally to Italy for silks and for gold and silver thread used to embroider clothing. To eliminate this outflow he resorted to sumptuary legislation. There were many precedents for this in France, but Sully's Calvinist background may have influenced his preference for these measures. He prided himself on wearing only the simplest of clothes. The Calvinist background of his kind, Henry IV, did not prevent the latter, however, from preferring a solution to the problems suggested by Barthélemy de Laffemas, his advisor in economic affairs. Rather than forbid the wearing of silks and thereby prevent the outflow of money to Italy, as Sully wished, the King favoured allowing silks to be worn but, above all, those manufactured in France. This policy gave a strong stimulus to the development of the French silk industry and, for that matter, to other luxury industries as well. For this reason the policy was carried forward most successfully by Jean Baptiste Colbert in the second half of the seventeenth century. Thus, instead of outlawing luxuries, France to her great profit became Europe's foremost producer of luxuries and also became the subject of envy and hatred of other European countries.

Paris became the centre of fashion during the seventeenth century. This was true to some extent even while Spanish and Dutch styles were still the vogue during the earlier part of the century. Beginning with the second half of the century, however, Paris' domination became increasingly obvious and self-conscious. Regularly every month Parisian mannequins called Pandoras (*bambola* in Italian and 'fashion babies' in English), were completely dressed in the latest fashion, and toured European capitals, not even impeded by war.[21] Who dictated the style at this time is not clear. Louis XIV consciously tried to influence it, but he was certainly not anywhere near as successful as were Madame de Pompadour in the eighteenth century and, from the 1770s to the French Revolution, Queen Marie Antoinette. The latter, in combination with her principal clothes supplier, Marie-Jeanne (better known under her assumed name Rose) Bertin, who was often called the unofficial minister of fashion, were the unquestioned fashion leaders of their time.[22] Under their aegis, there was a regular frenzy for variety and originality in style, resulting in great exaggerations in dress.[23] Such exaggerations often have resulted in major changes in style.[24] A new costume cycle did begin in the 1790s for which the French Revolution was largely responsible.

Paris was the intellectual leader of seventeenth- and eighteenth-century Europe. How did she become the leader in fashion as well? It was not only because of the Pandoras or even the court life in Versailles, emulated as it was all over the continent, that France influenced, to the point of controlling, the fashion in dress. Equally influential were the French journals. The *Mercure Gallant*, founded in 1672, may have been the first fashion magazine; it included illustrations and information on fashion. Late in the eighteenth century, other journals appeared both in France and abroad: *Galerie des Modes* and *Courier des Modes* began publication in France in the 1770s and *Cabinet des Modes* and *Magasin de Modes* in the mid-1780s; *Galery of Fashion* in the 1790s in England; and, in the same decade, *Journal des Luxus und der Moden* and *Journal für Fabriken, Manufakturen, Handlung, Kunst, und Mode* in Germany.[25] Fashion had gained a strong hold over people.

Although fashions might depend to some extent on overt leadership, their acceptance has been difficult to impede or control by legislation. Yet, this was attempted repeatedly, as has been suggested, and above all in late seventeenth-century France. The government of Louis XIV tried to aid French industry and prevent the outflow of bullion through clothing ordinances. Its most conspicuous attempt in this direction, and at the same time its greatest failure, was in trying to prevent the use of printed cottons in order to preserve the French silk industry. Thousands died or were sent to the galleys for infractions of these rules.[26] It is somewhat ironic that all this was done to aid the manufacture of silk, which a century before had been in a position analogous to that of cotton in the eighteenth century. Similar attempts were made elsewhere, especially in England, where they were even less successful than in France. England's Calico Act of 1720 may not have been called a sumptuary law, but its purpose was little different from many such laws enacted elsewhere in eighteenth-century Europe. Even in England, however, there were some demands for outright sumptuary laws to prevent the outflow of money for 'luxuries'.

Sumptuary laws did exist in a number of European countries until well into the eighteenth century. In general, however, it can be said that their doom was sealed during this century possibly, as John Martin Vincent suggests, by the increasing individualism and economic freedom of the time.[27] Moreover, the Mercantilist spirit was also a strong contributor. Its biggest contribution in this direction might have been in that it divorced these laws from moral and social connotations and employed them solely for the furtherance of the national economies in question. Clothing ordinances became for the Mercantilists merely another weapon akin to their favourite one of prohibiting imports. In short, they were primarily concerned with the outflow of bullion. If a new fashion came into vogue, they preferred producing the necessary goods within the country to prohibiting their use altogether.

The eighteenth-century economic writers were, as has often been stated, production minded; less emphasis has been placed on their attitude toward consumption.[28] In one form this problem is another aspect of the question of production. The opinion became more common that people worked best when they could increase their level of consumption through higher wages. This was opposed to the position held by many that low wages, near the subsistence level, were the necessary whip for maximum output. High wages they agreed would allow workers to purchase what had been up to then luxury goods.[29] Not only would this raise the production of such goods, but it would also provide a broader market for them. This in turn would be an incentive for manufacturers to expand production. This seems to have happened in England, where it aided the Industrial Revolution significantly. England was a society with some degree of vertical social mobility in which the fashionable articles of the rich could eventually filter down to the lower classes. As an eighteenth-century English writer said, 'a state . . . [in which] fashion . . . [has] uncontrolled sway' holds the promise of prosperity. The desire for luxuries may have been another important concomitant of the Industrial Revolution. It may have been a lure for some people to make them willing to submit to the discipline of factories, where the opportunities for higher wages existed.[30]

In general as the eighteenth century wore on, Mercantilists and other writers who concerned themselves with economic subjects began to approve the production and consumption of luxuries but took a strong stand against the importation of such goods. Along with David Hume they felt that excessive luxuries were an evil, but still preferable to none at all, so long as they were produced within the country.[31] Neither they nor Hume were willing to go to the extreme of Bernard Mandeville who saw the dirty streets of London as necessary so that luxury could employ 'a million of the poor and odious pride a million more'.[32] This argument found strong opposition in the English economist Sir James Stuart and in Jean Jacques Rousseau, who saw the material needed for luxuries diverted from necessities and thus harmful rather than beneficial to the poor.[33]

Some were not even much concerned that fashionable goods had to be bought abroad, although they did prefer the home product. If a luxury item had to be imported, however, it should at least come from a country that bought from one's own. In the case of Germany, this meant that imports from France should not be purchased but that imports from England and Holland were permissible.[34] Moreover, no exceptions were to be made for aristocrats and royalty who would, of course, consider the right of purchasing foreign cloth a part of their privileged position in society. Now in the eighteenth century they were to be required to set the good example that the rest of society was to emulate. The German princes, for example, wrote a contemporary German writer, should be the first to do without French fashion goods.[35] This was also the attitude of Hapsburg officials in proposing sumptuary laws during the eighteenth century.[36]

A tendency toward social equality can thus be observed, though it would be folly to assert that class distinctions had ceased or that the upper class was willingly giving up its prerogatives in dress. It merely means that the nobility was being required to contribute in this way to the common effort toward economic development. As the officials of the Hapsburg commercial council (*Hofkommerzienrat*) pointed out in 1761, one could hardly expect the common people to wear domestically manufactured cloth if the court and the monarch did not.[37] That was also the reason why Duke Leopold of Tuscany (reigned 1765–1790), later Emperor Leopold II (reigned 1790–1792), felt it necessary to warn his nobility against excess in luxury.[38] Similarly, the ruling of the Swedish king, Gustav III (reigned 1771–1792), which ordered the wearing of a national costume made of Swedish cloth, had an egalitarian character although its specific purpose was to aid the woollen industry.[39] This was also true of the Polish sumptuary law of 1776, one of the last on record in Europe. It enjoined all, irrespective of rank, to wear Polish goods though the various classes were assigned different styles of apparel.[40] A report on this law appeared in a German Physiocratic journal, which strongly inveighed against it. The writer felt that its prohibitive character eliminated foreign competition and was therefore harmful inasmuch as all competition was a necessary spur to high production.[41] That this Physiocratic journal stood for economic freedom need not occasion surprise; but its friendly attitude toward industry as opposed to agriculture made it quite different from its French counterpart. The French Physiocrats opposed sumptuary laws, but they were displeased with luxury, except in the products of the soil. They felt that free competition rather than laws could check ostentatious living.[42] On this point the German Physiocratic journal also differed. It favoured luxury as an incentive to work and, in one article, enunciated the principle that 'ever-recurring extravagance is the fundamental principle of the welfare of society (*ein sich beständig erneuernder Aufwand . . . [ist] ein unumgängliches Bedingniss der gesellschaftlichen Glückseligkeit*).'[43]

Whether of Physiocratic, Mercantilist, or other persuasion, economic writers by the end of the eighteenth century generally accepted the positive role of fashion and luxury in a country's development.

The effect that the democratization of fashion and luxury had on business is hard to judge in precise terms. Yet there is abundant proof that fashionableness provided the incentive for many important industries. One need only point to the French silk industry centred in Lyons or the so-called French fine cloth industry at Sedan, Elboeuf, and Abbeville. In England, the 'New Draperies' introduced by Dutch and Flemish artisans satisfied a demand for lighter and more sumptuous goods. And the greatest success story of all has to be mentioned, the production of printed cotton fabrics in England. These fabrics all took the route from fashion for the few to consumption for the many and wider markets. To these examples may be added specific instances such as Verviers and Montjoie (both in modern Belgium) which became great centres for cloth production in the eighteenth century by watching the latest fashions. The Rococo style in men's clothing called for lighter, pastel colours and Verviers and Montjoie catered to that demand.[44]

In the case of England and Belgium, it was businessmen who discovered the opportunities and exploited them. In France, however, it was the government which was prominently engaged in the creation of new business. Most of continental Europe followed the French rather than the English model. The reason may have been, as a high Hapsburg official pointed out in the 1760s, that the spirit of enterprise was not as yet well developed.[45] It might be added that many continental national economies were backward compared to England and the Netherlands in terms of technological skills, business techniques, and capital. Prussia, Russia, and the Hapsburg monarchy, among others, used the power of government to encourage, direct, and finance new enterprises so that fashion goods and luxuries need not be bought abroad. In using these methods, they copied France in order to oppose her. They hoped to have to purchase less from that fount of fashions. Unfortunately for them, they were often not successful; the new goods produced by less skilled hands could not compete with the French articles. Moreover, part of the intrinsic attraction of fashion goods was that they came from abroad, especially from France, It was only natural, therefore, that when Marie Antoinette came from Austria to meet her bridegroom, the Paris fashion house of Rose Bertin outfitted her.

The case of Rose Bertin deserves further comment. She was a retail merchant who sold ready-to-wear garments and hats. Her store exerted leadership in the field of fashion, and she exercised this leadership in consultation with Marie Antoinette.[46] Without her connections, Rose Bertin could hardly have become the outstanding *marchande de modes* of the 1770s and 1780s. The risks were tremendous, but many girls, so Platière asserted, were drawn into the business.[47]

Ready-to-wear clothing, today associated primarily with the mass market, may have been born in the demand for fashion goods, as Sombart asserted. On the other end of the scale, the used-clothing business undoubtedly also received a strong stimulus therefrom. It is the nature of fashionable goods to become quickly obsolete. Since, in many cases, they were still in good condition when discarded, they found their way to the used-clothing market. This type of business was also fostered by the military. Possibly even before discarded fashion goods came to the used-clothing market, used uniforms did.

The ramifications of fashion and luxury, as has been shown, were fairly widespread. During the century and a half prior to the French Revolution of 1789, both fashion and luxury increased in scope and in social penetration. They represented a significant determinant of the democratization of society. Furthermore, they laid a basis for the Industrial Revolution which for its mass production needed mass markets. At the same time they introduced an instability that became characteristic of many national economies.

To stem the tide of fashion and luxury with legislation proved to be a total failure even when the punishment for infraction was great. Generally during this period such sumptuary laws had as their purpose to aid the national economy, though many writers and government officials recognized that they were ineffectual. Nevertheless, they had changed their character significantly since the Middle Ages when morality and social distinction were their primary goals. Such legislation was considered an important aid to business by many in the seventeenth and eighteenth centuries when government participation in the economy and initiative in economic development were considered important. By the beginning of the nineteenth century, however, the ideas of the French Physiocrats on the appropriate role of government were waning before the novel economic thought of Adam Smith. Sumptuary legislation disappeared apace.

References

1. Wilfrid Hooper, 'The Tudor Sumptuary Laws', *English Historical Review*, vol. 30 (July 1915), pp. 448–49.
2. Frances E. Baldwin, *Sumptuary Legislation and Personal Regulation in England* (Baltimore, 1926), pp. 46–47.
3. John M. Vincent, *Costume and Conduct in the Laws of Basel, Bern, and Zurich, 1370–1800* (Baltimore, 1935), p. 42.
4. *Gentleman's Magazine*, vol. 8 (April, 1738), p. 191.
5. Werner Sombart, *Luxus und Kapitalismus* (München & Leipzig, 1922), pp. 203–205.

6. Max von Boehn, *Die Mode: Menschen und Moden im Mittelalter* (München, 1925), pp. 203–204.
7. Ibid., p. 174.
8. Max von Boehn, *Die Mode: Menschen und Moden im siebzehnten Jahrhundert* (München, 1913), p. 139.
9. Boehn, *Mittelalter*, p. 201.
10. Thorstein Veblen, *The Theory of the Leisure Class: An Economic Study of Institutions* (New York, 1912), p. 126.
11. Sombart, *Luxus*, pp. 68–69.
12. Max von Boehn, *Die Mode: Menschen und Moden im sechzehnten Jahrhundert* (München, 1923), p. 149.
13. Max von Boehn, *Die Mode: Menschen und Moden im achtzehnten Jahrhundert* (München, 1923), p. 208.
14. Joseph A. Schumpeter, *History of Economic Analysis* (New York, 1954), p. 324 n. This appears to have been the purpose of a French ordinance of 1633 which attempted to control dress to prevent the ruination of the courtiers. Michèle Beaulieu, *Contribution à l'Étude de la Mode à Paris: Les Transformations du Costume Élégant sous le Règne de Louis XIII (1610–1643)* (Paris, 1936), p. 81.
15. Boehn, *Mittelalter*, pp. 241–42.
16. *Gentleman's Magazine*, vol. 9 (January, 1739), p. 28.
17. Caroline A. Foley, 'Fashion', *Economic Journal*, vol. 3 (Sept. 1893), p. 465.
18. Sombart, *Luxus*, pp. 68–69; Vincent, *Costume*, p. 49.
19. Boehn, *Sechzehntes Jahrhundert*, p. 174.
20. Henri J. L. Baudrillart, *Histoire du Luxe Privé et Public* (Paris, 1880–1881), vol. 4, pp. 11–23.
21. Boehn, *Achtzehntes Jahrhundert*, p. 128. The practice of having two such puppets began in the first half of the century—one large and one small. Beaulieu, *Contribution*, p. 11.
22. Emile Langlade, *La Marchande de Modes de Marie Antoinette: Rose Bertin* (Paris, n.d.), pp. 56–57. There is an English edition of this book, *Rose Bertin: The Creator of Fashion at the Court of Marie Antoinette*, adapted from the French by Angelo S. Rappoport (London, 1913).
23. Roland de la Platière, *Encyclopédie Methodique, Manufactures, Arts, et Métiers* (Paris, 1785), p. 133.
24. Dwight E. Robinson, 'Fashion Theory and Product Design', *Harvard Business Review*, vol. 36 (Nov.–Dec., 1958), p. 128 (*see* chapter 27).
25. Boehn, *Achtzehntes Jahrhundert*, p. 238. *See* also André Blum, *Histoire du Costume: Les Modes au XVIIᵉ et au XVIIIᵉ Siècles* (Paris, 1928), pp. 74–75.
26. Eli F. Heckscher, *Mercantilism*, trans. by Mendel Shapiro (2 vols., London, 1935), vol. I, pp. 172–73.
27. John M. Vincent, 'Sumptuary Legislation', *Encyclopedia of the Social Sciences* vol. 14, (New York, 1948), p. 466.
28. A. W. Coats, 'Changing Attitudes to Labour in the Mid-Eighteenth Century', *Economic History Review*, Second Series, vol. 11 (Aug., 1958), pp. 35–51.
29. Joseph J. Spengler, 'Mercantilist and Physiocratic Growth Theory', in Bert F. Hoselitz (ed.), *Theories of Economic Growth* (Glencoe, 1960), pp. 19–20. *See also* E. A. J. Johnson, 'Unemployment and Consumption: The Mercantilist View', *Quarterly Journal of Economics*, vol. 46 (Aug. 1932), pp. 698–719.
30. Elizabeth W. Gilboy, 'Demand as a Factor in the Industrial Revolution', *Facts and Factors in Economic History* (Cambridge, Mass., 1932), pp. 628–29.
31. David Hume, *Writings on Economics*, ed. by Eugene Rotwein (Madison, 1955), p. 11. Also, Johann Heinrich Ludwig Bergius (ed.), *Policey-und Cameral Magazin* (Frankfurt a/M, 1773), vol. 7, pp. 180–205.
32. Bernard Mandeville, *The Fable of the Bees; or, Private Vices, Public Benefits* (Edinburgh, 1777), vol. 1, pp. vii, 13.
33. Carl Landauer, *Die Theorien der Merkantilisten und der Physiokraten über die oekonomische Bedeutung des Luxus* (München, 1915), pp. 50, 104–106.
34. Johann Jacob Marperger, *Das Neu-eröffnete Manufakturwarenhauss* (Hamburg, 1704), pp. 13–15.
35. Ibid., p. 13.

36. Adolf Beer, 'Zwei Handschreiben von Maria Theresia über den Luxus', *Zeitschrift für Sozial und Wirtschaftsgeschichte*, vol. 1 (1893), pp. 341–48.
37. Hofkammerarchiv (Vienna), Boehm. Commerz, fasc. 100, red no. 890, f. 28ff.
38. *Ephemeriden der Menschheit*, vol. 18 (Sept. 1782), pp. 365–67.
39. Ibid., vol. 4 (Jan. 1778), pp. 87–90.
40. Ibid., vol. 3 (Feb. 1777), pp. 158–75.
41. Ibid., p. 170.
42. *Ephemerides du Citoyens* (1767), part 1, pp. 223ff.
43. *Ephemeriden der Menschheit*, vol. 9 (May 1781), p. 528.
44. Ernst Barkhausen, *Die Tuchindustrie in Montjoie, ihr Aufstieg und Neidergang* (Aachen, 1925), p. 34.
45. Hofkammerarchiv (Vienna), Boehm. Commerz, fasc. 101/1, red no. 891, 14 April 1761.
46. Langlade, *Marchande*, pp. 56–57. Marie-Jeanne (Rose) Bertin was apprenticed to a *marchande de mode* in Abbeville named Barbier who wanted to set up business in Paris with Rose. When Barbier's husband refused to go along, Rose went by herself in 1770 and Barbier joined her later after the latter's husband died. Barbier married M. Tetard, *negotiant au drop et fournisseur de la Reine*, in Paris, and the Tetards gave Bertin credits and supported her financially in other ways. Pierre de Nouvion and Emile Liez, *Un Ministre des Modes sous Louis XVI: Mademoiselle Bertin* (Paris, 1911), pp. 22–28.
47. Platière, *Encyclopédie*, p. 135.

Chapter 7

THE LIMITS OF FASHION CONTROL*
by Nancy Koplin Jack and Betty Schiffer

A further analytical study of more contemporary fashion trends in line with the Kroeber and Richardson tradition, looking specifically at skirt lengths.

The national scene in 1947 was enlivened by the interesting and sometimes amusing revolt among some women—and men—against the New Look. The issue raised illustrated one facet of a very fundamental social problem, namely the relative contribution of leader and follower in collective behaviour or, to state it more scientifically, the relative contribution of the norm creators and the conforming population in any pattern of mass behaviour. The present study was an attempt to formulate this problem in a way which would render it amenable to scientific treatment. The question raised was this: what are the relative or reciprocal roles of those who set the fashions—the designers—and those who are supposed to follow them—the women in the street? Or, stated differently, what are the limits within which norm creators—in this case fashion designers—must remain if they are to be followed?

The implications of this question ramify widely. They lead, in the political field, to such questions as: how much control can dictators actually impose on followers? How much control can any law impose on people even in a democracy? How much can advertising or propaganda change man's behaviour? What in brief are the limits, if any, within which any control system in any field must operate, if it is to secure conformity?

In the political and legal field, exact methods of measuring these limits have not yet presented themselves, so that instead of objective research we have chiefly impassioned arguments for or against control and laissez-faire. In the absence of scientific data, such arguments are usually more likely to be emotional than to be disinterested.

There is, however, in the field of fashion control, a set of data—pictures—which, while faithfully reflecting pattern and conforming behaviour, can be statistically manipulated and thus exploited for purposes of finding, or at least exploring, answers to the above questions.

A. L. Kroeber was one of the first to use fashion data to establish the fact of orderliness in the evolution of human culture.[1] More recently he and Jane

* From the *American Sociological Review*, vol. 13 (American Sociological Association, 1948).

Richardson have presented data on six aspects of women's formal dress over a period of three centuries.[2] They measured length of skirt, length of waist, length of *décolletage*, width of skirt, width of waist and width of *décolletage*. They found that:

'It is evident that the basic features of style as distinct from more rapidly fluctuating mode, being taken for granted at any given moment, are largely unconscious in the sense that they are felt as axiomatic and derivations are made from them, but they are not tampered with, except again unconsciously.

This in turn seems to imply that the role of particular individuals in moulding the basic dress style is slight. The influence of creative or important individuals is probably largely exerted on the accessories of transient mode. How great it is there, has never been objectively examined, and would be difficult to investigate. Historians of fashion may be partly right or mainly fictitious in the influence they assign to Marie Antionette, Récamier, Eugénie, and the various Princes of Wales. The reverse is much more likely, that individuals conform to the style which they find in existence, operate in minor ways within its configuration, and at times of coincidence receive false credit for 'causing' one or more of its features. . . . So far as individuals are concerned, the total situation seems overwhelmingly to indicate that their actions are determined by the style far more than they can determine it. . . .

Definitely significant is the fact that there are periods of high and low variability of style. These come out much alike whether it is a matter of variations of yearly averages from the five-year moving mean, or of variations of individual dresses from the year's mean. . . .

The best explanation that we are able to suggest for these phenomena is that of a basic pattern of women's dress style, toward which European culture of recent centuries has been tending as an ideal. This pattern comprises amplitude in most dimensions, scantness or medium value in others. As these proportions are achieved there are equilibrium, relative stability, and low variability. The pattern may be said to be saturated. All other times, most or all of the proportions are at the opposite extreme, which may be construed as one of strain, and variability rises high. This basic or ideal pattern, for Europe of the last two or three centuries, requires a skirt that is both full and long, a waist that is abnormally constricted but in nearly proper anatomical position, and *décolletage* that is ample both vertically and horizontally. . . .

We have deliberately avoided explanation of our phenomena in terms of psychological factors such as imitation, emulation, or competition, which are a stock explanation: the leaders want to surpass the mass, so they keep going one step farther, until a physical limit is reached, when they turn about and head the procession back. We do not deny that such psychological motivations may be operative. We do believe that as explanations they are conjectural, and scientifically useless, because, to date at least, they depend on factors which are unmeasurable and undefinable. On the contrary, we think we have shown that through behaviouristic and inductive procedures operating wholly within the socio-cultural level, functional correlations can be established for such supposedly refractory cultural manifestations as style and fashion changes.'

Interesting and useful as these data used by Kroeber and Richardson are, they are definitely limited so far as answering certain basic theoretical questions is concerned. For example, dealing only with women's formal attire, they automatically limit themselves to a restricted segment of the population. They deal with only a small and numerically insignificant class. Nor do they tell us what even this class was actually wearing, that is, whether the fashion plate or models were followed by women or not.*

The present study was conceived, therefore, as a more intensive analysis of the reciprocal roles of leader and follower, that is, of norm creator and conformist, in just one measurable aspect of mass behaviour, namely dress length.

The Method

Three series of measurements were secured for the 19-year period 1929–47. These measurements were limited to length of skirt as the most feasible fashion detail for study and as more amenable to precise measurement than other details like silhouette, shoulder angle, fullness of skirt, height of waist, etc. The three series were selected to represent the top level of fashion design, a middle level, and, thirdly, the average woman, that is, the woman in the street. The first two constituted the norms of behaviour set by fashion, the third, the response or degree of conformity of actual women. *Vogue* magazine was selected to represent the first of these levels and *The Woman's Home Companion* was chosen as representing a mid-way point, that is, high fashion modified for the woman-in-the-street. (As it turned out, this hypothesis with respect to the two journals was incorrect. The *Woman's Home Companion*, instead of representing a modification of extreme fashion, turned out to be more extreme than *Vogue*. In the periods of long skirts, it showed lower hemlines than did *Vogue*; in the period of short skirts, it showed a higher hemline than did *Vogue*. It tended to raise and lower hemlines faster than did *Vogue*. Except for the period 1945–47, *Vogue* tended to lie between *Woman's Home Companion* and the woman-in-the-street so far as length of skirt was concerned.)

It was far more difficult to secure data representative of the woman-in-the-street. After much searching, it was decided to select *Review of Reviews, Literary Digest, Outlook-Independent* for the period 1929 through 1936 and *Life* magazine from 1937 to 1947. Photographs were used instead of drawings, to avoid the distortions introduced by the artist. One picture was selected for each month. Figures were selected solely on the basis of measurability of the garment displayed and were limited to those modelling street clothes. The selection was wholly random in the sense that any style might be displayed on a model standing in a measurable position. That is, there was no reason to suppose that any one length had a better chance than any other to be modelled

* Our own experience leads us, further, to question the comparability of measures based on plates. We found that the anatomical distortions in fashion drawings were such that they could not be used. The artist presents a figure elongated in the femur and more slender than actual women. If the distortion were uniform, it could be adjusted. But it does not seem to be identical in all cases. Only photographs of actual women were stable enough to render measurements reliable. Dealing with figures as small as fashion plates renders even a tiny error very serious.

by a figure fulfilling the requirements of selection. In the case of the woman in the street, there was often no choice at all, there being only one usable picture for the entire month. When any one observation appeared to be out of line, a second measurement was taken, and the average of the two was used. This occurred 16 times through the three series.

After experimenting with a number of measuring techniques, all of which proved defective,* the method finally selected was to proceed as follows: (1) a photograph was† chosen which showed as unequivocally as possible the anchoring or base points required for measuring, namely (a) the 'v' at the throat and (b) the weight-bearing foot (this was usually the rear foot); (2) two horizontal lines were drawn parallel to the top (or bottom) of the page, one through the 'v' of the throat and one touching the lowest point (usually the toe) of the weight-bearing foot; (3) five lines were drawn at right angles to the first two lines: one from the 'v' of the throat, two touching the outermost points of the hemline and two lines bisecting the divisions thus created; (4) the distance from the base line to the 'v' of the throat was used as the denominator;‡ (5) the numerator was computed by measuring all five of the vertical lines from top to skirt, the results added together and divided by 5; (6) the resulting fraction was changed to percentage form, and, in order to make the graphic representation low for long hemlines and high for short hemlines, this percentage was subtracted from 100 to secure the final value. Thus, the final value was:

$$v = 100 - \sum_{n=1}^{n=5} x \frac{5}{y}$$

The method was tested by having each investigator measure the same five figures independently. When the results of these independent measures were compared, it was found that three of the five agreed 100 per cent, the other differing only one point in the second decimal place.

As a second test, each of five pairs of students, briefed on the method, measured models independently. When the results were compared, it was

* Before the final successful method was achieved, the following trials were made: (1) use of the knee-to-ankle measurement for the denominator and the knee-to-the-skirtline as the numerator; (2) use of waist-to-ankle as a denominator and waist-to-skirtline as numerator; (3) use of distance from the hollow of the neck to the heel of the weight-bearing foot as the denominator and the distance from the hollow of the neck to the bottom of the skirt as the numerator; (4) use of a line drawn from the collar bone to the inside ankle of the weight-bearing foot (axis of the body) as the denominator and for the numerator an ellipse drawn around the skirt edges, crossed with an axis. (Suggested by Mrs Scott of the Art Department, The Pennsylvania State College.) The first of these methods was discarded because of the subjective judgement involved in locating the knee; the second method was discarded because of the subjective element involved in locating the waistline; the third method was eliminated because one measure did not seem to be sufficient to give a true picture of the length of the skirt. The fourth trial was unsuccessful due to the subjective element involved in locating the inside ankle of the weight-bearing foot.

† Drawings were not used because of the artists' distortion.

‡ At the end of the measuring process, a short-cut method was found; namely, that of placing transparent graph paper over the figures and counting the squares rather than measuring the lines. (Suggestion was made by Mr Gunther Cohn of the Franklin Institute of Philadelphia, Pa.)

TABLE 1 *Least-squares Lines for Length of Skirt for Three Series: Vogue Models, Women's Home Companion Models, and Woman-in-the-Street* (see text for details)

(i)	V (*Vogue*)	$y = 26 - 0.34x$	(Jan. 1929–Dec. 1931)
	WHC (*Woman's Home Companion*)	$y = 25 - 0.34x$	(Jan. 1929–Apr. 1932)
	WS (*Woman-in-the-Street*)	$y = 24 - 0.23x$	(Jan. 1930–Jan. 1932)
(ii)	V	$y = 20 - 0.03x$	(Jan. 1932–Dec. 1935)
	WHC	$y = 19 - 0.04x$	(May 1932–Jan. 1936)
	WS	$y = 23 - 0.01x$	(Jan. 1932–Jan. 1936)
(iii)	V	$y = 26 + 0.19x$	(Jan. 1936–July 1939)
	WHC	$y = 28 + 0.22x$	(Jan. 1936–May 1940)
	WS	$y = 24 + 0.27x$	(Jan. 1936–Aug. 1940)
(iv)	V	$y = 31 + 0.02x$	(Aug. 1939–Dec. 1942)
	WHC	$y = 33 - 0.12x$	(May 1940–July 1942)
	WS	$y = 30 + 0.06x$	(Aug. 1939–July 1942)
(v)	V	$y = 31 - 0.02x$	(Jan. 1943–July 1945)
	WHC	$y = 32 - 0.014x$	(July 1942–June 1945)
	WS	$y = 32 - 0.04x$	(July 1942–June 1945)
(vi)	V	$y = 27 - 0.28x$	(July 1945–Dec. 1947)
	WHC	$y = 30 - 0.23x$	(July 1945–Dec. 1947)
	WS	$y = 29 - 0.14x$	(July 1945–Dec. 1947)

found that in each of three pairs they were identical, and in two, practically so, giving a reliability of 0·99. These checks were taken as a fair index of the objectivity of the method used.

Results

Three types of analysis of the above described data confirm the generalization that the follower, in this case the woman-in-the-street, exerts a definable limit to control pressures. In this specific instance, she permitted herself to be pushed just so far, but no farther. Within certain limits, she was very amenable to control; beyond those limits, she was not.

The three types of analysis were: (1) time-series analysis; (2) ordinary frequency distribution analysis; and (3) deviation analysis.

(1) *Time-series analysis*

The data were plotted along a time abscissa and least squares lines fitted to them. (Fig. 1.) Since the purpose was not to delineate fashion cycles but to analyse the relationship between trends, there was no attempt to fit complex curves. A series of straight lines fitted to certain periods, determined by inspection, was used instead. All three series showed in a general way the same trends, namely: (1) a lowering of hemlines, 1929–32; (2) a low hemline plateau, 1932–36; (3) a gradual raising of hemlines up to 1939; (4) a high hemline, 1939–42; (5) a high hemline plateau during the period covered by L-85, the wartime order restricting the use of materials, 1942–45; and (6) a descending hemline, 1945–47.

It will be noted that the WS series tended to descend at a slower rate than either of the other two series in both of the downward periods. Thus the slope of the WS line was only −0·23 in the first of these downward periods in contrast to −0·34 for the WHC and the V series; and it was only −0·14 in the second downward period (1945–47) as compared with −0·23 and −0·28 for the WHC and the V series. On the other hand, in the one period of ascending hemlines, the WS series rose more rapidly ($b = +0·27$) than the other two ($b = +0·19$ for V, $+0·22$ for WHC). This suggests a reluctance to lower hemlines on the part of the woman-in-the-street—a resistance to long skirts—and a readiness

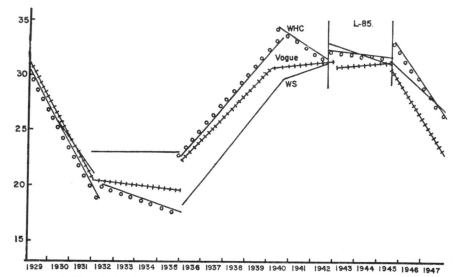

FIG. 1. Trends in skirt lengths as prescribed by fashion magazines and as worn by the woman-in-the-street, 1929–47.

to raise hemlines—a preference for short skirts. In part this may, of course, reflect the greater ease with which skirts may be shortened without purchasing new garments and the difficulty of lengthening skirts.

However in the low hemline plateau of the middle thirties it will be noted that the woman-in-the-street did not wear her skirts as long as those prescribed by the fashion magazines. In the high hemline period of the late thirties and early forties, on the other hand, she wore her skirts slightly longer than those prescribed by the fashion magazines. These results can scarcely be the result of strictly economic factors, that is, ease of shortening compared with difficulty of lengthening skirts; they seem to point to a genuine braking effect on the part of the woman-in-the-street to extremes in length. The period covered by the war order L-85 represents an artificially transfixed fashion situation imposed by law and is not, therefore, pertinent to our analysis at this point.

(2) Frequency distribution analysis

Figure 2 (a–c) shows the three series thrown into frequency distributions. It will be noted that each one is bi-modal, containing both a short-skirt and a

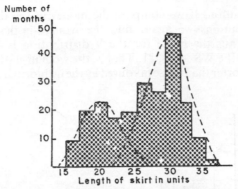

FIG. 2a. The distribution by months of skirt lengths shown by *Vogue* magazine, 1929–47.

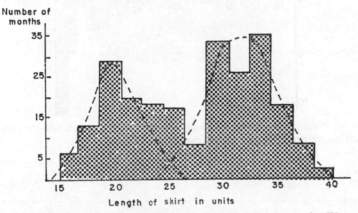

FIG. 2b. The distribution by months of skirt lengths shown in *Women's Home Companion* magazine, 1929–47.

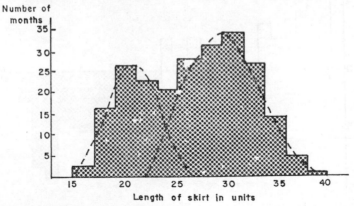

FIG. 2c. The distribution by months of skirt lengths shown by the woman-in-the-street, 1929–47.

153

long-skirt distribution. If we compare the modes in the three series for the long-skirt distributions we again find the woman-in-the-street exerting a limiting effect. Thus the mode for the V distribution is 19, for the WHC series, 20, but for the WS series, 21. That is, the woman-in-the-street tended to wear her skirts shorter than those favoured by the fashion magazines. However,

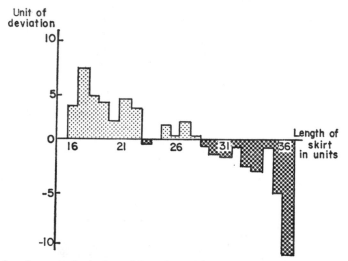

FIG. 3a. Average deviation of length of skirt of the woman-in-the-street from length prescribed in *Vogue* magazine, 1929–47.

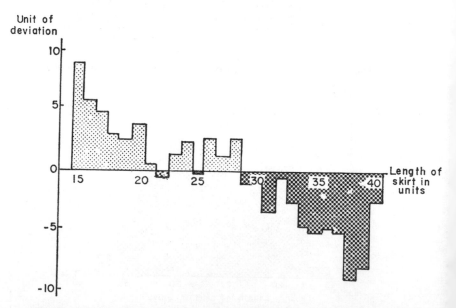

FIG. 3b. Average deviation of length of skirt of the woman-in-the-street from length prescribed in the *Woman's Home Companion*, 1929–47.

if we compare the modes for the short-skirt distributions, we find that the WS series shows a longer mode—29—than either of the fashion magazines—33 for WHC and 30 for V. When fashion 'dictated' long skirts, that is, the woman-in-the-street lengthened her skirts, but not so low as prescribed by the fashion 'dictators'. At both extremes of length, then, the woman-in-the-street exerted a braking effect.

(3) *Deviation analysis*

Figure 3 (a, b), however, brings out most clearly the limiting effect exerted by the woman-in-the-street. The abscissae in 3a and 3b represent the length shown in *Vogue* and *Woman's Home Companion* respectively. The ordinates represent the average deviation, or amount of nonconformity, shown by the WS series from the length prescribed by the fashion magazines. When, for example, V was showing hemlines of 17 units, the average deviation of the WS was almost 7 units; when V was showing hemlines of 24 units, the average amount of nonconformity of the WS series was zero; when V was showing hemlines of 37 units, the average deviation of the WS series was −11. The rank-order correlation between nonconformity and fashion model was +0·31 for the 16 to 22 interval, +0·16 for the 23 to 28 interval, and +0.65 for the 29 to 37 interval. A similar but even more marked pattern revealed itself for the relationship between the WS series and WHC series, the rank correlation for the 15 to 21 interval being +0·89, for the 23 to 28 interval, zero, and for the 29 to 40 interval, +0·63. For the 29 to 39 interval—that is, disregarding the last item—the rank-order correlation was +0·90.

In other words, the more extreme the 'dictated' hemline, short or long, the greater the non-conformity of the woman-in-the-street. If the prescribed length of skirts got much shorter than 30 units or longer than 20 units, she did not tend to follow. She showed a preferred range of, roughly, about 20 to 30 units. Within that range, she conformed to the pattern set by the fashion magazines. Outside that range, she balked and resisted. Fashion designers and creators could 'dictate' freely within an acceptable range; they could not so successfully 'dictate' outside of that preferred range.*

For a woman 5 feet 6 inches tall, the preferred length was roughly 14 inches from the floor, for the woman 5 feet tall, about 12 inches.†

Implications

These results suggest that there are decided and clear-cut limits within which fashion controls may operate in a given population, in a given period of time. The fashion dictator does not appear to be free to impose his will without restrictions. He must, it would seem, remain within certain bounds or he will

---

* One is reminded of the story told of Henry Ford, Sr., who is reported to have told his stylists that they could make Fords any colour just so long as it was black. Or the story of the man in the French Revolution who looked out of the window and then, turning to his host as he grabbed his hat, cried out, 'I have to go. There goes my mob. I have to follow them for I am their leader!'

† That is, allowing one foot for the head, and assuming 25 to be the preferred length, this would mean a quarter of the distance from floor to V of neck, as the distance from floor to hemline most preferred.

not be followed. The contribution of the followers appears to be rather marked. By their inertia, they seem to circumscribe the dictator's power.

The question now arises as to whether or not we can measure with equal precision the limits to other than fashion controls. What, for instance, are the precise limits within which legal controls can operate? Propaganda controls? Advertising controls? Data for answering these questions objectively are not readily available. But when they are found and exploited we shall know a good deal more about the processes of social control than we do at the present time.

References

1. A. L. Kroeber, 'On the Principle of Order in Civilization as Exemplified by Changes of Fashion'. *Amer. Anthropoloist*, 21, New series (1919), pp. 235–263.
2. *Three Centuries of Women's Dress Fashions* (Berkeley, University of California Press, 1940). (*See* Chapter 3.)

Chapter 8

CONSUMER FASHION*
by Caroline A. Foley

This early contribution exemplifies the economists' approach to fashion. Its concern for diffusion of fashion ideas is remarkable, and its bibliography to early contributions throughout Europe is of considerable value.

The study of the consumer, which is once more occupying the attention of economic science in England, is more disinterested and genuine than it was in the past. It is a study of the consumer as such. Two centuries ago and less he was appraised through the spectacles of trade and from the standpoint of national defence. His tastes were prone to go wavering over sea after strange gods. As the Athenian's lust for the East and the Teuton's craving for Italy, so was the Briton's hankering after the products, 'guises', and fashions of his Celto-Latin neighbours. It is the subject of comment, warning and rebuke from the days of the Plantagenets, that our countrymen 'haunted so much unto the folly of strangers'.[1] Strangers meant mostly the French. When French supremacy arose on the decay of that of Spain, the seductiveness of French example and taste became doubly dangerous, and to yield to it became unpatriotic as well as improvident. Economists and social reformers took up the burden of the encyclopaedic chronicler and preacher. ''Tis better for England,' wrote Defoe, 'that we should drink all Turnip-wine, or any wine, than that we should drink the best wine in Europe and go back to France for it. At present the Gust to French wines is laid by and the gross Draght of the whole Nation is upon Portugal wines. These the Portuguese sell us for our Manufactures . . . all that ready Money we us'd to pay the French for their Wine, Brandy and Vinegar is sav'd in our Pockets.' (*A Review of the Affairs of France*, No 86, 1704.)[2] Readers of economic history know that there are few writers, from Bacon[3] down to the days of Adam Smith, who do not discourse after this sort when on the subject of foreign trade. There was not only the expansion of commerce tempting young democracy to take what it fancied and not perhaps what, economically and politically, it ought, so that as early as the days of Elizabeth 'from the towne to Westminster alonge, every Streate' was full of French and 'Millen' shops displaying goods 'able to make any temperate man

* From the *Economic Journal*, vol. 3 (1893).

to gase on them and to buy somewhat, though it serve to no purpose necessarie.'[4] There was besides at the other end of the balance a dexterous State policy exploiting this British weakness and using its own creative and purveying skill to ends of aggrandizement.[5] Hence in early economic theory the dynamic of wants and tastes, even when belief in paternal State functions waned, was not likely to be neglected.

Peace, steam and factory, proletariat and means of subsistence, diverted attention to production and population. But the working man has been for some time asserting that he is not a machine, but has tastes and likes to be in the fashion, even though fashion may turn and rend him as it abandons his employer's business.[6] He too is a consumer, 'temperate', it may be, yet apt 'to gase and to buy somewhat', and influence the fluctuations in demand. There is no further excuse for neglecting a thoroughgoing examination of those fluctuations.

Nevertheless that factor in these movements, which, if it is not the most potent, is at least the most characteristic and typical of all, inasmuch as it is the expression of the very spirit and instinct of variability itself, receives never more than a sentence or a paragraph of consideration in modern economic treatises. Mill, Cairnes and Fawcett do not condescend to the economics of fashion; and yet the last was of opinion that 'in political economy, as in many other sciences, the causes which produce disturbing fluctuations require a more careful investigation than those causes whose action is more constant and more undeviating'.[7] Cournot believed that all human societies were tending towards a final, stable, persisting order, and that the effectual regulating of every demand was to hasten the blessed time when history should be no more, because we should all live according to scientific laws;[8] but it does not appear that he coped with the regulation of fashion. Thorold Rogers only alluded to the 'unintelligible fickleness' of fashion to groan and pass by.[9] Of living economists General Walker and Professors Sidgwick and Marshall graze the fearful subject with hasty comment, the Cambridge scholars viewing it from the standpoint of Production and Consumption respectively. Professor Menger examines the phenomenon of Inconstant Demand, but selects for special mention only domestic arrangements against fire, and, for country dwellers, the Family Medicine-chest.[10] Dr Roscher,[11] however, and Hermann[12] inquire and classify with a more curious regard; and in England Professor Foxwell, in his valuable inquiry into the causes of trade and labour fluctuations, has ranged fashion amongst the third of his three dual groups of change-elements, namely, as a special cause of price movement peculiar to each particular commodity.[13] It is true that he too, seeing in fashion a mere matter of bonnets, associates the mental procedure beneath them with that of 'earthquakes and such inscrutable dispensations of nature'. Yet seismology advances, and so has his faith in the pervasion of law. Economic historians may some day heed Edmond About's warning that the history of modern industry, under the penalty of serious omission, will have to consecrate a chapter to the influence of caprice over labour.[14] Meanwhile the results of a rough analysis, and of a few first-hand inquiries, presented in a very condensed form, may be of interest.

It may not be wholly superfluous to distinguish fashion forthwith from custom, usage, or taste. Tastes, whether concerned with the what or the how of our wants, convey more or less the implication of an aesthetically sufficient reason: custom or usage may be based on comfort or morality. But when anything is wanted on the ground that it is fashionable a rational basis seems farther to seek. An errant instinct obtruding into the lines of motived conduct is not unnaturally judged to be irrational, and the philosophy that identified the irrational with the shifting and impermanent has not died out since the day when it was put into the mouth of Nature attacking Fashion. '*Vous affectez si fort le changement, dont la sagesse est ennemi capitale . . . la raison est toujours uniforme et invariable.*'[15] This implication of a more or less incessant tendency to change best characterizes fashion when viewed together with taste and usage as modes in which a society is satisfying its various wants, and is recognized and emphasized by French definitions of 'mode'.[16] For the English language fashion is current usage; for the French *l'usage n'est qu'une longue mode*. Mode is *le goût mobile, usage passager*. Fashion cannot claim to express such changes in habits and modes of life as are due to fresh discoveries and to improvements in taste and comfort as such, nor from those consequent on change in physical or social environment. They may all involve corresponding changes in fashion, but when eliminated they will leave a residuum of variableness in wants not accounted for, yet which, together with the complementary fact of a *general* conformity to that variableness, make up the phenomenon of fashion properly so-called.

Inquiry into the data requisite to explain an economic phenomenon would be out of place here. It must suffice merely to assert them. The cosmic law of rhythm, which seems to affect consumption generally,[17] and manifests itself in the individual through the law of variety in wants; and a nexus of social factors: love of distinction, imitation, and the effort after equalization, together with the unconscious effort to express the spirit of the age, in proportion as it impresses itself more deeply now in one, now in another, centre of civilization, —these being granted, we have man actuated by what Fourier called picturesquely *la passion papillonne*,[18] or as Montaigne defined him, 'vain, diverse and undulating' (*Essays*, I). The 'flitting' from one mode to another of the influential few becomes impressive and prevailing when multiplied into the 'sequaciousness' of the many, or when, if larger periods be considered, the selections made in mode and material are discerned as making for some expression of social consciousness.

Further, the increasing systematization in fashion, i.e. the order of its changes and their diffusion in European and other centres of civilization, is the outcome of several special conditions, some positive, e.g. a high development of commercial and social intercourse between nations having relatively identical ideals of culture,[19] together with advanced productive skill and practical arts; some negative, e.g. the absence of political and social barriers to the general adoption of the new modes.

Thus conditioned fashion, or any given fashion, comes to be both for consumer and purveyor an element on the one hand of complication, on the other of simplification. The field for the selective play of the consumer's choice is so great, that purveyance is rendered very speculative. On the other hand, where his choice settles, demand is certain to be both prompt and extensive.

Fashion in Consumption

From this standpoint, for purposes both of historic and present-day inquiry, it might prove useful to define fashion somewhat more specifically, by ranking it not so much as a class of wants under such heads as necessaries, comforts, or luxuries, but as rather a coefficient of any of these, so that it appears as a want *in* wants. It may enter even into necessaries; in comforts and still more, perhaps, in luxuries it becomes a coefficient of a higher power. There is of course less scope for change in primary and definite needs, nevertheless there is no one commodity, unless pure air and pure water be considered as relative exceptions, which admits of being produced in one *mode* only. Hence the love of variety and its social liabilities, as sketched above, finds even in necessaries its opportunity, e.g. in the form and flour of loaves or in the shape of a boot.[20]

When nature ceases to be peremptory in her requirements, choice is ampler and fashion more influential. Experience incites to fresh experiments in forms of utility, and though there are regulative forces limiting selection, fashion often traverses these triumphantly or else, as their coefficient, exploits them, so to speak, and may even convert them into excesses of taste depriving them of their purity and dignity.[21] At this higher power fashion has been ranked as one of the four principles of luxury,[22] and as the expression of refined sensuality, opinion or caprice, creating unreal wants.[23]

On the other hand, and by writers of the same nationality, fashion has been frankly and warmly defended. It has not only checked sloth and slovenliness,[24] and fostered refinement, but also stimulated imagination, fire and facility in the adaptation of matter to use (*à bien tourner les choses*.)[25] Its essential element, love of change and mobility of taste, is the great incentive and *primum mobile* of all progress,[26] breaking the bonds of custom by creating fresh needs or modes of need, and if judiciously cultivated through its periodic manifestations in the individual, as it makes itself felt moderately every hour, and keenly every second hour, might banish what is the curse of civilization—excess both of work and play, and *ennui*.[27]

Viewed thus as a potent coefficient in demand, fashion has (1) a history to be traced and (2) present manifestations to be investigated.

(1) In the former connection, Dr Schäffle sees a course of evolution, by which 'custom in wants, locally homogeneous and temporarily stable, has become fashion distributed in space and transient in time'.[28] This does not, or should not, mean that in the transition new psychological or sociological factors have been combined with the older coefficient custom. Where customs are stable, the innovatory instinct is latent or extremely circumscribed by rigid external conditions and by undeveloped, or, it may be, diverted imagination. A barbarian and a West European man may dress with equal uniformity. The former has in his raiment a very definite set of social symbols, and a limited range of skill in production. The latter has mainly stripped his vesture of symbolism and is circumscribed as to its variability by an active life of wear, tear, and hurry. The dress of a 'lady', in Europe and America, is still expressive of her more leisured life and less diverted imagination. But now she also has girded up her loins to work, and is to that extent gravitating towards a more appropriate and relatively stable 'costume'.

160

But however the economic historian views the phenomenon of fashion, he will find that, rooted as it is in elemental soil, it is absent from no society or social epoch.[29] 'Every epoch', as M. Havard has said, 'has colours and contours which it prefers, forms which it affects symbols which it venerates.'[30] Every epoch, too, has ebullitions of sentiment, whims and fantasies to indulge in, is emulous within each caste, or class, or smaller group, is prone to follow and apt to produce leaders. Every nation has its own geographical position, social temperament, and political development to express. Every individual, assimilating his own social medium, tends to modify it according to his own individuality, circumstances, and the direction of his activities. And vibrations in social consciousness naturally find most facile expression in such human products as constitute the most intimate adjuncts of life and best lend themselves to mobility of taste.

The association of stability with all ancient customs is to some extent based on the scantiness of such contemporary records as have been till recently accessible. Epochs which have long stood out from the obscurity of the past have been treated too much as 'rigid unities' of relatively unchanging manners.[31] De Laveleye found in the taste for change the distinctive scourge of this epoch, because, forsooth, Greek vases before, and catacombs after, A.D. 1, show figures clad alike.[32] But it is impossible to read of Terence's fashionable mothers,[33] and of Plautus's enumeration of annual change in smart stuffs and colours, or of the attendant troop of dunning tradesmen,[34] and retain the belief in the modernness of fashion.[35] Dr Roscher judges that fashion was very constant in the days of Charlemagne, because clothing was dear.[36] Julius Lessing, however, points to that monarch's sumptuary laws passed to check the rage for Italian fashions.[37] Before the end of the fourteenth century change in tastes had become frequent and extensive.[38] The frequent denunciations of contemporary writers, who saw all class distinctions waning in the imitative scramble after new modes of dress, point to permanence and stability as rather the ideals of the few than the habit and tendency of the many,[39] and reveal also the influence of changing taste on the conditions of production. 'At this time,' says the Limburg chronicler in 1380, 'the fashion in raiment was so changed, that he who last year was a master-tailor, became in a twelvemonth a labourer.'[40] The comments in the second half of the sixteenth century on swift changes of fashion, culminating in Montaigne, Shakspere, and Jonson, multiply too greatly to need mention. The idea of a periodical recurrence in specific tastes had already been put forward.[41] The organisation of dress and manners in the seventeenth century by Louis XIV,[42] and the relatively unsuccessful attempt in the same direction by Charles II,[43] throw light on the inception of fashions, though to what extent the example of the courts were followed throughout each of the two countries is not so clear. In France the launching of a taste has devolved mainly on to the stage[44] and uncrowned leaders of society: in this country the example of Royalty is followed only within a very narrow circle.

(2) The examination of present economic conditions has to estimate Fashion in its modern developments as in various ways influencing consumption, and therewith the personal and national budget. It may tell, e.g. (a) on the quality, or kinds, of wealth consumed, (b) on the relative quantities of the same, (c) on the rapidity of consumption.

11

(*a*) Inasmuch as in fashion both change, as such, and social distinction are aimed at, demand is likely to vary in the direction of *contrast*. Changes in the substance and shape of clothing and adornment abound with illustrations of this tendency, but the law also holds good in every kind of taste, pursuit, and cult.

Through the resisting influence of habit, however, the change may be of the nature of a development—in other words, a variation along the same line of choice. And this, as will be shown, may make all the difference to the producer, for the new supply may be effected by adaptation of the same productive apparatus.

Further, as an expression of the effort after equalization, fashion, in diffusing itself outwards and downwards, involves deterioration in quality through adulteration, reproduction in coarser material, and coarser methods of production. When every woman wishes to wear silk, cotton admixture is lavishly used even in a proportion of 9 to 1.[45]

Again, as expressing the drift of some social impulse, fashion selects some class of materials, forms and colours in preference to others. Dress, it has been pointed out,[46] has to subserve three objects, viz., practical, aesthetic, and symbolical. The last, in the savage, is compassed by tattoo marks, war paint, feathers, scalps, etc., as well as the distinctive dress of the sexes, and tends to change with the 'spiritual currents' (*geistige Strömungen*) and 'world-moving ideas' of the *Zeitgeist*. This view is best illustrated by historic contemplation, such as was afforded by the collection of hats at the Vienna Exhibition, 1873, ranging over 200 years, from the formal Spanish hat of the sixteenth century to the swashing plumed sombrero of the Thirty Years War, when the military type became normal, and again from the succeeding courtly peruke and cocked hat of French supremacy to the French Revolution, when Franklin's black-lacquered Dutch 'matelot' hat from New York,[47] and the British *redingote, couleur de suie des cheminees de Londres*,[48] were adopted as emblems of constitutional liberty in France, and of political expansion or Wertherism in Germany.

(*b*) This is too patent a fact to need dwelling on. Typical of many other products is such evidence as the following: The English demand for silks had certainly fallen off. Why? 'Because for the moment the fashion for wear is against silks.'[49]

(*c*) Under this head reference may be made to the now forgotten lectures of Storch, who distinguished, besides nature and use as causes of the consumption of wealth, opinion, which destroys the value of wealth independently of matter.[50] Shakspere had already expressed the truth more picturesquely: 'The fashion wears out more apparel than the man.' J. B. Say was also epigrammatic, if not picturesque, in asserting that fashion, by condemning what is still not only fresh, but perhaps also pretty and comfortable as well, impoverishes the state both in what it consumes and in what it does not consume. Through the distribution and prolonged consumption of whilom fashionable goods in other classes of society, as well as in the colonies, by means of the second-hand trade, the truth of this epigram is limited in application to the budget of the individual fashionable consumers.[51] It is none the less true that fashion throws for the 'sequacious' consumer a glamour over the product in vogue often irrespective of beauty, convenience, or fitness, and which as it fades causes the same product to be the more hastily superseded in proportion as those qualities are absent.

Fashion, as affecting consumption in quality, quantity, and rapidity, finds limitations[52] to its power in such forces as beauty, convenience, fitness, the efficacy of which varies according to social temperament and culture. 'If the inconstancy of modes shortens the term of consumption of certain articles, the taste of the beautiful in the arts prolongs that of some others.'[53] So, according to Junghanns,[54] does the love of comfort in Germany. A perception of fitness in adapting consumption to circumstances of life and means will further restrict the range of variability. And custom, as shown in costume, uniform or livery, may withstand the seduction of change even for centuries.[55] Hygienic principles, again, may proscribe what is actually or potentially the fashion. And philanthropy and patriotism, morality and religion, let alone economy, have all been brought to bear as regulative principles of careless innovation or excess in tastes and manners. Fashion, on the other hand, has often rendered such principles yeoman's service by developing them as *their* coefficient, so that it may become equally fashionable to frequent evangelical revival meetings as to buy Irish laces.[56]

Viewed in its effect upon expenditure, fashion, by increasing some values and lowering others, has been held as self-equating with respect to the national budget,[57] although, as was pointed out at first, this opinion was not held in the so-called mercantile phase of political economy. In private expenditure, on the other hand, fashion favours economy or extravagance according as the consumer is concerned to lead, or simply follow, in fashionable departures, or again, to cultivate an independence of taste. Modern production, on the 'mass' pattern and ready-made system renders it cheaper to buy not what is coming, but what is just come, into fashion. For the individual to anticipate mass-production, or else to demand, careless of the drift of fashionable tendencies and consulting only his own taste, involves a greater outlay. A price prohibitive for the million, and often out of proportion to the cost of production, is still in most cases the main guarantee of the fashion-leader's brief monopoly: as it was when Locke wrote: 'Things of fashion will be had . . . whatever rates they cost, and the rather because they are dear.'[58]

Fashion in Production and Distribution

The anxious purveyor to fashionable needs has been shown to be as ancient a figure in history as fashion itself. Nor is rapidity of change a new difficulty he has to contend with. Annual and even more frequent changes are alluded to by medieval writers, and though the conditions of modern production, commerce, and diffusion of knowledge tend possibly to make the changes 'more frequent and rapid of late years',[59] the producer's 'fashion-difficulty' is intensified rather by division of labour and specialization of machinery, international competition and the wage-question, than by any feverish acceleration of pace in *la papillonne*. A century ago, when the first fashion journal was started fortnightly in Paris, the editors defied German pirated editions, because they could not be brought out till three weeks after the genuine issue, by which time the fashions depicted would have varied again![60]

As affecting trade and industry to-day, fashion is assigned a place (if a small one) by modern economics, under the head of trade risks, fluctuations of industry, or variations in production. Mobility and fancy have permeated the whole field of demand, so that principles, once governing the production of articles of luxury only, apply now to the majority of forms and many of the materials in supply. Makers and purveyors, some more, some less, have now, at an unprecedented degree of rivalry, national and international, to study both how to supply what people want, and to win them to want what they supply.[61] As in the struggle for life and wealth generally, so in coping with fashion, provision, with prompt adaptation to, and modification of, the fluctuating conditions, in which they must sink or swim, are the main elements of success. Fashion, as involving changes often hard to foresee and of uncertain duration, tends to aggravate 'the incessant small vibrations of industry';[62] fashion as involving far-reaching conformity, together with a highly centralized process of inception and radiation, simplifies the work of supply and reduces the cost of production.[63] The problem of the supplier is to transform the intensified element of risk from a possible cause of disaster into a stepping-stone to success. When fluctuation and impermanence are not thoroughly accepted as the normal state of modern trade, a relatively durable fashion may lead to maladjustment.[64] Anything introducing rigidity into production enhances the jeopardizing power of fashion. Adaptability and versatility, both mental and manual,[65] have to cope with high specialization of machinery and skill, as well as with the necessity for mass-production in order to the realization of profit.[66]

Owners and cultivators of land are not exempt from this species of risk, though to a relatively small extent, fashion affecting the mode of the product to a much greater extent than the substance. Viticulture, sericulture, horticulture in its more refined products, and the management of ostrich farms, are liable to be affected by changes in fashion.[67] Teraminta's dismissal of an admirer because he did not drink claret[68] points to a taste once, and since, favouring French viticulture. Again the ostrich feathers imported into this country had declined between 1880 and 1889 in the proportion of $5:2$; the weight in that of $2 \cdot 5:2$.[69] The fashion of going up to London 'to learn the fashions' and of absenteeism generally, in so far as it is due to fashion, has been considered prejudicial to rural prosperity. The fancy of a poet foresaw that the introduction of coaches would ruin England in leather, ash trees, and young horses.[70]

In the tactics of the manufacturer the symptoms (1) of a vacillation in demand raise the problem—What can I 'bring out' to attract it? (2) of a favourable turn—What can I do to get or keep ahead in the race? (3) of a recoil—Can I turn out what is now in demand with such plant, machinery and hands as I have? Favour at flood tide involves the further question, How long will it last? Can it be sustained by devising developments? Ebb tide brings the uncertainty as to whether the recoil be transient or practically permanent. In some such attitude he has to confront demand with its coefficient of fashion, and, armed with 'money, wits, and perseverance', compass the capture of the lucky *conjunctur*.[71] 'Wits' he partly embodies in superiority of machinery, of designing, i.e. in the faculty of taking a lead in designs which 'sell', of dyeing and finishing, and finally in that fine, commercial *flair*, which leads to 'hits' rather than to 'misses'. By this quasi-instinct he lays his hand upon the pulse of taste, and, interpreting its movements, is able in some degree to 'reduce the play of chance' in his business arena.[72] Unless fashion be seriously held to be above, or beneath, law, the importance of such far-seeing augury to the *entrepreneur* is obvious, and indeed is admitted by some.[73] British manufacturers of silk and other articles of female dress are content to follow in the wake of France, a course which is fraught with no less danger than that of the French creator,[74] though it is not impossible, by close observation of the inception of a taste, and estimation of the average rate of diffusion both in time and space, to anticipate its final stage, as a want of the million, and reap a rich harvest of profit.[75]

Exact estimate of the effect of fashion on the fortunes of an industrial centre or firm is complicated by the intermixture of other causes. Of nineteen merchants and manufacturers among those who gave evidence before the Commission of Inquiry into the Depression of Trade in 1886—an inquiry which negatively absolved fashion as a cause of that specific depression—all, while not professing to distinguish between the causes of change in taste, admitted that such changes were one of the greatest difficulties they had to contend with though some (woollen manufacturers) contended that adaptation to demand without radical change of machinery was often possible, and also that by avoidance of large stocks, danger was frequently to be averted.[76] The silk and lace manufacturers were naturally more emphatic as to the powerful influence of fashion.[77] Injury through absence of prevision and enterprise was admitted by one of the latter.[78] By another the fruits of Lister's marvellous inventive skill and adaptation were attributed to exceptional luck.[79] Bradford, Paisley and Coventry in Great Britain, and St Etienne[80] and Lyons in France, are instances of centres which have suffered economic fluctuations, aggravated, if not wholly created, by fashion. Taken collectively, such movements in textile industry are molecular and self-compensating, but this is not productive of consolation for some molecules.[81] A centre may often adapt itself to a new industry. Till about 1850 one-third of the population of Paisley was engaged in manufacturing psuedo-Indian shawls; now thread, starch, engineering, and shipbuilding have sprung up instead of that defunct industry, and trade, being on a broader basis, is less liable to severe fluctuations. Coventry has ceased to concentrate itself on anything so 'chancy'[82] as ribbons, and has realized locally unprecedented fortunes in cycles, besides developing other trades. 'Lister's' spin thread when plush and velvet are 'sluggish'.

Procedure in adjustment to, and creation of, new demand is in keeping with the development of modern democracy. Dress seems at one time to have been imposed, and then suggested, from above, speaking socially. Now the sovereign people's tastes are besieged simultaneously and *en bloc* by shop windows, advertisement, fashion paper, and pattern. Louis XIV, when he determined in 1655 that perukes should be worn, in one day named forty-eight court perruquiers and founded a guild of 200 wig-makers. To reinstate the waning taste, wig-makers solicited George III not to wear only his own hair.[83] The *marchand des modes* was a recent specialization in trade when the *Encyclopédie* was appearing (1705)[84]—a purveyor to the wealthy and elegant minority. Now the *Grands Magasins* may go with their own developments to the public direct, and cater for them from head to foot.[85] And so long as elasticity is compassed by the purchase of lighter stock and shorter quantities, mobility of taste is to the purveyor as desirable as mobility of the price of stock to the broker and jobber. This has been rendered patent to the laity by the census of the retail drapery trade effected during the last two winters by the weekly organ, *The Wholesale Draper*, in which the absence of a more or less radical change in the shape of mantle or dress is very generally reported as of disastrous effect.[86]

As affected by fashion the interests of the wage-earner are *solidaire* with those of the employer in so far as the former is an adaptable machine. Rigidity, whether through bad generalship, over-specialized skill, want of technical versatility, or any accidents of combination, is fraught with intimate peril for rank and file. The vicissitudes of Spitalfields and Coventry silk-weavers are historical, and the latter, inadequate to take to cycle-making, fell into destitution or emigrated.[87] Nevertheless fashion was only one factor in these fluctuations. It was more responsible for distress occasioned by the decay of the Irish cottage industry of hand-embroidered muslin.[88] Versatility, on the other hand, appears in the habit of St Etienne men, as reported by M. de Lanessan, of getting taken on in other local industries when the ribbon-trade is slack. Interesting insight into the effects of fashion on woman's work in the East of London, e.g., in ostrich feather trimming,[89] and other trimmings, such as fringe,[90] fur-sewing, and artificial flower-making, is afforded by Miss Collet's contribution to *Life and Labour in London*, vol. 1. Sudden cessation of employment is not alone disastrous; a slowly waning taste may involve degradation in skill and wages.

The worker whose skill is, or borders on, that of artistic handicraft is affected by fashion in proportion as he ministers to a want which is substantially inconstant. A skilled West End tailoress will profit by every new departure, adapting her skill better than the old Limburg tailors. The Christmas card painter, on the other hand, has suffered severely.

Instances might no doubt be multiplied *ad infinitum*. I have attempted only a brief economic digest of a very wide subject; and, mindful of Bacon's exhortation, that 'it is not good to look too long upon these turning wheels of vicissitudes, lest we become giddy', desist.

References

1. John of Glastonbury, cf. *The Book of Costume* (London 1847), p. 55.
2. Cf. also Defoe's *Weavers' Riots against Calicoes* and *An Humble Proposal to the People of England for the increase of their Trade*, &c., in W. Lee's *Daniel Defoe*. Also Berkeley, *Querist*, pp. 141, 144.
3. *Letter to Villiers*.
4. *A Compendious or Brief Examination of certain ordinary complaints*, by W. S. 1581, pt. 2, cf. *Britannia Languens*, § viii.
5. Cf. Joshua Gee, *The Trade and Navigation of Great Britain considered*, p. 22, and Samuel Fortrey, *England's Interest and Improvement*. Also *Britannia Languens*. § xii. Cf. too Thorold Rogers, *Industrial and Commercial History of England*, on Colbert's policy, p. 186.
6. Cf. Report of Industrial Remuneration Conference, 1885, pp. 242, 176.
7. *Manual*, p. 84.
8. *Théorie des Richesses*, 1863, p. 52.
9. *Pol. Econ.* p. 78.

10. *Grundsätze*, p. 37.
11. *Pol. Econ.* § ccviii, &c.
12. *Staatswissenschaftliche Untersuchungen*, pp. 98–100.
13. *Irregularity of Employment and Fluctuations of Prices*, pp. 36, 37, 67.
14. *La Vieille Roche*, pt. II, cp. ii.
15. *Dialogue entre la Mode et la Nature* (Paris, 1656).
16. *'Les modes changent, les mœurs ne changent point'. Le Théophraste moderne*, Anon. (Paris, 1700).
17. Cf. Mr Spencer's *First Principles*, § 87; and *Principles of Sociology*, vol. 2, pt. iv, cp. xi.
18. *Le Nouveau Monde Industriel*, § I, 1 and 2.
19. 'Fashion is the costume of European culture', in J. von Falke, *Costümgeschichte*, Introd.
20. According to Mr Giffen it influences an important 'conventional necessary', viz., currency. *See The Case against Bimetallism*, p. 220.
21. 'It is a universal law that whatever pursuit, whatever doctrine, becomes fashionable, shall lose a portion of that dignity which it had possessed while it was confined to a small but earnest majority and was loved for its own sake alone.'—Macaulay, *History of England*, p. 3.
22. Baudrillart, *Histoire du Luxe*, 1879, p. 7 *et seq*.
23. J. B. Say, *Traité d'Economie politique* (1841), p. 4.
24. *Les Lois de la Galanterie*, in Quicherat, *Histoire du Costume*. (Fashionable persons were required to wash their hands every day and their face nearly as often.)
25. *Dialogue entre la Mode et la Nature*.
26. Baudrillart, op. cit. p. 10.
27. Fourier, *Le Nouveau Monde*, loc. cit. Cf. also Berkeley, *The Querist*, p. 20.
28. *Das gesellschaftliche System der menschlichen Wirthschaft* (1873), vol. 3, p. 343.
29. Cf. Darwin, *Descent of Man*, vol. 2, p. 383; Westermarck, *History of Human Marriage*, p. 274; pp. 165–86.
30. *L'art à travers les Mœurs*, (1884).
31. Fr. Studniczka, *Beiträge zur Geschichte der altgriechischen Tracht* (Vienna, 1886). Herman Weiss. *Kostümkunde*, pt. ii. Moyr, *Ancient Greek Female Costume*.
32. *Le Luxe*, p. 26.
33. *Eunuchus*, ii, 4.
34. *Epidicus*, ii, 2 : *Aulularia*, iii, 10.
35. Cf. G. Duplessis, *Costumes Historiques*, Introduction.
36. *Pol. Econ.* § ccxxv.
37. *Der Modeteufel* (Berlin, 1884).
38. Viollet-le-Duc, *Dictionnaire du Mobilier Français*, vol. 1, p. 357, f.n. Chaucer *The Persone's Tale*. John of Glastonbury, loc. cit. H. de Knyghton (Twysden, 2729), (1388), 'unusquisque imitabatur alium et nitebatur inducere noivorem gysam', &c. *'The Knight of the Tower'*, (1371), Harl. Lib. No. 1764. More, *Utopia*, bk. 1. Jost Amman, *Gynaeceum*, 1586. Rohrbach, *Trachten der Völker*, pp. 187–90. Louandre, *Hist. du Costume*, vol. 1, 173. The 'jointed baby', 'Mademoiselle', or fashion-doll of the *Spectator* (No. 277), seems to have been in vogue in the fourteenth century, if not earlier. Challamel, *Histoire de la Mode en France*. Robida, *Ten Centuries of Toilette*.
39. Cf. Occliff, *Dialogus inter Occliff et Mendicum*, MS. Harl. Lib. 4,826. 'Allas where is this worldlys stabilnesse?' *et seq*.
40. *Limburger Chronik* (Marburg, 1828).
41. Drant, *A Medicinall Morall*, 1566.

> 'Fashions in all our gesterings
> fashions in our attyre,
> Which (as the wyse have thoughte) do cum,
> and goe in circled gyre.'

42. Two centuries earlier, Charles VII had been petitioned to create a ministry of fashion. Quicherat, op. cit. Cf. Ary Renan, *Le Costume en France*, p. 127.
43. Cf. Evelyn, *Tyrannus, or the Mode*; 'a triffe in which Evelyn advocated a particular kind of costume, the like of which the King adopted some few years afterwards at his court' (Diary, ed. 1879, p. xli). See also Miscellaneous Writings, ed. 1825, p. xiii, and Pepys' Diary for 8, 13, 15 October and 22 November 1666.

44. Cf. Lessing, op. cit. Challamel, *Histoire de la Mode en France*, p. 5 (1875). Illustrated by the case last autumn at Paris of Mme. Rodriguez *v.* Mlle. Brack *modiste* versus *danseuse*.
45. Report on Depression of Trade (1886), p. 7507.
46. Kleinwächter, *Zur Philosophie der Mode* (1880). J. von Falke, *Zur Cultur und Kunst (Costüm und Mode)* (1878).
47. Also the English *Chapeau Jockai*.
48. *Magasin des Modes nouvelles françaises et anglaises*, 1786–7.
49. Report on Depression of Trade (1886), pp. 7350–51.
50. *Cours d'Economie politique*, vol. 4, p. 1.
51. In the last century fashionable people largely purchased decorative china with discarded smart clothing. Viz., Addison, *The Lover*. At the present day the house-to-house flower-trade has to some extent superseded the china.
52. 'So long, observe, as fashion has influence on the manufacture of plate so long, you can't have the goldsmith's art in this country.' Ruskin, *The Political Economy of Art*, pp. 60 *et seq*. 'It may be stated generally that the principles of such eminent purveyors as Mme Elise and Messrs Worth and Poole are hostile to those of the artist. In the Aesthetic Republic . . . they . . . would starve.' P. Fitzgerald, 'The Art of Dressing and of being Dressed', *Art Journal*, vol. 187, p. 293. Cf. also Falke, *Art in the House*, on the monotonous prevalence, once fashionable, of *red* in English dining-rooms. The revival of the need and sense of beauty in dress and other adjuncts has fared hardly through the vagaries of its 'aesthetic' foster-parents, nevertheless the resultant economic effect affords a reply to the charge made by fellow-subject and foreigner against the English, of being the most arti-ficial and conventional of nations, viz. that it was only in London, till quite recently, that a woman could purchase for daily wear artistic clothing, made independently of fashion, at the very centre of fashion's dispensary.
53. Storch, op. cit.
54. *Der Fortschritt des Zollvereins* (1848), pp. 27, 28, 50, 51.
55. Hearn, *Plutology*, p. 450–1. Cf. Storch, op. et loc. cit. on the Japanese attributing a different nationality to Russian travellers, at different periods, owing to the altered mode of wearing the hair.
56. D. Nisard says somewhere '*La mode dans les choses de la littérature n'est souvent que l'excès d'une disposition vraie*'. Cf. Mr Strachey's Report on the German tariff reform of 1879, (C. 4530, 1884–5, lxxxi, p. 28) that the demand for the various articles which com-pose the wardrobe of the '50,000 fanatics', of 'Jaeger's system', has been sufficient to give a stimulus to the spinning of carded yarns, in compensation to the increasing demand for combed, mixed, and mungo yarns. Again, Paris orders for German fancy leather goods have been cancelled after outbursts of French patriotism.
57. Roscher, *Principles of Political Economy* (New York, 1878), sec. ccviii.
58. *Some Considerations of the Lowering of Interest* (1692), pp. 93, 94. For a contrasted emulation to secure cheapness, cf. Junghanns, op. cit. pp. 57, 58. Cf. also H. S. Foxwell, op. cit., p. 69.
59. Report on Depression of Trade, p. 6343. Article by Ada Heather Bigg, *Nineteenth Century* (7 Feburary 1893).
60. *Magasin des Modes nouvelles françaises et anglaises*, cahier 4, (20 Dec. 1786). Cf. also Montesquieu's, *Lettres Persanes*, xcix, and Purchas, *Microcosmus* (1627), cp. xxv.
61. Mr Graham Wallas sends me a note from the MSS of Francis Place, to the effect that in a strike in the leather breeches trade, 1793, the masters prevailed on their customers to wear stuff breeches, to make which they substituted other tailors in place of the strikers. At an earlier date legislation would have been resorted to to assist an industry; cf. the case of 'illegally covered buttons' in the eighteenth century, *The Warehouseman and Draper*, 11 March 1893; also W. Lee, *Daniel Defoe's Life*, &c., bk. iv, p. 57. For a strike of *con-sumers*, cf. W. Lee, op. cit. bk. ii, 'Women's Complaint against the Weavers' pp. 132–142.
62. Walker, *Wages Question*, p. 179.
63. Hermann, op. cit. p. 100: Roscher, op. cit. Schäffle, op. cit.
64. Cf. the manufacture of steel for crinolines, Thorold Rogers, *A Manual of Political Economy*, p. 78. Also the case of the stay-makers, when women 'thought proper to throw off their bodice'. *Essay on Political Circumstances of Ireland* (1798), pp. 89–90; of the buckle-makers, &c., Malthus, *Essay*, bk. iii, cp. xiii, and the hair-powder trade, *Ann. Reg.* (1759), p. 179.

65. Cf. Mr Strachey's Report (p. 4530, 1884–5, lxxxi), pp. 27, 30: 'Our manufacturers will not emerge from a certain traditional groove of hardness, heaviness, and durability. . . . Roubaix manufacturers adapt themselves much more quickly than English makers to any change of fashion.' But Crefeld and Elberfeld are now quicker than the French, p. 42. The German is better educated and more enterprising.

66. A Birmingham engineer writes: 'In the face of the present keen competition, to enable a manufacturer to produce an article at a price at which he can sell he is obliged to make a quantity of one article at a time. . . . A change in fashion will often prevent his finding a market for the goods, and he more often than not has to sell at much less than cost. Take, e.g., the trade in standard lamps you mention. This branch of trade has found work in the past year for a number of hands, but there are not nearly so many sold now, and a manufacturer is glad to dispose of his stock at a low price to get rid of them.'

67. The fur-trapper's fortunes are not exempt. Decline in demand for finer furs often reduces the Hudson Bay Company's dividends, cf. Report for 1890.

68. *Spectator*, No 277.

69. Mulhall, *Dictionary of Statistics*. Through the German Consul at Port Elizabeth I am informed that the price of a pair of good ostriches has fallen in ten years from £250 to £25.

70. Taylor the water poet, 'The world runs on wheels' (1623).

71. Cf. Leroy Beaulieu. *Répartition des Richesses*, p. 299.

72. Leroy Beaulieu, op. cit., p. 302.

73. As a Lyonnese manufacturer said: 'That something, which in the world of fashion is only an indefinite sentiment, in fact a mere predisposition, we endeavour to render palpable, to give it a strongly pronounced character and assign it a name. Therefore it is that with us fashion is so paramount: the objects of industry, the commencement of a season, exactly chime in with, and anticipate the predispositions of society.' (Mr Dyce's Report to the Board of Trade of Schools of Design, and *Edinburgh Review*, vol. 90, p. 481.)

74. Cf. Report on Depression of Trade, pp. 7279–7284.

75. A letter in my possession describes a successful career of this kind, in which a north country manufacturer cultivated the friendship of a great French modiste, and by fresh machinery anticipated the diffusion of a fashion among the million, which took place in the third year after its inception, by producing the article at a cheap price in advance of other competitors on the same plane.

76. Insisted on especially by a German from South Scotland, pp. 5376 *et seq.* Another manufacturer, of the same opinion, made an exception in the case of the great swerve of fashion from woollen goods to worsteds, pp. 4880–91.

77. Cf. an account of Webster and Co.'s hat manufactory in a publication entitled *Leicester in 1891*, 'The smallest alteration in shape (of silk hats) means an extensive outlay in blocks, it being necessary to obtain new sets for each fashion that comes up, and a shape once discarded, seldom, or never, comes before the public again in precisely the same form.'

78. Appendix A, 10.

79. 7292–93.

80. Cf. Edmond About, *La Vieille Roche*, op. et loc. cit.

81. A Yorkshire millowner writes: 'In the crinoline days Bradford dress goods from English wools were in great demand. When ladies preferred clinging fabrics (cashmeres, &c.) the advantage went to the soft goods of France (which are now largely made in Bradford). When mohairs and alpacas were in fashion, Bradford by its yarns got the advantage. When braids are fashionable, Bradford benefits. When calico prints were much in fashion, Bradford suffered; on the other hand it obtained advantage from the demand for *mousseline de laine*.'

82. Mrs Tulliver: 'Crowns are so chancy' (i.e. of bonnets).

83. *Ann. Register*, 1765.

84. V. vol. X. *Mode*.

85. Cf. J. Lessing, *Der Modeteufel*, of the pushing in this way of Mülhausen printed cottons at Paris.

86. To this interest is due the intermittent revival of the argument that fashion is good for trade, witnessed in last winter's press, and prominently urged at many an earlier date, e.g., *Magasin des Modes nouvelles* (November 1786).

87. Mr. Shufflebotham, of Coventry, informs me that some found employment in the elastic web trade.
88. *Journ. Statist. Soc.*, vol. 24, pp. 515–17.
89. 'Changes in fashion have thrown the feather-curlers out of work or reduced them to work on half time', p. 444.
90. 'Fringe is out of fashion, and fringe-makers suffer accordingly, if they have no alternative occupation', p. 417, also pp. 423, 454.

Chapter 9

FASHION*
by Georg Simmel

This early contribution is a sociological classic. Fashion is seen as a form of imitation and so of social equalization, but, paradoxically, in changing incessantly, it differentiates one time from another and one social stratum from another. It unites those of a social class and segregates them from others. The elite initiates a fashion and, when the mass imitates it in an effort to obliterate the external distinctions of class, abandons it for a newer mode—a process that quickens with the increase of wealth.

The general formula in accordance with which we usually interpret the differing aspects of the individual as well as of the public mind may be stated broadly as follows: We recognize two antagonistic forces, tendencies, or characteristics, either of which, if left unaffected, would approach infinity; and it is by the mutual limitation of the two forces that the characteristics of the individual and public mind result. We are constantly seeking ultimate forces, fundamental aspirations, some one of which controls our entire conduct. But in no case do we find any single force attaining a perfectly independent expression, and we are thus obliged to separate a majority of the factors and determine the relative extent to which each shall have representation. To do this we must establish the degree of limitation exercised by the counteraction of some other force, as well as the influence exerted by the latter upon the primitive force.

Man has ever had a dualistic nature. This fact, however, has had but little effect on the uniformity of his conduct, and this uniformity is usually the result of a number of elements. An action that results from less than a majority of fundamental forces would appear barren and empty. Over an old Flemish house there stands the mystical inscription, 'There is more within me'; and this is the formula according to which the first impression of an action is supplemented by a far-reaching diversity of causes. Human life cannot hope to develop a wealth of inexhaustible possibilities until we come to recognize in every moment and content of existence a pair of forces, each one of which, in striving to go beyond the initial point, has resolved the infinity of the other by mutual impingement into mere tension and desire. While the explanation of some aspects of the soul as the result of the action of two fundamental forces

* From *The American Journal of Sociology*, vol. 62, No. 6 (University of Chicago Press, May 1957). Originally published in *International Quarterly* (New York), vol. 10 (October 1904). By kind permission of Dodd, Mead & Co.

satisfies the theoretical instinct, it furthermore adds a new charm to the image of things, not only by tracing distinctly the outlines of the fact, but also by interpreting the vague, often enigmatic, realization that in the creation of the life of soul deeper forces, more unsolved tensions, more comprehensive conflicts and conciliations have been at work than their immediate reality would lead one to suppose.

There seem to be two tendencies in the individual soul as well as in society. All designations for this most general form of dualism within us undoubtedly emanate from a more or less individual example. This fundamental form of life cannot be reached by exact definition; we must rest content with the separation of this primitive form from a multitude of examples, which more or less clearly reveal the really inexpressible element of this duality of our soul. The physiological basis of our being gives the first hint, for we discover that human nature requires motion and repose, receptiveness and productivity—a masculine and a feminine principle are united in every human being. This type of duality applied to our spiritual nature causes the latter to be guided by the striving towards generalization on the one hand, and on the other by the desire to describe the single, special element. Thus generalization gives rest to the soul, whereas specialization permits it to move from example to example; and the same is true in the world of feeling. On the one hand we seek peaceful surrender to men and things, on the other an energetic activity with respect to both.

The whole history of society is reflected in the striking conflicts, the compromises, slowly won and quickly lost, between socialistic adaptation to society and individual departure from its demands. We have here the provincial forms, as it were, of those great antagonistic forces which represent the foundations of our individual destiny, and in which our outer as well as our inner life, our intellectual as well as our spiritual being, find the poles of their oscillations. Whether these forces be expressed philosophically in the contrast between cosmotheism and the doctrine of inherent differentiation and separate existence of every cosmic element, or whether they be ground in practical conflict representing socialism on the one hand or individualism on the other, we have always to deal with the same fundamental form of duality which is manifested biologically in the contrast between heredity and variation. Of these the former represents the idea of generalization, of uniformity, of inactive similarity of the forms and contents of life; the latter stands for motion, for differentiation of separate elements, producing the restless changing of an individual life. The essential forms of life in the history of our race invariably show the effectiveness of the two antagonistic principles. Each in its sphere attempts to combine the interest in duration, unity, and similarity with that in change, specialization, and peculiarity. It becomes self-evident that there is no institution, no law, no estate of life, which can uniformly satisfy the full demands of the two opposing principles. The only realization of this condition possible for humanity finds expression in constantly changing approximations, in ever retracted attempts and ever revived hopes. It is this that constitutes the whole wealth of our development, the whole incentive to advancement, the possibility of grasping a vast proportion of all the infinite combinations of the elements of human character, a proportion that is approaching the unlimited itself.

Within the social embodiments of these contrasts, one side is generally maintained by the psychological tendency towards imitation. The charm of imitation in the first place is to be found in the fact that it makes possible an expedient test of power, which, however, requires no great personal and creative application, but is displayed easily and smoothly, because its content is a given quantity. We might define it as the child of thought and thoughtlessness. It affords the pregnant possibility of continually extending the greatest creations of the human spirit, without the aid of the forces which were originally the very condition of their birth. Imitation, furthermore, gives to the individual the satisfaction of not standing alone in his actions. Whenever we imitate, we transfer not only the demand for creative activity, but also the responsibility for the action from ourselves to another. Thus the individual is freed from the worry of choosing and appears simply as a creature of the group, as a vessel of the social contents.

The tendency towards imitation characterizes a stage of development in which the desire for expedient personal activity is present, but from which the capacity for possessing the individual acquirements is absent. It is interesting to note the exactness with which children insist upon the repetition of facts, how they constantly clamour for a repetition of the same games and pastimes, how they will object to the slightest variation in the telling of a story they have heard twenty times. In this imitation and in exact adaptation to the past the child first rises above its momentary existence; the immediate content of life reaches into the past, it expands the present for the child, likewise for primitive man; and the pedantic exactness of this adaptation to the given formula need not be regarded offhand as a token of poverty or narrowness. At this stage every deviation from imitation of the given facts breaks the connection which alone can now unite the present with something that is more than the present, something that tends to expand existence as a mere creature of the moment. The advance beyond this stage is reflected in the circumstance that our thoughts, actions, and feelings are determined by the future as well as by fixed, past, and traditional factors: the teleological individual represents the counterpole of the imitative mortal. The imitator is the passive individual, who believes in social similarity and adapts himself to existing elements; the teleological individual, on the other hand, is ever experimenting, always restlessly striving, and he relies on his own personal conviction.

Thus we see that imitation in all the instances where it is a productive factor represents one of the fundamental tendencies of our character, namely, that which contents itself with similarity, with uniformity, with the adaptation of the special to the general, and accentuates the constant element in change. Conversely, wherever prominence is given to change, wherever individual differentiation, independence, and relief from generality are sought, there imitation is the negative and obstructive principle. The principle of adherence to given formulas, of being and of acting like others, is irreconcilably opposed to the striving to advance to ever new and individual forms of life; for this very reason social life represents a battle-ground, of which every inch is stubbornly contested, and social institutions may be looked upon as the peace-treaties, in which the constant antagonism of both principles has been reduced externally to a form of co-operation.

The vital conditions of fashion as a universal phenomenon in the history of our race are circumscribed by these conceptions. Fashion is the imitation of a given example and satisfies the demand for social adaptation; it leads the individual upon the road which all travel, it furnishes a general condition, which resolves the conduct of every individual into a mere example. At the same time it satisfies in no less degree the need of differentiation, the tendency towards dissimilarity, the desire for change and contrast, on the one hand by a constant change of contents, which gives to the fashion of today an individual stamp as opposed to that of yesterday and of tomorrow, on the other hand because fashions differ for different classes—the fashions of the upper stratum of society are never identical with those of the lower; in fact, they are abandoned by the former as soon as the latter prepares to appropriate them. Thus fashion represents nothing more than one of the many forms of life by the aid of which we seek to combine in uniform spheres of activity the tendency towards social equalization with the desire for individual differentiation and change. Every phase of the conflicting pair strives visibly beyond the degree of satisfaction that any fashion offers to an absolute control of the sphere of life in question. If we should study the history of fashions (which hitherto have been examined only from the view-point of the development of their contents) in connection with their importance for the form of the social process, we should find that it reflects the history of the attempts to adjust the satisfaction of the two counter-tendencies more and more perfectly to the condition of the existing individual and social culture. The various psychological elements in fashion all conform to this fundamental principle.

Fashion, as noted above, is a product of class distinction and operates like a number of other forms, honour especially, the double function of which consists in revolving within a given circle and at the same time emphasizing it as separate from others. Just as the frame of a picture characterizes the work of art inwardly as a coherent, homogeneous, independent entity and at the same time outwardly severs all direct relations with the surrounding space, just as the uniform energy of such forms cannot be expressed unless we determine the double effect, both inward and outward, so honour owes its character, and above all its moral rights, to the fact that the individual in his personal honour at the same time represents and maintains that of his social circle and his class. These moral rights, however, are frequently considered unjust by those without the pale. Thus fashion on the one hand signifies union with those in the same class, the uniformity of a circle characterized by it, and, *uno actu*, the exclusion of all other groups.

Union and segregation are the two fundamental functions which are here inseparably united, and one of which, although or because it forms a logical contrast to the other, becomes the condition of its realization. Fashion is merely a product of social demands, even though the individual object which it creates or recreates may represent a more or less individual need. This is clearly proved by the fact that very frequently not the slightest reason can be found for the creations of fashion from the standpoint of an objective, aesthetic, or other expediency. While in general our wearing apparel is really adapted to our needs, there is not a trace of expediency in the method by which fashion dictates, for example, whether wide or narrow trousers, coloured or black scarfs shall be worn. As a rule the material justification for an action coincides with its general adoption, but in the case of fashion there is a complete separation of the two elements, and there remains for the individual only this general acceptance as the deciding motive to appropriate it. Judging from the ugly and repugnant things that are sometimes in vogue, it would seem as though fashion were desirous of exhibiting its power by getting us to adopt the most atrocious things for its sake alone. The absolute indifference of fashion to the material standards of life is well illustrated by the way in which it recommends something appropriate in one instance, something abstruse in another, and something materially and aesthetically quite indifferent in a third. The only motivations with which fashion is concerned are formal social ones. The reason why even aesthetically impossible styles seem *distingué*, elegant, artistically tolerable when affected by persons who carry them to the extreme, is that the persons who do this are generally the most elegant and pay the greatest attention to their personal appearance, so that under any circumstances we would get the impression of something *distingué* and aesthetically cultivated. This impression we credit to the questionable element of fashion, the latter appealing to our consciousness as the new and consequently most conspicuous feature of the *tout ensemble*.

Fashion occasionally will accept objectively determined subjects such as religious faith, scientific interests, even socialism and individualism; but it does not become operative as fashion until these subjects can be considered independent of the deeper human motives from which they have risen. For this reason the rule of fashion becomes in such fields unendurable. We therefore see that there is good reason why externals—clothing, social conduct, amusements—constitute the specific field of fashion, for here no dependence is placed on really vital motives of human action. It is the field which we can most easily relinquish to the bent towards imitation, which it would be a sin to follow in important questions. We encounter here a close connection between the consciousness of personality and that of the material forms of life, a connection that runs all through history. The more objective our view of life has become in the last centuries, the more it has stripped the picture of nature of all subjective and anthropomorphic elements, and the more sharply has the conception of individual personality become defined. The social regulation of our inner and outer life is a sort of embryo condition, in which the contrasts of the purely personal and the purely objective are differentiated, the action being synchronous and reciprocal. Therefore wherever man appears essentially as a social being we observe neither strict objectivity in the view of life nor absorption and independence in the consciousness of personality.

Social forms, apparel, aesthetic judgment, the whole style of human expression, are constantly transformed by fashion, in such a way, however, that fashion—i.e., the latest fashion—in all these things affects only the upper classes. Just as soon as the lower classes begin to copy their style, thereby crossing the line of demarcation the upper classes have drawn and destroying the uniformity of their coherence, the upper classes turn away from this style and adopt a new one, which in its turn differentiates them from the masses; and thus the game goes merrily on. Naturally the lower classes look and strive towards the upper, and they encounter the least resistance in those fields which are subject to the whims of fashion; for it is here that mere external imitation is most readily applied. The same process is at work as between the different sets within the upper classes, although it is not always as visible here as it is, for example, between mistress and maid. Indeed, we may often observe that the more nearly one set has approached another, the more frantic becomes the desire for imitation from below and the seeking for the new from above. The increase of wealth is bound to hasten the process considerably and render it visible, because the objects of fashion, embracing as they do the externals of life, are most accessible to the mere call of money, and conformity to the higher set is more easily acquired here than in fields which demand an individual test that gold and silver cannot affect.

We see, therefore, that in addition to the element of imitation the element of demarcation constitutes an important factor of fashion. This is especially noticeable wherever the social structure does not include any super-imposed groups, in which case fashion asserts itself in neighbouring groups. Among primitive peoples we often find that closely connected groups living under exactly similar conditions develop sharply differentiated fashions, by means of which each group establishes uniformity within, as well as difference without the prescribed set. On the other hand, there exists a wide-spread predilection for importing fashions from without, and such foreign fashions assume a greater value within the circle, simply because they did not originate there. The prophet Zephaniah expressed his indignation at the aristocrats who affected imported apparel. As a matter of fact the exotic origin of fashions seems strongly to favour the exclusiveness of the groups which adopt them. Because of their external origin, these imported fashions create a special and significant form of socialization, which arises through mutual relation to a point without the circle. It sometimes appears as though social elements, just like the axes of vision, converge best at a point that is not too near. The currency, or more precisely the medium of exchange among primitive races, often consists of objects that are brought in from without. On the Solomon Islands, and at Ibo on the Niger, for example, there exists a regular industry for the manufacture of money from shells, etc., which are not employed as a medium of exchange in the place itself, but in neighbouring districts, to which they are exported. Paris modes are frequently created with the sole intention of setting a fashion elsewhere.

This motive of foreignness, which fashion employs in its socializing endeavours, is restricted to higher civilization, because novelty, which foreign origin guarantees in extreme form is often regarded by primitive races as an evil. This is certainly one of the reasons why primitive conditions of life favour a correspondingly infrequent change of fashions. The savage is afraid of strange appearances; the difficulties and dangers that beset his career cause him to scent danger in anything new which he does not understand and which he cannot assign to a familiar category. Civilization, however, transforms this affection into its very opposite. Whatever is exceptional, bizarre, or conspicuous, or whatever departs from the customary norm, exercises a peculiar charm upon the man of culture, entirely independent of its material justification. The removal of the feeling of insecurity with reference to all things new was accomplished by the progress of civilization. At the same time it may be the old inherited prejudice, although it has become purely formal and unconscious, which, in connection with the present feeling of security, produces this piquant interest in exceptional and odd things. For this reason the fashions of the upper classes develop their power of exclusion against the lower in proportion as general culture advances, at least until the mingling of the classes and the levelling effect of democracy exert a counter-influence.

Fashion plays a more conspicuous role in modern times, because the differences in our standards of life have become so much more strongly accentuated, for the more numerous and the more sharply drawn these differences are, the greater the opportunities for emphasizing them at every turn. In innumerable instances this cannot be accomplished by passive inactivity, but only by the development of forms established by fashion; and this has become all the more pronounced since legal restrictions prescribing various forms of apparel and modes of life for different classes have been removed.

Two social tendencies are essential to the establishment of fashion, namely the need of union on the one hand and the need of isolation on the other. Should one of these be absent, fashion will not be formed—its sway will abruptly end. Consequently the lower classes possess very few modes and those they have are seldom specific; for this reason the modes of primitive races are much more stable than ours. Among primitive races the socializing impulse is much more powerfully developed than the differentiating impulse. For, no matter how decisively the groups may be separated from one another, separation is for the most part hostile in such a way, that the very relation the rejection of which within the classes of civilized races makes fashion reasonable, is absolutely lacking. Segregation by means of differences in clothing, manners, taste, etc., is expedient only where the danger of absorption and obliteration exists, as is the case among highly civilized nations. Where these differences do not exist, where we have an absolute antagonism, as for example between not directly friendly groups of primitive races, the development of fashion has no sense at all.

It is interesting to observe how the prevalence of the socializing impulse in primitive peoples affects various institutions, such as the dance. It has been noted quite generally that the dances of primitive races exhibit a remarkable uniformity in arrangement and rhythm. The dancing group feels and acts like a uniform organism; the dance forces and accustoms a number of individuals, who are usually driven to and fro without rhyme or reason by vacillating conditions and needs of life, to be guided by a common impulse and a single common motive. Even making allowances for the tremendous difference in the outward appearance of the dance, we are dealing here with the same element that appears in the socializing force of fashion. Movement, time, rhythm of the gestures, are all undoubtedly influenced largely by what is worn: similarly dressed persons exhibit relative similarity in their actions. This is of especial value in modern life with its individualistic diffusion, while in the case of primitive races the effect produced is directed within and is therefore not dependent upon changes of fashion. Among primitive races fashions will be less numerous and more stable because the need of new impressions and forms of life, quite apart from their social effect, is far less pressing. Changes in fashion reflect the dullness of nervous impulses: the more nervous the age, the more rapidly its fashions change, simply because the desire for differentiation, one of the most important elements of all fashion, goes hand in hand with the weakening of nervous energy. This fact in itself is one of the reasons why the real seat of fashion is found among the upper classes.

Viewed from a purely social standpoint, two neighbouring primitive races furnish eloquent examples of the requirement of the two elements of union and isolation in the setting of fashion. Among the Kaffirs the class-system is very strongly developed, and as a result we find there a fairly rapid change of fashions, in spite of the fact that wearing-apparel and adornments are subject to certain legal restrictions. The Bushmen, on the other hand, who have developed no class-system, have no fashions whatsoever—no one has been able to discover among them any interest in changes in apparel and in finery. Occasionally these negative elements have consciously prevented the setting of a fashion even at the very heights of civilization. It is said that there was no ruling fashion in male attire in Florence about the year 1390, because every one adopted a style of his own. Here the first element, the need of union, was absent; and without it, as we have seen, no fashion can arise. Conversely, the Venetian nobles are said to have set no fashion, for according to law they had to dress in black in order not to call the attention of the lower classes to the smallness of their number. Here there were no fashions because the other element essential for their creation was lacking, a visible differentiation from the lower classes being purposely avoided.

The very character of fashion demands that it should be exercised at one time only by a portion of the given group, the great majority being merely on the road to adopting it. As soon as an example has been universally adopted, that is, as soon an anything that was originally done only by a few has really come to be practised by all—as is the case in certain portions of our apparel and in various forms of social conduct—we no longer speak of fashion. As fashion spreads, it gradually goes to its doom. The distinctiveness which in the early stages of a set fashion assures for it a certain distribution is destroyed as the fashion spreads, and as this element wanes, the fashion also is bound to die. By reason of this peculiar play between the tendency towards universal acceptance and the destruction of its very purpose to which this general adoption leads, fashion includes a peculiar attraction of limitation, the attraction of a simultaneous beginning and end, the charm of novelty coupled to that of transitoriness. The attractions of both poles of the phenomena meet in fashion, and show also here that they belong together unconditionally, although, or rather because, they are contradictory in their very nature. Fashion always occupies the dividing-line between the past and the future, and consequently conveys a stronger feeling of the present, at least while it is at its height, than most other phenomena. What we call the present is usually nothing more than a combination of a fragment of the past with a fragment of the future. Attention is called to the present less often than colloquial usage, which is rather liberal in its employment of the word, would lead us to believe.

Few phenomena of social life possess such a pointed curve of consciousness as does fashion. As soon as the social consciousness attains to the highest point designated by fashion, it marks the beginning of the end for the latter. This transitory character of fashion, however, does not on the whole degrade it, but adds a new element of attraction. At all events an object does not suffer degradation by being called fashionable, unless we reject it with disgust or wish to debase it for other, material reasons, in which case, of course, fashion becomes an idea of value. In the practice of life anything else similarly new and suddenly disseminated is not called fashion, when we are convinced of its continuance and its material justification. If, on the other hand, we feel certain that the fact will vanish as rapidly as it came, then we call it fashion. We can discover one of the reasons why in these latter days fashion exercises such a powerful influence on our consciousness in the circumstance that the great, permanent, unquestionable convictions are continually losing strength, as a consequence of which the transitory and vacillating elements of life acquire more room for the display of their activity. The break with the past, which, for more than a century, civilized mankind has been labouring unceasingly to bring about, makes the consciousness turn more and more to the present. This accentuation of the present evidently at the same time emphasizes the element of change, and a class will turn to fashion in all fields, by no means only in that of apparel, in proportion to the degree in which it supports the given civilizing tendency. It may almost be considered a sign of the increased power of fashion, that it has overstepped the bounds of its original domain, which comprised only personal externals, and has acquired an increasing influence over taste, over theoretical convictions, and even over the moral foundations of life.

From the fact that fashion as such can never be generally in vogue, the individual derives the satisfaction of knowing that as adopted by him it still represents something special and striking, while at the same time he feels inwardly supported by a set of persons who are striving for the same thing, not as in the case of other social satisfactions, by a set actually doing the same thing. The fashionable person is regarded with mingled feelings of approval and envy; we envy him as an individual, but approve of him as a member of a set or group. Yet even this envy has a peculiar colouring. There is a shade of envy which includes a species of ideal participation in the envied object itself. An instructive example of this is furnished by the conduct of the poor man who gets a glimpse of the feast of his rich neighbour. The moment we envy an object or a person, we are no longer absolutely excluded from it; some relation or other has been established—between both the same psychic content now exists—although in entirely different categories and forms of sensations. This quiet personal usurpation of the envied property contains a kind of antidote, which occasionally counter-acts the evil effects of this feeling of envy. The contents of fashion afford an especially good chance for the development of this conciliatory shade of envy, which also gives to the envied person a better conscience because of his satisfaction over his good fortune. This is due to the fact that these contents are not, as many other psychic contents are, denied absolutely to any one, for a change of fortune, which is never entirely out of the question, may play them into the hands of an individual who had previously been confined to the state of envy.

From all this we see that fashion furnishes an ideal field for individuals with dependent natures, whose self-consciousness, however, requires a certain amount of prominence, attention, and singularity. Fashion raises even the unimportant individual by making him the representative of a class, the embodiment of a joint spirit. And here again we observe the curious intermixture of

179

antagonistic values. Speaking broadly, it is characteristic of a standard set by a general body, that its acceptance by any one individual does not call attention to him; in other words, a positive adoption of a given norm signifies nothing. Whoever keeps the laws the breaking of which is punished by the penal code, whoever lives up to the social forms prescribed by his class, gains no conspicuousness or notoriety. The slightest infraction or opposition, however, is immediately noticed and places the individual in an exceptional position by calling the attention of the public to his action. All such norms do not assume positive importance for the individual until he begins to depart from them. It is peculiarly characteristic of fashion that it renders possible a social obedience, which at the same time is a form of individual differentiation. Fashion does this because in its very nature it represents a standard that can never be accepted by all. While fashion postulates a certain amount of general acceptance, it nevertheless is not without significance in the characterization of the individual, for it emphasizes his personality not only through omission but also through observance. In the dude the social demands of fashion appear exaggerated to such a degree that they completely assume an individualistic and peculiar character. It is characteristic of the dude that he carries the elements of a particular fashion to an extreme; when pointed shoes are in style, he wears shoes that resemble the prow of a ship; when high collars are all the rage, he wears collars that come up to his ears; when scientific lectures are fashionable, you cannot find him anywhere else, etc., etc. Thus he represents something distinctly individual, which consists in the quantitative intensification of such elements as are qualitatively common property of the given set of class. He leads the way, but all travel the same road. Representing as he does the most recently conquered heights of public taste, he seems to be marching at the head of the general procession. In reality, however, what is so frequently true of the relation between individuals and groups applies also to him: as a matter of fact, the leader allows himself to be led.

Democratic times unquestionably favour such a condition to a remarkable degree, so much so that even Bismarck and other very prominent party leaders in constitutional governments have emphasized the fact that inasmuch as they are leaders of a group, they are bound to follow it. The spirit of democracy causes persons to seek the dignity and sensation of command in this manner; it tends to a confusion and ambiguity of sensations, which fail to distinguish between ruling the mass and being ruled by it. The conceit of the dude is thus the caricature of a confused understanding, fostered by democracy, of the relation between the individual and the public. Undeniably, however, the dude, through the conspicuousness gained in a purely quantitative way, but expressed in a difference of quality, represents a state of equilibrium between the social and the individualizing impulses which is really original. This explains the extreme to which otherwise thoroughly intelligent and prominent persons frequently resort in matters of fashion, an extreme that outwardly appears so abstruse. It furnishes a combination of relations to things and men, which under ordinary circumstances appear more divided. It is not only the mixture of individual peculiarity with social equality, but, in a more practical vein, as it were, it is the mingling of the sensation of rulership with submission, the influence of which is here at work. In other words, we have here the mixing of a masculine and a feminine principle. The very fact that this process goes on in the field of fashion only in an ideal attenuation, as it were, the fact that only the form of both elements is embodied in a content indifferent in itself, may lend to fashion a special attraction, especially for sensitive natures that do not care to concern themselves with robust reality. From an objective standpoint, life according to fashion consists of a balancing of destruction and upbuilding; its content acquires characteristics by destruction of an earlier form; it possesses a peculiar uniformity, in which the satisfying of the love of destruction and of the demand for positive elements can no longer be separated from each other.

Inasmuch as we are dealing here not with the importance of a single fact or a single satisfaction, but rather with the play between two contents and their mutual distinction, it becomes evident that the same combination which extreme obedience to fashion acquires can be won also by opposition to it. Whoever consciously avoids following the fashion, does not attain the consequest sensation of individualization through any real individual qualification, but rather through mere negation of the social example. If obedience to fashion consists in imitation of such an example, conscious neglect of fashion represents similar imitation, but under an inverse sign. The latter, however, furnishes just as fair testimony of the power of the social tendency, which demands our dependence in some positive or negative manner. The man who consciously pays no heed to fashion accepts its forms just as much as the dude does, only he embodies it in another category, the former in that of exaggeration, the latter in that of negation. Indeed, it occasionally happens that it becomes fashionable in whole bodies of a large class to depart altogether from the standards set by fashion. This constitutes a most curious social-psychological complication, in which the tendency towards individual conspicuousness primarily rests content with a mere inversion of the social imitation and secondly draws in strength from approximation to a similarly characterized narrower circle. If the club-haters organized themselves into a club, it would not be logically more impossible and psychologically more possible than the above case. Similarly atheism has been made into a religion, embodying the same fanaticism, the same intolerance, the same satisfying of the needs of the soul that are embraced in religion proper. Freedom, likewise, after having put a stop to tyranny, frequently becomes no less tyrannical and arbitrary. So the phenomenon of conscious departure from fashion illustrates how ready the fundamental forms of human character are to accept the total antithesis of contents and to show their strength and their attraction in the negation of the very thing to whose acceptance they seemed a moment before irrevocably committed. It is often absolutely impossible to tell whether the elements of personal strength or of personal weakness preponderate in the group of causes that lead to such a departure from fashion. It may result from a desire not to make common cause with the mass, a desire that has at its basis not independence of the mass, to be sure, but yet an inherently sovereign position with respect to the latter. However, it may be due to a delicate sensibility, which causes the individual to fear that he will be unable to maintain his individuality in case he adopts the forms, the tastes, and the customs of the general public. Such opposition is by no means always a sign of personal strength.

The fact that fashion expresses and at the same time emphasizes the tendency towards equalization and individualization, and the desire for imitation and conspicuousness, perhaps explains why it is that women, broadly speaking, are its staunchest adherents. Scientific discretion should caution us against forming judgements about woman 'in the plural'. At the same time it may be said of woman in a general way, whether the statement be justified in every case or not, that her psychological characteristic in so far as it differs from that of man, consists in a lack of differentiation, in a greater similarity among the different members of her sex, in a stricter adherence to the social average. Whether on the final heights of modern culture, the facts of which have not yet furnished a contribution to the formation of this general conviction, there will be a change in the relation between men and women, a change that may result in a complete reversal of the above distinction, I do not care to discuss, inasmuch as we are concerned here with more comprehensive historical averages. The relation and the weakness of her social position, to which woman has been doomed during the far greater portion of history, however, explains her strict regard for custom, for the generally accepted and approved forms of life, for all that is proper. A weak person steers clear of individualization; he avoids dependence upon self with its responsibilities and the necessity of defending himself unaided. He finds protection only in the typical form of life, which prevents the strong from exercising his exceptional powers. But resting on the firm foundation of custom, of what is generally accepted, woman strives anxiously for all the relative individualization and personal conspicuousness that remains.

Fashion furnishes this very combination in the happiest manner, for we have here on the one hand a field of general imitation, the individual floating in the broadest social current, relieved of responsibility for his tastes and his actions, yet on the other hand we have a certain conspicuousness, and emphasis, an individual accentuation of the personality. It seems that there exists for each class of human beings, probably for each individual, a definite quantitative relation between the tendency towards individualization and the desire to be merged in the group, so that when the satisfying of one tendency is denied in a certain field of life, he seeks another, in which he then fulfils the measure which he requires. Thus it seems as though fashion were the valve through which woman's craving for some measure of conspicuousness and individual prominence finds vent, when its satisfaction is denied her in other fields.

During the fourteenth and fifteenth centuries Germany exhibits an unusually strong development of individuality. Great inroads were made upon the collectivistic regulations of the Middle Ages by the freedom of the individual. Woman, however, took no part in this individualistic development: the freedom of personal action and self-improvement were still denied her. She sought redress by adopting the most extravagant and hypertrophic styles in dress. On the other hand, in Italy during the same epoch woman was given full play for the exercise of individuality. The woman of the Renaissance possessed opportunities of culture, of external activity, of personal differentiation such as were not offered her for many centuries thereafter. In the upper classes of society, especially, education and freedom of action were almost identical for both sexes. It is not astonishing, therefore, that no particularly extravagant Italian female fashions should have come down to us from that period. The need of exercising individuality in this field was absent, because the tendency embodied therein found sufficient vent in other spheres. In general the history of woman in the outer as well as the inner life, individually as well as collectively, exhibits such a comparatively great uniformity, levelling and similarity, that she requires a more lively activity at least in the sphere of fashion, which is nothing more nor less than change, in order to add an attraction to herself and her life for her own feeling as well as for others. Just as in the case of individualism and collectivism, there exists between the uniformity and the change of the contents of life a definite proportion of needs, which is tossed to and fro in the different fields and seeks to balance refusal in one by consent, however acquired, in another. On the whole, we may say that woman is a more faithful creature than man. Now fidelity, expressing as it does the uniformity and regularity of one's nature only in the direction of the feelings, demands a more lively change in the outward surrounding spheres in order to establish the balance in the tendencies of life referred to above. Man, on the other hand, a rather unfaithful being, who does not ordinarily restrict dependence to a relation of the feelings with the same implicitness and concentration of all interests of life to a single one, is consequently less in need of an outward form of change. Non-acceptance of changes in external fields, and indifference towards fashions in outward appearance are specifically a male quality, not because man is the more uniform but because he is the more many-sided creature and for that reason can get along better without such outward changes. Therefore, the emancipated woman of the present, who seeks to imitate in the good as well as perhaps also in the bad sense the whole differentiation, personality and activity of the male sex, lays particular stress on her indifference to fashion.

In a certain sense fashion gives woman a compensation for her lack of position in a class based on a calling or profession. The man who has become absorbed in a calling has entered a relatively uniform class, within which he resembles many others, and is thus often only an illustration of the conception of this class or calling. On the other hand, as though to compensate him for this absorption, he is invested with the full importance and the objective as well as social power of this class. To his individual importance is added that of his class, which often covers the defects and deficiencies of his purely personal character. The individuality of the class often supplements or replaces that of the member. This identical thing fashion accomplishes with other means. Fashion also supplements a person's lack of importance, his inability to individualize his existence purely by his own unaided efforts, by enabling him to join a set characterized and singled out in the public consciousness by fashion alone. Here also, to be sure, the personality as such is reduced to a general formula, yet this formula itself, from a social standpoint, possesses an individual tinge, and thus makes up through the social way what is denied to the personality in a purely individual way. The fact that the demi-monde is so frequently a pioneer in matters of fashion, is due to its peculiarly uprooted form of life. The pariah existence to which society condemns the demi-monde, produces an open or latent hatred against everything that has the sanction of law, of every permanent institution, a hatred that finds its relatively most innocent and aesthetic expression in the striving for ever new forms of appearance. In this continual striving for new, previously unheard-of fashions, in the regardlessness with which the one that is most diametrically opposed to the existing one is passionately adopted, there lurks an aesthetic expression of the desire for destruction, which seems to be an element peculiar to all that lead this pariah-like existence, so long as they are not completely enslaved within.

When we examine the final and most subtle impulses of the soul, which it is difficult to express in words, we find that they also exhibit this antagonistic play of the fundamental human tendencies. These latter seek to regain their continually lost balance by means of ever new proportions, and they succeed here through the reflection which fashion occasionally throws into the most delicate and tender spiritual processes. Fashion insists, to be sure, on treating all individualities alike, yet it is always done in such a way that one's whole nature is never affected. Fashion always continues to be regarded as something external, even in spheres outside of mere styles of apparel, for the form of mutability in which it is presented to the individual is under all circumstances a contrast to the stability of the ego-feeling. Indeed, the latter, through this contrast, must become conscious of its relative duration. The changeableness of those contents can express itself as mutability and develop its attraction only through this enduring element. But for this very reason fashion always stands, as I have pointed out, at the periphery of personality, which regards itself as a *pièce de résistance* for fashion, or at least can do so when called upon.

It is this phase of fashion that is received by sensitive and peculiar persons, who use it as a sort of mask. They consider blind obedience to the standards of the general public in all externals as the conscious and desired means of reserving their personal feeling and their taste, which they are eager to reserve for themselves alone, in such a way that they do not care to enter in an appearance that is visible to all. It is therefore a feeling of modesty and reserve which causes many a delicate nature to seek refuge in the levelling cloak of fashion; such individuals do not care to resort to a peculiarity in externals for fear of perhaps betraying a peculiarity of their innermost soul. We have here a triumph of the soul over the actual circumstances of existence, which must be considered one of the highest and finest victories, at least as far as form is concerned, for the reasons that the enemy himself is transformed into a servant, and that the very thing which the personality seemed to suppress is voluntarily seized, because the levelling suppression is here transferred to the external spheres of life in such a way that it furnishes a veil and a protection for everything spiritual and now all the more free. This corresponds exactly to the triviality of expression and conversation through which very sensitive and retiring people, especially women, often deceive one about the individual depth of the soul. It is one of the pleasures of the judge of human nature, although somewhat cruel withal, to fell the anxiousness with which woman clings to the commonplace contents and forms of social intercourse. The impossibility of enticing her beyond the most banal and trite forms of expression, which often drives one to despair, in innumerable instances signifies nothing more than a barricade of the soul, an iron mask that conceals the real features and can furnish this service only by means of a wholly uncompromising separation of the feelings and the externals of life.

All feeling of shame rests upon isolation of the individual; it arises whenever stress is laid upon the ego, whenever the attention of a circle is drawn to such an

184

individual—in reality or only in his imagination—which at the same time is felt to be in some way incongruous. For that reason retiring and weak natures particularly incline to feelings of shame. The moment they step into the centre of general attention, the moment they make themselves conspicuous in any way, a painful oscillation between emphasis and withdrawal of the ego becomes manifest. Inasmuch as the individual departure from a generality as the source of the feeling of shame is quite independent of the particular content upon the basis of which it occurs, one is frequently ashamed of good and noble things. The fact that the commonplace is good form in society in the narrower sense of the term, is due not only to a mutual regard, which causes it to be considered bad taste to make one's self conspicuous through some individual, singular expression that not every one can repeat, but also to the fear of that feeling of shame which as it were forms a self-inflicted punishment for the departure from the form and activity similar for all and equally accessible to all. By reason of its peculiar inner structure, fashion furnishes a departure of the individual, which is always looked upon as proper. No matter how extravagant the form of appearance or manner of expression, as long as it is fashionable, it is protected against those painful reflections which the individual otherwise experiences when he becomes the object of attention. All concerted actions are characterized by the loss of this feeling of shame. As a member of a mass the individual will do many things which would have aroused unconquerable repugnance in his soul had they been suggested to him alone. It is one of the strangest social-psychological phenomena, in which this characteristic of concerted action is well exemplified, that many fashions tolerate breaches of modesty which, if suggested to the individual alone, would be angrily repudiated. But as dictates of fashion they find ready acceptance. The feeling of shame is eradicated in matters of fashion, because it represents a united action, in the same way that the feeling of responsibility is extinguished in the participants of a crime committed by a mob, each member of which, if left to himself, would shrink from violence.

Fashion also is only one of the forms by the aid of which men seek to save their inner freedom all the more completely by sacrificing externals to enslavement by the general public. Freedom and dependence also belong to those antagonistic pairs, whose ever renewed strife and endless mobility give to life much more piquancy and permit of a much greater breadth and development, than a permanent, unchangeable balance of the two could give. Schopenhauer held that each persons's cup of life is filled with a certain quantity of joy and woe, and that this measure can neither remain empty nor be filled to overflowing, but only changes its form in all the differentiations and vacillations of internal and external relations. In the same way and much less mystically we may observe in each period, in each class, and in each individual, either a really permanent proportion of dependence and freedom, or at least the longing for it, whereas we can only change the fields over which they are distributed. It is the task of the higher life, to be sure, to arrange this distribution in such a way that the other values of existence require thereby the possibility of the most favourable development. The same quantity of dependence and freedom may at one time help to increase the moral, intellectual, and aesthetic values to the highest point and at another time, without any change in quantity but merely in distribution, it may bring about the exact opposite of this success. Speaking broadly, we may say that the most favourable result for the aggregate value of life will be obtained when all unavoidable dependence is transferred more and more to the periphery, to the externals of life. Perhaps Goethe, in his later period, is the most eloquent example of a wholly great life, for by means of his adaptability in all externals, his strict regard for form, his willing obedience to the conventions of society, he attained a maximum of inner freedom, a complete saving of the centres of life from the touch of the unavoidable quantity of dependence. In this respect fashion is also a social form of marvellous expediency, because, like the law, it affects only the externals of life, only those sides of life which are turned to society. It provides us with a formula by means of which we can unequivocally attest our dependence upon what is generally adopted, our obedience to the standards established by our time, our class, and our narrower circle, and enables us to withdraw the freedom given us in life from externals and concentrate it more and more in our innermost natures.

Within the individual soul the relations of equalizing unification and individual demarcation are to a certain extent repeated. The antagonism of the tendencies which produces fashion is transferred as far as form is concerned in an entirely similar manner also to those inner relations of many individuals, who have nothing whatever to do with social obligations. The instances to which I have just referred exhibit the oftmentioned parallelism with which the relations between individuals are repeated in the correlation between the psychic elements of the individual himself. With more or less intention the individual often establishes a mode of conduct or a style for himself, which by reason of the rhythm of its rise, sway, and decline becomes characterized in fashion. Young people especially often exhibit a sudden strangeness in behaviour; an unexpected, objectively unfounded interest arises and governs their whole sphere of consciousness, only to disappear in the same irrational manner. We might call this a personal fashion, which forms an analogy to social fashion. The former is supported on the one hand by the individual demand for differentiation and thereby attests to the same impulse that is active in the formation of social fashion. The need of imitation, of similarity, of the blending of the individual in the mass, are here satisfied purely within the individual himself, namely through the concentration of the personal consciousness upon this one form or content, as well as through the imitation of his own self, as it were, which here takes the place of imitation of others. Indeed, we might say that we attain in this case an even more pronounced concentration, an even more intimate support of the individual contents of life by a central uniformity than we do where the fashion is common property.

A certain intermediate stage is often realized within narrow circles between individual mode and personal fashion. Ordinary persons frequently adopt some expression, which they apply at every opportunity—in common with as many as possible in the same set—to all manner of suitable or unsuitable objects. In one respect this is a group fashion, yet in another respect it is really individual, for its express purpose consists in having the individual make the totality of his circle of ideas subject to this formula. Brutal violence is hereby committed against the individuality of things; all variation is destroyed by the curious supremacy of this one category of expressions, for example, when we

186

designate all things that happen to please us for any reason whatsoever as 'chic', or 'smart', even though the objects in question may bear no relation whatsoever to the fields to which these expressions belong. In this manner the inner world of the individual is made subject to fashion, and thus reflects the aspects of the external group governed by fashion, chiefly by reason of the objective absurdity of such individual manners, which illustrate the power of the formal, unifying element over the objective rational element. In the same way many persons and circles only ask that they be uniformly governed, without thinking to inquire into the nature or value of the authority. It cannot be denied that inasmuch as violence is done to objects treated in this way, and inasmuch as they are all transformed uniformly to a category of our own making, the individual really renders an arbitrary decision with respect to these objects, he acquires an individual feeling of power, and thus the ego is strongly emphasized.

The fact that appears here in the light of a caricature is everywhere noticeable to a less pronounced degree in the relation of persons to things. Only the noblest persons seek the greatest depth and power of their ego by respecting the individuality inherent in things. The hostility which the soul bears to the supremacy, independence, and indifference of the universe gives rise—beside the loftiest and most valuable strivings of humanity—to attempts to oppress things externally; the ego offers violence to them not by absorbing and moulding their powers, not by recognizing their individuality only to make it serviceable, but by forcing it to bow outwardly to some subjective formula. To be sure the ego has not in reality gained control of the things, but only of its own false and fanciful conception of them. The feeling of power, however, which originates thus, betrays its lack of foundation and its fanciful origin by the rapidity with which such expressions pass by. It is just as illusionary as the feeling of the uniformity of being, which springs for the moment from this formulating of all expressions. As a matter of fact the man who carries out a schematic similarity of conduct under all circumstances is by no means the most consistent, the one asserting the ego most regularly against the universe. On account of the difference in the given factors of life, a difference of conduct will be essential whenever the same germ of the ego is to prevail uniformly over all, just as identical answers in a calculation into which two factors enter, of which one continually varies, cannot be secured if the other remains unchanged, but only if the latter undergoes variations corresponding to the changes of the former.

We have seen that in fashion the different dimensions of life, so to speak, acquire a peculiar convergence, that fashion is a complex structure in which all the leading antithetical tendencies of the soul are represented in one way or another. This will make clear that the total rhythm in which the individuals and the groups move will exert an important influence also upon their relation to fashion, that the various strata of a group, altogether aside from their different contents of life and external possibilities, will bear different relations to fashion simply because their contents of life are evolved either in conservative or in rapidly varying form. On the one hand the lower classes are difficult to put in motion and they develop slowly. A very clear and instructive example of this may be found in the attitude of the lower classes in England towards the Danish and the Norman conquests. On the whole the changes brought about affected the upper classes only; in the lower classes we find such a degree of fidelity to arrangements and forms of life that the whole continuity of English life which was retained through all those national vicissitudes rests entirely upon the persistence and immovable conservatism of the lower classes. The upper classes, however, were most intensely affected and transformed by new influences, just as the upper branches of a tree are most responsive to the movements of the air. The highest classes, as everyone knows, are the most conservative, and frequently enough they are even archaic. They dread every motion and change, not because they have an antipathy for the contents or because the latter are injurious to them, but simply because it is change and because they regard every modification of the whole as suspicious and dangerous. No change can bring them additional power, and every change can give them something to fear, but nothing to hope for. The real variability of historical life is therefore vested in the middle classes, and for this reason the history of social and cultural movements has fallen into an entirely different pace since the *tiers état* assumed control. For this reason fashion, which represents the variable and contrasting forms of life, has since then become much broader and more animated, and also because of the transformation in the immediate political life, for man requires an ephemeral tyrant the moment he has rid himself of the absolute and permanent one. The frequent change of fashion represents a tremendous subjugation of the individual and in that respect forms one of the essential complements of the increased social and political freedom. A form of life, for the contents of which the moment of acquired height marks the beginning of decline, belongs to a class which is inherently much more variable, much more restless in its rhythms than the lowest classes with their dull, unconscious conservatism, and the highest classes with their consciously desired conservatism. Classes and individuals who demand constant change, because the rapidity of their development gives them the advantage over others, find in fashion something that keeps pace with their own soul-movements. Social advance above all is favourable to the rapid change of fashion, for it capacitates lower classes so much for imitation of upper ones, and thus the process characterized above, according to which every higher set throws aside a fashion the moment a lower set adopts it, has acquired a breadth and activity never dreamed of before.

This fact has important bearing on the content of fashion. Above all else it brings in its train a reduction in the cost and extravagance of fashions. In earlier times there was a compensation for the costliness of the first acquisition or the difficulties in transforming conduct and taste in the longer duration of their sway. The more an article becomes subject to rapid changes of fashion, the greater the demand for *cheap* products of its kind, not only because the larger and therefore poorer classes nevertheless have enough purchasing power to regulate industry and demand objects, which at least bear the outward semblance of style, but also because even the higher circles of society could not afford to adopt the rapid changes in fashion forced upon them by the imitation of the lower circles, if the objects were not relatively cheap. The rapidity of the development is of such importance in actual articles of fashion that it even withdraws them from certain advances of economy gradually won in other fields. It has been noticed, especially in the older branches of modern productive industry, that the speculative element gradually ceases to play an influential role. The movements of the market can be better overlooked, requirements can be better foreseen and production can be more accurately regulated than before, so that the rationalization of production makes greater and greater inroads on chance conjunctures, on the aimless vacillation of supply and demand. Only pure articles of fashion seem to prove an exception. The polar oscillations, which modern economics in many instances knows how to avoid and from which it is visibly striving towards entirely new economic orders and forms, still hold sway in the field immediately subject to fashion. The element of feverish change is so essential here that fashion stands, as it were, in a logical contrast to the tendencies for development in modern economics.

In contrast to this characteristic, however, fashion possesses this peculiar quality, that every individual type to a certain extent makes its appearance as though it intended to live forever. When we furnish a house these days, intending the articles to last a quarter of a century, we invariably invest in furniture designed according to the very latest patterns and do not even consider articles in vogue two years before. Yet it is evident that the attraction of fashion will desert the present article just as it left the earlier one, and satisfaction or dissatisfaction with both forms is determined by other material criterions. A peculiar psychological process seems to be at work here in addition to the mere bias of the moment. Some fashion always exists and fashion *per se* is indeed immortal, which fact seems to affect in some manner or other each of its manifestations, although the very nature of each individual fashion stamps it as being transitory. The fact that change itself does not change, in this instance endows each of the objects which it affects with a psychological appearance of duration.

This apparent duration becomes real for the different fashion-contents within the change itself in the following special manner. Fashion, to be sure, is concerned only with change, yet like all phenomena it tends to conserve energy; it endeavours to attain its objects as completely as possible, but nevertheless with the relatively most economical means. For this very reason, fashion repeatedly returns to old forms, as is illustrated particularly in wearing-apparel; and the course of fashion has been likened to a circle. As soon as an earlier fashion has partially been forgotten there is no reason why it should not be allowed to return to favour and why the charm of difference, which constitutes its very essence, should not be permitted to exercise an influence similar to that which it exerted conversely some time before.

The power of the moving form upon which fashion lives is not strong enough to subject every fact uniformly. Even in the fields governed by fashion, all forms are not equally suited to become fashion, for the peculiar character of many of them furnishes a certain resistance. This may be compared with the unequal relation that the objects of external perception bear to the possibility of their being transformed into works of art. It is a very enticing opinion, but one that cannot hold water, that every real object is equally suited to become the object of a work of art. The forms of art, as they have developed historically —constantly determined by chance, frequently one-sided and affected by technical perfections and imperfections—by no means occupy a neutral height above all world objects. On the contrary, the forms of art bear a closer relation to some facts than they do to others. Many objects assume artistic form without apparent effort, as though nature had created them for that very purpose, while others, as though wilful and supported by nature, avoid all transformation into the given forms of art. The sovereignty of art over reality by no means implies, as naturalism and many theories of idealism so steadfastly maintain, the ability to draw all the contents of existence uniformly into its sphere. None of the forms by which the human mind masters the material of existence and adapts it to its purpose is so general and neutral that all objects, indifferent as they are to their own structure, should uniformly conform to it.

Thus fashion can to all appearances and *in abstracto* absorb any chosen content: any given form of clothing, of art, of conduct, of opinion may become fashionable. And yet many forms in their deeper nature show a special disposition to live themselves out in fashion, just as others offer inward resistance. Thus, for example, everything that may be termed 'classic' is comparatively far removed from fashion and alien to it, although occasionally, of course, the classic also falls under the sway of fashion. The nature of the classic is determined by a concentration of the parts around a fixed centre; classic objects possess an air of composure, which does not offer so many points of attack, as it were, from which modification, disturbance, destruction of the equilibrium might emanate. Concentration of the limbs is characteristic of classic plastics: the *tout ensemble* is absolutely governed from within, the spirit and the feeling of life governing the whole embrace uniformly every single part, because of the perceptible unity of the object. That is the reason we speak of the classic repose of Greek art. It is due exclusively to the concentration of the object, which concentration permits no part to bear any relation to any extraneous powers and fortunes and thereby incites the feeling that this formation is exempt from the changing influences of general life. In contrast to this everything odd, extreme and unusual will be drawn to fashion from within: fashion does not take hold of such characteristic things as an external fate, but rather as the historical expression of their material peculiarities. The widely projecting limbs in baroque-statues seem to be in perpetual danger of being broken off, the inner life of the figure does not exercise complete control over them, but turns them over a prey to the chance influences of external life. Baroque forms in themselves lack repose, they seem ruled by chance and subjected to the momentary impulse, which fashion expresses as a form of social life. But still another factor confronts us here, namely, that we soon grow tired of eccentric, bizarre or fanciful forms and from a purely physiological standpoint long for the change that fashions outlines for us.

I have had occasion to point out above that the *tempo* of fashion depends upon the loss of sensibility to nervous incitements which are formed by the individual disposition. The latter changes with the ages, and combines with the form of the objects in an inextricable mutual influence. We find here also one of the deep relations which we thought to have discovered between the classical and the 'natural' composition of things. The conception of what is included in the term natural is rather vague and misleading, for as a rule it is merely an expression of value, which is employed to grace values prized for different reasons, and which has therefore been uniformly supported by the most antagonistic elements. At the same time, we may limit the term 'natural' from a

190

negative standpoint by a process of exclusion, inasmuch as certain forms, impulses and conceptions can certainly lay no claim to the term; and these are the forms that succumb most rapidly to the changes of fashion, because they lack that relation to the fixed centre of things and of life which justifies the claim to permanent existence. Thus Elizabeth Charlotte of the Palatinate, a sister-in-law of Louis XIV, exceedingly masculine in her ways, inspired the fashion at the French Court of women acting like men and being addressed as such, whereas the men conducted themselves like women. It is self-evident that such behaviour can be countenanced by fashion only because it is far removed from that never-absent substance of human relations to which the form of life must eventually return in some way, shape, or manner. We cannot claim that all fashion is unnatural, because the existence of fashion itself seems perfectly natural to us as social beings, yet we can say, conversely, that absolutely unnatural forms may at least for a time bear the stamp of fashion.

To sum up the peculiarly piquant and suggestive attraction of fashion lies in the contrast between its extensive, all-embracing distribution and its rapid and complete disintegration; and with the latter of these characteristics the apparent claim to permanent acceptance again stands in contrast. Furthermore, fashion depends no less upon the narrow distinctions it draws for a given circle, the intimate connection of which it expresses in the terms of both cause and effect, than it does upon the decisiveness with which it separates the given circle from others. And, finally, fashion is based on adoption by a social set, which demands mutual imitation from its members and thereby releases the individual of all responsibility—ethical and aesthetic—as well as of the possibility of producing within these limits individual accentuation and original shading of the elements of fashion. Thus fashion is shown to be an objective characteristic grouping upon equal terms by social expediency of the antagonistic tendencies of life.

Chapter 10

CHARACTER AND DIRECTION OF FASHION MOVEMENTS*
by Paul Nystrom

This extract from Nystrom's classic analysis of the economics of fashion explores the way in which fashion movements can be diffused downwards through social strata. This so-called 'trickle effect' has been a dominant issue in fashion marketing for nearly fifty years.

What, then, determines the choice of styles in the making of a new fashion? Do fashions tend to follow certain highways and reject others, and if so what are the reasons for the choice of these highways? If these questions can be answered much progress will have been made toward a rational explanation of fashions. In this chapter an attempt will be made to list and describe the factors that guide and influence the character and direction of fashion movements.

These factors may be classified under three general headings, namely: (a) outstanding or dominating events; (b) dominating ideals which mould the thought and action of large numbers of people; and (c) dominating social groups that rule or lead and influence the rest of society.

Dominating Events

Under the head of dominating events, the first and most important illustration to be given was that of the World War which, of course, overshadowed every other occurrence in modern times. Its influence on fashions was profound. Millions of civilians changed from ordinary apparel to military dress, generally somber khaki, significant of the serious business of war. Most men left at home became more conservative about dress. Less attention was given to apparel by both men and women, and a general slowing up of all fashion movement characterized the period. The apparel of women was likewise deeply influenced by the war. Millinery, coats and dresses, as well as shoes, took on a military appearance. The use of braids, buttons and tailored effects was emphasized. There was a distinct trend, during this period, toward mannish costumes.

Following the war, particularly in France and England and to some extent in this country, fashions were deeply subdued in the spirit of mourning over

* From *Economics of Fashion* (New York, Ronald Press Company, 1928).

the many loved ones who had been lost in the war. Women's apparel remained dominantly black during 1919 and 1920 throughout the fashion world.

Whenever a great misfortune occurs, its effect on fashion movement is instantaneous and far-reaching. In Japan when an emperor or some other member of the royal household dies, it is a fixed custom that the entire nation should go into mourning, so that the fashion movements in existence prior to this event are completely checked by the adoption of mourning costumes of the people.

In America particularly, and similarly in the colonies of European nations, the visits of famous people from Europe have often brought notable effects on fashion. In 1823 the United States was visited by Lafayette, who during the Revolution aided the American cause. By this time he was quite an old man with the conservative tastes of a cultured Frenchman who looked back to the régime of Louis XVI and Queen Marie Antoinette, rather than forward to more modern influences. Similarly, his dress represented conservative French style rather than the more vigorous and possibly less artistic dress that was coming into use in France and elsewhere in the 20s. However, Lafayette's visit affected fashions extensively, in that many features of his attire were followed by women as well as by men, thus helping to maintain the conservative French influence in American dress for at least five or six years longer than it might otherwise have been maintained, had it not been for his visit.

In 1851 another distinguished visitor, Louis Kossuth, Hungarian patriot, visited the United States, practically as the nation's guest. Everywhere he went he was received with enthusiasm and every mark of honour. One of the most important effects of his visit was a change in style, and the adoption of a new fashion in men's hats. At the time of his visit American men of all classes very generally wore stiff, hard, high hats, the 'chimney pot hat'. Louis Kossuth came to this country wearing a soft felt or velour hat such as worn at the time by Hungarians as a part of their national costume. This men's soft hat impressed American men so much that they began to adopt its use, so that by 1860 probably half of the men in the country were wearing soft hats.

In 1860 another distinguished visitor arrived in the United States, Albert Edward, Prince of Wales, later King Edward VII of England. Prince Albert Edward appeared at many public gatherings and functions in this country, and at these wore a double-breasted, broadcloth frock coat that came nearly to the knees. This type of frock coat was new to most Americans and struck their fancy, with the result that for thirty years following this visit the Prince Albert coat continued to be the standard style for men, for formal occasions.

There seems to be considerable reason for the belief that the people of this country do not now adopt and follow fashions by imitation of famous visitors to such a great extent as formerly. During the last score of years there have been many princes, dukes and even an occasional king or queen, but in no case have they left with our people such positive fashions as did Louis Kossuth in 1851, and Prince Albert Edward in 1860.

The visit of the Prince of Wales in 1924 was hailed by commercial interests as a wonderful opportunity for the promotion of new fashions. Through ambitious commercial enterprise, it was known in advance of his visit to this country what styles of clothing he would wear. Both tailoring and manufacturing institutions accordingly made their plans for the promotion of these styles to the American public. Among the items so offered were Glen Urquhart plaids, blue shirts and snap brim hats, all of which were worn by the Prince of Wales. All of these undoubtedly received much sales impetus from the Prince's visit, as well as from the stronger commercial promotion accompanying the Prince's visit, but it does not seem that any one of the three offered anything very revolutionary in change from what had been in use before. The raw edge hat brim was not a new feature in American hat styles, blue shirts had certainly been worn before his visit, and Glen Urquhart plaids were not greatly different from other plaids that had been offered and sold to American men for business and sport wear for at least twelve years preceding.

Queen Marie of Roumania visited the United States in 1927. Much interest developed among commercial concerns dealing in women's fashion, over the possible effect on American fashions. With the possible exception of some increased sale and use of jewelry, particularly of 60- and 72-inch pearl necklaces, it would be difficult to point to any concrete effect whatsoever on fashions produced by this famous Queen's visit. American women were generally very much interested in what Queen Marie wore. Her taste was admired, but no widespread imitation of what she wore followed among American women.

Another type of dominating event that exercises a very great deal of influence over fashion movements are the art vogues that occasionally sweep over the world. Art itself is, of course, influenced by fashion. Therefore it is not surprising that the application of any particular style of art to apparel, home furnishings and automobiles should form a very important place in fashion movements.

From the standpoint of its influences on fashion, the most remarkable art movement in modern times came out of Russia in connection with the Russian ballet, together with music and decorations accompanying the ballet. The Russian ballet first appeared in Paris in the season of 1909–10. Parisians and visitors from other parts of the world who happened to be in Paris that year received the Russian ballet with storms of applause. During the period from 1910 down to the opening of the World War, the Russian ballet was presented in most of the principal cities of Europe and of America as well.

The Russian ballet was undoubtedly one of the early sources of the so-called modern art movement. Its significance is so great to this movement that the names of its leaders are worth while mentioning. Diaghilev was the guiding and organizing genius who staged the productions. Fokine devised the dances. Bakst provided the scenery and costumes. The incomparable Pavlowa, who was one of the early dancing stars, is known in almost all parts of this country.

The Russian ballet not only introduced a new type of music and dance, but also a new form of decoration, quite definitely departing from the classic standards that had previously dominated in the western art world. The use of lines, lights and colours, in unconventional ways, constituted a new note in decorative effect that is gradually becoming a fashion in the art world and is being carried over into apparel, furniture, interior decoration, automobiles, jewelry, glass, pottery and many other applied and useful arts. The modern art movement has shown marked development, and undoubtedly possesses additional important potentialities for the future. Its influence will well bear watching for its effects on fashions for several years to come.

Fashion has also been very much influenced by Spanish art since the World War, but more particularly from 1921 down to 1925. The rich colour effects secured by modern Spanish artists have served as an effective supplement to the Russian art. The modern art movement undoubtedly owes much to Spanish art, and Spanish art has been the inspiration for several fashion motives during the last ten years, such as the use of rouge, certain types of hair dressing, softening the line of the feminine silhouette, and so on.

As an illustration of the effect on fashion of more or less accidental events, one may mention the discovery of the tomb of Tut-Ankh-Amen in Egypt in 1923, and the curious interest manifested during 1924 in the treasures found in this tomb. The publication of the illustrations of ancient Egyptian art found in this tomb excited all classes of people very extensively, and resulted in widespread success and adoption of the so-called Tut-Ankh-Amen styles in many lines, such as in fabric designs, in millinery, in jewelry and other accessories.

World's fairs have had important effects on fashion. For example, the Centennial Exhibition held in Philadelphia in 1876 brought together a collection of exhibits from all of the arts, including fabrics, articles of home furnishings, such as furniture, draperies, carpets, silverware, china, glass, and so on. For many years preceding 1876, the people of the United States had been intensively occupied in rebuilding the resources of the country that had been broken down by the Civil War, in developing the new West, in building railroads, in opening up vast farming areas, in digging mines, cutting down forests and otherwise preparing the country for civilization, but in this close work with the crude elemental forces of nature, interest in the arts and particularly in the applied arts had been allowed to decline. The period from 1860 down to 1885 was one in which the public interest in art was probably at the lowest level it has ever reached in this country. The masses of people apparently took less interest in clothing, in personal appearance and in the furnishings of their homes than at any period previous or since.

The Centennial Exhibition served to mark the turning point in awakening public taste in the arts. People, particularly from the middle and far western portions of the country, who had gained material prosperity from their contact with nature, from mining, lumbering, stock-raising, farming and railroad building, came to this exposition. What they saw opened their eyes and taught them to appreciate finer things in fabrics, apparel, furniture, home furnishings and other lines of goods used in the arts of living, goods that had formed but a small part of their thought up to that time. What they saw and learned from these exhibits they carried back home with them to their respective communities, and gradually changes began to be made to correspond to the new ideals expressed by the exhibition. It would be difficult to overestimate the far-reaching effects of the Centennial Exhibition on the common life of the people. The influence of this exhibition continued over a period of several years following.

The World's Columbian Exposition in Chicago in 1893 likewise had a marked influence on the consumption habits of the people of this country, but the movement for more art and luxury in the common life had already well begun, so that the Chicago Exposition served more to emphasize and promote, rather than to set off new trends. New fashions came into existence as a result of the Chicago World's Fair, but these for the most part were in minor details and smaller changes, rather than in revolutionary character.

One noteworthy exception must be mentioned. The Chicago World's Fair was a remarkable achievement from an architectural standpoint. There had been but little progress in the arts of building from the period of 1860 down to 1893. Office buildings, stores, factories and all varieties of domestic architecture were generally ugly in design. The beautiful architecture at the Chicago World's Fair started a new and welcome fashion in building. People who visited the Chicago World's Fair gained new standards in architecture which they were not slow in putting to use in the various parts of the country. The Chicago World's Fair buildings and grounds were planned and laid out by artists and architects who were imbued not only with classic ideals and education, but with the needs of modern life as well, so that something of a neo-classic result was obtained embodying both excellent classic art and modern convenience.

Public buildings and the larger structures for business purposes were the first to carry out and follow the examples set by the Chicago World's Fair, but by the beginning of the twentieth century the wave of fashion in architecture had reached domestic buildings of all types.

Another interesting effect on fashion resulting from the Chicago World's Fair was the re-establishment of the influence of Paris in women's apparel. Following the breakdown of the French Second Empire under Louis Napoleon and Eugénie in 1870, France lost considerable influence over fashion for women in the United States. Paris fashions continued to be reported in the fashion journals of the 80s and early 90s, but importation of Paris gowns to this country dropped to almost nothing.

Several Paris dressmakers united in sending an exhibit of fashionable apparel to the Chicago World's Fair. This exhibit attracted considerable attention, and at the close of the Fair was sold to a leading American department store. Prior to this not more than a half dozen American stores, if that many, had established regular buying of Paris style goods for their American customers. Following the exhibit at the Chicago World's Fair, within a short time several department stores began to send buyers to Paris regularly.

There have been many expositions and world's fairs held in various cities in Europe as well as in this country since 1893. Each has no doubt contributed its share of influence in the development of fashions, but with one exception, probably none of them has had such outstanding effects as the two that have been mentioned here. These two, the Philadelphia and the Chicago Fairs, came at critical or timely periods in the development of the country, so that the changes following were highly remarkable.

The exception referred to in the foregoing paragraph was the 'International Exposition of Industrial and Decorative Arts,' held in Paris in 1925. Modern art and its application to the products of industry had been developing for several years before this exposition in practically all of the western countries. In some lines it seems that this new art had been carried even farther than in

France. There were many critics who, in looking over the field of practical art, began in 1923 and 1924 to suggest that France was losing its leadership even in the creation of apparel styles. Paris met this challenge effectively by holding this exposition, and by inviting the exhibition of articles of all kinds embodying modern art from all countries in the world.

Many nations participated in the Paris exposition. Notable exhibits were made by Czechoslovakia, Germany, Belgium, the Scandinavian countries, Italy, and even Russia. The United States was not represented. Individuals as well as industries from many other parts of the world made their artistic contributions to this exhibition. As indicated by the title, it was essentially an exhibition of industrial and decorative arts; thus there were shown a great many lines of merchandise representing practically all classes of consumers' goods in which style fashion interest is always a dominant factor.

The interest that had developed in modern art before 1925 was given a great deal of impetus by the exposition. It was visited by a large number of people, including business men and women as well as artists and craftsmen, all of whom carried their impressions of the exposition back to their own localities, and began to apply them in various ways. Since the International Exposition of Industrial and Decorative Arts was held in Paris, modern art has spread very widely. It has been applied in a great many ways and the present trend seems to be toward a much wider application and use. It looks as if modern art, so called, represents the beginnings of a fundamental fashion which may well become a very important cycle, extending all over the world before it gives way to some new movement.

Since the exposition was held in Paris, there have been many minor exhibitions and displays of modern art in various other places, in connection with art museums and in business institutions. In 1927, R. H. Macy and Company conducted an extensive exhibit of home furnishings in the modernistic art note. In 1928, Lord and Taylor, Inc., and several other stores in the United States held exhibits of home furnishings and other goods in which the modern art influence was uppermost.

Dominating Ideals

Among the dominating ideals that have been influential at one time or another in the past, there may be mentioned the classic Greek ideal of pure beauty, or art for art's sake, in which utility was subordinated to efforts to secure the highest emotional appeal to the human sense of beauty. The Roman ideal of order and efficiency likewise produced its effect on fashion, differing extensively from that of the Greek ideal, even at the same time of history. The Roman ideal, however, continued for several hundreds of years after classic Greek art influence had disappeared as the dominating force in Europe.

The religious ideals of the world have in like manner influenced the consumption and arts of life of the people very greatly. A religion, for example, such as that of the Hindoos, raises an ideal of quiet contemplation for its subjects in which, naturally, consumption takes a very minor place, for consumption is primarily an activity or a function of activity. The pursuit of fashion is contrary to a life of contemplation.

While the ideals taught by Jesus were of universal brotherhood, sympathy and compassion, the religion of the Christians for a long period of time was characterized by a strong interest in a future life, quite definitely at the expense of interests in present life, and a desire to save people from going to Hell by inquisition and force if necessary. Preparation for life in another world became the dominant aim of life in this, with the result that the common activities of the present life were looked upon as a means rather than as the end of life. In consequence, the ordinary arts of life, such as affect food, clothing, shelter, were given minor consideration. Interest in the fine arts, in so far as they were utilized at all, extended solely to their application to religious subjects, such as in the architecture of churches, sculpture, painting and carving of religious subjects, and so on. Clothing and home furnishings for the masses of the people remained very primitive, and followed the lines of custom. There appears to have been very little change in fashion over long periods of time. Traditions ruled. Interests in developing the arts naturally declined to a mimimum. It was altogether a dark age so far as fashion was concerned.

The rise of modern western nations has been accompanied by the development of certain political philosophies such as support republican forms of government and democracy. There are students who think this development culminated at the time of the World War. There is neither time nor place here to speculate in detail on the future of this great fashion in political thinking. This digression may be pardoned. What strange irony of fate if the war waged for the purpose of making the world safe for democracy, should have marked the beginning of the end of this ideal of government.

The development of the western nations has carried with it the upbuilding of ideals of national greatness in which the functions of citizenship have been emphasized and stressed. Patriotism, as a necessary part of citizenship, has become a great fashion, extending from loyalty to the local community up to a loyalty for state and nation. These ideals have been influential in many ways on the arts of living and the fashions affecting them. One might mention the interest taken by every nation struggling to make the most of itself in developing its home industries and arts.

Whatever the outcome may be as to the ideals of citizenship, certainly the national walls erected are not sufficient to prevent the interchange of styles and arts. There is nothing quite so international in present-day life as fashion. While it may have been possible in times past to count on the people of the country to follow the fashions developed within that country, legislative edicts aiming at such results in these days have but little effect. For example, in 1924 Mussolini urged that Italian women should wear apparel designed and made in Italy. Mussolini's outburst seems to have had little or no effect in spite of the fact that probably no person in modern times has commanded the power and influence that Mussolini has over the people of Italy. Rulers of other nations as well as church dignitaries have attempted national or local modifications of fashions, but the results have apparently never been impressive.

In certain periods of history, and in certain countries, ancestor worship has prevailed. In modified degree one finds something of this among the western nations as well as in China and Japan which are usually given as examples of countries in which this ideal prevails to the greatest extent in modern times. Under the ideals of ancestor worship, respect for age and for the traditions of the past dominates the thought and activities of the people. Custom, ritual and formalism take the place of change, and fashion tends to move slowly under these conditions.

The opposite ideal of ancestor worship is represented in youth movements which characterized other periods of history. In an era in which ideals of youth are dominant, respect for age and custom declines, interest in the activities of youth, such as athletics, games, sports, adventure and all outdoor activity, increases. As fashion moves but slowly in periods when ancestors or older generations dominate, so in periods of youth movement, fashion tends to rapid change.

As one looks back over the history of civilization, there appears to have been a ceaseless conflict of ideals for supremacy. Some ideals were worked out and applied in highly practical ways, while others, perhaps highly desirable, obtained practically no influence whatsoever. Many of such ideals or philosophies of life have never progressed beyond the stage of theory. Among these may be mentioned such ideals as general or universal kindliness taught by many great leaders, the ideal of the simple life that has been offered to humanity again and again by great philosophers, beautiful living frequently urged by teachers and artists as a solution of the problems of human life, complete all-round development which was the educational ideal of the classic Greeks, humility of spirit taught to the English for an entire generation by one of its greatest school masters, Matthew Arnold.

Desirable as these ideals may have been, for the most part they never obtained a position of sufficient importance to sway or influence the thought or manner of living of any important part of society. These ideals are simply mentioned here to indicate the variety of philosophies which have been devised, and which have been offered but for some reason or other have never become the ruling fashion.

Dominating Groups

Among the dominating groups that affect the manner of living of society, one may mention those who occupy positions of power or leadership over others, such as royalty and nobility, the government officers and the heads of the army and navy as found in most nations. Kings, queens and princes have set the fashions for their subjects for ages, and while there have been exceptions, up to the last century, most of the people looked to their ruling classes for suggestions and for leadership in their fashion movements. As has already been pointed out, the power of ruling classes over the arts of living as practised by the masses of the people has apparently declined. Mention is made here of this power because of its historic importance.

As indicated under our consideration of dominating ideals, periods of ancestor worship are characterized by domination of social groups made up of older people. Parents and the older generations set the standards under these conditions for the imitation of children and of younger people. It is interesting to note how the pendulum swings from varying degrees of ancestor worship to youth movements, and back again. During the past twenty-five years, and particularly since the World War, the western nations have experienced a very strong youth movement, an interest in the activities of youth, the manner of living of youth, and so on. During an earlier period, say from 1860 down to 1900, the interests of the masses of people seemed to have centred in maturity, in things dignified by age. Appointments to high official political positions, high positions in business, particularly in places requiring contact with the public, went to older men and to persons appearing mature. The era was characterized by an effort on the part of both men and women to make themselves appear mature by the art of dress.

In all probability the present youth movement will in time decline and may then be followed by another era of several years in which maturity and age may have a more important place in the social scheme than it has at present.

For at least the past one hundred and fifty years the possession of wealth and the power to use such wealth have been the most important factors, not only in the business field but in social life as well. Even during eras of youth worship, or of ancestor worship, wealth serves as a background, and in combination with the other factors dominates the thoughts and activities of the time.

It may be possible to indicate in somewhat greater detail just how the factor of wealth and the power of the groups possessing wealth influence the character and direction of fashion movement, and in this the views expressed by Veblen in 'The Theory of the Leisure Class' will be followed quite closely.

If wealth and the possession of wealth are important determining factors in the field of fashion, then it may be assumed that the fashion, whatever it may be, must demonstrate the presence or possession of that wealth. There are, in general, two ways in which wealth may be demonstrated. The first is by means of habits of life that will indicate to the social world that the consumer need not work for a living, or, as Veblen expresses it, proving the possession of wealth by *conspicuous leisure*. The second method of demonstrating the ownership of wealth and power in its use is by means of *conspicuous consumption*. In every case in which the power of wealth is dominant either one or both of these methods of demonstration of wealth is likely to appear.

The reader is referred to Veblen's work for a complete development of this thought. Only a few suggestions concerning its implications are offered here.

In former periods when slavery formed a part of the social and economic organization of nations, obviously certain forms of labour came to be considered degrading, and suitable only for slaves to perform. The stigma attached to these forms of labour has, to some extent, continued down to the present in spite of the fact that the institution of slavery has disappeared from practically all nations.

Under the complex economic organizations of the present time, there is always the tendency to classify the various kinds of work according to their desirability, not from the standpoint of utility, but rather from the standpoint of the honour or dishonour connected with them. Thus all forms of simple manual labour of the unskilled type have been generally accorded the lowest place in this classification. Next have come those kinds of work that might be classified as semi-skilled and then the skilled trades and occupations. Higher up the social scale one finds types of work, such as clerical positions, in which it is possible for the worker to wear better clothing, white collars and creased pants. Still farther up the scale come the supervisory and executive as well as the professional occupations.

The arrangement of work in grades is, of course, largely artificial, for it would be very difficult for anyone to prove by any method of logic that the work of a salesman in a retail store, or a clerk in a bookkeeper's department, is any higher or more useful, or more necessary in any way to society than the work done by a farmer out in the field, or a ditch digger in the street. There is no question, however, of the fact that society does evaluate the positions held by the salesman and the clerk as more socially desirable.

In consequence of this development of grades of work according to social importance, the means of consumption, such as dress, automobiles and street front architecture, are employed to prove that those who are in the so-called lower groups of work really belong in the higher groups, and so on upward to the true leisure class which is under no economic obligation to do any kind of useful labour whatsoever.

Thus from a social standpoint, that clothing is most desirable that indicates that its user belongs to one of the higher occupation groups, or does not have to do any useful work at all. Millinery, such as is generally sold and worn by women, garments made of delicate material requiring careful use to prevent destruction, high silk hats and even derby hats are examples of clothing which tend to incapacitate their wearers from engaging in any form of labour except that which most closely approximates leisure activities. Even the coat and vest worn by men is unsuited for work and there are very few men, when called upon to do any active labour, who do not divest themselves of these garments and put on something more suitable for the purpose. The spotless white collars of the clericals are clear illustrations of the desire to prove by means of clothing that the wearer does not have to perform dirty manual labour. The creases in the trousers, the high polish of the shoes, the cane and the watch and chain are in their own way silent but effective testimonials of their wearer's social position in the scale referred to above. Even in the matter of eye-glasses there is the eloquent suggestion in the frailty of the frame, or in the complete lack of frame, as in the case of the pince-nez which proves that the user could not possibly engage in any active manual labour and wear these glasses. The high heel and tight shoes worn by women, the application of paint and powder, which would be disgusting and demoralizing if the person were engaged in manual labour of a degree causing profuse perspiration, are other effective illustrations of the same point.

That this principle is recognized by competent advertising and sales promotion men is evident from the fact that rarely ever does one see high-class advertising of clothing for either men or women illustrating the use of such clothing in connection with the performance of any useful or economic labour. Advertising illustrations for clothing as a rule depict the atmosphere of social life, sports and other leisure activities. It probably would be a mistake to attempt to sell apparel with any appeal of possible use in work. The aim is obviously to produce the illusion or effect that the prospective wearer will be able to prove his high social position by the clothing offered for sale.

Illustrations of conspicuous consumption may also be found in plentiful number in the field of fashion goods. In the present evolution of industrialism, much of the old order of aristocracy, built on owership of land and holding of influential political offices, has given way to the influence of people in charge of large industrial and commercial enterprises. In the old aristocracy made up of landed gentry, it was entirely possible to develop and live up to a philosophy of life in which leisure should occupy the highest place, but in modern industrialism this is not so easy. Important work cannot be given up to assistants or other employees. The big business executive must stay on the job. So power, social and economic, has passed into the hands of business men who are active. Under modern conditions business men must continue in harness or lose their power and perhaps their businesses as well.

This movement began more than a century ago and has grown more and more important since the beginning of the twentieth century, and more particularly since the end of the World War. If at any future time it should be possible to standardize the processes of production and of distribution and work out standards of supervision of these processes, then it again may be possible for the owners to withdraw from their businesses to a life of comparative leisure as the landed estate owner formerly did. In the meantime the balance of power among all of the social classes seems to be held by active business men.

Conspicuous leisure is directly impossible for the big business man. Consequently, the leisure activities are usually left to be carried on by his wife and his sons and daughters. Conspicuous consumption serves the purpose much better. Magnificent and splendid balls, parties and dinners are the most common forms of impressing one's associates of the possession of power and wealth. Giving large sums of money to causes more or less worthy, endowments for institutions that bear the names of their donors, the purchase of expensive art works, particularly such works for which there is keen competition in the market, are other marked evidences of conspicuous consumption.

One of the influential urges in many cases causing the purchase of automobiles is this desire to prove one's social position, from the standpoint of ownership of wealth, by this act of conspicuous consumption. As Veblen so effectively shows, homes are built with the view of impressing the outside world. More attention is usually given to the front than to the back, and the reception rooms and guest rooms are more artistically and expensively furnished and decorated than those parts which serve the immediate family, and more particularly than those parts that serve for utility, Large, well-kept, close-clipped lawns are illustrations of conspicuous consumption. The cultivation of expensive flowers and shrubs, regardless of their intrinsic beauty, is another of many forms of expression of the principle. The use of expensive material in the production of apparel and home furnishings, and of platinum instead of gold for jewelry, are additional illustrations.

In line with this principle that consumption must be expensive and wasteful, there have grown up a number of current maxims or adages which convey the same idea. For example, the expression 'better grade' almost always means more expensive grade. 'A cheap coat makes a cheap man' and 'cheap and nasty' are common expressions. The struggle of people who are not wealthy but who have been imbued with the honorific qualities of expensive goods, who try to keep up in competition with their neighbours, is pathetically illustrated by their claim that when they do purchase they buy only 'the best'.

One may construct a business rule from this analysis to the effect that a style, to succeed as a fashion, must have qualities that advertise either conspicuous leisure or conspicuous consumption for the user.

In such articles as garments, in order that there may be a chance of high success as a widely adopted fashion, they must look as if they were not intended for any useful labour and must carry the suggestion that their wearers belong to the higher vocational classes or to the leisure classes, and in the second place, they must look as if they cost a lot of money. In other words, as the slang expression goes, they must 'look like a million dollars'.

It is not enough, however, that these rules be applied crudely, for, while people with limited education and training in the art of consumption may be satisfied with gaudy displays of expense, with more social experience and education obtained in one way or another, groups of people who have acquired wealth and who seek to express themselves through the medium of conspicuous consumption, learn that the crude displays are not nearly so effective as displays contrived with some artistic effect. The cruder displays are but the first steps in the evolution of securing the most effective social results from conspicuous consumption. So, as the knowledge and experience of such individuals or groups increases in the art of consumption, the expression of expensiveness becomes ever more subtle. What was formerly applied in gilt and gaudy colours will tone down in order to secure effects which, however, are fully as expressive of expensiveness to those who know. The leadership of those who not only have wealth and the power to use it, but at the same time know how to use it artistically and recognize its artistic use in others, is more willingly accepted than the leadership of any other group of people today.

In a society such as that in which we live at the present time, the possession of wealth is admittedly highly important for its influence in giving the individual position and power and means for self-expression. The possession of wealth and knowledge of how to use it is perhaps one of the most effective methods of overcoming feelings of inferiority described in a former chapter. The effective use of wealth as a means of impressing others calls for some artistic ability, so that instead of shouting to the world from the housetops about its possession, individuals must demonstrate it through the ownership and use of such things as fine wearing apparel, high-powered automobiles, fashionable houses and furnishings. All of these goods, which are of course strongly affected by fashion, are therefore to be used in such a way that they will give the impression of wealth.

Here then are two important rules regarding fashion. If wealth is as much a dominating factor as has been suggested here, then in the creation of new designs and in the promotion of new styles in development of fashion, the styles should go as far as possible in proving that the owner does not have to work for a living. Secondly, to become a successful fashion, a style must appear expensive, not crudely, but artistically if possible, but always expensive. The degree of artistry, of course, will depend upon the sophistication of the people who are to be impressed by the style. To put this in another way, commercial interests attempting to promote fashions are almost certain to fail if the goods or styles they offer do not suggest conspicuous leisure and conspicuous expensiveness.

In this chapter there have been discussed three classes of factors that influence the character and direction of fashion movements, viz., dominating events, dominating ideals and dominating groups. Present fashions are affected by all three. Under dominating events there are still the after-effects of the World War and the influence of the modern art movement. Under dominating ideals comes the very forceful influence of the current youth movement. Under dominating groups the most influential in our time are the people of wealth who also have acquired the subtle art of artistic spending. One may find a fairly complete explanation of fashion of the present time by reference to the effects of these three great factors.

Chapter 11

A NOTE ON THE TRICKLE EFFECT*
by Lloyd A. Fallers

Nystrom's concept of fashions trickling through society is discussed and extended. The differential rate of diffusion is emphasized as a fundamentally important characteristic of fashion.

Much has been written—and much more spoken in informal social scientific shop talk—about the so-called 'trickle effect'—the tendency in U.S. society (and perhaps to a lesser extent in Western societies generally) for new styles or fashions in consumption goods to be introduced via the socio-economic *élite* and then to pass down through the status hierarchy, often in the form of inexpensive, mass-produced copies.

In a recent paper, Barber and Lobel have analysed this phenomenon in the field of women's clothes.[1] They point out that women's dress fashions are not simply irrational shifts in taste, but that they have definite functions in the U.S. status system. Most Americans, they say, are oriented toward status mobility. Goods and services consumed are symbolic of social status. In the family division of labour, the husband and father 'achieves' in the occupational system and thus provides the family with monetary income. Women, as wives and daughters, have the task of allocating this income so as to maximize its status-symbolic value. Since women's clothing permits much subtlety of expression in selection and display, it becomes of great significance as a status-mobility symbol.[2] The ideology of the 'open class' system, however, stresses broad 'equality' as well as differential status. The tendency of women's dress fashions to 'trickle down' fairly rapidly via inexpensive reproductions of originals created at fashion centres helps to resolve this seeming inconsistency by preventing the development of rigid status distinctions.[3]

In the widest sense, of course, the 'trickle effect' applies not only to women's dress but also to consumption goods of many other kinds. Most similar to women's dress fashions are styles in household furnishings. A colleague has pointed out to me that venetian blinds have had a similar status career—being introduced at relatively high levels in the status hierarchy and within a few years passing down to relatively low levels. Like women's dress styles, styles in household furnishings are to a substantial degree matters of taste and their adoption a matter of 'learning' by lower status persons that they are status

* From *The Public Opinion Quarterly* (Autumn, 1954).

relevant. The trickling down of other types of consumption goods is to a greater degree influenced by long-term increases in purchasing power at lower socio-economic levels. Such consumers' durables as refrigerators and automobiles, being products of heavy industry and hence highly standardized over relatively long periods and throughout the industries which produce them, are much less subject to considerations of taste. They do, however, trickle down over the long term and their possession is clearly status-relevant.

The dominant tendency among social scientists has been to regard the trickle effect mainly as a 'battle of wits' between upper-status persons who attempt to guard their symbolic treasure and lower-status persons (in league with mass-production industries) who attempt to devalue the status-symbolic currency. There is much truth in this view. Latterly we have observed a drama of this sort being played out in the automotive field. Sheer ownership of an automobile is no longer symbolic of high status and neither is frequent trading-in. Not even the 'big car' manufacturers can keep their products out of the hands of middle- and lower-status persons 'on the make'. High-status persons have therefore turned to ancient or foreign sports-cars.

It seems possible, however, that the trickle effect has other and perhaps more far-reaching functions for the society as a whole. Western (and particularly U.S.) society, with its stress upon the value of success through individual achievement, poses a major motivational problem: The occupational system is primarily organized about the norm of technical efficiency. Technical efficiency is promoted by recruiting and rewarding persons on the basis of their objective competence and performance in occupational roles. The field of opportunity for advancement, however, is pyramidal in shape; the number of available positions decreases as differential rewards increase. But for the few most competent to be chosen, the many must be 'called', that is, motivated to strive for competence and hence success. This, of course, involves relative failure by the many, hence the problem: How is the widespread motivation to strive maintained in the face of the patent likelihood of failure for all but the few? In a widely-quoted paper, Merton has recognized that this situation is a serious focus of strain in the social system and has pointed to some structured types of deviant reaction to it.[4] I should like to suggest the hypothesis that *the trickle effect is a mechanism for maintaining the motivation to strive for success, and hence for maintaining efficiency of performance in occupational roles, in a system in which differential success is possible for only a few*. Status-symbolic consumption goods trickle down, thus giving the 'illusion' of success to those who fail to achieve *differential* success in the opportunity and status pyramid. From this point of view, the trickle effect becomes a 'treadmill'.

There are, of course, other hypotheses to account for the maintenance of motivation to strive against very unfavourable odds. Perhaps the most common is the notion that the 'myth of success', perhaps maintained by the mass-communications media under the control of the 'vested interests', deceives people into believing that their chances for success are greater than is in fact the case. Merton seems to accept this explanation in part while denying that the ruse is entirely effective.[5] Somewhat similar is another common explanation, put forward, for example, by Schumpeter, that though the chances for success are not great, the rewards are so glittering as to make the struggle attractive.[6] Undoubtedly both the 'success myth' theory and the 'gambling' theory contain elements of truth. Individual achievement certainly *is* a major value in the society and dominates much of its ideology, while risk-taking is clearly institutionalized, at any rate in the business segment of the occupational system. Taken by themselves, however, these explanations do not seem sufficient to account for the situation. At any rate, if it is possible to show that the system *does* 'pay off' for the many in the form of 'trickle-down' status-symbolic consumption goods, one need not lean so heavily upon such arguments.

It seems a sound principle of sociological analysis to assume 'irrationality' as a motivation for human action only where exhaustive analysis fails to reveal a 'realistic' pay-off for the observed behaviour. To be sure, the explanation put forward here also assumes 'irrationality', but in a different sense. The individual who is rewarded for his striving by the trickling-down of status-symbolic consumption goods has the *illusion*, and not the *fact*, of status mobility among his fellows. But in terms of his life history, he nevertheless *has* been rewarded with things which are valued and to this degree his striving is quite 'realistic'.[7] Though his status position *vis-à-vis* his fellows has not changed, he can look back upon his own life history and say to himself (perhaps not explicitly since the whole status-mobility motivational complex is probably quite often wholly or in part unconscious): 'I (or my family) have succeeded. I now have things which five (or ten or twenty) years ago I could not have had, things which were then possessed only by persons of higher status.' To the degree that status is *defined* in terms of consumption of goods and services one should perhaps say, not that such an individual has only the *illusion* of mobility, but rather that the entire population has been upwardly mobile. From this point of view, status-symbolic goods and services do not 'trickle-down' but rather remain in fixed positions; the population moves up through the hierarchy of status-symbolic consumption patterns.

The accompanying diagram illustrates the various possibilities in terms of the life-histories of individuals. The two half-pyramids represent the status hierarchy at two points in time (X and Y). A, B, C and D are individuals occupying different levels in the status hierarchy. Roman numerals I through V represent the hierarchy of status-symbolic consumption patterns. Between time periods X and Y, a new high-status consumption pattern has developed and has been taken over by the *élite*. All status levels have 'moved up' to 'higher' consumption patterns. During the elapsed time, individual C has 'succeeded' in the sense of having become able to consume goods and services which were unavailable to him before, though he has remained in the same relative status level. Individual B has been downwardly mobile in the status hierarchy, but this blow has been softened for him because the level into which he has dropped has in the meantime taken over consumption patterns previously available only to persons in the higher level in which B began. Individual D has been sufficiently downwardly mobile so that he has also lost ground in the hierarchy of consumption patterns. Finally, individual A, who has been a spectacular success, has risen to the very top of the status hierarchy where he is able to consume goods and services which were unavailable even to the *élite* at an earlier time period. Needless to say, this diagram is not meant to represent the actual status levels, the proportions of persons in each level, or the frequencies of upward and downward mobility in the U.S. social system. It is simply meant to illustrate diagramatically the tendency of the system, in terms of status-symbolic consumption goods, to reward even those who are not status mobile and to provide a 'cushion' for those who are slightly downward mobile.

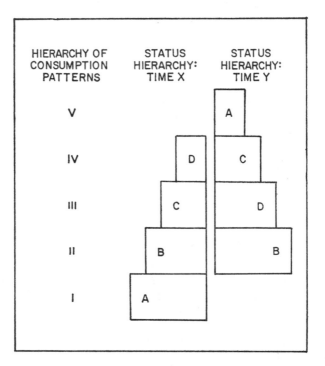

FIG. 1.

Undoubtedly this view of the system misrepresents 'the facts' in one way as much as the notion of status-symbolic goods and services 'trickling down' through a stable status hierarchy does in another. Consumption patterns do not retain the same status-symbolic value as they become available to more people. Certainly to some degree the 'currency becomes inflated'. A more adequate diagram would show both consumption patterns trickling down and the status hierarchy moving up. Nonetheless, I would suggest that *to some degree* particular consumption goods have 'absolute' value in terms of the individual's life history and his motivation to succeed. To the degree that this is so, the system pays off even for the person who is not status-mobile.

This pay-off, of course, is entirely dependent upon constant innovation and expansion in the industrial system. New goods and services must be developed and existing ones must become more widely available through mass-production. Average 'real income' must constantly rise. If status-symbolic consumption patterns remained stationary both in kind and in degree of availability, the system would pay off only for the status-mobile and the achievement motive would indeed be unrealistic for most individuals. Were the productive system to shrink, the pay-off would become negative for most and the unrealism of the motivation to achieve would be compounded. Under such circumstances, the motivational complex of striving-achievement–occupational efficiency would be placed under great strain. Indeed, Merton seems to have had such circumstances in mind when he described 'innovation', 'ritualism', 'rebellion', and 'passive withdrawal' as common patterned deviations from the norm.[8]

This suggests a 'vicious circle' relationship between achievement motivation and industrial productivity. It seems reasonable to suppose that a high level of achievement motivation is both a cause and a result of efficiency in occupational role performance. Such an assumption underlies much of our thinking about the modern Western occupational system and indeed is perhaps little more than common sense. One British sociologist, commenting upon the reports of the British 'Productivity Teams' which have recently been visiting American factories, is impressed by American workers' desire for status-symbolic consumption, partly the result of pressure upon husbands by their wives, as a factor in the greater 'per man hour' productivity of American industry.[9] Greater productivity, of course, means more and cheaper consumption goods and hence a greater pay-off for the worker. Conversely, low achievement motivation and inefficiency in occupational role performance would seem to stimulate one another. The worker has less to work for, works less efficiently, and in turn receives still less reward. Presumably these relationships would tend to hold, though in some cases less directly, throughout the occupational system and not only in the sphere of the industrial worker.

To the degree that the relationships suggested here between motivation to status-symbolic consumption, occupational role performance, and expanding productivity actually exist, they should be matters of some importance to the theory of business cycles. Although they say nothing about the genesis of up-turns and down-turns in business activity, they do suggest some social structural reasons why upward or downward movements, once started, might tend to continue. It is not suggested, of course, that these are the only, or even the most important, reasons. More generally, they exemplify the striking degree to which the stability of modern industrial society often depends upon the maintenance of delicate equilibria.

The hypotheses suggested here are, it seems to me, amenable to research by a number of techniques. It would be most useful to discover more precisely just which types of status-symbolic consumption goods follow the classical trickle-down pattern and which do not. Television sets, introduced in a period of relative prosperity, seem to have followed a different pattern, spreading laterally across the middle-income groups rather than trickling down from above. This example suggests another. Some upper-income groups appear to have shunned television on the grounds of its 'vulgarity'—a valuation shared by many academics. To what degree are preferences for other goods and services introduced, not at the upper income levels, but by the 'intelligensia', who appear at times to have greater pattern-setting potential than their relatively low economic position might lead one to believe? Finally, which consumption items spread rapidly and which more slowly? Such questions might be answered by the standard techniques of polling and market analysis.

More difficult to research are hypotheses concerning the motivational significance of consumption goods. I have suggested that the significance for the individual of the trickling down of consumption patterns must be seen in terms of his life-history and not merely in terms of short-term situations. It seems likely that two general patterns may be distinguished. On the one hand, individuals for whom success means primarily rising above their fellows may be more sensitive to those types of goods and services which must be chosen and consumed according to relatively subtle and rapidly changing standards of taste current at any one time at higher levels. Such persons must deal successfully with the more rapid devaluations of status-symbolic currency which go on among those actively battling for dominance. Such persons it may be who are responsible for the more short-term fluctuations in consumption patterns. On the other hand, if my hypothesis is correct, the great mass of the labour force may be oriented more to long-term success in terms of their own life-histories—success in the sense of achieving a 'better standard of living' without particular regard to *differential* status. Interviews centred upon the role of consumption patterns in individuals' life aspirations should reveal such differences if they exist, while differences in perception of symbols of taste might be tested by psychological techniques.

Most difficult of all would be the testing of the circular relationship between motivation and productivity. Major fluctuations in the economy are relatively long term and could be studied only through research planned on an equally long-term basis. Relatively short-term and localized fluctuations, however, do occur at more frequent intervals and would provide possibilities for research. One would require an index of occupational performance which could be related to real income and the relationship between these elements should ideally be traced through periods of both rising and falling real income.

References

1. Bernard Barber and Lyle S. Lobel, ' "Fashion" in Women's Clothes and the American Social System', *Social Forces*, vol. 31, pp. 124–131. Reprinted in Reinhard Bendix and S. M. Lipset, *Class, Status and Power: A Reader in Social Stratification* (Free Press, 1953), pp. 323–332. (*See* chapter 20.)
2. It is not suggested that women are *solely* in charge of status-symbolic expenditure, merely that they play perhaps the major role in this respect. See also: Parsons, Talcott, *Essays in Sociological Theory* (Free Press, 1949), p. 225.
3. Our thinking concerning the status-symbolic role of consumption patterns owes a great debt, of course, to Veblen's notion of 'conspicuous consumption' and more recently to the work of W. L. Warner and his colleagues.
4. R. K. Merton, 'Social Structure and Anomie', reprinted as Chapter IV, *Social Theory and Social Structure* (Free Press, 1949).
5. Ibid.
6. J. A. Schumpter, *Capitalism, Socialism and Democracy* (Harpers, 1947), pp. 73–74.

7. By 'irrationality' is meant here irrationality *within the framework of a given value system*. Values themselves, of course, are neither 'rational' nor 'irrational' but 'nonrational'. The value of individual achievement is non-rational. Action directed toward achievement may be termed rational to the degree that, in terms of the information available to the actor, it is likely to result in achievement; it is irrational to the degree that this is not so.
8. R. K. Merton, op. cit.
9. W. C. Balfour, 'Productivity and the Worker', *British Journal of Sociology*, vol. 4, No. 3 (1953), pp. 257–265.

Chapter 12

A REBUTTAL TO THE
'TRICKLE DOWN' THEORY*
by Charles W. King

*For centuries, the 'trickle down' theory has prevailed in the fashion
literature as the basic model descriptive of the fashion adoption process.
The central question is, does the 'trickle down' theory accurately reflect
contemporary fashion behaviour? In this paper, the applicability of the
traditional theory is challenged. The 'trickle down' theory is critiqued,
empirical data refuting the notion is presented, and a counter approach
to the fashion adoption process is developed.*

The oscillations and vagaries of fashions in women's apparel have been the
topic of social critics for centuries. A sizable body of literature has developed
in fashion based on over three hundred years of conceptual commentary and
anecdotal evidence. Collectively, these contributions have become the core of
modern day 'fashion theory'.

What is known as fashion theory, however, is more an amorphous network of
concepts than an integrated paradigm predictive of modern fashion behaviour.
The loose conceptual framework is organized around a basic model of the
fashion adoption process—the 'trickle down' theory of fashion adoption.
The theory unfortunately lacks contemporary validation in empirical research.
Virtually none of the proponents of the 'trickle down' process have tested the
details of the model. Historically, specific anecdotal evidence supporting the
traditional notion has been limited. Even in the era of the consumer survey,
published studies of fashion behaviour are scarce.

In this project, fashion adoption has been attacked as a specific type of
innovative behaviour within the broader contexts of social change and product
innovation. Contemporary innovation research and methodology have been
applied in the fashion adoption context. Specifically, the project has involved
an exploratory consumer survey of the consumer change agents—the innovator
(the early season buyer) and the influential (the opinion leader) in the fashion
adoption process within the product category of women's millinery. The
central theme of the research is that the traditional fashion adoption process
model—the 'trickle down' theory—does not reflect contemporary fashion
behaviour.

* From Proceeding of AMA Conference: *Towards Scientific Marketing* (American
Marketing Association, 1963).

The 'Trickle Down' Theory

What is the 'trickle down' theory? The flavour of the theory can be most fully appreciated by quoting directly from its supporters. Though the theory has been implied by many early economists such as Rae,[1] Foley,[2] and Veblen,[3] one of the first detailed presentations was made by Simmel,[4] a sociologist:

'Social forms, apparel, aesthetic judgement, the whol style of human expression are constantly transformed by fashion, in such a way, however, that fashion—in all these things—affects only the upper classes. Just as soon as the lower classes begin to copy their style, thereby crossing the line of demarcation the upper classes have drawn and destroying the uniformity of their coherence, the upper classes turn away from this style and adopt a new one, which in its turn differentiates them from the masses; and thus the game goes merrily on. Naturally, the lower classes look and strive toward the upper, and they encounter least resistance in those fields which are subject to the whims of fashion; for it is here that mere external imitation is most readily applied. The same process is at work as between the different sets within the upper classes, although it is not always as visible here. . . .'

Barber in more recent research on social stratification has emphasized the 'trickle down' process in women's clothes,[5] and Robinson argues essentially the same vertical flow notion, modifying it slightly to include horizontal movement within particular social strata:

'. . . any given group (or cluster of groups forming a class) will tend to take its cues from those contiguous with it. Horizontally fashions will spread outward from central loci; and vertically—the more important consideration—any given group will tend to adopt as its mentor not the highest distinguishable group, but, rather, those immediately above it. In consequence of the vertical contiguity of class groupings, new fashions tend to filter down by stages through the levels of affluence. The process of discarding any fashion will be a mere reflex of its proliferation. For an object of fashion to lose its meaning for the topmost class, it is only necessary for it to be taken up by the secondmost and so on down the line.[6]

In essence, then, the vertical flow hypothesis simply states that the upper socio-economic classes adopt fashions first in the time dimension as symbols of distinction and exclusiveness. In the course of inter-intra class competition, the lower classes, each and in turn, emulate and follow the upper class leaders. At a certain level of adoption by the lower levels the syndrome of styles becomes vulgarized and is discarded by the upper class in favour of a new set of fashion symbols. The 'trickle' is again activated and the process repeats itself.

For the sophisticated marketer and social scientist, this discussion of the vertical flow hypothesis may have added little in terms of substantive knowledge. The purpose of the detailed quotations from these theorists has been to highlight the similarity of the fashion adoption process model among different writers over time (Simmel wrote in 1904, Robinson in 1961). Despite a changing social and business environment, the conceptualizations have remained essentially static in theme and detail for at least sixty years.

216

A Rebuttal to 'Trickle Down'

The basic question is, does the 'trickle down' theory accurately describe the contemporary fashion adoption process? The traditional notion is vulnerable. The historical evidence quoted by the early theorists strongly indicates the vertical flow process may have been functional in earlier periods in different types of class structures. The modern social environment, mass communications, and the fashion industry's manufacturing and merchandising strategies, however, almost impede any systematic vertical flow process.

Changing Social Environment

During the past 30 years in the United States, social and economic 'levelling influences' have changed the entire profile of the consumer market. The once obviously structured class system has changed; class lines are clearly drawn only at extreme points on the social class continuum. As a result of the levelling influence, a much broader slice of the population can afford to be in fashion. The traditional value of material and craftsmanship in labelling social position still exists. But quality apparel is now within the reach of more people. The population's affluence reverberates through other facets of the theory also.

Impact of Mass Media

Mass communication media rapidly accelerate the spread of fashion awareness and influence mass market endorsement. The traditional upper class fashion leader directing the lower levels is largely short-circuited in the communication process. Within hours after the exclusive Paris and American designers' showings, the season's styles have been passed to the mass audiences via newspaper and television. The mass media 'fashion seminars' also reflect the short-cutting of upper class influence in a direct sense. The woman's fashion page universally geared to 'middle majority', the 'woman's problems' columns, the fashion journals, and the broadcast media's fashion programmes provide detailed 'what to wear' and 'how to wear it' instruction aimed directly at the mass market buyer. The traditional process of vertical personal transmission is again challenged.

Fashion Industry Manufacturing and Merchandising

Fashion industry manufacturing and merchandising methods actually impede any vertical flow process of fashion adoption.

Fashion adoption is a process of social contagion by which a new style or product is adopted by the consumer after commercial introduction by the designer or manufacturer. Though gradual long term secular trends in apparel fashions have been documented,[7] the actual consumer adoption decision is made within the time dimension of a season. Though historically, the fashion seasons have roughly paralleled climatic seasons, in recent years fashion merchandisers have tended to accelerate the transitions from season to season. In women's apparel, the season is typically three to six months in length.

As a merchandising strategy, designers and manufacturers strive to differentiate products between comparable seasons over time. Though classic styles and silhouettes may carry over, new styles are introduced and colours and fabrics

217

changed. Therefore, the adoption of a new fashion entails a shift within the population from the styles appropriate at a given time the previous year to the new style offerings. Individuals make the adoption decisions at different speeds and at different times. The aggregate fashion cycle for a style is an expression of this continuum of adoption.

The net impact of operating within the time dimensions of a season is to compress the adoption process into a blur. The rapidity of adoption dictated by the fashion season directly challenges the operationality of the 'trickle down' process.

The lag time for vertical flow of fashion adoption at the consumer level is almost non-existent. From creation to mass market introduction, there may be virtually no opportunity for vertical flow. Paris fashions pose a good example. Many of the Paris designers are concentrating almost exclusively on 'originals' for the mass fashion industry. In 1957, an estimated 30 per cent of Paris *haute couture* volume was accounted for by manufacturers and retail syndicate and store buyers.[8] In these cases, there is little upper-class style endorsement supporting mass market adoption. In 1960, for further support, the August showings in Paris that were purchased or leased by American concerns were flown to the United States on the same plane on 23 August. On 5 September, New York fashion houses introduced the fall collection of copied Paris originals to the fashion press. Following five days of manufacturing and merchandise preparation, Macy's, Gimbels, and other leading New York department stores introduced the 'popular priced' fall fashions to the consumers.[9] Again, where was the vertical flow process and upper class initiation and lower class emulation?

In the area of product design, the consumer moves from one extreme of virtually no choice in fashion selection to the other extreme of wide freedom of choice. The fashion industry defines basic colours, fabrics, and silhouettes for all price lines for a given season months before the season actually gets underway at the retail level. Once the basic dimensions of a season's fashions are set, a multiplicity of contemporary and classic styles are introduced. These decisions are certainly the result of a vast distillation of fashion design experience, success, and failure. These product decisions are rarely the result of empirical research beyond review of last season's trends.

Theoretically, the consumer can select from a wide range of current and classic designs and still be entirely 'in fashion' regardless of the particular selection she makes. The consumer has comparative freedom across styles to satisfy personal tastes and physical features with little social penalty.

Product differences between price lines are almost exclusively quality based rather than design based. The same basic silhouettes, materials and imitations, and colours are featured in each broad price range. The higher priced lines tend to be merely of higher quality in material and craftsmanship. Styling may be more versatile and creative in the higher priced lines because of the wider profit margins. The obvious differences, however, are difficult to recognize once the economy lines are excluded.

The time factor in retail merchandising impedes much vertical flow except on a very rapid basis. In fact, modern retailing almost guarantees simultaneous adoption of the same basic styles across status levels. The volume fashion manufacturing and retailing industry operates essentially in the same way and on the same basic seasonal schedules in the higher priced and in the lower priced categories. The season's styles at each price level tend to be introduced at approximately the same time. In millinery, departments introduce new season items at essentially the same time in the seasons. Stores at all price levels tend to follow basically the same fashion calendar in fashion promotion.

Why Continued Support of the Theory

Given these contradictions of the vertical flow process, how does the notion marshal support from sophisticated fashion theorists?

The confusion is, in part, a product of using the fashion industry as a source of information.[10] Defining the broad fashion innovation process as the entire range of activities from conceptualization of a new style through detailed design to market introduction, a vertical flow definitely operates *within* the industry. The character of that process is entirely different from the consumer reaction outlined by Simmel and others.

The three elements of the innovation process—manufacturers, trade channel buyers, and consumers—represent a great filtering system. The three elements or sub-systems operate as interdependent yet independent evaluation and adoption centres. The manufacturers select a finite number of styles to feature from an almost infinite array of possibilities. The trade channel buyers then select a sampling of styles for ultimate sales from the universe of lines offered by all manufacturers. The consumers then adopt a sampling of these selections and endorse them as accepted fashions.

Within the industry subsets, a vertical flow exists also. The exclusive and famous designers are watched closely and emulated by lesser designers. Major manufacturers are studied and copied by smaller and less expert competitors. Design piracy is a well established competitive strategy.

In describing the consumer fashion adoption process, industry spokesmen are surprisingly uninformed.[11] An enigmatic 'fashionable woman' guides many fashion managers. Others refer to the all pervasive importance of celebrity endorsement in influencing fashion trends. Some recognize the mass market influence but understand little of its complexity.

In modest defence of the vertical flow supporters, it must be granted that some upper class influence undoubtedly exists. The question really is: does it dictate market behaviour as predicted by the theory? In one segment of the market, a narrowly defined vertical flow can be recognized. The small, chic, and very wealthy upper class indirectly influences styles through the private designer. The social *élite* nurture the private designers through their patronage. More importantly, the private designers test new styles with this group and adapt successful trends for mass market showings. The garment manufacturers' and retail buyers' offerings, then, are partially distillations of upper class taste. Therefore, an indirect and hazy 'vertical flow' process might be considered at work.

This type of function, however, falls far short of the all pervasive social status emulation outlined by Simmel, Barber, Robinson, and others. To use this evidence in defence of the traditional vertical flow theory may be theoretically but pragmatically irrelevant.

If this limited interpretation of the 'trickle down' process is to be applied then there is no current fashion adoption theory. The great adoption function occurs within the mass market. This limited interpretation gives no explanation of mass market adoption. What goes on there? This is the crucial question to fashion management and social scientists.

Research Design

The research described here has involved an exploratory consumer survey of the key figures in fashion adoption, the innovator (the early buyer) and the influential (the opinion leader). The context has been confined to the product category of women's millinery and the geographical area of Metropolitan Boston. The field research was conducted immediately following the close of the Fall (1962) millinery season.

The millinery buying context has proved particularly suitable to fashion adoption research. Millinery is recognized as a highly fashion oriented item of women's apparel. Fashion change occurs semi-annually and is an accepted social phenomenon. Involvement in millinery adoption is high and almost all women can discuss the adoption process with some expertise.

The cornerstone of the project involved inclusion of the time of adoption as the critical variable in the research design. Respondents were qualified on a continuum of adoption based on their Fall buying behaviour. The objective was to segment the adoption continuum into independent parts as accurately as possible within the financial constraints. Time of adoption was defined as the month of first purchase of a hat during the Fall season. The adoption decision was not defined as adoption of any specific style but merely purchase in time since the consumer can 'adopt' from a wide range of styles within the season's merchandise and be 'in style' regardless of the specific selection. The 'early' and 'late' buyers were operationally defined:

(1) 'early' buyers: late August or September purchasers representing the first 35 per cent of the Fall season's buyers.
(2) 'late' buyers: October through mid-January purchasers representing the latter 65 per cent of the season's buyers.

The field research involved two phases: a brief telephone interview, and a one hour personal interview with selected respondents.

Based on the Metropolitan Boston Telephone Directory, a random cluster sampling procedure was used to select 1,934 adult women, who were classified into the adopter categories. Of these, 303 respondents in the early and later buyer categories were selected and personally interviewed to probe their general fashion and hat adoption processes in detail, including coverage of an extensive array of demographic, psychological, social, and mass communication and personal influence variables.

Rejections of the 'Trickle Down' Theory

The empirical data support rejection of the 'trickle down' theory of fashion adoption in this product context. Two broad questions central to the theory have been analysed:

(1) Are the early buyers, in fact, the high status '*élite* esotery' depicted by the vertical flow notion?

(2) Are early buyers more influential than late buyers in dictating fashion adoption?

The tradition theory implies a form of personal influence in which the high status, early buyers directly influence the lower status, later adopters in the interpersonal network of information transmission.

Socioeconomic Status of the Adopter Categories

The socioeconomic status of the respondents was measured on three levels: total annual family income, husband's occupational status, and self designated or perceived social class position. The three measures are obviously highly intercorrelated but each taps a somewhat different dimension of social status. The three measures produced essentially identical results.

The basic conclusion to be drawn from the analysis of social status was that early buyers were consistently higher status than late buyers *but* the early buyers were not 'upper class'. Specifically:

(1) In terms of annual family income, 59 per cent of the early buyers had income under $9000 per year; 19 per cent had income of less than $6000.

(2) In terms of husband's occupational status, 62 per cent of the early buyers were 'middle class' or lower; 33 per cent were 'lower middle class' or lower.

(3) In terms of respondent's perceived class position, despite the expected clustering of reports in the 'middle class', 16 per cent of the early buyers located themselves in 'lower middle' or 'lower class' social positions.

Is this group of early buyers the '*élite* esotery' the traditional theorists have labelled as the fashion innovators initiating the 'trickle down' process?

Personal Influence and the Adopter Categories

Even if the early buyers were assumed to meet the status requirements for the '*élite* esotery', the second question of personal influence in fashion adoption must be answered. Admittedly, the early buyer does levy some visual influence through displaying the season's fashions early in the season. In turn, because of the reliance of retailers on early season sales as a guide to later season inventory purchases, the early buyer exercises influence over retail inventories. The issue here, however, centres on the early buyer's role as a personal influential in the interpersonal network of information transmission.

As a first step in the anaylsis, 'influentials' were identified in two contexts: general fashion and hat buying. In the general fashion context an influential was anyone who had 'been asked her advice' or 'offered any suggestions' on fashions recently or felt she was 'more likely' to be asked than any of her friends. The hat influentials were those respondents who felt they were 'more likely' to be asked their advice about hats than their friends. This approach to identifying influential opinion leaders has frequently been used in other contexts.[12]

Reliance on personal interactions in information receiving and transmitting is high, particularly in the general fashion context. Approximately 73 per cent and 25 per cent of the respondents relied on personal interactions in the general fashion and hat buying contexts respectively. The lower incidence of interaction in hat buying is largely a result of narrowing the reporting context from broad fashion to the specific product category of women's millinery.

Given the role of personal influence and the identification of influentials, three dimensions were explored in measuring the dynamics of influence exercised by early versus late buyers:

(1) The frequency of interaction by the influentials within adopter groups.
(2) The number of influentials within the adopter group.
(3) The status compatibility between the receiver and the influential in the reported interactions.

There were no significant patterned differences in the frequency of reported interactions by influentials in the early versus late adopter groups as indicated in Table 1. It should be noted that only the interactions from the general fashion context are reported in Tables 1 and 4. Too few interactions were fully

TABLE 1 *Comparison of Early v. Late Buyers by Influence Interaction Frequency General Fashion Context*

	Early Buyer	Late Buyer
Number of Interactions Per Influential	1·06*	1.10
Base Number of Influentials	66	86

* i.e., Early buyer influentials reported 1·06 interactions per influential.

reported in the hat context to justify detailed presentation. The general pattern reflected by the data in the two contexts, however, were essentially identical.

Recognizing the importance of the level of influence, the analysis has concentrated on the influentials within the adopter groups. Though the early buyers have been found to be well distributed across the class structure rather than 'upper class', supporters of the 'trickle down' theory could argue that the influence in the early buyer group was concentrated in the upper income sector. If this were the case, greater credence might be given the 'trickle down' concept.

To attack this hypothesis, the adopter groups were divided into high, medium, and low income subsets. To eliminate the impact of the slightly larger number of higher income respondents in the early group, the percentage of respondents qualifying as influentials within each income subset was calculated. As presented in Table 2, in both the general fashion and hat buying contexts, influence was not concentrated in the early buyer, high income subset.

TABLE 2 *Comparison of Early and Late Buyers by Incidence of Influence within Income Subsets—General Fashion and Hat Buying Contexts*

Family Income	General Fashion Context		Hat Buying Context	
	Early Buyer	Late Buyer	Early Buyer	Late Buyer
Under $6000	50%*	41%	4%	13%†
$6000 to $8999	50%	51%	17%	10%
$9000 or more	51%	62%	10%	21%

Note: Percentages do not add to 100%.
* i.e., 50% of the early buyers reported 'under $6000' income qualified as influentials in the general fashion context.
† i.e., 13% of the late buyers reported 'under $6000' income qualified as influentials in the hat buying context.

In the general fashion context, the early buyers within each income subset had essentially identical probabilities of being influentials. In the hat buying context the early buyer, middle income respondents had a somewhat higher probability of qualifying as influentials. Nor were the early buyer, high income respondents more influential than their late buyer, high income counterparts. In fact the late buyer, high income subset had more per capita influence in both contexts than any other subset—further refutation of the 'trickle down' theory.

A logical question would be: are early buyers in total more influential than late buyers? The basic data presented in Table 3 indicate that in both the general fashion and hat buying contexts, the percentage of respondents qualifying as influentials within the early buyer and late buyer groups was essentially identical. Though the general incidence of influence was lower in the hat context, the relationship of the adopter categories remained the same. Clearly in contradiction to the traditional theory, the early buyers were no more likely to be influentials than late buyers.

A critical blow to the traditional 'trickle down' notion is provided when the early and late buyer groups are weighted according to their relative importance in the Fall hat buying market. By definition, the early buyer group (August

TABLE 3 *Comparison of Early and Late Buyers by Incidence of Influence General Fashion and Hat Buying Contexts*

Respondents Qualified as:	General Fashion Context		Hat Buying Context	
	Early Buyer	Late Buyer	Early Buyer	Late Buyer
Receiver	23%	23%	14%	16%
Influential	49%*	51%	11%†	14%
Uninvolved	28%	26%	75%	70%
Total	100%	100%	100%	100%
Base	135	168	135	168

* i.e., 49% of the early buyer group qualified as influentials in the general fashion context.
† i.e., 11% of the early buyer group qualified as influentials in the hat buying context.

and September buyers) represented 35 per cent of the total buyers, and the late buyers represented 65 per cent of the market. Therefore, since the two adopter groups had essentially identical levels of influence *within* the categories, weighting for market importance indicated there were 86 per cent more late buyer influentials compared with early buyer influentials in the total Fall season hat buying population. In direct contradiction to the 'trickle down' theory, the total impact of influence by late buyers was markedly greater than that of early buyers.

The third question to be answered centres around the interpersonal interaction itself. Who talks to whom? The traditional notion would predict that influentials influence those lower in social status and receivers receive from those higher in social status than themselves. In the personal interview, each time an interaction was reported, a series of questions was asked concerning the referent with whom the respondent had talked. The referent's husband's occupation was defined and compared with the respondent's husband's occupation as the basis for the status compatibility measure.

Analysis of non-family interactions is presented in Table 4. Though some 'trickle' might be read into the data, the basic conclusion is that the vast majority of receiving and influencing interactions by both early and late buyers were between individuals of the same social status. Personal transmission of fashion information moves primarily horizontally rather than vertically in the class hierarchy.

TABLE 4 *Comparison of Early and Late Buyers' Non-Family Interactions by Social Status Compatibility—General Fashion Context*

Referent Compared to Respondent	Receiving Interactions*		Influencing Interactions*	
	Early Buyer	Late Buyer	Early Buyer	Late Buyer
Referent of higher social status	16%†	11%	13%‡	—
Referent of same social status	80%	82%	74%	86%
Referent of lower social status	4%	7%	13%	14%
Total	100%	100%	100%	100%
Base number of Interactions	25	27	23	35

* 'Receiving' interactions were those where the respondent primarily received information: in 'influencing' interactions the respondent *gave* advice.

† i.e., in 16% of the 'receiving' interactions, the referent had a higher social status than the respondent in the early buyer group.

‡ i.e., in 13% of the 'influencing' interactions, the referent had a higher social status than the respondent in the early buyer group.

A New Approach to Fashion Adoption

The critique and rejection of the 'trickle down' theory have set the scene for a counter theory—a 'mass market' or 'trickle across' scheme of fashion adoption. The purpose of this discussion is not to present a highly structured or detailed paradigm in the tradition of the deductive method. Rather, the objective is to draw the data presented earlier into a broad conceptual scheme descriptive of modern adoption behaviour. The scheme represents only a loose framework of notions but is a first step toward a more definitive model of the adoption process.

In essence, the 'mass market' or 'trickle across' theory of fashion adoption centres around four broad arguments:

(1) Within the fashion season, the social culture and the fashion industry's manufacturing and merchandising strategies almost guarantee adoption by consumers across socioeconomic groups simultaneously in the time dimension.

(2) Consumers theoretically have the freedom to select from a wide range of contemporary and classic styles in the season's inventory to satisfy the dictates of their physical features and personal tastes.

(3) The innovators and influentials play key roles in directing fashion adoption and represent discrete market segments within social strata.

(4) The transmission of information and personal influence 'trickles across' or flows primarily horizontally within social strata rather than vertically across strata.

The basic contribution of this scheme is to refocus on the horizontal versus the vertical flow and on the major consumer change agents—the innovator and the influential—in the adoption process. Though some vertical flow undoubtedly exists, it does not represent the dominant movement in adoption. Given simultaneous adoption across socioeconomic strata and freedom of choice among consumers, the innovators and the influentials tend to direct fashion adoption within social strata.

In general, the functions of the innovator and the influential appear to differ. The innovator is the earliest visual communicator of the season's styles for the mass of fashion consumers. The influential appears to define and endorse appropriate standards. Both the innovator and the influential are performing advisory functions but the nature of the advice and the respective power are different, For example, in a particular social network, the influential may define the dress appropriate for the bridge party, cocktail party, etc. The innovator, in turn, may present the current offerings consistent with these broad standards. The separate role of the innovator and the influential are graphically supported by the concentration of the influentials in the late buyer sector of the total Fall millinery market.

Within this framework, the horizontal flow concept is fundamental. When the new fashions are introduced, the innovators and influentials play out their roles within social strata. Given initial introduction across social strata, adoption processes are operative simultaneously within different strata. An abundance of anecdotal evidence exists illustrating products and fashions that have received wide acceptance within some social strata, but have not been successful at other levels.

The new conceptual approach has important implications for fashion management. Though the fashion industry typically segments the market on price dimensions, merchandisers deal in aggregate terms within specific price ranges. To be sure, fashion merchandisers often 'sense' style and colour trends with uncanny accuracy and intuitively segment markets in this manner. More precise segmentation, however, is rare.

The 'mass market' model suggests a form of 'functional' segmentation. The innovators and the influentials are identified as discrete market segments within social strata. These groups represent prime sales targets themselves. More importantly, however, they represent the key links to the volume fashion market. Obviously, the fashion manufacturer and merchandiser should cultivate these market segments and utilize them in expediting the fashion flow.

Summary

The central theme of this research has been that the traditional fashion adoption process model—the 'trickle down' theory—does not reflect contemporary fashion behaviour. Based on a consumer survey of adoption in women's millinery, the empirical data indicated that the innovators or early buyers in the fashion season were not an '*élite* esotery' of upper class consumers. Nor were the early buyers the dominant personal influentials in the adoption process. In contrast, the fashion influentials were concentrated in the late buyer group. Based on the anecdotal and empirical evidence, the 'mass market' or 'trickle across' scheme has been presented. The major contribution of this approach is the emphasis on the horizontal flow of adoption within strata and the roles of the innovators and the influentials in the process.

While the scheme is based on research in the product category of millinery, the conclusions have relevance for the entire area of fashion adoption. The specific identity and profile of the innovators and the influentials may vary with fashion products. The adoption process outlined in this paper, however, seems applicable across fashion products. Utilization of the scheme by fashion merchandizers is contingent upon identification of the innovator and influential market segments within specific contexts. The scheme does represent a general analytical approach to the mysteries of fashion adoption more descriptive of modern adoption behaviour than the traditional 'trickle down' theory.

References

1. John Rae, *The Sociological Theory of Capital* (London, Macmillan Company, 1834), Chapter 13, and Appendix I.
2. Caroline R. Foley, 'Fashion', *Economic Journal*, vol. 3 (1893), p. 458. (*See* Chapter 8.)
3. Thorstein Veblen, *The Theory of the Leisure Class* (New York; Macmillan, 1912).
4. Georg Simmel, 'Fashion', *American Journal of Sociology*, vol. 62 (May 1957), pp. 541–558. (Reprinted from the International Quarterly, vol. 10 (October 1904), pp. 130–155.) (*See* Chapter 9.)
5. Bernard Barber, *Social Stratification* (New York, Harcourt, Brace and Company, 1957), p. 150.
6. Dwight E. Robinson, 'The Economics of Fashion Demand', *The Quarterly Journal of Economics*, vol. 75, no. 3 (1961), p. 376.
7. For example, see A. L. Kroeber, 'Order in Changes in Fashion (1919)', *The Nature of Culture* (Chicago, University of Chicago Press, 1952), pp. 332–337; Jane Richardson and A. L. Kroeber, 'Three Centuries of Women's Dress Fashions: A Quantitative Analysis', *Anthropological Records* (October, 1940), pp. 111–153; Agnes Brook Young, *Recurring Cycles of Fashion, 1760–1937* (New York, Harper and Brothers, 1937). (*See* Chapters 3 and 4.)

8. 'Yield from High Fashion is Low: Paris Haute', *Business Week*, (16 February 1957), pp. 68–70.
9. 'Bringing Paris Fashions Down to the Mass Market', *Business Week* (20 August 1960), pp. 72–77.
10. Robinson, for example, relied heavily on fashion industry interviews. No formal consumer research was reported.
11. Based on approximately 30 interviews with major millinery manufacturers, retail syndicate and retail buyers, and leading fashion journalists and researchers.
12. See Elihu Katz and Paul F. Lazarsfeld, *Personal Influence* (Glencoe, Illinois, The Free Press, 1965); and Everett M. Rogers and David G. Cartano, 'Methods of Measuring Opinion Leadership', *Public Opinion Quarterly*, vol. 26, no. 3 (Autumn 1962), p. 135.

Chapter 13

THE FORCES OF FASHION*
by J. C. Flugel

'See'st thou not, I say, what a deformed thief this fashion is? How giddily he turns about all the hot bloods between fourteen and five and thirty . . . ?'

*'All this I see, and I see that the fashion wears out more apparel than the man. But art not thou thyself giddy with the fashion too, that thou hast shifted out of thy tale into telling me of the fashion?'—*Much Ado About Nothing, III, iii.

This paper, in its turn, is the psychology classic in the field of fashion.

'La Mode est la déesse des apparences', Mallarmé tells us. Fashion, we have been brought up to believe (and generations of writers in a myriad of journals have contributed to this belief), is a mysterious goddess, whose decrees it is our duty to obey rather than to understand; for indeed, it is implied, these decrees transcend all ordinary human understanding. We know not why they are made, nor how long they will endure, but only that they must be followed; and that the quicker the obedience the greater is the merit. To contemplate in an unprejudiced and scientific manner the nature and activities of this divinity is as difficult as any other psychological investigation in the domain of religion; when one is not a worshipper, one tends all too easily to become a scoffer, and neither attitude befits the scientist. If the writers in the technical journals of La Mode preach as true believers, the small number of outside students resemble atheists rather than agnostics, and can ill conceal their joy at ridiculing the mysteries that others venerate. Mindful of this double danger, it is now our task to approach the goddess without fear or rancour, and to study, so far as we are able, with unbiased judgement and unclouded vision, her origin, her essence, and her edicts.

In pursuance of this programme we will first investigate *why* fashion exists in the modern world; we must, that is, examine the psychological and social causes that have originated it and that maintain it. We will then pass to the question as to the actual agencies through which fashion works, studying also the psychological functions and limitations of these agencies—in other words the *how* of fashion. Finally, we will contemplate the *what* of fashion by reviewing a few of the concrete ways in which its influence is felt.

* From *The Psychology of Clothes* (Hogarth Press, 1930). Reprinted by permission of the Author's Literary Estate and the Hogarth Press Ltd.

The Why of Fashion

There can be little doubt that the ultimate and essential cause of fashion lies in competition; competition of a social and a sexual kind, in which the social elements are more obvious and manifest and the sexual elements more indirect, concealed, and unavowed, hiding themselves, as it were, behind the social ones. We have already seen that decoration has a sexual and a social value, attractive (according to the prevalent taste) and striking forms of ornamentation being useful both for purposes of sexual allurement and as signs of rank, wealth, or power—following the convention that the more elaborate and decorative the costume, the higher the social position of the wearer. So long as the system of 'fixed' costume prevails, each social grade is content to wear the costume with which it is associated. But when the barriers between one grade and another become less insuperable, when, in psychological terms, one class begins seriously to aspire to the position of that above it, it is natural that the distinctive outward signs and symbols of the grades in question should become imperilled. As we have already had occasion to remark in another connection, it is a fundamental human trait to imitate those who are admired or envied. At the stage of social development in question, those in a given social stratum have learnt not only to admire, but as a rule to envy also, those who are above them; they therefore tend to imitate them; and what more natural, and, at the same time, more symbolic, than to start the process of imitation by copying their clothes, the very insignia of the admired and envied qualities?

If this were all that happened, the significant sartorial distinctions would merely tend to become abolished by a gradual appropriation by the lower social ranks of the styles affected by the wealthy and the powerful (a process which, as certain sociologists—notably Herbert Spencer—have pointed out, tends frequently to take place in the case of titles—as in Spain, where every beggar is a *caballero*). But the higher social classes on their side are naturally unwilling to abandon the signs of their superiority.* They can endeavour to retain their sartorial distinctiveness in two ways: either by passing sumptuary laws forbidding to others the use of their own special garments; or else by the abandonment of these garments, which are in danger of losing their distinctive value now that they are being copied, and by the adoption of a new form of dress which shall re-establish the desired distinction. Since the method of sumptuary laws, though often tried, seldom if ever proves effective, recourse must sooner or later be made to the second method. And thus fashion is born.

* Some writers on fashion, again following Herbert Spencer, distinguish two motives for the imitation involved in fashion—which may be briefly described as reverence and the desire for equality respectively. It is clear, of course, that some element, if not of reverence, at least of admiration, is always necessary for this imitation; we do not willingly imitate people except on this condition. The imitation of a fashion is always in one sense a compliment to those from whom it is copied. Occasionally, too, the element of desire for (at any rate certain specific forms of) equality or similarity may be almost or quite absent (as, for instance, in the case of wearing a high collar in obsequious imitation of a potentate who has himself adopted one to hide a scrofulous neck). But if this were generally so, the imitated would feel little need to create a fresh distinction for themselves, and fashion (as a continuous movement) would come to an end through the permanent adoption of the imitated style by all concerned. The element of rivalry, therefore, seems essential to the continuance of fashion.

There is now a movement from both ends; one from the lower social ranks in the direction of those who stand higher in the scale, and another from these latter away from their own former position, which has now become fashionably untenable. It is this double movement which essentially constitutes fashion, and is the ground of the perpetual variation to which 'modish' costume is subject.

When the double movement is thoroughly established, it manifests itself not only in the community as a whole, but also within each individual member of the community. For practical purposes it may be said that our view of separate social classes corresponding, so to speak, to the pursued and the pursuing, is little more than a convenient abstraction. Almost every individual partakes to some extent of both characters, the one or the other predominating according to his circumstances, ambitions, and abilities. The paradox of fashion is that everyone is trying at the same time to be like, and to be unlike, his fellow-men —to be like them in so far as he regards them as superiors, to be unlike them (in the sense of being more 'fashionable') so far as he thinks they are below him. Inasmuch as we are aristocratically minded and dare to assert our own individuality by being different, we are leaders of fashion (for we all exercise some influence, however small); inasmuch as we feel our own inferiority and the need of conformity to the standards set by others, we are followers of fashion. Here again, from the point of view of the individual, the essentially unstable nature of fashion becomes apparent.

As already indicated, fashion implies a certain fluidity of the social structure of the community. There must be differences of social position, but it must seem possible and desirable to bridge these differences; in a rigid hierarchy fashion is impossible. But it is of course not necessary that fashion should infect at once the whole of a community. Indeed, in most cases it probably began among a relatively small section towards the top of the social scale, and for long periods its more striking manifestations were found only among the aristocracy, particularly among those whose life was spent in courts and capitals, the common people meanwhile dressing in costume which approximated more to the traditional or 'fixed' type. But with the rise, first of a bourgeoisie and then of a democracy, fashion spreads inevitably downwards, until finally the whole community is more or less involved—as is the case with nearly all progressive countries of today. But with the attainment of complete democracy, the conditions become once again less favourable for fashion.* When every man is as good as his fellows, there are no superior social strata left to imitate, and it would seem as though the race of fashion must end, since those behind have definitely caught up those in front. Actually, however, the race tends to be prolonged by the fact that the aristocracy of fashion—an aristocracy which is essential to its existence—changes as political and social development proceed. In most countries today it is no longer entirely an aristocracy of nobility or wealth. These still furnish in many cases an indispensable foundation, but they are supplemented by further very varied elements, to which the demimonde, the stage, Bohemia, the world of sport and motoring all furnish

---

* As they are also in the relatively anarchic state of some very primitive societies. Thus it has been said that Bushmen have no fashions, while Kaffirs have: the presence of fashion among the latter being connected with their well-marked social differentiation (Mustoxidi).

contributions. In the case of men's clothes especially, it is perhaps even true that changes occur as much from below as from above, since the upper social circles have become so very wedded to the idea of a more or less stereotyped correctness, which only permits of variation within very narrow limits; thus in London it is the 'bloods' of Whitechapel rather than those of Mayfair who are reintroducing colour, the riders of the humble bicycle rather than of the aristocratic horse who have begun to popularize the 'Byron' collar.

Meanwhile there have come into play a number of fresh influences tending to maintain fashion. Among the most important of these is one of a definitely economic order: as fashion has spread downwards into all classes, large and powerful commercial interests have become involved and great industries have been built up to supply the constant stream of novel garments that fashion demands. This again supplies a stimulus at both ends of the fashionable scale. On the one hand, modern means of mass production and improved methods of transport and distribution have made it possible to supply copies of all the newest and exclusive models rapidly, in great numbers, and at relatively low prices, so that women of moderate means in small provincial towns can wear clothes of practically the same design as those that were introduced by the leaders of fashion in the great cities only a few weeks before. At the same time, increased facilities for rapid locomotion and for travel have brought people in all parts of a country, and indeed in most Europeanized parts of the world, into much closer touch with the great centres than was formerly the case, so that they have far better opportunities of learning at first hand the latest changes of fashion in these centres. Meanwhile, too, a multitude of special journals has sprung up, all aiming at the stimulation of interest in these changes. Thus the movement of fashion is hastened from below. To meet this increased speed of imitation, a constant supply of new models must be produced for the benefit of the leaders, in order that they may preserve their distinction. The whole march of fashion is thus accelerated, and the consequent more rapid turnover in clothes, though perhaps of doubtful benefit to the community as a whole, is of advantage to the clothing industries, which not unnaturally endeavour to maintain it, employing for this purpose all the arts of modern salesmanship; arts which are constantly in use for suggesting that this or that style is out of date and that some new garment of fresh design must be acquired on pain of being hopelessly behind the fashion.

This economic tendency towards rapid change of fashion is assisted by the fact that modern clothes tend on the whole to be less durable than those of many former periods. By some writers this fact has been brought into connection with the better environmental conditions of modern civilized life, and especially of urban life. The shoes, for instance, that we can wear in modern towns with their carefully paved streets would have been quite unsuitable for the street conditions that existed in most towns two hundred years ago; we do not need the thick boots that were then the only safe or convenient form of footwear in which to cross the muddy sewers with which the streets of that period abounded. Nevertheless, our thinner shoes wear out more quickly and have to be replaced the sooner; and since we have in any case to purchase new ones, we may as well gratify our vanity by getting such as are in the latest fashion. This is undoubtedly true of many present-day articles of dress, contrasting, as they do, strongly, in this matter, both with many former fashions and with clothing of the 'fixed' type. (Cf., for instance, the stuff of modern 'modish' dresses with the much more durable materials of which 'national' dresses and uniforms are made.)

The general tendency to rapid change in recent times, though it admittedly depends to some extent upon factors of an economic order, has been philoso-phized by certain authors, who have seen in it only one particular manifestation of the generally increased rapidity of social and scientific development in modern life. It is a commonplace that human evolution proceeds slowly at first and thereafter with ever greater speed. The earlier inventions, such as the use of stone and metal tools, took many thousand years to be worked out and generally applied. Motoring, aviation, cinematography, the gramophone, the wireless, have all come into general use in the course of two or three decades. Corresponding to this rapidity of change in our environment, we have become less conservative, more intolerant of the old and more enamoured of the new, a mental tendency which can best express itself in changing tastes as regards clothing (which, by its very nature, is in any case less lasting than are most other forms of applied art). The old no longer inspires us with the same sense of veneration as it did; we are inclined to be revolutionary and iconoclastic, and to look forward ever hopefully (though our hope is not always reasonable) towards the new. In so far as there is truth in this view, our changing fashions may indeed be looked upon as symbolic of our changing outlook upon many other things.

We saw in Chapter VII [not reproduced here] that, from the beginning of the nineteenth century onwards, men's clothing has been distinguished from women's by its greater uniformity and its relative lack of the decorative element. This difference we regarded as an effort to reduce competition among men. In harmony with this view is the fact that sex differences are nowhere more appar-ent than in the field of fashion. Almost everything that we have here said about fashion applies in a lesser degree to men than it does to women. Men's fashions change far less rapidly than women's (so great indeed is the difference, that a twenty or thirty years' old suit can easily be worn in public without exciting comment, whereas a woman's dress of equal age would make the wearer an object of universal curiosity and ridicule). Such changes as occur from year to year affect small details only instead of whole designs. The economic interests at work are adjusted far more to a state of relative permanence than to a con-dition of violent and continual change, and have made little attempt to exploit the advantages of rapid variation; even the materials used are, to a large extent, more durable, so that the need for replacing outworn garments is less often felt. On all these scores, as well as on the ground of its great uniformity, men's dress is less 'modish' and more 'fixed' than women's. Indeed, in many of their aspects (e.g. attire for formal occasions, for the evening, and for many sports) men's clothes occupy about the same position with regard to types as do some of the 'occupational' clothes of which we spoke in the last chapter. As in the case of these latter, there is some small individual choice in minor details (the shape of a collar or the size and colour of a tie), but none at all as regards general cut, proportions, or design.

In the case of men the elimination of competition by means of clothes has thus very greatly reduced the influence of fashion. A question of great interest is whether women are likely to follow in the same course in the near future. Several factors point in this direction, e.g. (1) the relative victory of mass production over exclusive design, a victory which is tending steadily to reduce the difference between the leaders of fashion and the ordinary rank and file, so that the social distinctiveness of dress is becoming as negligible as it is with men; (2) the ever-increasing socialization of women, a tendency which subjects them to the same influences as those which led to the reduction of clothes-competition among men (one already notices that in some fields, e.g. sport, women's costume has become almost as standardized and 'occupational' as that of men). Against this, however, there are at least two other important factors to be taken into consideration, (1) the great influence of the economic interests which stand to lose by a reduction of the role of fashion and which can be counted on to combat any tendency to such reduction by all the means within their power; (2) the fact that women's greater participation in social life and undoubted greater sense of social values has not led to any great reduction in their Narcissism. At any rate our traditions still sanction, and indeed approve, a much greater and more open manifestation of Narcissism among women than among men. Now it is true that Narcissism need not necessarily find expression in fashion (since it is only indirectly connected with competition) but, given the present conditions, it is comparatively easy for the commercial influences to exploit Narcissism in the interests of fashion. This matter of women and fashion is, indeed, one of the many fascinating sartorial problems on which it would be rash, even to the point of foolhardiness, to prophesy. We can only point out the chief influences that seem to be at work, and watch their interplay.

The How of Fashion

But if all this throws at least some rays of light upon the question of why new fashions are produced, it does not tell us how they are produced. This latter question is admittedly one that is extremely difficult to answer. It is indeed the central mystery of fashion. Individual fashions are, in their origin, almost as elusive as some other social products, such as the rumours or jokes that pass from mouth to mouth, and of which it is seldom if ever possible to trace the source. The general notion is that fashions are originated by some mysterious authority resident in Paris; and the investigations of those few economists who have deigned to turn their attention to the subject* would seem to show that there is much truth in this idea. For very many years a large proportion of women's fashions have indeed been born in Paris; partly, it would seem, in the studios and offices of a few big firms, and partly in the private workshops of a few independent designers, who may sell their ideas to these firms or occasionally to private clients.† It seems, therefore, that on the producer's side the predominant influence lies with a relatively small group of individuals. But though fashions travel quickly, they have to pass through the hands of many

* I have found the most useful to be Sombart.
† The most interesting recent description of the intimate working of the dress-making industry in Paris with which I am acquainted is that of Roubaud.

individuals before they have reached out to all corners of the earth, and here, as elsewhere (as, for instance, in the case of rumours), each individual tends to be responsible for some small change.

In any case, however, the producers of fashion as a group are not so all-powerful as the writers of the theological literature of fashion, in their more inspired utterances, would lead us to suppose. To create a fashion it is not sufficient to make a new design. For the design to become a fashion, it must be worn, and not merely at a mannequin parade. It is natural, therefore, that the wearers should have some say in the launching of new fashions. Here too, however, a predominant influence would seem to be exercised by a relatively small group of individuals, though a larger and less homogeneous group than that in the case of the producers. In the early days of modern fashion, this influence came chiefly from the members of royal and aristocratic houses. In later years, however, even before the Great War shattered the last remains of kingly power in so many parts of the world, the royal ladies had largely lost their supremacy. The Empress Eugénie is usually considered to have been the last of the long dynasty of royal fashion leaders, and their place has been taken by a much larger number of more varied individuals. Royal influence has lasted longer in the case of men's clothes, and the British royal family has still some power within this sphere. It is probable, however, that any kind of eminence, of whatsoever sort, is capable of being used to mould fashion. In his day Beau Brummell exercised an immense influence by acquiring a reputation for perfect taste. To take a recent instance, one from the field of sport, there can be little doubt that Suzanne Lenglen was very largely responsible for the complete revolution in women's tennis dress that took place after the war, a revolution that was not without important effects on women's costume generally. More recently still (in the summer of 1929) tennis has seen the battle of the bare legs. Feeling ran high, and the authorities at Wimbledon felt called upon to issue a manifesto, though couched in the discreetest terms. Everyone waited eagerly to see what Miss Helen Wills would do. She appeared in stockings, and all others did the same. But, here again, we can scarcely doubt that, had she elected to play without them, many would have copied her, and in the warm summer that followed, the advocates of uncovered calves would have scored a very decisive triumph.

Nevertheless, fashions cannot be entirely accounted for in terms of individuals, either on the side of the producers or the wearers. For a new style of dress to become fashionable, it must in some way appeal to a large number of people. The mysterious dictates of Paris are, as a matter of fact, by no means always obeyed. During the last twenty years quite a number of new designs have been launched which have seldom seen the light of day outside the fashion shops. One was the harem skirt, which was introduced under the very highest auspices but which completely failed. No greater success was met by the attempt to introduce striking asymmetrical effects, such as a *décolletage* lower at one side than the other. A more recent and interesting instance concerns the length of skirts. If we are to believe M. Jean Patou,[1] the short skirt cannot boast the illustrious parentage of *La Haute Couture*. 'Born from the brain of some Boeotian', as that master has it, its legitimacy has never been officially recognized, but this did not prevent its triumphal progress through the world.

It is obvious, therefore, that in dealing with fashion, we have to consider not only the individual creators of clothes but the group mentality of those who wear them. This group mentality offers some fascinating problems for the social psychologist. It has often been held that successive fashions express in some way the 'spirit of the age'; but when it comes to describing in detail how this spirit manifests itself in fashion, the explanations offered are often vague and disappointing. Indeed, it would probably require a much more thorough study (with the collaboration of the historian and the sociologist) before we could explain the full social significance of the detailed changes of fashion from one year to another. Nevertheless, the significance of certain main changes over long periods seems fairly clear. Let us consider very briefly a few epochs in modern history.

If we glance, in the first place, at the costumes of the Renaissance, we seem to find the great release of human energy which characterized that period mirrored, as it were, in its fashions. In men's clothing emphasis was given to strength and muscular development by closely fitting garments that exhibited all the play of the muscles. The coverings of legs and arms were, indeed, so tight that they had to be slashed at the joints to permit of freedom of movement; but these slashes were made the means of elaborate ornamentation with the help of multi-coloured cloths and ribbons. The age indulged in an orgy of colour, which was not afraid of crudeness. There was, indeed, no false modesty about that period; the cod-piece worn by men for no less than fifty years is perhaps the most audacious piece of clothing that has ever been invented, while the women followed suit by endeavouring to produce the appearance of being always pregnant.

Compared with this crude but intensely vital exuberance, the eighteenth century was a period of artificiality and refinement, in which the glittering ceremoniousness of court life held undisputed sway. Vivid colours were banned in favour of pale tints and powder. In its somewhat exotic magnificence costume bore but little resemblance to the actual human form.

At the close of the eighteenth century and the beginning of the nineteenth, we see again a striking change. All artificiality was swept away; the ideal now was to follow Nature. The Empire costumes of the period are strikingly simple, and make no serious attempt to represent the human body as other than it is. Here, as at other periods, democracy had no use for the gorgeous and complicated trappings which had flourished in a preceding age of absolutism and of highly accentuated class distinctions.

As the nineteenth century wore on, the ideas of class superiority and fastidious refinement once again became attractive and found its expression in a relative artificiality and exuberance of clothing (though this time the movement was confined to women). Finally, a return to greater frankness and sincerity, combined with a great upward movement of democracy in recent years, has brought us back to another period of simplicity and exiguousness in costume.

The real existence of some influence of the *Zeitgeist* upon costume is corroborated if we compare costume with architecture and the internal decoration of houses. As we pointed out in an earlier chapter, there is a certain parallelism, both of function and of psychological significance, between our clothing and our houses, so that we should expect that the psychological influences that guide our fashions in dress would also affect our styles of building and of decoration. Here again we can only draw attention to the general existence of such a parallelism and illustrate it by a few examples.

To deal first with interior decoration: the desire for classical simplicity which showed itself in dress at the beginning of the nineteenth century is mirrored in the severe and classical style of the furniture and equipment of that period—a style which differed strikingly from the more ornate treatment of the classic that was in vogue during the previous century. The return to a greatly increased elaboration of costume in the mid-Victorian period was accompanied by what now seems to us the over-detailed ornamentation of the Victorian drawing-room, whereas our modern preference for simplicity of dress has been followed once again by a taste for relatively simple interiors.

The case of architecture is complicated by the fact that buildings are by their nature much more permanent than dress, so that any given generation has for the most part to live among the architectural products of its fathers or fore-fathers. Nevertheless, there are some striking correspondences here also. We can scarcely fail to see in the long lines of Gothic a parallel to the elongated shapes of medieval dress. The fussiness of the Rococo style in architecture is correlated with the detailed elaboration of dress of the same period. The early nineteenth century, so intensely classical in the spirit of its costumes, be-queathed us many buildings also in the classic style. The Victorian era, it is true, failed to produce or reproduce any distinctive style of architecture, so it is difficult to trace the correspondence here (unless we recognize as such the equal tastelessness—as it now seems to us—of its buildings and its fashions).* On the other hand, we may perhaps be justified in seeing a parallel between the plain, wide-windowed, open style of post-war factory or office building and the relatively simple style of modern dress, which has no ornamental compli-cations and seeks to hide no secrets.†

After this excursion into group psychology as manifested in the spirit of the age, let us turn once more, in conclusion, to the problem of the origin of individual fashions. We can perhaps now see a little more clearly, at least in general terms, how it is that the influence of the leaders and initiators is limited. We can at least surmise with some show of plausibility that the harem skirt (which doubtless hoped to satisfy the long manifested hankering after a discreet and unobtrusive bifurcated garment) failed because of its associations with a social system that was definitely antagonistic to the aspirations of women at a

* May it perhaps be that the aesthetic failure, both of Ruskin's Gothic revival and of the subsequent pseudo-Elizabethan style of domestic architecture, was partly because both were utterly foreign to the spirit of the age—a fact that shows itself in the absence of any corre-sponding sartorial fashions?

† Several writers, including among quite recent ones Gerald Heard, have drawn attention to interesting parallels between individual garments and parts of buildings, e.g. between roofs, spires, and domes and certain corresponding forms of head-dress, between the long factory chimneys of the industrial era and the long tubular trousers of the same period. Entering into greater detail, Mr Heard reminds us that, as Gothic windows and arches became gradually less pointed until they reached the rather extreme flatness of the Tudor period, the pointed effects in clothes characteristic of later medievalism gradually gave place to an in-creased breadth. The high-pointed head dress was replaced by a low, broad one, and pointed toes by an extremely broad-toed shoe, the Sableton. In fact the whole style of clothing tended to accentuate the breadth of the body.

time when they were fighting for a vote. Were European women to identify themselves with their relatively unemancipated Turkish sisters, just at a period when these latter were beginning to look westwards in envious admiration of the liberty already won in that direction? We can surmise too that such an apparent anomaly as the hobble skirt achieved its temporary vogue by appealing to the ideal of slimness—an ideal that was itself associated with the growing importance of youth and the corresponding growth of a youthful ideal. We can see too (and with much greater clarity) why it was that the war, with its sudden introduction of the ideal of work and activity, swept away the hobble skirt, which so seriously hampered movement. It is easy to understand also that the short skirt was something in the nature of a triumphant gesture of freedom on the part of women (who had achieved an unprecedented self-confidence and an unexampled admiration as workers during the war); and that, at the same time, it represented the final apotheosis of the youthful ideal, now that youth itself had definitely acquired its freedom and come into its heritage; and how that, this being so, Paris was powerless to prevent its progress. It might be, as M. Patou said, 'la négation même de toute véritable élégance', but it has not been elegance, but youth, freedom, and activity that have been the dominant ideals of these post-war years.

New fashions, if they are to be successful, must be in accordance with certain ideals current at the time that they are launched. Women must see in the new fashion a symbol of an ideal that is before them—though of course, as with other symbols, there need be no conscious realization of its true significance. This does not mean that the personality of the launcher is unimportant. We have already shown good reason to think otherwise. It means, however, that the influence of the initiating personality is efficient only so long as the persons to be influenced can see in what is proposed, so to speak, the incarnation of their own ideals. In the language of psycho-analysis, they must project their own super-ego on to the person who exercises the suggestive influence.[2] The use of suggestion, in the launching of a fashion, as in any other case, depends partly upon the intrinsic prestige of the suggester and partly upon the effective value of what he suggests. Beau Brummell was such an important figure in the world of fashion because he knew better than any other how to create the ideal of unobtrusive elegance and perfect taste—the most satisfactory form of sartorial exhibitionism that was still permitted to men since the right to the more blatant displays of earlier periods had been lost. Miss Wills had far more influence on tennis costume than other women, for another reason—her special ability within the field of tennis itself. She might have created a triumphant bare-legged mode, where others would have failed. But there are obvious limits to

* Of course there is also such a thing as negative prestige. A fashion may be killed in its infancy by being adopted by persons whom it is considered undesirable to imitate. The classical instance of this was the sudden disappearance of 'bloomers' in 1851, when a London brewery dressed all their barmaids in nether garments of this type. Another (and in a sense more literal) method of killing fashions was by associating them with public executions—in the persons either of the executed or the executioner. In Queen Anne's reign there was considerable pother about women appearing in the street in their nightgowns. But this fashion speedily came to an end when a woman was executed in a garment of this description. In the terminology of the behaviourist, the habit was 'deconditioned' by being thus brought into association with an event of such a painful character.

her power; she could not have introduced such a mode twenty years earlier, however well she played. The fashions to be introduced must not be too remote from the sentiments and aspirations of the time. But there is a direct relationship between the prestige of the launcher of fashions and the degree of difference that he can bridge in his attempted innovation. The greater the innovation (either in a progressive or a retrograde direction) the greater the personal prestige that is necessary to introduce it. The Prince of Wales succeeded in brightening men's evening attire by the introduction of white waistcoats. He did not succeed in creating a new fashion when he wore a pullover with a smoking-jacket. Popular as he is, the incongruous associations of the two garments caused too big a shock for the new combination to be adopted. Very big changes (and this was a startling change in view of the intense conservatism of men's dress) can only be accepted if at the same time there is a corresponding change in the ideal. The ideal of men's clothing has become so 'fixed' that to produce an innovation of this magnitude is an undertaking of the greatest difficulty.

At the present moment (early in 1930) two bold attempts at the modification of existing ideals are being made; one (relating to men) of an open nature; the other (relating to women) more insidious. The Men's Dress Reform Party in England is trying definitely to induce a relatively big and sudden change by the inculcation of fresh ideals. On the other hand, the *Haute Couture* has embarked on a more subtle campaign to abolish the ideals of youthfulness, activity, and naturalness that have distinguished women's fashions in recent years. Paradoxically enough, men are being urged to imitate certain aspects of women's dress (i.e. its lightness, simplicity and freedom) at the same time that women are being induced to abandon these aspects. The situation is not without a certain piquant interest for the psychological student of dress, and we shall have more to say with regard to both movements before we take leave of the reader.

References

1. Interview in *La Liberté* (12 Dec. 1929).
2. Cf. E. Jones, 'The Nature of Auto-Suggestion', *International Journal of Psycho-Analysis* (1923), vol. 4, p. 293.

Chapter 14

FASHION LEADERS*
by Elihu Katz and Paul Lazarsfeld

This extract from their classic book on Personal Influence looks particularly at process of influence in fashion adoption. Gregariousness emerges as significantly related with fashion 'exporting' or leadership.

More than in marketing, fashion is an arena of constant change. In fact, the essence of being 'in fashion' is the making of right changes at the right time. About two-thirds of the women in our sample told us they had recently made some fashion change—in clothing, or cosmetics, or the like, and most of them said that personal influences had in some way entered into the making of their decisions. Here as before, our problem is to locate the opinion leaders—the leaders of change—in this arena.†

Where are the fashion leaders concentrated? Do they emerge throughout the life-cycle or do they congregate in a particular life-cycle position? Are they high up on the status ladder or are they represented equally on every status level? Are they more gregarious than the non-leaders or is gregariousness not a major factor here? Answering these questions, we shall learn not only about some of the distinguishing characteristics of the fashion leader, but also something about participation in the fashion market as well.

The Girls: Life-Cycle Position and Fashion Leadership

Let us begin here with life-cycle position—the factor that proved most discriminating in the case of the marketing leader. The general accent on youth and youthfulness among men and women in America leads us to expect that fashion leadership might be more typical of girls than of matrons. These young women are single; many of them are on the market for dates and marriage, and fashion is of obvious advantage in these markets. But, even if fashion is a concern to most women, it is more likely to have a greater sway among the girls than among the mothers of children since girls may well have fewer interests competing for their time, energy and finances. According to this view, marriage, as the realization of one goal of fashion participation, would be

---

* From *Personal Influence* (The Macmillan Co., Free Press, 1955).

† Leaders are here defined as (a) those women who indicated on both interviews that they had recently been asked their advice on some matter—in this case, a matter relative to clothes, cosmetics, etc., and (b) those who said, on only one interview, that their advice had not been asked, but who considered themselves 'more likely' than others to be consulted for fashion advice.

associated with a decrease in fashion activities and leadership; motherhood, as a competing interest and activity, would also be accompanied by a further decrease in such fashion leadership; and matronhood, which for most women involves a withdrawal from youth-oriented fashion competitiveness, should be associated with least fashion advice giving. And, in fact, the life-cycle typology which represents these major stages is strongly related to fashion leadership. Here are the figures:

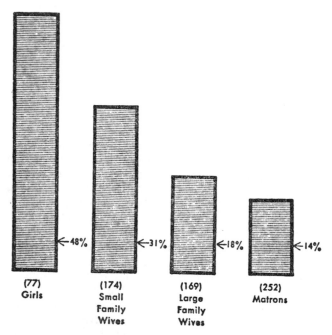

FIG. 1. Fashion leadership declines with each step in the life-cycle.

Each successive life-cycle position is associated with a declining leadership rate: among the girls, almost five out of ten, but among the matrons, only one in ten, is a fashion opinion leader. This direct relationship between fashion leadership and the life cycle emphasizes the cumulative effects of age, marriage, and motherhood on a woman's chances for leadership in this area.

In the case of marketing, we had no measure of interest or involvement. Perhaps it is even reasonable to make the assumption that there is a near universality of involvement—at least among married women—in the daily problems of selecting food for the family table. In any event, we did not emphasize the possibility that those life-cycle types which produced fewer leaders were not concerned with or interested in marketing. In the arena of fashions, however, we cannot assume universality of interest or involvement. Intuitively, one feels that there must be sharp variations not only in fashion leadership but also in advice-seeking, and in fashion interest generally, among the life-cycle types.

Does Interest Determine Leadership?

In our interviews, we asked three questions which may serve as an index of fashion interest. We asked (1) Do you feel it is very important, moderately important, or not important at all to be in style?; (2) Have you recently changed anything about your hairdo, type of clothes, cosmetics, make-up or any other change to something more fashionable?; and (3) How many new dresses have you bought or made since the beginning of last summer? (twelve months earlier). Answers to these three questions are indicative, we think, of a woman's attitude toward the importance of being in fashion. What is more, these questions are intentionally phrased in such a way that the income factor is not of appreciable significance. A change to a new perfume costing fifty cents or to a shorter skirt priced at a few dollars is just as much a fashion change as the shift to a $50 perfume or to an expensive, new Paris creation. Here is the way replies to the three questions are distributed:

TABLE 1 *Replies to Three Questions Indicating Interest in Fashion*

(1) Important to be in style?	
Very important	37%
Moderately important	55%
Not important	8%
(2) Made a recent Fashion change?	
Yes	56%
No	44%
(3) How many new dresses bought or made?	
7 or more	29%
5–6	27%
3–4	25%
1–2	13%
None	6%
Totals (=100%)	(711)

We combined answers to these three questions into a scale simply by ranking women according to whether their answers, in each case, indicated 'high' or 'low' fashion interest and then by counting the total number of 'high' answers.* A woman who ranked 'high' on two or three of the questions was considered to have an overall 'high interest' in fashion. Given this measure of interest,

---

* On the first question (importance of being in style), women who answered 'very important' were ranked 'high'; an affirmative answer to the second question (recent change) ranked 'high'; and a report of 5 or more new dresses on the third question ranked 'high'. An overall rank of two or more 'high' answers was considered 'high interest', as follows:

		Cases
3	'high interest'	18%
2		33%
1		30%
0		19%
	Total (=100%)	(711)

now we can ask whether or not a woman's life-cycle position is associated with the degree of her expressed interest in fashion.

TABLE 2 *Interest in Fashion Declines With the Life-Cycle*

Life-Cycle Type	High Interest	Total (=100%)
Girls	80%	(77)
Small Family Wives	59%	(173)
Large Family Wives	56%	(169)
Matrons	34%	(252)

Clearly, fashion interest is highly correlated with the life-cycle. It is at its peak among young, single women (the girls); it decreases by one-third among married women under 45 regardless of the size of their families; and it falls sharply among married women over 45 (the matrons). We can say that high fashion interest is a majority characteristic among women under 45 and a minority characteristic of women 45 and over.

This distribution of fashion interest along the life-cycle generally parallels the distribution of fashion leadership. It directs us to ask whether leadership may not simply be a by-product of interest—that is, perhaps the more interested a woman is in fashions, the more likely she is to be a fashion leader. That there is a strong relationship between fashion interest and leadership is evident in Table 3.

TABLE 3 *Interested Women Are More Likely To Be Fashion Leaders*

Interest Scores	Fashion leaders	Total (=100%)
3 (high)	49%	(129)
2	28%	(235)
1	13%	(212)
0 (low)	4%	(135)

Proportionately, there are twelve times as many fashion leaders among the highly interested women as there are among women who are completely uninterested in fashion. At the upper extreme of interest, close to half of the respondents are opinion leaders in fashion matters; at the lower extreme only 4 per cent are fashion leaders.

This strong relationship between interest and leadership forces us to reopen the question of the relationship between fashion leadership and the life-cycle. We must ask, in other words, whether the varying concentrations of leadership which we observed above (Figure 1) is something more than simply a reflection of the different concentrations of interest among the different types of women. Thus, it may be that a woman's chances for fashion leadership are determined exclusively by the degree of her fashion interest and that life-cycle type enters the picture only by virtue of the differing amounts of interest characteristic of the several different life-cycle positions. If this is the case, then a comparison of women of differing life-cycle types who have an equivalent amount of interest should reveal an equal incidence of opinion leadership; thus, matrons, for example, should emerge as fashion leaders as often as girls, provided only that they express an equal amount of fashion interest.

TABLE 4 *Fashion Leadership Still Varies With the Life Cycle Even When Interest in Fashion is Controlled*

| | | Fashion Leaders | | |
| | | Small Family | Large Family | |
Interest*	Girls	Wives	Wives	Matrons
High	55% (62)	46% (102)	20% (95)	27% (84)
Low	20% (15)	10% (71)	16% (75)	7% (168)

* High interest consists of 2 or 3 'high' replies; low interest is 1 or 0 'high' replies. See footnote page 233.

Table 4 does not bear out our conjecture at all. That is, life-cycle variations in leadership do not disappear by any means when women of differing life-cycle positions, but equally high interest, are compared.*

Somehow, then, we must account for why a girl with high fashion interest is so much more likely to be asked her advice than a matron with equivalently high interest. In other words, we must ask what there is about being a single, unmarried woman with a high interest in fashion that provides so much more opportunity for fashion leadership than that provided a married woman over 45 whose interest in fashion is just as great. Or, again, why are small family wives with high fashion interest so much more likely to be fashion leaders than equally interested large family wives?

The Flow of Influence: Two Approaches

The clue to the answer, we think comes with remembering that any influence exchange, any act of advice-giving, takes two people. Thus, a matron who is highly interested in fashions may be eager and 'ready' to give advice, but she must have somebody to give it to. Now, who is that going to be? Other matrons? Very few of them, we saw, are interested in fashions. Younger women? Their fashion problems are likely to be quite different than hers. Here, then, we have a situation where an individual's predisposition to lead in a given realm is not 'activated' because there are no followers available to her.

Not so with the girls, of course. Among the girls, the traffic in fashion advice must be very heavy. Judging from the extensive interest in this realm that almost all the girls profess, we have reason to believe that the 'demand' for fashion leadership among groups of girls is very lively. Thus, the chances that a girl with high interest will be consulted by another girl seems particularly

* The irregular results on the low interest level together with the relatively small differences suggest the hypothesis that position in the life-cycle cannot appreciably affect a woman's leadership chances if she herself is *not personally interested*. It appears, in other words, that the effect of life-cycle position as a predisposing factor for leadership is maximized on the level of high fashion interest and almost, but not quite, obliterated on the low interest level.

great. This presumes, of course, that girls are leaders and followers for each other. But even if we assume that fashion advice-giving often crosses life-cycle lines, there is still considerably more reason to believe that it is the old who come for advice to the younger rather than vice versa. This should be the case, first of all, because the American fashion market is so manifestly geared to youth; thus, the girls are surely the *avant garde* of fashion change. And there is a second reason, too, which is worth considering: Imagine a woman looking for some fashion advice and suppose that she does not quite know whom to ask. Now, although she does not personally know a fashion consultant, she may very well know (as we do from Table 2) that almost 8 out of every 10 girls are highly interested in fashions and that the same is true for only one-half of the wives and one-third of the matrons. Where would she go? Clearly, to the girls. Presuming that some such knowledge about the concentration of fashion interest is widespread in the community, it stands to reason that an interested woman—and hence, someone at least theoretically capable of giving advice—can be located much more readily among the girls than among older women. The maxim, of course, is to look where you know there's a concentration of what you're looking for.

Among the large and the small family wives, the story is not so neat. Both types of women have almost equal interest in fashion but while the small family wives have almost as many leaders as the highly interested girls, the large family wives have as few as the uninterested matrons. The explanation in this case seems also to have something to do with the accessibility of advice-seekers. While we have no evidence on this point, our guess is that small family wives may have more rapidly changing fashion trends to keep up with, and at the same time, fewer everyday problems of other sorts to engage their attention. That there is such a large concentration of marketing leaders among the large family wives is some evidence for this point, but, of course, our whole interpretation must be put to the test of future research.

In any event, as we have been noting throughout our explanation, we are making the assumption—and only the 'follow-up' data will permit us to test it—that fashion influencing tends to take place most of all among women of similar life-cycle position. Thus, when we explained that the concentration of high fashion interest among the girls generates many advice-seekers which, in turn, generates many advice-givers, we made it clear that we were assuming that girls tend to influence other girls. In other words, fashion give-and-take tends to be carried on, we think, primarily among life-cycle peers.

All this, of course, presumes that these life-cycle categories we have created—girls, matrons, etc.—are, in a sense, real-life 'groups' in that girls really associate with other girls, matrons with matrons, etc. If we proceed with this presumption that this, in fact, is the case, we can suggest an approach to tracing the flow of influence which we have not considered so far. Let us examine this new approach before turning again to the 'follow-up' data with which we have already become familiar—the limitations of which we have also noted—in the previous chapter.

The 'Export' Index. The new approach is readily explained. It proposes that the rate of opinion leadership in any group will be determined by two social forces. The first force is the level of interest—the 'saliency'—of a given topic for the members of the group. High 'saliency' would lead, of course, to much intra-group advice-seeking and leadership with reference to that particular topic. The second force is the 'attractiveness' of the group as an advice-giving source for members of other groups. Thus, the proportion of opinion leaders in a group may be said to have two components reflecting (1) the degree of interchange on a given topic carried on by members of the group among themselves and (2) the extent of their interaction with members of other groups with reference to this area.

Now what we want to know is how much of the opinion leadership which emerges in a given group serves members of the same group and how much of it is 'exported' to other groups. This is the problem which we seek to answer directly with our follow-up data and, more indirectly, with the data at hand. For if the rate of opinion leadership in a group is the resultant of 'saliency' plus 'attractiveness', since we have measures for both leadership rate and 'saliency' we ought to be able to deduce 'attractiveness'—the extent to which others come calling on a given group for advice.

Consider the fashion realm. The measure of fashion interest with which we have been dealing may be taken as a measure of the 'saliency' of fashions for any group. What we can do, then, is to examine the extent to which the opinion leader rate for each group parallels or deviates from the 'saliency' rate and we will take the extent of this variation as a measure of the group's 'attractiveness'. For example, if in a given group the proportion of women who are fashion leaders compared with women who are highly interested exceeds the average value of this proportion for our total population, we may infer that the leaders of this group satisfy not only their own group's leadership needs but are attractive as sources of influence to members of other groups as well. In other words, we would conclude that the 'excess' of leadership (over that which a given measure of 'saliency' would 'require') is exported'.

To carry out this idea, we must first compute a ratio of fashion leadership to fashion interest for the sample as a whole. Altogether, 155 of 672 respondents concerning whom we have sufficient information are fashion leaders, and 345 of the 672 are highly interested. The ratio 155:345 is 0·45, meaning that for every two highly interested women, taking the sample as a whole, there is slightly less than one fashion leader. Now, if we divide our sample once again into groups, we shall expect to find that some groups maintain this 'average' ratio—that is, they will have about two highly interested women for every one fashion leader—while other groups exceed the average or fall behind it. Where a group maintains the 'average' ratio, we shall infer that its leader supply is just about equal to its internal demand for leadership based on the 'saliency' of the topic for the group. Where a group exceeds the 'average' ratio—that is, where the leadership rate is relatively larger than the rate of interest—we shall infer that this group not only supplies its own leadership needs, but is approached by other groups for leadership as well. Where the leadership rate falls behind the interest rate, we shall infer that the group has not enough leadership even for itself and presumably, therefore, turns to others.

To make things easy, we can compute an index where the 'average' ratio—

0·45 in this case—is equal to 'one'. Then, for each group, we can compute the ratio of leaders to highly interested people, and, translating the resultant ratio into our index, we shall find that some groups exceed 'one', and some groups fall behind. Let us try this for the four life-cycle groups in the realm of fashion:

TABLE 5 *Fashion Leadership is 'Exported' by the Girls*

	Ratio of Fashion Leadership to Fashion 'Saliency' (The 'average' ratio for the entire sample = 1·00)
Girls	1·33
Small Family Wives	1·18
Large Family Wives	0·71
Matrons	0·93

The girls exceed the 'average' ratio most of all; the large family wives fall far behind; while the small family wives and the matrons hover near the 'average'. In accordance with the interpretation we have been suggesting, these results would seem to mean that the small family wives and the matrons have just enough leadership in their own ranks to satisfy the amount of interest present in their groups. The large family wives, for their part, seem for some reason to have less than the quota of leaders their interest would appear to require.* The girls, on the other hand, have an overabundance of leaders, from which we propose to infer that the girls satisfy not only their own demand for fashion advice but also provide leadership for others. The girls, in other words, meet the demand for fashion advice in their own internal market and 'export' advice as well.

The Follow-Up Story. Now that we have examined this new way of looking at things, let us return to the more familiar follow-up data to seek further corroboration for our story. If our appraisal of the situation is correct we should find that (1) fashion influencing tends to take place most of all among life-cycle peers, and (2) in those fashion exchanges that do take place between women of different ages, that the younger women are more often influentials than influencees. Let us, therefore, look at these flow-of-influence data remembering that they deal not with life-cycle as such but with age, and that they cannot, for reasons already mentioned, be treated as more than 'suggestive'.

Of the follow-up interviews that were completed, 33 were with fashion leaders who were named by some member of their own families, and 125 were with non-family influentials. Let us consider the handful of intra-family influence incidents first:

Within the family—if we can make any statement at all from the few cases in Table 6—less than half of all influential-influencee pairs are of the same age.

* This suggests that in the realm of fashions the large family wives may be a less self-contained 'group' than the others.

TABLE 6 *The Flow of Fashion Influence Among Age Groups Within the Family*

| Her Fashion Leader's Age is | Influencee's Age is | | | |
	15–24	25–44	45+	Totals
15–24	4	4	6	14
25–44	5	9	—	14
45+	2	1	2	5
Totals	11	14	8	33

(We shall see, below, that this figure is larger for extra-family influences.) And when family members of different ages do exchange influence, the influence tends to flow somewhat more from young to old than from old to young; this is as we expected. This is particularly clear for the women over 45 whom we may assume have grown children; three-fourths of these (6 of 8 cases) are influenced by women aged 15–24.

TABLE 7 *The Flow of Fashion Influence Among Age Groups Outside the Family*

| Her Fashion Leader's Age is | Influencee's Age is | | | |
	15–24	25–44	45+	Totals
15–24	27	12	2	41
25–44	13	32	9	54
45+	2	14	14	30
Totals	42	58	25	125

But Table 7—reporting on the flow of influence outside the household—does not corroborate our expectations. It is true that we find greater age homogeneity here between influential and influencee—about six of every ten influence pairs are age peers—but among the women who did cross age lines in quest of fashion advice, the direction of influence was no more from young to old than it was from old to young. Thus, while we may say that age peers are the predominant source of influence, we do not find confirmation for our expectation that younger people would be more likely to be influential for their elders than vice versa.

It is not immediately clear why these follow-up data do not support the 'export' data of Table 5. Except for the slight intra-family trend reported in Table 6, then, we are left with the suggestion of the 'export' data that fashion influence travels from young to old but with no direct confirmation from the interviews with influential-influencee pairs themselves.

It is interesting, finally, to observe what a small part men play in everyday fashion advice-giving. Of the many hundreds of women who credited some recent fashion decision they had made at least partly to the advice of some other individual, only 13 named men, and of these, 11 were husbands. Men are spectators rather than direct participants in the changing world of fashions;

such influence as they do have is the indirect and passive influence of members of the audience. They do not often make so bold as to give direct advice.

Gregariousness and Fashion Leadership

Along with the life-cycle, a second factor that proved discriminating in the case of marketing leadership was the gregariousness index. This relationship also holds true for opinion leadership in the arena of fashion:

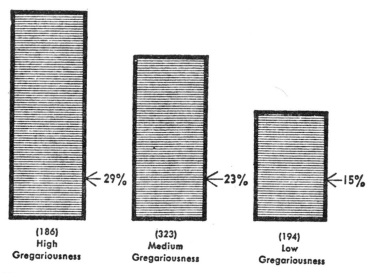

FIG. 2. Fashion leadership increases with increasing gregariousness.

The rate of fashion leadership is twice as great among the highly gregarious as among those who score low on gregariousness. The woman with many social contacts is most likely to be a fashion leader, if only because of her greater opportunities to lead. But in the field of fashion there is another reason why more highly gregarious women should more frequently emerge as fashion leaders. The reason is that gregariousness itself is not merely an index of the volume of contacts a woman has, but an indication, also, of the character of her interests. The highly gregarious woman, we think, is likely to be sensitive to the impression she makes on others. She is concerned with interaction and integration among varying groups and individuals, and one of the ways she expresses this is by being in style. This would mean that, compared to the socially isolate, gregarious women have a greater opportunity to be asked for fashion advice not only because they are more accessible to advice-seekers, but also because they are under a kind of pressure to be more concerned with and active in the fashion market. If this is the case in fact, we should expect it to be reflected on our fashion-interest index.

Table 8 bears out our contention to some extent only; surprisingly, the relationship is by no means as strong as we had anticipated. Fashion interest is stimulated by gregarious activity, we may conclude—but not very much.

TABLE 8 *Gregarious Women are Somewhat More Interested in Fashion*

Gregariousness Score	High Interest	Total (=100%)
High	56%	(178)
Medium	54%	(323)
Low	43%	(174)

Apparently, apart from her personal involvement in fashion, the social demand made on the highly gregarious woman to be *au courant* makes for the increased likelihood of her being a fashion influential. In other words, even if she is not very interested, the gregarious woman, by virtue of the gregariousness is somewhat more likely to be asked for fashion advice.*

Again, then, we see that the psychological factor of high personal interest does not by itself create opinion leadership. Leadership involves also the social context in which the woman with high interest moves. In connection with the life-cycle, it will be recalled, we found that highly interested girls were quite likely to become fashion leaders, but that equally interested matrons were not; in the present instance, where interest is almost equally divided among the three gregariousness levels, we find that the highly gregarious woman is quite likely to become a fashion leader while the ungregarious woman is not. Thus, as we suggested in connection with the earlier observation, there would seem to be a contextual factor operative here, too: It is not enough for a woman to be highly interested; to be a leader she must have contact with other people who (1) are seeking leadership and (2) who recognize her qualities as appropriate for the kind of leadership desired. It is important, so to speak, to be in the right context at the right time.

That gregarious women provide influence for others more often than they accept influence in return can be surmised from the measure of 'export' leadership which was introduced earlier in this chapter. Here, again, we can take the 'average' ratio of leadership-to-interest for the sample as a whole, make it equal to 'one', and then see how each of the three 'groups' of differing gregariousness compares with the 'average'.†

TABLE 9 *Fashion Leadership is 'Exported' by the Highly Gregarious*

	Ratio of Fashion Leadership to Fashion 'Saliency' (The 'average' ratio for the entire sample = 1·00)
High Gregariousness	1·24
Medium Gregariousness	1·02
Low Gregariousness	0·81

* Even among women with low fashion interest, 17 per cent of the highly gregarious, but only 5 per cent of the ungregarious, are opinion leaders.

† The ratio for the sample as a whole is 0·42. The very slight difference from the 0·45 ratio reported for the sample as a whole in the case of life-cycle results from the slight variation in total number of cases for whom we have information in the two instances.

The women with low gregariousness have less than enough leadership to satisfy the degree of interest in fashion which prevails in their midst while the middle group corresponds almost exactly to the 'average' in its leadership-interest ratio. Only the women with high gregariousness have an 'excess' of leadership which, according to our interpretation, means that this group is 'attractive' for other groups in this realm of fashion and thus, in addition to satisfying its own internal demand for fashion give-and-take, 'exports' some advice as well.

Now that we have seen the relevance of life-cycle position and of gregariousness for fashion leadership, it might be interesting to consider the combined effects of these two factors on a woman's chances for leadership. What difference does it make for fashion leadership if, for example, a girl is low in gregariousness and a matron is high? Our expectation is that gregariousness will be most important as a stimulus to fashion leadership for women whose life-cycle types provide least opportunity, or inclination, for fashion participation and leadership, that is, for the large family wives and for the matrons. These are the women whose household-anchored life cycle positions impose objective restrictions on the extent and intensity of their participation in the fashion-market—restrictions of time, energy and money and restrictions on 'social location' relative to others who are interested. When such a woman is highly gregarious, however—that is, if her extra-household interests are sufficiently strong and the opportunity to pursue them sufficiently great—we expect that she, unlike her less gregarious life-cycle peers, will be active in the fashion market and will have a better chance, too, for opinion leadership.

By the same token, gregariousness scores are not very likely, we would expect, to make very much difference in the chances that a girl has for fashion leadership. For while gregariousness may be a major stimulus to the fashion activity of family-anchored and older women, the universal urge among girls toward fashion participation may perhaps be intensified by increased gregariousness but certainly not completely dependent on it. Small family wives, too, compared with the large family wives, are likely to be more active in fashions and more inclined toward leadership even when they are not highly gregarious. In other words, we are suggesting that among the girls, whose natural inclination to fashions is greatest, being a fashion leader should depend least of all on being highly gregarious, while for each subsequent life cycle type, this condition for fashion leadership should become increasingly important.

To test this hypothesis we have only to sub-classify women in each of the four life-cycle types, according to their gregariousness—this gives us twelve groups of women—and then see how fashion leadership varies among them.

In the following table, those groups of women who have a better than average chance* to be fashion leaders are identified by an 'x'. The pattern of these crosses indicates clearly that with the progression of the life cycle, a high degree of gregariousness becomes a more important condition for a woman's chances for leadership in fashion.

All girls, whatever their gregariousness, small family wives only if they are

* As was explained earlier, we mean by 'a better than average' chance for leadership that the ratio of leaders to non-leaders in a given group exceeds the ratio of leaders to non-leaders in the sample as a whole.

TABLE 10 *Better-Than-Average Chances for Fashion Leadership According to Life Cycle Type and Gregariousness*

| | | Life Cycle Type | | |
| | | Small Family | Large Family | |
Gregariousness Score	Girls	Wives	Wives	Matrons
High	×	×	×	×
Medium	×	×		
Low	×			

at least moderately gregarious, and large family wives and matrons only if they are highly gregarious, have a better than average chance to be leaders in fashion. For older and/or family-anchored women, then, a high degree of gregariousness is a necessary condition for a good chance at fashion leadership. The quantity and quality of social contact expressed in a high degree of gregariousness seems to act as the equivalent of youth and its accompanying freedom from family responsibilities, in stimulating participation in fashion and fashion leadership.

Social Status and Fashion Leadership

So far, then, we have seen that the two factors which are paramount in pointing to concentrations of marketing leaders—life-cycle and gregariousness—are also proving to be major keys for an understanding of fashion leadership, despite the considerable differences between the two arenas. Now, we shall turn to the third factor—that of social status—to see whether it plays any role in determining who shall be the fashion leaders.

When most people speak of fashion leaders, they mean the glamorous women who first display the expensive fashions. However true this may be, we are interested in another type of fashion leader: the woman who is influential face to face. In such relations, we may be sure, the fashion leader is not necessarily the most glamorous woman, but rather a woman known personally to the advice-seeker, a woman to whom she can feel free to turn for advice. Thus, the two women, the adviser and the one advised, are not likely to be separated from each other by a wide gap in their social standing. They are, rather, more likely to move in generally similar social circles. Moreover, we suggested earlier, that in looking for advice, women are likely to turn to those who face problems like their own and this fact would reinforce the likelihood that the advice-seeker would seek out fashion leaders within her own status level. Following this view, we should find that fashion leaders exist on all social strata, and that influence rarely crosses status lines.

Even so, one can argue that there still remains some reason to believe that status-linked factors do produce differences in the incidence of fashion leadership. Women on the low- or middle-status levels may not emulate café society directly, but they may express their desire for social mobility by consulting the taste of women just a little above them in status but still within their own social orbit or its outskirts. If this is the case, and if our data are sensitive enough on this point, we should find that fashion leadership is not equally distributed but that the higher status levels have the greater proportions.

Furthermore, even if leadership does not tend to cross status lines, it may be that a greater concern with fashion, and a greater participation in fashionable activities is characteristic of the higher statuses. Similarly, there may be differential value attached to being in style on the several status levels. Should any or all of these be the case, we will find increasing proportions of fashion leaders on each succeeding status level. If, however, fashion interest is relatively evenly distributed among the status levels, and if women predominantly tend to look to others like themselves for advice, we shall find equal proportions of fashion leaders on each status level. Figure 3 should have an answer for us:

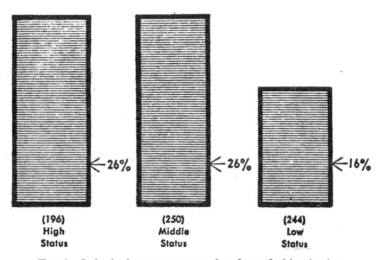

FIG. 3. Only the low status group has fewer fashion leaders.

According to our data, there are as many fashion leaders on the middle status level as on the high, but somewhat fewer on the low status level; the difference between the lowest level and the two higher levels is 10 per cent. In other words, the differences in fashion leadership among the status levels are not very great, and their peculiar distribution leaves us in doubt about the proper interpretation to invoke. If from the difference between the low and middle status we decide there is an increase in the rate of leadership with an increase in status, we are forced to pose the question: Why is there no comparable difference between the middle and the high levels? But even this question demands interpretation: We may ask either why there are so few leaders on the high level—where we most expect them—or, alternatively, why there are so many on the middle level. Let us look into this matter more closely. Perhaps we can find our clue, again, by examining the distribution of interest in fashion on these three levels.

Each higher status level contains a somewhat greater proportion of women interested in fashion. This finding suggests to us that our attention should be directed to the high status group rather than the middle one. In other words, the interesting problem does not seem to be why there are so many middle

TABLE 11 *Interest in Fashion Increases With Each Step Up the Status Ladder*

Social Status Level	Per cent with High Interest	Total (=100%)
High	61%	(191)
Middle	53%	(253)
Low	42%	(237)

status fashion leaders but why, given their greater interest, there are not more fashion leaders among the high status group.

There seems to be only one way to answer this question: The women of high status, with all their interest in fashion, simply talk about it less. We can think of two reasons why this might be so. First of all, for such women, fashion may be only one item on a relatively more elaborate agenda of informal conversation and everyday activity. Public affairs, charity work, women's clubs, etc.—in short, all the involvements of the higher status woman—may crowd out fashions as a subject of conversation and advice-giving. Secondly, it may be that there is even some deliberate unconcern with fashion talk among women of this status level. Although there is great fashion interest among such women, perhaps is is not considered good gamesmanship to ask for advice, or good taste to proffer it.

While we have no data to test this interpretation adequately, it is interesting, perhaps, to point out that this type of interpretation is the same one we have employed at several previous points. Immediately above, it will be recalled, we suggested that the lower incidence of fashion leaders in the ranks of older women, women with large families and women with low gregariousness—even when these women have high fashion interest—may be explained by the fact that they are not so likely to come into contact with others who are interested and, thus, who are seeking advice. In the same way, we are suggesting now that it is a similar contextual factor which explains the lower proportion of fashion leadership on the high status level. Here, however, this contextual factor is not a generally low level of interest but rather, we think, a general avoidance of fashions as a subject for discussion.

Our 'export' measure, in effect, summarizes some of what we have been saying:

TABLE 12 *Only Middle Status Women 'Export' Fashion Leadership (but even they don't 'export' very much)*

	Ratio of Fashion Leadership to Fashion 'Saliency' (The 'average' ratio for the entire sample = 1.00)
High Status	1·00
Middle Status	1·14
Low Status	0·88

Table 12 indicates that the leaders among women of high status are just enough to satisfy the extent of fashion interest among those women. The low status level, on the other hand, would seem to have a slight predominance of interest over leadership indicating that, to some extent, they must seek out others' leadership to satisfy the extent of their concern with fashions. Only the middle status group has a predominance of leadership over interest. To a slight extent, then, we may say that the middle status women are attractive enough for others—presumably women of lower status—to 'export' some amount of leadership, although the major conclusion of this table would seem to be that fashion leadership within each stratum seems relatively self-contained.

We have been assuming, of course, that women discuss fashions with others like themselves. But the 'follow-up' data will bear this out.

TABLE 13 *The Flow of Fashion Influence Among Status Levels Outside the Family*

Her Fashion Leader's Status is	Influencee's Status is			
	Low	Middle	High	Totals
Low	5	7	3	15
Middle	17	47	11	75
High	2	13	17	32
Totals	24	67	31	122

Fifty-seven per cent of all influence transactions outside the family went on between women of equal social status. Only the low status women went outside their class to any appreciable extent. Furthermore, when influence did cross status lines, it did not travel very far: almost invariably it was an exchange between women of immediately adjacent status levels. This, of course, means that the middle status level is called on somewhat more and thus the table shows—comparing the 'totals' this time—that the middle status group is the only one with more influentials (75) than influencees (67).* Although this difference is hardly dramatic, the findings of this table are directly in line with what Table 12 had led us to anticipate.

The Joint Role of Status Level and Gregariousness

So far, we have seen that status plays some part—although not a very important one—in determining the incidence of opinion leadership; we saw that there were somewhat larger numbers of fashion leaders on the high and middle status levels as compared with the lower. Now, before we leave the subject of status, we must ask ourselves whether perhaps variations in the extent of gregariousness may not account for this difference. It will be recalled that this was the case in marketing; that is, the emergence of a greater proportion of marketing leaders on the upper status levels was shown to be a mere reflection of the greater opportunity for gregariousness available to upper-status women. Is this the case, too, in fashions?

* We are again employing here the measure of social status (A,B,C,D) attributed by our interviewers to influential and influencee.

TABLE 14 *Status Level and Gregariousness Are Equally Important as Determinants of Fashion Leadership*

| | Fashion Leaders | | |
Gregariousness Score	High Status	Middle Status	Low Status
High	22%	36%	24%
Medium	31%	24%	17%
Low	21%	17%	11%

While Table 14 does tell us something more about the relationship between social status and fashion leadership when gregariousness is held constant, it tells us something unexpected, too, which is of primary importance. The reader will recall the main point of Figure 3, that the highest status level —which has the highest fashion interest—shows no more fashion leadership than the middle status level and in Tables 12 and 13 we have just seen that the upper status level does not 'export' at all. Table 14 provides us with another clue to the interpretation of these relationships; the table indicates that it is among the most gregarious women on the high status level that the drop in fashion leadership takes place. This is in marked contrast to the other two levels where the women with highest gregariousness have the greatest opportunities for leadership. That the glamorous women of highest status and highest gregariousness fall behind in fashion leadership seems to lend weight to the suggestion we ventured earlier: These are the women who do not talk much about fashion. Perhaps, as we suggested earlier, it is because the range of their interests is broader and fashion is only one of many concerns; perhaps it is because it is somehow not 'smart' to talk about fashion and to give and take fashion advice. At any rate, the very women whom popular imagery would point to as the most likely fashion leaders fall behind other groups in this respect.

Other than this one group which is high in both status and gregariousness there are two noticeable trends in Table 14: (1) as status level increases so does the proportion of opinion leaders; (2) as gregariousness increases so does the proportion of opinion leaders. In sum, this table clarifies very much. It tells us, first of all, about the major exception we pointed out above. And, secondly, we learn that, for all other groups, gregariousness as well as social status each contribute modestly, and independently, to the incidence of fashion leadership.

The Flow of Fashion Influence: A Summary

To sum up, we may say that—just as in marketing—fashion leadership is dependent most of all on life-cycle type; the difference in the proportion of fashion leaders among the several life-cycle positions is especially sharp. But whereas in marketing, leadership was concentrated among the large family wives, in fashions the girls are the key influentials.

In marketing, only gregariousness has a share along with life-cycle in determining the incidence of opinion leadership. In fashion however, social status must also be taken into account—although its role is uneven. High gregariousness and high status conspire to produce an actual drop in anticipated leadership, and this goes some distance, we think, in closing in on an adequate interpretation for our observation that the highest status level revealed no more leadership than the middle level. The lowest status level, on the other hand, yielded fewer leaders than the others and with the one important exception noted above it would appear that even when gregariousness is controlled, social status has some part in making for concentrations of fashion leaders.

Again, as in marketing, we find a fairly high degree of similarity of age and social status as between influential and influencee. When fashion influence does cross age lines, however, it is not at all clear that it travels from young to old as we had expected. While our 'export' index would seem to support this expectation, and follow-up interviewing with influentials *within* the family support it, too, the extra-household influence pairs who were followed-up do not. When influence travelled across status lines, it stemmed somewhat more from women of middle status than from others and when it was exchanged between gregariousness levels, it was somewhat more likely to emanate from women of higher gregariousness.

Chapter 15

THE DIFFUSION OF FASHION*

by Ingrid Brenninkmeyer

The author offers a comprehensive review of the field of diffusion theory as it relates to fashion. The bibliography is valuable in that it encompasses a considerable amount of European work. The fashion cycle is also analysed and the limits imposed to fashion forms identified and described.

The clothing habits of an individual are the result of group life. Our outlook on clothes is first formed by the primary group into which we are born; the ideas of parents, relatives, neighbours, playmates and school companions have a formative influence. Later on in life, secondary social groups with which we come into contact, such as professional associations, social committees, community clubs and even the social strata into which one marries or those people in whose company one spends one's leisure hours, all play a part. The original ideas of childhood are rejected for the ideas of the new group; sometimes some traditional ideas are retained whilst others are dispelled, often a compromise is made between the new and the old. This depends largely on the role that the individual plays or aspires to play in group life, in the associations to which he or she belongs. Every person has a role to play in society. Often an individual is a member of more than one group at the same time, and has a different function to fulfil, that is a different role to play in each group. Social function calls for an appropriate manner of dress. Not only do our natural looks, talents or the things we have learned in professional life or social intercourse have a decisive influence on the way we dress, but also the valuation of our dress-appearance in the groups in which we move. Public opinion acts as censorship. Approval and admiration will encourage behaviour of the same kind; disapproval or disdain will tend to bring about a change in dress.

We see, therefore, that fashion is a social and psychological problem. It is the problem of the individual in society.[1] Translated into the language of fashion, this means the problem of dressing to be seen by other people, 'For the apparel oft proclaims the man'.[2] We must guard against studying fashion either only from the point of view of the individual as the early psychologists indicated, or only from the point of view of the structure and function of society as a whole as many sociologists would have us do. Fashion has both a

---

* From *The Sociology of Fashion* (Ph.D. Thesis, University of Lausanne 1963).

psychological and sociological aspect; it is the result of individual aspirations and necessities as they are formed by the social system with which the individual comes into contact. To neglect either of these two elements or not to see their interdependence would be to misunderstand the essence of fashion.

The reaction of the individual personality to things fashionable, the parts played by the leaders and followers of fashion and the phenomenon of the spread of mass fashions can only be explained as social psychological inter-actions. An understanding of these micro-sociological group problems of present day life is essential before examining the significance of different historical fashions in a broader, macro-sociological context.

Instinctive Attitudes and the Resulting Characteristics of Fashion

'The group to which an individual belongs is the ground for his perceptions, his feelings and his actions.'[3] It is in group life that the individual character is formed. 'By group we mean any collection of human beings who are brought into social relationships with one another.'[4] Every social relationship involves attitudes; these are subjective reactions within the individual regarding objects of interest.[5] Love, hate, pride and humility, for example, are attitudes; friend, enemy, school and dress connote interests. Social relationships concern both attitudes and the interests to which they are related. Fashion as an object of interest, gives rise to certain definite reactions. Such things as the impulse to imitate and the desire to differentiate oneself from others are typical attitudes proper to all people who endeavour to be fashionable. Changeability, period-icity and psychological insistence are phenomena following from these funda-mentally competitive attitudes. Surprisingly enough, all people whether leaders or followers, have basically the same attitudes to fashion; it is more a matter of intensity and rate of adaptation that marks the difference between the fashion instigator and the fashion adherent. The unfashionable person will wear very similar clothes to the fashionable only of inferior quality and make and at a much later date, when the fashionable set have already discarded these gar-ments, once worn with so much enthusiasm, for something new. Because so much of our behaviour seems to be dictated by the unconscious, early writers and non-specialists tend to see all manners of behaviour not so easily accounted for, fashion included, as the result of a few deep-rooted instincts. Hofstätter points out that there are practically no fixed and fast instincts,[6] they all result from what we have learned in society. Social life is responsible for the shaping of interests: they are formed through the desires and needs which the environ-ment and nature impose on an individual. Hofstätter, therefore, considers it more correct to speak about 'instinctive attitudes' rather than 'instincts' which give the false impression of fixed and unchangeable. Fashion is definitely a matter of great changeability, depending on all kinds of structural and historical influences. It is in no way rigidly fixed, and the instinctive attitudes underlying its development change according to the social pattern of the times. In the following pages fashion is examined in its contemporary form. What is stated is mainly applicable to feminine clothing which is far more changeable and unsteady than its masculine counterpart. Competition is perhaps the most typical attribute of present day fashion.

260

Competition: Imitation and Differentiation

G. Simmel, writing in 1914, analysed fashion as a combination of two antagonistic attitudes; 'the fusion with our social group and the accentuation of the individual'. Fashionable imitation results from the desire to appear original without oneself having the inspiration of creativeness or having to bear personal responsibility for the success or failure of the actions performed. Differentiation expresses the impulse to stand out in our surroundings without seriously offending against the prevailing social norms.

Most normal individuals consciously or unconsciously have the itch to break away in some measure from a too literal loyalty to accepted custom. They are not fundamentally in revolt from custom but they wish somehow to legitimize their personal deviation without laying themselves open to the charge of insensitiveness to good taste and good manners. Fashion is the discreet solution of the subtle conflict. The slight changes from the established in dress or other forms of behaviour seem for the moment to give the victory to the individual, while the fact that one's fellows revolt in the same direction gives one a feeling of adventurous safety. The personal note which is at the hidden core of fashion is superpersonalized.[8]

Imitation and differentiation taken together are two complementary elements of social competition in group life. 'Social life is the battleground of these two principles and their reconciliation.'[9] The imitator never copies in very detail. He or she copies with the idea of being slightly different or even slightly better than the other people in the social group. Woman, in particular, never wants to be exactly like the others. If she has the misfortune to wear the same garment as someone else on some special occasion, she will immediately change her clothes or disappear no matter what it costs.

The whole of fashion history could be written as the interplay of these two competitive attitudes. New fashions arise when the differentiation attitude gains the upper hand; present day fashions are consolidated when the need for social conformity plays the greater part. Too much of one attitude evokes the other as a series of reactions upon reactions. Social recognition in the group to which the individual wants to belong is the goal aimed at by this behaviour.

There is a difference as to the proportions in which these two elements are present in different types of people. Leaders of fashion are far more unstable and susceptible to change; differentiation plays the greater part in their ideas. Followers of fashion have a greater tendency to imitation, and the unfashionable or homely part of the population practicially only imitate and have no original ideas in their clothing. Out of these two attitudes, competitive imitation and competitive differentiation, the characteristic fickleness of fashion arises.

Fickleness of Fashion

The inconstancy and changeability of fashion is due to its irrationality and superficial tendencies. 'Fashion taken in a broad sense, in so far as it is determined by changing daily happenings, is the form of life; it has taken on the meaning of the moment and consequently a certain superficiality and instability characterize it.'[10] What James Laver calls the 'pleasures of vicissitude'[11] adds

261

tremendously to the enjoyment of life. Fads, crazes, 'fashion moods' and 'fashion follies' within the fashion of the day bring short lived amusement. People who always do the same things and wear the same clothes, are themselves bored and make life boring for others. Zest for life leads to a love of change. 'We like to be different from ourselves of last year, we also like to be different from our friends and neighbours of this year.'[11] In all human beings there is a tendency to become tired of sensations that are repeated constantly.[12] The main stream of life may run its uninteresting regular daily course, but we look for our amusement and variety in the superficial, in such things as fashion. To counteract the superficial in quickly changing fashions 'there is on the other hand the development of a greater flexibility of the mind, which is encouraged by the need for rapid adaptability, as also an increase in the enjoyment of life, fashion is often a welcome blessing, counteracting the dreary paralysis often caused by daily worries and economic troubles.'[13] Nevertheless if we look at all these supposedly superficial elements of fashionable dress throughout the years, we will find that even in their irrationality, they tell the story of the cultural ups and downs of the years considered.

Popularity Periods

Every fashion is in existence for a certain period of time and nobody knows exactly when or why its popularity suddenly arises and then almost as quickly as it came, fades away. Fashion has been compared to the waves of the sea 'long before one wave has finished its course, new ones are being formed, which follow or overtake the first one.'[14] The length of the fashion period is partly dependent on the speed with which the new fashion wave spreads among the population. This again is dependent on the economic possibilities and social structure of the groups concerned. When the expansion has been completed or practically completed through imitation, the desire of differentiation arises anew and another popularity period furthering a different fashion ensues. The popularity of certain fashions is due to what Hofstätter calls the 'dominating role of an unsatisfied need.'[15] The neglect of some essential element of decoration over a long period of time will lead to a vigorous revival. The need that has drastically been denied satisfaction will claim its rights all the more vehemently. The sudden upsurge of many fashions can be explained from such frustrations; when a shortage of material has been dominant for some time, the next period will bring voluminous clothes; thick textures are followed by thin textured material; pointed shoes by round or square shoes. Nevertheless no-one can forecast the length of the popularity period or exactly what will follow. Shakespeare already said 'See'est thou not, I say, what a deformed thief this fashion is.'[16] In spite of studying the past, one never knows what to expect in the future.

Psychological Insistence

'Fashion is a regulating system of its own kind which distinguishes itself from other regulating systems (such as custom, usage, convention, morals and law) only in degree and not through other essential differences.'[17] Fashion is a strict mistress; social vanity or the desire for prestige or recognition are the motives bringing about adherence to her rules. 'Fashion has a compulsory character'[18] writes Hofstätter. He gives fashion the third place in his spectrum of the social order in which he distinguishes five types of generally accepted social regulative measures.[19] Fashion plays a dynamic role in the process of social change. She insists on obedience. Those people who scorn her dictates become outcasts of society. A certain amount of adherence is absolutely essential for acceptance in group life. People who ignore fashion entirely are considered queer, abnormal, lifeless and anti-social. We are not free to be totally unfashionable. '. . . generally, fashion is not considered to be a limitation of personal freedom. What has become a matter of course, is experienced as if it were our own free choice. The experience of choosing is not impaired by the fact that the final result is almost exactly the same as that chosen by many, in fact by almost all other people.'[20] We are free to do as the others do and if we willingly follow fashion in the spirit of our age, our obedience appears to us to be freedom. Fashion is not as authoritative as custom or law, but it has a psychological force, its laws are unwritten but if disregarded ostracism from the group is the ensuing punishment.

Competitive imitation and competitive differentiation are the two most characteristic attitudes of fashion. Their interplay necessarily gives rise to fickleness and changeability, which works itself out in popularity periods of different lengths. Psychological insistence, springing from the human need to be accepted in the social group, ensures the success of each great fashion wave.

Fashion Leaders and Adherents

In order to understand the diffusion of fashion, we must first consider the roles played by those social groups most directly connected with its propagation. Group structure consists of an interwoven pattern of intrinsically connected social roles.[21] This is of major importance for both fashion leaders and fashion adherents. A social role can be defined as 'the sum of the diverse elements of conduct expected of an individual, on which the behaviour of other group members is based.'[22] It does not matter who plays the roles, but it is very important that the roles are played. Group structure necessitates the division of functions or roles among its members. On their capability depends the successful functioning of well-integrated group life. The larger the group, the more complicated will be its structure. This in turn necessitates a greater number of specialized roles. The 'complexity of our own culture is mirrored to a large extent in the phenomenon that we can be at the same time members of diverse overlapping groups, and an understanding of our actions and attitudes presupposes a knowledge of the positions which we hold in those various groups.'[23] Hardly anyone lives only for clothes. A person is nearly always a bundle of various social roles and has diverse functions to fulfil in society. The roles of wife, mother, secretary, teacher, writer, nurse, dressmaker and hostess can all be played by the same person. The various social worlds in which people live their lives are the realities to which they suit their clothes. The influence of these many social groups shape fashion; that is the reason why fashion is so often called a mirror of society.

Every group has a typical structure which is built up for the attainment of the group purpose in accordance with its norms. The fashionable world has its own specialized groups with their roles of leaders and adherents connected by an intricate web of innumerable interwoven relationships. In this world of fashion, the fashion instigator has an all important function to fulfil.

Fashion Instigators

G. M. Homans describes a leader as 'he whose behaviour most closely corresponds to the group norms.'[24] A fashion leader would, therefore, be one who has grasped the meaning of the *Zeitgeist* and can interprete this in '*verstofflichte Gedanken*'.[25] 'Only that person can influence fashion, who is talented enough to understand the unconscious flow of the taste of the times and who is at the same time able to anticipate this taste in advance.'[26] To understand the *Zeitgeist* it is necessary to live and work where the heritage of bygone culture and the art of present day living are together present in a concentrated and harmonious form. It is in this atmosphere and only in this atmosphere that fashion can develop. This is the reason why Paris is the centre of 'La Mode'.

Parisian Fashion Leadership. Paris is today the fashion centre of the world. This is due to a number of factors; the ideal, geographical location of the city, which is the meeting place of the rich and fashionable people of the world, the numerous art collections and art schools, and the large number of artists specializing in textile and jewellery designing. Paris is the centre of jewellery production, toilet articles, costume jewellery, delicate perfumes and all kinds of fashion accessories, such as: belts, buttons, buckles, handbags, gloves, artificial flowers, feathers, beads, hats, ribbons and many other items. The international market for the buying and selling of works of art is there. The ability and training of the French worker is meticulous and thorough. In the industrial area of Paris, in 1928, 300,000 workers of a total of 1,200,000 people employed in clothing and allied trades in the whole of France, worked in Paris.[27] One quarter of the population of Paris was employed in clothing. The midinettes, of which there are thousands, are known for their exact work. They begin as young girls in their teens and are taught the handicrafts of cutting, fitting and sewing.[28] In 1928, there were already 80,000 dressmaking shops in Paris, more than in the whole of the United States at that time. They produced 500–1,000 models a year. In this atmosphere of art, industry and 'savoir vivre', fashion is born. 'The craftsmanship and artistic ability of the Frenchman is as remarkable as his talent for improvisation; his inborn sureness of taste and his feeling for aesthetic values.'[29] Maggy Rouff aptly describes the atmosphere in which the fashion instigator finds his inspiration. 'One collects day after day all the artistic and fanciful impressions thrust upon us by the world about us. There come pell-mell: a gala concert, a vexation, a book, sometimes alcohol or narcotics, or even both, snobbish obstinacy, or real enthuisasm. Four times a year clothes are made from these various impressions.'[30] Truly fashion is the 'Child of thought and thoughtlessness.'[31]

The origins of the Parisian dress-making trade go back to at least the mid-Fifteenth Century. Nationalistic and mercantilistic ideas formed the shelter under which industries serving fashionable demands grew up. The French rulers, who considered dependence on other nations for manufactured goods humiliating and deplorable, strove to make France a great, self-supporting nation and did everything in their power to strengthen the economic armoury of their land. Louis XI welcomed silk weavers from Italy and also imposed prohibitive import duties to foster the expansion of the French silk industry. Francis I with the help of his Florentine wife, brought manufacturers of Italian silks and brocades to France. He offered special liberties to Italian workers to attract them within the French borders. Catherine de Medici introduced the art of lace making, the manufacture of parasols and fans and the distilling of perfumes.[32] She was also responsible for the use of sugar and liquors as well as what is nowadays known as the French art of cooking.[33] Henry IV continued to encourage the raising of silkworms, and subsidized immigrant makers of Venetian glass, Persian rugs, Turkish carpets, Flemish tapestries and apparel for the court aristocracy.[34]

Nevertheless it was under Louis XIV and Colbert that France became the fashion centre of Europe. Mercantilistic practices were used to further this end. The term mercantilism was coined by Adam Smith to 'identify the policies by which the early modern state tried to create a reservoir of economic resources, to stimulate a variety of occupations, to reduce dependence on the industries, ships, or traders of other countries, to build up a large national income, and thus create a fiscal counterpart to a politically powerful state.'[35] Colbert, son of a Reims cloth merchant, gathered together all the plans and expedients of his predecessors for a prolonged attempt to establish an entirely self-sufficing national economy. Gold or money for his King, who continually had such great pecuniary demands, was the aim of his policy. Trade and industry became the most important factors of Colbert's mercantilistic economy. 'These manufactured articles', wrote Colbert, 'yield at the same time returns in money, which is, in one word, the only aim of commerce, and the only way of increasing the greatness and power of this state.'[36] To foster the industries which he most urgently wanted developed, Colbert used many methods: encouragement through the giving of honours or monetary rewards; regulation through the Code de Commerce which set forth exactly what was to be produced and by which methods it was to be manufactured; protection by raising import duties on manufactured goods; and company promotion through state subsidized enterprises at home and the foundation of trading companies in the colonies.[37] Colbert's greatest success, however, the results of which well outlasted his time, was the establishment of those industries supplying the wants of the King and his court. The manufacture of mirrors, porcelain, gobelins, furnishing materials, ribbons, hosiery, lace, gold and silver thread and brocade were encouraged on a vast scale. Although the ensuing wars momentarily ruined much of Colbert's work, later generations revived and further developed what he had founded. All Europe admired French luxury products, they bought them and even tried to copy them. As Colbert said 'With our taste let us make war on Europe and through fashion conquer the world.'[38]

Since the days of Louis XIV French fashions have dominated society. Besides the establishment of industries necessary for luxurious apparel and fashionable accessories, the Sun King lightened the guild regulations which up to that time only permitted tailors to practise both dressmaking and tailoring. Very soon, 1,700 independent dressmakers were present in Paris. In 1773, Rose Bertin, dressmaker to Queen Marie Antoinette set up a dressmaking establishment in the Rue St Honoré called the 'Grand Mogol.'[39] Once a month she sent little dolls dressed up in the latest fashions to many foreign courts; to Spain, Portugal, Russia, England, Scandinavia, Germany, Italy, Constantinople and America.[40] This was the first famous dressmaking establishment with international connections. By this time France had won the cultural hegemony of the Western World.[41] The *savoir-vivre* of the French was copied in high society everywhere, in the U.S. just as in Europe. The courts of Louis XVIII, 1841–24, Charles X, 1824–30, and Louis Philippe, 1830–48, were all centres of 'La Mode'. It was not extraordinary for two hundred balls to be held on the same evening in Paris.[42] Just think of the inspiration and industry needed for so many different evening dresses to be worn at the same time.

In 1858 the first modern dressmaking establishment was set up by Charles Worth,[43] often called the grandfather of fashion. He was an Englishman who had served his apprenticeship at Swan and Edgar's Department store in London. In 1846 he went to Paris to work in the silk house Gagelin. In 1858 he formed a partnership with a Swede, named Bobergh, who had worked in the ladies tailoring business in the Rue de la Paix. Princess Metternich, wife of the Austrian Ambassador, became a customer, then later the Empress Eugenie in 1859. In 1870, Bobergh retired from business and Worth continued alone with his two sons. His son, Jean-Philippe was a great designer, trained by the painter Corot. Worth, through his use of rich materials, revived the Lyon silk industry which had been having a bad time. He introduced the custom of mannequins to show off his new designs. The idea of selling export models originated at Worths, as also the idea of selling models to be copied.[44] This is the first connection between the Haute Couture and mass production. The house of Worth is now in the fifth generation, which is exceptionally long for a fashion house.

After Worth came many other famous establishments such as: Paquin 1890–1914, who favoured the modern art trend and engaged Bakst, the Russian painter as a designer;[45] the Callot sisters with their neutral colours and straight sheath dresses;[46] Doucet, who dressed Sarah Bernhardt and was at the same time a famous art collector;[47] Paul Poiret, who began as a designer at Doucets and later set up his own establishment, was greatly influenced by Diagilev and the Russian Ballet and the charm of oriental gowns.[48] Other well-known houses are Lanvin-Castillo, Jacques Heim, Pierre Balmain, Givenchy, Guy Laroche, Pierre Cardin, Nina Ricci, Michel Goma, Alex Grès, Jean Patou and Christian Dior. All these fashion leaders lived and worked in the atmosphere of Paris. No matter from what nation or what class of society they came, they all found their inspiration in this city, in its tradition, its art, its life and its industry.

What are the qualities of a fashion leader? Above all the fashion leader has the personality of an artist, an artist of clothes. Like all artists, his ability is inborn; the feeling for clothes cannot be taught; either a man possesses the flare or he is without it. Of all the visual arts, the clothes designer has most in common with the painter who also works with colour and form. Deep in his personality, the fashion leader like the painter, must possess an intense feeling for the beautiful in the tangible world of present day culture, and have the desire to express what he feels in his own medium of clothes making. The fashion leader handles something that is in constant motion and far more fleeting than the work of the artist. The designer must have completely mastered the technical side of dressmaking and have an innate feeling for colour harmonies, the balance and arrangement of parts, the matching of different or similar materials and a feeling for rhythm "as a regular or measured repetition of some feature such as a line, a surface or a mass."[49] He must be able to create illusions to get across his ideas such as: width, height or depth. And above all he must be able to subordinate all these artifices and techniques to one general unified effect, so that he expresses one idea in a harmonious whole which is momentarily beautiful, whether the wearer is in motion, walking or dancing, or static, just posing or sitting. Just as the artist lives in his creations, so the fashion leader must exist in clothes; 'he lives clothes, he sleeps clothes, he dreams clothes.'[50] It is the passion of his life.

Besides this the fashion leader's feeling or taste must change every season; he is not allowed to remain hovering over one favoured style. He must have a strong and sure sense of the development in clothes. This is one of the hardest things to grasp; it requires a continued changeability of taste in a certain direction. The majority of designers fail to develop a progressive adaptability. Fashion does not wait for them, but goes on to something new. Because of this tendency to become stereotyped in style, so many model houses or fashion leaders are ruined; and those newcomers, who have understood the next step on the road of fashion-development, take over their places until they too suffer the same fate as their predecessors. It is very seldom that a person has a continuous sensitive feeling for the new and the coming, and can at the same time leave the just 'passé' behind. Those designers who can do it are the geniuses of fashion; but usually designers understand one, two or a few fashions and then their capability for comprehending the new is finished. It seems to be a law of human nature that a person is only capable of a few deep experiences. Life is too short and consumes too much of our vitality for more. Because of this limited capacity of man and the impossibility of inheriting the artistic flare of fashion, the majority of the Haute Couture establishments seldom survive the death of their founders. 'Just as the firms of art dealers in the majority of cases, depend entirely upon the personality of the man who gave the firm its name, they are seldom inheritable like trade and industry in general, so in the same way the most prominent Fashion houses are dependent on the personality of their founder.'[51] The dressmaking establishment depends solely on the personality and talent of the fashion leader. Nevertheless the fashion itself has little to do with the person. It is practically a matter of historical necessity. But the originality and beauty of the individual creations depends on the personal interpretation of the designer. It does not matter who designs the fashion; if one man cannot do it, fashion will find her right promoter. Fashion is democratic, she desires appropriate interpretation regardless of rank, birth or heredity.

The role of the fashion leader is, therefore, skilfully to design models for the select group of rich women who will later be imitated by other groups in the long hierarchy of fashion diffusion, to be a symbol for the modern manner of appearance, to make the fashion of the moment seem so attractive and expressive of the momentary mood in living that all people recognize it, admire it and aspire to follow in its wake. Fashion is the expression of a mass mood. The fashion

267

leader must be as sensitive as an artist and grasp this mood, express it in a harmonious design, matched by suitable material and colour, and, in modern times, organize its production. Sometimes one man fulfils all of these functions; other times the functions are divided up between two people or a group of people. Both elements of artistry and business are necessary to the successful fashion leader. Nevertheless the artistic element is the more important, the business side can be seen to by someone more capable in that sphere. For example the two sons of Charles Worth divided these functions between them: Jean-Philippe Worth was responsible for the designing, while Gaston Worth saw to the business transactions.[52] The same can be seen at Christian Dior, where Marcel Boussac looks to the business interests, while first Christian Dior, then Yves Saint Laurent and now Marc Bohan does the designing.

As we have seen the French dressmaker is above all an artist, not interested in the making of money. Nevertheless this art is so fleeting that it must be sold or it entirely loses its value. For this reason it has come about that the couturier welcomed the aid of the fabric manufacturer; without this aid the Haute Couture could not exist at all. It is quite easy for a fabric manufacturer to gain control of a dress-making establishment.

'Dressmakers . . . need an enormous amount of credit from the manufacturers from whom they buy. Paris couturiers are the display windows for the French fabrics. For every good model of a given fabric designed and made by a top designer, the fabric house sells many times the model's value in yardage. They sell the material not only through the designer's house, but through the other houses who copy the model in Paris, England, South America, the World. French fabric manufacturers make such for Vionnet, something else for Molyneux; another for Schiaparelli. Of course he keeps Vionnet in business, even if a bad collection one year; everyone knows a designer has an off season now and then. But if four off seasons in a row, Finis. Collect the bills, goodbye Vionnet. Give credit to a new one. Build her up'.[53]

We see therefore, that it is the business interests of the French fabric manufacturers that keep the Haute Couturiers going. Without their business acumen, this trade of top designing would probably have died a natural death a long time ago. Artistry and money making are seldom bedfellows. But these big businessmen never tire of searching for artists who are capable of fashioning the right stuff for sale at the right time. They cannot do without this advertising propaganda for their materials. Thus a fruitful alliance has grown up between the artist who creates momentary beauty and the businessman who is profit-minded.

Besides Paris other capital towns have influenced fashion, but have never attained the importance of the French capital. In the Eighteenth Century England had a profound influence on men's clothing.[54] The suit that men wear nowadays is derived from the riding costume made in London for the English country gentlemen. But women's fashions were decided in France. At the end of the first world war, Berlin and Vienna both deliberately tried to take over the leadership of fashion without success.[55] Their action was motivated by nationalistic reasons; they disliked being under the fashion dictatorship of France. For some Americans it is a mystery why New York with its enormous dressmaking industry is not the fashion centre of the world.[56] Why do wealthy American women always want to buy Paris models? The crux of the matter is that fashion finds its inspiration only in the partnership of present day culture and leisurely living. This needs to be backed by expert handicraft and all the allied fashion industries. New York cannot compare with Paris for cultural opportunities or for leisurely living. Possibilities for mass production alone do not make fashion. Individual inspiration is the essential. There is little time left for original ideas in the rush of this huge metropolis, where the loss of a quarter of a minute means the loss of many dollars. Italy, in recent times, has influenced fashion. Ideas for hairstyles, shoes, men's suits, beach-wear have often come from Rome and Florence. These ideas have been surprisingly tenacious in spreading through Western Europe. Nevertheless the fashionable world still looks to Paris, where individuality in the making of clothes has become a standing tradition.

The Intermediary Role of Mass Production. Mass production can be looked upon both as a leader and a follower of fashion. Mass production is the primary follower of fashion because it copies the models of the Haute Couture; it is, at the same time, a secondary leader of fashion because clothes are made which are worn by the majority of the population. For most people mass-produced clothes are practically the only clothes they see and wish to buy.

The early Haute Couturiers dressed only individual women of the upper-set who had the means and the figures to be beautifully clothed. The couturiers understood only these kinds of women and were not interested in women who were less wealthy and less good looking. Mass-production finds its inspiration in this atmosphere of artistic individual dressmaking, and twice a year in January and August, manufacturers from all over Europe and the United States go to Paris to discover what is suitable for the next season. 'Of all the dressmaking establishments in Paris, probably not more than two hundred merit the title of Haute Couture. Only about twenty-five of them are highly important at any time, the rest are copyists.'[57] In the 1920s and 1930s it was very difficult to obtain copies of Parisian models. The models themselves were extremely expensive. Under French law it is possible for the couturier to register designs in the Chambre Syndicale de la Couture Parisienne and obtain the protection of this authority in case of attempted stealing of his models.[58] This practice was totally unknown in other European countries and America. In those days American and German manufacturers obtained French models either through the illegal means of copyhouses or with the help of sketchers. Copy houses were small dressmaking establishments selling copies of the models put out by the Haute Couture.[59] This was against the law, and in case of sudden inspection a double set of books was kept to avoid supplementary taxation. Model dresses were obtained from customers in financial stress, mistresses of rich men or from foreign buyers. Clothes were often loaned to be copied and then given back. The exactness of the copy was a matter of price. A really good copy costs about a half of the original model. A sketcher, on the other hand, was a person who went with the buyer to the Paris shows and afterwards drew what she had seen from memory. A good sketcher averaged about fifteen sketches per collection. After the show she was rushed to her office in a taxi and quickly sketched all that she remembered. Such people were employed by manufacturers and buyers of department stores. Nowadays most copyists seem to work for the American market. Also models bought in Paris are lent out to be copied in New York, thus cheating the French dressmaker of his just reward. Often the copy is a perfect imitation. It can only be distinguished from the original by the invisible, indelible ink marking used to counteract cheating. It only becomes visible when the garment is placed under ultra-violet rays.[60]

After the Second World War, a new wind stirred the atmosphere of Parisian dressmaking. Marcel Boussac, the French cotton millionaire, wanted to revive an old dressmaking establishment with its old glory. Christian Dior, a then unknown personality, who had once been an art dealer and possessed the friendship of many artists, among them Christian Bérard,[61] dreamed of starting a more feminine fashion. He believed in founding a small atelier and creating clothes of refined luxury for the upper-set; he did not believe in reviving an already dead business. Surprisingly enough Marcel Boussac gave Dior the financial backing and allowed him to found his own establishment under his own name. Dior chose the little hotel on the corner of number 30 Avenue de Montaigne and had it adapted for his purposes. In 1947 he started business with four women, who knew the fashion world well, as his advisers and 85 employees. He created the 'new look' tearing out the stiff square shoulders and replacing them by a softer, rounded line, lengthening the skirts many inches and increasing their volume. In spite of hard times and the food shortage in Europe, the 'new look' established itself everywhere. Dior and Boussac did not stop at top fashion; they founded a whole industry around it. The house of Dior spread into the neighbouring buildings; 28 new dressmaking ateliers were opened and the number of employees grew to 1,500.[62] In 1954 eight Christian Dior companies existed in France and foreign countries, including 16 participating firms. Branches of Christian Dior were opened in New York, London and Caracas.[63] Dior did not only work for the upper-set. He also put his name on fashion accessories so that those women who could never buy a model dress, could at least buy gloves, stockings, a scarf or a necklace with the Dior label. In the neighbourhood of his dressmaking establishment he opened the Dior boutique where tourists could buy all kinds of accessories such as perfume 'Miss Dior' and 'Diorama'. Dior stockings are made in Lippstadt, Germany; Dior gloves in London; Dior costume jewellery in Pforzheim and Dior scarves and furs complete the picture.

The main business of Christian Dior commences with the selling of models at the fashion shows twice a year. Sometimes a model is sold 100 times. At every fashion show about 200 to 250 models are shown. Dior sells 400 tickets for admittance; with them he covers the technical costs of the show. A buyer from overseas can do one of three things: he can buy a paper pattern of the model, but he may not label it Christian Dior; or he can buy a canvas copy and change it to suit his purposes naming it 'Original-Christian-Dior-Copy'; or he can buy the original model in material which is the most expensive and is permitted to label it 'Christian Dior'. The more the buyer buys, the greater discount he receives from Dior. Crowds of busily sewing midinettes are responsible for the quick finishing of the garments so that the buyer can soon travel home with his new models safely in his suitcase. Exact drawings and reproductions of the new fashions are first allowed to appear a month after the fashion shows. The Chambre Syndicale de la Couture Parisienne to which all important model houses belong, supervises the keeping of this set term. In these four weeks the manufacturers make up the clothes, and exact reproductions and photos of the models first appear in the papers and magazines at the same time that the models are shown in the shop windows. Dior exports 65 per cent of his clothes to foreign lands, 40 per cent to the United States, and 33 per cent is sold in Paris. He sells perfume in 87 countries.[64]

To help the manufacturer with his time problem, Christian Dior sells his name to business partners in different countries. Dior demands a yearly sum of money and in return sends these manufacturers 20 to 30 original patterns and a great deal of vignettes. The manufacturer can change these designs as much as he likes and has the right to label them 'Vignette Christian Dior' even if the clothes in question have very little to do with the original Dior model. The patterns and vignettes sold thus are the same as those shown at the January and August fashion shows.[65] This can give rise to embarrassing situations such as the possibility of the wife of the Director of a department store and the little shop assistant both wearing the same Parisian model dress with the label 'Model Haute Couture' sewn on inside. The main difference being that the original model is far more expensive than the copy. Nevertheless practically only an expert can tell the difference between the two. This state of affairs has led recently to great dissatisfaction among American department buyers who demand the old exclusiveness of the Haute Couture.

Christian Dior can be called the modernizer of the Haute Couture. Unlike the couturiers of the 20s and 30s who desired to keep their trade totally exclusive and only for the high society, Christian Dior recognized the importance of mass-production and the advantages obtainable for both the manufacturers and the Haute Couturier himself if they worked together. Thus the Haute Couture ensures its leadership of fashion and at the same time makes a sizable profit selling to manufacturers over the whole world; this is quite impossible if a model house only sells to a few exclusive clients. The manufacturer has far less trouble to get the desired models twice a year on time for production and he can now offer his wares with the selling bate of 'Paris Original' sewn on to it. No need for the complicated stealing of the 20s and 30s. Most of the Haute Couture are following in the steps of Christian Dior; they are no longer totally exclusive. Jacques Fath was one of the first to seek a connection with the manufacturer. In 1948 he made a contract with Joseph Halpert of New York, giving Halpert the right to sell thousands of dresses under the name of 'Fath'.[66] Fashion is becoming international. It still finds its inspiration, as all art does, in individual artistic creation, but its expansion is taken care of through the joint leadership of the Haute Couture working together with the manufacturers of many countries. 'For the fashion creator a new and by no means a less valuable task has arisen, which he can only fulfil in co-operation with the now highly developed clothing industry. Since the rapid dwindling of the couture houses, the mass-production industry has taken over the increasingly responsible role

271

of mediator between the Parisian fashion houses and the consuming public.'[67] Dior has borne this thought in mind when creating his designs. Balenciaga created the sack; Dior simplified and adapted it for the masses.[68] He tried to make his designs suitable to the needs of a great consuming public. This he understood well. It is now the question whether Marc Bohan can carry on his work or will the house of Dior suffer the fate of most fashion houses, and slowly die now that its founder is in the grave.

This new co-operation between the Haute Couture and mass production has nevertheless certain inherent dangers for the Haute Couture. The Haute Couture must avoid becoming only a superior kind of model house for cheaper ready-to-wear. The race after money and markets must not be allowed to kill the artistic spirit of the Haute Couture and thus degrade fashion. Haute Couture and mass production are not the same thing; they are two totally different ways of clothing women. Haute Couture is born in luxury and leisure and is above all the result of individual artistic inspiration. It is closely linked to aesthetic values and is an expression of contemporary culture. It aims at clothing the body of one particularly beautiful woman. Mass production has the far more material function of clothing the masses at a reasonable price and of finding models which will sell by thousands to cloth the bodies of thousands. It is the function of mass production and not of the Haute Couture to choose a design or to adapt the creations of the Parisian Model Houses to match the taste of the public at large. The role 'of mediator' should be left to those who understand mass taste, to the mass production industry. It would be a great pity if in the future years the Haute Couture were to forget its high calling and descend the social scale. It would mean the degrading of fashion and the end of Parisian exclusiveness.

Fashion Adherents

Strictly speaking, everyone except the Haute Couture of Paris is today a fashion follower. A fashion adherent is one who dresses according to the ideas of the time dictated to him by someone else. The most ardent followers of fashion are people who have a zest for living, a capability for enjoying material things; usually with a certain amount of sensuality and are not tied down by customs and conventions. These quick adherents of fashion play the part of fashion leaders in the group in which they move. The mass of fashion-followers seldom directly copy the Paris models, but rather the leaders of the group to which they belong. These leaders are in reality the followers of some other more advanced group from outside their own party. And if we follow this hierarchy of group-copying back to its origin we arrive at the Haute Couture of Paris. A fashionable person can both be a leader in one group and at the same time a follower of a more advanced group. Fashion adherents can be examined from two points of view: the type of person most susceptible to 'La Mode' and the income group in which these types are most likely to predominate.

Social Exhibitionism.
Social exhibitionists are the prime fashion followers. At bottom they are lovers of adventure and luxury, hating the monotony of everyday life and ordinary clothing. G. Simmel defines the essence of adventure; 'Indeed the form of an adventure is characterized in a very general way by the

fact that it falls out of the normal context of life ... it is like an island in life, the beginning and end of which are determined by its own formative power, and not like the parts of a continent according to the boundaries on this side or that.'[69] For the social exhibitionist each startling dress is an adventure undergone to shock the onlookers. By her clothes she hopes to attract adventure and excitement into her life. This seeking for the exceptional and this desire to experience something new is equally to be found in an artistic nature, 'Then it belongs to the nature of a work of art to cut a piece out of the never ending, continual flow of opinions or experiences; or to remove it from its rightful place between present and future, and to give it a self-sufficient form as if determined and kept together from within.'[70] This is true of fashion as it is of painting and for this reason only an artistic nature can understand fashion. The successful fashion exhibitionist has something of the artist and something of the adventurer in his make-up. The attitude of differentiation is developed to the extreme, usually on a narcissistic basis.

Social exhibitionism predominates in youth, in those seeking erotic adventure and in social misfits. Youth has a far more subjective and momentary approach to life than the more advanced age groups.[71] Old age is by contrast objective, coming from the past and going to the future and consequently far less susceptible to fashion which is the glorification of the passing moment. Since the Second World War, fashion has become exceedingly young: in the Unites States college girls and teenagers have their own way of dressing. The age at which girls start to wear lipstick and high heels becomes earlier each year. This is due to the quicker oncoming of maturity and the influence of industrial town life. Before the First World War and between the two world wars, fashion was considered the right of the young married woman, girls should be simply clad without much fuss. Times have changed, youth has come into its own and daughters now tell their mothers what they should wear.

Besides being an accompaniment of youth, exhibitionist clothing is the companion of illegitimate love. W. Sombart in his *Luxus und Kapitalismus* explains luxury as a phenomenon arising together with the free love of the courtesan and the cocotte. A man will buy his illegitimate love far more beautiful things than he will his wife. Free sexual relationships and luxury go together.[72] Havelock Ellis, who took a great interest in prostitution, is convinced that the motives stimulating women to this kind of existence are love of life, desire for luxury, feminine vanity and love of change rather than erotic or monetary reasons.[73] A passionate woman cannot be satisfied by these brief relationships. Nevertheless the sexual element is part of the adventure, otherwise a man will not take a girl out in a luxurious way and buy her beautiful clothes. The prostitute is the exact opposite of the housewife, who is tied to house and family and usually has little time or interest left over for fashion. The prostitute can live for fashion and enjoy the fun of exceptionality by being so extremely up-to-date.

There is a third group of people who are adamant followers of fashion. Social misfits, people who do not fit into any group structure, outsiders of the group, who try to establish their place within the group through fashionable clothing. Such people as the *nouveaux riches*, persons with physical deficiencies or inferiority complexes resulting from little education or trying to live in a social group which is of a higher milieu than that from which they originally come. Such people try to hide the selfconsciousness arising from their defects behind the cover of fashion. They think that fashionable attire will make up for the lack of other properties essential for acceptance in group life.

Income Groups. Fashion exhibitionists are nowadays usually found either at the top or the bottom of the financial scale. Fashion can only develop in an atmosphere of liberty and freedom from restraint. This is present to a greater degree in the higher and lower income groups, seldom in the middle range. 'Little by little a grotesque fashion hierarchy comes into being. The few rich women of the world, who have their clothes made in the houses of the Haute Couture, are dressed according to the latest fashion in unique garments of the finest workmanship and of the best materials. On their heels follow those women who are clothed in copies of the latest fashion, whose wardrobe is characterized by this or that seasonal detail or fashion colour. Between these two groups is the middle income section, consisting of those critical customers who cannot afford the Paris originals and do not like the department store styles; they strive to find a valuable and relatively timeless kind of ready-to-wear.'[74] The higher incomes have so much surplus means that even after amply fulfilling other consumption demands, they can still afford all kinds of fashionable eccentricities. Their money gives them economic freedom and in the eyes of the less wealthy a certain right to do things that ordinary people would not do. It depends solely on their love of adventure and artistic sense whether such women are fashionable or not. At the other end of the scale are those people without means; they are free because they have nothing. Unlike the middle class, who usually have ideas about what is appropriate and suitable to their station in life, the masses of wage-earners in the towns have no such values. When the young boy or girl earns money, it will be spent on what they most want. He may buy a motorcycle and she will buy, what she has always wanted, plenty of clothes in the latest fashion. Although she lives in a tiny attic without central heating or comfort, she will have her many pairs of pointed shoes, flimsy nylon underwear, short skirted dresses and she will willingly pay for the latest high topped Italian hairstyle. When, on her day off, she goes out in her newly bought finery, she feels like the queen of the town. The middle class, on the other hand, considers this attitude irresponsible and unseemly. The bourgeois lives out of past values for the future. One should dress appropriately and never buy too highly fashionable clothes as they could be unwearable the next season. Conservative and classical styles are the best as they can be worn for a longer period of time. The bourgeois income is mapped out in advance by social conventions; a certain standard of living, parties, clubs, theatre, holidays abroad, education of children in a certain milieu are all a 'must'. In the mind of the middle income groups there is little room left for experimental fashions, risks are out of the question, the bourgeois always plays safe. The wage-earning proletariat do not care about social prestige; they buy what they fancy and enjoy life here and now. Even in the country where people and ideas are less mobile, this attitude is pushing its way in.

This new kind of social structure began to take shape after the Second World War. Before this time kings and queens, aristocrats, upstarts from the lower classes, who became the mistresses of famous men; dandies and actresses, and at one time even the wealthy bourgeoisie, all have been primary fashion adherents at some time in history. After two world wars, people believe less in security and absolute values. The masses of wage-earners in the towns, emancipated from the social norms of their elders through their economic independence, are out for enjoyment. The upward trend of the trade cycle with its many opportunities for work, encourages spending. So we get for the first time in history, fashions most quickly taken up and spread through the world by the young wage-earning class; narrow-legged trousers, pointed shoes, high-headed hairstyles and short skirts were all first worn by the lower income groups. Hairdressers, shop girls, waitresses, and factory workers all had the new fashions in no time. The middle class income groups, even though they do not like imitating what is socially under them, slowly find themselves forced to follow.

Fashion Determination

The primary leadership of fashion is today still dependent on individual artistic inspiration and designing of the Haute Couture in Paris, which works together with the manufacturers of mass-produced clothes, who form the secondary leaders of fashion. Mass-production fulfils the role of a middleman between the Haute Couture and the final consumer. The role of fashion leadership, no matter who fulfils it, is vital for all manufacturers in the fashion trade. They need to know what is the trend in clothes and what to produce next. This knowledge saves time and lessens risks. Paris with its handicraft, its culture, its *savoir-vivre* is the centre of fashion instigation. As long as this city retains its feeling for the present and what is coming, it will remain the place where fashion designers seek their inspiration, otherwise it will forfeit its power of fashion instigation. Primary fashion followers are always, in some way, social exhibitionists. Nevertheless fashion today no longer follows the leadership of individual people. 'Today fashion is more of a social or popular movement in which the imitation is largely of types and ideals, rather than of persons.'[75] Brigitte Bardot's style of dressing is popular because she incorporates what the modern girl wants to look like. She is not admired for her own personality, only for the portrayal of a fashion ideal. 'What the notables wear apparently means less and less to the masses of intelligent fashion-conscious women, unless these same notables are themselves apparelled in the current fashions of the day.'[75] The notables have become bourgeois minded. Kings and queens sit on their tottering thrones and try to behave as they think the masses would like to see them behave; they dress to be approved by the crowds; they are no longer free to do as they like. Every movement is prescribed by tradition and social conventions which must not be broken. The free atmosphere and love of adventure so apparent in the European courts of former times have disappeared. Royal clothing reflects this change; dress is prescribed for them and no longer made by them. 'Fashion leadership is no longer the result of birth or position.'[76] Nowadays there are highly fashion conscious social groups, no longer individuals. Two groups predominate: the wealthy few 'who have sufficient leisure and are free from restraint and custom; they have good taste, artistic sense and a desire for pre-eminence in style and fashion';[77] and the wage-earning class who have few intellectual interests and no particular purpose in life, they are free from conventions and very near to momentary things, to fashion.

The question has often been asked who makes the fashion, the producer or the consumer. In the light of what has been said, it may be seen that no person alone makes the fashion; fashion is above all the result of historical development; it is the result of all those interwoven elements which collectively make history. The spirit of the age determines fashion. The individual artistic nature who has grasped the meaning of the *Zeitgeist* and can translate it into clothing designs, suggests fashion. Manufacturers of mass-produced clothes convey these suggested forms to the consumers, and it is the consumers who have the last word to say. Ultimately fashion depends on consumer choice. The public at large censure fashion. If they buy the new modes, they have expressed their approval; if they decline they have shown their disapproval. Paris and Mass-production can do what they like; the public taken collectively, is closer to the *Zeitgeist* than the individual designers or manufacturers. The will of the majority is decisive.

'Business cannot stop the train of fashion, or turn it backward or change it in some other way.'[78] In 1909 when tighter skirts were becoming fashionable, manufacturers invented the 'panier skirt' with much bunching of material at the back and sides to try to sell more material. This skirt required 50 per cent more stuff than the then worn straight skirts. A big drive was started in Paris; Parisian dressmakers of international repute created the models; leading actresses in Paris and New York were engaged to wear the skirts. Well-written articles appeared in fashion magazines. Retailers sold the skirts, department stores put them in their windows, pattern houses designed patterns for thrifty housewives. Much energy and money was put into the campaign. But all to no avail, it was a great failure, the consumer was not interested.[79] It is futile to try and change a major trend in fashion demand; no amount of sales promotion can do any good. The spirit of the age bends all to its will. The same can again be seen in the Autumn of 1958 when Yves Saint Laurent tried to re-introduce longer skirts.[80] Longer skirts were not in the air, and no fashion designer, no matter how gifted he is, can change the trend of fashion and the trend of fashion was short. Manufacturers bought Yves Saint Laurent's skirts and cut off many inches before trying to sell them. The wage-earning part of the population anticipated the new fashion trend; they cut their skirts shorter than Paris and in the next season the whole of the Haute Couture obediently followed the trend, shortening all skirts. Neither mass production nor the Haute Couture can change the logical development of fashion.

The Spread of Fashion

The expansion of Fashion is a phenomenon of collective behaviour. In the past, the subject of crowd psychology received little sympathetic attention and authors writing on this subject were liable to confuse terms.[81] The word 'masses' has been applied to such varied things as: unpremeditated, quickly-passing throngs of people, the population problem or the common people as opposed to high society. The use of the same term to denote such different subjects of discussion has led to much perplexity. The unorganized 'mass', best described as an unrelated collection of individuals, becomes a 'crowd' when these individuals are subjected to the same influences and come into communication with each other. Le Bon describes the characteristic qualities of the individual succumbed to crowd sentiments, 'We see, then, that the disappearance of the conscious personality, the predominance of the unconscious personality, the turning by means of suggestion or contagion of feelings and ideas in an identical direction, the tendency to immediately transform the suggested ideas into actions; these, we see, are the principal characteristics of the individual forming part of a crowd.'[82] Fashion used to be condemned in the same way. Early writers denied the crowd any positive qualities; they looked upon all mass phenomena, that is anything to do with large quantities, as a sign of degeneration, ultimately leading to a decline of culture. For Hofstätter 'the masses presuppose a transitional stage in the conversion of a crowd into minor groupings.'[83] Human achievements have always grown out of some kind of group structure. 'The human invention is the flexibly orientated group.'[84] The crowd ceases to be a danger or a negation once it becomes part of well-integrated group life. Seen from this point of view, the problem of the masses seems first of all to be a problem of social structure. Revolutions come about when the inflexible norms of old groupings no longer suit present-day living conditions. People break out, band together under a leader to rid themselves of the antiquated customs and regulations. Order is restored when a new workable group structure has been established. The existence of unorganized masses is proof of the lack of well-organized group life. In modern times, this problem can only be solved by the establishment of a hierarchy of functionally mobile groups.

What has this to do with fashion? Fashion shows forth the structure of society. By looking at the clothes of different nations and peoples, we can see whether an integrated group structure is actualized or not. In most of Europe and the United States fashion has spread to all parts of the population, showing that there must be some kind of satisfying group organization. People obviously earn money, do not have too many material worries and are interested in the newest things; otherwise they would not be fashionably dressed. In other countries, mainly in Eastern lands, Southern Italy and Spain, and Latin America tattered clothing and rags are to be seen, signifying poverty and discontent. Where there are rags, group organization is not satisfactory; the problem of the masses still predominates. Revolutions and social unrest are latent.

The masses have not always been condemned. Aristotle, in the third book of his Politics,[85] considered it better for them to have the right of decision rather than the minority of the refined. The masses judge works of art more realistically than the art critic. One person understands this point, the next another point, and the next yet another. Taken collectively the whole of the work receives its just appraisal. It is the same with fashion; the public evaluate it and through their collective decision override what might be the erring decision of an individual. Together they judge whether a certain manner of dressing is the right expression of their feeling for life as they experience it at the moment. Fashion reflects the cultural surroundings from which it springs. The speed and depth of its expansion, the quality of its designs and materials, the differentiation of its models and its penetration of certain groups in preference to others, shows forth the type of society in which it is born.

The Diffusion of Fashion

At no time in history has the diffusion of fashion reached such extended limits as in the present. More people than ever before are fashionably dressed in the latest styles. Industrial town life has given rise to numerous opportunities for enjoying the present and coming into close contact with the new things that are just coming. The population at large sees more fashion, has greater possibilities for acquiring it, and is encouraged to do so by numerous means of mass communications. Fashion as 'the socially approved sequence of variation on a cultural theme,'[86] adds immeasurably more to the pleasures of modern life.

Modern Mobility. Society is today more mobile in every sense of the word. The industrial civilization of large cities in which the egalitarian doctrine reigns supreme is gradually blotting out differences of rank, class and wealth. Numerous opportunities for work with good pay are to be found in the city and plenty of possibilities for buying an endless variety of consumer goods. People change their jobs far more frequently than at the beginning of the century. Whole groups of people are mobile. Families move from the country to the town, from one town to the other and from this land to that. The individual who is born, lives and dies in the same place is becoming a fast disappearing rarity. A person is no longer rigidly fixed in a predestined place on the social scale; he can climb or descend the ladder of prestige. Social merit rests on quite a different basis than in earlier times in history. Ours can be called the age of 'meritocracy'. He who achieves most in some specialized field of human endeavour merits the admiration and praise of his fellow men till someone better than he surpasses him and takes over his place.

In the fluid atmosphere of the industrial city, fashion plays a great part. Town life is the ideal fashion encourager. Fashion is visible everywhere; in crowded streets, in buses, trams, trains and taxis. Italian coffee bars and French boulevard cafés house much day-time chic. Fashion is seen as it was never seen before. As was first pointed out by René König,[87] electric light does its part, giving us the colourful fashion scene even at night and in the early hours of the morning in dance halls, ballrooms and exclusive night clubs; in the cinema, theatre and the concert hall. Since the days of Charles Ritz, who with his chef, Escoffier, persuaded the aristocracy and the rich that parties held in restaurants could be just as enticing as those given in private homes, these places have played a major role in the deliberate showing off of fashion. Hotel lounges have become a stage for displaying clothes; fashionable ladies sip delicate cups of tea in the Ritz in Paris, the Plaza in New York, the Dorchester in London; each jealously eyeing the other to see who is the most elegant. In the numerous cocktail bars, which are an American invention, men whet their appetites and women seductively hide their charms under the cover of voluminous mink stoles. Luncheon and dinner parties are given in hotels by elegantly-clad hostesses to further the pleasantries of social life. Gourmands, accompanied by fashionably dressed ladies who decorate the other half of the table, are fed by experienced restaurateurs. Fashion and luxurious living go hand in hand. More free time is spent outside the home. Modern methods of transportation convey masses of people to the city-centre in the evening and out again. Every income group can have its share of amusement.

Fashion is also diffused to the countryside and the seashore. Travellers and holiday makers bring the newest modes all through the world. In the summer, the Riviera, the Adriatic Coast, and the Costa Brava display hundreds of different bathing suits; spring fashions can be seen at the races, at Ascot or at Longchamp; and in the winter the newest ski fashions are on view in numerous Alpine resorts. Fashion is everywhere where there is a love of living. What K. Lewin calls social, bodily and intellectual locomotion of groups and individuals is steadily on the increase.[88] The social field in which a person moves is far more varied and less well defined than that of the elder generation This fluidity of social life has led to a lot of experimentation with fashion. Just as etiquette is less formal, so the do's and dont's of fashion are less rigid, allowing the individual greater liberty of choice. Horizontal and vertical mobility are great stimulators of fashion.

Fashion Availability. The rising standard of living due to better pay and shorter working hours does much to make fashion available for the masses. Women are no longer slaves of the household; small modern apartments with few children and little furniture and all kinds of electric devices for washing, cleaning and cooking shorten the hours of household drudgery, leaving more time for the care of beauty and the buying of clothes. Nowadays most women want to appear young and good looking no matter what age or what income group they belong to. This is quite a new outlook on life;[89] due partly to the longer life expectancy of the population at large, to the possibilities offered by modern cosmetics, hairdyes and foundation garments, and also to the security offered by the expectancy of old age pensions. Women do not want to be put on the shelf after having lived only half of their lives. The idea that elderly women should wear only sombre colours, use no make-up and have sedate hairstyles and practically retire from social life to the benefit of the young, is outlived. Women of all ages want to look young and desirable. They go on trying to be fashionable till they reach the grave. Often we have the strange experience of seeing a group of what appear to be young girls from the back, then, when they turn around we discover that in spite of short skirts and high heels, they are really quite advanced in years. This kind of thing is, however, more likely to occur in the United States where elderly women dress in younger styles and have better groomed hair than in Europe. Nevertheless this attitude to life is also appearing on this side of the Atlantic. Besides spreading to the older generation, fashion has come to the young; the age at which children start to appear fashionable comes sooner and sooner. The working classes who have grown in self respect and have more money than they have ever had before, look upon fashion as a necessity of life. Fashion has widened its boundaries, becoming available for practically all of the population.

Fashion Propaganda. Ideas about fashion are spread through the population by organized means of mass-propaganda. In the technical and industrial age in

279

which we live, the possibilities of influencing masses of people are innumerable. Propaganda can be defined as 'any and all sets of symbols which influence opinon, belief or action on issues regarded by the community as controversial.'[90] Individuals are always on the outlook for what they should have, do, or look like, to fit into the appropriate group structure. The majority of modern people who no longer live under the influence of ancestral tradition or according to the dictates of some inner principle are neither 'tradition-directed types' nor 'inner-directed types' as D. Riesman would say, but are open to all kinds of different ideas and changeable notions.[91] Such 'other-directed types' of human beings are the ideal objects of both political and economic propaganda. Modern leaders of mass-production make ample use of all methods of influencing the consumer public. 'Fashion is a satellite of public opinion.'[92] According to David Riesman consumption and free time are most important for the 'other-directeds'.[93] The modern woman, who is very fashion conscious and open to all the influences thrust upon her by the manufacturer of clothing, will spend plenty of time window-shopping to look at clothes and prices, or while away an afternoon at a fashion show. Whereas fashion shows used to be the privilege of exclusive shops, nowadays even the cheaper stores have fashion parades to inform their clients what is on the market. Modern woman is susceptible to all kinds of propaganda. She peruses newspapers, current periodicals, advertisements and films to discover what are the trends in fashion. She wants to wear what other people would like to see her in; she wants to like what it is fashionable to like, so as to fit in to the framework of social life. The social structure as 'an inclusive society with its subgroups all of them pervaded by living, dynamic opinion-trends, memories of the recent past, various and frequently opposed interests, formulated beliefs and principles',[94] is confronted with the work of various agencies of information and suggestion, acting on the specific hopes and fears of the onlookers. Moreover it must not be forgotten that the people who write the newspapers, speak to us on the radio, decorate the shop windows and make the fashion-photos are members of the same society for which they accomplish these things; they, also, are part of the network of public thinking, and, therefore, equally under the influence of the popular trend.

Public opinion a hundred years ago, must have been something vastly different from what it is today. Possibilities for the intercommunication of minds have increased by leaps and bounds. In 1896, the newspaper, the *Daily Mail* appeared as a general agency for the spread of information.[95] The radio started its life in 1920, when the Westinghouse Electric Company of East Pittsburgh broadcast the results of the Harding election.[95] Daily newspapers with their advertisements do much to bring the newest styles under the eyes of the public. Modern advertising tries to awaken mass demand. 'Mass advertising is based on the great similarities of human nature and on the uniformity of psychic reactions under similar conditions.'[96] The levelling of incomes, widespread education and the ever increasing similarity of living conditions of masses of city-dwellers has greatly contributed to making the population as a whole susceptible to the same kind of propaganda. The feeling that we are all in the same boat, every woman has household chores to perform, increases the possibility of crowds of people identifying themselves with the same elegant female on the placard, each feeling that that attractive woman on the poster could be herself, helps to hurry on a wave of fashion buying. Fashion advertisements in newspapers, shop-windows and cinemas can reach a far greater quantity of people at the same time than ever before.

Above all the fashion magazine has an important function to fulfil. In France these periodicals directly serve the interests of the fashion industry. They diffuse ideas to encourage the selling of French clothes. These magazines appeared prior to and after the First World War and have since profited immensely from the improvements in the techniques of photography and graphic illustration. Writers like Cocteau, Giraudoux and Colette; painters like Raoul Dufy and Christian Bérard helped to fill the pages.[97] In 1912, Lucien Vogel started the *Gazette de Bon Ton* which is now out of print, but, in its time was a great stimulus for other newcomers. In 1917 *Vogue* appeared in America. In 1921 it was edited in French and later followed the English edition. *Vogue* under the leadership of Edna Woolman-Chase, has become a magazine of major importance. With *Harper's Bazaar* it is the most exclusive American fashion magazine.[98] Dress patterns for home-made clothing were started in Germany, they are now made in great quantities everywhere and thrifty housewives can thus also try to be fashionable.

Since the turn of the century, the art of photography has steadily improved. Fashion photography began in 1920s–1930s. It has now become one of the most important means of fashion propaganda to be seen in the magazines and newspapers. The cinema is practically a living photograph, a continual encouragement to imitation. Young people try to look like James Dean, cut their hair like Marlon Brando, be nonchalant like Jean Gabin, do their hair like Brigitte Bardot, look slim like Audrey Hepburn, or be voluptuously rounded like Marilyn Monroe and Gina Lollobrigida. In the future television, due to the possibilities offered by Telstar and other satellites which will surely follow, may well take over many functions of the film and the photograph. People will be able to see the newest fashions parade on the screen in their own homes without even taking the trouble to go out to the cinema or await the arrival of the latest fashion magazine.

There is a definite relation between fashion and politics. Until the French Revolution political power and fashion leadership went together. Powerful European rulers such as Francis I of France, Philipp II of Spain and Louis XIV of France led the fashion of their country and often of the whole of Europe. They tried to control fashion through numerous sumptuary laws and taxes. Fashion went with political power. During the years following the French Revolution practically every successful war brought a new fashion; military uniforms were usually copies of the victor's clothes.[99] In 1813 'coats à la Blücher'; 'boots à la Wellington'; 'hats à la Platow' were fashionable.[100] When, in the middle of the Eighteenth Century France defeated Italy, most nations adopted French uniforms. The American Civil War was fought in French uniforms. In 1859, after the Austrian war, 'magenta' and 'Solferino blue' suddenly became fashion colours; 1853–56 'Crimean green' (taken from the green of the Islamic flag) and the 'ash grey' of Sebastopol were worn. In the Russo-Japanese war, Japanese kimonos and Russian blouses were copied; in the Bulgarian-Turkish war, Bulgarian colours and embroideries were widely used.[101] In 1863 'Solferino blue' was replaced by 'Mexican blue' reflecting the interests of France. 'Metternich green', from the Tyrolean Alps, also had its day. The defeat of France and the victory of the Prussians in 1870 brought a modified spiked helmet. After the battle of Sadowa in 1866, 'Bismarck brown' flooded Paris. There were many shades depicting Bismarck in varied moods such as orange for an 'angry Bismarck'.[102]

With the oncome of modern specialization and democratic methods of government, when kings and queens are practically powerless, and heads of State change every few years being only installed for a short period of time, fashion is no longer at home in this unstable atmosphere. Fashion goes with power. Consequently fashion is nowadays with the people. Clothing reflects the manner of life of the population; in Europe it is individualistic, in the United States mass-produced, in Russia it is proletarian and suited to a population that is continually goaded on to work and has little time for the development of individualistic characteristics.

The political structure of a country is the form in which social life is enclosed. Politics are a frame around life. They are a boundary within which certain things are permitted or forbidden. Thus politics may prohibit fashions as in present day Russia, or promote fashion, as in seventeenth century France under the influence of Colbert's policies. But just as the state cannot make culture so the state cannot make fashion. Culture and its offspring fashion, are reflectors of the life within the State. They develop out of the interplay of numerous complex factors which collectively shape the pattern of social life. Fashion is never made by the State, it is only encouraged or retarded by it but never instigated.

The Fashion Cycle

The growth and decline of fashions among the population is one of the most difficult things to understand. No research has led to any definite results which could form a basis for the prediction of future clothing. Psychological causes play a great part in the fashion cycle, making the exact study of the ups and downs of these movements very difficult to grasp. Just as we cannot prophesy the future of world history, so we cannot predict future fashions which are a reflection of the history that is yet to be. Fashion changes can be considered from two points of view: the long-run changes or the general trend of clothing development, and the short-run or seasonal fluctuations. A. L. Kroeber recognized that the details of fashion are quick to change but the general line evolves over a long period of time.[103]

Long-Run Fashion Changes. If we open a book of historical costumes and ponder the long-run trends of clothing through the ages, we become aware of the steady evolution of clothes and the continual recurring symbolism, which bear evidence of the continuity of fashion. 'This constancy is due to the historical structure of human consciousness'.[104] Fashion does not come out of the blue; one thing is the logical development of another. Fashion is a historical process expressed in dress.

The Evolution of Clothes. It is amazing how much tradition a person carries about with him in the clothes that he wears. For those who are aware of it, they are a constant reminder of the past. Men's clothing, which has practically become a uniform, shows forth many vestiges of ancient times. The hatband was originally a fillet worn in olden days to keep the headcloth fixed securely on the head.[105] The silk bow inside the back of a man's hat used to be threaded around the lining to make the hat fit more securely when riding.[106] Plumes, feathers and other decorations are always worn on the left side of the hat so as to be out of the way of the sword or any other weapons that the rider might use.[107] Braid stripes on men's evening trousers are left-overs from the days when trousers were too tight for the leg to pass through. They had to be buttoned and the braid was used to hide the fastening.[108] Slits on the bottom of the back of men's coats come from the seventeenth century when men went riding in their coats and could separate the two back pieces, buttoning them up at the waist so as to be out of the way when seated astride. Side pockets are vestiges of the hole through which the hilt of the sword used to be passed.[109] Nowadays often only the flap is left. Buttons on the end of sleeves of men's jackets come from the days when sleeves had to be opened to be put on; the buttons are now purely decorative. Cuffs on coat sleeves and trouser legs are reminders of the old habit of turning the sleeves and trousers of uniforms back so that the lining showed. This was done to protect the material.[110] Not only have many of the decorative details of our clothing evolved from the past, but also the garments worn on ceremonial occasions are rooted in tradition. 'The more important the ceremonial, the more ancient the clothing.'[111] Historical costumes are worn at both State and ecclesiastical functions. The coronation of kings and queens or the opening of parliament are performed in traditional dress. Ecclesiastical vestments often originated in Roman times; the alb coming from the Roman tunica alba, the amice used to be a Roman neckcloth and the chasuble derived from the Roman paenula, a garment worn by soldiers and people of lower rank.[112] The black gown of the barrister was introduced as mourning for Queen Mary II and has never been discarded since that day.[113] Academic dress, such as the 'pileus quadratus' dates from the fifteenth century; originally such garments were part of clerical costume. Wedding dresses and mourning attire are rooted in local custom. They are part of our cultural heritage, handed down from one generation to the next. The evolution of clothing is proof of the historical continuity of the human race.

Symbolism in fashion. 'A symbol is a trait of actuality that for the sensuously-alert man has an immediate and inwardly-sure significance, and that is incommunicable by process of reason.'[114] Symbolism in clothing is of two kinds; it is either phallic or significant of world-feeling. Phallic symbolism is limited to a relatively small range of possibilities which come and go in cycles very similar to the changes of 'erotic zones' discussed in the first part of this thesis. In phallic symbolism, the shoe has always been very important. The jewish word for wife and shoe is identical. A Bedouin form of divorce is 'she is my slipper, I have cast her off.'[115] In the Bible, the casting of a shoe over land was symbolical of conquering it. Old shoes are thrown after newly weds to bring them luck. In Russia, wives used to remove their husband's shoes to show their subservience as part of the wedding ceremony.[116] In Bulgaria the bridegroom makes a present of money to the relatives of the bride so that they can buy her

283

shoes for the wedding. This is called shoe money. In the Middle Ages, the points of shoes became exceedingly long; their phallic symbolism can be seen by the Church's vehement condemnation of this fashion. High headdresses such as the hennin in the fifteenth century and the wigs of the eighteenth century were morally denounced.[117] Phallic symbolism in clothes is part of the conflict between exhibitionism and modesty. Those people who are on the outlook for such symbols will find them everywhere; in pointed toes and high heels, in buttons passing through button holes, in ties, in hats, in sharp finger-nails, in the designs and shapes of feminine clothing. Innocent people often wear these fashion details, having no idea about the feelings that they may arouse in a sensitive onlooker.

Clothing is not only symbolic of sex but also of world-feeling. 'Dress is the outward expression of a man's state of mind.'[118] Each historical age has brought forth very different ideas from those who went before them and those to come after them. History has its symbols; 'woman is the mould into which the spirit of the age pours itself, and to those with any sense of history, no detail of the resulting symbolic statue is without importance.'[119] Clothing is symbolic of the values and aspirations of an age. 'The biologist from a fragment of bone can reconstruct the entire primeval beast, the student of clothes and the accessories that go with them, from the broken handle of a fan, from a cameo or a shoe buckle, can build up a convincing picture of a bygone age. Josephine's Egyptian brooches enshrine the oriental ambitions of Napoleon, the enamelled surface of a rococo snuff-box reflects the entire age of Louis XV. These things are more than relics—they are symbols, and the crinoline is as much a monument as the Albert memorial.'[120]

'Fashion is but the prevailing style of art either in pure or applied forms.'[121] Fashion and art are both expressions of the *Zeitgeist*. 'Art has been defined as *exaggeration à propos*, and the artist knows what to exaggerate. In the same way elegance is essentially exaggeration à propos, and its successful practice is as instinctive in its operations and as magical in its effect as the work of art.'[122] Most fashion creators are steeped in the art of their times; through them the impressionistic colours and ornaments of the Belle Epoche; the interior decoration and new printed designs of the Art Nouveau grasped by Paul Poiret; modern simplicity understood by Gabrielle Chanel; surrealism expressed in the creations of Elsa Schiaparelli, who was a great friend of Salvador Dali, have all found their way into clothing.

Of all the arts portrait painting is most closely related to fashion. Great portraits have brought forth many a symbol of personality 'summing up within itself and intelligently presenting the essence of that great man and the significance of his being.'[123] Portraits arise in a culture where the individual personality is especially valued. Other cultures where personality plays a lesser part, as for instance in Eastern countries, individualistic fashions and consequently portraits have not developed to the same degree as in the West. They do not have the urge to become a personality which is so deeply rooted in the West. The memories of personalities held fast for all time in pictures have inspired many a modern fashion designer. So, according to the *Figaro Litteraire*,[124] Yves Saint Laurent in the winter 1958/59 found his inspiration in the Renaissance portraits; in a Dürer sketch, a Vermeer's portrait of a lady reading, a Pisanello of a Florentine lady for an evening dress, a Goya picture of the Marquess de la Merced in black tulle. Other couturiers copied the high waists and accentuated knees of the Directoire as portrayed in a Gérard picture. Painting will always be an inspiration for fashion. Nowadays we have photography and films to help us collect the relics of our time. But none of these media have the depth or the atmosphere of oil.

'Changes in women's dress foreshadow changes in interior decoration, which in their turn foreshadow changes in architecture', writes James Laver.[125] If we look at the history of architecture and at the history of dress, we will find many similarities between buildings and clothes; the turban of Eastern church dignitaries is shaped like a mosque, a Siamese head-dress is like a votive spire in that country.[126] The hennin is similar to a gothic pinnacle. A knight's helmet in the Middle Ages resembles a gothic arch, the Assyrian mitre a Chaldean zigurat, the slashings of trunk hose in the sixteenth century the Elizabethan table leg, the Fontange headgear a William and Mary chair, the crinoline the domes of the Crystal Palace exhibition hall of 1862, and the straight square lines of 1928 fashions the Empire state building in New York.[127] In our own time, modern slim-heeled shoes and narrow-legged trousers resemble the legs of all kinds of modern furniture; the tucking up of bedspreads to reveal the legs of beds is analogous to short-skirted fashions.

There is always a time-lag in the appreciation of fashions and art. The most recent is usually despised. This despicableness is not fixed but is 'like a cloud moving over an expanse of sky. Things pass from the despised category to the second hand category into the glory of the antique.'[128] They are still too near to be understood. The modes of 1920 which used to be disliked in the war years are now more distant and no longer considered bad taste. Daughters have started rummaging amongst their mothers' old clothes; perhaps there was something in them after all.

Short-Run Fashion Changes. Besides the long run course of fashion as demonstrated by the steady evolution of garments, springing up and being worn until they gradually fade away as useless ornaments, and the significant symbolism which portrays, over a long series of years, the changing erotic suggestion and worldly aspirations of different generations, besides this there are the short-run fashion changes about which so little is really known and so much is spoken.

The fashion cycle consists of 'the rise, culmination and decline of popular acceptance of a style.'[129] There are two distinct movements in the spread of fashion.[130] The first period is marked by hesitation; one wants to be fashionable but not too quickly in case the new fashion turns out to be a false alarm. The primary fashion adherent, in each community or group, takes the lead enthusiastically and enjoys herself being ahead of all the others, making both male and female heads turn in amazement. This situation may last a few weeks, its length varies. Thereafter the fashion wave gathers momentum, spreading with growing speed within each community, through the different groups and subgroups diffusing through the masses, till it reaches its climax. How long this process of growth will continue no-one exactly knows. A fashion's death is certain once it has spread through the whole population. Thereafter comes the decline in the form of a new fashion which drives out the once popular style.

The fashion cycle can be influenced by many factors. It can be broken by catastrophes of some kind such as war, earthquakes or severe weather changes.[131] In some cases, the fashion that has not reached its climax is continued at a later date. For example in the winter 1960/61 fur hats for both sexes were becoming popular, then there was an abnormally warm period lasting for many weeks which abruptly broke this cycle. It is quite likely that in the next winter this fashion will again be taken up. However we must not forget that consumer buying declines faster than consumer use.[132] In the beginning of the cycle the curve of buying drops, but the curve of wearing is slower in the descent. People wear clothes sometime after buying them. To look just at what the majority of people on the street are wearing can be very deceptive when trying to discover the direction of the style. It looks as if a fashion is in full swing, whereas in reality it may be on the way out. What the few exceptions wear is often more important, they are the future. A fashion cycle is sometimes indefinitely lengthened; articles of continued use remain in fashion for long periods of time till something better comes.[133] The wristwatch has remained since the 1890s, nylon stockings since the Second World War, the rubber bathing cap for over thirty years.

Modern sales are times of consolidating fashion. All stimulants are used to spread the fashion among the consuming public. From a business point of view this is a very good thing. Not only are large quantities sold but the sooner the fashion spreads through all of the population, the sooner they will be bored by it and want something new. Sales used to be a method of getting rid of otherwise unsaleable articles at low prices. Modern sales are entirely different, huge quantities of goods are manufactured at low prices especially for the sales, helping to popularize the styles among the population and give them added enjoyment from fashion.[134] The unsaleable objects in the out-moded shops have a steadily declining chance of being sold when better things are to be had at modern sales.

Research on the different phases of the fashion cycle is a very difficult problem. Those people who could give the most information are least inclined to do so. Private enterprise with its competitive outlook on fashion keeps its successes and failures a secret and the academic investigator cannot count on much help from this quarter. Generally speaking the fashion cycle follows the trade cycle. One thing is, however, of particular interest: the beginning of a depression helps to increase the sales of mass-produced clothes, causing a considerable slide of the general demand curve for mass-produced fashion to the right. In a depression the higher income groups, who used to be able to afford model dresses and individual dressmaking, turn to mass production for cheaper wear. This enlarges the number of customers in such shops and helps to popularize mass-produced clothes. In the depth of the depression, of course, all business is lamed, but afterwards a certain percentage of those once higher incomes will continue to buy ready-to-wear. The depression taught them the value of mass production. This was often the case in the 1920s and 1930s.

What factors affect the speed and expansion of the fashion movement? Modern quickly changing fashions are only possible where there is a large population, much industrial activity enabling the production of large quantities of cheap goods, high earnings with rising purchasing power for families, widespread education which increases earning power and general interests, rapid and cheap means of communication and transportation. The current philosophy of life, expressed in social, political, moral and religious ideas encourage or retard the fashion movement. Democratic, tolerant philosophies are more conducive to fashion than an aristocratic, class-conscious outlook on life. The strictness of customs, morals and religion always slow down fashion. Fashion develops fastest in a fluid social structure, where tolerance, equality of opportunity and individual liberty in all spheres of life predominate.

Scientific Analyses of the Fashion Cycle. Occasionally attempts at analysing the fashion cycle with the aid of mathematical instruments have been made. Nevertheless these attempts have seldom yielded fruitful results. The studies made by A. L. Kroeber and recently those suggested by R. Barthes deserve closer attention.

One of the first and the most well-known studies concerning changes of forms in the fashion world is that undertaken by A. L. Kroeber.[135] Contrary to R. Barthes, who aims at examining the short period of one year, Kroeber made a diachrony of seventy-five years. Since fashion is a fact of numbers and manufactured objects can be more easily measured, Kroeber decided to make an inquiry into the principles guiding fashion. He wanted to discover what underlies change. If the principle of change could be determined for one simple object of clothing, it could later be applied to other, more changeable kinds of dress. Kroeber made a study of woman's full evening dress, which he thought to vary little in purpose and only slightly each season. The material of the dresses examined was always silk. Superficial parts and trimmings were disregarded; the change being therefore only stylistic. Kroeber made a statistical study of these changes. In order to do this, he had eight measurements taken:

Four for the length:

1. The total length of the figure from the centre of the mouth to the tip of the toes.
2. The distance from the mouth to the bottom of the skirt.
3. The distance from the mouth to the minimum diameter across the waist.
4. The depth of the *décolletage* from the mouth to the middle of the corsage edge in front.

Four for the width:

1. The diameter of the skirt at the hem.
2. The maximum diameter of the skirt at any point above the base.
3. The minimum diameter in the region of the waist.
4. The width of the shoulders; more accurately the width of the *décolletage* across the shoulders.[136]

These measurements were taken ten times every year. They were selected at random from different fashion volumes so as to avoid subjective selection. Kroeber made this diachrony for a period which began in 1844 and ended 1919. The data was obtained from the fashion journals *Petit Courrier des Dames* till 1868, then *Harper's Bazaar* till 1918, 1919 was taken from the March number of *Vogue*. Kroeber converted the absolute numbers obtained into percentage

287

ratios proportional to the length of the entire figure. Then these percentage figures were averaged for each year and plotted in charts.

This experiment revealed many interesting results. The width of the skirts in 1844 was 57 per cent of the body length. Then it fluctuates for many years reaching the extreme in 1859; in the crinoline, the flare of the skirt exceeded the height of the person. In eight years the skirt diameter had nearly doubled. From 1859 a progressive reduction of width was observed during fifty years. In 1908 the basal diameter was for the first time below fifty inches. In 1911, it was only twenty-three inches. From 1918–1919 twenty to twenty-three inches was usual. The average width, for seventy-six years was 65·3 inches, which measurement was recorded between 1852–1878. Kroeber speaks of a correlation between the width and the length of the skirt. A short skirt may be full or narrow, but a tight one will scarcely reach the ground on account of the inconvenience which results when walking. (Kroeber, writing in 1919, had not yet seen the tight long evening dresses with a slit down the side, so often worn in the 1930s.) The rhythmic period for a certain style of skirt length was considered to be a third of that for the width; about thirty-five years as compared with a century. The diameter of the waist fluctuates irregularly, but a short waistline always coincides with its enlargement. The periods of lowering or increasing the *décolletage* was found to be nearly three times as long as that for the rising of the corsage, which usually takes place by sudden leaps. The general course of the width of the *décolletage* is similar to that of the basal skirt width, with the probability of an even longer period.

Kroeber compares these several different rhythms of change, 'The pulsation of the width of women's skirts which is symmetrical and extends in its up and down beat over a full century . . .' can be compared to 'an analogous rhythm in skirt length, but with a period of only about a third the duration.'[137] The waistline curve may alter, following a normal curve in a seventy-year period, and a possibility that the width of shoulder exposure varies in the same manner, but with the longest rhythm of all. If the continuity of a tendency in one direction for seventy years establishes a periodicity of about a century and a half, the change in this feature of dress seems to follow a symmetrically recurrent plan. The 'conspicuous externalizations of fashion alter very fast. But the major proportions of dress change with slow majesty, in periods often exceeding the duration of human life.'[138] The development and decline of dress fashions are not symmetrical, the elements of civilization are wholly unrelated, the changes are unique.

Kroeber's conclusions might have been very different if he had examined other periods of fashion history. 1844–1918 was primarily the time of wide skirts and bourgeois fashions. The years 1918–1993, the next seventy-five years, will show very different ratios between such factors as skirt width and skirt length. Already in the 1920s knee length skirts and boyish modes produced a totally different picture with their own typical relationships between the individual parts of garments. The slow majesty of change seems to have given way to playful experimentation. Kroeber did not find a definite deterministic principle underlying fashion. The examination of a certain period of history only gives results concerning that particular period. One cannot easily apply these results to other periods without first examining them in detail.

An important fact concerning the fashion cycle has recently been brought to the fore in an article '*Le bleu est à la mode cette année*' by Roland Barthes.[139] This author is of the opinion 'that the abundance of forms upon which the entire mythology of fashion is based, is an illusion'. Let us first examine the train of thought by which R. Barthes comes to the above conclusion. This essay seems to have been written as a result of the author's extreme displeasure on reading fashion journals in which two totally different realities, written language and physical objects, which do not belong to the same order of things, are brought into close contact. The author goes on to analyse the semantic character imposed on fashion in these journals; he states that a relationship is set up between a concept (springtime, youth) and a form (an accessory, blue). The former he names '*signifié*' and the latter '*significant*'. These *signifiés* and *significants* have no necessary connection; there is no reason why '*pour le déjeuner de fête à Deauville*' a '*canezon*' should be worn or '*pour le thé dansant à Juan-les-Pins*' a '*décolleté bateau*'. The fashion journal purposely brings these two different domains together in a procedure of elementary signification; in what may be considered a lexicographical style. The phraseology of the fashion journal imbues the sign with a function, attempting to give the fashion of the moment an eternal guarantee. Consequently fashion is, so to speak, astride two systems at the same time; it is based on language (the forms of clothing) and on a meta-language (the literature of fashion).[140] This does not simplify appearances. Fashion, as opposed to the simple system of linguistics, is subject to a double system of analysis.

The author, who wants to discover the fundamental elements of fashion, tries to do this by turning to the semeiological method. He wants to get away from the economic method, which only considers categories such as 'articles of clothing' which are too wide and blur his analysis. He coins the term '*vestème*' which he has taken from morphological theory.[141] A *vestème* is a '*morphème vestimentaire*'. The concept is easier to understand if we first examine the term *morphème*. A *morphème* is the smallest unit of a language; a word, a root, affix or inflective ending: -men, run, pro-, -ing, -ess.[142] Apply this to the language of clothes and a *vestème* must mean the most elementary features which can be put together in different ways to compose a dress. Buttons, material, belt, collar, sleeves, skirt, pleats are all significant elements which can be part of a dress. The establishment of a list of *vestèmes* can best be organized by first seeking out the generic *morphèmes*: material, colour, design; then by collecting all the homogeneous classes of *signifiants*. Each of these classes constitutes a sort of syntagmatic unity, forming part of a special order. They are to be collected under such headings as: place of attachment of the piece of clothing (head, neck, hips, waist, shoulders), or clothing details (collar, pockets, pleats, borders, frills). This soon enables the formation of a paradigm, an arranged list of the main items with their opposites to help clarify their exact nature in a systematic order.

The author then explains that the number of possible *signifiés* in the fashion world, even though each *signifié* may have many *signifiants*, are few. When the *signifié* is not explicit but implied, so to speak in the air, it is fashion itself. This *signifié*, fashion, may be either named '*le bleu est à la mode*', or carried over by a succession of contingent *signifiés* (accessory = spring = fashion) or neither named nor carried over, but implied, it is the expression of a universal *signifié*, applicable to all the *signifiants* in use. The *signifié* fashion constitutes a general field of signification. The author suggests setting up a methodological inventory, a '*machine pour faire la mode*' which would serve as a mathematical registration of the variety of forms. If this machine were to be synchronized for one year, it would become evident that the abundance of forms, which are so apparent in the fashion journals, is really a mythical concept, in other words a deception. Fashion could be reduced to a finite number of recurring forms which appear in changing combinations. These changing combinations are the essence of 'newness' of fashion, whereas the number of forms is necessarily limited.

This idea is similar to the recent discussion by chess experts who suggest the establishment of an electronic machine which could be fed with magnetic bands registering all moves that could possibly be made. A human being playing against the machine is bound to lose as the machine automatically produces the best counter-moves. Nevertheless it is questionable whether such a machine would produce all the optimal possibilities, or whether the human mind would still find other solutions. The problems arising with a fashion machine are similar and even more complicated; this is due to the continual flux of fashion, the great variety of possible combinations in individuals and in groups and the many exceptions that are likely to appear.

R. Barthes' conclusion that the abundance of forms is a mythical deception is followed by the phrase, '. . . a shocking truth for an industry based entirely on the exaltation of an unceasing neology.'[143] Mr Barthes' statement that the fashion industry is not conscious of the finiteness of forms is unacceptable. If anyone has considered the recurring elements in dress, it is the manufacturer and not the designer. The latter is an artist and believes in the originality of his creations. But for the practical-minded manufacturer or businessman, this fact of basic forms is a trade secret. He does not tell anyone about it, but he knows it very well. His rationalized methods of production are based on this idea. Nevertheless, in order to sell his wares he supports the mythological deception which is created by the fashion designer and furthered by the fashion journals. It would do the manufacturer no good to inform his clients, for example, that the new bell-shaped skirt, which supposedly gives an air of youth, is practically the same as that worn a few seasons ago; his object is not to encourage the thriftiness of the consumer, but rather to awaken the desire for the new in order to sell more goods. The manufacturer has standardized patterns for all kinds of garments and parts of garments; he knows exactly what he has sold in the past and how he made it. When a new mode comes, he knows to adapt what he has to the new requirements. He does not start from scratch each time. His productive methods have to be rational, he has to keep down costs. Rationalization of procedure saves time and energy, labour and material. Mass production, due to the necessity of keeping costs low, is forced to find basic shapes. Those people who believe in the illusion of the abundance of forms are the majority of the consuming public. They are people who have had no connection with the fashion industry or with the history of costume and dressmaking. They judge by experience. As R. Barthes says, the human memory of forms is very short. Most people are not historically minded; they register mentally only those styles that they themselves have seen in their lifetime, and each time that something new appears in the fashion journal, they are overwhelmed by what seems to them to be a multitude of new shapes.

The idea of combining linguistics with fashion is for the manufacturer purely a matter of sales technique. The fashion journal is, next to the shop window, the best method of advertising new fashions. The magazine reaches a great number of people; the sketch shows what a new article of clothing looks like and the words explain the effect that a person clothed in this garment will have in certain surroundings. By a process of identification with the mannequin in the photo, the individual is encouraged to buy. No woman will buy a dress simply because it is beautiful; for her it is very important that clothing should be suitable to the occasion and to her personality. She does not want to appear ridiculous. Just as the sales girl in the shop tells a customer where and when a certain kind of dress is being worn, so the explicit *signifiés* in the magazine reassure the latent consumer about this point. For the designer and the manufacturer the relationship between the *signifié* and the *signifiant* is purely psychological; they have, of course, never thought about the semeiological aspect.

By far the most difficult and by far the most questionable term in R. Barthes' article is that of the *vestème*.[144] Mr Barthes, in order to explain clearly his theory, does not side-track, and consequently he avoids all the problems connected with the *vestème*. Nevertheless, these cannot be overlooked. As A. L. Kroeber says, in the fashion world 'the variety of phenomena to be examined are qualitative, whereas a workable law or deterministic principle must be quantitative.'[145] This is the crux of the many difficulties arising in connection with fashion. Fashion is intimately bound up with numbers. A fashion does not exist until it has borne the test of numbers. In so far it can be very misleading to study fashion solely in the light of the utopian fashion journals. Of the models sketched in the journals, many of the styles will be worn by the masses, but there are always some which will not be accepted by the public. They are failures. This is analogous to literature; of the new books published in one year, many will be sold, only a few become best-sellers, and some are destined to remain on the racks. Not every dress created by a designer is a success. An inventory of *vestèmes*, taken from the journals, where the models sketched have not yet been tried out in life, must somehow solve the problem of either registering only those *signifiants* which become reality and not those which are only suggested, or it must at some later date re-examine the finished list of *vestèmes* and remove those which time has shown to have been insignificant.

Another problem is that the *vestèmes* do not all have the same value. Some *vestèmes* play a dominant role, while others succumb to the influence of the important ones. There is so to speak a hierarchy of values. One class of *vestèmes* which may be dominant during a series of years can suddenly lose its importance and instead of being dominant become subordinate. The rhythm of change of the many *vestèmes* in relation to the *signifiés* and in relation to each other also vary at different rates. Generally speaking, the shortest cycle of change is concerned with accessories, the middle length with generic classes as colour, material and design, and those traits which combine to make up the general silhouette are the longest to remain fixed.[146]

The paradigm, which results from classifying the various *vestèmes*, is likewise subject to continual change. As the relationship between *signifié* and *signifiant* alters, different sets of opposites will appear. There are periods in which opposites are more definitely and more strictly defined. In a hierarchical or class-conscious society clothing is subject to a strict set of rules, whereas in modern, mobile times, many of these distinctions have been watered down. Nowadays an elegant dress with a matching jacket could be worn at the office, at morning coffee, at luncheon, at teatime and even to a cocktail party. This can be said of many garments in the modern world. In one year 'drap-satin' may signify evening and be opposite to tweed which is suitable for the morning. But this can suddenly change. It will be remembered that in 1953 tweed cocktail dresses with a large *décolleté* and a tweed jacket to match for street wear, were fashion. At the same time the normal tweed suit was still being worn. The variation of possible combinations is often totally unexpected and not subject to rigidly opposed distinctions. There is always a danger in establishing hard and fast terms when talking about something that is continually changing. It is questionable whether clothing can be examined from the point of view of precise and clear definitions. It is not of the same nature as philosophy or law. Fashion is not an exact science, it is largely intuitive. Its forms and meanings are far less definite and rigid, and they often change before they have been fully understood. The possibility of an inventory of *vestèmes* is easier to consider from a static viewpoint; when looking at the past it is possible to examine the syntagmatic or special unity of the parts once used. But when the continual flux, which has become so prominent in our time, is taken into consideration, the whole problem becomes very much more complicated.

That the abundance of forms in fashion is an illusion can also be proved by other methods than that proposed by R. Barthes. When we consider the basic shape of the human body, the spirit of the age which determines the *signifiés* of fashion and the development of dress-making techniques we realize that the forms of fashion are limited by these factors.

The human body has a certain construction and this construction only allows for certain kinds of draping and dressing. Clothing can only be supported on the head, shoulders and hips; legs and arms, hands and feet can also be covered. Besides these fundamental limitations resulting from the shape of the object to be covered, aesthetic considerations also play a part. Certain proportions are more pleasing to the eye than others, and fashion will often vary from one extreme to the other, but it always tends to come back to the basic laws of harmony. Perhaps this bears some relation to the Euclidean law of the Golden Section, which insists that a certain ratio of proportion of the frontal plane of a figure is most aesthetically satisfactory; the smaller length or area being to the larger as the larger is to the whole.[147] Because of this certain possible combinations are incompatible with the universal sense of good form intuitive to human nature. The individual growth or stature of a person also limits his or her suitability for certain styles. A dark-haired, fat person should be differently dressed than a slim, blond type. The laws of elegance require that the fashionable element be combined with the suitable.

The second limitation to the abundance of forms in the fashion world is the spirit of the times. No culture is receptive of all possible forms. Every age has its own leading ideas with its own world-view which constitutes its culture and these presuppose certain forms to the exclusion of others. Oswald Spengler speaks of each culture as having its own kind of mathematical theory which is expressed in its architecture and applied arts.[148] Dressmaking, which is based on geometric design, is also dependent on such ideas. The long, flowing garments of former times or the rich ornamentation of the Renaissance which we are technically capable of making, do not fit into our moden world. These

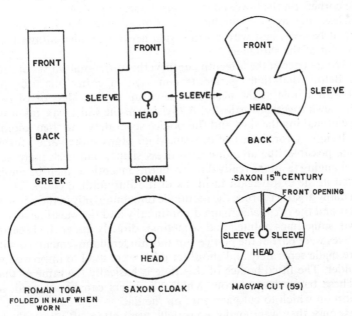

FIG. 1.

possible forms are ruled out by the kind of world-feeling of our age. Just so the masses of the inhabitants of India, who live in the throes of the caste system, are totally unsuited for our kind of dress. It does not fit in with their outlook on life. The possible and the actual in fashion rarely coincide.

Dress design and cutting evolve from geometric shapes, from circles, rectangles, squares and triangles, as already mentioned in Part I of this thesis, but of course, with many changes through the ages.[149] The level of technical dressmaking knowledge reached is always a limitation of the possible forms of dress that can be worn in a certain historical epoch. The Greeks formed garments from rectangles, circles and segments of a circle; the rectangle being the basis of the chiton, and the circle that of the cloak.

The circle is more limited in its uses than the rectangle, but it can form a useful outer covering when folded just above the half as in the Roman toga. Later, in Saxon times, a hole was made in the centre for the head to go through. The next step in evolution is to cut in from the circumference using fastenings, still

293

later holes are cut to put the arms through, finally wedge-shaped pieces are cut in from the circumference which form the sleeve as in the fifteenth century cloak. Interesting effects can be brought about by moving the hole for the head forward or to the side. In the thirteenth and fourteenth centuries the semicircle was used for a cloak which reached to the ankles. 'The more purely geometric draperies are in form, the better they are in use.'[150] Many more shapes are born of the rectangle than of the circle. The Greek chiton consisted of one long rectangle folded in half with a hole in the centre for the neck. Later, what is now known as the 'Magyar cut' developed; wedge-shaped pieces were cut up from the corners on the lower edge as may be seen in fifteenth century dresses. Nevertheless, the magyar cut has only limited uses, lacking slope on the shoulder, it behaves best with a long wide neckline, which allows it to drop on to the flat of the shoulder.[151]

In the last quarter of the fifteenth century, the horizontal waist cut came into fashion. Before that time, garments consisted of either one long piece of material with a hole at the neck and sewn up at the sides, or of two long rectangles sewn together vertically. A division at the waist was unknown. The discovery of making the skirt and the bodice separately and then joining them was revolutionary for the art of dressmaking. Many more varied forms were thus made possible; the abundance of dress shapes had been increased. Our quickly changing fashions really date from this invention; their beginning was manifested in the extravagant fashions of the Burgundian court. The bodice takes on many abstract forms, the rectangle remaining only in the construction. The collar and the décolleté changed continually and the waistline travelled up and down, sometimes pointed and sometimes directly under the breasts. First of all sleeves were part of the bodice but this hindered movement, so with time they were made separately and shoulder darts were used to improve the fit of the shoulder. The fitted bodice of this time is basically the same as that used today. These basic shapes, from which all others can be adapted, are the foundation on which to cut garments on the flat.

Sleeves, once they were made separately, were often left unattached to the garment, permitting numerous pairs of sleeves to be worn with the same dress. Their forms vary, sometimes they are made from one piece and sometimes from two. The armholes which they match are cut wider or narrower according to the fashion. The European peasant blouse is made up of six rectangles, gathered and sewn together, the smocking takes care of the extra fullness at the neck. Out of this developed the raglan sleeve; it is characterized by the diagnonal cut which removes the unwanted fullness and gives a better fit.[152] This shape allows greater variation.

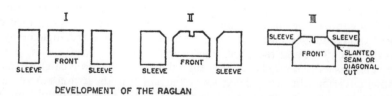

DEVELOPMENT OF THE RAGLAN

FIG. 2.

The skirt is based sometimes on a circle and sometimes on a rectangle. For many centuries it was a straight length of material gathered at the waist, or often it consisted of a series of rectangles which were sewn together. In the sixteenth century the skirt was opened up in front, showing the rich petticoats underneath. In the reign of Elizabeth I, a series of straight lengths were often pleated into the waist. The seventeenth century brought the draping back of the opened skirt, which merged into the fitted bodice. The circle is the basis of many skirt forms. Two thirds of a circle produce the partially flared skirt. A fitted skirt falls within one third of a circle, a slight curve fitting it to the hip. To obtain the waist curve for the circular skirt, one sixth of the waist measure gives the radius; for the semiflare, one fourth of the waist measure gives the radius, while for the fitted skirt a half of the waist measure is needed, but placed seven inches below the waist. These skirt patterns can be used as basic shapes for adaptation purposes.

We see therefore, that geometric shapes form the basis of all dressmaking; circles, squares, rectangles and triangles have to be continually used. Because the geometric shapes bear more definite relation to the grain of the material, they are more satisfactory than abstract forms.[153] The type of material used is of great importance; linen, wool, silk and nylon are each suitable for different kinds of clothing. They cannot all be treated alike and they do not lend themselves to the same kind of workmanship.

It is in England that the strict geometric lines of dressmaking have been most fully developed, in such garments as the gentleman's suit or the ladies classic *deux-pièces*. The French, on the other hand, even though their forms ultimately rest on the same geometric basis, are more likely to follow their fancy; they model their creations directly on the figure, which results in a softer and more exquisitely moulded garment, fitting the owner in minute detail.[154]

The abundance of the possible forms of clothing is dependent on the level of technical development in the drafting, cutting and sewing up of materials. This develops chronologically, not according to a set of hard and fast rules. The basic shapes are few, but the possible adaptations are numerous. Thus a conclusion similar to that of R. Barthes is reached by following another train of thought.

The fact that the abundance of forms is far less great than appears to the uninformed person can be seen by considering a few examples from the history of fashion. If we examine the development of the sleeve or the shoe, we see that what looks like an ever-changing variety can be worked down to a few fundamental forms from which other forms are solely an adaptation or an enlargement.

Sleeves as we know them did not exist in Greek and Roman times; they were simply part of the fold or drapery of the rectangular or circular unsewn garment. Later the desire for comfort inspired people to cut away the superfluous material under the arms, so that only a rectangular piece of material covering the arms was left. This could be joined underneath, forming the first cut sleeves which were used in ancient Egypt, Persia and Assyria.[155] Later sleeves were cut as a separate rectangle and sewn onto the dress, which was also rectangular. The Middle Ages took over the long, close-fitting sleeves of Byzantium. In the eleventh and thirteenth centuries, the dolman sleeve, a large cape-like sleeve which was cut in one piece with the body of the dress appeared, also the bellow sleeves which were gathered at the cuff, having a long vertical slit through which the hand could pass. In the eleventh century sleeves which were wide and turned back to reveal the ornate cuff were fashionable. With time they became long and pointed; the points grew until under the influence of Burgundy they practically reached the ground.[156] The mancheron or false hanging sleeve appeared; it became fashionable to wear an under sleeve, which was often part of the chemise, and an over sleeve which was detachable and could be tied or hooked to the bodice. In the thirteenth century the sleeve was for the first time fitted to an oval shaped armhole. The leg of mutton sleeve became popular, it was very wide at the shoulder and tapered down to the wrist. In 1625 sleeves were puffed below the elbow and later slashed. In 1680 large cuffs were fashionable for men.

Till the end of the Seventeenth Century, men and women wore what was essentially the same kind of sleeve. From then on men's sleeves take on the classical shape that has hardly changed till today. For women a great variety of shapes appeared: the bishops sleeve, wide and gathered at the cuff; the amandis sleeve, tight cuffed at the wrist; the beret sleeve, made from a wide circle of fabric; the Donna Maria sleeve, full and puffed below the elbow and then tight towards the wrist; the Dubarry sleeve, puffed above and below the elbow; the Gabrielle sleeve, full from the shoulder to the elbow, then fairly full to the middle of the forearm, ending in a deep cuff with a lace band. Popular were also the demi-gigot sleeve, full at the top, but tight from the elbow to the wrist; the mamaluke sleeve, reaching to the wrist; the Marie sleeve which was full and tied at intervals forming puffs; the Montespan sleeve with a full upper and lower part, a band at the elbow and ruffles extending over the forearm.[157]

The 1830s saw the pagoda sleeve, shaped like a funnel tight at the top and gradually widening at the wrist with several ruffles and the Pompadour sleeve which was elbow length and edged with ruffles.[158] These many kinds of sleeve were continually used in the fashions of the nineteenth century. In 1900 greater simplicity in sleeve making appeared; the kimono sleeve which was a return to the simple rectangle and the raglan sleeve with an extremely large opening at the armhole became fashion. In recent times not many new forms appeared, the only one being the leaving off of the sleeve in summer dresses and cocktail wear. Otherwise, the raglan, dolman, high puff and long simple sleeve are used most frequently.

To sum up, sleeves which are given such importance and such various picturesque names can be reduced to a few basic forms. Either they are part of the bodice, such as the sleeves of the Middle Ages or they are made separately from rectangular or circular pieces of material and sewn to the bodice later. One of the most important variations is concerned with the width of the armhole which can reach from the waist to the neck at its widest or only just allow enough room for the arm to pass through at its narrowest. The length of the sleeve can vary from the short sleeve just covering the shoulder to the long sleeve which practically reaches to the ground. The sleeve can of course be slim or voluminous. The set-in sleeve which is sewn in later, allows for more variations. It can be narrow or straight as in the man's suit jacket, or it can be very wide, the main variation consisting in playing about with the puffs, putting them up as in the Montespan sleeve, or down as in the gigot sleeve, or making an even variation of a row of puffs as in the Gabrielle sleeve, or one huge puff as in the bishop's sleeve, which reaches from shoulder to wrist.[159] Under and over sleeves add richness to the total appearance; slashings and transparency can give an interesting effect. Sleeves are modified by the shape of the shoulder, either bombasted, square, slanting or naturally shaped, or by the decoration at the sleeve bottom consisting of the cuff which can be wide or narrow, braided or buttoned and the great variety of ruffles, lace, ribbon, velvet, fur and other trimmings which can be used to ornament this piece of apparel. These elements are basic. The variety of forms is practically always an adaptation of one or some of them; varying according to which '*vestèmes*' are modish in the period considered. Sleeve shapes seem to be so multifarious because of the wealth and variety of ornamentation which often hides their relatively simply construction.

The history of the shoe leads to similar results. Sandals, consisting of a sole with straps, are found among the primitives, the Greeks and the Romans. In the Middle Ages, the slipper with a pointed toe appeared; the poulaine reached such an extreme form, that the long pointed toe had to be fastened to the knee. Clogs were worn as a protection against the mud; also the galoche, consisting of a wooden platform with ornamental fastenings. The fourteenth and fifteenth centuries saw the ankle-length boot. Rounded wide toes appeared, later to be followed by square ones in the Renaissance. Shoe roses, which were made of puffs or ribbon, were popular as ornaments. All sorts of boots were worn in the seventeenth century; the bucket-top boot (wide and often topped with a broad cuff), the jack-boot, which was large and heavy reaching to the knee.[160]

Under Louis XIV of France, high red-heeled shoes with buckles and straps came into fashion. Before this time shoes with heels were unknown.[161] From 1665–1720 long, square toes were popular, thereafter the rounded point. At this time, men's and women's shoes, which had always been the same, start to vary. 1774 brought the lower heel for men and high pointed heels for women, set with jewels and enamel. The Greek sandal and ballet slipper came in during the years of the 'Graecomania'. Men wore black kid pumps with a short vamp and a buckle. In 1804, women had a small wedge heel. The toe alternates between rounded, pointed and square shapes. A high, ankle shoe with a square heel, short tongue and latchet, as well as Hessian and Wellington boots were favoured by men. In 1835 the conservative men in France adopted the heavy sole and square toe, the extremists wearing the pointed toe. In the 1860s the front lacing of the shoes came in. Boots and shoes became lower. From 1868–1889 side buttoning, lacing, or an elastic inset became fashion. Patent leather shoes were popular for street wear.

1900 marks the beginning of modern shoe production.[162] The new methods of manufacture made it possible to produce many more forms at the same time. Men still wore the vamp with a pointed toe, the high laced shoe for winter, the white canvas shoe for summer and patent leather for dancing. Women wore the high buttoned boot, patent leather shoes with a cloth top, pumps for summer and low-heeled shoes for walking. In 1910 the pump with the horizontal strap appeared. In 1914, Oxfords were gradually displacing the high shoe formerly worn by men. Women favoured the baby Louis heel, having a medium or low height, with very pointed toes. Boots were practically out of the picture. From 1928–1939 the platform shoe, consisting of cork layers, appeared. During the war, low and high-heeled Oxfords were worn by women. Shoes had heavy, square, medium heels and rounded toes. Many kinds of shoe were worn; high heels for dressy occasions and flat shoes for casual wear. In 1958 the pointed toe and slim heel came into fashion under Italian influence.

Like the sleeve, footwear can be reduced to basic elements. There are boots, shoes and sandals. Shoes can be high like a boot, or scantily made of straps like a sandal; the different levels of variation between the two extremes depending on use; the weather, sport, profession and war play a role. And of course fashion has a great influence. The toes of footwear always vary between pointed, square and rounded. Nevertheless, there does not seem to be a logical or definite sequence in this change. Pointed toes are usually closed, square and rounded forms lend themselves more easily to the influence of the sandal, becoming open or strapped according to the fashion. Closed shoes can be decorated with buckles, artificial flowers, jewels or abstract ornamentations. Heels can be high, medium or low, thick or thin, square, rounded, concave or convex shaped. The body of the shoe may be ornamented, of different materials or colours, cut out in ornamental shapes or plain. Fastenings, more often seen on boots, can vary between lacing, buttons, straps, clasps, zippers and elastic inlets. Boots have ornamented cuffs, made of different materials or of fur. Different combinations of these basic elements make up the shoe line. Other variations are due to changes in material, colour scheme, design and ornamentation.

R. Barthes' statement that 'the "renewing" of fashion is essentially due to the apparent novelty of combinations, not to the change of traits'[163] is very true. We have seen that the abundance of forms can be reduced to basic elements, this being due to the anatomy of the human body, the spirit of the times and the standard of development reached in the art of dressmaking. Kroeber, who was one of the first to make an experiment with fashion, sought a deterministic principle; but he did not come to any really significant results; we do not learn much by being told that the ratio of change between the width of the skirt and the width of the *décolleté* averages so and so much in seventy-five years. R. Barthes, who has adopted a new method of approach, suggested the *vestème*, which has, perhaps, greater possibilities for research. In the article '*Le bleu est à la mode cette année*', the concept of the *vestème* seems to be a somewhat complicated term, so many kinds of classification are made. This would probably be clarified by an attempt at making such a synchrony for one year. One could then examine the results of the experiment and see whether this method bears promise of further developments. The idea of examining the '*unité syntagmatique*' of clothing could be very enlightening; fashion has seldom been examined academically from the point of view of the combination of minute parts of garments. It would be interesting to find out which kind of basic sleeve shape is being combined with which colour, kind of material, frills, cuffs and shoulder form in one year; or what shape of shoe is being placed together with which material, colour, toe, heel and ornamentation. When looking at the history of the sleeve and the shoe, it becomes apparent that the many features making up these articles of clothing in each century, are in reality '*vestèmes*' in the sense of R. Barthes. If some enterprising individual would take the time and the trouble to study these combinations in detail, he might come to interesting conclusions concerning the long- and short-run fashion cycles. With time it might become necessary to establish a macro-diachrony consisting of the comparison of several years and even centuries of the same type of clothes. This would show to what extent the abundance of forms is an illusion and exactly how useful a scientific analysis of this type could be.

Conclusion

The clothing habits of mankind, are, for those who can understand their language, a reflection of the needs and aspirations of a society. The individual learns to dress in the primary group. Clothing mirrors the social psychological influences of group life. The fashions of many individuals, of the masses, living in various groups, reflects those group interactions and interdependencies which form the way of life of a social structure, showing up its cultural values and deficiencies. 'Mass-phenomena are mechanisms of social change. They initiate innovation and the transformation of norm systems and social structures.'[164] The changes brought about by short- and long-run fashion cycles, taken collectively, show forth the manner of social change. By studying the trend of fashion developments through the centuries, we can obtain a realistic and convincing picture of social history and its determinants.

References

1. E. K. Francis, *Wissenschaftliche Grundlagen soziologischen Denkens* (Dalp-Taschenbücher, Bern 1957), p. 26.
2. Shakespeare, *Hamlet*, Act I, Sc. III.
3. G. W. Allport, Introduction to *Resolving Social Conflicts* by K. Levi (N. Y. 1948), p. vii.
4. R. M. MacIver and C. H. Page, *Society* (London, 1953), p. 213.
5. Ibid., p. 24.
6. P. Hofstätter, *Einführung in die Sozialpsychologie* (Stuttgart, 1959), pp. 180–213.
7. G. Simmel, *Philosophie der Mode* (Berlin, 1914), p. 6.
8. E. Sapir, 'Fashion', in: *Encyclopaedia of Social Sciences* (1930), vol. 5, p. 140,
9. Simmel, op. cit., p. 8.
10. F. Huber, *Die Mode und die Frau* (Wien (w. y.)), p. 9.
11. J. Laver, *Dress—How and Why* (London, 1950), p. 66.
12. P. Nystrom, *The Economics of Fashion* (N. Y., 1928) (*see* Chapter 10).
13. A. Elster, *Handwörterbuch der Staatswissenschaften*, 4. Auflage, Bd. 6, p. 610.
14. J. Dreier, *Die Mode als betriebswirtschaftliches Problem*, Diss. (Köln, 1957), p. 12, quoted from A. Rasch, *Die Entwicklung der Mode* (Tübingen, 1910).
15. P. Hofstätter, *Einführung in die Sozialpsychologie* (Stuttgart, 1959), p. 14.
16. Shakespeare, *Much Ado About Nothing*, Act III, Scene III.
17. R. König, *Mode in der menschlichen Gesellschaft* (Zürich, 1958), p. 113.
18. Hofstätter, op. cit., p. 60.
19. Ibid., p. 61.
20. Ibid., pp. 60–2.
21. Francis, op. cit., p. 63.
22. Hofstätter, op. cit., p. 319.
23. Ibid, p. 304.
24. Francis, op. cit., p. 80—describing the theory of Homans, G. C. Homans, *The Human Group*, 1950.
25. N. Stern, *Mode und Kultur* (Dresden, 1915)—'cloth-made thoughts'.

299

26. A. Elster, 'Wirtschaft und Mode', in: Jahrbücher für Nationalökonomie und Statistik, 3. Folge, 46. Band, p. 200.
27. Nystrom, op. cit., pp. 167–8.
28. Ibid., p. 191.
29. P. Schuppisser, 'Das Modezentrum Paris', in: Mode in der menschlichen Gesellschaft (Zürich, 1958), p. 269.
30. M. Rouff, Philosophie der Eleganz (München, 1956), p. 155 ff.
31. Simmel, op. cit.
32. M. Davenport, The Book of Costume (N. Y., 1949), p. 474.
33. W. Sombart, Luxus und Kapitalismus (Leipzig, 1922), p. 116.
34. H. Heaton, Economic History of Europe (N. Y., 1948), p. 294.
35. Heaton, op. cit., p. 225.
36. Clément, P., Lettres, Instructions et Mémoires de Colbert, Tome 11 (Paris, 1863), p. 268.
37. Heaton, op. cit., p. 295.
38. N. Stern, Die Weltpolitik der Weltmode (Stuttgart, 1915), p. 12.
39. Schuppisser, op. cit., p. 269.
40. Ibid., loc. cit.
41. Ibid., p. 270.
42. Ibid., loc. cit.
43. Nystrom, op. cit., p. 203.
44. Schuppisser, op. cit., p. 272.
45. Nystrom, op. cit., p. 208.
46. Ibid., p. 209.
47. Schuppisser, op. cit., p. 273.
48. Ibid., p. 306.
49. Nystrom, op. cit., p. 115.
50. G. Evers, Spielregeln der Mode (Düsseldorf, 1949), p. 29.
51. Article 'Mode', in: Der Spiegel, 12. Jahrgang, Nr. 39, 24 (Sept. 1958), p. 49.
52. Schuppisser, op. cit., pp. 284–5.
53. E. Hawes, Fashion is Spinach (N. Y., 1940), pp. 108–9.
54. Laver, 1950, op. cit.
55. F. Huber, Die Mode und die Frau, Wien (w. y.), p. 63.
56. Hawes, op. cit.
57. Nystrom, op. cit., p. 189.
58. Ibid., p. 191.
59. Hawes, op. cit., p. 38.
60. Christian Dior, Christian Dior et Moi (Paris, 1956), pp. 150–151.
61. Schuppisser, op. cit., p. 358.
62. Article 'Mode,' op. cit., p. 52.
63. Ibid., p. 53.
64. Schuppisser, op. cit., p. 359.
65. Article 'Mode,' op. cit., p. 53.
66. Schuppisser, op. cit., p. 359.
67. Ibid., p. 360.
68. Article 'Mode', op. cit., p. 55.
69. Simmel, G., 'Das Abenteuer', in: Philosophische Kultur (Leipzig, 1919), p. 8.
70. Ibid., p. 9.
71. Ibid.
72. Sombart, op. cit.
73. Ellis Havelock, Geschlecht und Gesellschaft—Grundzüge der Soziologie des Geschlechtslebens (Würzburg, 1910), p. 72.
74. S. Varenius, 'Mode als Verkaufsvehikel', in: Frankfurter Allgemeine Zeitung, Nr. 24, 28. (January, 1961).
75. Nystrom, op. cit., p. 32.
76. Ibid., p. 33.
77. Ibid., p. 34.
78. Ibid., p. 10.
79. Ibid., loc. cit.
80. Article 'Mode', op. cit., p. 49.

81. Francis, op. cit., p. 87.
82. G. Le Bon, *Psychologie des Foules* (Paris, 1895), p. 20.
83. P. Hofstätter, Gruppendynamik (Hamburg, 1957), p. 24.
84. Ibid., p. 21.
85. Aristotle, *Politics*, Book III.
86. MacIver and Page, op. cit., p. 364.
87. König, op. cit.
88. Lewin, K., Die Lösung sozialer Konflikte, Bad Nauheim 1953, p. 25.
89. König, op. cit., p. 265.
90. R. K. Merton, *Social Theory and Social Structure* (Illinois, 1951), p. 265.
91. D. Riesman, *Die einsame Masse* (Hamburg, 1958) (The Lonely Crowd).
92. Stern, Dresden 1915, op. cit., p. 212.
93. Riesman, op. cit.
94. W. J. H. Sprott, *Sociology* (Hutchinson's University Library, London), p. 117.
95. Ibid., p. 118.
96. K. Marbe, *Psychologie der Werbung* (Stuttgart, 1927), p. 58.
97. E. Arnet, '*Pionere, Boten und Richter der Mode*', in: *Mode in der menschlichen Gesellschaft* (Zürich, 1958), p. 243.
98. Ibid., p. 244.
99. J. Laver, *Taste and Fashion* (London, 1946), (*see* Chapter 22).
100. Stern, Dresden 1915, op. cit., p. 199.
101. Stern, Stuttgart 1915, op. cit., p. 14.
102. Schaefer, '*Oda, Metternichgrün und Bismarckbraun*, in: *Frankfurter Allgemeine Zeitung*, Nr. 60, 11 (März, 1961).
103. A. L. Kroeber, 'On the Principle of Order in Civilization as Exemplified in Changes in Fashion', in: *American Anthropologist*, N. S. xxi (1919), p. 258.
104. A. Vierkandt, *Die Stetigkeit im Kulturwandel* (Leipzig, 1908), p. 2.
105. W. H. Webb, *The Heritage of Dress* (London, 1907), p. 52.
106. Ibid., p. 56.
107. Ibid., loc. cit.
108. Ibid., p. 80.
109. Ibid., p. 26.
110. Ibid., p. 36.
111. Ibid., p. 184.
112. M. Davenport, *The Book of Costume* (N. Y., 1949), pp. 95, 96.
113. Webb, op. cit., p. 216.
114. O. Spengler, *Untergang des Abendlandes*, transl. by C. F. Atkinson (London, 1959), p. 163.
115. Webb, op. cit., p. 179.
116. Ibid., p. 177.
117. J. C. Flügel, 'Clothes Symbolism and Clothes Ambivalence', in: *International Journal of Psychoanalysis*, vol. 10 (London, 1929), p. 208.
118. P. Binder, *The Peacock's Tail* (London, 1958).
119. Laver, 1946, op. cit., p. 250.
120. Ibid., p. 262.
121. Nystrom, op. cit., p. 105.
122. Laver, 1946, op. cit., p. 249.
123. Spengler, op. cit., p. 259.
124. Article 'Mode', op. cit., p. 55.
125. Laver, 1946, op. cit., p. 266.
126. Webb, op. cit., p. 50.
127. Laver, J., Style and Costume, London 1948.
128. Ibid., 1946, op. cit., p. 262.
129. Nystrom, op. cit. p. 18.
130. Ibid., p. 36.
131. Ibid., p. 219.
132. Ibid., p. 22.
133. Ibid., p. 21.
134. König, op. cit., pp. 220–1.

135. Kroeber, op. cit.
136. Ibid.
137. Ibid., p. 258.
138. Ibid., loc. cit.
139. R. Barthes, 'Le bleu est à la mode cette année', in: Revue française de sociologie, Première année, no. 2 (1960) (see Chapter 17).
140. Ibid., p. 149.
141. Ibid., p. 154.
142. Britannica World Language Dictionary, Funk and Wagnall's International Edition (Chicago, 1960).
143. Barthes op. cit. p. 162.
144. Ibid., p. 154. 'Pour ces morphèmes vestimentaires, je proposerai le nom de "vestèmes"'; par analogie avec les 'mythèmes' de Cl. Lèvi-Strauss.
145. Kroeber, op. cit., p. 236.
146. Nystrom, op. cit., p. 29.
147. 'Golden Section', in: Britannica World Language Dictionary, op. cit.
148. Spengler, op. cit., p. 59.
149. R. K. Evans, Dress—the Evolution of Cut and its Effect on Modern Design (London, 1939), p. 11.
150. Ibid., p. 28.
151. Ibid., pp. 18–22.
152. Ibid., p. 60.
153. Ibid., p. 74.
154. R. Klein, Lexikon der Mode (Baden-Baden, 1960), p. 108.
155. Ibid., pp. 23–4.
156. C. Bradley, A History of World Costume (U.S.A., 1955).
157. Ibid.
158. N. Bradfield, Historical Costumes of England 1066–1936 (London, 1938).
159. Bradley, op. cit.
160. Ibid.
161. Klein, op. cit., pp. 333–6.
162. Bradley, op. cit.
163. Barthes, op. cit., p. 162.
164. Francis, op. cit., p. 84.

Chapter 16

THE DYNAMICS OF INNOVATION*
by Roy Hayhurst

The author takes a broader view of diffusion and innovation, extending his analysis to product fields not normally associated with fashion elements.

THE development and marketing of new products and services make substantial demands on the resources available to industry. The impetus for this activity derives essentially from industry's own needs: to maintain or improve levels of sales and profit in the face of increasingly shorter product life cycles or, given the competitive nature of competitive business, simply in order to survive. The innovatory behaviour of manufacturers must however be complemented by the development of new patterns of behaviour by consumers and, possibly, by distributors. Frequently, consumers are not prepared to innovate as the manufacturer would wish; this accounts in part for the hazards associated with the introduction of new products. As a result, a battery of techniques has been developed to assist in reducing the risks. It is the object of this chapter to examine these techniques briefly, to identify those areas where our knowledge is inadequate and to suggest promising directions for improvements.

Present Techniques for Analysis

The risks associated with new product introduction differ according to circumstance. A manufacturer of capital goods for industry or consumer durables is likely to make a substantial proportion of his total investment before any finished products have been produced. On the other hand, businesses which produce relatively inexpensive consumer goods, such as convenience goods or household products, may incur most of the total outlay in marketing expenses such as advertising and promotion. The methods which are used to evaluate the likely outcome of a product launch will vary accordingly. We shall be concerned here primarily with consumer goods and most of the techniques reviewed may be quite inappropriate to the situation of the industrial producer.

At the outset, it is necessary to remember that the application of techniques takes place within an organizational framework which can be highly structured or relatively informal. Although many firms are now adopting the Venture

* From *Exploration in Marketing Thought* (1969).

Group or Venture Manager concept, most still rely on new products being managed by executives who have line responsibility for existing brands. Behavioural problems often result, such as the conflict between a marketing manager's need to be aggressively optimistic in promoting the success of current products and to achieve a well balanced evaluation of the outcome of a new product. Controls may well have to be exercised by other managers; thus it is not uncommon to find that the subjective judgement applied to interpret information obtained from research is being applied in a disorganized fashion. This can be unfortunate, since it must be stressed that the prediction of consumer reactions to a new product depends on obtaining relevant information and thereafter ascribing the probabilities of occurrence to the various outcomes.

In the consumer field, programmes of evaluation frequently follow a logical sequence, starting with the initial testing of the new concepts which have been developed. This requires the presentation to potential consumers of the new product ideas, possibly in the form of a simple verbal statement or, at the other end of the scale, highly developed pictorial and verbal messages. Concept testing is normally used to compare a number of propositions and those which are best understood and are, on this simple basis, most acceptable to those interviewed may be approved for technical development. As pilot production quantities become available, it is usual to conduct one or more forms of product test. These may range from a simple office test designed to establish preference for perfumes or flavours etc., to much more ambitious placement tests by carefully selected samples of potential users, often on a comparative basis against the principal competitive product. Tests of this kind have many uses: they identify any major disadvantages of the new product, establish the relevance of promotional platforms and give an indication of the likely success of the new brand, given that all the other aspects of the marketing mix are effective in the market place. In order that the consumer can be persuaded to try the new brand, it will be necessary to achieve distribution and present an attractive proposition for consumer trial through effective pricing and promotional strategy. Other artificial features of product testing procedures may be observed: for example, the reliance on attitudes and preferences being expressed by only one member of the household, ignoring the decision processes which take place within the family.

The increasing use of test marketing activities has been prompted by the acknowledgement that, having tested and developed individual elements of the marketing mix in isolation and in artificial situations, it is then necessary to evaluate the effectiveness of the total marketing mix in the actual market. This is not always a reliable procedure; the experimental situation is disturbed by many variables, such as the difficulty of finding a geographical microcosm which is representative on all relevant dimensions, the dynamics of the market (particularly competitive activity) and the formidable problems of internal control. It is possible to take into account these recognized variables by weighting the final results; it is not however possible to make adjustments for variables which are either unrecognized or unquantifiable. A major area of this uncertainty lies in inadequate knowledge of consumer behaviour towards innovations.

Thus, the need for better knowledge of consumer behaviour towards innovations has been highlighted dramatically by instances of products whose users in a test market situation had quite different demographic characteristics from the consumers who represented the going market for the product after a period in national distribution.

Innovation and the Consumer

A new branch of the study of consumer behaviour has recently emerged to develop our knowledge of consumer behaviour towards innovations. Investigation into the Diffusion of Innovations has been notably encouraged by the work of Everett Rogers,[1] and later researchers have tried to apply the theories and concepts developed especially in the field of rural sociology within the broad stream of consumer innovation.

The elements of Diffusion may be viewed as:

1. The acceptance.[2]
2. Over time.
3. Of some specific item—an idea, practice or product.
4. By individuals, groups or other adopting units.
5. Linked to specific channels of communication.
6. To a social structure.
7. To a given system of values or culture.

Empirical investigation of these elements of the diffusion process has given us considerable insight into the dynamics of consumer innovation. Unfortunately, many of the important concepts and hypotheses have not been vigorously tested and the evidence is frequently ambiguous. However, it is worth looking at the principal elements in more detail.

For our purposes, we can consider acceptance as being continued use of a product, resulting from the individual's movement over time through the following stages:

(a) Awareness.
(b) Interest.
(c) Evaluation.
(d) Trial.
(e) Adoption (or Rejection).

Thus, the individual is seen to start with initial exposure to the innovation, where he is aware of it but not motivated to seek further information. A debate exists as to whether this stage is a passive act; it has been argued that awareness is not simply created by exposure but depends on the existence of a problem or need and a major variable here is the individual character of the product or market. From this primary stage the individual moves on to interest in the innovation, when he becomes purposive, and to an evaluation of the innovation, where it is assessed within his present or future situation and the decision is made to try or reject it. It is at this stage, where awareness and interest exist, that the influence of others at a personal level on a decision to try the product is probably most important, reinforcing the initial stimulus received from mass media sources. The fourth stage may be reached after this decision and, if the product fulfils the consumer's expectations, it is likely that he or she will repurchase and enter the final stage of adoption. Thus, this scheme describes the process within the individual in terms of a sequence, to which we can relate the manufacturer's measurement of awareness produced by advertising (stage *a*), initial trial (stage *d*) and repurchase (stage *e*).

Other schemes to portray the success of the adoption (or rejection) of an innovation have been proposed. The Lavidge and Steiner model[3] for example suggests a sequence of awareness, knowledge, liking, preference, conviction and purchase, thus breaking down Rogers' stage of adoption into a series of steps in the formation of favourable attributes towards the innovation. The common feature of these models is their implication of a consumer decision process between the stages of awareness and trial and the importance during this period of an individual's interpersonal reciprocal communication.

As far as the innovation itself is concerned, this need not be an idea or a product which is intrinsically new. If an existing product is being introduced to a new market segment—especially one geographically separate—it will be regarded by consumers as an innovation.

Considerable interest has been focused on ways of classifying innovations in order to identify variations in the processes of diffusion. Robertson[4] sees three basic groups:

1. A *continuous* innovation which has the least disrupting influence on established patterns of consumer behaviour. These are probably modifications and extensions of existing products, such as fluoride toothpaste and menthol cigarettes.
2. A *dynamically continuous* innovation, which has more disruptive consequences than continuous innovations. Even so, Robertson contends that innovations in this group do not generally alter established patterns and such examples are cited as electric toothbrushes and touch-tone telephones.
3. *Discontinuous* innovations involve the establishment of a new product and the formation of new behaviour patterns—such as television and computers.

Thus, the need to adapt consumer behaviour is seen to vary according to the perceived extent of innovation within the product or, we might add, within the associated communication.

Rogers[5] suggests that the diffusion system for a specific product will depend on five dimensions associated with the innovation as follows:

1. *Relative advantage:* as seen, for example, in terms of economic profitability or labour-saving.
2. *Compatibility:* or the degree to which the innovation is consistent with the values of the consumer and the norms of his or her group.
3. *Complexity:* or how difficult the innovation is to understand and use.

306

4. *Divisibility:* the extent to which an innovation may be tried on a limited basis.
5. *Communicability:* the results of some innovations are easily observable and may be more rapidly diffused to others. Thus, to take familiar examples, women's fashions and facial cosmetics will communicate more rapidly than, say, products employed in the preparation of food.

Later research has shown that the differences between innovations are of great importance in determining their acceptance by different social groups and the way in which they are adopted. Saxon Graham[6] showed that social classes accept innovations to the extent that the characteristics of the innovations and the cultural characteristics of the classes are compatible. Thus, higher socio-economic groups in the United States were found to be conservative in accepting television, whereas lower classes were conservative in accepting canasta. In the case of television, the rejecters differed from adopters in that they preferred active, participative recreational activities whereas with canasta the adopters were shown to possess markedly different features from rejecters, including a greater interest in active recreation, greater participation in card-playing and greater social intercourse. The higher status groups possessed the appropriate characteristics (apart from frequency of playing cards) to a much higher degree and were more prepared to adopt this innovation.

If we now look at further elements of the diffusion process, it becomes more difficult to find consistent findings and much more difficult to apply theory to the operational realities of introducing new products. A number of studies have examined the characteristics of distinct groups of consumers as to how they behave towards innovations. Most of the evidence suggests that individuals with common demographic characteristics do not behave in a consistent way towards all innovations. For every new product there will be a new group of innovative individuals who may have been slow to accept other innovations. Rogers, however, did begin to classify individuals according to when they adopted a number of selected innovations and went on to impute certain characteristics to each group. His five groups are:

		%
(a)	Innovators	2·5
(b)	Early Adopters	13·5
(c)	Early Majority	34·0
(d)	Late Majority	34·0
(e)	Laggards	16·0
		100

The size of each of these groups has been determined by laying off standard deviations from the mean time of adoption, the dimension of innovativeness being a normal distribution.

Having distributed the population who accept innovations into groups according to *when* the innovation was accepted. Rogers and later researchers have gone on to attribute certain characteristics to members of each group.

307

Innovators are seen as well-educated; their sources of information transcend the local community as they participate directly in national and local organizations. Early Adopters, have an above average education; they enjoy positions of leadership in the community and their levels of media exposure (especially printed) are above average. The third group, the Early Majority, are slightly above average in terms of education, are older and, although not leaders, are active members of organizations. They rely more than the two previous groups on *informal* sources of information. The major characteristics of the two latter groups are that they are progressively older and less well-educated.

The implication of these characteristics is that earlier adopters or innovators must act largely as a result of information derived from mass media sources of information, whereas later adopters may imitate the behaviour of these innovators, or at least allow their evaluation to be influenced by these leaders.

Thus, in a test market situation, the danger of relying on crude measurements of achievement is that sales may have been made largely to the earlier groups in the adoption scale, whereas the latter groups have not yet been attracted. There are arguments to suggest that innovators especially behave in a 'butterfly' manner, sampling a great number of innovations but remaining loyal to only a few, whereas other groups may need a longer time to be introduced to the trial stage—yet tend to remain more loyal and considerably more important for the success of the product in the medium and long term.

Later research has shown that we need to regard Rogers' scheme with a great deal of caution.

The question of the role of external agents in the communication process has also presented us with a series of fascinating concepts but conflicting evidence on the validity of the hypotheses which have been generated.

Katz and Lazarsfeld[7] first argued the importance of interpersonal communication in the sphere of Social and Political Attitudes as well as in Marketing and Fashion. The evidence of their study in Decatur, Illinois, revealed that there is considerable interpersonal traffic in marketing advice, views being exchanged about new products, the quality of different brands, possible shopping economies, and so on. Its existence might be expected but the survey disturbed conventional wisdom about the importance of information sources and the flow of this information, which instead of being transmitted via mass media to be accepted indiscriminately, was seen as influencing primarily only individuals within a group or community. These individuals, or opinion leaders, then represent the principal source of information *and* influence for the majority of their group. Thus, the relative roles of various influences on the housewife's decision to switch from one brand to another were, in order of importance, personal contacts, mass media, and sales personnel.

A much later study, which is probably more relevant to contemporary conditions, was reported by an American author in 1964,[8] who selected non-durable consumer products from food and toiletry areas, and carried out research in an in-store situation into exposure to information sources and the relative importance of these sources. A simple impact analysis was then derived showing first of all any exposure to an information source and secondly effective exposure, defined as one which respondents designated themselves as an important factor in the decision to purchase the product. The results were:

	Total exposure %	Effective exposure %
Television	57.6	17·2
Personal contacts	18·2	11·1
Sampling	26·3	17·2
Availability in store	11·1	4·0
Magazine advertising	5·0	2·0

The validity of the research method employed here, namely allowing respondents to designate important sources of information, may be questioned but nevertheless the findings suggest a number of important considerations. Thus, although television is a common source of information, its relative influence is apparently less great than consumer sampling. Personal sources of information although of low frequency, are relatively effective in precipitating behaviour.

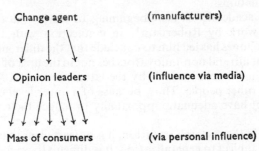

FIG. 1. Two-step communication system.

Comparative data for the United Kingdom is slight, although the New Housewife Survey carried out by J. Walter Thompson[9] does contain some findings on the source of discovery of new products by housewives aged 16–34 and the relative importance of recommendations by various external agencies. Briefly, these are that the principal sources of discovery are, in order, point of purchase, recommendation, advertising and sampling and that the recommendation is principally by friends, relatives outside the nuclear family and retailers.

The logic of the concept of opinion leaders in situations where innovatory behaviour by consumers depends substantially on interpersonal activity is that the relevant contribution of mass media messages is to influence the opinion leaders, who would then influence the majority by personal contact in a two-step communication system as depicted in Figure 1.

The practical problems of implementing this system are formidable. Firstly, it is unlikely that media can be discovered which apply selectively to a much higher proportion of opinion leaders and, more significantly, there is a continuing debate on whether opinion leaders are monomorphic, that is, influential in only one or two product fields, or polymorphic, in influencing others over a wide range of innovations.

Alvin Silk,[10] who carried out a study amongst self-designated opinion leaders, found that there was no significant overlap amongst them in five closely-related fields: dentist, electric toothbrush, mouthwash, toothpaste and regular toothbrush. The length of the continuing argument between those who contend that there are generalized opinion leaders and their opponents suggest that neither may have the truth, and that the influential members of the community exercise this influence in different degrees.

Early attempts to use interpersonal influence at the local level, by pinpointing community leaders through the membership of clubs and associations do not seem to have been successful, and the notable attempt by a media proprietor[11] to show that a newspaper was the most widely read amongst the active leaders in a community is thought not to have been repeated.

Thus although a manufacturer will take cognizance of the fact that his new product may gain sufficient consumer acceptance by a two-step process of communication, the present lack of knowledge makes it difficult to apply this knowledge in all contexts. However, individual commercial organizations are at present carrying out their own research to attempt to make this practicable in their own situations.

Research by academics is also beginning to clarify the confusion which exists. Recent work by Robertson[12] in connection with the adoption of touch-tone telephones has led him to conclude that the difference between those who innovate (at all) and non-innovators lies not in the area of information and awareness but in the relative lack by the latter group of a 'legitimating' reinforcement by other people. Thus, because of a lower level of social integration they do not have adequate opportunity to reduce their conflict between need and risk.

At this point in the research tradition, it is at least clear that the majority of findings are not subject to generalization. It is difficult to predict in advance the degree of innovativeness that consumers will impute to a new product. It is not possible to identify and communicate with either generalized innovators or generalized opinion leaders. In the future, our classification methods—in terms, for example, of groups of consumers with common psychological characteristics—may permit us to direct our new offering much more specifically to the initial target groups. For the present, however, we can concentrate on applying the concepts of diffusion research to our particular product.

If we concede that the traditional research procedures, such as concept testing and product testing, offer us only partial insights into likely eventual rates of acceptance, we might consider what scope exists for identifying and analysing the dynamic patterns of behaviour before a full-scale launch has been undertaken. Test marketing procedures do in fact very often allow this form of investigation. It was stated earlier that there are a number of problems associated with these procedures which may detract from the value of predictions which are made regarding subsequent national outcome. Nevertheless, a test market may offer an ideal opportunity for investigating the dynamic elements of the diffusion system for the new product under consideration. Even now, it is common for manufacturers to study specific elements—such as levels of awareness, usage and attitudes towards the new brand—but usually without attempting to integrate these data within an overall model of the diffusion system.

Early steps to model the process can of course be taken before a test market is begun. Information on how close the new product is considered to be to existing brands, the characteristics of users of existing brands and those attracted to the new entrant can be obtained at the product test stage. In addition, the promotional campaign which is developed will in itself partially structure the flow of information and persuasion. Within a test market, measurement of awareness levels, trial and repeat purchase levels and attitudes will form a base for forecasting the eventual pattern of diffusion. In addition, the sources of information and influences may be plotted. As a result, a fairly comprehensive model can be built up which can form the guidelines for the national introduction. Even then, it will be desirable to continue to monitor the test environment in order that important developments in the diffusion process can be identified and anticipated in those areas to which the new product has been recently introduced.

For the future, considerable research is now under way or planned into the diffusion processes of a wide range of products in the U.K. Studies are being carried out at the Management Centre of the University of Bradford into such fields as flour-milling equipment, ethical pharmaceuticals and numerically controlled machine tools in addition to a wide range of consumer goods. These will enable us to establish the universal elements of diffusion systems and to explain the differences which may be found. In the field of information and influence flows, research is now being carried out by a number of separate institutions, including television and print media companies. All this activity is attracting attention to the much neglected area of diffusion research.

References

1. E. M. Rogers, *The Diffusion of Innovations* (Free Press of Glencoe, 1962).
2. A full explanation of the terms used here may be found in: D. E. Cook, 'A Review of Some Methodological Aspects of Diffusion Research'. (University of Bradford M.Sc. Dissertation, 1970).
3. R. J. Lavidge, and G. A. Steiner, 'A Model of Predictive Measurements of Advertising Effectiveness', *Journal of Marketing* (25 October 1961), pp. 59–62.
4. T. S. Robertson, 'The Process of Innovation and the Diffusion of Innovation', *Journal of Marketing* (31 January 1967), pp. 14–19.
5. Rogers, op cit.
6. S. Graham, 'Class and Conservatism in the Adoption of Innovations', *Human Relations*, vol. 9, no. 1 (1956), pp. 91–100.
7. E. Katz and P. F. Lazarsfeld, *Personal Influence: the part played by people in the flow of mass communications* (Free Press of Glencoe, 1955).
8. G. H. Haines, 'A Study of Why People Purchase New Products'. Science, Technology and Marketing, 1966, *Autumn Conference Proceedings*, American Marketing Association.
9. J. Walter Thompson, *'The New Housewife'* (1967).
10. A. J. Silk, 'Overlap Amongst Self Designated Opinion Leaders: A Study of Selected Dental Products and Services', *Journal of Marketing Research*, vol. 8 (August 1966), pp. 255–259.
11. The Thomson Organisation, *The Active Leaders, A Readership Study of Wales, 1961*.
12. T. S. Robertson, 'Purchase Sequence Responses: Innovators vs. Non-Innovators', *Journal of Advertising Research*, vol. 8, no. 1 (1968), pp. 47–52.

311

Chapter 17

'LE BLEU EST À LA MODE
CETTE ANNÉE'*
by Roland Barthes

A note on research concerned with investigating certain outstanding similarities in fashion.

Whenever I read in a fashion magazine that 'this accessory signifies spring', or 'this costume' (I am here being confronted with a photograph) 'has a youthful and lissom line', or else that 'blue is the top fashion colour this year', I am forced to view such statements within a semantic framework: In every instance (whatever may be the roundabout use of metaphors in the statement) it is necessary to impose upon me (the reader) an equality between a concept (spring, youth, this year's fashions) and a form (the accessory, this costume, the fashion colour blue). In effect there is a connection between a sign and a meaning.

Of course it is not necessary that such a meaning be specified. If someone hints to me that: 'for an afternoon tea dance at Juan-les-Pins—the latest low neckline please' or 'for the celebratory luncheon at Deauville, a delicate creation', there exists a double connection since the afternoon tea dance does not require a low neckline, neither is a delicate creation obligatory for a luncheon party in Normandy. However, between the two terms there is an inter-connection (a tautology): the one refers to the other since the connection is of the citative kind. I am able at least, to discern some significance between them. This will also occur when a fashion magazine links one activity (a common-place festivity, Normandy lustre) with another (warm and heavy materials, an elegant and enveloping shape) by a simple process of affirmation. As yet I am not certain what clothing really signifies; I have therefore even less of a right to apply a method of linguistic analysis to it: however, the appropriateness of the method in terms of the objective will indicate the special significance of fashion (much more than is ever recognized) to its wearers.†

Because of the kind of wording which a fashion journal uses, the semiological character of these inter-connections is hidden. Sometimes it presents certain meanings (fashion, lissomness, spring) as the inherent qualities of particular

---

* From the *Revue Française de Sociologie*, vol. 1, No. 2 (Centre National de la Recherche Scientifique, 1960).

† I do not mean any clothes which are worn (even if they are in fashion) but only women's clothing as it is displayed both verbally and descriptively in fashion journals. Such clothing could be defined as a sort of 'utopia'.

313

forms or shapes to which it refers (perhaps suggesting that there is a kind of physical causality between fashion and the colour blue, or the accessory and spring).* Sometimes the opposite occurs. It relates the meaning to a simple purpose (i.e., a coat to travel in). Whether the trend is to causality or finality, the phraseology of the fashion magazine always tends surreptitiously to transform the linguistic element in clothing to a true-to-life or utilitarian one. Hence it lends to the proceedings a purpose or a function. In both cases, it becomes necessary to change a very arbitrary connection of a natural or technical kind. Briefly, a fashion garment is given a kind of gurantee concerning its use or necessity. The fashion magazine really uses only certain 'functional symbols': the function may never be separated from its symbol. The raincoat is a protection from the rain, but remains in another context a raincoat. This is the basic pre-requisite for all clothing: society considers it as unthinkable that any garment should remain purely functional. As soon as it is made up, it becomes inevitably part of a semantical exercise.

Therefore, the first task is to reduce the phraseology used in a fashion magazine. What is apparent is that there are very simple relationships (using a very simple model which allows comparison) between the sign and the meaning. Although these relationships may be elementary, they are not 'pure'. This is because signs are linked with a physical concept which is a continuum. I refer here to the actual area occupied by the article (a costume, a fold, a clip, gilded buttons, etc.), whilst the meanings (romance, rakishness, cocktail, the country, skiing, the young girl . . . etc.) are to me conveyed by a written or literary medium (even if it is bad, this does not change its place in the proceedings).†

This leads us to state that when they are taken to their ultimate position, the sign and the meaning in fashion garments are not really part of the same language. This is the tremendous distortion which is implicit within all fashion, and evidenced by its disconnected and divided structures (dealt with in a previous work[1]). Therefore the system's duplicity has an effect on both the language concerning the types of clothing, and the meta-language of fashion literature. This requires a double specification: the study of signs or symbols (for example the 'utopia' which they outline) as picked out from fashion mythology itself. On the other hand the study of the meanings (in fashion) is in

---

* 'Because' is one of fashion's favourite words. There is a curious symmetry between the contents of a fashion magazine (which tends to translate its ideas into a kind of causal equation) and the inverse in Logic, which refuses to see in connectives like 'because' and 'in order that' elements of truth. This separates them from logical computation, because they become, quite simply, too empirical.

However, if one places the problem in a totally semiological framework, the futility of any causal relationship (or final) between the sign and the meaning is apparent. This is well exhibited in the following (fictitious) example. Let us take a publicity image for a make of pipe, with an accompanying script of this kind: 'I'm at ease, I'm strong, I smoke a pipe'. The two inverse causalities here have the same impact, i.e., I am at ease because I smoke a pipe. I smoke a pipe because I'm at ease. Really there is only a single semantic relationship here.

† It is true to state that a sign or symbol is often relayed via a verbal description. However this is nothing more than a substitute for the image (the test here is that in photographs and drawings, the accompanying script is merely a 'double-take'). However, meaning only exists via a distinct language component.

314

the strictest sense the resultant of a semiology. Here I will ignore the former, in order to investigate the latter. I will only retain symbols in view of their importance to the signs themselves.

In the majority of other communication systems, the significant relationship does not occur principally in an analytical form. The system only constitutes a single sequence of meanings, without indicating their symbols. In effect a treatise will propose the words, but not the meaning of each word. If the decipherer of a language does not know it, and does not have a dictionary, he must work by slow stages, comparing the segments of the verbal sequence, and simultaneously manipulating them in a quasi-experimental way (testing connections). In the case of fashion, the tremendous variety of materials and meanings requires a methodical 'passing-down'. When meanings are presented to me on one side and symbols on the other, it is as if somebody has given me a textbook and a dictionary. In principle it is sufficient for me to use the signs and symbols to divine the meaning. Definition requires the isolation of important elements. If someone says 'blue is the top fashion colour', or that 'camellia indicates optimism', I will conclude that the colour and the dress are classes and groups of meaning.

It will be sufficient, therefore, to locate within each grouping those characteristics which when contrasted make up a meaning (blue/red? blue/white? camellia/pink?), in order to grasp the essential structure of fashion. In this programme we can recognize two phases of structural analysis: a listing of elementary groups or unities, and then the establishment of a kind of paradigm of relevant opposing forces for each group (unity). This will require on the one hand a form of spatial dissection or breaking down, and on the other a systematic construction. I will not consider here the first point, but will concern myself with the listing of formalized classings or groups.

It is of course much easier simply to set up a list using precisely stated relationships. Here I refer to the instance where the meaning is complemented by the image (or indeed the non-image). In such relationships both the symbol and the meaning form a part of the same language. Often, however, the fashion journal only indicates relationships where the meaning is entirely graphical (this daring costume, this elegant dress, this nonchalant two-piece). I have therefore no other means, other than intuitive ones, to decide what in this costume, this dress, or this two-piece signifies 'daring', 'elegance', or 'nonchalance'. The demonstrative article here (i.e., this/the[2]) refers to a general shape, and it is this which impedes the analytical precision required to isolate the key variables in fashion.

In all those relationships, which could be termed 'demonstrative' relationships, I am therefore really rather like a decipherer who must uncover similar elements which lie within a continuous message. The only method possible is to spot the repetitions. This permits me to see from which identical zone a message has come and appears therefore to have the same significance. It is exactly the same case for a fashion garment. It is necessary to see in each collection of photographs, which trait may be linked with a concept such as 'pertness' so that I can eventually infer that such and such a trait usually signifies pertness—or at least as far as my present interests are concerned—that there really is some fundamental connection.

315

This is just one of many difficulties. If, for example, I read that 'a white silk sweater with a square collar is very dressy' it is really impossible for me, without again using my intuition, to state which of these four elements (sweater, silk, white, square collar) are the meanings which assist in determining the concept 'dressy' or 'dressed up'. Yet another problem; is it only a single element which possesses significance, or is it on the other hand various rather meaningless factors which when combined have a significance? Here again it requires the slow method of using certain definitives which give the solution. I will perhaps learn, for example, that silk is a material synonymous with being 'well-dressed' or that the meaning can only be deduced within a framework comprising both materials and colours. In any case it is useful for me to note that the sweater, silk, white and the square collar could be the significant determinants. Above all else it helps to forecast a fifth determinant (without doubt important) which is a combination of all these four.

Or again another example might be of use to me. If after reading the other messages I am persuaded that the sweater is very rarely the meaning linked with the concept 'dressed up' or 'dressy', and that often it conceals an opposite symbol (sport for example), I will conclude therefore that the relationship presented to me is a paradoxical one. A certain number of determinants or characteristics (silk, white, square collar) misarrange the common-place signification of the sweater. It requires here some sort of regulation of the grammar used in fashion. But for the moment I will suggest only that here the sweater is not the meaning *per se*, it is the object effected by the meaning.

In principle the object which any signification in fashion aims to develop, should always be capable of definition. This is easy in those rather rare cases where the signification operates at a distance. Here the characteristic which is conveyed is physically separate from the article which is affected. For example: 'printed blouses lend a romantic air to the skirt'. The symbol here (printed blouses) is quite separate in its relation with the thing which it affects (the skirt). In the case of the white silk sweater, this distinction is much more difficult because the meanings are in some way incorporated within the article they are signifying. Often therefore the subject of the signification will not itself be indicated. It is really the total effect, the dress, the make up, even the personality which is the major determinant, and this can never really be specified.

The actual wording of any relationship will, however, often confuse the different functions. When, for example, someone talks to me about 'a costume with a blazer jacket for chilly days' I must see at the same time in this 'costume with a blazer jacket' both a meaning, and the subject of that meaning. In addition, such a wording has particular importance since it is also the foundation for meaning. We come upon here a new notion of importance. This will be illustrated in a very rare example where the three 'facets' are completely dissociated. Let us take as our example the sports cardigan when the *collar is fastened*. I will illustrate here three distinct ideas. The subject of the signification itself is the cardigan; the foundation for this is the collar; however, the real meaning here is the fastening of the collar itself. The foundation of any meaning occupies a great deal of space in any fashion guide. Sometimes they may be rather indefinite ('blue is in fashion'). However, for the most part a magazine will specify these. It is required to do so in those numerous instances where the significance is only apparent with 'the details' (a collar, the shape of the neck, the length of the sleeves, the positioning of a scallop neck-line etc). By definition the detail is subordinate to the article itself. The article supports the signification without really playing a part here either in whatever may be 'present' or whatever might subscribe to it. It is either a subject or a support to the meaning. Only the former really counts here. Even so it should be noted that a few instances do occur where the support (or prop) of the meaning is different from that (the object) which it affects.

But is there really a support for every kind of meaning? It is necessary here to think about language. It seems that at present language does not lend any support as such to a meaning. The word does not hold up the sense, since it is the sense itself. You cannot separate the sense from the word (as heard or illustrated) which conveys it. It is in this way, in accepting these limits, that structural linguistics has been able to improve upon itself. There really does exist a scheme or language which positions itself in such a way so that it doubles up the words and transforms the verbal chain into a basic support of sense. This is the kind of operation which elsewhere I have termed as 'writings'. In the writing of literature, for example, the wording has of course a literal sense and in this capacity, it closes itself to every possible dissociation concerning the subject and the sense. It is evidently a language. But this same wording has an additional meaning which is not the same as the words used; the symbol is literature itself. When I write a poem, I say certain things but *at the same time* I am intimating poetry itself.

It is somewhat similar in the case of fashion, although of course the literal sense in the majority of cases might here be defective, and therefore only a mythological sense will remain. In the 'language of clothing' the support of any meaning is really a rather withered or stunted indication. It is an inert and somewhat tamed vestige of a world where a sweater could quite literally signify ease or warmth—indeed rather the opposite to being 'dressed up'. This is because the fashion garment is part of a dual system. It is somewhat disconnected because there are additional secondary meanings which rest upon basic ones; these therefore will become increasingly less fundamental. Thus the system will contain these 'supports' or 'elements' of meaning containing simple semiologies, which will remain unknown.

A complete relationship should therefore give me at least three pieces of information: namely a meaning, a sign or symbol and a support of that meaning. Since such relationships are very numerous in the fashion magazine, I am able to make some kind of estimation using the model overleaf.

I am able to categorize constituents in two ways: by signs or meanings. This could be a very formidable choice[3] if I were using a great deal of matter with important statistical or empirical content. An example of this is linguistics. However, since the constituent is found in qualitative models, I am able to deal with the two categories easily. The first one will give me all the 'latent factors' in a single symbol. I will know that 'romantic' meanings are for example: muslin, lace, cambric, feather-stitching, fine linen, organdie flounces, veils and headbands. I am therefore in the position where linguistics should count the different distinctions of the plural (-s, they, their, etc). But where for

317

SIGN: 5 p.m.		SYMBOL: Satin Material
SUPPORT (BASIS) OF THE MEANING (OR SUBJECT WHICH IS AFFECTED BY IT) A Dress		
EXPRESSION OF THE SIGNIFICATION (THE PHRASEOLOGY) 'Giving an air of . . .'		Elle No. 611 Reference:

FIG. 1.

example the 's' is simultaneously an indication of the number, and of the person [Barthes gives the example here of the 's' in *'tu chantes'*. This is the singular, and the familiar form of 'you sing/you are singing' in French.], and equally organdie indicates the romantic air of a dress for semi-formal occasions. This leads me back to a context which may be spatial (the phrasing or the arrangement of the garment) or associative (the contrasts between you (singular) and you (plural) [Barthes uses 's' and 'ez'—the French forms for the singular/familiar and the singular/formal and plural for 'you'.] organdie and flanellete, for example).

It is really better at this point to set up homogeneous categories of meanings, without worrying about their substance (i.e., their signs or symbols). The symbol will not be referred to again until it becomes necessary to determine important variations within each of these categories. It is important first of all to locate the major generic 'latent factors' in fashion (I will deal with this in the middle section of this article).* If I collect together all relevant meanings linked with 'satin material' I will rapidly develop a general *'vestème'*: In the case of material, using a series of subsequent analyses applied to this, I can hope to open up a real paradigm (of which I cannot estimate the 'number'†), which will provide the appropriate contradistinction for example between satin and tweed (= morning).

These are the kind of determinants which I am trying to extrapolate. Often, however, a fashion magazine only gives me a single guideline (I term this 'an arbitrary vocabulary') when for example (in accordance with certain of its own mythological tendencies) it presents symbols as immovable essentials. For example, it will inform me that 'alpaca' represents 'summer' or that 'lace' represents 'mystery'. These are really almost eternal 'truths', whatever may be the other significations. In fact, the more arbitrary the law, the more imperative it becomes. However, knowledge of an 'arbitrary vocabulary' is

---

* I propose to use the word *'vestème'* as suitable for these 'latents'. This is analogous to Claude Levi-Strauss' *'mythèmes'*.

† Since I have not yet completely constructed the list of contrasts, I do not as yet know whether they are binary or complex.

insufficient because I cannot locate important counter-distinctions. The problem is very important because if I am satisfied with simple equations (alpaca = summer) I will be involved in substantiating the signification, and lose sight of the mythological determinant of the sign or symbol itself. In order to succeed in dispelling this 'arbitrary' and somewhat vague vocabulary (or guideline) which exists amongst the relevant counter-distinctions of fashion I propose, therefore, to reject the symbol in the mythological context.

Luckily, elsewhere, the fashion magazine will sometimes abandon such arbitrary vocabulary, and actually give certain arranged lists of counter-distinctions. In such cases I call these 'concomitant variations of symbols'. Any change in symbol means a change in meaning. I divide this into a minimum of four groups (two symbols and two meanings) which have between them a kind of harmony.* Let us take as an example 'a velvet hat with raw silk trimmings' (the basis of meaning); for the afternoon (sign/symbol I), it is decorated with 'two straw clasps' (meaning I); for the evening (sign/symbol II), it is decorated with 'three jet buttons' (meaning II):

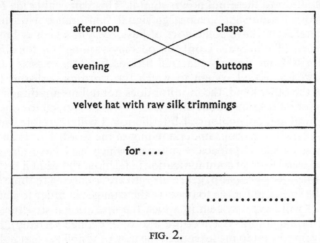

FIG. 2.

Usually the variation is shown by a conflicting contradistinction between symbols (sensible/amusing); but it can also apply to a whole range of conditions (dressy/very dressy/less dressy), occurrences (lunch/dinner/cocktails/5 p.m./10 p.m.) and events (a grand ball/an open air dance/a small dance/a private party). In one way the meaning is seen as almost encompassing a weak variation of the symbol. Subtle differences in the symbols ('more' or 'less dressy', for example) are accompanied by totally discontinuous meanings (the dress with or without a jacket).

These relationships are important because they develop the *'vestème'* stage together with the appropriate paradigm in a single stage. At the same time they uncover the unity within the framework, and contradistinction which generally accompanies it. An example might be the cardigan 'which is casual

* Here the harmony is a notion not unlike the unconnected character within a meaning. However, symbols are often quantifiable: 'dressy' and 'not so dressy' costumes, 'increasing capriciousness' etc.

319

according to whether the collar is open or fastened' (the collar is the meaning's support (basis) and the cardigan the subject which it affects). Here I am not only immediately confident that there is a *'vestème'*, i.e. the way in which to wear a garment (shortened here to: wearing)*, but in addition I know that the paradigm which is implied by this *'vestème'* will contain the contradistinction 'closed/opened'†.

It is necessary to use such concomitant variations within symbols in order to call attention once more to the particular structure of the language in fashion. It both resembles and differs from the spoken language. The spoken language is a very simple system (except when considering aspects of style, and 'wording'), but that used by fashion is a dual system. I will take into account this difference when comparing both of these with a third, extremely unrefined system, which has the advantage of being either double or single as required.

In one sector of a road signals system, I have command over three signs: red, green or orange. If anybody asked me what are the respective meanings of each, it will be necessary for me to note a certain number of times the responses in a real-life situation to these unknown stimuli. This will enable me to understand that red is a stop sign, green a go signal, and orange a warning. It is necessary therefore to have some sort of basic system which is linked with spoken language. (The message is only decoded by training.) On the other hand, if my monitor tells me directly that red forbids freedom to pass on, I have already acquired a second system in which the wording performs the relay action. If, on the other hand, the monitor does not tell me anything about the other signals (or informs me about them later) I will be entitled to consider that red is the natural and only colour of interdiction. I will, therefore, internalize a personal, somewhat spurious understanding of the word. This is an instance of 'arbitrary vocabulary' (alpaca = summer) which as I have already said, represents the usual form of communication in fashion. But what if my monitor tells me that the three signs (stop: get ready: go) are connected to three colours? Then it will be sufficient for me to observe the changes in order to understand the message. I will have a system in which the operational structure is quite obvious (even though this system could also be explained verbally). In effect, it is not really important to me (except in the case of visibility) that red, orange and green are significant. It is via the contrasts which they provide that I will be able to read the information system which is set before me. This kind of reasoning can equally be applied to the concomitant variations which I have developed.‡

* The way in which to wear a garment cannot really be shown by a simple list because it is linked with an institutional frame of reference. The fuzzy distinction between language and wording is again found here. In much the same way linguistics is only interested in the realities of language, and the semiology (semantics) of clothing is only concerned with normative determinants. Fashion clothing has this methodological advantage because it constitutes established forms of clothing in the most perfect form—since they are not worn in the usual way.

† A neutral term can already deal with this contradistinction (neither opened nor closed), it is 'side by side'. But since in fact 'side by side' is vouched for in a contradistinction like 'side by side/rolled up', we will need a four-factor function: 'rolled up/opened/closed/side by side'.

‡ How is red opposite to green? It could be said that the existence of a third or neutral factor (neither green nor red) increases the polarity between them.

I am now going to propose an initial listing of possible homogeneous classes or categories of meanings in fashion clothing. Each one makes up a kind of syntactic grouping (Saussure calls these definitive groupings). Essentially they are a series of spatial elements. Here is an initial list of these categories of '*vestèmes*':

— Material
— Colour
— Design

PARTS	DETAILS
(Defined according to appropriate relevance)	— Collars
— Head	— Sleeves
— Neck	— Pockets
— Shoulders	— Cut
— Hips	— Darts
— Midriff	— Fastenings
— Hands	— Folds
— Feet	— Hemming
	— Stitching
	— Ornamentation

— Wear
— Combinations of factors

Of course, each of these categories raises its own problems, which demand further explanation. Since I can only give here a brief outline of this systematic listing, I will only deal with two points.

I emphasize yet again that these categories are only concerned with providing an initial investigation of female clothing. I have not tried to class the different elements (or characteristics) of such clothing on aesthetic, anatomical, technical, commercial, terminological or even utilitarian (in the sense of usage) grounds, which have been suggested to me. I have only indicated the outstanding proviso of such and such an area, or of such an instance in clothing, which designates certain groupings. It is the sum of all these identical forms which makes up an explicit category or class. It follows, therefore, that these classes are at the same time very close to, and very far removed from, the type of classification of clothing which could ordinarily be conceived. It is very close because (it is not useless here to use this in the process of a 'specified' programme) the meanings of fashion clothing are evidently linked (in a certain way)*— to a practice in clothing which groups meanings, and which reflects the primary techniques in use (i.e., even if some kind of stitch is a sign or symbol, this does not discard the instrumental function of stitching). It is very far removed in the sense that clothing does not sell itself (taking here the current division of clothing into items) according to what it symbolizes. There are no large department stores with 'meanings' counters[4]. An idea of this ambiguity when considering the '*vestème*' will be shown in the following example (defined

* The connection between technical practices in clothing and the organization of its meanings is linked with the problem indicated in Reference 3.

321

according to its appropriate relevance)[5]. The part of clothing and the total item are linked within the same category. In principle they are discrete factors. But since the commercial classification categorizes the items on the basis of a complex combination of different criteria (using the vertical and horizontal axes of the body, the utility, the kinds of yoke, the existence of a characteristic detail, etc.) I do not need to remember what the article symbolizes (i.e., that which differentiates it from other meanings in terms either of simple substance* or of a particular detail). It follows that important groupings are often larger or smaller than the commercial item. Here the shoulder line could have an obvious general meaning according to whether it is for a top-coat, cape, waterproof or jacket. On the other hand, it could be much less obvious (the upturned or straight collar). The inverse of this is the item (a jacket or a skirt) which could be without any meaning whatsoever. The first task therefore in studying fashion clothing (also the most unwieldy because of the commercial character of the only terminology which we can use here) is to break down the concept of the item *per se* in order to be able to grasp the extremely variable semiological (semantic) factors.

The second very general comment I would like to make concerning the categories is the following: the only thing that the '*vestème*' itself substantiates is that it is completely linked with two kinds of structure, that of the propositions and that of the system. On the one hand it is an essential within the fashion cycle. On the other, the part which it plays has evolved by the removal of other determinants which contradict it. If we return to the example of the shoulders, although these are in themselves a part of the garment, they form together with the other pieces a combination whereby the resultant syntagmatic effect is achieved (Hjemslev-Togeby)†. The 'layer', however, can only be located within a single grouping. However within this same grouping 'the shoulder piece' opens itself to a paradigm which is without any real sense since it excludes everything else. An anorak is a syntagmatic unit where it meets the appropriate clothing at the hips (skirt or trousers). It is also a systematic unit where it is set against another shoulder piece of the same 'layer' category (a car-coat, for example). Therefore the '*vestème*' always has a double role. This is an extensive one since it is seen in a definite situation (topological) and it is intensive since it dresses what is virtually a paradigm of contradictory factors.

---

* One is able to predict a contradiction here in terms of the past itself: i.e. PRESENCE/ABSENCE. Taking as our example accentuation at the shoulders (termed E), under certain conditions, we perceive:

$$E+ \quad \text{(for women)}$$
$$E- \quad \text{(for men)}$$

† One of the difficulties of any structural analysis of clothing is its bi-dimensional component. The parts are related at one and the same time to both a horizontal and vertical axis (i.e., breadth and length). I have called these 'strata' (hat, scarf, jacket, skirt, shoes) in the case of vertical components, and 'layers' in the case of horizontal components (for men—vest/shirt/jacket/coat). Of course 'strata' have a much greater semantic importance than 'layers' since the semiology refers to this almost by definition. The problem becomes more complicated where: (1) certain 'layers' are only partially seen (high-necked shirts); (2) the 'layers' are not permanent: a jacket can be either external or internal (i.e., under a coat). However, an item is completely indicated according to the strata and the layer which it occupies.

Until now the symbols which I have described have always led back to some explicit sign. As I have again indicated, this is like giving signs within the meta-language of a literature. These signs are not numerous since the sphere from which they are drawn is very narrow.* However, if we remember that a sign has almost always several meanings, then the fashion garment gives the impression of being swarming with shapes. What is really happening?

Here it is useful to reflect upon the whole range of characteristics to which a fashion magazine does not ascribe any importance, or to which it does not attribute any explicit meaning. (The meaning remains 'in the air'.) We can dissemble, for example, a shirt-waister by enumerating its characteristics (poplin with white dots on a yellow background, high neckline, gathered pockets etc.) without linking these to any preconceived concept. The sign apparently seems to be defective. However, in every instance where the magazine simply describes, and does not give any explanation, it is always necessary to reinstate a sign which will constitute in itself the fashion.† Thus these apparently defective equations are important meanings because anything which is being expressed is not without meaning.

Fashion, like any other phenomenon, uses therefore a sign. The only difference being that the others are temporary and always stated. The sign 'fashion' is permanent and found under three guises: expressly indicated (blue is fashionable); expressed by supportive contingent signs (accessory = spring = fashion)‡; neither stated nor conveyed but implicit (a dress in crisp poplin, etc.). This is a quite universal sign. It could be said (here borrowing one of Logic's own expressions) that for every equation (whether implicit or otherwise) using the language of clothing's own vocabulary, fashion constitutes a survey of meaning.[6]

It literally follows that within this meta-language, through which the fashion magazine is able to convey certain equivalences, the symbol for fashion is itself delivered through a unique meaning which is quite self-sufficient. I will call this the 'influential determinant'. Every detail noted, and shape created (in effect every facet of clothing), from the moment when it is indicated, is reflected in the symbol 'fashion'. Therefore I can, and I must, treat everything which is said in the fashion magazine virtually as a meaningful element, which creates certain notations and ideas, and incorporates them within my own formal classifications. If they are appropriately placed therein, then the resultant general meaning will coincide to some extent with the development of more specific meanings. Hence an extensive but reasonably uniform listing is assured.

Is this listing (of meaningful forms and shapes) an exhaustive one? Firstly it is necessary to recall that the purpose of this research was comparative, and it was only concerned with those characteristics and forms observed during a

---

* It is probable that the signs themselves are organized within large typological classes: town/country; dressed-up/casual; day/evening, etc.

† Of course fashion should always be extended in its temporal sense: blazer = spring this year.

‡ In a more restrained way a 'psychological' sign can convey a circumstantial sign: a certain overcoat = travel, and via the intermediary of this sign = ease.

single year.* Therefore it is models rather than methods which are developed. After a characteristic is recorded, it is no longer necessary to compute the number of times it appears. A common characteristic is no more significant than one which is more rare. It is not the existent quantity of a shape or form which is notified, but its connection or relationship with other forms.

Logically, therefore, after a certain time the list of important forms is saturated. Although for practical purposes this is never achieved, if the general structure is correctly established, then no single shape—no matter which—is unforeseen. It is of course always possible to encounter a new sign, but if the formalised classes have been accurately drawn up, it should be possible to accommodate it in one or other of these.

Any 'revival' in fashion is therefore really dependent upon the apparent innovation within combinations, and not the result of any change in ideas. The '*vestèmes*' are limited in number (and probably there is little opportunity for augmentation).† The total number of combinations is consequently limited. Furthermore, since certain combinations are impossible because of particular rules concerning inconsistencies, this total number is further reduced. In effect, the swarm of shapes and forms, which is the basis of the mythology which surrounds fashion ('whimsy', 'taste', 'invention', 'intuition', 'inexhaustible change', etc.) is really an impossible illusion. This is because since the synchrony is so short, the process of using combinations easily overloads human memory. It would require the construction of some kind of mathematical memory[7] for fashion (equally at the level of a micro-diachrony) with the relevant shapes and movements shown in a limited and computable manner. This might prove quite unpleasant for an industry founded entirely upon the extollation of an incessant neology, but extremely useful in order to understand how an ideology rests upon reality.

References

1. *Mythologies* (Seuil, Paris, 1957).
2. It is not clear in traditional grammar texts how this type of demonstrative participle should be classified. The most useful work is by Damourette and Pichon, *Essay on the Grammar of the French Language 1911–27* (d'Artrey). See the chapter concerned with what the authors terms 'the area of importance of the nominal substantive' (vol. I, Ch. 6).
3. This is not the same thing as describing a structure, using its meanings and symbols. Meanings could be developed via a genetic process. Symbols might perhaps evolve where there is an endogenous organization of meaning? Remarkably enough, B. Mandelbrot has asked this same question in: *The Logic, Language and Theory of Information* (Paris, P.U.F., 1957), p. 63.
4. It could be useful to compare the organization of fashion 'meanings' and the categorization of clothing items in the mail order catalogue of a department store. The problem of these classifications (or taxonomies) has been dealt with by Mandelbrot (op. cit., p. 57) following Zipf and G. Herdan.

* Between synchronization in the strictest sense (fashion during a year) and large-scale diachrony (as studied by Richardson and Kroeber) there is a place for a micro-diachrony which would attempt to structure the variations of a single '*vestème*' during several years: for example, skirt lengths. This micro-diachrony is possible because meanings in fashion originate from a rule and not from use (the opposite to language).

† Remember that I have here studied certain categories of '*vestèmes*' not the '*vestèmes*' themselves, which would require a more systematic analysis.

5. The criterion: 'appropriate relevance' concerning an item of clothing comes from ethnology (A. Leroi-Gourhan, *The Environment and Techniques*, p. 208). This does not hinder any coincidence with the criterion of meaning or other element which determine the limits of Western dress.

6. R. Blanché: *Introduction to Contemporary Logic* (Paris, A. Colin, 1957), p. 138.

7. If the line is the resultant of a certain number of '*vestèmes*', it seems, in cybernetic terms, like the notion of a machine—'a long calculation on a succession of different operations (phonemes)' (Mandelbrot, op. cit., p. 44).

Chapter 18

FASHION: FROM CLASS DIFFERENTIATION TO COLLECTIVE SELECTION*
by Herbert Blumer

The author reviews the contemporary importance of fashion in society and emphasizes its expanding domain, a point made implicitly by Roy Hayhurst's contribution in chapter 16.

Deficiencies of Fashion as a Sociological Concept

This paper is an invitation to sociologists to take seriously the topic of fashion. Only a handful of scholars, such as Simmel (1904), Sapir (1931), and the Langs (1961), have given more than casual concern to the topic. Their individual analyses of it, while illuminating in several respects, have been limited in scope, and within the chosen limits very sketchy. The treatment of the topic by sociologists in general, such as we find it in textbooks and in occasional pieces of scholarly writing, is even more lacking in substance. The major deficiencies in the conventional sociological treatment are easily noted—a failure to observe and appreciate the wide range of operation of fashion; a false assumption that fashion has only trivial or peripheral significance; a mistaken idea that fashion falls in the area of the abnormal and irrational and thus is out of the mainstream of human group life; and, finally, a misunderstanding of the nature of fashion.

Fashion Restricted to Adornment. Similar to scholars in general who have shown some concern with the topic, sociologists are disposed to identify fashion exclusively or primarily with the area of costume and adornment. While occasional references may be made to its play in other areas, such casual references do not give a proper picture of the extent of its operation. Yet, to a discerning eye fashion is readily seen to operate in many diverse areas of human group life, especially so in modern times. It is easily observable in the realm of the pure and applied arts, such as painting, sculpture, music, drama, architecture, dancing, and household decoration. Its presence is very obvious in the area of entertainment and amusement. There is plenty of evidence to show its play in the field of medicine. Many of us are familiar with its operation in fields of industry, especially that of business management. It even touches

* From *The Sociological Quarterly*, vol. 10, No. 3 (Summer 1969).

such a relative sacred area as that of mortuary practice. Many scholars have noted its operation in the field of literature. Its presence can be seen in the history of modern philosophy. It can be observed at work in the realm of political doctrine. And—perhaps to the surprise of many—it is unquestionably at work in the field of science. That this is true of the social and psychological sciences is perhaps more readily apparent. But we have also to note, as several reputable and qualified scholars have done, that fashion appears in such redoubtable areas as physical and biological science and mathematics. The domain in which fashion operates is very extensive, indeed. To limit it to, or to centre it in, the field of costume and adornment is to have a very inadequate idea of the scope of its occurrence.

Fashion as Socially Inconsequential. This extensive range of fashion should, in itself, lead scholars to question their implicit belief that fashion is a peripheral and relatively inconsequential social happening. To the contrary, fashion may influence vitally the central content of any field in which it operates. For example, the styles in art, the themes and styles in literature, the forms and themes in entertainment, the perspectives in philosophy, the practices in business, and the preoccupations in science may be affected profoundly by fashion. These are not peripheral matters. In addition, the nature of the control wielded by fashion shows that its touch is not light. Where fashion operates it assumes an imperative position. It sets sanction of what is to be done, it is conspicuously indifferent to criticism, it demands adherence, and it by-passes as oddities and misfits those who fail to abide by it. This grip which it exercises over its area of operation does not bespeak an inconsequential mechanism.

Fashion as Aberrant and Irrational. The third deficiency, as mentioned, is to view fashion as an aberrant and irrational social happening, akin to a craze or mania. Presumably, this ill-considered view of fashion has arisen from considerations which suggest that fashion is bizarre and frivolous, that it is fickle, that it arises in response to irrational status anxieties, and that people are swept into conforming to it despite their better judgement. It is easy to form such impressions. For one thing, past fashions usually seem odd and frequently ludicrous to the contemporary eye. Next, they rarely seem to make sense in terms of utility or rational purpose; they seem much more to express the play of fancy and caprice. Further, following the classic analysis made by Simmel, fashion seems to represent a kind of anxious effort of *élite* groups to set themselves apart by introducing trivial and ephemeral demarcating insignia, with a corresponding strained effort by non-*élite* classes to make a spurious identification of themselves with upper classes by adopting these insignia. Finally, since fashion despite its seeming frivolous content sweeps multitudes of people into its fold, it is regarded as a form of collective craziness.

Understanding the Character of Fashion

Nevertheless, to view fashion as an irrational, aberrant, and craze-like social happening is to grievously misunderstand it. On the *individual side*, the adoption of what is fashionable is by and large a very calculating act. The fashion conscious person is usually quite careful and discerning in his effort to identify the fashion in order to make sure that he is 'in style'; the fashion does not appear to him as frivolous. In turn, the person who is coerced into adopting the fashion contrary to his wishes does so deliberately and not irrationally. Finally, the person who unwittingly follows a fashion does so because of a limitation of choice rather than as an impulsive expression of aroused emotions or inner anxiety. The bulk of evidence gives no support to the contention that individuals who adopt fashion are caught up in the spirit of a craze. Their behaviour is no more irrational or excited—and probably less so—than that of voters casting political ballots. On its *collective side*, fashion does not fit any better the pattern of a craze. The mechanisms of interaction are not those of circular transmission of aroused feelings, or of heightened suggestibility, or of fixed preoccupation with a gripping event. While people may become excited over a fashion they respond primarily to its character of propriety and social distinction; these are tempering guides. Fashion has respectability: it carries the stamp of approval of an *élite*—an *élite* that is recognized to be sophisticated and believed to be wise in the given area of endeavour. It is this endorsement which undergirds fashion—rather than the emotional interaction which is typical of crazes. Fashion has, to be true, an irrational, or better 'non-rational', dimension which we shall consider later, but this dimension does not make it into a craze or mania.

The observations that fashion operates over wide areas of human endeavour, that it is not aberrant and craze-like, and that it is not peripheral and inconsequential merely correct false pictures of it. They do little to identify its nature and mode of operation. It is to this identification that I now wish to turn.

Simmel: Fashion as Class Differentiation. Let me use as the starting point of the discussion the analysis of fashion made some sixty years ago be Georg Simmel. His analysis, without question, has set the character of what little solid sociological thought is to be found on the topic. His thesis was essentially simple. For him, fashion arose as a form of class differentiation in a relatively open class society. In such society the *élite* class seeks to set itself apart by observable marks or insignia, such as distinctive forms of dress. However, members of immediately subjacent classes adopt these insignia as a means of satisfying their striving to identify with a superior status. They, in turn, are copied by members of classes beneath them. In this way, the distinguishing insignia of the *élite* class filter down through the class pyramid. In this process, however, the *élite* class loses these marks of separate identity. It is led, accordingly, to devise new distinguishing insignia which, again, are copied by the classes below, thus repeating the cycle. This, for Simmel, was the nature of fashion and the mechanism of its operation. Fashion was thought to arise in the form of styles which demarcate an *élite* group. These styles automatically acquire prestige in the eyes of those who wish to emulate the *élite* group and are copied by them, thus forcing the *élite* group to devise new distinctive marks of their superior status. Fashion is thus caught up in an incessant and recurrent process of innovation and emulation. A fashion, once started, marches relentlessly to its doom; on its heels treads a new fashion destined to the same fate; and so on ad infinitum. This sets the fundamental character of the fashion process.

There are several features of Simmel's analysis which are admittedly of high merit. One of them was to point out that fashion requires a certain type of society in which to take place. Another was to highlight the importance of prestige in the operation of fashion. And another, of particular significance, was to stress that the essence of fashion lies in a process of change—a process that is natural and indigenous and not unusual and aberrant. Yet, despite the fact that his analysis still remains the best in the published literature, it failed to catch the character of fashion as a social happening. It is largely a parochial treatment, quite well suited to fashion in dress in the seventeenth, eighteenth, and nineteenth century Europe with its particular class structure. But it does not fit the operation of fashion in our contemporary epoch with its many diverse fields and its emphasis on modernity. Its shortcomings will be apparent, I think in the light of the following analysis.

Modernity and the Selection Process. Some years ago I had the opportunity to study rather extensively and at first hand the women's fashion industry in Paris. There were three matters in particular which I observed which seem to me to provide the clues for an understanding of fashion in general. I wish to discuss each of them briefly and indicate their significance.

First, I was forcibly impressed by the fact that the setting or determination of fashion takes place actually through an intense process of selection. At a seasonal opening of a major Parisian fashion house there may be presented a hundred or more designs of women's evening wear before an audience of from one to two hundred buyers. The managerial corps of the fashion house is able to indicate a group of about thirty designs of the entire lot, inside of which will fall the small number, usually about six to eight designs, that are chosen by the buyers; but the managerial staff is typically unable to predict this small number on which the choices converge. Now, these choices are made by the buyers—a highly competitive and secretive lot—independently of each other and without knowledge of each other's selections. Why should their choices converge on a few designs as they do? When the buyers were asked why they chose one dress in preference to another—between which my inexperienced eye could see no appreciable difference—the typical, honest, yet largely uninformative answer was that the dress was 'stunning'.

Inquiry into the reasons for the similarity in the buyers' choices led me to a second observation, namely, that the buyers were immersed in and preoccupied with a remarkably common world of intense stimulation. It was a world of lively discussion of what was happening in women's fashion, of fervent reading of fashion publications, and of close observation of one another's lines of products. And, above all, it was a world of close concern with the women's dress market, with the prevailing tastes and prospective tastes of the consuming public in the area of dress. It became vividly clear to me that by virtue of their intense immersion in this world the buyers came to develop common sensitivities and similar appreciations. To use an old but valuable psychological term, they developed a common 'appreception mass' which sharpened and directed their feelings of discrimination, which guided and sensitized their perceptions, and which channelled their judgements and choices. This explains, I am convinced, why the buyers, independently of each other, made such amazingly identical choices at the fashion openings. This observation also underlines a point of the greatest importance, namely, that the buyers became the unwitting surrogates of the fashion public. Their success, indeed their vocational fate, depended on their ability to sense the direction of taste in this public.

The third observation which I made pertained to the dress designers—those who created the new styles. They devised the various designs between which the buyers were ultimately to make the choices, and their natural concern was to be successful in gaining adoption of their creations. There were three lines of preoccupation from which they derived their ideas. One was to pour over old plates of former fashions and depictions of costumes of far-off peoples. A second was to brood and reflect over current and recent styles. The third, and most important, was to develop an intimate familiarity with the most recent expressions of modernity as these were to be seen in such areas as the fine arts, recent literature, political debates and happenings, and discourse in the sophisticated world. The dress designers were engaged in translating themes from these areas and media into dress designs. The designers were attuned to an impressive degree to modern developments and were seeking to capture and express in dress design the spirit of such developments. I think that this explains why the dress designers—again a competitive and secretive group, working apart from each other in a large number of different fashion houses—create independently of each other such remarkably similar designs. They pick up ideas of the past, but always through the filter of the present; they are guided and constrained by the immediate styles in dress, particularly the direction of such styles over the recent span of a few years; but above all, they are seeking to catch the proximate future as it is revealed in modern developments.

Taken together, these three observations which I have sketched in a most minimal form outline what is significant in the case of fashion in the women's dress industry. They indicate that the fashion is set through a process of free selection from among a large number of competing models; that the creators of the models are seeking to catch and give expression to what we may call the direction of modernity; and that the buyers, who through their choices set the fashion, are acting as the unwitting agents of a fashion consuming public whose incipient tastes the buyers are seeking to anticipate. In this paper I shall not deal with what is probably the most interesting and certainly the most obscure aspect of the entire relationship, namely, the relation between, on one hand, the expressions of modernity to which the dress designers are so responsive and, on the other hand, the incipient and inarticulate tastes which are taking shape in the fashion consuming public. Certainly, the two come together in the styles which are chosen and, in so doing, lay down the lines along which modern life in this area moves. I regard this line of relationship as constituting one of the most significant mechanisms in the shaping of our modern world, but I shall not undertake analysis of it in this paper.

Fashion and the Élite. The brief account which I have given of the setting of fashion in the women's wear industry permits one to return to Simmel's classic analysis and pinpoint more precisely its shortcomings. His scheme elevates the prestige of the *élite* to the position of major importance in the operation of fashion—styles come into fashion because of the stamp of distinction conferred on them by the *élite*. I think this view misses almost completely what is central to fashion, namely, *to be in fashion*. It is not the prestige of the *élite* which makes the design fashionable but, instead, it is the suitability or potential fashion-ableness of the design which allows the prestige of the *élite* to be attached to it. The design has to correspond to the direction of incipient taste of the fashion consuming public. The prestige of the *élite* affects but does not control the direction of this incipient taste. We have here a case of the fashion mechanism transcending and embracing the prestige of the *élite* group rather than stem-ming from that prestige.

There are a number of lines of evidence which I think clearly establish this to be the case. First, we should note that members of the *élite*—and I am still speaking of the *élite* in the realm of women's dress—are themselves as interested as anyone to be in fashion. Anyone familiar with them is acutely aware of their sensitivity in this regard, their wish not to be out of step with fashion, and in-deed their wish to be in the vanguard of proper fashion. They are caught in the need of responding to the direction of fashion rather than of occupying the privileged position of setting that direction. Second, as explained, the fashion-adopting actions of the *élite* take place in a context of competing models, each with its own source of prestige. Not all prestigeful persons are innovators—and innovators are not necessarily persons with the highest prestige. The *élite*, itself, has to select between models proposed by innovators; and their choice is not determined by the relative prestige of the innovators. As history shows abundantly, in the competitive process fashion readily ignores persons with the highest prestige and, indeed, by-passes acknowledged 'leaders' time after time. A further line of evidence is just as telling, namely, the interesting instances of failure to control the direction of fashion despite effective mar-shalling of the sources of prestige. An outstanding example was the effort in 1922 to check and reverse the trend toward shorter skirts which had started in 1919 to the dismay of clothing manufacturers. These manufacturers enlisted the co-operation of the heads of fashion houses, fashion magazines, fashion commentators, actresses, and acknowledged fashion leaders in an extensive, well organized and amply financed campaign to reverse the trend. The im-portant oracles of fashion declared that long dresses were returning, models of long dresses were presented in numbers at the seasonal openings, actresses wore them on the stage, and manikins paraded them at the fashionable meeting places. Yet, despite this effective marshalling of all significant sources of prestige, the campaign was a marked failure; the trend toward shorter skirts, after a slight interruption, continued until 1929 when a rather abrupt change to long dresses took place. Such instances—and there have been others—provide further indication that there is much more to the fashion mechanism than the exercise of prestige. Fashion appears much more as a collective groping for the proximate future than a channelled movement laid down by prestigeful figures.

Collective Selection Replaces Class Differentiation. These observations require us to put Simmel's treatment in a markedly different perspective, certainly as applied to fashion in our modern epoch. The efforts of an *élite* class to set itself apart in appearance takes place inside of the movement of fashion instead of being its cause. The prestige of *élite* groups, in place of setting the direction of the fashion movement, is effective only to the extent to which they are recognized as representing and portraying the movement. The people in other classes who consciously follow the fashion do so because it is the fashion and not because of the separate prestige of the *élite* group. The fashion dies not because it has been discarded by the *élite* group but because it gives way to a new model more consonant with developing taste. The fashion mechanism appears not in response to a need of class differentiation and class emulation but in response to a wish to be in fashion, to be abreast of what has good standing, to express new tastes which are emerging in a changing world. These are the changes that seem to be called for in Simmel's formulation. They are fundamental changes. They shift fashion from the fields of class differentiation to the area of collective selection and centre its mechanism in the process of such selection. This process of collective selection represents an effort to choose from among competing styles or models those which match developing tastes, those which 'click', or those which—to revert to my friends, the buyers— 'are stunning'. The fact that this process of collective selection is mysterious —it is mysterious because we do not understand it—does not contradict in any way that it takes place.

Features of the Fashion Mechanism

To view the fashion mechanism as a continuing process of collective selection from among competing models yields a markedly different picture from that given by conventional sociological analysis of fashion. It calls attention to the fact that those implicated in fashion—innovators, 'leaders', followers, and participants—are parts of a collective process that responds to changes in taste and sensitivity. In a legitimate sense, the movement of fashion represents a reaching out for new models which will answer to as yet indistinct and in-articulate newer tastes. The transformation of taste, of collective taste, results without question from the diversity of experience that occurs in social inter-action in a complex moving world. It leads, in turn, to an unwitting groping for suitable forms of expression, in an effort to move in a direction which is consonant with the movement of modern life in general. It is perhaps unnecess-ary to add that we know very little indeed about this area of transformation of collective taste. Despite its unquestioned importance it has been scarcely noted, much less studied. Sociologists are conspicuously ignorant of it and indifferent to it.

Before leaving the discussion of fashion in the area of conspicuous ap-pearance (such as dress, adornment, or mannerism), it is desirable to note and consider briefly several important features of the fashion mechanism, namely, its historical continuity, its modernity, the role of collective taste in its opera-tion, and the psychological motives which are alleged to account for it.

Historical Continuity. The history of fashion shows clearly that new fashions are related to, and grow out of, their immediate predecessors. This is one of the fundamental ways in which fashion differs from fads. Fads have no line of historical continuity; each springs up independently of a forerunner and gives rise to no successor. In the case of fashion, fashion innovators always have to consider the prevailing fashion, if for no other reason than to depart from it or to elaborate on it. The result is a line of continuity. Typically, although not universally, the line of continuity has the character of a cultural drift, expressing itself in what we customarily term a 'fashion trend'. Fashion trends are a highly important yet a much neglected object of study. They signify a convergence and marshalling of collective taste in a given direction and thus pertain to one of the most significant yet obscure features in group life. The terminal points of fashion trends are of special interest. Sometimes they are set by the nature of the medium (there is a point beyond which the skirt cannot be lengthened or shortened [see Richardson and Kroeber, 1947; Young, 1937]); sometimes they seem to represent an exhaustion of the logical possibilities of the medium; but frequently they signify a relatively abrupt shift in interests and taste. The terminal points are marked particularly by a much wider latitude of experimentation in the new fashion models that are advanced for adoption; at such points the fashion mechanism particularly reveals the groping character of collective choice to set itself on a new course. If it be true, as I propose to explain later, that the fashion mechanism is woven deeply into the texture of modern life, the study of fashion in its aspects of continuity, trends, and cycles would be highly important and rewarding.

Modernity. The feature of 'modernity' in fashion is especially significant. Fashion is always modern; it always seeks to keep abreast of the times. It is sensitive to the movement of current developments as they take place in its own field, in adjacent fields, and in the larger social world. Thus, in women's dress, fashion is responsive to its own trend, to developments in fabrics and ornamentation, to developments in the fine arts, to exciting events that catch public attention such as the discovery of the tomb of Tutankhamen, to political happenings, and to major social shifts such as the emancipation of women or the rise of the cult of youth. Fashion seems to sift out of these diverse sources of happenings a set of obscure guides which bring it into line with the general or over-all direction of modernity itself. This responsiveness in its more extended form seems to be the chief factor in formation of what we speak of as a 'spirit of the times' or a *Zeitgeist.*

Collective Taste. Since the idea of 'collective taste' is given such an important position in my analysis of the fashion mechanism, the idea warrants further clarification and explanation. I am taking the liberty of quoting my remarks as they appear in the article on 'Fashion' in the new International Encyclopedia of the Social Sciences V (1968: 341–345).

'... It represents an organic sensitivity to objects of social experience, as when we say that "vulgar comedy does not suit our taste" or that "they have a taste for orderly procedure". Taste has a tri-fold character—it is like an appetite in seeking positive satisfaction; it operates as a sensitive selector, giving a basis for acceptance or rejection; and it is a formative agent, guiding the development of lines of action and shaping objects to meet its demands. Thus, it appears as a subjective mechanism, giving orientation to individuals, structuring activity and moulding the world of experience. Tastes are themselves a product of experience; they usually develop from an initial state of vagueness to a state of refinement and stability, but once formed they may decay and distintegrate.

334

They are formed in the context of social interaction, responding to the definitions and affirmations given by others. People thrown into areas of common interaction and having similar runs of experience develop common tastes. The fashion process involves both a formation and an expression of collective taste in the given area of fashion. Initially, the taste is a loose fusion of vague inclinations and dissatisfactions that are aroused by new experiences in the field of fashion and in the larger surrounding world. In this initial state, collective taste is amorphous, inarticulate, vaguely poised, and awaiting specific direction. Through models and proposals, fashion innovators sketch out possible lines along which the incipient taste may gain objective expression and take definite form. Collective taste is an active force in the ensuing process of selection, setting limits and providing guidance; yet, at the same time it undergoes refinement and organization through its attachment to, and embodiment in, specific social forms. The origin, formation, and careers of collective taste constitute the huge problematic area in fashion. Major advancement in our knowledge of the fashion mechanism depends on the charting of this area. . . .'

Psychological Motives. Now, a word with regard to psychological interpretations of fashion. Scholars, by and large, have sought to account for fashion in terms of psychological motives. A perusal of the literature will show an assortment of different feelings and impulses which have been picked out to explain the occurrence of fashion. Some students ascribe fashion to efforts to escape from boredom or ennui, especially among members of the leisure class. Some treat fashion as arising from playful and whimsical impulses to enliven the routines of life with zest. Some regard it as due to a spirit of adventure which impels individuals to rebel against the confinement of prevailing social forms. Some see fashion as a symbolic expression of hidden sexual interests. Most striking is the view expressed by Sapir in his article on 'Fashion' in the first edition of the Encyclopedia of the Social Sciences VI (1931:139–141); Sapir held that fashion results from an effort to increase the attractiveness of the self, especially under conditions which impair the integrity of the ego; the sense of oneself is regained and heightened through novel yet socially sanctioned departures from prevailing social forms. Finally, some scholars trace fashion to desires for personal prestige or notoriety.

Such psychological explanations, either singly or collectively, fail to account for fashion; they do not explain why or how the various feelings or motives give rise to a fashion process. Such feelings are presumably present and in operation in all human societies; yet there are many societies in which fashion is not to be found. Further, such feelings may take various forms of expression which have no relation to a fashion process. We are given no explanation of why the feelings should lead to the formation of fashion in place of taking other channels of expression available to them. The psychological schemes fail to come to grip with the collective process which constitutes fashion—the emergence of new models in an area of changing experience, the differential attention given them, the interaction which leads to a focusing of collective choice on one of them, the social endorsement of it as proper, and the powerful control which this endorsement yields. Undoubtedly, the various feelings and impulses specified by psychologists operate within the fashion process—just as they operate

335

within non-fashion areas of group life. But their operation within fashion does not account for fashion. Instead, their operation presupposes the existence of the fashion process as one of the media for their play.

The foregoing discussion indicates, I trust, the inadequacy of conventional sociological and psychological schemes to explain the nature of fashion. Both sets of schemes fail to perceive fashion as the process of collective selection that it is. The schemes do not identify the nature of the social setting in which fashion arises nor do they catch or treat the mechanism by which fashion operates. The result is that students fail to see the scope and manner of its operation and to appreciate the vital role which it plays in modern group life. In the interest of presenting a clearer picture of these matters, I wish to amplify the sketch of fashion as given above in order to show more clearly its broad generic character.

Generic Character of Fashion

It is necessary, first of all, to insist that fashion is not confined to those areas, such as women's apparel, in which fashion is institutionalized and professionally exploited under conditions of intense competition. As mentioned earlier, it is found in operation in a wide variety and increasing number of fields which shun deliberate or intentional concern with fashion. In such fields, fashion occurs almost always without awareness on the part of those who are caught in its operation. What may be primarily response to fashion is seen and interpreted in other ways—chiefly as doing what is believed to be superior practice. The prevalence of such unwitting deception can be considerable. The basic mechanism of fashion which comes to such a clear, almost pure, form in women's dress is clouded or concealed in other fields but is none the less operative. Let me approach a consideration of this matter by outlining the six essential conditions under which fashion presumably comes into play.

Essential Conditions of Its Appearance. First, the area in which fashion operates must be one that is involved in a movement of change, with people ready to revise or discard old practices, beliefs, and attachments, and poised to adopt new social forms; there must be this thrust into the future. If the area is securely established, as in the domain of the sacred, there will be no fashion. Fashion presupposes that the area is in passage, responding to changes taking place in a surrounding world, and oriented to keeping abreast of new developments. The area is marked by a new psychological perspective which places a premium on being 'up to date' and which implies a readiness to denigrate given older forms of life as being outmoded. Above all, the changing character of the area must gain expression or reflection in changes in that subjective orientation which I have spoken of under the term 'taste'.

A *second* condition is that the area must be open to the recurrent presentation of models or proposals of new social forms. These models, depending on the given areas of fashion, may cover such diverse things as points of view, doctrines, lines of preoccupation, themes, practices, and use of artifacts. In a given area of fashion, these models differ from each other and of course from the prevailing social forms. Each of them is metaphorically a claimant for adoption. Thus their presence introduces a competitive situation and sets the stage for selection between them.

Third, there must be a relatively free opportunity for choice between the models. This implies that the models must be open, so to speak, to observation and that facilities and means must be available for their adoption. If the presentation of new models is prevented the fashion process will not get under way. Further, a severe limitation in the wherewithal needed to adopt models (such as necessary wealth, intellectual sophistication, refined skill, or aesthetic sensitivity) curtails the initiation of the fashion process.

Fashion is not guided by utilitarian or rational considerations. This points to a *fourth* condition essential to its operation, namely, that the pretended merit or value of the competing models cannot be demonstrated through open and decisive test. Where choices can be made between rival models on the basis of objective and effective test, there is no place for fashion. It is for this reason that fashion does not take root in those areas of utility, technology, or science where asserted claims can be brought before the bar of demonstrable proof. In contrast, the absence of means for testing effectively the relative merit of competing models opens the door to other considerations in making choices between them. This kind of situation is essential to the play of fashion.

A *fifth* condition for fashion is the presence of prestige figures who espouse one or another of the competing models. The prestige of such persons must be such that they are acknowledged as qualified to pass judgement on the value or suitability of the rival models. If they are so regarded their choice carries weight as an assurance or endorsement of the superiority or propriety of a given model. A combination of such prestigeful figures, espousing the same model, enhances the likelihood of adoption of the model.

A *sixth* and final condition is that the area must be open to the emergence of new interests and dispositions in response to (a) the impact of outside events, (b) the introduction of new participants into the area, and (c) changes in inner social interaction. This condition is chiefly responsible for the shifting of taste and the redirection of collective choice which together constitute the lifeline of fashion.

If the above six conditions are met, I believe that one will always find fashion to be in play. People in the area will be found to be converging their choices on models and shifting this convergence over time. The convergence of choice occurs not because of the intrinsic merit or demonstrated validity of the selected models but because of the appearance of high standing which the chosen models carry. Unquestionably, such high standing is given in major measure by the endorsement and espousal of models of prestigeful persons. But it must be stressed again that it is not prestige, *per se*, which imparts this sanction; a prestigeful person, despite his eminence, may be easily felt to be 'out-of-date'. To carry weight, the person of prestige must be believed or sensed to be voicing the proper perspective that is called for by developments in the area. To recognize this is to take note of the importance of the disposition to keep abreast of what is collectively judged to be up-to-date practice. The formation of this collective judgement takes place through an interesting but ill-understood interaction between prestige and incipient taste, between eminent endorsement and congenial interest. Collective choice of models is forged in this process of interaction, leading to a focusing of selection at a given time on one model and at a different time on another model.

Fashion and Contemporary Society

If we view modern life in terms of the analytical scheme which I have sketched, there is no difficulty in seeing the play of fashion in many diverse areas. Close scrutiny of such areas will show the features which we have discussed—a turning away from old forms that are thought to be out-of-date; the introduction of new models which compete for adoption; a selection between them that is made not on the basis of demonstrated merit or utility but in response to an interplay of prestige-endorsement and incipient taste; and a course of development in which a given type of model becomes solidified, socially elevated, and imperative in its demands for acceptance for a period of time. While this process is revealed most vividly in the area of women's fashion it can be noted in play here and there across the board in modern life and may, indeed, be confidently expected to increase in scope under the conditions of modern life. These conditions—the pressure to change, the open doors to innovation, the inadequacy or the unavailability of decisive tests of the merit of proposed models, the effort of prestigeful figures to gain or maintain standing in the face of developments to which they must respond, and the groping of people for a satisfactory expression of new and vague tastes—entrench fashion as a basic and widespread process in modern life.

The Expanding Domain of Fashion. This characterization may repel scholars who believe that fashion is an abnormal and irrational happening and that it gives way before enlightenment, sophistication, and increased knowledge. Such scholars would reject the thought that fashion is becoming increasingly embedded in a society which is presumably moving toward a higher level of intelligence and rational perspective. Yet, the facts are clear that fashion is an outstanding mark of modern civilization and that its domain is expanding rather than diminishing. As areas of life come to be caught in the vortex of movement and as proposed innovations multiply in them, a process of collective choice in the nature of fashion is naturally and inevitably brought into play. The absence or inadequacy of compelling tests of the merit of proposals opens the door to prestige-endorsement and taste as determinants of collective choice. The compelling role of these two factors as they interact easily escapes notice by those who participate in the process of collective choice; the model which emerges with a high sanction and approval is almost always believed by them as being intrinsically and demonstrably correct. This belief is fortified by the impressive arguments and arrays of specious facts that may frequently be marshalled on behalf of the model. Consequently, it is not surprising that participants may fail completely to recognize a fashion process in which they are sharing. The identification of the process as fashion occurs usually only after it is gone—when it can be viewed from the detached vantage point of later time. The fashions which we can now detect in the past history of philosophy, medicine, science, technological use and industrial practice did not appear as fashions to those who shared in them. The fashions merely appeared to them as up-to-date achievements! The fact that participants in fashion movements in different areas of contemporary life do not recognize such movements should not mislead perceptive scholars. The applications of this observation to the domain of social science is particularly in order; contemporary social science is rife with the play of fashion.

The Social Role of Fashion. I turn finally to a series of concluding remarks on what seems to be the societal role of fashion. As I have sought to explain, the key to the understanding of fashion is given in the simple words, 'being in fashion'. These words signify an area of life which is caught in movement—movement from an out-moded past toward a dim, uncertain, but explorable immediate future. In this passage, the need of the present is to be in march with the time. The fashion mechanism is the response to this need. These simple observations point to the social role of fashion—a role which I would state abstractly to be that of enabling and aiding collective adjustment to and in a moving world of divergent possibilities. In spelling out this abstract statement I wish to call attention to three matters.

The *first* is a matter which is rather obvious, namely, that fashion introduces a conspicuous measure of unanimity and uniformity in what would otherwise be a markedly fragmented arrangement. If all competing models enjoyed similar acceptance the situation would be one of disorder and disarray. In the field of dress, for example, if people were to freely adopt the hundreds of styles proposed professionally each year and the other thousands which the absence of competition would allow, there would be a veritable 'Tower of Babel' consequence. Fashion introduces order in a potentially anarchic and moving present. By establishing suitable models which carry the stamp of propriety and compel adherence, fashion narrowly limits the range of variability and so fosters uniformity and order, even though it be passing uniformity and order. In this respect fashion performs in a moving society a function which custom performs in a settled society.

Second, fashion serves to detach the grip of the past in a moving world. By placing a premium on being in the mode and derogating what developments have left behind, it frees actions for new movement. The significance of this release from the restraint of the past should not be minimized. To meet a moving and changing world requires freedom to move in new directions. Detachment from the hold of the past is no small contribution to the achievement of such freedom. In the areas of its operation fashion facilitates that contribution. In this sense there is virtue in applying the derogatory accusations of being 'old-fashioned', 'outmoded', 'backward', and 'out-of-date'.

Third, fashion operates as an orderly preparation for the immediate future. By allowing the presentation of new models but by forcing them through the gauntlet of competition and collective selection the fashion mechanism offers a continuous means of adjusting to what is on the horizon.* On the one hand, if offers to innovators and creators the opportunity to present through their models their ideas of what the immediate future should be in the given area

---

* The recognition that fashion is continuously at work is, in my judgement, the major although unintended contribution of Simmel's analysis. However, his thesis that the function of fashion is the oscillating differentiation and unification of social classes seems to me to miss what is most important.

of fashion. On the other hand, the adoption of the models which survive the gauntlet of collective selection gives expression to nascent dispositions that represents an accommodation or orientation to the immediate future. Through this process, fashion nurtures and shapes a body of common sensitivity and taste, as is suggested by the congeniality and naturalness of present fashions in contrast to the oddness and incongruity of past fashions. This body of common sensitivity and taste is analogous on the subjective side to a 'universe of discourse'. Like the latter, it provides a basis for a common approach to a world and for handling and digesting the experiences which the world yields. The value of a pliable and re-forming body of common taste to meet a shifting and developing world should be apparent.

Conclusion

In these three ways, fashion is a very adept mechanism for enabling people to adjust in an orderly and unified way to a moving and changing world which is potentially full of anarchic possibilities. It is suited, *par excellence*, to the demands of life in such a moving world since it facilitates, detachment from a receding past, opens the doors to proposals to the future, but subjects such proposals to the test of collective selection, thus bringing them in line with the direction of awakened interest and disposition. In areas of life—and they are many—in which the merit of the proposals cannot be demonstrated, it permits orderly movement and development.

In closing, let me renew the invitation to sociologists to take fashion seriously and give it the attention and study which it deserves and which are so sorely lacking. Fashion should be recognized as a central mechanism in forming social order in a modern type of world, a mechanism whose operation will increase. It needs to be lifted out of the area of the bizarre, the irrational and the inconsequential in which sociologists have so misguidingly lodged it. When sociologists respond to the need of developing a scheme of analysis suited to a moving or modern world they will be required to assign the fashion process to a position of central importance.

References

H. Blumer, 'Fashion' in *International Encyclopedia of the Social Sciences*, vol. 5 (N.Y., Macmillan, 1968), pp. 341–5.
K. and A. Lang, *Collective Dynamics* (N.Y., Crowell, 1961).
J. Richardson and A. L. Kroeber, 'Three Centuries of Women's Dress Fashions: a Quantitative Analysis', *Anthropological Records*, vol. 5 (1947), pp. 111–53. (*See* Chapter 3.)
E. Sapir, 'Fashion' in *Encyclopedia of the Social Sciences*, vol. 6 (N.Y., Macmillan, 1931), pp. 139–41.
G. Simmel, 'Fashion', *American Journal of Sociology*, vol. 62 (1957), pp. 541–58. (*See* Chapter 9.)
A. B. Young, *Recurring Cycles of Fashion: 1760–1937* (N.Y., Harpers & Brothers, 1937). (*See* Chapter 4.)

Chapter 19

WHAT MAKES FASHION?*
by Hardy Amies

The author traces the institutional structure of the fashion trade in which he works—particularly men's clothing. The relative influence of designer, manufacturer, and boutique is carefully weighed and a wealth of experience drawn upon to illustrate the points made.

Many of us are aware that Fashion appears in many things other than clothes; in architecture, in furniture and indeed in most of the applied arts. For the purpose of this lecture, however, I intend only to talk of clothes; but I shall be talking of clothes for both men and women.

Chanel said, '*La mode a deux buts: le confort et l'amour. La beauté c'est quand on y arrive.*' Lamely translated, I read this to mean 'Fashion has two objects; comfort and seduction. Beauty follows when both are achieved.' We need not discuss comfort at great length, for we northerners know that we have to clothe ourselves to keep ourselves warm. *Seduction* in clothing is, however, a fascinating subject; and let me say outright that I subscribe entirely to the seduction principle in Fashion: a principle which has been so ably and interestingly discussed by our own Mr James Laver and Mr Quentin Bell. I am certain that men and women dress themselves in order to make themselves attractive. Many of course think that they are more attractive if they are not dressed fashionably. I think we need not discuss at great length the sex element in clothing. We know that it is bad manners, and therefore unattractive, to be too sexily dressed in every-day life, and it is obvious that strategic exposure of certain parts of the body is a trick of dressing of woman which would be out of place in men's apparel. Men, on the other hand, can use other wiles. They can make themselves look rich and important, and thus attractive prospective husbands. Women, of course, can make themselves look rich and important to help themselves get their man, or at least keep their man this way. By being fashionably and expensively dressed, they can give themselves confidence.

Gregariousness enters into it too, I think, particularly to-day. People want to appear fashionable because they want to appear in the swim; they want to belong; they want to be 'with it'; they don't want to appear to be alone.

* From the *Journal of The Royal Society of Arts* (June 1964). By permission of Hardy Amies and The Royal Society of Arts.

Fashion is a constantly changing thing because we know instinctively that a true aid to seduction must change before the tricks are 'rumbled' or worn out.

The motives of these needs and satisfactions are probably in many cases complicated, and I am quite inadequately equipped to give you satisfactory explanations of them. I trust all the same that I shall be able to stimulate certain trends of thought which will allow you to draw, in many instances, your own conclusions.

A second aspect will also occur during this talk. This is that I hope to be able to show you that a dress designer is not just a frivolous person catering for the whims of rich women, but is someone who, properly used, can play a part in the industrial life of this country.

These words are purposely weighed for, in reading the literature regarding the Royal Society of Arts which your secretary has so kindly sent to me, I see that the title of your Society is 'The Royal Society for the Encouragement of Arts, Manufactures and Commerce'. This somewhat secondary aspect of my talk is therefore, I think, of importance to the Society.

Thirdly, I should like to point out to you that it so happens that this month I celebrate my thirtieth anniversary as a dress designer, This is perhaps of no real importance except to me personally, but I should like to tell you that I do consider your asking me to address your Society as a great honour, not only to me but to my trade, and by pointing out that I am celebrating this thirtieth anniversay I do so merely to accentuate, for one brief moment, the fact that I bring some authority based on experience.

The Couturier. Let us plunge right into some explanations of the machinery of fashion: I am a Couturier; a French word for which there is absolutely no adequate English translation.

A Couturier is a head dress designer who is the boss, in every sense of the word, of a Couture House. What part he plays in the financial side of the House will depend on his temperament. Many famous Couturiers are fairly uninterested in this side of the business, concentrating more on the artistic, but no good Couturier can neglect the commercial aspect. I have explained Couture as being 'less than art and greater than trade'.

I have also often had to answer the question as to why there are more successful men Couturiers than there are women. The answer lies in the fact that the Couturier *is* the boss, and I think that most people, particularly in the tough life of commerce today, prefer a man boss to a woman boss. There have been, and there still are, famous women Couturiers—for instance, Madame Chanel and Madame Schiaparelli—but both have one limitation, in that they design clothes which are very clearly for one type of woman, namely the type of woman that they themselves are. A man dress designer can take a more objective view of womankind, and design, therefore, for many more types of woman.

A Couture House. Haute Couture implies High Sewing, and it is an understood thing that, in a Couture House, you find the finest type of sewing by hand. At the head of the House you have the Couturier flanked possibly by a financial

342

director who may have a full job within the House, or, if it is a small one, may be engaged part-time. This financial director must occupy himself with the balance of ultimate yearly profit as a percentage of the capital involved. The Couturier himself, as his House expands, will probably need one, two or

FIG. 1. Dinner dress for autumn–winter 1963 by Hardy Amies.

three assistant designers who work roughly in the same relation as assistant painters did to the great masters in their studios. In other words, they will carry out the details of the design as laid down by the Couturier.

A well established Couture House has seldom a staff of less than a hundred, very often of two hundred, and in the case of a great international House in

343

Paris, such as Dior, it can be as high as a thousand. Here let me dispose also of another question which I am sure will run through your minds during the course of this talk; Paris is more important than London as a Couture centre because there are more Couture Houses in Paris and because, on the whole,

FIG. 2. Day dress for spring–summer 1964 by Hardy Amies.

these are larger than those in London. Geographically Paris is more the centre of Europe than London is. Paris is still the centre of luxurious fashion in all its aspects. Couture has to be fed by specialized cloth merchants even if we exclude weavers. It must have at its disposal button makers, flower makers and ribbon makers, all of whom are centred in Paris.

A Couture House in accordance with its importance will therefore have five or six, or even double this quantity of head fitters with their attendant workrooms. I will not weary you with a list of all the other staff, mannequins, packers, counting house, and, very important, the stock-keeper of the cloth. All these departments form the orchestra of which the Couturier is the conductor. To change the simile, this is his family and he is the father. The whole of the House must be permeated with his taste.

FIG. 3. Crêpe dinner dress for spring–summer 1964 by Hardy Amies.

Fitters and Cutters. We then come to the production side of the business, which is headed by the fitters and cutters. These are of tremendous importance. On the tailoring side, the cutter/fitter will almost certainly be a man. On the dressmaking side, of course, it is a woman. To avoid confusion, I will refer to them both as fitters. The fitter's role is twofold. Firstly, he or she will cut the models designed by the Couturier or his studio. (It is rare that the Couturier will himself cut, although on occasion he may do so to demonstrate a new sleeve or indeed a new cut, but it should be borne in mind that the fitter has often many more years of experience of cutting than has the Couturier.) Models will, however, be closely supervised by the Couturier in any case. This work takes place only at the times of making collections. Once the collection is launched—that is to say twice a year—the fitter will cut and fit customers. The fitter will therefore also be the head of a workroom. A workroom of skilled seamstresses or tailoresses will be backed up by a little army of assistants who stitch the less important parts of the dress, and who are training to climb up the trade at the top of which there is the fitter. A well balanced workroom usually consists of some twenty or thirty persons. A good fitter has in addition therefore to be a good workroom manager because, within the House, a workroom is considered as a tiny unit which has to be reasonably self supporting; in other words, it has to produce enough clothes to balance the workroom wages. Only in this way are costs kept within control.

The fitter also has a close personal relationship with the customer. The confidence the customer feels in the fitter helps to build up the clientèle: for Couture customers pay for fit as well as for design.

The Vendeuse. In the French tradition, the sales staff of the House are known as 'vendeuses'. Their job is to interpret the Couturier's idea, as demonstrated in the Collection, to the customer; to guide the customer in her choice from the Collection and to supervise the fittings of the customer. The balance between the power of the vendeuse and the power of the fitter is very important.

The Collection. Collections, as you know, are produced in January for the Spring and in July or early August for the Autumn and Winter. These times are not chosen arbitrarily, but because rich women find them most convenient for ordering their clothes for the coming Season. They order early because they know it will be several weeks before their order can be delivered. The Collection is really an exhibition on living models of the ideas that the Couturier puts forward as suggestions—and I emphasize the word—for his customers. The success of the Collection depends on how acceptable these suggestions are.

I should like to make two points here. When I say 'rich women' I mean women of substance rather than of extravagance. These ladies maintain a wardrobe to help them carry out the duties that fall on them in the position they may occupy by birth, by marriage or by their profession. If they are regular Couture customers, their wardrobe will have cost quite a deal of money, and no one wishes completely to abandon a wardrobe each Season. They will buy clothes in order to keep their wardrobe in good shape and repair. New clothes must therefore not be too conspicuously different from what they already have, but different enough to give them the pleasurable feeling of having something new. The second point is this: certain of the suggestions in the Collection are bound to be more acceptable than others. In other words certain models are copied more than others. In this way you get what we call 'winners'. It is fallacious to think that a Couturier produces original and new designs for each customer. The Collection is, in a certain sense, a series of experiments, and experiments on customers would not only be wearisome to the customer, but uneconomic to the Couturier. For time in a Couture House, which in a sense is a dress factory situated in the heart of a great city, is a very expensive operation. There follow therefore further points:

(a) Many customers choose exactly the same dress, but each model in the Collection has attached to it, as it were, patterns of the same material as the model but in different colours. The vendeuse will help the customer to choose the colour considered most suitable. There is of course a tremendous bias towards the colour in which the model is displayed.

(b) In the ordinary course of their lives, customers don't mind meeting, at certain functions, other women wearing identical dresses. They rarely look identical. All sorts of small details have probably been altered by the skilled fitter, advised by the expert saleswoman. Accessories such as hats, shoes and gloves, and almost certainly jewellery, help to present a different picture to the world.

There are two final very important points. It is this leaning towards certain popular models that makes one of the important foundations of fashion. Secondly, you will see that it is the customer who ultimately decides this fashion. The picture of the Couturier as a dictator must be exploded. He can suggest in his Collection the lengthening of skirts, but wise customers supported by a wise vendeuse will order the dress to be made with a skirt length considered by the vendeuse and the customer to be most acceptable. With a good Collection there should be no conflict.

The Clientèle. There cannot be a Couturier without a clientèle. As Managing Director of Lachasse, where I started life as a designer, I gained the confidence of certain customers; a nucleus of a clientèle. It is rare to engage a new vendeuse who has not already a clientèle. Fitters too have a clientèle; people for whom they have successfully cut and made before. All these elements will fuse together when a new House opens and will grow as the years progress. Couture relies much more on personal recommendations than is ever dreamed possible. A vendeuse will jealously guard her clientèle, and will be very indignant if recommended customers are not sent to her directly they set foot in the House. Again, this building up of the clientèle will necessarily influence the designs of the Couturier over the years. He will find himself perhaps satisfied commercially, and very often artistically, if he feels that he is giving service to his customers rather than indulging in extravagant expressions of his own artistic idea. To illustrate the point, people often ask, 'Why don't you open a House in Paris?' The simple answer is, 'Because I have no clientèle there'.

The Press. It seems to me that the wise heads of our great national Press have sensed the ever-increasing interest of readers in Fashion, and have therefore devoted an ever-increasing space in their newspapers to it. Since Haute Couture is the great vehicle for the launching of new ideas in Fashion, it follows that the Couturier can enjoy a great deal of publicity. Certainly publicity is of vast importance to a new House or even to a new designer working within a House. It is exciting and exhilarating. But a wise Couturier must see that he is not caught too much in this trap. If he gets bad publicity, a bad review of his Collection, the confidence of his clientèle will be shaken, although not always mortally so, for the faithfulness of the clientèle to the vendeuse, and indeed to the fitters, can often save the finances of his House for at least a Season. Nor must he be too impressed by good publicity if the customers' reactions don't produce satisfactory sales.

The best is a balance. There must be in the Collections enough advanced and interesting models to satisfy the Press, and enough basically intelligent clothes to satisfy the customers. A model that does both does sometimes happen. It is the Couturier's dream.

The Boutique. It is not very hard for you to imagine that a Couturier often has moments of depression when he feels that he is working in an outmoded and anachronistic medium; making clothes of his own design to measure in the middle of a modern city. The price today of a plain wool dress made in such a system is approximately £80; of a tailored suit approximately £120. Very many women can only afford to have a few such garments for their wardrobes and supplement the rest by Ready-to-Wear clothes. We sensed this change some twelve years ago and therefore opened a Boutique where customers could buy Ready-to-Wear clothes bearing the name and imprint of our own hand-writing. The making of such clothes being partly by machine is an operation in many aspects very different from Haute Couture. We therefore had to use workrooms slightly away from the main stream of the West End. The success of our Boutique clothes, offered as they were to our own private clientèle in the first instance, persuaded us to put part of the Boutique clothes on a whole-sale basis.

The Ready-to-Wear. Let us discuss the Ready-to-Wear in more detail and see where it differs from Haute Couture.

From the outset you are making clothes to be sold off-the-peg with the minimum of alteration. This latter point is important when designing; clothes must be uncomplicated and easy to alter. It would be unpractical, for instance, to have a decorated hem-line to a skirt because it could not be easily altered.

Sizing is very important. This is a technical matter and it doesn't really come into the design picture. There is much debate as to the desirability of a national standard of sizing. It should be noted in passing that the sizing standards of expensive Ready-to-Wear vary somewhat from cheaper clothes. They are usually longer waisted and, on the whole, made with a taller woman in mind.

A designer for the Ready-to-Wear usually has less skilled cutters at his disposal than has a grand Couturier. Cutters for the Ready-to-Wear are expensively paid for their skill in making basic patterns rather than inventing new cuts. Their mind is rightly geared to mass production. Apart from desiring to see high fashion presented in an inspiring way as Haute Couture tries to do, wholesale dress manufacturers and their designers like to go to the great Couturiers to buy new cuts. This saves the expense of attempting them at home; an operation they feel they cannot do very well in any case.

In the case of a House like my own, the cuts in the Couture are available for the Ready-to-Wear business to use. Some cuts, of course, particularly those of a classic nature, are used for several seasons with or without minor adaptations.

It is difficult to give an adequate picture of the excitement caused by the bi-annual migration of buyers from all over the world to a fashion centre like Paris at the time of the Collections. It is good for manufacturers as well as designers to have a change of scene and environment, as well as the inspiration of seeing the new clothes themselves. Here again, it is the appeal that the clothes make to the buyers that is a great source of fashion.

Ready-to-Wear Collections on the whole are presented in roughly the same way as are those of the Couture, perhaps with a little less attention to glamour and on a more down to earth basis. For instance, it is not usual to choose accessories for a wholesale Collection with such care. The Collections are offered to the buyers in the same way as a Collection in the Couture is offered to the private clientèle.

It is very important to note the difference in the timing of the Collections. Wholesale Spring Collections open in November. This is arranged deliberately for the wholesaler to get his orders in from the buyers during the month of November, so that he can cut the initial orders in December and January for delivery in February in time for the Spring Campaign in the shops. There is no way of getting round this date question. In order to cut the orders on an economic basis, the wholesaler must assemble a large portion of his orders and cut on some form of bulk basis. You will find therefore in practice that after a week to ten days of showing the wholesaler will withdraw from his Collection models which only attract a very low portion of orders. The more he concentrates his selling on a smaller number of models, the more happy will be his bank balance at the end of the Season. The cutting of small orders and execution of special orders must be left until the pressure on the workrooms is relieved.

Continuing the story of the timing, I must draw your attention to this fact: the Ready-to-Wear Collections for the Spring come out in November before the Haute Couture Collections in January. It is therefore impossible for the Haute Couture Collections to influence the corresponding Season. In other words, Spring can only influence Autumn and vice versa.

I must also emphasize here the all-important influence of the buyer, for she usually is the filter through which fashion passes. A buyer is someone who ultimately is very rigidly controlled and influenced by the profits her department makes. She must buy what she thinks she can sell rather than what she personally likes or what she personally believes in.

Export. Exports comprise a side of the buisness which is often high-lighted by the Press. The export picture of the Ready-to-Wear is comparatively simple. Export buyers buy roughly in the same way as do the home buyers. The export buyer will of course be influenced by the climatic conditions of her home country, and where—as in Scandiavian countries, for instance, or certain parts of the east coast of the United States and Canada—the conditions are roughly the same as ours, there is no problem.

349

But when it comes to exporting models in the Couture Collection the picture is slightly different. The biggest buyer, and the most sought after, is the U.S.A. There is in New York a very powerful Ready-to-Wear organization catering for a continent populated by people with money to spend and where clothes are used more as a status symbol than they are anywhere else in the world. But this Ready-to-Wear organization in the United States has grown very rapidly to maturity and has produced excellent designers of its own. It is exciting and stimulating and flattering to a designer in a very large degree to sell to overseas buyers. You feel that you are in the world-class fashion, competing at Wimbledon, as it were, rather that at County Week. But it should be borne in mind that, when export buyers are present, say at the January Openings, they require the delivery of their models to take place within two or three weeks, otherwise the models are useless to them. For the rest of the months of March, April, May and June, until the July Collections come round again, the big and expensive machinery of a Couture House must be kept fully, and above all, profitably occupied. Export selling is therefore very much the icing on the cake, and you can have a very nice cake without any icing at all, although it may be a little dull, and dullness is not compatible with fashion. But it is the models that are sold for export to the United States which probably receive the greatest publicity in the expensively produced glossy magazines such as *Vogue* and *Harper's*. Great care and expense is lavished on such photographs, and the combination of publicity, commerce and art which ensues is undoubtedly one of the factors which makes fashion.

Design. I have spent some time in trying to explain to you my ideas of the machinery of women's fashion, and I have only in passing referred to design proper. I must therefore make some points in this connection.

The Haute Couturier must design for his clientèle, which tends to be basically middle aged and somewhat conservative in outlook. His duty is to make his customers look appropriately dressed for their station in life, as expensively as, or rather more expensively than, this station warrants, and, above all, he must make them look as young as possible. He must also, and this is an obvious point, make them feel that they are fashionably dressed even if they are not demonstrating revolutionary fashions, which few of them today want to do.

I have purposely given the impression that the fashions demonstrated in the Ready-to-Wear are really adaptations of those originally launched in the Haute Couture. This is primarily true in what is called the more expensive end of the trade, that is to say, relatively high priced Ready-to-Wear, but, when it comes to cheaper clothes, and particularly those designed with the young in mind (I refer to the young woman of from 18 to 30), there is today some distinctively original designing going on which really owes little allegiance to the Haute Couture. It is not possible for me to go into this side of fashion too deeply or to discuss its origins. It would seem to stem from the desire of the young to make a new protest against the past.

Old standards of quality, cut and even attractive colours are often deliberately abandoned. I think most of these tendencies are exciting and quite healthy. What is curious, however, is that they are so striking and so emphatic that they do influence Haute Couture. I should think that now is probably the first time in the history of fashion that the expensive clothes have been influenced by the cheap.

Cloth. To complete my story I must refer to cloth, for this is the raw material from which our fashions are made. In practice, cloth manufacturers produce their collections and present them to the Couturier or to the wholesale designer for his choice. The designer is therefore regularly confronted by a collection of cloth some weeks or months before his Collection has to be completed; but the very tempo of his life may not give him time to have any preconceived ideas. The viewing of the collection is, however, followed by the necessity for him to make up his mind so that the cloth may be woven, and this forces him to canalize his ideas. Sometimes there is time to order special colours; sometimes there is not. I think it fair to say in general, however, that there is enough cloth to satisfy his demands without going to special designs.

The demands for Haute Couture as regards cloth are very special. It is of course obvious that the quality and designs must be of the first order, but very important too is the question of service, for, by tradition and for economic necessity, a Couture House only buys the cloth to execute an order once the order is placed by the customer. It stands to reason that if you show a Collection of some eighty models with, say, five different colour variations available for each model, the Couture House would not like to start the Season with four hundred bolts of cloth, some of which, indeed a great part of which, may be in new and rather revolutionary colours. There is in Paris a whole army of fabric makers dedicated—and I use no other word—to the service of the Couture, and it is on these sources that the London Couturier must rely, for the decline in the number of important Couture Houses in London has led to the decline among merchants in London dealing with the Couture. This may be a misfortune for the British or Scottish weaver, but it allows the London Couturier to be in very close contact with the Paris Couture, for it will be seen that we are drawing our raw materials from the same sources. For instance, an important French cloth merchant will often fly over to see a London Couturier to show his cloth collection, whereas the day before he has been showing it to a French Couturier. A designer draws great inspiration from his cloth. An inspired Couture cloth collection can spark off a lot of dormant ideas, and, if there is an English Couturier as actively minded as a French, you will get the same tendencies appearing in both collections. This makes us feel, when we think about it, very close to Paris, and I look on my House as being as important a part of the world fashion Haute Couture picture as a French House of similar importance. We do not and cannot compete with the giants like Balenciaga and Dior, but we can be a tree not ashamed to stand in the same orchard.

Subsidiary Designing

It is fair to say that the direct financial reward to a Couturier is really not in correct proportion to the effort expended in his taste and invention, and the years of painstaking skill of his fitters and sales staff. The basic reasons, I think, are that fundamentally one of his stock-in-trades is extravagance—only in an extravagant atmosphere can you persuade customers to be extravagant—

351

and secondly that it is practically impossible to achieve a fair basis of costing when you are going to sell. You are selling perfection—not only your idea of perfection, but the idea of perfection of the customer and, what is worse, of the customer's friends, husband and relations when she gets the dress home. If a Couture dress customer has an evening dress with thirty yards of chiffon in the skirt, and, when she gets it home, decides that the dress would look better shortened by half an inch, you will have to do it for her free of charge. You are also, however careful, always experimenting and always taking a risk when you launch your Collection. Someone said it was like having to pass an examination twice a year: an examination which becomes more exacting the older you get. So it has always been understood, particularly in Paris, that a Couture House should seek a more stable form of income by dealing in what I call Subsidiary Designing. The most obvious example of this is the scent business. Many famous French Houses have scent businesses either wholly or partly owned by the Couture House, which, as regards hard money, are far more important than the Couture House itself.

The London Couturier is denied this advantage for the simple reason that London is not the important centre of the scent business that Paris is. We have, however, very flourishing Boutiques, some of which are supported by a Ready-to-Wear business. Here we score over the French for the simple reason that Ready-toWear businesses in London are basically better organized than those in Paris.

Some years ago, too, Monsieur Jacques Fath, followed closely afterwards by Monsieur Dior, gave his attention to designing men's ties, which were put on sale in the Boutique. I was able to follow suit, and here I immediately felt the advantage of being in London, which is still so much the centre of the men's fahion trade (however important may have been, and may be, certain influences from Italy, and, in a less marked degree, from America). This gives me, I think, a natural opening to talk to you about designing for men.

Designing for Men. As I have said, it all really started with my designing men's ties for the Boutique. These proved ultimately so successful that we were quickly encouraged to offer the ties on sale on a wholesale basis. They are now on sale on such a basis throughout the world, and we export to some thirty-two countries. I must, however, make one thing clear. In all my undertakings for men I manufacture nothing myself, for in every case I work in close collaboration with an existing firm, using their machinery of manufacture and selling. It would be manifestly impossible for me and my staff to control such an elaborate machinery ourselves, and on the whole I am more than happy with the arrangements we have made. In all cases, we have very carefully worded contracts which give me neat but firm artistic control over the products produced, and of course, in most cases, the actual designs emanate from me or from the staff I have under my control. One further thing should be pointed out. My men's clothes are basically much cheaper than my women's, and are deliberately aimed at a moderately mass-produced market.

I hope it does not sound too casual if I say that I seem to have drifted into my career as a woman's dress designer. I was of course, as I have explained, in some ways born into it. But what I did in those early days was certainly done very unselfconsciously, almost naturally if you will. I went into the men's side not only with a great deal of practical experience gained through designing clothes for women, but I was able to go into it consciously and clearly, and, before actually plunging into design, was able to take a dispassionate view of the immediate past and the urgent present.

Structure of Men's Trade. It is interesting to look at the structure of men's trade, bearing in mind the picture that we have of the women's.

(1) *Savile Row.* The business of the high class men's bespoke tailoring which are referred to, conveniently and generically, as Savile Row, represent the pinnacle of the trade; and what goes for Savile Row also goes for similar businesses in Italy, America and elsewhere. There will, I think, always be bespoke tailoring as long as any sort of personal and private wealth is permitted. The influence on design of such establishments has, however, declined seriously since the disappearance of public figures like the actor Jack Buchanan and indeed the Prince of Wales, who were correctly considered leaders of fashion. Although Savile Row is the equivalent to Haute Couture on the women's side, it is always at the disadvantage of not being able to hold seasonal fashion shows. It has thus never been asked to be an authority, but has been merely a vehicle for executing the fashionable ideas of its private customers.

(ii) *Manufacturers.* I have no available figures, but it is certain that the men's trade in the Ready-to-Wear section has grown out of all proportion to the decline in the bespoke section. In other words, men all round probably have bigger wardrobes. But, if we accept this fact, as we must, we must also accept the fact that a great deal of the responsibility for design must devolve on the manufacturer of Ready-to-Wear clothing and his designers.

(iii) *The Multiple Tailor.* I must just mention this group, first because it is a peculiarly British phenomenon, although the actual system was invented in the U.S.A.; secondly because I am given to believe that some 50 per cent of the male population of this country dress with multiple tailors, and, thirdly, because I am so intimately connected with one of the finest myself. The principle is, as you know, quite simple. The customer orders a suit from a multiple tailor, where care is taken to give him all his requirements exactly as would be done by a bespoke tailor, but the suit itself, although hand cut individually for each customer, is made by hand with the minimum of fittings. By this method, using the same cloth as would a bespoke tailor, the price to the customer is reduced to as low a proportion as a quarter, and, on an average, to about a third. It must, however, be mentioned, since we are talking about fashion, that, because of the necessity for laying down clearly the customer's requirements and interpreting these desires in a shop, say, in Bournemouth and transmitting them to a factory in Leeds, and because the customer is possibly not able to express his desires very clearly himself without precise help from the salesman—some unification of design is very necessary. In other words, the customer is persuaded to make his choice from a fairly limited number of alternatives.

Design. When I came into the field, I saw that there were several very strongly felt influences.

First, the influence of the young, which had already been most noticeably demonstrated by the Teddy boys immediately after the war. There is no time to go into the psychological and social background of the upsurge of a fashion demonstration by the young and non-established classes. It was too picturesque and too marked to be anything other than admired. It must be noted in passing that this influence came from cheap clothing which ultimately influenced the expensive. We have remarked on the same tendencies in the women's trade.

Another factor was the influence from America and Italy, the latter being much the stronger of the two. It would seem that the Italian manufacturers, and indeed the minor bespoke tailors, of which there are such a quantity in Italy, were able to get more quickly off the mark with new designs after the war than were the still restricted British. Our men and women, rushing happily to foreign travel, breaking the enclosure of our war-beseiged island, seized quickly on these new ideas. In all these influences there was one main factor: a much closer fitting trouser, which must have echoed somewhere the smartness of our own cavalry officers, and which fitted in very precisely with the lines of the American blue-jean, which gains the universal approval of all men with youthful figures, even on remote Greek islands. When I started to design, I knew that the Italian look with its short jacket would not do. The correct way to set off the narrow trouser was to have a longer and more skirted jacket. From this there evolved a look which had something to do with the traditional look of the English gentlemen. It seemed perfectly right, therefore, to develop such a way of thinking.

Basic Differences. It is interesting perhaps to glance for one moment at the basic differences between designing for men and for women.

In designing for women, particularly for day clothes, practical considerations play some part, but of course such considerations are always subservient to others which are far from practical. For instance, skirts for women which only just cover the knee, supported as they are by very flimsy and often fragile nylon stockings, are hardly practical, but these form a basis for modern women's designs. But a man's suit cannot change radically unless our way of life, which is basically urban and basically commercial, also changes. It is now often perfectly permissible for a man to wear a sweater on occasions for which he would have thought it utterly unsuitable before the war, but he will shortly turn to his jacket because it carries his keys, his money, his notebook, his fountain pen, his driving licence if not his handkerchief.

Therefore it can be said that practical considerations are of more importance in men's designs than in women's. I am also aware of certain hierarchical principles. These have been very ably expounded by Mr James Laver in several of his books on costume and in a paper given to your Society. It seems of course that a man often likes to show his station in life by his clothes, although this may be done subtly; for instance, a banker likes to look like a banker; so of course do a lot of other people.

Aesthetically, after considering the question of the skirt for day clothes, on examination it will be found that women's designs have to make the dress a frame or background to the face. The face of a fashionable women is a very complicated piece of machinery on which much time and money is expended; the made-up lips, the carefully and heavily painted eyes all tend to make a complicated pattern; often so complicated that a perfectly plain neck line is the only answer—an answer all the more necessary when you add earrings and often a very elaborate hairdressing. As regards the body, the lines are fluid; very fluid indeed at this very moment when loose dresses, even if very carefully cut so as not to be sack-like, are very fashionable. In contrast to this fluidity, a man's costume is comparatively rigid; suits certainly are. And I had difficulty at first in persuading a man to take a fully cut back to a raglan overcoat, but I am succeeding. The lines of men's suits are all designed and cut to reproduce or accentuate, if it exists, a muscular and virile body.

When it comes to the question of accessories—and by this I mean garments which supplement basic costume, which in the case of a man is the suit—a principle does appear which is common to both men and women; namely that these supplementary garments, such as hats, shoes, ties and shirts, must eventually harmonize, and by this I don't mean necessarily harmonize in colour (that's another story), but I do mean harmonize in line. This harmonizing of line is, I think, a very comforting thought, and it encourages me to think that there is hope for the human race; a hope which is often dimmed by the sight of multitudes of men dressed in murky grey suits and even murkier grey raincoats. Viewing the history of fashion, and looking at the eccentric lines of a woman's costume of, say, 1924 (a little beige kasha dress which is above the knee and a cloche hat over the eyes), you will find that by 1926 she will have found absolutely the right accessories—the string of pearls, and the beige glacé strap shoes. Exactly the same automatic reactions to accessories takes place in the men's world. But now the men's world has moved swiftly and emphatically into a consciousness of being in the fashion business rather than in garment manufacture.

I am now the designer or consultant designer for firms manufacturing men's ties, handkerchiefs, scarves, shirts, pyjamas, dressing gowns, socks, pullovers, and all other kinds of knitwear, and hats; apart from the important operation that I do in men's suits and overcoats. This list can be shown in a less formidable light when you consider that all these things can be made to fall automatically into the same line. Having chosen your colours for ties, for instance, it is not difficult to apply the same to socks; the line of the collar of a jacket will affect the line of the shirt; narrow trousers are completed by elastic-sided boots without the interruption of laces; and the whole is topped by a high crowned forward tilting hat.

I am now given the opportunity for designing for the whole man, and, if this is successful, it may be my most important contribution to fashion history.

Designing for Industry. It is not without interest, I think, to note that a Couture House can make use of its taste and experience by applying fashion to industrial garments. It is obvious that in the course of time fashion creeps into such garments as the wearers, particularly if they are female, will make their own adjustments to, to bring such garments into fashion, in the same

355

way that a prima donna, even when she is dressed in period costume, will arrange her hair in a way which she considers most becoming; that is to say fashionable; and it takes great skill and tact on the part of a period designer to persuade her to do otherwise.

During the past twelve months, my House has had a number of commissions for garments which would not ordinarily fall within its sphere of activity. It has designed uniforms for female factory workers employed by one of the largest grocery concerns in this country; uniforms for male nurses in a well known mental institution and in a large London Hospital Group; for female nurses in a London Hospital Group; uniforms for the male and female staff of an important new London hotel, and for waiters in a chain of modern eating houses. It has also designed the robes for the Chancellor, Vice-Chancellor and Pro-Chancellor of a new English university.

Summary
1. Fashion is a constantly changing means of seduction.
2. The Couture is basically a bespoke operation where the female customer bespeaks a dress to be made as she wants it.
3. The Couturier experiments with new designs which he proposes to the customer and tries to coax her to accept, using all the magic and the power he possesses.
4. The wholesale dress manufacturer is prepared to accept the lead of the Couturier, and is indeed often happy to do so. He then has to coax the store or shop buyer into being a satisfactory medium and channel between the designer and the public who buy the dress as distinct from ordering it.
5. The man's garment manufacturer can today get little lead from bespoke tailors, and finds the responsibility for men's design falling on his shoulders: a responsibility which he often finds onerous and perplexing; a sensation which is now more marked than ever, as the men's trade becomes daily more aware of the fact that it is actually in a fashion business.
6. The Press is a very useful ally in all these cases.
7. All dress designers, either Couture or wholesale, are part of a commercial operation, and they must fail or succeed by these standards. If a designer does not feel that the better a dress is designed the better it sells, he ought not to continue to besmirch an honourable trade with his cynicism or defeatism.
8. All dress design, both male and female, is influenced today by designs destined for the young, which are therefore necessarily inexpensive. This influence is felt even at the most expensive end of the business: a feature of fashion which appears for the first time in the history of fashion.
9. Fashion can and does enter into industrial clothing design.
10. The biggest influence in fashion is our way of life. This is more evident in men's fashions than in women's.
11. Fashion is what is worn.

And all this, as Hamlet says, 'with a bare bodkin'.

Chapter 20

FASHION IN WOMEN'S CLOTHES AND THE AMERICAN SOCIAL SYSTEM*
by Bernard Barber and Lyle S. Lobel

Any concept of irrationality in fashion is rejected by the authors. The function of clothing and the meaning of fashion in society are explored. Age, sex and social class are examined as discriminating criteria in the determination of fashion diffusion.

In social science usage, 'fashion' is still an overgeneralized term. One writer lists the following 'fields of fashion': values in the pictorial arts, architecture, philosophies, religion, ethical behaviour, dress, and the physical, biological, and social sciences. 'Fashion' has also been used in reference to language usages, literature, food, dance music, recreation, indeed the whole range of social and cultural elements. The core of meaning in the term for all these different things is 'changeful', but it is unlikely that the structures of behaviour in these different social areas and the consequent dynamics of their change are all identical. 'Fashion', like 'crime', has too many referents; it covers significantly different kinds of social behaviour.[1]

The description of 'fashion' behaviour suffers also from treating 'fashion' as socially 'irrational'. 'Fashion' is usually grouped with 'fads' and 'crazes'. Robert Merton has shown how many kinds of patterned social behaviour have latent, or unintended, as well as manifest, or purposed, consequences for the social systems in which they exist. This distinction, he says, often 'clarifies the analysis of seemingly irrational social patterns'.[2] We shall confine ourselves to 'fashion' in American women's clothes and show that this behaviour is not at all socially 'irrational' when seen in relation to the American class structure, age-sex roles, and economic system.†

The field of 'fashion' in American women's clothes is an area of rich, accessible, but still largely unexploited empirical materials.[3] Our data have been taken primarily from a rough content analysis of 'copy' in several women's 'fashion' magazines. 'Fashion copy' is part successful social analysis, part unexamined social sentiment; and its dual nature reflects and successfully affects, all at the same time, the social structuring of 'fashion' behaviour.

* From *Social Forces*, vol. 32 (University of North Carolina Press, 1952).

† We ignore the psychological dimension of 'fashion' behaviour. The writer of the following Wallach's Store advertisement in *The New York Times* is obviously playing on this theme: 'Psycho-analysis has helped some men to overcome obstacles and gain new confidence. So has good tailoring.'

We have studied the 'fashion copy', the advertisements, and some of the stories in *Harper's Bazaar*, *Vogue*, *Ladies' Home Journal*, and *Woman's Home Companion* for the twenty-year period, 1930–1950. *Mademoiselle* (for college girls and young white collar women workers) was studied from its first issue, in 1935, to 1950. *Seventeen* (for teenagers from thirteen to seventeen) was studied from its first issue, in 1944, to 1950. *Harper's Bazaar* and *Vogue* are written for 'the trade' and for the higher reaches of the social class system: upper middle and upper; *Ladies' Home Journal* and *Woman's Home Companion* are written for the middle and lower parts of 'the middle classes'. We shall see that these magazines define 'fashion' differently from one another.

The Social Functions of Clothes and the Meaning of 'Fashion'

In all societies, the clothes which *all* people wear have at least three (mixed latent and manifest) functions: utilitarian, aesthetic, and symbolic of their social role.[4] In all societies, clothes are more or less useful, more or less handsome, and more or less indicative of their wearer's social position. We shall be primarily concerned here with the independent role-symbolic functions of clothing, but this will require us to see the interdependence of these functions with the utilitarian and aesthetic ones. 'Pretty' clothes for the teenage girl in American society, for instance, are defined by her social role, especially by her presumed sexual innocence.

Just a few comparative illustrations of role-symbolic functions of clothes may be useful. In France, during the centuries prior to the Revolution, when class position was clearly defined as a matter of law, there was detailed *legal* prescription of the relation between social rank and style of dress. Silks, traditionally an emblem of elegance, could be worn only by princesses and duchesses; ladies of high rank alone were permitted to wear muffs of fur or fine materials. When it wanted to abolish all class distinctions, during the Revolution, the General Assembly abolished all laws relating to distinction in dress.[5] Or, to take one more example, in Classical China, the mandarin showed his class position and his abstention from manual labour by his ankle-length gown and his long fingernails.[6]

It should be noted, in passing, that the symbolic function of clothes in society is only a specific phrasing of the more general sociological fact about all consumption. As Talcott Parsons has put this fact, 'Though the standard of living of any group must cover their intrinsically significant needs, such as food, shelter and the like, there can be no doubt that an exceedingly large component of standards of living everywhere is to be found in the symbolic significance of many of its items in relation to status.'[7] This general point is, of course, the rationale behind Chapin's living-room equipment scale for social class status.[8] The clothing style which is considered serviceable, appropriate and becoming in one social role and 'style of life' is not so for every role and life pattern.

We may now give a preliminary definition of 'fashion' for present purposes, a definition which will be expanded by the rest of our analysis. 'Fashion' in clothes has to do with the styles of cut, colour, silhouette, stuffs, etc., that are socially prescribed and socially accepted as appropriate for certain social roles, and especially with the recurring changes in these styles.

Fashion in Women's Clothes and the American Class System

The functions of consumption in the American class system. The American social class system approximates the open-class 'ideal type' of institutionalized class structure, in which moral approval is placed on mobility from lower to higher social class. The primary criterion of a man's social class status (and that of his wife and dependent children) is his occupational position. Occupational achievement is the primary determinant of social mobility. One of the chief, but by no means the only, index of relative rank of occupational position and achievement is money income and capital wealth. Hence the great symbolic significance of *all* consumption in American society. At least on first glance we all apply the following social equation: consumption equals wealth or income, wealth or income equals occupational position, occupational position equals social class position, and, *therefore*, consumption equals social class position. Even when this consequence is not intended by any particular consumer, his consumption has this latent function. The kind of house a man owns, the kind of car he drives, where he sends his children to college, etc. etc., all have symbolic significance for his social class status.

In the American class system, women take their class status, by and large, from their relationship to men: unmarried young women from their fathers, adult married women from their husbands. Hence the symbolic significance of women's consumption. The way a woman furnishes her house, the clothes she wears, 'put in evidence', as Veblen said, 'her household's ability to pay'.[9] Not wholly, but in important measure, it is the 'office of the woman to consume vicariously for the head of the household', that is, the adult male job-holder.[10] However, this is not at all the passive, uncontrollable function it is often alleged to be. Women can perform the consumption function in general, the buying and wearing of clothes in particular, more or less effectively. Not only can a wife's good taste enhance a little her family's social status, but her skill in maximizing the number and quality of the clothes she acquires on a given budget also counts. We shall see that some women know devices for such maximization that others do not: making their own clothes, buying 'seconds' and manufacturers' overstock, and patronizing 'bargain' stores.

Despite the stereotyped complaints and ridicule in jokes and cartoons about wives' conformity to fashion, there is good evidence that husbands as well as wives know the functions of women's clothes consumption. A poll conducted by the *Woman's Home Companion* (April 1947) yielded some comments which indicate this. One woman says, for example, 'My husband says I don't spend enough and don't represent him fairly'. Certainly the writers of 'fashion copy', ever sensitive to the sentiments of their readers, take the class-symbolic functions of women's dress for granted:

'If at first you don't succeed, change the way you dress.'[11]

'Clothes for climbing, or what to wear on your way up the ladder; to build that graciousness which leads first to charm and eventually to financial advancement, proper, attractive clothes are a sound investment.'[12]

In American society, all but a few groups are oriented to social mobility and therefore also to the functions in women's clothes 'fashions' for mobility. So at least we may infer from the vast volume of 'fashion copy' addressed to the American people. In all newspapers there are pages of advertisements for women's 'fashionable' clothing, editorial 'fashion' pages or columns, and, in the large cities, the newspapers periodically issue 'fashion supplements'. The general circulation magazines, like *Life*, pay a great deal of attention to 'fashion'; almost every issue has something directly or indirectly about it. Several magazines specialize in 'fashion' and all the general women's magazines maintain regular 'fashion' sections or features. The general women's magazines stress that 'fashion' is available to all. In its regular 'How America Lives' series, for instance, the *Ladies' Home Journal* portrays the 'fashion' consciousness of the relatively poor (a woman whose family has an income of under $2,000 a year) and of the ordinary farm family.[13]

The dilemma of equality and difference in the class system. In concrete social fact, American society has been a relatively close approximation to the 'ideal type' of an open-class system. A great deal of social mobility actually exists, so that social class boundaries, especially as between any few adjacent social classes, are somewhat vague. The American class system is a finely graded continuum of strata rather than a series of sharply separated ranks with little mobility between them. The result of this kind of class structure, in combination with American egalitarian values, has been the possibility of asserting the equality and similarity of everyone in the society, despite the actual class differences which exist. The ideology of equality and the social fact of difference are not so obviously inconsistent that they cannot seem to square with one another.

'Fashion' in women's clothes plays its part in helping to resolve this dilemma of equality and difference. Marked dress differences are not appropriate in the American class system, so one strong tendency in 'fashion copy' is to stress the similarity of appearance among women of all class levels. Here are some typical expressions:

'There goes an American . . . the classless way they dress. Filing clerk and company president's wife, the same nylons, little hats, tweed suits, navy-blue dresses.'[14]

'A democracy of government achieves also the only democracy of fashion in the world.'[15]

In women's clothes themselves, the most easily observable characteristics of what is currently 'new' are provided for all social levels. For example, hem length, one of the most noticeable characteristics of a dress, is always the same for all social classes. Many women can easily raise and lower hem length as it fluctuates from year to year and thus stay 'in fashion'. But to have the 'fashionable' silhouette, fabric, and colour, the aid of the 'fashion industry' is necessary and here is where difference as well as equality enters. The 'fashion industry' is founded upon the 'trickle down' pattern, which makes possible both gross similarity and subtle difference in 'fashion', and thus helps resolve the dilemma of equality and difference in the class system. As usual, 'fashion' writers know the social score, 'In fashion . . . a "trickle" system exists; a silhouette starts in the couturier collections, slowly trickles down through all the strata of ready-to-wear....'[16]

This is how the 'trickle' system works. When Paris couturier 'openings' are held each season, American 'fashion industry' representatives are present, together with those few American women who buy their clothes in Paris and serve as 'style leaders' for the whole society. American designers immediately adapt the newest Paris couturier 'fashions' for the very high-priced ready-to-wear market. It should be noted that American dresses sell in a price range from $1,500 to less than $5. The true mass production dress, priced under $25, is cut out by the hundreds. Fewer copies are made of the medium- to high-priced dresses, cut and finished individually. At the highest price, relative exclusiveness is possible and is offered:

'Fashions, cut one at a time, but ready for you to wear. Limited editions. She wears a ready-to-wear "name" dress with the same pride that a Frenchwoman has made to order a "name" dress ... upper bracket ready-to-wear ... enough ahead of the general fashion to assure long wearing.'[17]

As the new styles, set by Paris and first imitated by the designers of expensive 'limited editions', gain wider favour, the designers of each lower price range include the new 'fashion' points as best they can in the lines they create, in response to actual or anticipated demand from those on lower class levels. As the 'fashion' trickles down, fabrics become cheaper and mass production necessary. But even at the lower price and lower social levels, there is an attempt to avoid complete uniformity. Manufacturers try to distribute their job lots over a wide geographical area, including only a limited number of dresses of the same style, fabric, and size in a shipment to any one city, any one retailer. When a general style has 'trickled down' through all levels, the 'fashion' must change. The universalization of what started out as distinctive cheapens its symbolic value. A new change, a new 'fashion' symbol, is necessary.

For the most part, the 'trickle' system does not result in a progressive imitation of exact models in all the strata of ready-to-wear. There are real differences. For example, to indicate difference, reliance is often put on *patently* expensive materials, 'You won't see them elsewhere, for both fabrics are exclusive with us.'[18] However, American technical proficiency is continually producing good imitations of the finest fabrics, so there is a continual search for the *obviously* better and more expensive. Despite real differences, the lower-priced stores are driven to advertise the identity of their goods with the best. They may even claim, 'An exact Molyneux copy'. This encourages the lower social strata to buy what is 'trickling down', but it also encourages the upper strata to look for something new, something 'more fashionable'. The following tale is probably a modern myth, with important functions for the trickle system:

'... we parted with approximately four weeks' salary for a little sheaf of fine wool with crepe. It was distinctive, expensive, original. We were distinguished, elegant, proud. Two weeks later we saw the sheaf—cheapened but very recognizable, on Sixth Avenue (at a price!), and in subsequent weeks we followed it on its downward path all the way to Fourteenth Street and a raging popularity at six-ninety-five. Result: discard....'[19]

The 'trickle' system is perpetuated because the American class system makes some women continually seek for symbols of their difference from those just below them in the class system and at the same time makes other women continually seek for symbols of their equality with those just above them in the class system.

Social class differences in definitions of 'fashion'. We must abandon the stereo-type of complete standardization in American women's 'fashions'. Although there is a certain similarity at all class levels, there are also important differences. Let us consider some of the different phrasings of the 'fashion' theme that are used in 'fashion copy'.

At the top of the American social class system are those families where lineage, or family connections extending back one or more generations, counts in addition to present occupational position. These are the 'old money' families with established pre-eminence of social status. At this topmost level, where there is little need to compete for status through consumption, women may even maintain a certain independence of current changeful 'fashion'. Their quality clothes can remain roughly the same for several years. They can stress the aesthetic functions of clothes somewhat at the expense of 'fashion's' dictates. 'Individualists . . . Mrs. Byron C. Foy . . . who even in this era of wide skirts is seen at night in severe, high-waisted dresses. . . .'[20] At an extreme, one may even be queer and eccentric in one's dress, like the old ladies on Beacon Street in Boston. A woman in this highest social class position might have written: 'There is grace and charm in continuity. There is vulgarity in sudden, constant change.'[21] So far as it is uniform, the taste of these women is more British than French. It runs to tweeds, woollens, and it avoids the 'daring' so characteristic of French fancy dress. This symbolic identification with the British upper classes reveals a concern for birth distinction and English heredity as against the distinction of occupational achievement. Advertisements appealing to this taste stress adjectives like 'aristocratic', 'well-bred', 'distinguished', or phrases like 'a fox and hounds flare at the hip'.[22]

In the social class just below the 'old money' families we find most of the 'high fashion', Paris-conscious style leaders whom we have already mentioned. Their clothes symbols are related to wealth and high living rather than to family connection. Cosmopolitan, Parisian French styles express their values better than do conservative British modes. Yet, since they are aware of the class above, perhaps trying to gain entrance into it, these women seek to combine opulence with 'quiet elegance'. 'Fashion copy' for this group stresses the *pose* of assured distinction, effortless superiority, and inbred elegance. The recurrent symbols of prestige are sophistication and chic; the word 'glamour' is never used, for 'glamour' is 'cheap'. These women read *Vogue* and *Harper's Bazaar*, where they can at once learn about 'high style' and get advice about displaying some of the 'aristocratic' clothes symbols effectively. Especially they are cautioned against the *nouveau riche* sin of obvious ostentation: 'No woman of taste wishes to appear as though she had spent a great deal of money on her clothes. . . . The desired effect is price-tag anonymous. . . .'[23]

That is, one must actually spend a great deal on clothes, but one must not too obviously appear to have done so. This is a lesson which these women can also learn from a good 'fashion' store. Witness the comment of an executive of one such store:

'New millionaires from the oil fields of East Texas came to Neiman-Marcus (in Dallas). Their tastes began to be moulded and shaped by the clothes they wore and the furniture and décor selected for their homes, and in a relatively brief period it was difficult to distinguish them from any "old" money group in America.'[24]

In the middle and lower middle classes, the groups that read the *Ladies' Home Journal* and *Woman's Home Companion*, 'fashion' has a different meaning. There is a distaste for 'high style', for what is 'daring' or 'unusual'. When the *Woman's Home Companion* polled its readers on the question, 'Are women interested in Paris fashions?' there were many negative answers. 'To extreme,' said some; 'not the kind of clothes you can P.T.A in or afternoon shop in—they would be laughable in our community,' said others.[25] 'Respectability' is the standard, not 'breeding' or 'effect'. Clothes are conservative but 'smart', and 'smart' is what everyone else in one's social class is wearing. 'Everybody is wearing it' would never be a selling point in *Vogue*, but rather, 'The *élite* are wearing it.' The *Ladies' Home Journal* prefers the former appeal:

'Popularity plus. . . . Like an album of popular tunes, these clothes and their near cousins are sweeping across the country. The simple fact that thousands of women are choosing them for important spots in their wardrobes indicates their rightness, their universal becomingness.'[26]

At first sight, then, it may appear incongruous that their magazines refer all the time to 'glamour' and especially to 'Hollywood glamour'. But it turns out, on closer view, that 'glamour' does not mean 'slinkily sexy' but only 'femininely pretty'. And Hollywood movie stars are appropriate clothes models because Hollywood does not set 'fashion'. The Hollywood stars usually wear clothes that are 'in fashion' and not ahead of it.

We can compare upper with middle class definitions of 'fashion' in another way, by noting the appropriate role models that are used in 'fashion copy'. For the higher classes, socially prominent, sophisticated, chic women like Mrs Harrison Williams (a perennial 'style leader') and the Duchess of Windsor are featured. These women have the 'New York look', they are cosmopolitan symbols. For the middle classes, the wives of well-known businessmen or politicians are more suitable models: women like Mrs Earl Warren, Mrs Thomas E. Dewey. These ladies are attractive; they go to church; they are concerned with the cares of home, husband, and raising a family. The clothes they wear picture:

'A wardrobe for a busy life: house-wife, mother—an all-purpose glamour wardrobe to use as a working plan—kitchen, bridge, P.T.A., Sunday church, "dress up" . . .'[27]

Age-Sex Role Structuring of American 'Fashion'

The various meanings of 'fashion' are defined not only by the class system but also by American age-sex role structuring. Girls become aware of this, for instance, when they struggle with their parents for permission to wear their 'first black dress', a symbol to both mothers and daughters of an age-sex role in which sexual enticement is permissible. Hence the unsuitability of such a symbol to young girls.

College girls. 'Fashion copy' for college girls is written with an overwhelming emphasis on the appropriateness of 'casuals' and 'classics' in clothes styles. This seems to be a reflection of the college girl's temporary but socially structured removal from the need to display her social class status. It is no social accident, for example, that the extremes of 'casualness'—blue jeans, shorts, rough outdoor clothing—are found at the Eastern women's colleges, where there is relatively great social class homogeneity and where there are no potential mates to impress. Nor is it chance that the same girls who are 'casual' on weekdays are painfully or beautifully 'in fashion' when they engage in weekend, off-campus dating. 'Style leaders' and models come from within the college girl group itself. Each year, for this reason, *Mademoiselle* sponsors contests for clothes designs created by and for college girls. Each August, a 'college board' takes over the production of the fall college issue of *Mademoiselle*. Department stores also set up 'college boards' at this time of the year, and they hire college girls to sell other college girls the 'fashionable' uniform.

'Fashion copy' for college girls frowns on 'sexy' clothes even for dating. Feminine attractiveness in this age-sex role is defined by such terms as 'romantic', 'demure', 'pert', and 'simple'. 'Look natural. Your man expects to see you, not a clothes horse. A simple, becoming dress is preferable to something vampish, shoot-the-bank roll, or high fashion.'[28]

Clothes should bring out a college girl's softness, femininity, intelligence, and good companion qualities.

Teenagers. Many of the same features hold for precollege, teenage 'fashion' behaviour:

'High school girls of America: your clothes are pretty but not too different from the other girls. . . .'[29]

'How to be a heart-breaker: Put on your prettiest smile, your palest pastel—skirt soft, full, and feminine, the little sleeves draped, the bodice embroidered with sweet posies. . . .'[30]

Physical sexual appeal is not 'nice' for teenagers, says the 'fashion copy' written for them. In a story appearing in *Seventeen*, for instance, a tale is told of the success of a girl who wears a dress with 'simple neck and cunning little sleeves' and who 'looks her age': innocent, sweet, and young at a dance where the other girls have tried to look older than their years.[31] At this age, sophistication connotes 'cheapness'. *Seventeen* campaigns against it with parables like this one:

'Sixteen years old apiece. Connie's so lovely it hurts . . . but Gloria weighs more with her makeup on—her tortured pompadour, dowager jewels, and sophisticated femme fatale gown will land her on Wallflower Row.'[32]

The twelve-to-seventeen-year-olds are at an age when 'fashion', in its most usual loose meaning, is not at all 'fashionable'. They must be taught to suppress their incipient interest in adult women's 'fashion' for the time being and conform to the appropriate symbols of their own age-sex role.

Women's 'Fashion' and the American Economic System

One notable consequence of the treatment of 'fashion' behaviour as 'irrational' has been the neglect of its connections with the American economic system.[33] We shall only touch briefly on a few relevant points.

The most obvious thing to be said is that it is American mass production which makes 'fashion' available on all social class levels. But, note, mass production is not an independent, one-way 'cause': there is an interaction of social structures here. That is, the class structured and pervasive desire to stay 'in fashion' has encouraged the 'fashion industry' to develop its technical and organizational virtuosity. Mass consumption, in women's 'fashion' as in other things, is cause as well as effect of mass production. We can see this the more clearly if we compare the United States with France. In France too there is 'conspicuous consumption', but it is 'fundamentally different' from the American pattern.[34] French women's clothes consumption stresses quality of goods, personalization of the relation between producer and consumer, and individuality. This requires French textile manufacturers to make vast numbers of different materials, and each woman selects her own material carefully and makes it up herself or has it made for her by a small dress-maker. In this way, individualized consumption makes mass production of materials or clothes impossible. This is the typical situation for most French industry. American industry has a more favourable situation for its mass production because of the existence of socially structured mass consumption. Of course, as compared with other American industries, the American 'fashion industry' is not at all highly organized for mass production.[35] The demand for women's 'fashion' is much less standarized than, say, the demand for automobiles or men's suits or canned foods. But, as compared with its French counterpart, the American 'fashion industry' is based on mass production. The relative degree of individualization of consumption is always important for the possibility of more or less mass production.

There are other examples of this interdependence between 'fashion' behaviour and the American economic system. For instance, at all income levels but the very highest ones, women need to get the most for their money so that they can maximize their claim to social class position. For this reason, women's magazines at all class levels include regular advice on how to make a limited clothes allowance secure as much as possible of what is currently 'fashionable':

'Even your best friends won't know how few clothes you've got if you plan at least part of your wardrobe around separates.[36]

'She dresses on an allowance, and people wonder how she does it. She competes successfully with any woman in the room, and her answer is that she makes her own.'[37]

Each magazine provides its readers with the benefit of its own shopping expeditions, marking its discoveries variously: 'Lots for Little', 'Scoops of the Month', or 'The Well Spent Dollar'. For what Walter Firey has called the 'shopping pattern' is a much more common practice, probably, than 'making one's own'.[38] American women spend a great deal of time 'shopping', that is, in comparing the clothes sold by different stores in order to get the most for their money. One of the aids to the 'shopping pattern', and one of its consequences at the same time, is the concentration of retail stores in an accessible location so that comparisons may be made efficiently and in the shortest time.

For some women, especially those in the large cities, there are still other ways of maximizing the returns on one's clothing allowance. Some women can shop at out-of-the-way stores which undersell their more accessible competitors who are paying more for rent in central locations. In New York, for example, Klein's and Ohrbach's, which are in less costly locations, which offer none of the more expensive customer services, and which have a very large volume, sell 'fashionable' clothes to the energetic and the knowing at the lowest possible price. Some women can buy 'seconds'—clothes with a slight damage that is usually unnoticeable but which still cannot be sold in more respectable stores. In Boston, Filene's Basement Store specializes in 'seconds'. Or, finally, some women can buy at stores which are known to be outlets for manufacturers' surpluses. Filene's Basement does this kind of merchandising also, and so too do such stores as Klein's and Loehmann's in Brooklyn. In these several ways, the women who know what the current 'fashion' is, either from reading the magazines or first 'shopping' in better stores, can get clothes which would otherwise be beyond their means. This is part of what we meant when we said above that the American woman's share in 'conspicuous consumption' was not a wholly passive one.

Conclusion

'Fashion', we may now say in summary conclusion, is not socially 'irrational'. It means several different things, even in regard to women's clothes alone; and all its different meanings are socially and culturally structured. 'Fashion' behaviour has functions, latent as well as manifest, for many different aspects of the American social system.

References

1. Cf. E. H. Sutherland, *White Collar Crime* (N.Y.: The Dryden Press, 1949).
2. R. K. Merton, *Social Theory and Social Structure* (Glencoe, Ill.: The Free Press, 1949), p. 64 and Ch. 1 entire.
3. For some excellent sociological journalism on the economics of the 'fashion industry', *see* 'Cloak and Suit', *Fortune Magazine*, (June 1930), pp. 92–100; Ibid., 'The Dressmakers' of the U.S.' (Dec. 1933), pp. 36–41; *ibid.*, 'Adam Smith on Seventh Avenue' (January 1949), pp. 72–79.
4. For a general discussion of these three types of functions of any culture-object and a specific application to a different area of behaviour, see Bernard Barber, 'Place, Symbol and Utilitarian Function in War Memorials', *Social Forces*, vol. 28 (1948), pp. 64–68.
5. E. B. Hurlock, *The Psychology of Dress* (N.Y. 1929), p. 66. See also, Elinor G. Barber, 'The position of the Bourgeoisie in the Class Structure of 18th Century France', unpublished doctoral dissertation, Radcliffe College, 1951, esp. Ch. 5, The Bourgeois Way of Life.
6. Max Weber, *The Religion of China*. Trans. and ed. by H. H. Gerth (Glencoe, Ill.: The Free Press, 1951), pp. 156, 161ff.
7. Talcott Parsons, *Essays in Sociological Theory* (Glencoe, Ill.: The Free Press, 1949), p. 180.

8. F. S. Chaplin, *Measurement of Social Status by the Use of the Social Status Scale* (Minneapolis, 1933). Also on the symbolic function of house furnishing, see Irving Roscow, 'Home Ownership Motives', *American Sociological Review*, vol. 13 (1948), pp. 751–55. Despite its limitations, Veblen's analysis of this sociological problem is still very much worth reading. See A. K. Davis, 'Veblen on the Decline of the Protestant Ethic', *Social Forces*, vol. 22 (1944), pp. 282–286. On Veblen, see also Merton, op. cit., pp. 69–70.
9. Thorstein Veblen, *The Theory of the Leisure Class* (reprint, New York: The Modern Library, 1934), p. 180.
10. Ibid.
11. *Ladies' Home Journal* (November 1934), p. 32.
12. *Mademoiselle* (July 1939), p. 71.
13. *Ladies' Home Journal* (September 1940), p. 62; (March 1945), p. 132.
14. *Vogue* (1 February 1950), p. 125.
15. *Vogue* (1 February 1938), p. 87.
16. *Harper's Bazaar* (February 1949), p. 112.
17. *Vogue* (1 February 1948), p. 184.
18. Saks-Fifth Avenue Store advertisement in *Harper's Bazaar* (January 1931), p. 8.
19. *Mademoiselle* (January 1936), p. 64.
20. *Vogue* (15 May 1938), p. 262.
21. *Harper's Bazaar* (June 1947), p. 100.
22. *Harper's Bazaar* (November 1946), p. 180.
23. *Vogue* (15 October 1945), p. 87.
24. H. S. Marcus, 'Fashion is My Business', *Atlantic Monthly* (December 1948), p. 44.
25. *Woman's Home Companion* (May 1949), p. 12.
26. *Ladies' Home Journal* (April 1947), p. 60.
27. *Woman's Home Companion* (October 1948), p. 22.
28. *Mademoiselle* (July 1945), p. 104.
29. *Seventeen* (September 1944), p. 46.
30. *Mademoiselle* (January 1946), p. 108.
31. 'First Formal' (May 1945), p. 167.
32. *Seventeen* (October 1944), p. 34.
33. But see references in footnote 3 above.
34. David Landes, 'French Business and the Businessman: A Social and Cultural Analysis', in E. M. Earle, (ed.), *Modern France* (Princeton: University Press, 1951), esp. pp. 343ff.
35. *Fortune Magazine*, 'Adam Smith on Seventh Avenue' (January 1949), pp. 72–79.
36. *Woman's Home Companion* (January 1946), p. 54.
37. *Vogue* (1 February 1938), p. 89.
38. Walter Firey, *Land Use in Central Boston* (Cambridge: Harvard University Press, 1947) pp. 254–259.

Chapter 21

CARS AND CLOTHING:
UNDERSTANDING FASHION TRENDS*
by William H. Reynold

Keeping attuned to fashion trends is crucial to the success of companies in many industries. This article explains that fashion trends can be detected fairly easily if the marketer is aware of certain factors which help to determine whether a particular innovation will go on to become an accepted fashion. According to the author, fashion trends may be of two types which facilitate the prediction of peaks in fashion popularity and the point in time when the trend is likely to die out.

Many manufacturers of consumer goods must contend with the problem of fashion in their planning of new products. A fashion cycle is not quite the same thing as a product life cycle. For instance, it appears that colour television in a few years will supplant present black-and-white sets. This will occur, however, not because of a change in taste or fashion, but because of fundamental technological progress leading to an improved product at not too great a difference in price. Fashion, though, is a different matter. Words like 'fickle' and 'whimsical' are used in discussing it. A little common sense is in order.

The Detection of Fashion Trends

Contrary to what one might think, it is extraordinarily easy to detect fashion trends. For instance, in recent years it has been obvious to everyone—even to junior high school girls no more than 13 years old—that skirts were becoming shorter. Detecting the existence of this trend required no more than an intuitive plotting of points on a line. Only a few points were necessary to plot a line showing the direction of the fashion trend.

Sometimes, of course, difficulties can be encountered in plotting fashion trend lines. What kinds of measures, for instance, should be used in sketching the trend toward the increasing use of pop and op (and psychedelic) art in advertising? One answer would be to count inches of print advertising using these visual devices. How many ads in the current issue of a popular magazine show the influence of pop art? How many in the previous issue?

One reason why this works is that fashion is necessarily *public*. A secret fashion is a contradiction in terms. A designer hoping to start a new fashion

* From the *Journal of Marketing*, vol. 32 (American Marketing Association, July, 1968).

may, of course, try to keep his designs under cover until they are launched. This is a risky practice, however, since a new fashion usually requires some kind of concerted effort from a number of designers. The midiskirt—which reaches midway between the knee and ankle—will not catch on until several firms have taken up the idea. Firms in fashion industries thus (a) try to find out what their competitors are doing and (b) sometimes deliberately 'leak' information on their own plans in the hope that competitors will follow them. It is a rare fashion which is a surprise to the people in a certain field.

Another reason why counting works—and why designers do not have to worry too much about missing a particular bandwagon—is that fashions tend to persist much longer than most people think. Pontoon styling—which is a term used to designate a car with a flat rear deck, a flat front hood, and a midships passenger compartment—dominated automobile design from 1949 to about 1965. The shift dress has been around for a decade. (We are not speaking here of fads, which are distinguished from fashion changes in that they are short-lived, bizarre, and often restricted to a coterie.)

A fashion trend can often be detected by judgement alone. Any aware person looking at ads in the middle sixties would have noted that pop, op, camp, and psychedelic art were increasingly influential in advertising.

The phrase 'aware person' in the previous paragraph should be emphasized. Management-type people are often very insensitive to their cultural environment. Managers and executives tend to spend their evenings going through their briefcases instead of exposing themselves to current 'happenings.' Even if his firm produces a product influenced by fashion, the businessman is often the last to know that fashion is changing. The successful executive simply does not have time to attend art shows, read non-professional books, leaf idly through teenage magazines, or keep up with movie news. A designer, for instance, might have noted that Richard Burton wore a neck chain at the Venice Film Festival in 1966 and that male pop singers were wearing beads and neck chains still earlier. These are the obscure items in the news that the businessman is likely to miss. The current trend to neck chains for men would have been apparent to an aware designer two years ago.

The designer interested in launching a *new* fashion trend obviously cannot point at evidence of this kind. The stylist who *first* put fins on the Cadillac had very little assurance that the style would be widely accepted. He could have suggested that the public might be becoming fin-conscious because of the influence of aircraft design, since there were a great many more airplanes at the time than before World War II. In starting a trend, however, counting is rarely productive, and other kinds of evidence must be used in guessing whether or not a new style is going to become a fashion. (Some rules of thumb useful in this guessing operation are reviewed later in this article.)

Horizontal and Vertical Trends

Fashion trends may be of two kinds which are called here horizontal and vertical. A horizontal trend would be exemplified by a fashion adopted progressively by more and more people, but which does not change a great deal in the process. Turtleneck sweaters might be an example. They have become increasingly common, but still look about the same as they did 50 years ago.

Purely vertical fashion trends are rare, but would be exemplified by a fashion which does not spread through the general population and remains restricted to a 'coterie', but which changes progressively in a specifiable direction before it is superseded. Full plate armour, for instance, became increasingly more decorated, more convoluted, and less functional throughout the sixteenth century. At the same time, fewer and fewer people were wearing full plate armour.

Most fashion trends exhibit both horizontal and vertical movement. Fins in automobile design are an illustration. They first appeared on the Cadillac in the late forties and then spread (horizontally) to other cars. Concurrently, fins became larger and more conspicuous, and were thus consequently also a vertical trend.[1]

Mini-skirts are another instance. They became shorter as they became more popular.

It is useful for the marketer to know that most fashion trends show both horizontal and vertical movement. There are two reasons. One is that it makes trends easier to detect; movement in two directions is more likely to be noted than movement in only one. Second, the fact that fashion trends move both horizontally and vertically makes it easier to predict peaks and the point in time when the trend is likely to die out.

Fashion and taste interact.[2] One obtains distinction by expressing advanced taste *within* a fashion and not by espousing a completely different fashion. (This is the reason why fashions are usually vertical as well as hortizontal). If Baroque music is popular, for instance, one can demonstrate superior taste by liking only certain examples of this kind of music—only 'the very best Baroque,' but not by open admiration of Wagner.

When a fashion in musical taste has reached a point at which *only* one composer's compositions are acceptable, it is very probable that a change in the fashion is imminent. Dwight E. Robinson[3] (with others, including H. H. Hansen[4]) has insisted that all fashions come to an end in this kind of 'excess' or 'extremes'. The Gothic arch was carried as far as the technology of the time permitted and was then superseded. The Renaissance lace ruff reached an impossible apogee in Elizabethan times and was then abandoned.

Another reason why fashion trends are vertical as well as horizontal and go through a series of directional changes before being superseded, may lie in Herbert Simon's model of the search process as an element in the rationality of the 'satisficing man'[5]. His argument is that it is really impossible for people to optimize, if only because time is infinite and the alternatives that might be considered in a particular situation are not. Instead, a man or a firm confronted with a problem will choose the most satisfactory of the several alternative solutions that come to mind. If none is satisfactory, the man or the firm will 'search' for new alternatives.

It is suggested here that Simon's satisficing model applies to the designer—the man who 'invents' fashion—as much as to firm or to the consumer.

Confronted with fins as a fashion in automobile design, the satisficing stylist will first consider enlarging them, then canting them and decorating them with chrome; he will consider totally new elements of design only if all of these immediate possibilities prove unsatisfactory. If he comes to the conclusion that everything that can be done with fins has already been done and that further exploitation of them is impossible, he might well seek at that point some new fashion to take their place.

Defining Excess

Observing the direction in which a fashion is moving (and its speed), one can sometimes guess the movement when the fashion will have reached the point of no return. The problem lies in trying to predict how extreme a fashion must become before it is abandoned.

Mini-skirts again furnish an excellent instance. One would have thought—considering social mores and the history of short skirts—that mid-thigh would be the point at which the trend to shorter skirts would have to stop. In fact, the concomitant fashion of leotards and tights made skirts much shorter than this to satisfy the requirements of modesty.

On the other hand, some fashions are clearly self-limiting, if only for technological reasons. Turning to the automobiles again, two of three long-term trends which have governed automobile styling since at least the middle twenties came to an end in the early sixties. The third would have been expected by an astute observer to have ended at the same time, but did not. These three trends were toward:

> length and lowness
> increased use of glass
> integrated design.

The first two trends ended; the third did not (for reasons which will be explained).

Length and Lowness

Cars for many years were longer and lower in each successive model year. Length and lowness, in effect, were styling ideals. Until very recently, a long low car, other things being equal, was likely to be a better car. A low car has a lower centre of gravity, is more stable, holds the road better, and is less likely to turn over. Until V-8's supplanted the big-in-line engines of the past, a long hood was necessary to accommodate a powerful engine. For this reason—and

TABLE 1 *Over-all Length and Height (in Inches) of Ford and Chevrolet Cars**

Year	Ford Length	Height	Chevrolet Length	Height
1963	209·9	55·5	210·4	55·8
1961	209·9	54·8	209·3	55·5
1959	208·0	56·0	210·9	56·2
1957	207·7	57·1	200·0	59·9
1955	198·5	61·0	196·1	60·3
1953	197·8	62·3	195·7	63·2
1951	197·3	63·2	197·4	63·3

* Even numbered years are skipped. Based on unpublished analysis made in 1963 by the author.

because roominess is reflected in increased length—big, powerful, expensive cars tended to be long.

Once established, the trend became self-perpetuating. Models introduced in 1930 were longer and lower than those introduced in 1925; 1935 models were still longer and lower. Progress in automobile styling meant that each succeeding new model should be longer and lower than the preceding model.

By 1960, ordinary passenger cars had become about as long and as low as they could get. Longer cars simply would not fit into garages, and lower cars involved impossible headroom conditions. The trend stopped. Table 1 shows the overall length and height of Ford and Chevrolet cars from 1951 to 1963.

Glass Area in Cars

Second, there was a long-term trend toward increased use of glass, which also came to an end about 1960. In part, this trend was a response to improved glass technology and roof support engineering. Better visibility was another factor. There may also have been interaction with the general draft of design in other areas. Glass has been used more in construction, for instance.

The trend to increased use of glass, too, was self-perpetuating. Once it had been established that more glass meant a newer car, designers were forced to try to find ways to use more glass in each model. The two-door and four-door hardtops, with no centre roof support, became enormously popular in the 1950s. Compound windshields, which curved into the roof as well as from side to side, appeared on 1960 models.

Meanwhile, this increased use of glass began to pose difficult heating and cooling problems. Heavy tinting became necessary. The use of glass eventually peaked out. Table 2 shows the glass area in Ford and Chevrolet four-door sedans from 1957 to 1963.

TABLE 2 *Inches of Glass Area, Ford and Chevrolet Four-door Sedans**

| | Inches of Glass Area | |
Year	Ford	Chevrolet
1963	3723	4170
1962	3745	4196
1961	3792	4257
1960	4773	4687
1959	3655	4687
1958	3260	3498
1957	3260	3916

* Based on an unpublished analysis made in 1963 by the author. Exact figures later than 1963 are not easily available, but industry sources say there has been little change in recent years.

The termination of these two trends, length and lowness and increased use of glass, was predicted with remarkable accuracy as to date by people in the industry. Technology imposed limits.

The third trend, integrated design, was also confidently expected to terminate in the early sixties, but, as mentioned, failed to do so. In this case, however, the limits imposed were not technological. Instead, the prediction was based on a judgement as to how far the imagination of designers could carry a particular fashion. The designers proved able to carry it further than expected.

'Filling the Cube'

The trend in question was the steady movement since the 1920s toward integrated design and what has been called 'filling the cube'. Looking at cars over the past four or five decades, one can see that running boards have disappeared, headlights have been faired into fenders, and fenders have been faired into the basic shape of the car. Bumpers have become integral. License plates have been recessed. By 1960, it appeared that this trend had been carried about as far as it could go.

Recent automobiles suggest that the trend to integrated design is still in full swing. Designers seem simply to have shifted their attention from the elimination of excrescences to the elimination of extraneous design features on the *surface* of the car.

For example, the grille replaced the free-standing radiator many years ago, an instance of the long-term trend to integrated design. The grille itself, however, has been eliminated as a design feature on many current cars: The Corvair, the Corvette, the Avanti, the XKE Jaguar, and many European cars. The new plastic integrated grille and bumper painted to resemble ordinary sheet metal is a step in the same direction. Similarly, headlight and tail light pods disappeared long ago, but even after they had been faired into the body of the car, continued to exist as extraneous surface design elements. It is, consequently, another instance of the long-term trend toward integrated design that headlights are concealed on many current cars and that tail lights are camouflaged. Windshield wipers also are now concealed.

Finally, designers are moving away from the deeply gouged sculpturing which characterized cars in the early sixties according to D. R. Holls in the March 26, 1962 *Automotive News*. The trend to integrated design is still in progress.

The theory that a fashion ends in excess is thus valuable, as stated, but also dangerous. If the 'excess' is technological or functional, some reliance can be placed upon the theory as a predictor of fashion change. One should be extremely careful, however, in placing confidence in any 'excess' which is visual and aesthetic. Who would have thought that men's shoes in medieval France would have become so long that it would be necessary for men to tie the toes of their shoes to their knees or shins?

Factors to Consider

The real money in trend reading lies in early detection. The firm which sets a fashion or is early to exploit it can follow a skimming price policy with correspondingly high profits. At the same time, the firm which catches on to a new fashion in its early stages while its growth is accelerating (either horizontally or vertically) can often carve out a niche in the market which is more or less impregnable by the time competitors arrive on the scene. These competititors may force the early firm to lower its prices, but the early firm might well be able to maintain its share of the market untouched.

Nevertheless, deciding on the basis of only two or three points on a time series chart that a trend is present can be extremely risky. Granny dresses are an instance. When first introduced, they seemed to spread like wildfire, especially in Southern California which is often alleged to be a trend-setting area. A manufacturer who leaped into production of granny dresses, however, would have been gravely disappointed. First, other areas of the country did not show the same enthusiasm as Southern California, and the spread of the fashion was limited geographically. Second, the fashion did not spread beyond girls of junior high school age. Their older sisters and their mothers did not start wearing granny dresses. The spread of the fashion was thus limited to a single age group. Even the young girls who wore grannies often made them themselves. The fad collapsed quickly and never amounted to very much.

To jump on a bandwagon too early—before one knows where it is going—can lead to disastrous loss. If one waits too long, one can miss the bandwagon altogether. A firm must try to detect trends early and at the same time try to minimize risk by guessing at the shape of the curve a particular trend is likely to follow. There are a few rules of thumb that might be helpful in deciding whether a fashion innovation is likely to be a growing trend. All of the rules of thumb listed below are qualitative and heuristic rather than analytical and quantitative, and are less 'rules' than factors that people in fashion industries should take into account in their decision making.

First, does the innovation meet some genuine need or does it have some genuine functional reason for being? If so, it has a greater chance of success than simple gimmickry. For instance, the push-button transmission introduced on Chrysler products in the fifties offered no advantage whatsoever over the lever on the steering column and actually had some disadvantages. The driver had to remove his hand from the wheel to operate the buttons and sometimes confused the button with his heater controls. The buttons aroused some early interest, but never really became important.

Contrariwise, the shift dress seemed to fail in the late fifties, mainly because it was too radical a departure from earlier fashions. Nevertheless, it offered real benefits. It was easy to put on and take off, concealed bad figures and accentuated good ones, made confining girdles less necessary and was consequently more comfortable, was relatively inexpensive to produce and easy to run up on a home sewing machine, and was equally suitable as a house dress or for shopping. While it failed to catch on immediately, now, ten years later, it is still a dominant underlying theme in women's fashion.

Second, what is the nature of the long-term trends within which the particular fashion under consideration happens to exist? It has already been mentioned that automobile styling for many years was dominated by powerful trends that no manufacturer could really hope to buck successfully. Chrysler in the early fifties recognized that a short, high car offered many practical advantages and tried to fight the trend toward long, low cars. It failed, and it is that failure that marked the date of the beginning of Chrysler's subsequent long decline.

Third, look at past fashion cycles. Is the trend to close-fitting slacks for men approaching the limit? A glance back at the skintight doeskin breeches of Regency England will assure one that the current trend may have a long way to go.

375

Fourth, are there concurrent trends in other industries? One has been mentioned—glass in cars and glass in architecture. At the present time, psychedelic art is important in painting, music, lighting, fabric patterns, home furnishings, refrigerator design, and many other areas. The manufacturer who utilizes this trend is joining a wide-scale movement with many mutually reinforcing elements.

Fifth, are there self-limiting factors? These have already been discussed with emphasis on technological limits, but others should be considered. Is the fashion likely to be limited geographically? To a single age group? (Example: granny dresses.) To *avant garde* people only? (Example: John Cage compositions.)

Sixth, inspect the curve. How many points on the trend line can be plotted? A trend line with many points charted obviously warrants more confidence than one with only two or three. Do the points which can be plotted approximate a clearly defined line? A nice solid trend line looks better than one with jiggles in it. Is the curve accelerating or otherwise changing?

Seventh, consider the dicta of sociologists and anthropologsts on the factors influencing the adoption of a new product or practice. Is the fashion compatible with the norms, values, and techniques of the society (or at least lacking in obvious incompatibility)? How prestigious is the originator? How complex is the fashion? (That is, can one adopt it easily, or is some difficult learning process required?) Is the fashion communicable? (Will people become aware of it?) Is it divisible? (A 'divisible' new fashion product or fashion is one that can be tried piecemeal. Farmers will accept a new way of farming much more readily if they can try it out first on a single small piece of ground than if they have to replant an entire farm. Similarly, some fashions require that a wardrobe be completely replaced, while others are divisible and can be adopted by women in the normal process of buying one new garment after another.)[6]

Eighth, and perhaps most important, is any inside information available? One person or firm rarely makes a fashion by itself. The firm in a fashion industry must be aware of the institutional processes through which fashions are created. More simply, it must know what its competitors are planning.

A corollary of this eighth rule is that the nature of the fashion process probably varies in detail from industry to industry. A person able to predict fashion in cars, for instance, might find predicting fashion in jewelry or package design impossible.

Conclusion

To conclude on the same optimistic note with which this account began, it is not too hard to keep in touch with fashion trends. They are usually nakedly apparent, and ways more or less reliable exist to confirm those which are less apparent. The best of these is counting instances of a fashion through time.

One important point is that both the designer and the businessman have a contribution to make in the detection of fashion trends. The designer may suffer from 'cultural hyperaesthesia' and see trends where none exist. The businessman is rarely a member of the *avant garde* and may be inclined to drag his feet. Both are needed. The Mustang, for example, is a highly successful compromise between the advanced European designs proposed by the stylists

376

working on the car, and the more conventional American designs preferred by management.

That a Fashion moves both horizontally and vertically makes it easier to decide whether or not a trend is in the making. Two questions to be asked are: Is the incidence of the fashion in the population on the upswing? Is the fashion itself changing in some specifiable direction?

There are other factors to consider in evaluating whether a new fashion is likely to become popular. Is it functional? What long-term trends are operating? What is the character of past fashion cycles? Are there concurrent trends in other industries? Are there self-limiting factors? Can the fashion be adopted easily? What inside information is available?

Finally, the firm in a fashion industry has several built-in protections. One is that lead-times for many products are long enough that a firm is likely to hear about pending fashions even if it is not actually trying to do so. (And it usually is.) A related point is that fashions tend to persist longer than most people think. People keep refrigerators and washing machines for ten or more years, and this population of past products can inhibit rapid fashion change. This is true also of furniture and cars, and even, though to a much lesser extent, of women's clothes.

There is money to be made in understanding fashion, and money can be lost in misunderstanding it. Most of the time, however, fashion helps rather than hurts marketers.

References

1. William H. Reynolds, 'The Wide C-Post and the Fashion Process', *Journal of Marketing*, vol. 29 (January 1965), pp. 49–54.
2. Edward Sapir, 'Fashion', in *The Encyclopedia of Social Sciences*, vol. 6 (N.Y., Macmillan 1960), pp. 139–144.
3. Dwight E. Robinson, 'Fashion Theory and Product Design', *Harvard Business Review*, vol. 36 (November-December, 1958), pp. 126–138. (*See* Chapter 27.)
4. H. H. Hansen, *Costumes and Styles* (N.Y., E. P. Dutton, 1956).
5. James G. March and Herbert A. Simon, *Organizations* (N.Y., John Wiley and Sons, Inc.), pp. 140–141.
6. Everett M. Rogers, *Diffusion of Innovations* (N.Y., The Free Press, 1962), p. 124.

Chapter 22

TASTE AND FASHION SINCE THE FRENCH REVOLUTION*
by James Laver

James Laver is one of the great historians of fashion. His conclusions on taste and fashion are the result of a lifetime of study and research. His social acceptability scaling of fashions described here is now a widely accepted concept. His conclusions are drawn from fields beyond women's clothing and extend to furniture and wallpapers.

We have seen many seeming trifles take on an unexpected significance in the light of historical perspective. Only the superficial will consider such a subject a waste of time, for although the history of feminine elegance and the history of culture are not precisely the same thing, their courses are curiously parallel. It is useless for Puritans of every period to sigh for the simple, uncorrupted manners of their fathers. Every age has enjoyed what luxury it could, and the degree of its luxury has been, almost always, the measure of its civilization.

We need not here pause to investigate the moral questions involved; whether civilization in itself be good or bad is beside the point. We shall have done something to clear the ground if we can arrive at a satisfactory definition of elegance. What is this magical quality which some quite ugly women are able to make use of to enslave the world? What force lies in an inch more or an inch less of chiffon, in a waistline now high, now low, in complexions healthily brown or delicately pale, in legs long or short, in thighs massive or slender, in bosoms boyish or imperial?

The consideration of the smallest freak of fashion lands us inevitably into the discussion of the profoundest problems of human nature, into the obscurest corners of the history of social evolution.

Clothes, like the skins of animals, serve a double and somewhat inconsistent purpose. They are both self-protective and self-assertive. They serve to merge the individual in his environment, and are the most potent weapons of the recurrent parade of love. The tiger in the jungle and the broker in the City both assume the colour of their surroundings; while the brightness and beauty of fashion find their echo in the mating season of birds.

The biologist from a fragment of bone can reconstruct the entire primeval beast; the student of clothes and the accessories that go with them, from the

* From *Taste and Fashion*, (Harrap, 1937).

broken handle of a fan, from a cameo or a shoe-buckle, can build up a convincing picture of a bygone age. Josephine's Egyptian brooches enshrine the Oriental ambitions of Napoleon; the enamelled surface of a rococo snuff-box reflects the entire age of Louis XV; the jointed umbrella of an early Victorian lady implies a complete attitude to life. These things are more than relics—they are symbols, and the crinoline is as much a monument as the Albert Memorial.

Fashion is a very complex thing. Its rules are infinitely obscure, and one is almost forced back on the mystical notion that there lies some mysterious satisfaction in being in harmony with the spirit of one's age. In any period those are happiest who adapt themselves most completely to their surroundings, and woman is marvellously adaptable. She is soft and coquettish in the age of Greuze, Olympian in 1800, languishing in 1840, mysteriously medieval with the Pre-Raphaelites, perverse with the 'naughty nineties,' and boyish and athletic in the period which is just passing away.

Art has been defined as 'exaggeration *à propos*', and the artist is he who knows what to exaggerate. To know this beforehand is not so easy as it afterwards seems, for it implies an exact and instinctive vision of what are indeed the essential lines. In the same way elegance, or so it seems to me, is essentially exaggeration *à propos*, and its successful practice is as instinctive in its operation and as magical in its effect as the creation of a work of art.

The creation of fashion is now highly organized and commercialized; none the less the most skilful of Paris dressmakers can do no more than trim their sails to the prevailing wind. In 1928 they laboured in vain to bring in long skirts for evening dresses; in 1931 they laboured in vain who tried to keep them out. A hundred years hence grave historians will illustrate their account of the gradual subsidence of post-War hysteria by pointing to the more feminine modes which prevailed in the early nineteen-thirties. They will be justified, no doubt, but who can prophesy these things? The historical method is, after all, the safe one, and that is the method we have attempted to pursue.

There is nothing which is more surely part of ourselves than the decor of our lives. Even the much ridiculed male attire of the present day is expressive to the ultimate degree. It is industrialism modified by sport, just as the costume of an eighteenth-century nobleman represented gallantry controlled by etiquette, with relics of feudalism still clanking by his side. The costume of the period, even its male costume, is the mirror of the soul. How much more, then, must feminine costume, with its perpetual fluidity, express? We are assured by Wordsworth that:

> One impulse from a vernal wood
> May teach you more of man,
> Of moral evil and of good,
> Than all the sages can.

Tennyson expressed more or less the same sentiments concerning the 'flower in the crannied wall.' A more urban observer might, with equal justice, pick up from a woman's dressing-table, or from the floor of her bedroom, no matter what trifle. It would tell him more of woman than most of the sages can; and if it told him of woman it would tell him also of man, for man in every age has created woman in the image of his own desire. It is false flattery of women to pretend that this is not so. Woman is the mould into which the spirit of the age pours itself, and to those with any sense of history no detail of the resulting symbolic statue is without importance. To the true philosopher there are no trivialities.

In every period costume has some essential line, and when we look back over the fashions of the past we can see quite plainly what it is, and can see what is surely very strange, that the forms of dresses, apparently so haphazard, so dependent on the whim of the designer, have an extraordinary relevance to the spirit of the age. The aristocratic stiffness of the old régime in France is completely mirrored in the brocaded gowns of the eighteenth century. The Republican yet licentious notions of the Directoire find their echo in the plain transparent dresses of the time. Victorian modesty expressed itself in the multiplicity of petticoats; the emancipation of the post-War flapper in short hair and short skirts. We touch here something very mysterious, as if the Time Spirit were a reality, clothing itself ever in the most suitable garments and rejecting all others. One is almost driven back on the mystical conception of a *Zeitgeist*, who determines for us every detail of our lives, down to gestures, turns of phrase, and even thoughts.[1]

The striking thing about fashions is that they change, and in women's dress this change is so obvious that the word 'fashion' has come to be almost confined to changes in feminine costume. To prove that it should not be so confined is part of the purpose of this chapter, taste and fashion having a much wider range than is always readily admitted. But concerning the changes in women's dress there can be no room for argument.

The middle-aged among us may remember the days when our mothers, about to cross the road, were compelled to relinquish our small hands for a moment in order to gather their voluminous skirts from the ground to prevent them from trailing in the mud. As they did so there was the rustle of innumerable silk petticoats underneath, and even a glimpse of lace frill. Even the youngest can remember the excessively short skirts of 1927. Most of these styles are now so remote from the present day as to leave no doubt in the minds of anyone that fashion has changed. Why does it change?

The old-fashioned moralist's view—a view not quite extinct among the upper clergy—was that fashion changed because women were incurably frivolous and inconstant. '*La donna è mobile*. . . .' But we have seen that fashion's changes are never entirely arbitrary: they always have some inner historical significance, so that the inadequacy of the female character cannot be a complete explanation. Women themselves generally see in fashion's changes an ever-progressing evolution towards something more sensible in the way of dress. Most women, if questioned on this point, will give as their opinion that the fashions of yesterday were indeed ridiculous, and that the fashions of the present day are both beautiful and practical. Women were probably always of this opinion, and all that can be said about it is that it is a complete delusion. Practicality plays a very minor part in the formation of fashion. If it were not so women would not have worn crinolines in the days when buses and railway carriages were at their very narrowest; nor would they in the nineteen-thirties have groped for brake and accelerator through the confusion of a trailing evening skirt. They would have adopted something like the fashion of 1927, and kept to it for ever. The psychologists have come forward with another explanation, which is probably very much nearer the truth, however unflattering it may be to the ears of emancipated women.

There are probably now very few among those who have studied the subject of clothes, either from the anthropological or the psychological angle, who hold that the origin of clothing is to be found in the impulse of modesty. It is generally agreed that the main impulse among primitive people comes, on the contrary, from the desire for display, such display consisting in its most primitive forms of a decorative emphasis on those very parts of the body which modesty leads us to hide. Protection, as a motive for clothing, is now relegated to a very minor role, and sometimes dismissed as a mere rationalization of a process which has other causes. Even those who still hold that clothing had its origin in modesty are as convinced as their opponents of the sexual significance of bodily coverings of all kinds. But such sexual significance has, since men made the great renunciation at the end of the eighteenth century, been confined almost exclusively to female attire.[2] The sexuality of the female body is more diffused than that of the male, and as it is habitually covered up the exposure of any one part of it focuses the erotic attention, conscious or unconscious, and makes for seductiveness. Fashion really begins with the discovery in the fifteenth century that clothes could be used as a compromise between exhibitionism and modesty. The *décolletage*, however, which arose at this period has been dealt with in another chapter. It is sufficient here to note that the aim of fashion ever since has been the exposure of, or the emphasis upon, the various portions of the female body taken in series.

The main fact which emerges from the experiences of nudists in modern times is that while the imaginative contemplation of the naked body may be a highly erotic proceeding, the actual experience is exactly the reverse. It is not a matter of beauty or ugliness, but simply that the eye becomes so accustomed to the naked human body that it ceases to have any meaning to the imagination at all. Since the relaxations of prudery during the last ten years even the costumes of the lighter stage have exhibited the same law; in fact, men have become so used to seeing certain parts of the female body exposed that they no longer get any excitement out of the spectacle at all. In 1900 old gentlemen used to faint when they caught a passing glimpse of a female ankle. The modern young man can contemplate without emotion the entire area of the female leg and a considerable portion of the female stomach. In the nineteen-twenties, for the first time for many hundreds of years, the female leg was exposed to general view. The bust, however, also for the first time for many centuries, was not supposed to exist at all, and women who did not mind in the least exposing their lower limbs would have been embarrassed if called upon to wear a deep *décolletage*.*

* During the rehearsals of *Nymph Errant* at the Adelphi Theatre in 1933 the practice dress of most of the chorus girls consisted of a backless bathing costume. No one thought anything of this—least of all the girls themselves. But the day came for the dress rehearsal, and in one of the scenes it was found that Doris Zinkeisen had devised for the chorus a costume very like the male costume of 1830: tail-coat, trousers, waistcoat, etc. The front of the waistcoat, however, was cut low, so as to form a kind of *décolletage*. It was not a very startling *décolletage* —certainly no lower than would have been worn without any embarrassment by an *ingénue*

In short, the female body consists of a series of sterilized zones, which are those exposed by the fashion which is just going out, and an erogenous zone, which will be the point of interest for the fashion which is just coming in. This erogenous zone is always shifting, and it is the business of fashion to pursue it, without ever actually catching it up. It is obvious that if you really catch it up you are immediately arrested for indecent exposure. If you almost catch it up you are celebrated as a leader of fashion.

Granting, however, that this is an explanation of why fashions come in, it is not a complete explanation of why they go out, for in the eclipse of every fashion a large social—one might say snobbish—element is involved. The speeding up of fashion's changes during the last hundred years is due to several causes, chiefly to large-scale production and to the survival of snobbery into a democratic world.

The breakdown of the social hierarchy leaves every woman (for man has ceased to compete) free to dress as well as she can afford, with the result that the only possible superiority is the slight one of cut or material, or the short one of adopting a new fashion a little sooner than her neighbours. The latest creations of the great Paris *couturiers* are copied and duplicated almost as soon as they appear in the shops, so that the fashionable woman is forced to adopt something still newer in order to preserve her advantage. Fashion, in a word, filters steadily down in the social scale. The actual garments which express it become less and less attractive, owing to the use of poorer material and because they are less skilfully made. A fashion, therefore, very quickly becomes dowdy, and this is sufficient to induce women who can afford it to change it as quickly as possible. After a while it becomes worse than dowdy: it becomes hideous, and this may be confirmed by the simple process of showing to any woman a photograph of the dress which she herself wore ten years before.

In fact, the following list might be established. The same costume will be:

indecent	10 years before its time				
shameless	5	,,	,,	,,	,,
outré (daring)	1 year	,,		,,	,,
smart	—				
dowdy	1 year after its time				
hideous	10 years	,,	,,	,,	
ridiculous	20	,,	,,	,,	,,
amusing	30	,,	,,	,,	,,
quaint	50	,,	,,	,,	,,
charming	70	,,	,,	,,	,,
romantic	100	,,	,,	,,	,,
beautiful	150	,,	,,	,,	,,

In the race for chic—that is, for contemporary seductiveness—which is the essence of fashion, certain members of the community get left behind. These are either older women, who have given up the struggle, or poor women, women so poor that they cannot afford to struggle at all. That some duchesses are ill

of the eighties when attending her first ball. But there was a strike among the chorus against the indecency of this costume, and Mr Cochran was compelled to fill up the offending gap with gauze.

dressed, and that some women who are well dressed have not a penny in the bank, does not affect the argument. Contrary to the expectations of Liberal reformers in the nineteenth century, the more you abolish differences of caste and rank, the more desperate does the struggle for chic become, because it is only so that a woman can demonstrate superiority. In Russia for a short time this competition was abolished for sheer lack of materials, but it is apparent from all recent accounts of that country that fashions have already begun to make their return with growing prosperity. The visit of Mme Schiaparelli to Moscow in 1935 would have been quite unthinkable in 1925.

If a woman wishes to look young and rich—and what woman is there who does not desire both?—she must follow the fashion; for the only alternative is the following of a fashion which is already left behind. And this following of the fashion has been made very easy owing to the cheap manufacture of modern women's clothes. Hardly any time now elapses between the launching of a new model and its copying in the cheaper shops, and one of the main problems of the modern fashion-designer is to ensure a little breathing space for his creation in order to reap the financial benefit of it.

Sometimes the cheap manufacturers overleap themselves; a striking case of this was seen a few years ago with the little bowler hat for women, which was in all the cheap shops so quickly that it had no time to establish itself as a fashion, and disappeared in a week. But in general the facility with which clothes conform more or less to the latest fashion, and can be bought by even comparatively poor women, tends for obvious reasons to make fashions change ever more quickly. A similar influence is exerted by the fashion magazines.

The foregoing list shows quite clearly that there is no validity in our judgement concerning fashion until a certain period has elapsed: in short, there is a gap in appreciation; and it is the thesis of the present chapter that this gap in appreciation is not to be found only in questions of women's dress, but in every other matter of taste.

'There is no disputing about taste,' says the Latin tag familiar to every schoolboy; yet few of us would be willing to admit without argument that another man's taste is as good as our own. In point of fact there is and must be a very considerable disputing about taste, and much aesthetic discussion can by its very nature be nothing else. Of course, in every age there is a school of opinion which will not admit that aesthetic values are matters of taste at all. They can, we are told, be deduced from first principles, and this particular opinion was perhaps never so widespread as to-day. There is in the minds of our intellectuals a new thirst for the Absolute, a longing for the supposed certainties of medieval thought, a revival of Thomistic philosophy, so that one of the most highly regarded of our aesthetic mentors can begin a serious study of the arts with the phrase 'St. Thomas tells us that beauty is that which, being seen, pleases,' apparently oblivious of the fact that when St. Thomas tells us that he tells us nothing, seeing that the whole point at issue is, pleases whom, at what period, and for how long?

It is very difficult for any of us to adopt the view that there are no fixed standards in matters of taste. No one accepts willingly the idea of the relativity of judgement, and even more difficult to admit is the notion of the evolution of belief, especially one's own belief. Most of us believe, subconsciously or not,

384

that from the first there have been true believers and heretics, even in matters of taste. Yet taste, when we study its history, seems to be a fluctuating and changing thing, constantly developing, constantly taking new forms, and these changes in taste are not arbitrary. There are certain laws which appear to govern its development, and its evolution can be plotted.

It is generally agreed that people's taste, good or bad, is shown most clearly in the backgrounds of their lives, in the interiors which they have built up, in the furniture with which they have surrounded themselves, in the rooms they live in. Interior decoration, in fact, is generally accepted as the test of taste. Let us take a few examples.

Mr and Mrs A. have a maisonette in St John's Wood. They are both cultivated and modern in outlook, and although they have not much money they have succeeded in constructing a very pleasant home for themselves. They have plain distempered walls, straight-lined, open bookcases, chairs comfortable but without any unnecessary upholstery, covered not with flowering cretonnes, but with plain, coarse canvas. Their carpet is self-coloured, harmonizing with the tone of the room. Their lampshades are made of plain sheets of parchment. Their kitchen is all white tiles and labour-saving devices. On their walls they have one picture—a varnished Underground poster. Good taste.

Wealthy Mr B. has a flat in a mews in Mayfair. The style of his interior decoration may be shortly described as Spanish 'baroque'. His walls are completely plain; they may be whitewashed or rough-cast, and his furniture, although extremely complicated in design, has been carefully stripped so as to remove all traces of paint or gilding. He has one or two candelabra of elaborate beaten ironwork, such as may still be seen in Spanish churches. On a side-table he has a vase, containing paper altar flowers, waxed and highly stylized in shape. Once more, good taste.

Miss C. lives with her parents in Hampstead. The house must have been built at the end of the nineteenth century, and was probably decorated when her parents moved into it about 1905. It was then at the height of the fashion. A shelf runs round the heavily panelled walls at two feet above eye-level, and on this shelf reposes a series of art pots. There is an inglenook in the corner, and various built-in settees in the bow windows. Above the Dutch-tiled fireplace is a large sheet of beaten copper, figuring a Dutch windmill and a boat. Above this is a motto which reads, 'East—west, home's best,' or some similar copybook sentiment in praise of the domestic virtues. The part of the wall which is not covered with panelling is adorned with wallpaper, showing a curious writhing convolvulus pattern. The same *motif*, combined with that of a lady in flowing skirts, can be seen in the lamp standard, while from the middle of the ceiling hangs a beaten copper structure, with six pendant electric globes, cleverly constructed so as to appear like half-open flowers. Bad taste.

Old Mrs D. lives in an elaborate flat in Hans Crescent. There is a great deal of furniture, heavily gilded and upholstered in *petit point*. The style might be described as 1890 rococo. There is a good deal of china about, not only on the tables, but in cabinets constructed for the purpose. These cabinets have plate-glass fronts, most expensively cut and bevelled in rococo shape. The carpet is Aubusson, or a very passable imitation thereof. The ceiling has a most elaborate decoration of painted cupids. Bad taste.

Still older Mrs E. has a house in Wimpole Street, and the interior of this represented in its time the last word in high aesthetic culture. In fact, it has probably more right to the name aesthetic than any of the décors we have been describing, for it belongs to the age of the original Aesthete. There is a curious gimcrack medievalism about it: carved settees which seem to offer the discomfort of the medieval period without the solidity of its construction. The chairs have an unaccountable look of having been cut out of three-ply. Every room has a different Morris wallpaper. With all respect to the memory of Morris, most of us would be compelled to say 'Bad taste'.

Still older Mrs F. has a pure Victorian room. We will not pause to describe it in detail, but merely say that it is impossible to see the walls for the multitude of pictures, and impossible to see the furniture for the multitude of photographs scattered upon it. There can be only one verdict: bad taste.

Mr G. is a successful novelist. He prides himself upon being up to the minute. He has furnished a very attractive room entirely with *papier mâché* furniture. Inlaid in the *papier mâché* are Balmoral scenes, with wolves and baying hounds, or else garlands and wreaths of flowers in the taste of the forties. One would hesitate to call it good taste, perhaps, but 'definitely amusing—definitely'.

Mr H. lives at Brighton, in a Georgian house, which he has filled, after great trouble, entirely with Regency furniture. There is nothing displayed which could not have been there in 1830, except perhaps the ormolu structure supporting the lamp, which has been transformed with as little alteration as possible to take an electric globe. 'Not everbody's taste, you know, but definitely good.'

Viscount I., whose family was wealthy in the eighteenth century and has not had a penny since, has a country house some forty miles from London—all Chelsea porcelain and Chippendale furniture. We need not pause to describe it. Definitely good taste.

Mrs J., a rich American widow, has bought the perfect Queen Anne house in Westminster, and has restored it to its pristine condition. Good taste.

If the reader has followed this list of imaginary characters with some attention he will have made a rather curious observation. The good and bad marks are not scattered indiscriminately over the whole list. Instead, they group themselves rather too obviously to escape notice. We have some good ones in the beginning, breaking off sharply into wholly bad ones. Then, after a few more bad ones, we find an indeterminate country between the two, where good taste and bad taste shade off into one another. When we arrive at the eighteenth century we are striking the permanent abode of good taste.

Is this a true grouping, and, if so, has it any meaning? The usual answer, of course, is that the Victorian age was a particularly black spot in the history of taste. The decay of the crafts, we are told, the coming of mass-production in all its branches, Ruskinian Gothic, Pre-Raphaelite medieval snobbism, all combined to produce an age which had, in the strict sense, no taste at all, no sense of fitness, none of that instinct for harmony which was so strong in English decoration and furniture at the end of the eighteenth century. In fact, the explanation of the black patch lies entirely in the peculiar character of the Victorian era.

This is the popular view, but the more one examines the data available the less credible it becomes. For this black patch is not a steady period universally acknowledged and fixed for ever. On the contrary, it is like the shadow of a cloud moving over an expanse of sky. Ten years ago, for instance, it would have been almost impossible to find anyone who was willing to admit that the collection of *papier mâché* furniture inlaid with castles and moons in mother of pearl was anything but a personal idiosyncrasy. Now the dealers have apparently decided that these things have passed out of the despised category of second-hand into all the glory of the antique. A little earlier it would have been difficult to find anyone who admired Regency furniture. Now an admiration for Regency furniture is almost a test of good taste. It is plain that as we move forward in time the black patch of bad taste moves after us, separated from us always by an almost constant number of years. There is, in short, here, as in matters of dress, a gap in appreciation, and everything that falls into this gap is labelled for a while as bad taste.

If we now compare our results, dress on the one hand and interior decoration on the other, we shall find that though there is in each case a gap, in the case of dress the gap begins nearer to the present style and does not stretch so far back. The black patch ends, shall we say, about 1865. In interior decoration it ends somewhere about 1845.

There is one reason for this which seems so obvious that it can hardly be completely true. While dresses, with most persons of means, are contemporary or at least only six months or a year out of date, most people decorate their houses when they are first married, and not again until their children are grown up. Therefore most people grow up in an interior decoration which is almost a generation before their own. None the less, we can parallel the causes for changes in dress and for changes in furniture, and the result is to promote a certain scepticism as to the finality of any given style.

Most people who take any interest in such matters at all find such scepticism very hard to accept. They are nearly always convinced that the style of interior decoration at which we have just arrived is not merely one item in an endless series, but a final triumph of good taste over bad, and of common sense over stupidity. A few years ago the minds of all those who concern themselves with interior decoration were dominated by the magic word 'functionalism.'

Functionalism meant that nothing was to be useless—the decoration was to be reduced to a minimum: walls should be bare, the lines of furniture should be straight, the rooms in which we lived should look as much like laboratories or clinics as possible. The doctrine had the curious result also of persuading people that something square was *ipso facto* better than something round, and there were even produced square drinking-glasses and square spoons, the fact being ignored that neither of these two things was as functional as it had been in its traditional form.

The interesting fact is this, that functionalism as a doctrine was most potent about the year 1930, that is to say, when functional dress—very short skirts, straight lines, and bobbed hair—was already passing away in favour of a new style, consisting almost entirely of curves and with a definite flavour of the baroque. It has been plain, also, for the last few years that even in interior decoration the extremely rigid line, the excessive simplicity of functionalism, has been abandoned. Steel furniture, lack of pictures, absence of pattern in carpet and curtains—all these things have been given up in houses with some pretension to contemporary chic in favour of a style full of curves; old pieces of furniture have been unearthed and given places of honour; patterns have returned to furnishing fabrics. In short, interior decoration has already shown exactly the same development as was shown by women's dress between the years 1926 and 1930, but there was a time lag between the development of dress and the development of interior decoration.

If we now turn to architecture we shall find that the time lag is longer still. Many architects are even now putting up what might be described as short-skirted, short-haired buildings. The designers of new flats are still thinking in terms of functionalism, and many of them would assure the inquirer of their firm conviction that the final style in architecture had now been reached, that beauty was to be attained through simplicity, fitness for use and the rest. But this also is a delusion, and if anyone doubts this let him turn to any reliable account of recent artistic movements in Russia. For some years our advanced intellectuals have been pointing to Russia as the place where experiments in a new style could be carried out with the greatest freedom owing to the whole-hearted backing of the Government. We were led to believe that here the vagaries of fashion had at last been overcome, and the final style discovered suitable for the lives which we were all so shortly to be called upon to lead. For a whole decade it seemed as if the architecture of Russia had set firm like a jelly with a single mould. This was not fashion, we were given to understand—this was permanence, the permanence of the New World.

Alas for such theories! The Russians themselves have been the first to repudiate them. Indeed, it seems that there is only one thing that can make a style permanent, and that is poverty. As soon as Russia began to emerge from the more desperate straits caused, justifiably or not, by the gigantic Communist experiment it began to exhibit all those tendencies towards changes in taste which were supposed to be typical of the corrupt capitalist states of the West. Russia was already in the throes of a neo-Romanticism by the middle thirties. An article which recently appeared in *The Manchester Guardian* on architecture in Soviet Russia had the following significant passage:

'Protests have appeared in sections of the Soviet Press recently against professional and artistic Leftist tendencies. The very forms which for most of the post-Revolutionary years have been hailed abroad as a most striking and significant innovation, in the theatre, in music, in painting, in literature and architecture, are falling now under condemnation. . . . The reaction in the theatre came several years ago when the numerous imitators of the great Soviet experimental *régisseur*, Meyerhold, found themselves pulled up suddenly by a firm rein. . . . The attack has suddenly shifted to architecture. Under the title "Cacophony in Architecture" *Pravda* recalls that the struggle has been carried on for several years against a "vulgar primitivism" which has corrupted the style of Soviet architecture. The attack is clearly directed against the very type of structure which has become most solidly identified with the post-Revolutionary period in Russia.

Melnikoff's best-known work is the Moscow Municipal Workers' Club, finished in grey concrete, a combination of cubes and cylinders. This is now described in *Pravda* as ugly, but for years it has been one of the show places that foreign tourists have been taken to see, and pictures of it have been prominent in every collection of Moscow views. Melnikoff recently submitted a design for the proposed building of a Commissariat of Heavy Industry in Red Square opposite Lenin's tomb and the Kremlin, which calls for sixteen floors below the surface, forty-one storeys above, with outdoor staircases leading to the topmost storey.'

The critic describes these stairways as an absurdity in the snow and zero temperature of a Moscow winter. The western European builders, he says frequently turn their buildings into joyless, sunless barracks. As a typical example of this he cites the recently opened building of the Commissariat of Light Industry, one of a number in Moscow on which the French architect Corbusier worked during his stay in Russia.

It would seem therefore as if there were no final style in interior decoration and architecture any more than in women's dress, and it would also seem (although the idea must be accepted with some caution) as if the changes in women's dress foreshadowed changes in interior decoration, which in their turn foreshadowed changes in architecture. If this is so, then the fashions we have been considering in the present volume take on a new significance. Fashion, in short, is the spearhead of taste, or rather it is a kind of psychic weathercock which shows which way the wind blows, or even a weathercock with the gift of prophecy, which shows which way the wind will blow tomorrow.

What are these mysterious influences which mould in this fashion the clothes we wear and the very décor of our lives? They seem to be the sum at any given moment of human knowledge and human aspirations, the continuers, as it were, on the mental and spiritual plane of that evolution which has borne us from the single-celled creature to man; unconscious, like evolution itself, striving towards they know not what, but providing more than a hint to those who care to embark on the careful study of their vagaries for the plotting of the course of history. It is not suggested that their future course may be prophesied with anything approaching certainty over any long period of time, even the so-called Laws of Logic are here to be used with some discretion: but has not Bergson informed us that the Laws of Logic are only applicable to inanimate objects at rest? Fashion is not an inanimate object, and it is never at rest, a distinction it shares with life itself, of which it seems to be some special and significant manifestation.

References

[1] For a discussion of the philosophic implications of this problem see the present author's 'The Triumph of Time', in *Contemporary Essays* (London, 1933).

[2] For a full discussion of these problems see Dr. J. C. Flügels' *Psychology of Clothes* (International Psycho-Analytical Library, London, 1930).

Chapter 23

THE NATURAL HISTORY OF FADS*
by Rolf Meyersohn and Elihu Katz

The natural history of fads or fashions, a particular type of social change, is told as a succession of chronological stages, each characterized by the interaction among producers, distributors, and consumers. The process is thus: discovery of the potential fad, promotion by the discoverers and/or original consumers, labelling, dissemination, eventual loss of exclusiveness and uniqueness, and death by displacement.

The study of fads and fashions† may serve the student of social change much as the study of fruit flies has served geneticists: neither the sociologist nor the geneticist has to wait long for a new generation to arrive.

Fads provide an extraordinary opportunity to study processes of influence or contagion, of innovative and cyclical behaviour, and of leadership; this has been long recognized by social thinkers, most of whom tended, however, to regard fads and fashions as one form of permanent social change.[1]

To regard change in fads exclusively as a prototype of social change is to overlook several fundamental distinctions. In the first place, the process by which fads operate is typically confined to particular subgroups in society, and although fads may change violently and swiftly, the subgroup remains the same; the network of fad communication usually remains stable. On the other hand, patterns of communication that create new social movements—for example, a new religious sect—also create a new social structure; here both the content and the network of communication are new. This distinction is well made by Blumer, who points out that social movements, unlike fads, usually leave stable organizations in their wake:

* From the *American Journal of Sociology*, vol. 62 (University of Chicago Press, 1956/7). This is a publication of the Centre for the Study of Leisure of the University of Chicago which is supported by a grant from the Behavioural Sciences Division of the Ford Foundation. Some of the ideas presented in this paper were formulated several years ago in discussions with colleagues then at the Bureau of Applied Social Research, Columbia University, notably James Coleman, Philip Ennis, William McPhee, Herbert Menzel, and David Sills. We are also grateful to David Riesman and Mark Benney, both at the University of Chicago, for critical comments.
† We choose to ignore the distinction between the two concepts made by previous writers and perhaps most clearly stated by Sapir, who regarded fads as involving fewer people and as more personal and of shorter duration than fashions. He described a fad, furthermore, as 'something unexpected, irresponsible or bizarre' and socially disapproved (cf. Edward Spair, "Fashion,"' in *Encyclopaedia of the Social Sciences* [New York: Macmillan Co., 1937], vol. 3, 139–144). We apply both terms to transitory phenomena that involve a large number of people or a large proportion of members of a subculture.

391

'Not only is the fashion movement unique in terms of its character, but it differs from other movements in that it does not develop into a society. It does not build up a social organization; it does not develop a division of labour among its participants with each being assigned a given status; it does not construct a new set of symbols, myths, values, philosophy, or set of practices, and in this sense does not form a culture; and finally, it does not develop a set of loyalties or form a we-consciousness'.[2]

Popular music illustrates this distinction.* Every few months a new 'content' in the form of new hits flows through the same 'network' of distributors (disc jockeys, etc.) and consumers (primarily teenagers and other radio audiences). While an occasional song may attract some distributors or consumers who are not regularly a part of the system—for example, the recently popular song 'Morität' from Brecht and Weill's *Threepenny Opera* found high-brow listeners outside the regular music audience—these stray elements usually get out as quickly as they came in. The popular-music world as a whole remains unchanged and goes on as before to produce its continuous cycle of discontinuous hits.

Each new fad is a *functional alternative* for its predecessor: this hit for that hit, this parlour game for that one. On the other hand, the processes involved in broader social changes, such as religious conversions, an increase in the birth rate, or a movement toward suburban living, are too complex to permit simple substitution. Following Merton, who, in arguing against the functional indispensability of a social structure, points out that the range of possible variation is more relevant,[3] one may say that in fashion the range of functional alternatives is far greater than in other domains of social change.

Perhaps this is so because fashions are found in relatively superficial areas of human conduct—in the trivial or ornamental. Many more changes have occurred in the styling of automobiles (e.g., in the length of tail lights) than in their engines.[4] In a brilliant essay on fashion Simmel discusses the selective process whereby some cultural items are subject to fashion and others not, and he points out that the former must be 'independent of the vital motives of human action.'

'Fashion occasionally will accept objectively determined subjects such as religious faith, scientific interests, even socialism and individualism; but it does not become operative as fashion until these subjects can be considered independent of the deeper human motives from which they have risen. For this reason the rule of fashion becomes in such fields unendurable. We therefore see that there is good reason why externals—clothing, social conduct, amusements—constitute the specific field of fashion, for here no dependence is placed on really vital motives of human action.[5]

Triviality, of course, does not refer to the amount of emotion, affect, and functional significance surrounding an object but rather to its life-expectancy, its susceptibility to being *outmoded*. Every object has a finite and estimable lifespan; a pair of nylon stockings may last a few weeks, a dress a few years, an

* Examples in this paper which deal with popular music are based in part on the general conclusions of an unpublished study of disc jockeys carried out at the Bureau of Applied Social Research by William McPhee, Philip Ennis, and Rolf Meyersohn.

automobile a decade or two, a house much longer. It is one of the characteristics of fashion that replacement is made before the life-span ends. Such objects are acquired without regard for their durability. This is one definition of 'conspicuous consumption.'

Hence we arrive at one possible indication whether an item is a carrier of fashion. Simmel has illustrated this point very well:

'When we furnish a house these days, intending the articles to last a quarter of a century, we invariably invest in furniture designed according to the very latest patterns and do not even consider articles in vogue two years before. Yet it is obvious that the attraction of fashion will desert the present article just as it left the earlier one, and satisfaction or dissatisfaction with both forms is determined by other material criteria. A peculiar psychological process seems to be at work here in addition to the mere bias of the moment. Some fashion always exists and fashion per se is indeed immortal, which fact seems to affect in some manner or other each of its manifestations, although the very nature of each individual fashion stamps it as being transitory. The fact that change itself does not change, in this instance endows each of the objects which it affects with a psychological appearance of duration.'[6]

Since most fads are of a minority or subculture, they may of course exhibit contradictory or countervailing trends all at once. While the fashion system as a whole may rely on an incompleted life-span for a part of its *élan*, certain subsystems of fashions operate in the opposite way. Thus, the trend today may be to trade in perfectly usable automobiles; yet there are those who drive nothing but antique automobiles. Such people attempt to *exceed* the structural limits of this particular item, and their possessions are as much a part of the fashion system as the latest, newest, the 'most unique'.[7]

Several approaches to the study of fads can be distinguished. One is concerned with the function of fashion generally for society, groups, and individuals. There has been considerable interest in the question why one group rather than another is the carrier of certain fashions; for example, in most societies women are the agents of fashion in clothes, though occasionally, and particularly in deviant societies, it is the men. Simmel relates this to the presence or absence of a class system and/or the need to call attention to one.[8]

Fashions have also been examined in terms of their specific content, and many attempts have been made to relate a particular trend, style, or motif to a *Zeitgeist*, a 'climate of opinion', or an ideology. The unit under examination is a particular rather than a general fashion, as, for example, in the area of dress, in which a great many attempts have been made to relate style to *Zeitgeist*. Flügel has recorded a number of such connections, such as the shift after the French Revolution from clothes as display of ornament to clothes as display of body—which he attributed to the naturalism of the period.[9]

A third approach to fashion deals not with the content of fashions but with the network of people involved. A fashion 'system' may be seen in the interaction among producers, distributors, and consumers, which works as a spiral-like closed circuit. Studies have been made, on the one hand, of the several 'relay stations', the producers of fashions (such as the designers, the 'taste-makers'), and the media that serve them. On the other hand, there has been research on the economics of fashion and on the channels of information and advice that impinge on consumer decisions,[10] attention usually focusing on individual choices or 'effects' without emphasizing the flow from the mass media to groups and, within groups, from person to person. The latter can be done only by beginning with a specific fashion, A or B, tracing its diffusion, as in a fluoroscopic examination, from one consumer to the next.

A fourth approach to the study of fashions, one which differs from the three cited above, though it operates within their orbits, seeks to determine the origin of a given item, the conditions of acceptance by the first participants (the 'innovators'), the characteristics of those whom the innovators influence, the shifts from minority to majority acceptance, its waning, and where it goes to die. This is its natural history. The natural history of any phenomenon which is ephemeral and which comprises a specific content (e.g., popular music) with its particular network (e.g., the flow from song writers to publishing companies to record companies to disc jockeys to teenagers, to juke-box listeners, etc.) can obviously be studied. It is based on the premise that different *stages* of a fad can be isolated and studied. In the past this premise has been used in studies of crowds, race riots, lynching mobs, and even political movements, all of which have been described in terms of discrete evolutionary steps, isolated according to their patterns of person-to-person interaction.[11] Each stage, furthermore, has been described as paving the way for the next stage.

Fads and fashions, too, have been subjected to such analysis. Almost every text-book in social psychology points out how aspirants to social mobility continually try to pre-empt the symbols of higher status, thereby forcing their former holders to search ever for replacements. This is how the story of fashions and sometimes of all consumer purchasing, is usually told.[12] While it is certainly likely that one function of fashion is in the display of social ascent and that one network for its transmission is from the upper classes downward, the extent to which this traditional view of fashion remains valid cannot be told without refined empirical study—without tracing the diffusion of particular fads and fashions in time and through their relevant social structures.

In the continuing absence of such refined empirical data, this paper presents on the basis of crude observations some notes on the stages in the natural history of any fad; beginning at the point where some change has just begun to occur, it traces very roughly the fad's probably course.

Fads are not born but rediscovered. Where do new fads come from? In many instances they have existed all along but not as fads. For example, in the past several years a large number of songs that went under the collective title of 'Rhythm and Blues' rose to the top of the 'hit parade'. Now these songs and this type of music were not new. The music industry had known about them for many years, largely under the title 'race records'. They had been produced for consumption by a Negro audience, a number of small record companies and publishers devoting themselves almost exclusively to this market. Trade journals carried separate ratings for such music, ranking each new song according to its popularity within this special category.

Then, all of a sudden, 'rhythm and blues' songs invaded the general market, and 'feedback points' (including the disc jockeys, fan clubs, listings of sheet-music sales, record sales, juke-box sales, etc.) all began to indicate a new trend.* This particular new trend had existed for a good long time but in a different audience. It had been a little pocket in the music world as a whole which sustained it not as a fashion but as a 'custom'. What happened was that minority music was becoming majority music.

These majority social systems seem to feed many kinds of fashions to the majority. This is true not only of racial groups: the word 'minority' is here used in the sense of engaging only a small segment of the population. Some 'minorities' are more likely to be fashion-feeders, of course; the classic view of fashion assumes that a minority either in the upper classes or tangential to them engages in certain choices, and these are then 'discovered' and made fashionable by lower strata.

This process exists in a variety of fields. The hog-breeding industry, for example, has cyclical trends, and in time a number of 'dimensions' of hogs are altered in the prize-winning or champion hogs. Hogs may be well larded or have relatively long legs—results produced by variations in breeding. Some hog-breeders seem to ignore the going fashion, but most of them breed 'what the public wants', making appropriate annual changes in breeding. But every once in a while the mantle of fashion descends on one of the ignorers of fashion; he becomes the fashion leader, and his hogs set the style.†

In areas of life where 'new' products are in demand or vital to the continuation of the industry, such 'discoveries' are clearly more frequent. Since fashions serve a symbolic function and must be recognized in order to be transmitted, their greatest motility is likely to be found in those areas which are most visible. Thus, changes in dress are likely to be more frequent than in underclothes. Furthermore, the search for something new—what Simmel has called 'exceptional, bizarre, or conspicuous'[13]—will be greater there.

In the popular-music industry, where such a search is conducted on a monthly basis, the life-span of a 'hit' being approximately that long, new discoveries are essential. Hence, every pocket of the musical world is sooner or later 'discovered'. 'Rhythm and Blues' is one of many such pockets, if more successful than some of the others; for a time African songs were hits; South American music has followed this pattern; hill-billy music shows the same trend; even classical music was 'discovered' when suddenly the first movement of a Tchaikovsky piano concerto exploded all over America.

Minorities not only provide material to majorities but are also an integral part of the total system. Not only do they offer a protest—'If it goes well in Tangiers, maybe it has a chance here!'—but they are also a shelf and shelter for dangerous or threatening ideas. Mark Benney suggests that bohemias

---

* New trends are reported at least once a week. The uncertainty of prediction in combination with the fact that financial investments are made on the basis of such prediction bring it about that any and all shifts and flutters are exaggerated, and large-scale predictions are made for each and every one of them. This is of course true of all businesses, but many of them (e.g., the stock market) are kept from excesses by various control agencies (e.g., the Securities and Exchange Commission).

† This example draws on material presented in a term paper dealing with fashions in hog-raising, by Samuel R. Guard, graduate student, Committee on Communications, the University of Chicago.

serve this function. For urban societies their bohemias are a kind of social laboratory. Here something new can be tried out—because it is expected—without threatening either the bohemian minority or the urban population as a whole. The city watches, Benney suggests, and confers respectability on what it likes. Wrought-iron furniture, Japanese scrolls, charcoal-grey flannel suits, not to mention new literary forms and ideological movements, have indeed been bred in these quarters.

The tastemakers. While the community, the music industry, or the clothing world as a whole may watch and wait for new ideas in many places, the task of scouting seems to fall to one particular set of people. By the nature of their tasks, they must be intimately acquainted with two worlds, the majority and the minority. Fashions, for instance, are often transmitted by the homosexual element in the population or by others who have entree into different realms, Proustian characters who share the values of several groups.

A good example in the popular-music industry is the success of the current artist and repertoire director (the 'A&R Man') at Columbia Records, Mitch Miller. A concert oboist himself, he was thoroughly trained as a serious musician. With an established reputation and a semibohemian personality which manifests itself in harmless ways, such as the wearing of a beard and keeping odd hours, he has been able to utilize good judgement in the popular-music world not only by being better educated but by having a far broader range of minorities to draw on for inspiration. Thus he is familiar with the attributes of French horns and harpsichords, with echo chambers and goat bells, and has been able to use all to full advantage. One reason for his using esoteric 'effects' is that in the music industry any popular hit is immediately copied, but his arrangements have been made so complex by the use of such 'gimmicks' —as the music industry calls them—that imitation is very difficult. In addition of course, the gimmicks have given Columbia Records a unique reputation.[14]

In any case, certain individuals in society are equipped to scout for new ideas and products to feed the various fashion systems. What is perhaps more important is to examine the fate of the original producer of the particular minority 'custom' once it has been 'exported' and translated into a fashion.

The exporter becomes self-conscious. At some time in the past Parisian clothes were 'discovered' and made fashionable throughout 'society' in other countries. Before that, undoubtedly, a stable relationship existed between the Paris *couturières* and their customers, the designs were made with a very particular 'audience' in mind. In the course of 'discovering' these designs, one element which probably attracted the early innovators were precisely the product which emerged from this relationship. But, once discovered, what happened? As Simmel said, 'Paris modes are frequently created with the sole intention of setting a fashion elsewhere.'[15] The exporter becomes self-conscious, tries to appeal to his wider circle of customers, and *changes* the product. Another well-known example is found in oriental porcelain. In the nineteenth century, European art collectors 'discovered' Chinese and Japanese pottery, and in a very short time the potters began manufacturing 'export ware', creating an industry quite separate from the production of domestic 'china'. Another example is the shift from the 1954 to the 1955 MG car; the most popular British car in this country, the MG had been designed in a somewhat old-fashioned way, with a square hood; but recently the British Motor Company decided to build it more along the lines of the latest American styles

There are, of course, some occasions when the exporter does not become self-conscious. This would be most true where there is no return for more: composers who work fold songs into concert music, like Mozart, Beethoven, and Béla Bartók, do not affect the folk 'producers'.

What happens to the original consumers is not clear. Those who find their own customs—pizza or Yiddish melodies or canasta—becoming widely popular undoubtedly enjoy some sense of pride as well as mixed feelings about the inevitable distortions and perhaps yield to the temptation to make some accommodation from then on in the hope of being 'picked up' once again.

Statistical versus real fashions: a curse of pluralistic ignorance. Who can say that something is a fashion? Who knows about it? It may happen that a number of people in various parts of this country, for a variety of reasons, will all buy a certain item. They may all 'go in' for 'rhythm and blues' music or good musical sound reproduction or raccoon-skin caps, all unaware that others are doing the same thing.

Such situations, in which no one realizes that others are doing the same thing, probably occur all the time. They are similar to what social psychologists have called 'pluralistic ignorance', a state in which nobody knows that others maintain an attitude or belief identical with their own.[16] If this coincidence persists long enough, however, the point will be reached at which one cannot help noticing the unselfconscious, 'inner-directed' activity of large numbers of people in making identical choices.* At this point the phenomenon which had been statistical becomes a real fad; here another important stage is reached—the labelling of a fad.

The label and the coat tail. The birth of a fad is really accompanied by two labels; the phenomenon is given a name, and it is named as a fad. The fad is defined as real and in consequence becomes so.

Such a definition, however, must be made not only real but public. It must be translated from the specialized professional, business, or trade vocabulary into more popular terms—in short, into a label or a slogan.

While there are certainly plenty of labels which do not represent fads, there are no unlabelled fads or fashions. It is usually through the label that the fashion acquires fame—even beyond its consumer audience. Thus the 'New Look', 'hi-fi', 'motivation research', 'automation', and 'charcoal grey'.

The ground swell immediately after the labelling is caused partly by the activities of indirectly related enterprises. Machines that yesterday were ordinary phonographs and radios are suddenly called 'hi-fi'; coonskin headgear becomes Davy Crockett caps; a lever makes of an industrial machine

---

* An amusing portrayal of the consequences of large masses of people doing the same thing at the same time, such as crossing the George Washington Bridge on a Thursday afternoon, may be found in Robert Coates's short story, "The Law," a description of the law of averages and what might happen to it some day.

'automation'; an ordinary open-ended question converts a public opinion survey into 'motivation research'.

Thus the coat tails which dress the fashion. Although the original minorities —whether devotees of recordings of high quality and accurate sound reproduction or Negroes who have been hearing certain kinds of 'pop' music for years—may not recognize the $29.95 portable radio as 'hi-fi' or the ordinary hit of the week as 'rhythm and blues', the respective producers have found something that 'works', and every commodity within labelling distance has a chance to be included.

The flow. Where the various fashions find their victims depends on their specific nature. Beginning in the minority, the fad is 'discovered', then is labelled, and ultimately reaches the mass audiences. In the case of clothing, there is sometimes a stage, mentioned by Simmel and later by contemporary social psychologists and sociologists, which precedes or accompanies the labelling process, when the fashion is adopted by a group of acknowledged respectability. The fashion is perhaps borrowed from a fringe group within the society, or even outside it, and touted as an 'esoteric' discovery. But in a society such as ours very little can be kept private, and providing clues to 'better living', tips on the stock market, and advice on clothing, furniture, and virtually every other artifact is the professional job of all the media of communication. Thus, a product associated with a respected group or class is likely to spread, through being publicized, to other groups as well. From here it moves to groups which aspire to be like the advocates. These are not necessarily lower in status, although often so described. It may be that the lower group innovates—as in the 'do-it-yourself' fad, a phenomenon which all farmers and lower-income groups have been aware of all their lives—but it is more likely to be a somewhat esoteric group, as the bohemians who flocked to New York's Greenwich Village after World War I, followed by the middle class New Yorkers after World War II.

Regardless of the direction of the flow, for a time the original possessors of a fashion-to-be will maintain the fashion for themselves and their kind, for people of the same social status are more likely to hear about people of their own level, especially in the upper classes. But after a time the innovation will cross the boundary line of the groups who adopted it and pass into other groups, in the process losing some if its distinguished characteristics.

The old drives in the new. The story of fads is, then, one of constant change. And the changes themselves do not change, or at least not so much that they cannot be followed.

The process of change occurs necessarily at every point, leaving, as it were, a vacuum when the fashion departs for its next point. Eventually, the vacuum is filled, even to overflowing, by its successor. When a fad has reached full bloom, its distinguishing features become so blurred that some are totally lost. If everything is called 'hi-fi', nothing is high-fidelity. Furthermore, if more than just certain classes are *aficionados*, the self-conscious among the class-conscious will want something new for themselves.

Thus, at some point before a dress design hits the Sears-Roebuck catalogue, a sports car the secondhand automobile dealer, and a modern chair the suburban rummage sale, once again it is time for a change.

*The feedback.** Producers notoriously see an undifferentiated audience before their eyes. They tend so often just to count that they miscalculated demand.

William McPhee and James Coleman have suggested that, while one group may be oversaturated with a fad, another may be very receptive—and only accurate reporting (feedback) about each group can tell the whole story.[17] For example, since teenagers are the major purchasers of records and sheet music and the major investors in juke boxes, and since these three commodities are the major tests of demand consulted by the producers, teenagers can make or break a song. Disc jockeys also play a role in feedback, but it is primarily the 'top' jockeys with the large teenage followings who are the key informants. Yet there is another audience for popular music to whom the producers have almost no access—the daytime radio listeners: the housewives, travelling salesmen, commuters. Their tastes are thus inferred—of all places—from teenagers!

In other words, the skewed feedback of the music industry is responsible in part for the volatility of its fads; exaggerating as it does the tastes of an already erratic group considered as its primary audience, its fads fluctuate beyond all expectation. With perfect information, a normal distribution of tastes can be expected at most times and for most things. In certain industries, and among certain subgroups, the distribution is less likely to be normal in part due to the pressures for new commodities, to the superficiality of the appeals themselves, to the publicity accompanying every product, and, in the case of teenagers, to their unstable moods. When information comes only or largely from teenagers, who are at the fringes of the distribution curve, so to speak, then the music industry is rendered excessively phrenetic. Kurt and Gladys Lang, in studying the Chicago MacArthur Day parade of 1951, found that the television reporting of this rather slow-moving and dull event was systematically distorted to give the impression of a vast crowd, a glorious spectacle, and an unremitting enthusiasm.[18] Here, as in the case of the popular-music industry, the requirements to hold an audience from switching to another station or channel or losing interest in popular music or a given song force such emphasis on the manic.

Hence, while the feedback from consumer to producer makes, at first, for a frenzied increase in a fashionable product, it may also make for a more rapid saturation than is warranted or, if the gauge is placed somewhere else in society, for an oversupply.

References

1. The long-standing interest among social thinkers in fads and fashions is seen, for example, in Tarde, who contrasted fashion with custom and showed that the transformation of tradition and custom is made possible by the form of imitation known as fashion (*see* Gabriel Tarde, *The Laws of Imitation* (N.Y.; Henry Holt & Co., 1903), chap. vii). Sumner regarded a large array of human activities, beliefs, and artifacts as fashions and considered them essential determinants of the *Zeitgeist* (*see* William Graham Sumner,

* This word itself has become something of a fad!

Folkways (Boston: Ginn & Co., 1907), esp. pp. 194–220). Park and Burgess treated fashion as a form of social contagion and as one of the fundamental ways in which permanent social change is brought about (see Robert E. Park and Ernest W. Burgess, *Introduction to the Science of Sociology* (Chicago, University of Chicago Press, 1924), chap. xiii).

2. Herbert Blumer, 'Social Movements', in *New Outline of the Principles of Sociology*, ed. A. M. Lee (N.Y.; Barnes & Noble, 1946), pp. 217–218. While fashions do not create social organizations, there is some evidence that a new set of symbols, myths, etc., is apparently often built up in the course of a fashion movement. 'Bop talk', for example, could be considered a language built up by the participants of the 'bop' fad, and, although extrinsic to the music itself, it nevertheless contributed to 'we-consciousness'.
3. Robert K. Merton, *Social Theory and Social Structure* (Glencoe, Ill., Free Press, 1949), p. 52.
4. Eric Larrabee and David Riesman, 'Autos in America: Manifest and Latent Destiny', in *Consumer Behaviour*, vol. 3, ed. Lincoln H. Clark (N.Y.: New York University Press). (In press.)
5. Georg Simmel, 'Fashion', *International Quarterly*, vol. 10 (October 1904), p. 135. (*See* Chapter 9.)
6. Ibid., p. 152.
7. It is to such countervailing minority movements that Sapir applies the word 'fad'. A taste which asserts itself in spite of fashion and which may therefore be suspected of having something obsessive about it may be referred to as an individual fad' (ibid., p. 139).
8. Ibid., pp. 130–55. See also Talcott Parsons, 'An Analytical Approach to the Theory of Social Stratification', reprinted in *Essays in Sociological Theory Pure and Applied* (Glencoe, Ill.: Free Press, 1949), pp. 166–84; cf. Bernard Barber and Lyle S. Lobel, '"Fashion" in Women's Clothes and the American Social System', in *Class, Status and Power*, ed. Reinhard Bendix and Seymour M. Lipset (Glencoe, Ill.: Free Press, 1953), pp. 323–32. For an interesting historical discussion relating manners to milieu see Harold Nicolson, *Good Behaviour* (London: Constable & Co., Ltd., 1955).
9. J. C. Flügel, *The Psychology of Clothes* (London: Hogarth Press, 1930), chap. vii.
10. *See*, e.g., Elihu Katz and Paul F. Lazarsfeld, *Personal Influence* (Glencoe, Ill.; Free Press, 1956).
11. E.g., Blumer enumerated the stages of crowd behaviour as follows: from 'milling' to 'collective excitement' to 'social contagion' (*op. cit.*, p. 202).
12. The following may be a typical account: 'In recent years status objects of a technical kind have appeared in the home, such as washing, cleaning and polishing machines, and elaborate heating and cooking apparatus. In the United States appliances to provide an artificial climate in the home are the latest in a series of status-conferring devices', (Dennis Chapman, *The Family, the Home and Social Status* (London: Routledge & Kegan Paul, 1955), p. 23. A discussion of the importance of fads in television sets may be found in Rolf Meyersohn, 'Social Research in Television', in *Mass Culture*, ed. Bernard Rosenberg and David Manning White (Glencoe, Ill.: Free Press, 1957).
13. Simmel, Op. cit., p. 136. Cf. p. 166 in this issue.
14. In a recent essay on jazz and popular music, Adorno argued that its various forms, whether they be called 'swing' or 'bepop', are identical in all essential respects and distinguishable by only a few trivial variations, formulas, and clichés. He considers jazz a timeless and changeless fashion (Theodor Adorno, '*Zeitlose Mode: Zum Jazz*', *Prismen: Kulturkritik und Gesellschaft* (Frankfurt: Suhrkamp Verlag, 1955), pp. 144–61).
15. Simmel, Op. cit., p. 136.
16. Cf. Floyd H. Allport, *Social Psychology* (Boston: Houghton Mifflin Co., 1924).
17. 'Mass Dynamics' (an unpublished research proposal on file at the Bureau of Applied Social Research, Columbia University).
18. 'The Unique Perspective of Television', *American Sociological Review*, vol. 18 (February 1953), pp. 3–12.

Chapter 24

THEMES IN COSMETICS
AND GROOMING*

by Murray Wax

*Cosmetic and grooming practices are universal among human societies.
These practices may be analyzed according to casualness and control,
exposure and concealment, and plasticity and fixity. The modern
brassière illustrates the dialectic of exposure and concealment as well
as the plastic manipulation of the body. Permanent waving illustrates
the dialectic of casualness and control (manageability): the young
girl exemplifies casualness in grooming, the older woman, control.
Grooming is employed not merely in the service of sexuality but
primarily to denote the status and role of the person in relationship
to some audience.*

This paper deals with some practices concerning highly conscious, social
aspects of physical appearance, in particular the appearance of women.†
These go under the names of 'grooming' and 'cosmetics', and they involve
the manipulation of one's superficial physical structure so as to make a desired
impression upon others.‡ The manipulations include bathing, anointing, and
colouring the skin; cutting, shaving, plucking, braiding, waving, and setting
the hair; deodorizing and scenting the body; colouring or marking the lips,
hands, nails, eyes, face, or other exposed regions; cleansing, colouring, and
filing the teeth; moulding, restraining, and concealing various parts of the
body; and so on.

As a class, these activities are universal among human beings. Some of the
oldest artifacts discovered indicate the usage of cosmetics, for example, the
presence of red ochre in Cro-Magnon graves and the elaborate toilette sets

* From the *American Journal of Sociology*, vol. 62, No. 6 (University of Chicago Press,
1957).

† For the past several years I have been intensively occupied in market research and am
currently employed by a company that produces cosmetic and other items of personal care
for women. The notions presented in this paper are derived from my research experience
but, since the data and findings are the property of the client, cannot be offered in support
of my arguments; the reader must judge validity by his own experience.

‡ Excluded from this paper but involved in the phenomena here discussed are certain other
significant phenomena: gesture, facial expression, and demeanor as elements in the process of
communication (*see* several articles by Erving Goffman) and physique, carriage, gait, and the
development and tonus of the major muscles.

of the Egyptians. The Bible relates varied instances of the use of cosmetics: Esther and the other maids being prepared for King Ahasuerus and the anointing of Jesus in Bethany.

The cosmetic and grooming practices of other peoples sometimes appear to us as peculiar or outrageous (e.g., lip-stretching, foot-binding, tattooing, head-shaping, scarification), but in every case the custom can be understood as an attempt to modify or mould the superficial physical structure of the body into patterns considered attractive and appropriate to the status of the individual.

Apparently, there has been little analysis of the meaning of cosmetics by those in the sociological-anthropological profession.[1] Ethnographers have reported the tremendous variety of forms that personal ornamentation and grooming may take. More important, they have observed—and characterized as such—the association of patterns of dress and grooming with social status, noting how changes in dress and grooming are universally employed to denote the movement from one social status to another (infancy, childhood, sexual maturity, marriage, maternity, anility, death) or the assumption of special office (chief, priest, medicine man, Doctor's degree).

One of the main sources of literature on cosmetics and grooming is that of the moral critics. Throughout the recorded history of the West there have been repeated denunciations of the use of cosmetics. Isaiah's stern eschatology supplies the reader with both his attitude and a fair picture of how the sophisticated women of his time appeared:

'In that day the Lord will take away the bravery of their tinkling ornaments about their feet, and their cauls, and their round tires like the moon,
The chains, and the bracelets, and the mufflers,
The bonnets, and the ornaments of the legs, and the headbands, and the tablets, and the earrings,
The rings, and the nose jewels,
The changeable suits of apparel, and the mantles, and the wimples, and the crisping pins,
The glasses, and the fine linen, and the hoods, and the veils.
And it shall come to pass, that instead of a sweet smell there shall be stink; and instead of a girdle a rent; and instead of well set hair baldness; and instead of a stomacher a girding of sackcloth; and burning instead of beauty.[2]

(The prophet grants that the effect was 'beauty'.)

A more or less continuous line of critical commentary runs from the Old Testament through the medieval moralists to Shakespeare[3] ("The harlot's cheek beautified with plastering art")[4] and on to modern times. Evidently those who employed cosmetics were less vocal and less literary than their critics but equally persistent.

The themes of this criticism are, first, that women should be interested in more spiritual matters than the vanity of beautifying their physical appearance; second, that cosmetics make women more attractive to men and thus lead both parties from the path of virtue; third, that cosmetics are deceitful, inasmuch as they give women a better appearance than they natively have; and, fourth, a modern criticism,[5] that cosmetics are an instrument of the ubiquitous modern drive for conformity, in which all persons must look alike and act alike.

The Modern Use of Cosmetics

Some insight into the meanings of adornment, cosmetics, and grooming may be gained from three themes, expressed by opposing pairs of concepts: *casualness* and *control*, *exposure* and *concealment*, and *plasticity* and *fixity*. While these notions are not so clearly separable as might be required in a polished conceptual scheme—and, indeed, they may be but different aspects of the same theme—nonetheless, they will assist this preliminary study.

The brassière is a pointed illustration of the theme of exposure and concealment. On the one hand, the brassière is the principal one of several articles of clothing that serve to conceal the bosom from view. On the other hand, the brassière makes the bosom more conspicuous, so that, even beneath several layers of clothing, the onlooker can appreciate the feminine form. Many brassières are designed with the purposes of exposing and emphasizing certain portions of the body and skin while concealing others.

The brassière also illustrates the theme of plasticity: it moulds the bosom into forms that are considered attractive and elegant but that are found naturally, if ever, only among a few. Women differ in their emphasis on one or another of the opposing terms that compose a theme; for example, in discussing how they judged whether a brassière fitted, some said that they wished to feel a firm and definite, yet comfortable, lift, while others said that they made sure the garment fitted smoothly so that there would be no underarm exposure when they wore a sleeveless dress or blouse. Incidentally, the recent fashion in bosoms has called forth critical comment from social analysts in such terms as 'infantilism' and 'momism'. On the other hand, the current ideal of the full yet high bosom is more mature and more sane than past emphases upon the flat chest and virginal torso.

The themes of concealment and control are pungently illustrated by the current emphasis on eliminating the odours of the body and its products. Bathing and even sterilizing the skin, reducing the rate of and absorbing perspiration, and personal and household sanitary techniques have spread widely throughout our society as devices for reducing human odour. Happily, the more old-fashioned *plastic* theme (which aims at the positive enhancement of body odour) has not been affected; the consumption of perfumes and scents seems to be increasing.

The demand for control of body odour seems to be experienced in several kinds of situations, primary among which is the enforced intimacy of heterosexual office work. In the office, people live with one another in close physical proximity for more of their waking hours than they do with their families. This minimizing of human odours may be interpreted as part of the attempt to minimize the physical being and to emphasize the social role and office. Office workers must strive to interact with each other in official roles, with a restrained personal interest, rather than as physical intimates. While physical intimacy between office personnel may occur, it is exceptional and contrary to the folkways. This does not deny to business its share of the sexual wickedness of the world but simply notes the restraints that seem automatically to be

403

imposed when a small group of people must work hard together in the public eye.

The Permanent Wave as an Illustration

The way in which the motives for control and plasticity interlock and the efforts that women make to achieve the proper appearance are illustrated by modern 'permanent'-waving customs. About two-thirds of the white women in the United States had their hair permanent-waved last year. For most of these women it was more or less habitual; they had had the operation performed several times during the year. Most permanent waves are given at home, using kits that cost only a few dollars. The successful merchandising of the home wave kit has put the waving process within the economic reach of the large majority of American women, and most of them have accepted the invitation.

On the face of it, the situation is peculiar. The cold-waving process, employing thioglycolate salts, is simple in principle, but, in practice, much depends on the skill and care with which the operations are performed and on the condition of the hair. Most women have experienced or seen cases of over-processing that gave frizzy hair or of mis-processing that left no wave but dried the hair. Also, the waving process is unpleasant: while the odour of the waving lotion has been improved, the scent remains far from agreeable; the lotion is not kind to the skin; and the process is usually messy. Added to this is the uncertainty of the outcome.

When asked to describe what they seek, most women will answer, or accept the phrase, 'A soft, natural wave'. Since a majority of women have to go through the process just described in order to achieve this wave, it is difficult to agree that it is natural. But it has been a rather consistent cultural ideal of the West for some centuries that this type of wave is the natural and ideal kind of hair for women, while straight hair is natural and ideal to men. As a cultural ideal, it is as reasonable as many another, but it has little relation to sex-linked genes.

'Softness' of wave is likewise a loaded term. The student discovers painfully that a *soft wave* is by definition the kind of wave a woman wants, whether this be in fact the slightest of twists to the hair fibers or the most extreme rotation short of breakage. The soft wave is not an end in itself but only a proximate goal. Women wave their hair not merely for the wave per se but also because it gives them plastic control over their hair. Hair that is artificially or naturally curly has what women call "body" and may be arranged in an almost indefinite variety of coiffures. That curly hair thus becomes a plastic yet consciously controllable aspect of a woman's appearance is indicated by such expressions as "It will take a set" or "You can do something with it."*

Although they sound contradictory, plasticity and control actually require each other. Control is not possible unless there is some way to make a plastic arrangement or modification of the portion of the body, bringing it from a less

---

* In contrast, straight hair can be controlled but not so plastically. It can be imprisoned in a braid or a bun or cut so short that it is often considered unattractive or unfeminine ("the boyish bob"). Allowed to hang free, straight hair of any length is somewhat of a problem for its possessor and her intimates, although it can be beautiful.

to a more controlled state, and plasticity would be meaningless unless the rearrangement accomplished through plasticity could be fixed for some period of time.*

In permanent waving, women differ in their emphasis on sides of the plastic-fixed, casual-control themes. Some wish just enough wave to achieve some body and manageability and are fearful that too much curl will appear un-natural, that is, not casual. Others wish a wave that will enable them to keep their hair always neat and ordered; they do not want their hair to fly casually about. The firmer the wave, the easier it is to *manage* the hair and to keep it under control. Younger women constitute the largest market for loose, casual waves; older women, for tight, curly waves. Loose waves appear softer and more "feminine" but are more difficult to manage and can best be adapted to informal casual styles of grooming. Most women seek a compromise between the wave that is too soft to manage well and the wave that is so tight (con-trolled) that it appears unnatural or unfeminine, and many pursue the elusive goal of the soft wave and completely manageable hair.

Woman Makes Herself

Amongst some peoples the costume proper to the socially and sexually mature man or woman is relatively fixed. It may be a tattoo or a style of dress or of coiffure; but, whatever it is, it changes only slightly, if at all, unless the person moves into a distinctly different status. In the United States fixed dress and grooming are peculiarly distinctive of religious orders and some religious sects that cling to a stylized version of what was common and decent at the time that the sect or order was instituted.

Such fixity or rigidity of grooming practices is not characteristic of all peoples, and, particularly, it is not characteristic of the typical American woman, who, following the plastic theme, tends to view her body as a crafts-man or artist views his raw material. This is the matter which she can shape, color, and arrange to produce an object which, hopefully, will be at once attractive, fashionable, and expressive of her own individuality. Devices which increase her ability to mould her body (e.g., permanent waving) are received much as the *avant-garde* artist receives new techniques and modalities for his work.

The clearest expression of the (casual) plastic motif is afforded by the ideal of a girl in late adolescence. Continually experimenting with new styles of dress and grooming, she is in effect trying on this or that role or personality to see what response it will bring to her. She is most aware of new products and new styles, and she uses them to manipulate her appearance this way and that.

To some social observers, however, the teen-ager appears as the slave to fad and fashion and not as the experimenter. A more accurate formulation would be that the teen-ager follows fad and fashion—to the extent that she does, and not all do—because she is experimenting with herself and has not yet developed a self-image with which she can be comfortable. An older,

---

* Hair sprays, which are a technique for applying a fixative, usually a lacquer—which is, incidentally, flammable—to hair which has been set, may change habits of hair care, but they do not substantially alter the present analysis.

more stable woman, who knows herself and her roles and how she wishes to appear, can ignore fad and follow fashion at a distance.

A clear expression of the conceal and control theme is given by the woman who is striving to eliminate her femininity and reduce herself to an *office*. She tries to minimize her natural shape, smell, colour, texture, and movement and to replace these by impersonal, neutral surfaces. She is not opposed to cosmetics or grooming aids—indeed, she employs them vigorously for purposes of restraint and control—but she is critical of grooming aids when they are employed in the service of casual, exposed femininity. It is understandable that these types sometimes go with petty, bureaucratic authority, sitting as guardians of the organizational structure against the subversive influence of the less restrained of their own sex. It is interesting to compare these controlled women, who have reached the zenith of their careers, with the attractive girl who manipulates, rather than restrains, her appearance and employs it as an instrument for her upward mobility.

A different expression of plastic control, this time accompanied by a higher ratio of exposure, is afforded by those mature women who are engaged in the valiant battle against being classed as old. Our culture classifies old age as retirement from sexual, vocational, and even sociable activity, and the woman who is battling age is trying to prevent too early a retirement. She employs the techniques of grooming to conceal the signs of aging and to accentuate (and expose) the body areas where her appearance is still youthful. Some search hopefully for new techniques that will reverse the aging process in particular areas (e.g., 'miracle' skin cream), others are shining examples of self-restraint and self-discipline (e.g., diet and exercise), and still others become virtuosos in the use of plastic devices of grooming (e.g., hair colour rinses).

Interestingly, plastic control of grooming involves not only creativity but the application of the capitalistic ethic: beauty becomes the product of diligence rather than an inexplicable gift from the supernatural.* Thus, those with an interest in the elaboration of the grooming ritual (e.g., charm schools, cosmetic manufacturers, cosmeticians, beauty shops) issue advice that has a hortatory, even a moral, character. The woman is informed of the many steps she must take to maintain a "beautiful," that is, socially proper, appearance. She is praised when she fulfils every requirement and condemned for backsliding. It is ironic to compare this moral voice of modern society, with its insistence on perfect grooming, with the moral voice of the past as represented by Isaiah.

The Social Function of Grooming

There is also the social function of grooming, reported by the ethnographer: cosmetics and dress are often used to denote differences in status. So, in our

---

* Ichheiser notes that beauty may be "cultivated" or "denatured" and, further, that the socioeconomic position of the woman is important in facilitating or curtailing her access to the implements of cultivation (see Ichheiser's article cited above, n. 3). The mass-production society has reduced the differential due to socioeconomic position as far as access to cosmetic and personal care items is concerned. There remain significant differentials associated with ethnicity and income and perhaps most apparent in areas of aesthetic judgment (taste) and health so far as the present inquiry is concerned.

society, cosmetics help to identify a person as a female of our culture and, generally speaking, as a female who views herself and should be treated as socially and sexually mature. The girl who wears cosmetics is insisting on her right to be treated as a woman rather than a child; likewise, the elderly woman wearing cosmetics is insisting that she not be consigned to the neutral sex of old age.

To some critics modern grooming practices represent cultural demands for a high degree of conformity, but this is a view based on a limited study of the case and a limited knowledge of other cultures. Most societies have rather restricted notions of what are acceptable costumes for those who are socially and sexually mature. In this respect our society is less severe than most, and it is very unusual in the emphasis that it gives to individual expression in the designing of appearance. The woman who has the patience, the skill, and, most important, the eager and self-disciplined attitude toward her body can—even with limited natural resources—make of her appearance something aesthetically interesting and sexually exciting.

The question is sometimes raised, usually in the feature sections of newspapers: For whom does a woman dress—does she dress for men or women? We have observed that one indispensable kind of answer includes a reference to culture, or, more concretely, to the social situation. A woman dresses and grooms herself in anticipation of a *social situation*. The situations that require the most careful grooming are those in which her peers or social superiors will be present and which are not defined as informal (casual). The woman who is isolated from men who are her peers, for example, the suburban housewife, can "neglect her appearance." Her dress and grooming tend to be casual. When questioned, she replies defensively that she is "too busy" to worry about her appearance; but the career woman has far more demands on her time, newspaper feature editors notwithstanding. The point is that the career woman always has an audience of male and female peers alert to her appearance, while the housewife seldom has one.

It may seem as though the function of cosmetics and grooming in heightening the sexual attractiveness of one sex to the other has been neglected. This de-emphasis reflects the facts of the case, particularly as it is in modern society. Certainly, cosmetics and grooming practices are influential in courtship, and, moreover, novel practices seem to emerge within this relationship and spread to less sexualized areas of existence. (Thus it has happened that the grooming practices of courtesans have been adopted by respectable women.) But, while sexuality is thus basic to grooming, it cannot serve to explain grooming as a social activity any more than it can the American dating complex.

The function of grooming in our society is understandable from the perspective of *sociability*, not of *sexuality*.[6] A woman grooms herself to appear as a desirable sexual object, not necessarily as an attainable one. In grooming herself, she is preparing to play the part of the *beauty*, not the part of the erotically passionate woman. In this sense, cosmetics and grooming serve to transmute the attraction between the sexes from a raw physical relationship into a civilized *game*.

Some may carp at the game, feeling that activity should be functional and that beauty should therefore denote the superior female, the ideal sex partner and mother. Here the question becomes evaluative: Should cosmetics and grooming be judged as a form of *play*, engaging and entertaining its participants, or should they serve a nobler purpose? We leave Isaiah to confront the sculptor of the Cnidian Aphrodite.

References

1. There is a literature, particularly in German, on the nature of physical beauty (see, e.g., Gustav Ichheiser, 'The Significance of the Physical Beauty of the Individual in Socio-psychological and Sociological Explanation', *Zeitschrift für Völkerpsychologie und Soziologie*, 1928, a translation of which by Everett C. Hughes appears in Carl A. Dawson and Warner E. Gettys, *An Introduction to Sociology* (rev. ed.; New York: Ronald Press Co., 1935), pp. 749–53). This literature becomes relevant to the present problem to the extent that the analyst moves from considering 'natural' beauty to considering the 'artificial' creation or supplementation of physical beauty via cosmetics and grooming.
2. Isa. 3:18–24.
3. Gwyn Williams, 'The Pale Cast of Thought', *Modern Language Review*, vol. 45 (1950), pp. 216–18.
4. *Hamlet*, Act III, scene 1.
5. Note on 'Nails', *New Statesman and Nation*, vol. 14 (1937), pp. 245–6.
6. Georg Simmel, 'The Sociology of Sociability', translated from the German by Everett C. Hughes, *American Journal of Sociology*, vol. 55, (November 1940), pp. 254–61.

Chapter 25

FASHIONS IN CHRISTIAN NAMES
D. Sheppard

Christian names do have social significance, and perhaps particularly so in cultures where many families have the same surname, already a common situation in Wales. They have personal significance, too, for it has been shown that quite a lot of people regard Christian names as indicative of the type of person bearing them. The writer has shown that John is commonly thought of as trustworthy and Tony as sociable. Pre-conceptions of this kind can be strong enough to lead some people to dislike even their own names and in an enquiry by Mass-Observation one man is quoted as saying, 'I have been conscious of having a Christian name (Percy) which did not fit in with my character, and consequently have had to live down my name.'

Little is known about the reasons for choosing particular Christian names, but it is clear that fashion has its influence here, as in other spheres of human activity. Some data have been published to show what names are most commonly given to children and although no complete census of such names is published, a yearly census of names cited in *The Times* has been made by J. W. Leaver[1], while more recently the same has been done by Anne Wigley for names published in *The Guardian*[2]. These are of course special populations, because the readers of such papers come mainly from particular social classes and particular areas. What is more, many readers who could do so, do not choose to announce a child's birth in this way, while among those who do, half do not cite the names to be given to the child.

Table 1 shows the ten boys' names and the ten girls' names which occurred most commonly in *The Times* announcements in 1962. A comparison with similar data for 1947 (the first year that a census of such names was taken) shows that out of the nine most common names at that time, six were among the ten most common in 1962. A comparison of the nine most common girls' names in 1947 and the ten for 1962 shows seven names which occur in both lists. The names which were popular in 1947 but are less popular now are Anthony, Peter, Christopher, Jennifer and Diana.

Thus despite the fact that, according to the book *What Shall We Name the Baby?*[3], there are 1,640 girls' names and 1,480 boys' names to choose from, it is clear that marked and consistent preferences exist. This consistency becomes even more marked when one realizes that John has been top of *The Times* lists for every one of the sixteen years concerned, with David holding second place for nine of those years, while if the various versions of Ann are counted as one name, this, and the name Mary have been among the most popular three girls'

TABLE 1 *Most Common Names Given in 'Births' Announced in* The Times *in 1962*

Boys		Girls	
John	194	Jane	212
James	171	Mary	141
Charles	114	Anne	72 ⎫
Richard	110	Ann	45 ⎬
David	102	Elizabeth	104
William	101	Sarah	94
Mark	94	Caroline	82
Andrew	90	Louise	72
Michael	87	Catherine	66
Jonathan	82	Margaret	63
Nicholas	82	Susan	54

names in all sixteen years. In 1962, the most popular boy's name (John) was given to 11 per cent of the named boys, while the most popular girl's name (Jane) was given to 14 per cent of the named girls.

There have been changes, too. In some earlier years the name John occurred almost twice as frequently as the next most common boy's name, but this lead has now been decreased and, in 1962, John had only a 12 per cent lead over the next most popular boy's name. James has increased in popularity from being eighth in 1947 to second in 1960–2, while there has also been a trend for the name Charles to increase in popularity and for Anne to increase in popularity relatively to Ann, which suggests that readers of *The Times* were not insensitive to the Royal births of 1948 and 1950. However, the name Andrew has not been any more popular since 1960. Jane is another name which has increased in popularity from 1947 on, and this has been the most popular of all girls' names from 1957 to 1962.

The Times is read mainly by people living in London and the South and its readers are more concentrated in the upper social classes than are readers of *The Guardian,* who live mainly in London and the Midlands. There are similarities between the names chosen in that John has been first favourite among *Guardian* readers for eight out of the nine years for which names have been collected, with David as second most popular name for eight of those years. Jane, Ann, Anne and Mary are all popular, with Jane showing a gradual increase in popularity until this name topped the list in the years 1958–60 and again in 1962. Anne has increased in popularity relatively to Ann, but Charles was never a popular name with *Guardian* readers during this period and has

410

become less popular with time. The popularity of the name Andrew has not changed either.

Over the nine years for which comparisons are possible, an average of 7·1 boys' names occur both in *The Times* and *Guardian* top ten (or eleven) in each year. The average number for girls' names is 7·4. Usually, the order of popularity of the names given is more alike in the *Guardian* and *Times* lists when boys' lists for the same year are compared, than when girls' lists for the same year are compared: this applies for eight out of the nine years for which such a comparison can be made.

A source of names which represents all regions and all classes has been examined by Gray[4]. He made a list of the more common names in the electoral roll and these names are shown in Table 2. Because many electors do not give all their names in full for the register, consistency was assured by abstracting first names only. This could affect comparisons between this list and others, for *The Times* and *Guardian* lists cited here consist of all names given and there

TABLE 2 *Most Common Names Occurring in a Sample Taken from the 1958–9 Register of Electors for England and Wales*

Name Men with this first name, as a percentage of all men (477)		Name Women with this first name, as a percentage of all women (551)	
John	8	Mary	6
William	8	Margaret	4
James	5	Elizabeth	4
Thomas	4	Alice	3
George	4	Annie	3
Robert	3	Florence	3
Arthur	3	Doris	2
Charles	3	Ethel	2
Frederick	3	Dorothy	2
Edward	2	Edith	2
Walter	2	Phyllis	2
Alfred	2	Elsie	2
Leonard	2	Gladys	2
Leslie	2	Kathleen	2
David	2	Edna	1
Others	47	Others	60

411

is a marked and statistically significant trend for *Times* readers to be more likely to give multiple Christian names to their children than for the parents of electors in general to do this. In fact, Hall has recently claimed that the number of initiants a person has is a very sensitive indicator of that person's social class. However, for 1962, Leaver listed first names as well as all names given, and it is clear that the 'first names' in Gray's electoral roll list agree less well with the *Times* first names than they do with the *Times* list of all names.

Clearly there are marked differences between the names given in the electoral roll and those collected from birth announcements, and this seems unlikely to be due to differences between first names and others. Other possible explanations are regional differences, differences in social class, or changes in naming patterns which have occurred over the years.

Some evidence on this last aspect can be obtained by comparing data on births announcements with data on deaths announcements. If these are taken from the same newspaper, it can be assumed that regional or social class differences will be cancelled out. Table 3 shows data for deaths announcements in *The Times* in 1954, collected by Wilkins[5], as well as births announcements for the same year.

TABLE 3 *Most Common Names Given in Births and Deaths Announcements in* The Times *in 1954*

Male Names				Female Names			
Deaths		Births		Deaths		Births	
John	384	John	176	Mary	341	Mary	142
William	335	David	109	Margaret	191	Ann	56 }
Charles	258	James	93	Edith	189	Anne	85 }
Arthur	222	Charles	87	Alice	159	Jane	126
George	216	Michael	78	Ann, Anne, Annie	154	Elizabeth	95
Henry	177	Peter	74	Ethel	127	Susan	73
James	173	Nicholas	74	Elizabeth	118	Margaret	71
Thomas	161	Richard	73	Dorothy	116	Sarah	67
Edward	155	Christopher	60	Florence	116	Caroline	52
Frederick	150	Robert	59	Helen	116	Helen	38
Robert	150	William	59	(C) Katherine	114	Patricia	33
Herbert	94			Emily	81		

A comparison of these names shows that five male names remained in fashion, as well as five female names. At first sight, there would seem to be almost as much similarity here as there is when one compares names given in

1947 and 1962 births announcements. A closer look, however, suggests that there is in fact a greater difference between the names given in the births and deaths announcements, for names given in the 1947 births list probably nearly achieve the top ten in 1962, while it seems unlikely that some included in the 1954 deaths list were anywhere near the top ten for births in 1954. It seems unlikely that it was usual in 1954 for *Times* readers to inflict upon their children names such as Alice, Edith, Arthur or George.

An interesting feature is that the names taken from the electoral roll (see Table 2) are more like the names given in the *Times* deaths columns than the names given in the births columns. Ten out of the fifteen male names in the electoral roll list also occur among the twelve most common names in the deaths columns (for 1954) and nine female names are common to both lists. Only five male names and four female names are common to both the electoral roll list and the 1962 *Times* births lists and a comparison with births announced in the *Guardian* in 1962 shows three male names common to both the *Guardian* and electoral roll lists and three female names common to both.

Without further evidence, it is not possible to be sure about this, but it is possible that the greater likeness to the Deaths, as opposed to the Births column may imply that there is a lag, and the preferred names of the less privileged classes in the provinces only become similar to those of the elite at a considerably later date. An alternative explanation for the trend would be that electors in general do tend to give the same names to their children as do *Times* and *Guardian* readers, but it happens that in recent years fashions in names have been changing more rapidly.

A point of some interest in the electoral roll list is that the fifteen most popular male names account for a higher proportion (53 per cent) of the total male first names given to male electors than is the case with the fifteen most popular female first names (these represent 40 per cent of all first names). Data on first names given to children, cited for the year 1962 in *The Times*, shows a similar trend, though the difference is smaller. An intriguing feature of this particular *Times* list is that the names most commonly given when all names are taken into account are not always the most popular when only first names are considered. Thus the name John, always top of *The Times* list for all names, only holds tenth place in the list of first names, and Charles does not appear at all in the ten most popular first names. Among girls' names, Jane tops the list for all names but is only ninth in the list of first names, while Mary and Ann(e) do not appear at all in the list of the most common ten first names. Names such as Andrew, David, Sarah and Elizabeth are among the most popular in both lists.

So much for the evidence about fashions in names. Though there are many questions outstanding, it is clear that strong preferences do exist and that these change with time and probably vary with social class and region.

How do these fashions operate? Is there a 'core' of people who are unaffected by fashion and who will, say, always name children with one of the 'family names'? If so, how large a group is this? What starts off a fashion? A royal birth or a newly 'arrived' star will have an influence but few changes in fashion can be explained in these terms. What perpetuates a fashion? Unfashionable names may be ridiculed or given unfortunate associations in plays or books, but this will not always happen. How does news about a change in fashion spread? This is obvious enough in the case of publicity for say, a royal birth, but what happens in other cases? Do prospective parents look at the births announcements for inspiration, or do they learn what names are currently popular from conversation with other people with young families? What motivates people who follow the fashion? Do they deliberately try to do this, or is it just that increasing familiarity with a name focuses attention on it until people come to like it? This is not a simple issue, for few will want to inflict a child with a very uncommon name, yet one would not want to choose a name which is extremely common in the neighbourhood, or a name which has already been chosen for other children in close relatives' or close friends' families.

Clearly there is plenty of scope here for research, if anyone should wish to pursue it, and much could be learnt by questioning parents on this topic, though one might have difficulties in resolving certain of the problems by this means.

References

1. J. W. Leaver, Letters to *The Times*, 1948–63, normally published within the first two weeks in January of each year.
2. Anne Wigley, Letters to *The Guardian*, 1955–63, normally published within the first two weeks in January of each year.
3. W. Ames and S. A. Doody, *What Shall We Name the Baby?* (London, Hutchinson, 1934).
4. P. G. Gray, More about the electoral register. Paper given to the conference on Statistical Methods in Social Investigation, Cambridge, 1959.
5. A. E. Wilkins, Letter to *The Times*, 13 January, 1955, p. 9.

Chapter 26

THE SEAMLESS STOCKING SAGA
by David Midgley

The disappearance of fully-fashioned stockings, almost overnight, from the fashion scene is one of the most intriguing fashion sagas of recent years. This well documented account is based on an original report by the author working in collaboration with A. Halstead and T. Hutchings in the University of Bradford Management Centre's Fashion Dynamics Research Unit.

Pascal wrote: 'Fashion is a tyrant from which nothing frees us. We must suit ourselves to its fantastic tastes. But being compelled to live under its foolish laws, the wise man is never first to follow, nor the last to keep.'

In this study we shall attempt to look at the determinants of these 'foolish laws' as they relate to a particular fashion change, the change from the fully-fashioned woman's stockings to the seamless stocking. We will find that these determinants can be broadly grouped under threee headings, behavioural, economic and technological, and we will attempt to outline the causal hierarchy of these factors.

We shall try to identify how the 'fashion' moved—did it trickle down or up; who were the innovators and opinion leaders and how long was the period from invention to mass acceptance. In short, we attempt to relate this fashion change to the body of extant fashion theory, to see if this has any relevance to this particular change, and conversely to see if this change adds to general knowledge.

M. S. Ryan comments that the new synthetic fibres have changed fashions because of their ease of washing, and that new machinery for mass production has changed the type and quantity of garments owned by an individual. We examine here the implications of the development of nylon on the stocking industry, and the movement towards 'easier' living because of this new fibre technology. We shall examine the latter specifically from the point of view that the seamless stocking was easier to put on—no seams to worry about.

We shall also try to assess the arguments of Professor Blumer—do fashion editors influence fashion, do opinion leaders cater to the whims of the mass or do they manipulate them? How did the change diffuse to the public? Hugel states that the ultimate essential cause of fashion dies in competition—of a social and sexual kind. It is a fundamental human trait to imitate those who are admired or envied, so he argues, and the process of imitation starts by copying the clothes of higher social stratums. The upper stratas then abandon these styles and a new fashion is born. We will argue the converse, that the higher social groups cling to the older fashion of the fully-fashioned stocking and the younger, less economically established groups, start the new trend.

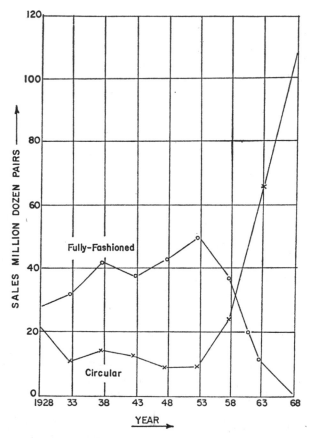

FIG. 1. The sales of fully-fashioned and seamless (circular) stockings in the U.S. from 1928 to 1968.

We examine the role played by the development of nylon fibre and the parallel developments in machinery innovation. While it has not always been possible to determine whether consumer demand gave the impetus to technology or whether the converse happened, we find that there is a definite pattern in their relationship.

We now look at the three aspects of the change to the seamless stocking—technological, economic and behavioural. Finally, we shall draw out what we consider are the causal relationships between these forces.

416

Technological Aspects

At the turn of the century in the U.S.A. 88 per cent of all womens' hosiery was produced in cotton. The remainder being mainly wool with a very small percentage being produced in silk. In about 1915, when hemlines started to rise, fashion and feminine vanity demanded sheer hosiery for the exposed leg which led to the increased usage of silk. Until the late 20s the sales of fully-fashioned and seamless stockings were roughly comparable.

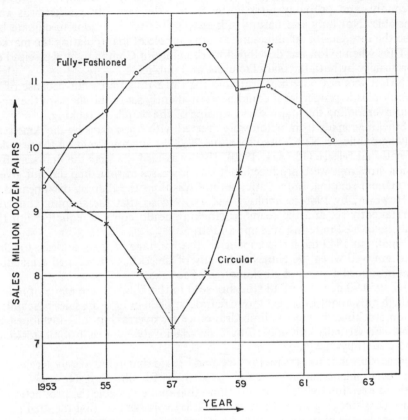

FIG. 2. The sales of fully-fashioned and seamless (circular) stockings in the U.K. from 1953 to 1963.

The method of knitting a fully-fashioned stocking was such that a flat blank was knitted and shaped to the leg by progressively dropping stitches. The stocking, after passing through the seaming operation, was thus shaped to all parts of the leg and especially the heel. This latter point was of prime importance to the consumer.

On the other hand, the method of knitting seamless stockings was such that stitches could not be dropped, shaping was achieved by reducing the stitch length. With the machinery at that time this meant that not only was the process time consuming and not suitable for mass production, but that little variation in shape between the top of the thigh and the heel was possible. This led to poorly fitting stockings, a fact which inhibited consumer acceptance. Throughout the 30s then, due to the above, the fully-fashioned silk stocking gained wider acceptance at the expense of the seamless.

Despite this wide acceptance, the silk stocking (accounting for about 90 per cent of all sales in the U.S.A. at this time) had several drawbacks. Firstly, it had a fairly short life span and dyeing tended to weaken the fibre, but secondly, and probably more importantly, the raw silk market was very unstable. Not only was natural silk susceptible to variations in climate but also the foreign silk manufacturers were capable of manipulating the market.

Thus when nylon was developed by the Dupont Company, it was seized on for hosiery by both the manufacturers and public.

Nylon was not only more durable than previous fibres but because of its thermoplastic properties it could be permanently set to the shape of the leg— thus overcoming the major disadvantage of the seamless stocking.

Stockings made from nylon were greeted with open arms by the American buying public. In New York city alone 72,000 pairs were sold on the first day of national release (15 May, 1940). 1940 was also the year the first seamfree nylon stockings were produced, but the processes at that time did not give a permanent shaping. In fact after several washings the shaping disappeared.

However, by 1946 technology had evolved so that the shaping could be permanently set and the seamless stocking could compete equally with the fully-fashioned in terms of shape and fit.

Finally in 1949 the last competitive disadvantage of the seamless stocking was removed when the Hanes Company of the U.S.A. developed a machine that produced a seamless stocking free of streaks.

By 1950 90 per cent of all stocking sold in the U.S.A. were made of nylon, though only about 18 per cent were seamless. Then in 1953 the sales of seamless nylon stockings began to climb dramatically, overtaking fully-fashioned by 1960, and virtually killing it off by 1966 when only 3 per cent of all stockings sold were fully-fashioned.

Regarding machine technology it could be said that nylon merely accelerated the developments already occurring to cope with silk fibre. However, while without question nylon is the one thing that made possible the production of a seamless stocking shaped to the foot, it is probable also that the final result could not have been accomplished without the simultaneous development of 400 needle equipment.

If we now turn and examine the state of fibre and machine technology in the U.K., all the evidence points to the fact that it was as advanced in 1953 as technology in the U.S.A. 1953 was the year the Board of Trade suspended controls on nylon yarn and allowed greater supplies to the home market. Yet while 1953 was the year the sales of seamless stocking started to soar in the U.S.A., those in the U.K. continued to decline, a decline that was not halted until 1957.

It was only then that the sales of seamless started to climb, overtaking fully-fashioned in 1960, the same year as in the U.S.A. Thus while sales climbed much

418

more rapidly than in the U.S.A., there was an initial four year lag from the technology and fibre supply being available, to the gaining of consumer acceptance in the U.K. This is directly comparable with the U.S.A. as while the technology and fibre supply there was available around 1950/51 acceptance was not gained until 1953.

So if we seek to explain the determinants of the change in fashion from fully-fashioned to seamless stockings we must look to deeper than purely techno-logical aspects; for, in both cases, the technological capacity to produce seamless stocking was available some time before the fashion gained wide-spread acceptance.

Economic Aspects

Under this heading we will first discuss general economic trends—the supply and demand of machinery and fibres—before going on to discuss price.

In the early years of the twentieth century there was a shortage of fully-fashioned machinery and hence sales of seamless stockings were greater than perhaps they would otherwise have been. In the early 20s this situation was rectified, especially in the U.S.A. where by 1924 manufacturers became concerned about the over-production of machines. Nonetheless, both in the U.S.A. and the U.K. growth continued until World War II.

During the war all types of stockings were extremely scarce. No money could be spent on machine building and what nylon was available was chan-nelled to war use.

After the war in the U.K. heavy emphasis was placed on the need to export, and because of the heavy subsidy for fully-fashioned it left the home market free to the seamless stockings. This, however, had the effect of increasing latent demand for the fully-fashioned because it made it appear a 'superior' article and after the lean years the consumer wanted to move back into the fashion prevalent at the time. By 1948 stocks of seamless hose were beginning to pile up.

In *Review of Textile Progress* in 1949 another reason for the superior image of the fully-fashioned stocking was advanced. By and large the fully-fashioned industry was in the hands of the large brand name manufacturers who had the resources to install the expensive fully-fashioned equipment. The manufacturers producing seamless hose were on the whole the smaller ones.

By 1950 about two-thirds of all the nylons produced in the U.K. were shipped overseas, and manufacturers were continually being asked why inferior nylons were being put on the home market. In fact in that year there was such a demand for fully-fashioned that consideration was given to large scale produc-tion of silk stockings again! Demand for seamless had waned—the Hosiery Trade Journal indicates the state of trade thinking in 1952.

'Despite the conviction that the circular hose trade (seamless) is doomed, Hinckley has not lost faith in this branch of stocking production. There is even some opinion in Hinckley that circular hose may well afford even better opportunity than fully-fashioned in the future.'

The supply and demand position began to change by 1955 when there were signs on the U.K. market that interest in seamless was reviving. It was voiced in the trade press that while fully-fashioned manufacturers were not unduly worried, they were expecting to have a more competitive time in the future. As late as 1957, however, we can read in the *Hosiery Trade Journal*. 'Many seamless hose manufacturers are now ready to abandon ship.' When seamless demand increased some trade journals, reviewing trends in America, noted that 10 years previously an American company had decided to put a major part of its resources into seamless in the face of an established fully-fashioned market.

This last example fits into the pattern of oscillating trade attitudes towards the possible future of the seamless stocking.

Whilst most resources were expended in response to consumer demand for the fully-fashioned, some companies did considerable work on the seamless against this tide of demand. To some extent this latter may have helped to improve the quality of the seamless stocking and hence stimulate, or at least prepare the way for the future demand.

As far as price is concerned it is interesting to study the price differentials between these two types of stockings and to what extent these differentials either stimulated or retarded the changeover. Here we can isolate three historical periods, pre 1945, 1945–55, and after 1955.

Pre 1945

Prior to 1920 circular knit (seamless) stockings predominated, retailing at about 50 cents in the U.S.A. compared with 70 cents for the fully-fashioned article. The higher price reflects the more involved manufacturing process for the fully-fashioned, which at that time had a far better fit and appearance than the seamless. It is likely that the higher prices became associated with superior quality at this time.

In the 1920s sales of fully-fashioned began to grow. The prices ranged from $2·75 to $17·50 per pair, the average being around $3. Nonetheless considerable numbers of seamfree were sold up to World War II, mainly because of their cheapness.

We believe it is during this period that consumers' opinion was consolidated. Fully-fashioned stockings were the superior product, they were also the more expensive one. We think that connotations of poor quality and an inferior product were then associated with seamfree stockings, these connotations were very strong—particularly in the U.K.

This brings us to the post-war years when nylon was available on a large scale for commercial utilization.

1945 to 1955

It was during this period that most of the fully-fashioned stockings produced in the U.K. were exported, leaving the home market mainly to the then inferior seamless stocking. This plus the coupon arrangements during rationing reinforced the consumers' attitudes to seamless stockings.

The average price per dozen of stockings leaving the manufacturer during this period was 63 shillings in 1953 increasing to 65 shillings in 1954. In this period the corrresponding value of seamfree went up from 31 shillings to 34 shillings. It was in this period of the early 50s that many technical developments occurred both in circular and fully-fashioned machinery. Developments

420

in the circular field contributed to greater cost reductions but for both these and fully-fashioned the knitting of finer deniers results in a higher proportion of rejects and higher handling costs. Raw material prices stabilized during this period.

Overall it seems likely that cost reductions were greater and more frequent for the seamless manufacturers though it is a little hard to judge on the evidence gained.

After 1955

The average price of seamfree decreased from 33s 6d per dozen in 1955 to 32s 7d in 1958. In the same period the prices of fully-fashioned decreased from 63s 7d to 54s 2d per dozen pair. This price decrease accompanied a marginal increase in sales from 1955 to 1958 whilst the sales of circular stockings decreased until 1957 and then started to increase.

Whilst this was the situation in the U.K., the changeover to seamless was well established in the U.S.A.; seamfree were selling at $1.75 per pair compared with 75 cents for fully-fashioned, i.e. seamfree were selling at higher prices than fully-fashioned.

In the U.K. in 1957 prices of fully-fashioned came under pressure from Italian imports. The quantities imported were not large but the fact that a chain store was offering them for sale at 4s. 11d. a pair was sufficient to bring the average price of home produced fully-fashioned stockings down by 19 per cent to 7 shillings.

The average price of seamfree stockings changed very little during this period and remained at about 5 shillings. With the increasing import of seam-less, whose prices were always several shillings cheaper than fully-fashioned, there was an increasing tendency to bring down the overall average price of stockings.

The price differential in this country between seamless and fully-fashioned had remained fairly stable for the immediate few years preceding 1957, at a level of 2s 6d to 3s per pair. Yet the fashion did not begin to spread until 1957. Certainly there were no drastic price changes which would immediately account for the growth in sales, particularly as seamless stockings had always been cheaper and as the price of fully-fashioned did not begin to drop markedly till after seamless were well established. Price then does not in itself seem a sufficient cause of the change, though undoubtedly the high price, high quality image of the fully-fashioned and the inferior image of the seamless was one reason why the change did not occur earlier.

It seems if we are to locate the stimulus, we must look further.

Behavioural Aspects

Under the previous two headings we have examined what may be called the more factual aspects of the change to seamless stockings. Under this heading we examine the sociological and psychological aspects of this change. Perhaps because the consequences of the change were not realized at the time they were happening, the process has not been very well documented, but we feel that enough evidence has been gleaned to fit the prices together to form a coherent picture. Once again it is useful to work at the situation historically in three periods 1900–38, 1938–46 and 1946–65.

1900 to 1938

When discussing the change in fashion from the fully-fashioned to the seamless stocking, we must be clear that the seamless stocking was not new in the 1950s. As we have said previously, at the beginning of the century the majority of stockings were seamless. Because the seamless stocking is not new is the major reason for examining this earlier period, in it are some very important clues to the change in consumer attitudes which occurred in the late 1950s.

These early stockings were not shaped and did not fit well, but this was irrelevant as with ankle-length skirts stockings were not visible. Thus stockings were utilitarian articles and not regarded as in any way a 'fashion' good.

When in the 1920s Paris decreed that skirts should be shorter then more attention began to be focused on the leg. Women started to look towards the fully-fashioned stocking, which at that time was the only type which could be fitted to the shape of the leg. Silk became the dominant fibre because of its sheerness which became to be perceived as attractive. 1922 was the year Paris shortened skirts, and 1923 was the year that the sale of fully-fashioned began to grow at the expense of seamless. It would appear that there is a very strong correlation between the skirt length being raised and the attention given to stockings as a fashion article.

The 20s was the period also that stockings began to be produced in the now familiar tan shades, prior to this they had been black or white. The implications of this can be seen in the advertisements of the time in Paris where a whole range of colours were associated with the 'nude' look. Nude stockings became a passion with variations such as 'French Nude' and 'Champagne'.

This desire for sheerness and the 'nude' look was to provide the hosiery industry with a headache. In 1929 the following appeared in one of the trade magazines:

'Startling news from Palm Beach. Since hosiery buyers have come to regard style trends at the southern winter resorts as indicative of what women through-out the country will wear the following spring, latest reports coming in from Palm Beach are somewhat disconcerting. It appears that some of the younger set, their craving for sheer hosiery unsatisfied by even the sheerest products of the fully-fashioned machines, have launched the sensational vogue of appearing in public without any stockings at all . . .!

This paragraph reflects what we consider paramountly important in this study. It isolates the fashion leaders in the American hosiery scene of the period and it crystallizes the start of developments which culminated in the swing to seamless hosiery thirty years later. This sort of statement throws light on the underlying sociological attitudes—a change was taking place in attitudes towards nudity. This was a continuing trend, in spite of the increasing sheerness of silk stockings and the promotion behind it. Younger women continued to go bare-legged in the summer despite comments such as appeared in *Hosiery and Underwear* in 1929: 'intelligent people equate barelegggedness with brazenness, even coarseness'.

In the 1930s Paris gave the lead to the lengthening of the skirt, which by 1934 had reached the ankles again. However, the fully-fashioned stocking had by now established itself firmly in the consumer's mind as a fashion article and the fact that skirts were longer had no effect on the increasing demand for fully-fashioned stockings.

In 1935 a conference was held in the U.S.A. by the hosiery associations to consider how they could persuade women to wear stockings during the summer. They came up with the promotional idea that with seamless stockings a woman would look as though she had no stockings on—just a nice tan on her legs. This was only a minor success as at the time seamless were technically far inferior to fully-fashioned. The odds were really against the success of the seamless as a substitute for the bare-leg or nude trend—the image was inferior, the fibre wrong and the knit too coarse.

In spite of these difficulties it had become apparent to some manufacturers what the prevailing social attitudes implied for hosiery, but the point was that fully-fashioned was associated with everything that meant quality and style in the mind of the consumer. It is of course a distinct advantage to look in retrospect at the complex attitudes which prevailed at the time because one is able to see how the incongruities were subsequently reconciled.

On one hand, substantial promotion, machinery development and product satisfaction had succeeded in putting the fully-fashioned article on a fashion pedestal; on the other the consumer showed a trend towards the bare-leg look, towards a stocking which revealed the leg itself, but the product which fulfilled this had been downgraded in its image and associations—quite simply it was not considered a 'fashion' article.

However, the bare-leg trend had not yet reached very high proportions and the fully-fashioned silk stocking was in very great demand. Investment was applied to produce better quality and sheerer stockings, a movement which continued until the advent of nylon in 1938. In the main, seamless stockings were only being sold where the demand for fully-fashioned could not be satisfied.

We now move to the second period after the invention of nylon.

1938 to 1946

The war period had two major effects on the hosiery trade. The first allowed radical changes in technology and the second accentuated an already existing trend.

The first was, of course, the advent of nylon. We think it would be correct to say that the change from fully-fashioned to seamless would never have occurred without the development of nylon (or another thermoplastic yarn of similar properties). Nevertheless this was not the main reason for the change to seamless stockings.

Secondly, the war period was a period when little attention could be paid to high fashion. The quality of materials was poor and various fibres were in exceedingly short supply. The period of fashion starvation accentuated the fashion image of fully-fashioned stockings immediately after the war. The seamless stocking after the war had an even shoddier image than before.

By 1943 consumers were complaining in America that there were no 'fashion' stockings to be found anywhere, and in a survey conducted at that time nylon stockings were high on the list of things women wanted after the war. In this survey the two main desired characteristics wanted in nylons were:

(1) sheerness; and
(2) fit at the ankles.

Not a great deal seems to have been recorded about attitudes towards hosiery during the period, because of more pressing issues, but there certainly was a tremendous desire being built up during the war by women to be able to indulge themselves again in these things that could re-emphasize their femininity.

The war period had also served to down-grade the seamless, mainly because the fully-fashioned was in such short supply but also because the quality of the seamless had been even poorer. By the end of the war the seamless stocking was firmly associated with a period of scarcity, a period where fashion was no longer relevant. The seamless stocking was an excellent example of a product with every possible thing wrong with its image as perceived by the consumer.

To illustrate the demand for fully-fashioned nylons which had built up during the war it is worth recalling that when they became available again there were scenes such as that in San Fransisco where 10,000 shoppers beseiged one store, halting traffic, and pushing in a window.

1946 to 1965

As we have pointed out, at the end of the war, there was a tremendous demand for nylon fully-fashioned stockings. We have also emphasized that the seamless stocking had a very poor image, an image which had suppressed demand to such an extent that manufacturers were not confident enough to invest in the new seamless technology, rather they would opt for the fully-fashioned.

There were in fact no technical impediments to the acceptance of seamless stockings from about 1946 on. Of course there were machine and yarn improvements subsequently but basically the tools to do a satisfactory seamless job were there. Why then was there a lag, especially when the consumer had visibly expressed a predisposition for a bare-leg look. The answer must lie with the image, indeed in 1947 seamless manufacturers were still having to insert a mock seam into most of their stockings to imitate the 'superior' article.

As the century moved into the 1950s the demand for fully-fashioned was at its height. A conference of hosiery manufacturers was held in 1950 and reported in *Knitwear and Stockings* of that year and the following is a quotation from that report: 'The popularity of seamless stockings has waned: women are fully-fashioned minded as never before. As a result, many makers of seamless wish to switch over, but their factories are often unsuitable for the accommodation of large units, and the capital outlay is formidable.' In May 1950 the same magazine forecast 'the end of circular-knit stockings' and maintained that fully fashioned are certain to be in greater demand.

Nonetheless we do find comment in the *Hosiery Trade Journal* that seamless were more attractive to young people and looked prettier on the leg—'not only are seamless easier to put on, but the legs appear to have no stockings at all.' Here we see the beginnings of the bringing together of the desire for

424

a bare-leg look and the possibility of this being satisfied by the seamless stocking. In the same year there appears the following comment in the American magazine *Hosiery and Underwear*: 'Women seem attracted by the sheerness of the seamless stocking and not having to straighten the seam'. From this can be detected another factor in the change—ease of wear. A year later the same magazine commented: 'Bare legs are the industry's major enemy. There is a trend in recent years towards more informal living and dressing.'

We are now at the date when the turning point was reached for the seamless stocking—1952–53. Sales of fully-fashioned had reached their peak in America, four years before this occurred in the U.K. Movement was taking place in the seamless world and these manufacturers were beginning to see the potential of their stockings as a weapon against the bare-leg trend. The U.K. journal *Knitwear and Stockings* of 1952 comments on the fact that the American manufacturers are waging an all-out war against the bare-leg bogey. The following year another U.K. trade journal commented on the rise in the U.S.A. of the seamfree and poses the question whether a similar swing would be likely to happen in the U.K.

British manufacturers were certainly becoming aware of a certain degree of swing towards seamless, but a subsequent edition of *Knitwear and Stockings* states that 'the attitude of women in this country towards seamfree is tainted with prejudice'. It then gives much the same reasons for this as we have given and goes on to say 'since the war nylon has revolutionized circular hosiery but the prejudice remains'.

On the American scene, the manufacturers began a concerted effort in promotion and advertising to deal with the bare-leg trend. Seamless stocking demand was on the increase and the following quotation from *Hosiery and Underwear* of March 1952 gives a pointer to what will turn out eventually to be the major determinant of the trend. Commenting on the demand for seamless the journal said: 'This is the entrance of a new crop of consumers—young girls who are just reaching the age for wearing stockings. The seamless has a strong appeal to these consumers'. The next month this same journal gave more evidence for the identification of this key market segment. 'Teenagers and the younger set have adopted the bare-leg habit as a fad. They are the ones we have to educate.' Clearly the problem area had been isolated and the American hosiery trade geared its promotion to this market segment with some success. Manufacturers had now realized that their job was to attempt to equate the 'bare-leg' with the 'seamless stocking'.

In April 1953 the following remark appeared in *Hosiery and Underwear*:

'We know of this trend to bare legs and because of the promotion of some companies, they equated the bare-leg look with seamless. Seamless can furnish the best suntan look of all. Some manufacturers obviously don't want to encourage the seamless trend, but it is necessary to sell what is demanded not try to go against it. The seamless stocking is now becoming the anti bare-leg formula.'

From 1953 to 1957 there was a concentrated effort in the U.S.A. by both the trade associations and individual manufacturers to promote the seamless

425

stocking as the answer to women's desire for a bare look. By the end of this period the seamless was launched and was soon to overtake the fully-fashioned in popularity.

A very important aspect of this advertising was the emphasis on the fashion features of the seamless stocking. This was vital because of the 'utilitarian' image which had been built up previously.

In the U.K. there was an awareness of the trends in America and also of the difference in attitude towards seamless stockings in the U.K.

'As far as seamless goes, the confidence of the buying public has gone. Also manufacturers seem to think that seamless is second best, but seamless are being enthusiastically received in the U.S.A. A publicity campaign for seamless has been successful in the U.S.A. because they made a super quality article and marketed it as a fashion article'—*Hosiery Trade Journal*, 1956.

Subsequently in the same year this journal noted, however, that there seemed to be a demand for seamless in the U.K. from young girls. *Knitwear and Stockings* gives some further evidence for the identification of the opinion leaders in this change. It states: 'At the moment it is the younger women and schoolgirls who are buying seamfree. The reason for the trend: insubstantial appearance—gossamer fine—filmy wisps. Conservatism has gone overboard and many fashion leaders can be seen in youthful bare-leg style. There are no seams to worry about.'

During the year 1957 the seamless stocking became very well established in the U.S.A. while in the U.K. there was an awareness of American experience and a realization that seamless stocking sales were increasing. The teenagers and young women had been identified as the opinion leaders in this change. Throughout 1957 and 1958 in the U.S.A. the fully-fashioned manufacturers tried desperately to stem the tide, even going to the extent of imitating seamless by putting invisible seams in their stockings. A survey done by Dupont at this time indicated that the seamless was favoured because of its bare-leg look. The subsequent years to 1966 show a drastic decline for the fully-fashioned to an annual sales figure of 3,200 thousand dozen pairs against 97,000 thousand dozen pairs of seamless. There has been an even further decline since, so that the fully-fashioned has disappeared from the American market. The next significant developments were the changes to tights and textured yarns.

The U.K. was behind the U.S.A. in the acceptance of seamfree by three to four years. Although there was a lot of comment in the trade journals of 1958 and 1959 about the trend in the U.S.A., there was also a considerable amount of uncertainty about what was really going to happen in the U.K. It is clear in retrospect that the same forces were at work in the consumer's mind in the U.K. as in America but because of the lower quality (both real and perceived) which has been identified earlier, there was still a reluctance on the part of the U.K. consumer to quickly accept the trend.

In 1957 in the *Hosiery Trade Journal*, a review appeared of the circular knit hose story in America, Europe and the U.K. The article reviewed the boom of seamless on the American market and the conservatism of the U.K. market.

426

The factors which it considered relevant to the success of seamless in America were:

(1) machinery
(2) the advent of nylon
(3) advertising
(4) relatively greater acceptance of novelty by the American teenager.
(5) the lead given by one large seamless hose manufacturer.

The quality aspect of the American seamfree is continually stressed, and the difference drawn out that in the U.K. manufacturers either did not or could not invest in new seamless plant; which resulted in the following: 'More and more it became apparent that the public was regarding the seamless stocking as the fully-fashioned article's poor sister. . . . Now if there is to be a revival of interest in the seamless stocking, not only a second best but also a poor quality stigma has to be overcome.' It is also quite surprising to read in the same article as late as 1957 that: 'Logical consideration of them, on the face of it, holds out little hope for a bare-leg trend in this country.' This article blames the unwillingness to invest in new equipment but totally under-estimates the underlying trend to the nude look, and the fact that at that time the seamless stocking was selling well to teenagers in the U.K.

Nonetheless there continued to be interest in the seamless and more favour-able comments began to appear:

'Seamfree do not have the formal appearance of fully-fashioned but they are particularly suitable for wear with informal and casual clothes. The fit has improved of late and concertinaed ankles are a thing of the past. The rather straight, slender leg has always looked better in seamless and this is possibly a factor which has contributed to their enormous popularity in the U.S.A. The seamless stockings are likely to be popular amongst teenagers. The price difference between these and the fully-fashioned stocking is enough to tip the scales in favour of seamless and then young legs are not so dependent on the flattery of the tapered heel and slimming seams.'—*Knitwear and Stockings*, 1958.'

'The bareleg fashion captivates the London models.'—*Hosiery Trade Journal*, March 1959.

Demand was now increasing and by 1959 the teenagers who had started buying seamless were a new generation not aware of the image of the pre-war seamless stocking. These consumers were those with no memory for prejudices —the fully-fashioned stocking to them was beginning now not to be associated with high fashion and high quality, but with the older age groups.

Although not nearly so well documented as the American market, we are led to the conclusion, from the available evidence, that the same trend for bare legs was to a large extent satisfied by the seamless stocking. It seemed to follow an almost identical pattern to the U.S.A. in the way the seamless stocking was launched as a seasonal, summer stocking in an attempt to combat the bare leg.

By 1960 *Knitwear and Stockings* records:

'Sales of seamless have rocketed up in the last twelve months. It has taken a long time to establish the bare leg look in Britain. Seamless meant regression not progress to English women who are not easily influenced by the American counterpart who led the new fashion. It was the teenagers here who set the fashion. Teenagers first buying nylons now buy seamfree and keep to them.'

In a survey conducted in the *Hosiery Trade Journal* in 1961 it comes out fairly clearly that there is a large swing to seamfree by teenagers.

Age	Fully-fashioned %	Mock Seam %	Seamfree %
15–19	13	7	80
20–29	46	6	48
30–39	62	9	29
40–49	59	12	29
50–59	61	14	25
60+	68	17	15
Total	50	10	40

In 1961 this journal also reviewed the factors it considered to have influenced the trend to seamless:

(1) Influence of the bare leg trend in the U.S.A.
(2) Desire to be 'in fashion'—at first London models were seen wearing fine gauge seamfree
(3) Price—an economic one
(4) Convenience—attractive to teenagers because of no seams
(5) Appearance—more sex appeal—view seems to be held by most younger women
(6) The cheap and inferior tag has now been lost by seamfree
(7) Vigorous advertising and promotion
(8) Quality—most important factor for the growth of seamfree.

Knitwear and Stockings in 1961 also corroborates the above reasoning to a large extent—it argues that the change was because:

(1) There was a desire among teenagers to copy America
(2) Shorter skirts revealed more seam to get crooked
(3) There was trading up of the seamfree stocking.

One comment in particular by a teenager sums up a lot of the argument: 'Mum wears fully-fashioned, so it's seamfree for me'.

By 1961 the seamfree was fully established on the U.K. market and the fully-fashioned on the way out. Like the American market, textured yarns and tights were the next major change. It is interesting to note, however, that manufacturers were going to make the same mistake in refusing to accept the trend towards these. The *Hosiery Trade Journal* of 1961 said: 'Textured seamfree stockings have not been widely promoted and trade interest is increasing. *They may never become a large part* of the stocking market, but do at least offer something to promote in a market short of promotional features.'

The sequel to the above is that in 1970, textured stockings constituted about 90 per cent of the market!

Conclusions

One of the most noticeable differences in today's hosiery industry is the great emphasis on fashion. This was not always so, during the first part of the century stockings were only a utility, now they have become part of the glamour of dress.

Grace Jones was a fashion expert in America during the period of the changeover to seamless stockings and it is claimed that she was one of the major instruments in effecting the change. It was said that she took the seamless stocking, a basement and low-end article, and put it on top. When asked how she accounted for the change, she gave a reply which covers many points of our study: 'Women tired of straightening seams. Nylon made possible sheer fitting stockings without seams. At the same time there was seamless knitting machinery development. The fashion merchandising techniques used in seamless promotion ignored its old image and built a new exciting image'. While giving some of the facts, this reply misses the major determinant of the change—the trend in consumer attitudes towards the nude look.

We have three main strands to consider—technological, economic and behavioural. Is it possible to list them in some causal hierarchy? Our findings suggest that all three played their part but we feel we could conclude the following.

The economic situation up to the time of the Second World War was such that the price differential between the fully-fashioned stocking and the seamless helped to create a quality image for the fully-fashioned. In the U.K. this image was enhanced during and immediately after the war by Government rationing and shortage of supplies. However we think that the poor image of the seamless stocking had more to do with technology than just price and demand factors. We must conclude that economic issues were secondary to consumer attitudes and technological progress.

The technological aspects of the study in one sense are the most important. If nylon (or a similar yard) had not been invented it would have been impossible to knit a circular stocking which could be shaped to the leg, and we would therefore not have had the fashion of the seamless stocking. Secondly, machinery development enabled a sheer non-streaky stocking to be knitted. Developments also meant that seamless stockings could be produced faster and faster, but above all these developments meant that the inferior image which was so ingrained in the consumer's mind could be demolished.

What is difficult to assess is the extent to which consumer preferences, evidenced by a demand for a bare-leg look, stimulated technological development or whether the technological improvements caused the consumer to upgrade the image of seamless stockings. In the initial stages of growth both sides seem to have contributed and then as demand began to grow it would appear that this demand gave the real impetus to further technological investment and innovation. We noted in our discussion earlier that although the

429

change could not have been successful without nylon and machine improvement—these factors were available about seven years before the change actually took place in the U.S.A., and about ten years in the U.K.

This leads us to the conclusion that although the technological aspects were absolutely necessary prerequisites of the change from fully-fashioned to seamless, they do not appear to be the cause of the change.

This brings us to the third main strand—the behavioural side. Before World War II, in fact in 1924, we identified an important event in Palm Beach—the beginning of the trend towards a nude look. This we suggest was a social movement of critical importance to the subsequent fashion change to seamless stockings. Also skirts had been raised and there seems to be a definite relation between skirt length and the attention focused on womens' legs, and the consequent desire for the nude look. At this stage technology was all important, for although the female consumer wanted the bare leg look, technology could not provide an answer.

After the war nylon was available and the consumer desire for the bare leg look continued. During the summer months the fact that teenagers and younger women were going without stockings caused a severe problem for the hosiery industry. Far-sighted manufacturers both of stockings and machinery worked on seamless development because they realized that the social move towards a nude look could be satisfied by a good quality, sheer, seamfree nylon stocking. The seamless stocking, however, had a pronounced and stubborn 'inferior' image which coupled with the bare leg trend led to intensive advertising and promotion, particularly in the U.S.A.

We propose therefore that the psychological barrier of the image of seamless stockings and the sociological movement towards a nude look were the chief determinants of the change to seamless, and this in turn prompted to a large extent machine and fibre improvement. However, it proved so difficult to eradicate this image that it was eventually the younger age groups, without any preconceptions of seamless stockings, who started the fashion both in the U.K. and America. It then permeated up to the older age groups—the ones who remembered pre-war seamless stockings.

The reasons the change was three to four years later in the U.K. would seem to be threefold:

(1) Seamless had a more pronounced 'inferior' image in the mind of the English consumer
(2) Supplies of nylon were not readily available until 1953
(3) Manufacturers were reluctant to invest in the new seamless technology.

Nonetheless, the same factors were at work in the U.K. as in the U.S.A. and by 1970 virtually all stockings produced in the U.K. were seamless. However, since seamless reached the majority another change in fashion has occurred, the change to tights, which supports the quotation: 'As soon as a fashion is universal, it is out of date.'

References

1. *Books*
P. Bleiss, *Marketing and the Behavioural Sciences.*

J. D. DeHann, *The Fully fashioned hosiery industry in the United States* (1956).
A. W. Eley, *Stockings*.
J. C. Flugel, *Psychology of Clothes* (1950).
A. Gold, *How to sell fashion* (Fairchild, 1968).
M. H. Grass, *History of Hosiery*.
L. Halliday, *The Fashion Makers*.
I. J. Haskell, *Hosiery through the years*.
A. G. Pool and Llewellyn, *The British Hosiery Industry—A study in Competition*.
R. Robson, *The Man-Made Fibres Industry* (1958).
M. E. Rooch and J. B. Elcher, *Dress, Adornment and the Social Order* (J. Wiley & Sons, 1965).
M. S. Ryan, *Clothing: A study in Human Behaviour* (Holt, Rinehart and Wilson, 1966).
E. M. Schenke, *The Manufacture of Hosiery and its Problems* (1935).
Taylor/Wills. *Pricing Strategy* (Staples, 1969).
The Hosiery Manufacturing Industry in North Carolina and its Marketing Problems.
F. A. Wells, *The British Hosiery Trade* (1935).
K. Young, *Handbook of Social Psychology* (N.Y., Appleton-Century-Crofts).

2. *Journals, Statistical Reports and other Publications*

British Clothing Manufacturer (1969).
British Nylon Spinners Stocking Business Survey 1957 to 1964.
British Productivity Council. 'Productivity in the Italian Stocking Industry' (published 1960).
Board of Trade Hosiery Working Party Report.
British Standards Institute, Consumer Advisory Council, 'Nylon Stockings Know How'.
Directory of Clothing Research, 1968.
Dupont Marketing Research Department. J. M. Mecredy, 'Nylon hosiery—A psychological study of consumers'.
Hosiery Abstracts (1956 to 1962).
Hosiery and Underwear (1917 to 1962).
Hosiery Times (1955 to 1963).
Hosiery Trade Journal (1946 to 1962).
Knitted Outerwear Times (1956 to 1961).
Knitwear and Stockings (1948 to 1962).
Manchester Guardian (8 September 1965)—K. Lewis, 'The Stocking Truth'.
Observer Colour Supplement (6 March 1966)—'Who sets the styles?'
Parlons Bas (1960 to 1963).
Review of Texile Progress (1949 to 1963).
Royal Society of Art Journal, vol. 112 (June 1964), p. 473. H. Amies, 'What Makes Fashion?'
Sociology and Social Research, vol. 41 (September–October 1956). W. F. Ogburn, 'Technology as Environment'.
Textile Institute and Industry, vol. 1, no. 1 (1963), p. 16. E. Kann, 'Man-Made Fibres and the Consumer'.
Textile Institute and Industry (April 1965). 'Consumer requirements in Womens Wear'.

Odd relevant issues:
  Textile Month
  Textile Organon
  Textile Manufacturer
  Textile Weekly
Twentieth Century, vol. 173 (Spring 1965), pp. 49–51. J. Holland, 'Fashion and Class'.
P. M. Prentice, 'An extended essay on the Hosiery Industry'.

Chapter 27

FASHION THEORY AND
PRODUCT DESIGN*
by Dwight E. Robinson

This contribution looks again beyond the conventional areas of fashion to explore the implications of fashion knowledge for successful marketing.

What rules govern changes in fashion—in women's apparel, as the classic case, and in all other industries?

What are the implications of these rules for styling policy and fashion leadership?

Has the trend toward architectural nudity and low, rambling homes reached the end of the road?

Is the emphasis on 'functional' furniture and 'streamlined' home appliances on the wane?

Will automobile styling revert to higher cars and greater interior comfort?

The history of succeeding styles observes a few unalterable rules which, even if they do not always appear to be firmly grasped by vice-presidents in charge of styling or by consumer researchers, are applicable to all industries. No matter whether the problem is selling cars, architectural plans, pedigree dogs, or dresses, the motives which prod consumers into continual revision of their tastes are essentially the same from commodity to commodity.

Despite all the current studies of consumer motivation, however, American management so far has generally failed to grasp the significance of the basic rules of style, or to realize the benefits to be obtained by applying them. Not enough attention has been paid to the underlying secrets of the women's apparel trade, the purest and oldest form of fashion expression, or to the possi-

* From 'Fashion Marketing', *Harvard Business Review*, vol. 36, No. 6 (1958). Published by permission of the President and Fellows of Harvard College.

AUTHOR'S NOTE: A substantial part of the research contributing to this study was made under a fellowship granted by The Ford Foundation. I wish to express my appreciation to Lois Wallace for valuable research assistance and to the large number of individuals in various fields of study or business related to styling who generously gave of their time for interviews. However, the views and other statements expressed are the writer's alone.

bilities of studying fashion as an independent behavioural phenomenon rather than as an adjunct to some other specialized area of study such as consumer psychology, economic demand, or industrial design.

Part of the explanation for these oversights may lie in a certain provincialism on the part of market researchers, including social scientists. While they have displayed a pronounced and growing tendency to advise product planners, designers, advertisers, and marketing executives in general as to the impressions they should or should not try to create in particular instances, all too frequently the researchers have based their advice solely on inferences drawn from the raw data obtained by questionnaires and by interviews, with little knowledge of the social dynamics of taste to guide them. Whether out of masculine disdain or befuddlement in the face of a subject which smacks of womanly vanity, only a few sociologists and psychologists have joined a much larger number of men of letters, museum curators, and the like, in exploring the basic theory of fashion.

As might be expected in the case of a game of appearances, so subtle is the realm of fashion, and so deceptive are the devices of those who make it what it is, that it demands the most single-minded attention from any person who would understand it. It is a world that is always creating misleading impressions, as if deliberately trying to trap the unwary or confuse those who lack the patience to unravel its threads by painstaking examination. Yet it will surrender its mysteries to patient inquiry no less readily than any other subject of human behaviour.

The Meaning of Fashion

The behavioural complex underlying all stylistic innovation—by this I mean all changes in design which are not purely the results of engineering advances —can conveniently be summed up under the single word *fashion*. And fashion, defined in its most general sense, is the pursuit of novelty for its own sake. Every market into which the consumer's fashion sense has insinuated itself is, by that very token, subject to this common, compelling need for unceasing change in the styling of its goods.

The reason for this is that the stimuli of fashion derive solely from the *comparisons* that consumers draw between new designs and the old designs they replace. No single style of design, no matter how brilliantly it is conceived, can claim any independent fashion significance at all, nor can it possess more than a fugitive lease on life.

Rule of excess. Paul Poiret, the top Paris couturier of the 1920s, once summed up his credo by declaring, 'All fashions end in excess'—a principle which is the beginning of wisdom for all who are concerned with style policy. He was aware that the overriding responsibility of the designer in a fashion market is the unending provision of novelty. Implicitly he recognized that one of the most exacting problems the stylist ever faces is that of deciding what to do when he has exhausted the possibilities of a current direction in styling emphasis. What does he do, for example, when the waistline, hemline, or any other line has been carried as far as it will go? It is here that the couturier must exercise to the utmost every ounce of his insight into the meaning of fashion.

As a couturier Poiret knew that the appetite for novelty, arising from the twofold insistence of the lady of fashion on preserving her inimitability from the onslaught of the vulgar and on demonstrating her affluence through unrelenting expenditure on newly cut costumes, is never satisfied with any one mode of presenting the figure. Fashions in dress design subsist on measures to

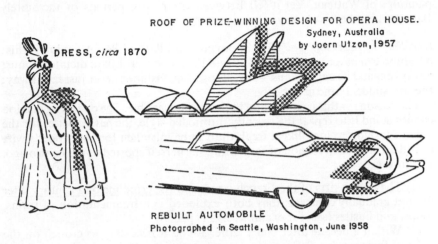

FIG. 1. Extremes in design.

Sources: the dress design comes from Henry Harald Hansen, *Costumes and Styles* (New York, 1956); the opera house roof design comes from Sigfried Giedion, *Architecture, You and Me* (Cambridge, Mass., 1958).

transform or to distort, whether through exaggeration or minimization, the shape and features of the human figure. To illustrate:

(1) The hoop skirts of the eighteenth century and the crinoline of the nineteenth ballooned to diameters of eight feet. As the hip line was exaggerated beyond the point of simply imperilling navigation to the point of making it literally impossible, the waistline was tightened to the point of suffocation and interference with digestion.

(2) In the interim, the Directoire and Empire periods around 1800, a contrary tendency toward undress was exploited. *La Parisienne's* test of the suitability of a pseudoclassical gown of transparent silk was to see whether she could easily draw it through a ring taken from her little finger. The last resort of modesty was flesh-coloured tights.

(3) The flapper of the Jazz Age, though she was in her turn the despair of her late-Victorian parents, never dashed about in quite the deshabille of Mme Récamier, but what she missed in transparency she made up for with leg display.

Whether, at a given time, the particular form of emphasis is toward padding out or constricting, toward concealment or exposure, once such a movement is launched it must be intensified each season, ensuring that the ultrafashionable will be able to disport themselves in more of a good thing than their less-favoured contemporaries. Indeed, this recurrent pattern can be traced back to even earlier centuries. The style of European costume associated with the French Regency (1715–1730) emphasized delicacy and restraint. Its graceful, free-flowing costume is best remembered in the airy, idyllic scenes depicted in the paintings of Watteau. Yet it fell between the ornate periods of the stately Baroque and the frivolously extravagant Rococo.

Corollary of Reversal. The most important corollary of Poiret's axion is this: a fashion can never retreat gradually and in good order. Like a dictator it must always expand its aggressions—or collapse. Old fashions never just fade away; they die suddenly and arbitrarily.

The reason for this is simple and logically inescapable. The one thing fashion cannot stand is to repeat the recently outmoded style, the *passé*. Better for the lady of fashion to look like a freak than to be mistaken for her grocer's wife dolled up in a cheap version of something she herself sported a year or two ago. For instance:

(1) The hoop skirts of the French court and the crinoline of a century later did not gradually contract: they both exploded in a fragmentation of trains, loops, and bustles (see, for example, fig. 1, p. 435).

(2) Within a decade after court ladies found it necessary to crouch on the floor of their coaches so as to accommodate their soaring head-dresses, Lady Hamilton (Nelson's Emma) was enthralling the court of Naples and eminent visitors such as Goethe with her 'classical attitudes', for which her main props were no more than her own silky curls, a few yards of gauze, and a pet dove or two. And it was not long before thousands of less notorious ladies were taking her cue.

(3) Again, a couple of generations later, after such devices as the bustle and the leg-of-mutton sleeve exhausted the expansionist tendencies of late-Victorian days, the shirtwaist and hobble skirt were suddenly introduced, clearing the way for the boyish skimpiness of the 1920s.

As we shall see later in greater detail, the rule that fashion never smoothly retraces its footsteps demonstrates itself even in the history of architecture, which is a particularly stern testing ground.

Look at what happened to the arch when, at the end of the late Gothic style, it had reached the extreme of pointedness. Did the Tudor architects, seeing that matters had reached a geometric impasse, decide to blunt it just a bit? Not at all. With unerring wisdom, they squashed it almost flat, making it a perfect frame for Henry VIII (see fig. 2). The royal tailors had, meanwhile, taken care to pad his already thick physique to something closely approaching a true square.

Classic Compromise. What lies behind these swift and extreme changes? If functional criteria could be more precisely defined, the game of fashion change might be interpreted as a series of departures from, and returns to, the norm of function. Unfortunately, this is not the case. Function is permissive. Even

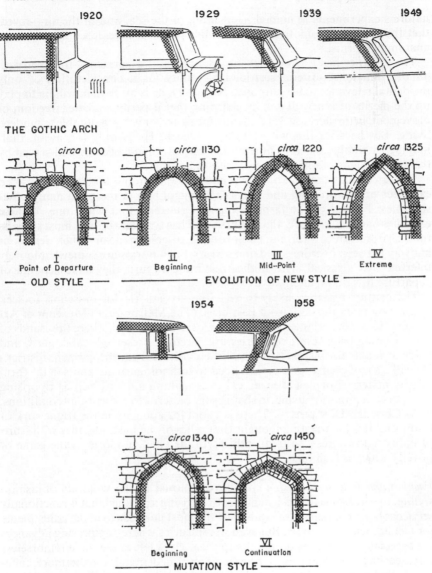

THE AUTOMOBILE WINDSHIELD

1920   1929   1939   1949

THE GOTHIC ARCH

circa 1100   *circa* 1130   *circa* 1220   *circa* 1325

I
Point of Departure

II
Beginning

III
Mid-Point

IV
Extreme

—— OLD STYLE ——   ———— EVOLUTION OF NEW STYLE ————

1954   1958

circa 1340   *circa* 1450

V
Beginning

VI
Continuation

———— MUTATION STYLE ————

FIG. 2. Illustrations of evolution and mutation of styles.*

The Gothic edifices from which models of arches have been taken are: (I) and
(II) Durham Cathedral; (III) Salisbury Cathedral; (IV) Ely Cathedral; (V)
Gloucester Cathedral; (VI) King's College Chapel, Cambridge.

* The tendencies shown here are, of course, highly simplified versions of complex realities.
As noted in the text, not only are exceptions always to be found, but old and new styles
usually 'fight it out' for dominance for many years. Also, let me assure architects that I intend
no new theory of the Gothic Style; the sketches are intended only to emphasize that stylistic
features tend to realize their potentials and then to be rapidly replaced by markedly different
forms.

nature's experiments in animals—on land, in the sea, and in the air—reveal that the laws of locomotion or mechanics permit a kaleidoscopic variety of anatomical forms.

The designer has learned that the usefulness of a garment—together with all the functional criteria surrounding utility—is a consideration of only incidental relevance to his purposes. Naturally, he is more than willing to play up the merits of a new design by claiming that it permits greater freedom of movement, better accentuates the feminine figure, or is more suitable to modern living. But he does this with tongue in cheek. He is only too aware that, judging by results, the aims of feminine coquetry have been as well served by the dress designs of one era as by those of another.

The safest thing that can be said of costume variation is that it veers between extremes of overdressing and underdressing, although there are many other variables. Perusal of the fashion journals suggests that when one of these extremes has been reached, the recourse that has typically proved most success-ful is swift return to a form of compromise, or golden mean, which lies about halfway between overdress and underdress. Such norms are somewhat loosely referred to as 'classical' styles in the dress trade. In turn, they serve as points of departure toward an alternative extreme.

The couturier is then likely to visit the art galleries or museums to seek inspiration from the designs of past eras. (The Metropolitan Museum of Art in New York, for instance, maintains a Costume Institute, where thousands of dresses going back several centuries are carefully preserved, catalogued, and made available for inspection by qualified visitors from the garment district.) He will also, of course, give careful heed to technological advances in the form of new materials or new mechanical dressmaking aids, as well as to arising needs of contemporary living, in shaping his patterns to present-day conditions.

As Christian Dior puts it, 'There is room for audacity in the framework of tradition.' It is an arresting thought that relics of the past, together with fruits of industrial progress, so frequently form the chief supports of the game of novelty which is fashion.

Fashion and Industrial Design. In sharp contrast to the volatility of fashion styling, the problems the designer faces in devising a product that is functionally serviceable are comparatively stable; at the most he needs to make adjustments for technological advances. But even in industries where engineering advances are especially rapid, they do not make themselves felt in the same remorseless way, season after season, as in the case of fashion demand. Furthermore, func-tion is obviously the sole basis for distinguishing one commodity from another.

Fashion, on the other hand, is concerned only with appearances, with decoration. While decoration must always to some extent adapt itself to the function of the article it embellishes, it is still very much an end in itself. It is in this respect that the problems involved in styling changes are essentially the same from industry to industry.

The American Home

A look at the home and its decoration will illustrate my thesis. In thus shifting our attention from dresses to buildings, we make a long leap from one of the most ephemeral forms of decoration to one of the most enduring. From this vantage point we can see the more stable, long-range forces operating on the mainstream of stylistic development. For the obvious reasons that houses are extremely durable and are major items of expenditure, a family's taste must necessarily be frozen for a long period of time, if not for a lifetime.

Fashion's Parallels. As far as the study of style changes is concerned, however, the differences between architectural trends and fashion trends should not be overestimated. Surprising as it may seem, the long-term society-wide swings between the two extreme poles of elaboration and ornamentation, on the one hand, and simplicity and functionalism, on the other, dominate the exterior and interior decoration of the home just as powerfully and unfailingly as they do costume. Despite the pronounced differences in durability between the two media, the timing of these swings in each case is almost exactly parallel. For example:

(1) When the Empire style succeeded the Rococo toward the end of the eighteenth century, 'noble simplicity' was as much the ideal in the fine arts, including architecture, as comparative undress was the fancy of the lady of fashion.

(2) The crinoline corresponded with the overloaded gingerbread façade in the heyday of Victorianism.

(3) The flapper of the 1920s witnessed the onslaught of the stripped-down, modernistic edifice.

True, fashions in dress, which can be discarded so readily, do exhibit a much greater frequency of short-term excursions and alarms, but there the difference ends.

Perhaps this over-all parallelism is not so surprising after all. As psychologists have pointed out, the symbolism inherent in the house and its furnishings is only one degree less intimate and personal than that of dress itself. It is hard to imagine that when people's tastes in architecture are bent on either simplicity or elaboration, they should adhere to the opposite of one or the other in their clothing. But the most telling consideration of all is that it appears to be the workings of the human memory rather than comparative durabilities of goods which determine the major fashion rhythm. After two generations have passed, few people will remember a once-popular but long-outmoded style. By that time, basic design features reminiscent of the old style can be reintroduced as if they were fresh and novel.

Succeeding Styles. What is more, we find that the reactions in taste which follow the excesses of either extreme tend to be almost as sharp and drastic in architecture and furnishings as in dress. The only difference is that, naturally enough, it takes a longer time to translate these taste changes into action— which is to say production—where the household is concerned.

Only a century ago (really a relatively short span in an art where style changes can scarcely be measured in terms briefer than generations) John Ruskin declared: 'Ornamentation is the principal part of architecture.'[1] That dictum sounds well-nigh incredible to those of us brought up in the ascendancy of Frank Lloyd Wright, Gropius, Le Corbusier, and their functionalist followers.

439

Yet thus did the acknowledged mentor of the most edified taste of his day herald the late-Victorian gingerbread.

However, it was only 40 years later, in 1892, that Louis Sullivan, the first American exponent of modernism, was writing that 'ornament is mentally a luxury, not a necessary', and that 'it would be greatly for our aesthetic good, if we should refrain entirely from the use of ornament for a period of years, in order that our thought might concentrate acutely upon the production of buildings well formed and comely in the nude.'[2]

Nudity versus Adornment. Sullivan's comment is a highly subtle one, for, in addition to his implied analogy with the history of dress, he left the door open to the return to a sense of the need for ornament. Indeed, this sense is activating leading architects of today such as Eero Saarinen and Edward Stone; witness, for example, their resort to vivid colours, varied textures, and fanciful contrivance of structurally nonrequisite patterns.

In a recent series of interviews, I found an overwhelming consensus among art experts and industrial designers that the functional school is already meeting its Waterloo in the monotony it has imposed on urban building and even on interior decoration. Our architects have come just about as close to architectural nudity as is either possible or endurable. Thus:

(1) Construction features which at one time may have served the cause of utility—the use of greater areas of glass for improved lighting is the most conspicuous example—are tending to become exaggerated to the point of perverting function through destruction of privacy, removal of protection from the sun, and so on.

(2) The 'sincere' demonstrations of what various structural features—girders, reinforced concrete, cantilevering—are capable of doing have been carried perilously close to mere displays of virtuosity and are made to assume shapes that are of no practical value whatsoever (see fig. 1). Ornament, once officially legislated out of existence, has cropped out again in the form of extreme displays of the marvels of engineering.

One-Level Living. So ingrained with us today is the notion that nothing can be new and modern unless it is also stark and shocking that it is hard to imagine any new style wave in housing not following the edicts of Gropius, Le Corbusier, and other 'modernists'. Yet that is just what is happening. Moreover, the new approach may prove to be something more profound than 'modernist' design, even though far less discordant with tradition and a great deal less strident.

In his valuable book, *The Tastemakers*, Russell Lynes concludes with no hesitation that as far as domestic architecture is concerned, the flat-roofed, cubistic, and glass-walled house has been almost totally superseded by something quite different, which, for want of a better name, he calls the 'ranch house.'[3] Indeed, it appears quite evident that Le Corbusier's modernistic concept, 'the machine for living,' though a few examples of it are still being built, is itself rapidly becoming outmoded.

The contemporary American house is the suburban house. The number of families who live in mid-city homes (outside of apartments) or who can afford a second house in the country is no longer significant. The tremendous change in living habits that has been wrought by the automobile and also by the demands that the great corporation places on the family breadwinner is as epochal in its own way as the change in the social structure which took place in eighteenth-century England.

What are the central tendencies of the contemporary suburban house? What have been its origins, and what is its future?

The fundamental feature appears to be 'one-level living' (a feature sometimes more a matter of semblance than reality, for living space is frequently provided at basement level or in a partially concealed second storey). This is accompanied by picture windows, a gently sloping, peaked roof, and rather muted reference to one or more of the styles of the architectural past—which the eclectic school of architects used to copy so literally in the 1920s—or, at times, a watered-down suggestion of functionalism. Houses of this type are already labelled 'modern' by the practising real estate agent, who is prone to refer to something in the Le Corbusier spirit as 'international'.

The search for the antecedents of structures of this type has been accompanied by a good deal of guesswork. Lynes, for example, mentions the pre-World War I bungalow (favoured because of its anticipation of the picture window and overhanging eaves), the California ranch house (although, in point of historical accuracy, the bunk house might be more apt), the Cape Cod cottage, the English cotter's croft, the Swiss chalet, and the Spanish-American mission. He might as readily have included the log cabin. It's a free country!

Synthetic Ramblers. Can the theory of fashion set forth here help explain the evolution of the one-level house? In general terms I think it can, although it must always be remembered that generalities are never all-sufficient and can be useful only insofar as they sum up the more relevant forces with reasonable accuracy and sense of proportion.

Ever since the 1890s and even before, the architect has been in flight from ornamentation. (Gingerbread and gewgaws had their last fling in the late-Victorian style of balloon-construction house somewhat dubiously dubbed 'Queen Anne'.) In the pursuit of simplicity, he has followed two alternate paths: (1) to the modernist functionalist school of design previously described; (2) to the eclectic school of architecture associated with such names as Richard Morris Hunt (who 'adapted' the French chateau to the aspirations of the American tycoon) and Stanford White and Ralph Adams Cram, both leaders in the revival of American Colonial. The antiquarian-minded eclecticists worshipped simplicity almost as reverently as the functionalists did.

From the very beginning of the flight from Victorianism, however, a number of architects and aesthetic critics of different mind worked both sides of the street at the same time. For example. William Morris, who of all men has the best claim to being the founding father of modern design, could never make up his mind as to whether to be antiquarian or functionalist. Noted English architects of the 1900s, like C. F. Annesley Voysey and Charles Rennie Mackintosh, carried on in the same synthetic vein. Equally significant, their houses tended to be low and rambling.

Perhaps they were the most prophetic, for the modern home is in their spirit (see fig. 3). From the motley suburbs of the 1920s, where a conflicting assortment of Tudor, Spanish, French Provincial, Mediterranean, and Colonial

441

THE RAMBLER STYLE (left column) TRIUMPHS OVER THE OPPOSITION (right column)

1. PIONEER RAMBLER

4. THE OLD ORDER

2. CONTEMPORARY RAMBLERS
STRONGLY TRADITIONAL

5. 'ECLECTIC' AND 'FUNCTIONAL' RIVALS
COLONIAL REVIVAL

3. CONTEMPORARY RAMBLERS
MINIMALLY TRADITIONAL

6. 'ECLECTIC' AND 'FUNCTIONAL' RIVALS
'MACHINE FOR LIVING'

FIG. 3. Some highlights in 60 years of domestic architecture*

vied with a radical minority of modernistic experiments, we have undergone
a pronounced synthesizing process.

Individual preference still accounts for the fact that any particular house of

* The close affinity between today's ramblers (2) and (3) and Voysey's (1), designed 60
years ago, is strikingly apparent. But for a very few stylistic differences related to different
social conditions, Voysey's design can be said to have anticipated the prevalent features of
contemporary domestic architecture: horizontality, simplicity, the ell plan enhancing the
rambling effect, view windows, overhanging eaves, and contrasting surface materials. Note
the fieldstone terrace so familiar today. In contrast, both the 'eclectic' (5) and 'functional-
modernistic' house (6) 'missed the boat' by retaining the verticality of the Victorian house (4).
This was common even in the case of deep-country dwellings.

The ascendancy of the rambler illustrates two points made in the text: first, that a fundamental style change generally represents a sharp though not diametric break with the past—
compare houses (1) and (4); second, that the new style fights a winning battle not only with
the old style but also with 'progressive' and 'traditional' departures from the latter.

Naturally, a few illustrations cannot tell the story. Between the main types shown here all
sorts of cross-currents have taken place.

442

suburbia may carry a trace of one or another of these styles, but such traces are subdued, and the structural outlines of every house—long, low, and rambling—are very much of a piece. The individual's preference, where he has a chance to exercise it, may be determined by his region or, perhaps even more, since furniture is the pith of the home, by the furniture he owns.

Vertical to Horizontal. To ask whether the contemporary house is descended from the bungalow, the ranch house, the cottage, or whatnot seems to be irrelevant. None of these would have entered the picture in the first place unless supported by deeper forces. It is more to the point, perhaps to ask whether one-level living may be in part a response to the cult of comfort, a recognition of the disappearance of live-in servants, or an attempt to reproduce in the suburbs the arrangement of the city apartment in which most exurbanites once lived.

But if my view of fashion reactions is substantially correct, the most relevant, as well as the simplest explanation, is that the low, rambling effect was a logical direction for architects to take in groping for a style markedly different from box-like, many-peaked domiciles of grandfather's day. If so, it is only too apparent that while the big guns on the battlefield of architectural doctrine were booming forth their conflicting dogmas, the unconscious desires of the public for something meaningfully new and different, but still not too out of kilter with traditional sentiments, were in a quieter but more profound way shaping the look of the future.

Such a conclusion does seem confirmed by the historical record, which shows that over the past 50 or more years the rambling house has steadily increased in frequency, no matter what style the designer told himself and his client he was working in.

Are fresh reactions against the simplified rambler in the making? Prediction, of course, does not follow automatically from analysis, largely because fashion may desert any particular variation for another. For example, the public and its architects may decide to leave the dimensions of the house as they are and concentrate rather on the introduction of new building materials, new colours, and the like. We can only suggest that after more than a half-century the trends toward architectural nudity and toward lowness have nearly reached the end of the road.

As early as 1954, in fact, home-building journals were beginning to report that in certain of the most populous areas of the country the 'split-level' house (defined as a dwelling 'with at least three separate levels, two of which are located one above the other, and all of which are one-half level apart in elevation') was actually outselling ranch types four to one.[4] This half-way, yet decisive, return to verticality and a more 'impressive' look is precisely what this analysis would lead us to expect.

Furniture and Appliances

The history of furniture demonstrates most notably that the central current of stylistic development—no matter how sharp its twistings and turnings—will carry elements of past and present.

The greater part of the public (and this is equally true at all levels of prestige

443

and income) is motivated just as surely by a sense of loyalty to traditional sentiment as it is by the desire for novelty or considerations of utility. Such loyalty is the backbone of cultural continuity, just as willingness to adopt new materials or mechanical advantages is the backbone of progress. These two driving interests will separate at times and at other times come together. Once again: 'There is room for audacity in the framework of tradition.'

Antique versus Modern. Whereas clothing is worn out and discarded, corrupted by moths, or hidden away in attics, neither the rage of the wrecker nor natural catastrophe ever completely obliterates the antique furniture of bygone eras. Because of its mobility, it offers the antique collector his golden opportunity —so that when most people hear the word *antique*, they think only of furniture. Consequently, the American house has been more profoundly influenced by past standards of design through its furniture (whether in the form of authentic period pieces or reproductions) than in any other way. To nomadic Americans, furniture has become the chief material means of symbolizing family continuity.

To refer to the stylistic significance of antiquities in a study of fashion reactions—reactions already defined as arising from the pursuit of novelty for its own sake—is far less paradoxical than may appear to be the case at first glance. A curio from the remote past is just as apt to be considered a novelty as a new gadget or an exotic rarity. Back in the 1920s, for example, the suddenly discovered charm of colonial furniture was as much a novelty to those who succumbed to it as was the scientific miracle of the radio or the mysterious fascination of mah-jongg.

The antique serves as the most effective reminder of the great style periods of the past. It appeals to the sentiments we associate with great traditions— especially if it dates from one of the pioneering eras (such as eighteenth-century England was in furniture) whose rich creativity in design entitles it to be called classical. But every generation, as it swings back and forth along the great rhythm between elaboration and simplicity, will exercise its own particular preferences among all the styles of the past and its own special ideas about how to express them. Some will prefer the simpler, some the more ornate. Some will want their antiques or their reproductions 'neat', others will want to doctor them up. In short, there are fashions in antiques as in everything else.

The furniture stores have for many decades stocked, side by side, 'traditional' pieces, consisting of more or less faithful reproductions, and 'modern' pieces, consisting largely of furniture featuring metal materials or newly treated forms of wood such as plywood, along with functional shapes based on theories of anatomical suitability.

Closer examination, nevertheless, will show that increasingly this apparent distinction has become less meaningful. More and more, the so-called modern has become dominated by pieces which, though they often show a significant degree of originality, conform essentially to eighteenth-century standards of proportion and symmetry. Common to both for the past half-century has been the great movement toward simplicity, one that only recently has begun to give indications of a shift in direction.

This drive toward simplicity is itself a reaction to the excesses to which the Victorians carried the initial impetus of the eighteenth century.

Exit Streamlined Appliances. It takes no expert to realize that the greatest godsend to the designers of home appliances in recent history was the discovery in aerodynamics of the value of the teardrop shape to the reduction of wind resistance. Streamlining was adopted with functional logic for vehicles in the various transportation fields first, and then was applied, without functional logic, to stationary household appliances ranging from the stove, refrigerator, and washing machine all the way down the scale to the toaster, alarm clock, and waffle iron.

Everything had to have rounded edges; everything had to look compact, sleek, and as if it were capable of going somewhere fast. Armed with the principle of streamlining, and some rather self-conscious claims to aesthetic cultivation which the factory-bound designers of grandma's coal range or grandpa's buggy lacked, the latter-day industrial designer succeeded in establishing a specialized form of big business.

Best of all, streamlining suggested its own ethical justification. It was advertised as symbolizing the modern American's enlightened determination to cast off the encumbrances of convention in order to forge a new, vital, and dynamic civilization. Of course, once designers had sold business leaders on the importance of ethical justification to support styling appeal, it got to be a habit. A leading industrial designer told me recently that most of his clients were not satisfied when he merely presented a design for their product which they or surveyed consumers found attractive. They demanded an ethic for it. 'So,' he went on, 'we give them an ethic. Ethic? That's a fashion, too.'

As anyone who looks at the advertisements knows, however, the streamlining of many household appliances has abruptly ceased in the last few years. The new refrigerators are almost all rectilinear with severely sharp edges; the fully rounded sides have disappeared. Fashion, unable to exploit streamlining indefinitely, did not permit a gradual lessening of the curves and bulges but demanded a jump to the geometric block shape.

Other recent alterations following the same principles have been the desertion of pristine, sanitary white enamelling in favour of an outburst of colour, and also an abandonment of hard metallic or vitreous surfaces with a clinical look in favour of richer textures. Natural grained woods are being lavishly used for kitchen cabinets.

About Face Detroit?

How does our theory of fashion leadership apply to automobile styling? The present turbulent state of affairs in the automobile market gives every indication that Poiret's nemesis of excess is once again in the process of making itself felt with decisive impact. This impact is portentous of great change for the shape and dimensions of the car body. This is evidenced not only by the current striking symptoms of shifts in the public's tastes but by what Detroit designers are saying and doing themselves.

The Long, Low Look. Automotive stylists are thoroughly aware that the dynamics of styling in their industry correspond closely with the experience of of other industries. A representative statement of their views can be found in a recent talk delivered by William M. Schmidt, executive stylist of the Chrysler Corporation:

'The low silhouette is the most important and universal key to contemporary design. Low, ranch-type houses are in demand. Low, modern furniture is handsome, comfortable, and popular. More and more household appliances are being designed with the low look in mind. Modern office buildings, hotels, shopping centres, and civic and cultural centres are being designed for the eye appeal of low parallel lines, rather than the vertical lines of another styling era. To fit into its surroundings gracefully, the automobile also must have a contemporary appearance.'[5]

It is extremely interesting in this connection to note that of recent years the styling divisions of the automobile manufacturers have established regular channels of communication with key people in the women's fashion trades, although so far the guidance they have sought has largely been confined to interior styling and colour and does not, as yet, appear to have been extended to the modelling of the body, the most important phase of exterior styling.

Detroit's decision to join the designers of household appliances in deserting streamlining for a relatively squared-off, boxy look a decision which became apparent no later than 1954, is already past history, and seems to have settled the question of contour for some time to come.

So there is no question about Detroit's awareness of general style trends. There can be little question, either, about its sophistication in the use of market research. Yet, as Detroit looks ahead of its model-conversion and production lead times, it sees a major dilemma in styling policy:

(1) Stylists recognize that the extreme limits on lowness imposed by the human physique are only a few inches away (something in the neighbourhood of 45 inches) and will come close to realization in the 1960 models. These models are already predetermined beyond anything more than superficial changes.

(2) It also seems unquestionable that the long-established styling tendency toward longer overhang cannot practicably be carried much farther. The analogy between this squashing effect and the tight lacing of the waist and the expansion of the skirt in the crinoline era is almost irresistible.

(3) In the same context, the tail fin—supposedly derived from the aeroplane tail—may be interpreted as a last resort of overextension, an out-cropping that, quite seriously, serves much the same purpose as the bustle or the train (see fig. 1). Although advertising claims have been made to the effect that fins serve the functional purpose of stabilizing a moving car in a cross-wind, I found few designers in Detroit willing to say there is much scientific support for these claims.

What should Detroit do now? If it cannot go much farther forward, should it gradually retrace its footsteps? I think not. Having utilized gradual compression and lengthwise expansion of the body as a means of differentiating new-model cars from old for so many years, it would be entirely self-defeating for the industry to start building them a few inches shorter or higher, say, in 1961. The reason? This would be tantamount to repeating the dimensional style characteristics of 1957 or 1958. The new cars would then be duplicates of silhouettes already cluttering up the used car lot, the last place Detroit wants to wind up.

As a matter of fact, the accuracy of this view has already been tested. In 1953 several models were introduced with bodies which were, in defiance of the main drift, *slightly* reduced in length. And the results, marketwise, were most unfortunate.

Invasion From Europe. It is all too easy to misinterpret the significance that the soaring popularity of foreign cars holds as an index of shifts taking place in the tastes of the car-buying public. The unlikelihood that the representative American family will ever be satisfied with a really small car is not so much a question for the style analyst as a matter of cold reason.

In the first place, the size of the typical European car is, after all, an accident of the European economy and tax laws. In the United States smallness has undoubtedly been welcomed as a novelty, but like all novelties it will wear off in time. Secondly, while the future may well hold a comfortable niche for the pint-size model as a second car (free, incidentally, of the taint of the used-car lot) or as a special purpose vehicle, nevertheless only 12 per cent of American motorists own two automobiles. In addition, this is a big country, where more money is spent on touring than on any other form of recreation. Such factual considerations point to the conclusion that the standard model will have to remain sizeable. (This does *not* mean, however, that it may not be made more compact.)

Naturally, it is with the styling features of foreign cars rather than with the mere factor of overall bulk that the fashion analyst is primarily concerned. Two features are unmistakably dominant:

(1) European manufacturers have exercised far greater freedom in experimenting with functional arrangements than Americans have: cars with a wide variety of engine types, cars with engines in the rear, three-wheel cars, and cars with doors in the front.

(2) In other foreign makes, a sharply contrasting feature is the theme of close adherence to traditional body designs. Whether we consider larger passenger cars like the Rolls Royce and Mercedes-Benz or sports cars such as the MG and Jaguar, it is equally clear that their designers have been faithful to styling features that they consider the classic hallmarks of their particular makes.

If the popularity of the imported cars is a meaningful symptom of where domestic fashions are tending—and any student of fashion knows that such symptoms may presage a whole future trend—we must recognize that the American motorist is looking for a change and is seeking it through the dual approaches of functional experiment and antiquarianism in much the same way he has been doing in residential architecture and in furniture.

Back to the 'Classics'? Nor need we confine our attention to the foreign car market for corroboration of this conclusion. The large domestic market in this country's own models of a bygone era—actually referred to as 'classics' in the automobile magazines—points in the same direction. For example, an Associ-

447

ated Press release, date-lined St Paul, Kansas, June 28, 1958, states that a 1904 Winton car was sold there for $3,400. Over the past ten or more years, a small but flourishing industry has sprung up to serve car hobbyists through the repair, rebuilding, and duplication of parts of antiquated models.

There are, then, many symptoms suggesting directions in which the taste of the automotive public is groping. Their very vitality attests to their significance. It was Poiret, too, who always insisted that in matters of fashion it is the consumer rather than designer or producer who is the ultimate arbiter. To try to understand the complex problem of evolving automobile design without paying heed to what is happening in this world of car hobbyists would be a misguided effort.

The new interest in antique cars points toward a revival of forms comparable to those that have not been seen since the early days of motoring. Spurred on by, but also benefiting from, its foreign competition, Detroit will look back for inspiration to its own great heritage, not as a musty copybook of bygone designs to follow slavishly, but as a treasury of suggestions to be blended with modern concepts and technical innovations. And, considering the role the human memory plays in governing the timing of fashion swings, it probably would be wise for today's designers to re-examine the vintages of not merely one but two generations past.

Indeed, the theory of fashion leaves no choice but to conclude that, barring only the unlikely contingency that the automobile body is abandoned as a medium of fashion appeal, there must shortly ensue a striking reorientation of the shape and silhouette of American cars. In the decade ahead they should show a pronounced tendency to move away from their present attenuated appearance toward something less sleek but more commodious and comfortable. Thus:

In view of the long trips of the American tourist, Detroit might well cock an eye at the stately European tradition of the grand tour. While the typical Detroit product is engineered for the world's best cruising performance (I have driven a pint-size European car on Germany's superhighways, and the experience is one I do not care to repeat), body design has become more and more out of tune with touring.

The tourist wants *room*—head room, leg room, luggage room—just plain room, without a lot of waste space under the hood and fenders. Here is an instance where function as an ideal can be put to good account. Let us also remember that an extremely low centre of gravity is functionally insignificant in the face of the scientifically gradual, banked curves of the modern throughway.

Drastic Changes. Summing up, the force of fashion's fundamental reactions between the extremes of simplicity and elaboration or horizontality and verticality are suggestive of basic shifts in the design of the American car. The unsuitability of gradual reverses in fashion trends suggests that when these shifts set in, they are bound to be sharp and decisive. We are moving toward ornamentation and stateliness and probably veering toward the upright look once more. Finally, if the lessons of experience in the styling changes of other products are to be repeated, the transformation which lies ahead will be implemented both by a wave of functional innovation and by a revival movement.

Detroit stylists are already looking in this direction, despite the advertisements and public relations releases dedicated to help sell the current models. I was interested to discover during a recent Detroit visit that any number of the designers there are not only avidly interested in the early history of automobiling but are also well-versed authorities on models of the past. None of them, for example, expressed any astonishment when I raised the question of the likelihood of a revival movement. It would, of course, be misleading to create the impression that Detroit has been thinking explicitly along the lines outlined in this article. No outside observer can expect to be vouchsafed the innermost secrets of any company's styling policy.

Design is an artistic and therefore a largely intuitive process, and automobile design is no exception. It is by no means visionary to foresee the possibility that the art historian of an unborn generation may look back not to our sculpture as much as to our automobile bodies as the United States' most meaningful aesthetic achievement in plastic expression during the mid-twentieth century. The new cars are bound to be, insofar as the concept of newness can be meaningfully defined at all, new. It will doubtless take a practiced observer to detect in them the fusion of traditional images and functional advance that our interpretation anticipates.

Conclusion

My aim has been to provide a springboard to a better understanding of a fascinating but perplexing area of decision making. I have sought to point out that fashion—the impulse underlying the dynamics of style—is both a less mystifying and a more profound force in social behaviour than is commonly supposed. Most authorities on fashion consider it an evolutionary process. In this I join them. Yet evolution relies on sudden mutations as much as, if not more than, small changes. For this reason, I have emphasized the sharply pronounced reactions which always seem to follow the extremes of styling.

Of course, I do not intend to put forward a formula or nostrum for the automatic prediction of style trends. History does not repeat itself any more neatly and prettily in styles than it does in any other sphere—business fluctuations, for example. My objective has been only to present a systematic exposition of a few of the insights that have long been the guideposts of fashion's most adept practitioners.

Nobody's crystal ball can show up the fashion future in complete detail. If it could, a lot of brain power would be unemployed; a lot of fun would go out of life. But this much is certain: the fact that an industry invests billions of dollars in equipment is no guarantee of a continued market for its products. Fashion is absolutely and callously indifferent to any monumental achievements in manufacturing proficiency. If anything, she takes capricious delight in nullifying man's industry—or pretenses to rationality. All of the fame and bulk of a leading textile, appliance, construction, or automobile company will not save it from fashion's dustbin if she so wills. She, and not the so-called fashion dictator—as Paul Poiret always professed—is the true autocrat; and only in a totalitarian state, where the consumer's taste is legislated by government edict, does she meet her match.

References

1. As quoted by Nikolaus Pevsner in *Pioneers of Modern Design* (New York, The Museum of Modern Art, 1949), p. 7.
2. Ibid., p. 13.
3. Russel Lynes, *The Tastemakers* (N.Y., Harper & Brothers, 1954), pp. 251–5, 270–1, and 350.
4. See, for example, 'What's Happening in Split Levels', *House and Home* (April 1954), pp. 110–124.
5. 'What Price Lowness?' presented at the Passenger Car Activity Meeting of the Detroit Section, Society of Automotive Engineers, 5 May 1958.

Chapter 28

HOW PREDICTABLE ARE FASHION AND OTHER PRODUCT LIFE CYCLES?*
by Chester R. Wasson

The author furthers the translation of fashion ideas to the wider area of marketing application, and particularly emphasises the need for tentative predictions based on life cycle analysis.

No aspect of marketing is so uncertain as the acceptance of new products, particularly those with a fashion element. Yet product introduction and fashion itself are such basic necessities for continued success that the gamble must be taken repeatedly. Clearly, a sound means of forecasting the onset of any popularity wave is needed, of predicting its course, and of recognizing the earliest symptoms of a forthcoming decline. Market planning needs a fundamental explanatory theory of the fashion cycle which would explain the clearly observable, ceaseless fluctuations and their subsequent course. The explanation can be sound only if based on known tendencies of human behaviour and on the way human motives, both innate and socially conditioned, cause people to react to the kind of stimulus called a new product. To be useful the theory also must indicate at the minimum the general direction of the next fluctuation and detect the timing of at least the first signs of a new swing.

The thesis of this paper is that already a suitable framework exists for such a theory. It can be drawn from the documented results of product acceptance research when interpreted in the light of human reaction to product offerings and the social psychology of perception and motivation. Furthermore, the theory is at least testable for some kinds of products and corresponds with the results of some proprietary research, unfortunately not published. If valid, this theory is the direct antithesis of the popular myth of 'created' fashion.

The Myth of Created Fashion

That fashion is a synthetic creation of the seller is an idea so entrenched that even marketing professionals are often blind to the observably low batting average of those who attempt such 'creation'. Even within the area of women's apparel, the fact most obvious to those who follow the news of new offerings is the diversity of their direction and the large numbers of 'dictated' designs

* From the *Journal of Marketing*, vol. 32 (American Marketing Association, July, 1968).

which fall by the wayside after every Paris showing. However, fashion is not limited to women's apparel, nor confined to matters of commercial exploitation.

There are fashions in politics and in business decision methods as marked as the documented cycles in styles of clothing and architecture.[1] A colleague once demonstrated similar cycles in religious interest in a study of church publications, and followers of the stock market are aware of the constantly changing identity of the 'glamour' stocks. Whether on the dance floor, in the dress shop, or in the business conference room, the 'in' thing changes with the calendar.

No seller can afford to ignore the state of the fashion cycle. Chrysler's misreading of the trend in taste caused real trouble for the firm on at least three occasions: with the 1934 Airflow Chrysler and DeSoto, with the unpopular early 1950s designs, and with the 'lean look' models of 1962. Ford's later correct reading of the trend gave the firm the well-publicized triumph of the Mustang introduction. In fact, even a superficial knowledge of the successes and failures of design introduction which dot the history of every major auto maker should long ago have convinced everyone that human behaviour is not subject to the easy manipulation assumed by the created-fashions myth. The acceptance of a fashion is but one aspect of the process of new product acceptance and rests on the same principles of individual and social behaviour.

Fashion, Product Acceptance, and Human Behaviour

Both fashions and fads are, of course, successful new product introductions. The distinction between the two is generally defined on an *ex post facto* basis—on the nature of their acceptance cycle. Fashions are generally thought to have an initially slower rise to popularity, a plateau of continuing popularity lacking in most fads, and a slow, rather than abrupt decline typical of the fad. (See Figures 1*a* and 1*b*.) The acceptance cycle of a fashion is thus considered the same as the accepted theoretical course of the normal product life cycle (Figure 1*a*). Such an empirical after-the-fact basis for distinction, however, deprives any theory of most of its potential utility. It cannot be used for rational market planning. To be useful the theory must distinguish fads from other new products *in advance* on the basis of measurable product attributes, which explain why a market development period might be unnecessary and why acceptance disappears at the very peak of the market. If such an explanation is possible, it should be possible to identify and predict in advance another class of products: a class which requires little or nothing in the way of early market development, but rises in an active growth market from the moment of introduction and then remains popular for long periods. (See Figure 1*c*.) Those who have observed any fashion-oriented market will also recognize the need to explain another related phenomenon with the same theory—the *classic*—the style which is never out of style for its market segment and is rarely the 'rage'.

To be really useful for product planning, a product acceptance theory should be based on known tendencies of individual and social behaviour and encompass in a single model an explanation of:

(1) Why and how any new product gains acceptance, and why about half of the seemingly well-screened and well-researched products fail.[2]

(2) Why some products must pass through a slowly accelerating period of market development of some length before sales catch fire whereas others zoom to early popularity from the start.

(3) Why some products succeed in attainment of a relatively solid niche in the culture, why the popularity of others tends to fluctuate, and why the popularity of fads collapses at their very sales peak.

(4) How and why classics exist in a fashion environment.

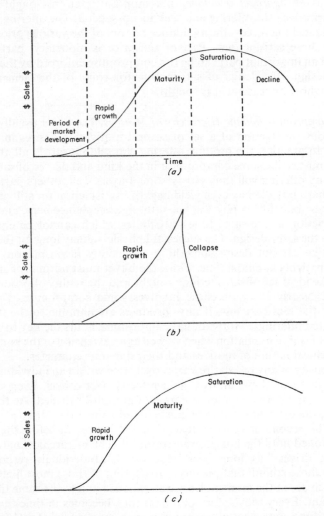

FIG. 1. The three types of product cycles. (a) The theoretical normal life cycle of a fashion or other new product. (b) Usual trajectory of a fad. (c) Apparent life cycles pattern of some new products for which the market seems to be waiting.

453

The behavioural basis for such an explanation starts with the managerial economics view of a product as a compromise bundle of attributes perceived by buyers as an inseparable set of sources of satisfaction and also of some offsetting dissatisfactions for times for a set of desires.[3] To gain the satisfactions, the buyer must pay some price—he must sacrifice some measure of time, money, and/or effort. Whether he moves toward possession of this offering depends on his personal evaluation of the net gain in satisfaction its possession will bring.

Expressed in these terms, an operant psychologist would recognize the purchase as an *approach-avoidance* reaction. Satisfactions sought cause the buyer to approach the offering and seek its possession. The offering, however, includes a repelling force—the avoidance factors of the various prices exacted to obtain those satisfactions. Part of the price is monetary, part is search effort, and an important part can be the compromise enforced by the nature of product design—the denial of satisfaction for some of the elements in the desire-set whose appeasement is sought.

Product Compromise and the Hierarchy of Motives. The buyer usually seeks the simultaneous satisfaction of a set of several motivating desires in making a purchase. In practice, the product offering can seldom satisfy all at the same time and must strike some compromise in the kind and degree of satisfactions offered. Any offering will thus satisfy some buyers well, others partially; and some, perhaps not all, may even yield negative satisfaction for still others. The dress may be bought for physical warmth, figure enhancement, and freedom from restriction at the same time—attributes which cannot be equally well satisfied in the same design. The successful physician may long for the qualities of a prestige car but desire something sufficiently inconspicuous to avoid offending patients at billing time. Thus, the buyer must normally compromise between the ideal set of satisfactions sought and the reality of product design potentials. Nearly every purchase involves some compromise. This is evidenced by the fact that few, if any, products are immune to the inroads of differentiated offerings. Motivational compromise holds the key to an understanding of fashion oscillation when viewed as an extension of the knowledge of the hierarchical nature of motives and their dynamic character.

The intensity of any one desire varies over time within an individual, and, at any given moment, some motives gain priority over others. Even such basic motives as hunger and appetite dominate only until satisfied. As the meal is consumed, the drive to eat is extinguished and some other drive assumes top priority. This second drive was already inherently present before the meal but was not evoked until the hunger was appeased. The hierarchical nature of the motivating drives has long been recognized.[4] Individuals respond most actively to those stimuli that promise satisfaction of those most highly valued drives which are at the moment least well satisfied and at the same time felt to be important. Every satisfactory purchase thus becomes in time the initiator of a search for a somewhat different offering to satisfy newly felt drives. Thus, this continual restructuring of the motivational hierarchy gives the basis for a model explaining fashion oscillation and furnishes a framework for prediction of its new direction:

'The popularity of design attributes in a given utility-bundle will oscillate because no one design can encompass in full measure all of the attributes in the desire-set. The oscillation will tend to be polar, swinging from one extreme to the opposite, because the satisfaction-yield span of any one design will extinguish the very drives which led to its adoption and bring to the fore those drives least well fulfilled by the design.'

Consider the example of the automobile design problem (Figure 2) and the oscillations of popular approval between the large and massive and the compact, relatively economical. The 1955 designs fulfilled all of the drives associ-

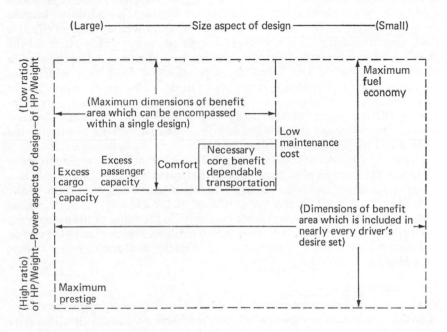

FIG. 2. The automobile design puzzle: how to get as much of what the driver wants in a single design.

ated with massive appearance and power. In developing these designs, the automobile industry had to leave some other drives less well satisfied—for example, low cost of ownership and maintenance and such ease-of-use aspects as parking and roadability. Once most drivers had acquired the highly ornamented mammoths they desired, attention began to focus on the drives whose satisfaction had been neglected, and size became an avoidance factor for many. Buyers became attracted by models offering high gasoline mileage, low physical and temporal depreciation, and ease of parking and handling. The sales of foreign makes which offered such attributes in abundance began a climb, and slowed down only when Detroit developed its own compacts in 1960. But the fickle customer, having a free choice of offerings giving most of what he desired, began to yearn again for the attributes associated with size, and the cycle restarted. By 1965, he was buying 'compact' models almost as large as the 1955 'big' cars.

However, the composition of the desire-set varies so much from one person to another that the explanation needs one further element to account for the completeness of most new-fashion adoption and the rapidity of its spread. That element is furnished by that human drive for social approval—the desire to be 'in the swim'. The result is an almost universal tendency toward over-adoption. Overadoption is painfully apparent with every extreme swing in the feminine fashion silhouette—the bandy-legged adopted mini-skirts which could only reveal physical deficiencies of the wearer. Overadoption became quite obvious in business management when organizations replaced an effective $300-a-month clerk with a $3,000-per-month computer which often did the clerk's job less efficiently. Overadoption has been documented in the studies of rural sociologists who found farmers adopting machinery which was uneconomic for their scale of operation.[5] The desire for social approval thus speeds adoption, but at the price of leading many to overadoption—to adoption of offerings which do not satisfy their desires well. The result is a considerable market segment which quickly develops an avoidance reaction to the fashion and triggers a decline from the peak.

The three principles of product acceptance—inherent purchase compromise, the changing hierarchy of motivation, and the tendency toward overadoption—furnish a necessary and sufficient explanation of the swings of fashion. However, they leave unexplained the existence of the classic—the style whose changes are minimal, but which remains always in the range of the acceptable. No theory of fashion can be adequate which omits an explanation of the classic and its appeal to a minority market which does not conform to major swings of fashion.

The Classic

The changeless, always acceptable classic is found in every recognized area of fashion. A woman can always feel comfortable in a tailored suit with a skirt line close to the knees. In automobiles, designs similar to the postwar Loewy-designed Studebaker still find a ready market around the world. The values placed by buyers on some security issues respond little to the gyrations of the bulk of those listed on the Big Board. Beige and off-white colours always sell well in automobiles and house paints. Such classics occasionally become the reigning fashion, but seldom are they 'the rage'.

What makes a classic? Observation seems to indicate that all classics are midpoint compromises and their buyers either have a special kind of personality or are prospects seeking only a few of the core attributes in the bundle for sale. The classic automobile design is neither starkly spartan not highly ornamented; it is roomy but not gargantuan. The classic colour is not found in the 'hot' red end of the spectrum nor at the icy blue extreme; it is moderately pleasing but not conspicuous. The classic gives some measure of satisfaction to nearly all of the desire-set of drives, and probably does so at the expense of complete satisfaction of any drives except those at the core of product's physical functions. The classic buyer, then, has to be a person seeking only the core function attributes (such as convenient transportation in a Volkswagen) or one who recognizes that compromise is necessary in any case and who has chosen a compromise least likely to develop over time. He most certainly must be an individual who does not value highly the satisfaction of the drive for new experience. Such a consumer is a poor prospect for any fad, but may well be an excellent early-market customer for innovations of major functional import which others would be slow to accept, since he feels little need for complete conformity. If so, he is important in the early adoption of those products which are slow to catch on at first. Certainly, the differences in the speed of acceptance of various kinds of offerings is one of the most obvious puzzles of new product introduction which must be explained.

Differences in the Early Acceptance Pattern and Their Explanation

As already indicated, some products follow the standard conceptual curve of the product life cycle, but others, particularly fads, leap-frog the early market development phase of this curve with a rocket-like ascent to popularity. Clearly, the marketing mix must differ with the kind of sales acceleration likely to be experienced. Also, different levels of resource commitment are needed for the product which undergoes an extended period of slowly developing sales and those which attain their market potential early. When black-and-white television became a commercial reality, even fly-by-night electronic firms could get a profitable market share, and those who knew how to build on their early success could and did carve out a permanent market niche. Waiting out the ten long years until colour television sales hit the growth phase, however, required the resources of an RCA.

A great many pairs of seeming anomalies can be cited from every kind of marketing operation. Soluble coffee existed for over a generation before World War II; and even when wartime developments brought its price down, six years were needed to develop the market potential. Frozen orange juice, another wartime beneficiary, rose from scratch to peak market in three years, as fast as facilities could be developed. The astonishing benefits of hybrid corn yields were not sufficient to get more than 6% of the farmers interested during the first six years on the market, although little else is planted today. However, another farm improvement—2-4-D and related insecticides were so avidly sought by farmers upon their release after the war that they became a real threat to health. Some textbooks take years to gain acceptance of the approach championed, yet Samuelson's *Economics* rose to quick dominance of the elementary course in colleges.

The anomaly disappears when we examine the value an adopter perceives in any product new or otherwise. To the purchaser, a product is only one element in the use-system which is the real source of the satisfaction of the desire-set. Products deliver their potential satisfactions only in the context of some established set of procedural habits organized around their use. Seed corn yields the sought-after crop only when procured, planted, cultivated, harvested and stored in a carefully planned and well-learned system of habitual practices. Television yields entertainment only when manipulated and viewed in another set of habit patterns.

457

The development of most habit patterns is a painful—or at least annoying—process for most of us. The extinction of one habit system leading to a satisfactory result and its replacement of another is even more so, as anyone who has gone from a three-speed manual automobile shift to a four-speed can testify. The degree to which a product offering involves habit pattern relearning will thus slow down its adoption. Conversely, innovative products which can simply replace old ones using the same set of procedures, or the same set simplified, should gain ready acceptance.

Good examples of products fitting neatly into existing procedures are the new insecticides, black-and-white television, and frozen orange juice. The new insecticides were applied by the same spray methods, with a similar timing, as the ones they displaced. They simply delivered a noticeably higher level of satisfaction—greater kill over a broader spectrum of pests. Black-and-white television entertained in the same way the movies did, by sitting and viewing a picture, but it avoided many nuisance steps—additional cost for every show, problems of travel, parking and getting tickets, and finding a desired seat position. Black-and-white television, too, simply delivered more value in the same system. (Eventually, of course, adoption of TV changed family living patterns. But such pattern changes were not a pre-condition for adoption.) Frozen orange juice fitted into kitchens long used to canned goods; the fact that it was frozen fitted into established perceptions of frozen foods being the equivalents of fresh ones. These products required no substantial learning of new habits or relearning of old. By contrast, hybrid seed corn, colour television, and instant coffee all involved learning of some sort.

Any new offering can pose the problem of one or more of three kinds of learning:

(1) Learning of a new sequence of motor habits (as in changing over from a three-speed shift to a four-speed, or from a wringer to an automatic washer);

(2) Learning to perceive new benefits as valuable and thus worth paying for (as in learning to appreciate the cornering qualities offered by the small sports car);

(3) Learning to perceive one's role in the use of the product as of less importance (as in the acceptance of an automatic transmission).

The acceptance of the use of hybrid seed required the learning of both a new sequential element and of the perception of relative value. Before its adoption, the farmer usually saved some of the better quality of the previous year's crop and replanted it. The use of hybrid seed meant the complete disposal of the crop and the repurchase of seed each year. (The farm journals of the period ran many an article warning farmers not to replant seed from hybrid crops.) Moreover, the seed he bought cost several times as much per bushel as the farmer received for the crop he sold. This resulted in a real value-perception problem.

The acceptance of colour television in 1955 required no change in motor or other use-habits, but did involve a substantial change in value perception. It required seeing that the mere addition of colour to the picture was worth hundreds of dollars—at a time when Technicolor movies had never achieved use in more than a minority of films. Colour also deprived the viewer of the satisfaction of closure—the supplying of missing details himself. Psychologically, successful closure heightened the satisfaction gained, and has probably always been an element of successful entertainment. The double-meaning joke get its whole point from the use of closure.

Soluble coffee certainly simplified the brewing process and required little in the way of motor learning. Once wartime experience had reduced its cost, any problem disappeared. But soluble coffee downgraded the home-maker's role; it required her to see her role in relation to mealmaking as less important. Coffee brewing is susceptible to individual skill, and many housewives pride themselves on their coffee. Acceptance of soluble coffee required admission that the housewife's kitchen role was less vital to family happiness than it had been. Is it any coincidence that the use of soluble increased with the growing acceptance of the housewife as a major contributor to the family's *outside* income?

The overnight successes of radically new products like Samuelson's *Economics* are explainable as examples of products filling a missing link in an already developed system. They are products for which the market has been waiting. Economists began to pay increasing attention to the macro aspect of economic theory in the early 1930s. By 1946, when Samuelson's first edition was published, many economists were orienting their courses entirely in this direction. Since no satisfactory texts were available, a well-done text, as Samuelson's was, could hardly help but succeed. Rubber tractor tyres provide a similar example. Mechanized farming became well established on the better-managed farms, but the steel-tyred tractors compacted the soil, could not be run over paved roads, and did not always furnish the desired traction. Once a satisfactory tyre was developed, the steel-wheeled tractor disappeared overnight. The supermarket was also a missing link in a developing food shopping and storing system. The automobile had widened the shopping range of the family; the need to park it called for a single stop. In addition, ownership of mechanical refrigerators was wide enough to eliminate the daily shopping trip. All that was needed was the foresight of a few independent entrepreneurs. Even though such missing link products do require learning of elements not required by the products they displace, the learning process is complete by the time of their introduction.

The rate of early-adoption acceleration is thus seen as contingent on the degree of learning required to accept and properly use any new offering. Both learning-content and attribute-compromise analyses are feasible, rendering the proposed model of product adoption speed and of fashion fluctuation subject to test and confirmation.

The Evidence of Testability

A model is valid if it has utility for prediction. The main recommendation for the proposed model is its testability—parts of it rather easily—and the fact that it is in harmony with some known successful proprietary unpublished private research predictions. Three kinds of evidence as to its validity can be cited:

(1) Such known proprietary research clearly demonstrates that taste and

fashion are predictable ahead of promotion and sales, and even in advance of design, on the basis of analysis of consumer reaction.

(2) It is possible to cite at least a few examples of situations in which a simple learning-content analysis would have greatly improved otherwise extensive research on product acceptance.

(3) Some limited observation and research has proved successful in prediction of a fashion cycle.

Sensing the Trend in Taste Ahead of Introduction. A sizable body of proprietary research has established the fact that rather simple, carefully administered checks of consumer reaction can reveal in advance which of an equally-promoted group of designs will succeed and which will fail. Dilman M. K. Smith[6] has sketched some of the results of successful Opinion Research studies in this area, some going back over three decades. The author of this article himself was able to develop a very simple ahead-of-the-season measure of relative demand in a line of dresses over 20 years ago—a test still in routine use by the employer for whom he developed it. A research director for a maker of permanent waves was able to alert his firm to a change in hair style tastes months before the change began to show up in beauty parlours and thus permitted a successful effort to buttress the firm's market position. Even more relevant was an unpublished Opinion Research triumph: the development of a new, instantly successful rug weave based on a revelation of an unsatisfactory consumer compromise. When research showed that housewives liked the texture of velvet rugs but were repelled by such a weave's tendency to show tracks, the firm advised a client to find a velvet weave which was trackless. After considerable prodding, designers came up with the sculptured wilton, which took off on a typical fast growth curve when introduced.

Unfortunately, understanding of consumer product acceptance has not gained much from this private research, since only fragments of a minor part could land in footnotable publications. The rest remains hidden in the files of those who pay for it and confined to conversations among a few research analysts. Confirmation of the learning content aspect of the proposed model, fortunately, does not always require access to any confidential data.

Learning Content and Prediction. The author has shown at length[7] elsewhere that use-systems learning requirements can be determined easily by means of simple comparison of flow diagrams—one diagram for the current means of obtaining the satisfaction desired and one for the system which would be the setting for use of the new product. Such a comparison quickly reveals both the advantages and the avoidance factors involved in adoption of the new. One need read only the preparation instructions on a pouch of dehydrated soup to discover why this thoroughly researched product was a market failure which cost Campbell's alone some $10,000,000 in unsuccessful promotion,[8] according to news stories. The flow diagrams reveal a tremendous time-and-effort price disadvantage for the dehydrated product relative to the canned concentrate. It should have been clear that the housewife would not pay such a price for the kinds of satisfactions expected from soup in the American diet pattern. It may well be much of the failure of carefully investigated new products traces

460

to the failure to investigate the learning-content requirements and the preparation-time price.

Perceptual-learning and value-learning requirements do not yield to as simple an analytical device as the flow chart, of course, but they are certainly possible to discover with currently available research techniques. And this singular aspect of the proposed model is manifestly testable against past history. Prediction of fashion oscillations is not so clearly testable against the past.

Checking Fashion Oscillation Predictability. Almost any hypothetical model must start with some classification and observation of past experience. But any model involving as many complex factors as the one proposed for fashion oscillation cannot be safely checked against history alone. This is true particularly when few observations from that past contain any substantial evidence of the psychological motives that buyers hope to appease with their adoptions. Most such observations have to be limited to studies in the fluctuations among physically measurable attributes which may or may not be the relevant items involved. The result can be a number of plausible but different explanations, each of which can be rationalized as fitting if the classifications and other data are carefully chosen. An acceptable theory must give more than a plausible explanation of past events: it must have pragmatic validity, be capable of predicting the future in some meaningful manner.

In this respect, the author can cite only a single documented successful prediction although he has attempted several others, unpublished, which have borne or are bearing fruit. As noted earlier, the author, writing in 1961 (for publication in 1964), traced the history of the swings in research fashion and noted that the current wave was at the peak of the recurrent mathematical emphasis. A swing to behavioural models and techniques was predicted. At the time of the analysis, the *Business Periodicals Index*[9] listed only two articles under 'Innovation', neither of them in marketing journals and neither of them on research into the process. Concurrently, one of the marketing publications turned down Lionberger's *Adoption of New Ideas and Practices* as 'not germane to the interests of' its readers. By 1965, both the Detroit and New York chapters of the AMA were holding New Products conferences, and 'diffusion theory' is now the current shibboleth.

One such prediction success, or any number of them, does not constitute the final test of validity, however. A sound theory in any field must dig beneath any coincidence between its predictions and subsequent events to explain why the events can be expected to occur in the manner observed. A sound theory must have construct validity, be based on behavioural constructs which themselves are capable of test and confirmation or modification. The theory offered above is just such a theory. It is possible to test it pragmatically— to make predictions as to the next direction of a fashion swing or as to the speed of adoption of a projected new product and then to observe the objective events. But this theory also postulates a specific behavioural mechanism as responsible for the observed patterns, a mechanism fairly well established in behavioural knowledge and subject to test itself. What is being proposed is thus no mere attempt to invent plausible behavioural labels to explain known observations. Rather, it starts from a series of established behavioural con-

461

structs derived independently of the kind of data to which they are being applied, and attempts to see if their implications fit the phenomena of fashion and product acceptance. This theory thus offers a framework for research into product acceptance in general as well as formulating an improvement for the practical problem of new product screening and testing.

Conclusion

Not only fashion, but product acceptance in general is far more predictable than is generally thought, providing we make full use of the basic concepts of a product as a compromise bundle of desire attributes, demand as a desire set based on social conditioning, and motives as existing in a dynamic hierarchy and constantly restructured in the very process of their appeasement. These concepts alone are adequate to explain both the existence of a constant oscillation in fashions and the directions these oscillations take. Fads are explainable within the framework of this model as products which satisfy solely a single utility-drive for new experience; thus they pose neither a learning requirement nor have much value once their newness has gone. The speed of adoption of products of any kind depends on the amount of required learning of three types: use-systems learning, value perception learning, and role-perception learning. All are researchable and describable in objective terms in advance.

References

1. Chester R. Wasson, *The Strategy of Marketing Research* (N.Y., Appleton-Century-Crofts, 1964), pp. 67–77.
2. *Management of New Products* (Chicago, Booz, Allen & Hamilton, 1960).
3. Edward H. Chamberlin, *Theory of Monopolistic Competition*, 8th edition (Cambridge, Mass., Harvard University Press, 1962), Appendix F, pp. 275–281; Chester R. Wasson, *The Economics of Managerial Decision* (N.Y., Appleton-Century-Crofts, 1965), pp. 55–87; and Chester R. Wasson, Frederick D. Sturdivant, and David McConaughy, *Competition and Human Behaviour* (N.Y., Appleton-Century-Crofts, 1968), pp. 4–25.
4. A. H. Maslow, 'A Dynamic Theory of Human Motivation', *Psychological Review*, vol. 50 (March, 1963), pp. 370–396.
5. Everett Rogers, *The Diffusion of Innovations* (N.Y., The Free Press, 1962), pp. 142–145.
6. Dilman M. K. Smith, *How to Avoid Mistakes When Introducing New Products* (N.Y., Vantage Press, 1964).
7. Wasson, Sturdivant and McConaughy, op. cit., pp. 83–91.
8. 'Campbell's Drops Red Kettle Line', *Advertising Age* (29 August 1966), p. 3.
9. *Business Periodicals Index* (N.Y., The H. W. Wilson Co., July 1961-June 1962), p. 378.

Chapter 29

THE IDENTITY OF WOMEN'S CLOTHING FASHION OPINION LEADERS*
by John O. Summers

This article analyses the characteristics of women's clothing fashion opinion leaders. The data suggest that substantial differences exist between fashion opinion leaders and non-leaders on a wide variety of demographic, sociological, attitudinal, communication, and fashion involvement measures.

Introduction

Central to the study of interpersonal communication has been the concept of opinion leadership, which proposes that some individuals exert a disproportionate amount of influence on the behaviour of others in some given topic area. A wide range of terms has been used to designate these individuals, including 'opinion leader' and 'influential'.

The research presented here represents an analysis of parts of an adoption and diffusion behaviour survey among female homemakers conducted in Marion County (Indianapolis), Indiana, in Spring 1967. The basic objective here is to identify and profile women's clothing fashion opinion leaders.

Characteristics of Opinion Leaders

The dimensions investigated in studies focusing on the identity of the opinion leader can be classified into three basic categories of characteristics: demographic, social and attitudinal, and topic-oriented.

The demographic characteristics of opinion leaders appear to be dependent on the topic context of interest.[1, 4, 7, 9, 10, 12, 20, 22, 29, 31] For example, status, income, and education have been positively associated with opinion leadership in studies such as those on community affairs, although they are unimportant in some other contexts. Furthermore, young women seem to dominate in fashion and movie-going, large family wives in marketing, older individuals in community affairs, and in some other areas age is not a factor.

Studies on social participation or gregariousness have shown a strong positive association with opinion leadership across topic contexts.[1, 12, 21] 'Cosmopoliteness' has been positively related to opinion leadership for decision areas where information from outside the immediate environment

* From the *Journal of Marketing Research*, vol. 1.7 (American Marketing Association, May 1970).

appears to be important.[12, 22, 25, 29] Research on interpersonal communication has largely ignored personality and attitudinal characteristics. However, of approximately 30 personality measures included in two studies of interest, only 'leadership' was found to be related to opinion leadership.[27, 31]

Interpersonal influence studies have consistently found interest, media exposure, and competence to be positively associated with opinion leadership.[1, 5, 9, 12, 19, 22, 26, 31] Opinion leaders' innovativeness has been shown to be a function of the group's norm: where it favours innovativeness, the relationship will tend to be positive.[5, 9, 13, 16, 22, 23, 24, 32]

Research Methodology

The research instruments for this survey of new product adoption behaviour included a personal interview questionnaire and four self-administered questionnaires. The random sample of 1,000 homemakers was based on a clustering design of 100 clusters of 10. Replacements for non-participating respondents were specified to be the female homemaker living next door to the primary respondent. The sampling procedure resulted in an overall response rate of 50 per cent for both primary and replacement respondents for the seven to nine-hour interviewing experience. For a discussion of the project, see Ref. 16.

The measure of opinion leadership used in this project was a modification of the six question self-designating method used by Rogers[28]:

OPINION LEADERSHIP SCALE

1. In general do you like to talk about _____ with your friends?
   Yes_____ 1   No_____ 2

2. Would you say you give *very little information, an average amount of information,* or *a great deal of information* about _____ to your friends?
   You give very little information   _____ 1
   You give an average amount of information   _____ 2
   You give a great deal of information   _____ 3

3. During the *past six months,* have *you told anyone about* some _____?
   Yes_____ 1   No_____ 2

4. Compared with *your circle of friends,* are *you less likely, about as likely,* or *more likely* to be asked for advice about_____?
   Less likely to be asked   _____ 1
   About as likely to be asked   _____ 2
   More likely to be asked   _____ 3

5. If you and your friends were to discuss _____, what part would *you* be most likely to play? Would you *mainly listen* to your friends' ideas or would *you try to convince them* of your ideas?
   You mainly listen to your friends' ideas   _____ 1
   You try to convince them of your ideas   _____ 2

6. Which of these happens more often? Do *you tell your friends* about some _____, or do *they tell you* about some _____?
   You tell them about some _____ _____ 1
   They tell you about some _____ _____ 2

7. Do you have the feeling that you are generally regarded by your friends and neighbours as a good source of advice about _____?
   Yes_____ 1   No_____ 2

The use of the self-designating method was necessitated by the fact that the project involved a random sample of 1,000 housewives in a county which contains over 200,000 households. Rogers' method was used because of evidence of its validity, reliability, and intuitive appeal.

Operationally, the characteristics under investigation may be categorized into five sets of variables: demographic and sociological variables, personality and attitudinal factors, mass media exposure, and involvement in women's clothing fashions.

A brief description of the variables included in each variable set is included in the Appendix.

The personality inventory questions, which involved two separate tests, were the product of previous research by Borgatta.[2,3] Some questions were modified slightly to make responses easier for the homemakers. Two attitudes and values tests were developed to construct attitudinal measures not included in standard personality tests, which might prove valuable in predicting opinion leadership and innovativeness. All of the items contained in the four tests involved a five-interval scale ranging from 'strongly disagree' to 'strongly agree'. Each test was factor analysed separately using principal components solution and orthogonal rotation with the varimax criterion.

Analysis

The use of cross classification provided an effective base for comparing the research findings of this project with those of other opinion leadership studies. The division of the opinion leadership scores into dichotomous categories was designed to approximate the percentage classified as fashion leaders by Katz and Lazarsfeld. The upper 28 per cent of the respondents were classified as opinion leaders compared with 23 per cent by Katz and Lazarsfeld, Ref. 14, p. 333.

The results are presented by variable set. The data are arranged in concentrations of opinion leaders, rather than direct leader v. non-leader comparisons. The higher concentrations of opinion leaders are often interpreted in terms of the differential characteristics of opinion leaders v. non-leaders (i.e., if opinion leaders were more concentrated in the younger age groups, they would be younger as a group than non-leaders).

Demographic Characteristics. Opinion leaders were found to be more highly concentrated among those segments of the samples which: (1) were younger, (2) had more education, (3) had higher incomes, and (4) had higher occupational status (Table 1). These findings are consistent with previous research by Katz and Lazarsfeld,[12] who found concentrations of transmitters among young unmarrieds, small-family wives, and the middle and upper social status groups, probably because of greater fashion interest and broader social contacts of these groups. However, a substantial number of opinion leaders exists at all levels of age, education, income, and occupational status, suggesting that although fashion leadership is more concentrated in certain demographic categories, it remains a widespread trait.

Sociological Characteristics. Sociological characteristics provide an effective

TABLE 1 *Concentration of Women's Clothing Fashion Opinion Leaders by Selected Demographic Characteristics*

Characteristics	Percentage concentrations of opinion leaders	Base	Level of significance
Age			
29 years and under	38*	229	$p < 0.001$†
30–39 years	31	221	
40–50 years	26	233	
50 years and over	21	293	
Education			
Less than a high school graduate	19	265	$p < 0.001$
High school graduate	28	384	
One or more years of college	36	328	
Income			
$5,999/year or less	18	213	$p < 0.001$
$6,000-$8,999/year	27	291	
$9,000-$11,999/year	34	252	
$12,000/year or more	33	220	
Occupational status (*Bureau of Census rating*)			
Low	22	400	$p < 0.001$
Medium	31	401	
High	35	176	

* Read: 38 % of the 229 respondents who were 29 years or younger were opinion leaders.
† The differences were statistically significant at the 0·001 level based on χ^2 analysis.

means of locating concentrations of women's clothing fashion opinion leaders (Table 2). Physical mobility, a measure of 'cosmopoliteness' characteristic of leaders in a number of topic areas, may allow the individual greater opportunity for exposure to new and different fashion ideas, which may in turn provide fashion information for social conversation. Social communications, affiliations with organizations, and participation in social activities represent three dimensions of gregariousness, which promotes social interaction and which has been linked with opinion leadership in all topic contexts in previous research findings. Organizational and social activities, two particularly strong determinants of opinion leadership in women's clothing fashions, can promote leadership in this category in at least three ways:

(1) they may require fashion involvement:
(2) they may create opportunities for visual gathering of fashion information relevant to social conversations concerning fashion; and
(3) they may involve social settings appropriate for transmitting fashion information.

Personality, Attitudes and Values Factors. As a group, the attitudes and values factors were more powerful predictors than the personality factors. Not only were a higher percentage of these variables statistically significant (78 per cent v. 50 per cent), but the differences in concentrations were also

466

TABLE 2 *Concentration of Women's Clothing Fashion Opinion Leaders by Sociological Characteristics*

Sociological characteristic	Percentage concentrations of opinion leaders			Level of significance
	Low	Medium	High	
1. Physical mobility	24*	28	34	$p < 0.01$†
Base	(383)	(312)	(282)	
2. Social communication	21	32	33	$p < 0.01$
Base	(330)	(432)	(214)	
3. Organizational membership	22	29	37	$p < 0.001$
Base	(361)	(384)	(232)	
4. Organizational participation	23	29	41	$p < 0.001$
Base	(461)	(339)	(177)	
5. Organizational offices held	27	29	39	$p < 0.05$
Base	(773)	(115)	(89)	
6. Organizational affiliations	23	26	38	$p < 0.001$
Base	(357)	(346)	(273)	
7. Participation in formal social activities	19	27	42	$p < 0.001$
Base	(397)	(305)	(275)	
8. Participation in informal social activities	19	28	40	$p < 0.001$
Base	(330)	(398)	(249)	
9. Participation in sporting activities	22	29	35	$p < 0.01$
Base	(360)	(286)	(330)	
10. Total social activity participation	16	29	42	$p < 0.001$
Base	(345)	(339)	(293)	

* Read: 24% of the 383 respondents scoring low on physical mobility were opinion leaders.

† The differences were statistically significant at the 0.01 level based on χ^2 analysis.

substantially greater (Table 3), suggesting the potential rewards for developing attitudinal inventories tailored to consumer behaviour research. Non-leadership was the one personality factor that was particularly predictive of opinion leadership in fashion. Opinion leaders were found in a substantially greater concentration (40 per cent) among respondents scoring low on non-leadership than among those scoring high on this factor (16 per cent). However, the two items loading highest on this factor were:

(1) I do not find it easy to speak publicly.
(2) I seem to be shy in many situations when I should really be speaking up.

The greater assertiveness and emotional stability of fashion opinion leaders may aid them in speaking out on topics in which they feel competent and in commanding respect for their ideas. Their self-perception as more likeable and less depressive may encourage their active participation in social conversations. The attitude and value 'non-leadership' factor, which was *not* composed of questions relating to 'speaking', produced results almost identical to its personality factor counterpart. This underlines the importance of the need to direct others in determining opinion leadership.

The 'competitive-exhibitionism' factor may be a particularly strong corre-

TABLE 3 *Concentration of Women's Clothing Fashion Opinion Leaders by Personality and Attitudes and Values Factors*

Personality inventory factor	Percentage concentrations of opinion leaders			Level of significance
	Low	Medium	High	
1. Responsible	25*	30	30	Not significant† (p > 0·05)
Base	(308)	(295)	(373)	
2. Emotionally stable	24	27	33	p < 0·05
Base	(317)	(298)	(361)	
3. Assertive	26	23	37	p < 0·001
Base	(330)	(326)	(319)	
4. Likeable	22	30	32	p < 0·01
Base	(320)	(330)	(326)	
5. Depressive/self deprecating	35	26	23	p < 0·001
Base	(345)	(331)	(300)	
6. Impulsive	28	29	27	Not significant (p > 0·05)
Base	(305)	(333)	(338)	
7. Non-leadership	40	30	16	p < 0·001
Base	(312)	(323)	(341)	
8. Self-control	28	32	25	Not significant (p < 0·05)
Base	(331)	(339)	(306)	
9. Anti-social	28	26	32	Not significant (p > 0·05)
Base	(324)	(364)	(288)	
10. Non-intellectual	30	27	28	Not significant (p > 0·05)
Base	(365)	(310)	(310)	

Attitudes and values factors	Percentage concentrations of opinion leader			Level of Significance
	Low	Medium	High	
1. Competitive-exhibitionism	17	26	42	p < 0·001
Base	(339)	(321)	(316)	
2. Negative attitudes toward risk and change	35	28	21	p < 0·001
Base	(328)	(343)	(305)	
3. Progressive-attention seekers	20	30	35	p < 0·001
Base	(334)	(302)	(340)	
4. Shyness and personal uncertainty	35	28	21	p < 0·001
Base	(324)	(339)	(313)	
5. Local gregariousness	19	29	37	p < 0·001
Base	(345)	(289)	(342)	
6. Self-confidence	20	27	38	p < 0·001
Base	(319)	(349)	(308)	
7. Non-leadership	42	23	19	p < 0·001
Base	(344)	(308)	(323)	
8. Dissatisfied/non-confident	27	30	27	Not significant (p > 0·05)
Base	(317)	(352)	(307)	
9. Active	25	30	30	Not significant (p > 0·05)
Base	(310)	(322)	(344)	

* Read: 25% of the 308 respondents scoring low on the factor 'responsible' were opinion leaders.
† The differences were not statistically significant at the 0·05 level based on χ^2 analysis.

TABLE 4 *Concentration of Women's Clothing Fashion Opinion Leaders by Mass Media Exposure*

Media exposure	Percentage that rarely or‡ never reads	Percentage concentrations of opinion leaders			Level of significance
		Low	Medium	High	
1. Radio listening	—	28*	26	31	Not significant†
Base		(392)	(331)	(254)	(p > 0·05)
2. Television watching	—	25	28	30	Not isgnificant
Base		(105)	(552)	(320)	(p > 0·05)
3. Book readership	—	24	30	30	Not significant
Base		(325)	(254)	(398)	(p > 0·05)
4. General interest magazine, mass appeal readership	20	27	34	29	p < 0·05
Base	(135)	(366)	(257)	(218)	
5. General interest magazine, intellectual appeal, readership	26	38	33	32	Not significant
Base	(731)	(61)	(72)	(113)	(p > 0·05)
6. News magazine readership	25	34	30	39	p < 0·05
Base	(644)	(129)	(105)	(98)	
7. Home magazine readership	20	25	35	36	p < 0·001
Base	(201)	(362)	(233)	(179)	
8. Women's magazine readership	18	31	25	36	p < 0·001
Base	(224)	(259)	(203)	(295)	
9. Women's fashion magazine readership	20	40	53	63	p < 0·001
Base	(661)	(212)	(74)	(30)	
10. Romance magazine readership	28	25	24	34	Not significant
Base	(752)	(92)	(66)	(67)	(p > 0·05)
11. Total magazine readership	—	21	26	37	p < 0·001
Base		(300)	(329)	(348)	

* Read: 28% of the 392 respondents scoring 'low' on radio listening were opinion leaders.
† The differences were *not* significant at the 0·05 level based on χ² analysis.
‡ This column only applies to specific magazine groupings.

late of opinion leadership in the area of fashion because the concept of fashion involves display or exhibition. Also, the act of influencing others, independent of the topic context, may be considered competitive and exhibitionistic. Self-confidence also may be a characteristic of opinion leadership in all topic contexts and not just in fashion; it may be that in order to advise others an individual must first have confidence in himself and his ideas. That opinion leaders scored higher on the 'local gregariousness' factor than non-opinion leaders provides further support for similar findings reported in the socio-logical and social activities sections. Opinion leaders must be involved in social interaction to function.

Tendencies toward being progressive, outgoing (less shy), and susceptible to change may render fashion opinion leaders more 'interesting' conversation-alists, which may provide them with larger and more attentive 'audiences' for fashion information. As a group, the attitudes and values factors were par-ticularly effective in locating fashion opinion leaders. Many of these factors represent new dimensions of analysis in opinion leadership and appear to be applicable to a wide variety of topic contexts, since most appear to have little direct connection with the area of fashion.

Media Exposure. Radio listening, television viewing, and book readership had no apparent effect in determining opinion leadership in women's clothing fashions, while total magazine readership was strongly related to this trait. However, radio, television, and books read for pleasure are media which are largely entertainment and not information-oriented. Furthermore, as broad media categories they are neither selective in their content nor in the audiences they attract. Women's fashion magazines represented the one category in which opinion leaders were dramatically more concentrated in the highest-exposed group, supporting previous research in which opinion leaders tended to be more exposed to mass media in general and substantially more to media specializing in their area of influence. Following this theme, readership of home and women's (general interest) magazines, which have substantial fashion con-tent on both clothing and home furnishings, were strongly positively associated with opinion leadership in women's clothing fashions.

However, approximately half, 132 (20 per cent of 661) of 275, of the opinion leaders rarely or never read any women's fashion magazines, and there were substantial numbers of opinion leaders who scored 'low' on home and women's (general interest) magazine readership, demonstrating that no single medium is sufficient to reach this group.

Fashion Involvement. Involvement in women's clothing fashion represents the strongest of the five variable sets in determining opinion leadership. Results of opinion leadership versus interest, venturesomeness, knowledge, and receiving fashion information from friends demonstrate the opinion leaders' greater involvement in their area of influence (Table 5).

Opinion leaders perceived themselves as much more interested in women's clothing fashion than non-leaders, suggesting that interest is a primary stimu-lus for social conversation in the fashion context.

Opinion leaders were more concentrated among those who 'enjoyed testing

470

TABLE 5 *Concentration of Women's Clothing Fashion Opinion Leaders by Selected Fashion Involvement Variables*

Fashion interest	Percentage concentrations of opinion leaders	Base	Level of significance
Which ONE of these statements best describes your reactions to changing fashions in women's clothes?			
I read the fashion news regularly and try to keep my wardrobe up to date with the fashion trends.	63*	56	$p < 0.001$†
I keep up to date on all fashion changes although I don't always attempt to dress according to these changes.	36	557	
I check to see what is currently fashionable only when I need to buy some new clothes.	18	116	
I don't pay much attention to fashion trends unless a major changes takes place.	9	202	
I am not at all interested in fashion trends.	4	45	
Venturesomeness in women's clothing fashions			
I enjoy testing and experimenting with new women's clothing fashions just out.	76	76	$p < 0.001$
I prefer to wait until the new women's clothing fashions have been out for a while and see if they are going to be popular before I buy them.	29	292	
I prefer to buy women's clothing fashions that are classic styles, that are always in style, and are well accepted.	22	609	
Perceived knowledge about women's clothing fashions			
Low	14	260	$p < 0.001$
Medium	23	404	
High	46	312	
Receiving information from friends—specific (During the past six months, has anyone told you about some women's clothing fashions?)			
Yes	35	688	$p < 0.001$
No	12	288	

* Read: 63% of the 56 respondents who 'read the fashion news regularly . . .' were opinion leaders.
† The differences were statistically significant at the 0·001 level based on χ^2 analysis.

and experimenting with new clothing fashions just out'. However, venture-someness in women's clothing is not necessary to opinion leadership. Of the 275 respondents designated opinion leaders, 134 (22 per cent of 609) said they "prefer to buy women's clothing fashions that are classic styles, that are always in style, and are well accepted.' When asked to evaluate their knowledge regarding nine specific women's fashions, opinion leaders scored significantly higher (46 per cent) than non-leaders (14 per cent).

Opinion leaders are frequently recipients as well as transmitters of fashion information. Only 35 (12 per cent of 288) of the 275 women's clothing fashion leaders said they had *not* been told about some women's clothing fashion during the last six months. They may imply either that a chain of opinion leaders exists or that interpersonal communication involves more equal roles for the participants than previously supposed.

Implications

The women's clothing fashion opinion leader represents a discrete and significant market segment to the fashion marketer. Based on cross-classification analysis, fashion opinion leaders were differentiated from non-leaders on a variety of demographic, sociological, attitudinal, communication, and fashion involvement measures. Opinion leaders can be integrated into marketing strategy on at least two dimensions:

(1) Fashion opinion leaders represent a significant target market with high sales potential for the fashion marketer;
(2) They represent important change agents in disseminating fashion information during the fashion season.

By the operational definition used in this research, the fashion opinion leader group represented 28·3 per cent of the sample. More importantly, this group has more potential need for fashion products, because of greater participation in all types of social activities which requires a broader and more current fashion wardrobe. The higher income of this group reflects their ability to purchase clothing fashions appropriate for their status and life style.

Women's clothing fashion opinion leaders are also important as a market segment beyond their individual purchase capacity. They are also change agents in the diffusion process, perceiving themselves as more innovative than non-opinion leaders. This role of introducing new fashions is supported by their greater visibility resulting from their more active participation in social activities. Furthermore, they talk more to other people about fashions, which complements and reinforces their visual display of new fashions. They provide additional data concerning current fashion trends and interpret these trends in terms of their immediate social environment.

To effectively integrate this market segment into marketing strategy, the marketer must not only reach these individuals through the mass media but should also tailor the communication message: (1) to persuade opinion leaders, and (2) to be transmittable in interpersonal channels. Although women's fashion magazines represent a particularly effective medium for reaching fashion opinion leaders, no single source can be relied on to reach all of this group. The transmissibility of the message involves the inclusion of a copy theme consistent with the fashion opinion leader's perception of herself, and factual data which can be talked about and is of interest to her social group.

APPENDIX

Individual Variable Sets

Demographic Variables
1. age
2. education
3. income
4. occupational status

Sociological Variables
1. physical mobility (i.e., number living locations, travel, etc.)
2. social communications (via telephone, letters and cards)
3. organization membership
4. organization participation (time spent per month)
5. organization offices held
6. organization affiliations (a summary of membership, participation and offices held)
7. participation in formal social activities (plays, concerts, cocktail parties, etc.)
8. participation in informal social activities (visiting and entertaining friends, coffee klatches, etc.)
9. participation in sporting activities (as a spectator and participant)
10. total social activity participation (formal, informal and sports)

Personality and Attitudinal Factors, Personality Inventory, Borgatta
Test 1:
1. responsible (accepts responsibility, is mature, etc.)
2. emotionally stable (is not nervous or emotional, does not get upset easily, etc.)
3. assertive (is frank and outspoken, wants others to follow, etc.)
4. likeable (is friendly, pleasant, etc.)

Test 2:
1. depressive/self deprecating (often feels blue and sad, moods go up and down, etc.)
2. impulsive (rarely thinks things out, likes to make quick decisions, etc.)
3. non-leadership (doesn't take the lead in groups, doesn't find it easy to speak publicly, etc.)
4. self-control (doesn't get upset easily, has 'self-control,' etc.)
5. anti-social (not nice to people doesn't like, most people are boring, etc.)
6. non-intellectual (doesn't enjoy reading books, doesn't like discussions about serious problems, etc.)

Attitudes and Values Inventory, King and Summers
Test 1:
1. competitive-exhibitionism (likes to be the centre of attention, feels must win in discussions, etc.)

473

2. negative attitudes toward risk and change (likes to do things the old way, doesn't like to take chances, etc.)
3. progressive—attention seeker (likes to do new and interesting things, likes to get people's attention, etc.)
4. shyness and personal uncertainty (likes to keep in the background, feels uncomfortable in social groups, etc.)

Test 2

1. local gregariousness (gets together with friends frequently for coffee, entertains in home, etc.)
2. self-confidence (feels independent, is confident of personal ability, etc.)
3. non-leadership (doesn't like to be considered a leader, almost always goes along with the group, etc.)
4. dissatisfied/non-confident (gets bored quickly, likes to do things differently, etc.)
5. active (likes to do many different things, feels it is important to have activities outside the home, etc.)

Mass Media Exposure

1. radio listening
2. television watching
3. book reading
4. general interest magazine, mass appeal, readership (*Life, Look, Saturday Evening Post*, and *Reader's Digest*)
5. general interest magazine, intellectual appeal, readership (*Atlantic Monthly, National Geographic, New Yorker, Saturday Review*, and *Harper's Review*)
6. news magazine readership (*Business Week, Newsweek, Time*, and *U.S. News and World Report*)
7. home magazine readership (*Better Homes and Gardens, Good Housekeeping, House Beautiful*, and *American Home*)
8. women's magazine readership (*Family Circle, Ladies Home Journal, McCall's, Pagent, Redbook*, and *Women's Day*)
9. women's fashion magazine readership (*Glamour, Harper's Bazaar, Mademoiselle, Vogue*, and *Seventeen*)
10. romance magazine readership (*Modern Romance, Modern Screen, True Confessions*, and *True Story*)
11. total magazine readership (all magazines listed above)

Involvement in Women's Clothing Fashions

1. fashion interest
2. venturesomeness in women's clothing fashions
3. perceived knowledge about women's clothing fashions (scaled knowledge about specific fashions listed)
4. receiving fashion information from friends

References

1. Bernard Berelson, Paul Lazarsfeld, and William McPhee, *Voting: A Study of Opinion Formation in a Presidential Campaign* (Chicago: University of Chicago Press, 1954).

2. Edgar F. Borgatta, 'A Short Test of Personality: The S-ident Form', *Journal of Educational Research*, vol. 58 (July–August 1965), pp. 453–456.
3. Id., 'A Very Short Test of Personality: The Behavioral Self-Rating (BSR) Form', *Psychological Reports*, vol. 14 (February 1964), pp. 275–284.
4. Richard O. Carlson, *Adoption of Educational Innovations* (Eugene, Oregon: The Centre for the Advanced Study of Educational Administration, University of Oregon, 1965).
5. James S. Coleman, Elihu Katz, and Herbert Menzel, 'The Diffusion of an Innovation Among Physicians', *Sociometry*, vol. 20 (December 1957), pp. 253–270.
6. Id., *Medical Innovation: A Diffusion Study* (N.Y., Bobbs-Merrill Company, Inc., 1966).
7. Paul J. Deutschmann and Wayne A. Danielson, 'Diffusion of Knowledge of the Major News Story', *Journalism Quarterly*, vol. 37 (Summer 1960), pp. 345–355.
8. W. J. Dixon, ed., *BMD Biomedical Computer Programs* (Los Angeles; University of California Health Sciences Computing Facility, 1965).
9. Frederick Emery and Oscar Oeser, *Information, Decision and Action: A Study of the Psychological Determinants of Changes in Farming Techniques* (N.Y.; Cambridge University Press, 1958).
10. Frederick C. Fliegel, 'Farm Income and Adoption of Farm Practices', *Rural Sociology*, vol. 22 (June 1957), pp. 159–162.
11. Elihu Katz, 'The Two-Step Flow of Communication: An Up-to-date Report on an Hypothesis', *Public Opinion Quarterly*, vol. 21 (Spring 1957), pp. 61–78.
→ 12. Id., and Paul Lazarsfeld, *Personal Influence* (Glencoe, Ill.: Free Press, 1955).
13. Elihu Katz and Herbert Menzel, *On the Flow of Scientific Information in the Medical Profession* (New York: Columbia University Bureau of Applied Social Research, 1954).
14. Charles W. King and John O. Summers, 'Dynamics of Interpersonal Communication: The Interaction Dyad', in Donald F. Cox, ed., *Risk Taking and Information Handling in Consumer Behaviour* (Boston: Graduate School of Business Administration, Harvard University, 1967).
15. Id., *Interaction Patterns in Interpersonal Communication* (Lafayette, Indiana: Institute for Research in the Behavioural Economic and Management Sciences, Purdue University, 1967).
16. Id., *The New Product Adoption Research Project: A Survey of New Product Adoption Behavior Across A Wide Range of Consumer Products Among Marion County, Indiana Homemakers* (Lafayette, Indiana: Institute for Research in the Behavioral, Economic and Management Sciences, Purdue University, 1967).
17. Id., 'Overlap of Opinion Leadership Across Consumer Product Categories', *Journal of Marketing Research*, vol. 7 (February 1970), pp. 43–50.
18. Id., 'Technology, Innovation and Consumer Decision Making', *Proceedings*, Winter Conference, American Marketing Association (1967), pp. 63–68.
19. Paul F. Lazarsfeld, Bernard Berelson, and Hazel Gaudet, *The People's Choice* (New York: Columbia University Press, 1944).
20. Herbert F. Lionberger, 'Community Prestige and Choice of Sources of Farm Information', *Public Opinion Quarterly*, vol. 23 (Spring 1959), pp. 110–118.
21. Id., 'The Relation of Informal Social Group to the Diffusion of Farm Information in a Northeast Missouri Farm Community', *Rural Sociology*, vol. 19 (September 1954), pp. 233–43.
22. Id., 'Some Characteristics of Farm Operators Sought as Sources of Farm Information in a Missouri Community', *Rural Sociology*, vol. 18 (December 1953), pp. 327–338.
23. C. Paul Marsh and A. Lee Coleman, 'Group Influences and Agricultural Innovations: Some Tentative Findings and Hypotheses', *American Journal of Sociology*, vol. 61 (May 1956), pp. 588–594.
24. Herbert Menzel, 'Innovation, Integration and Marginality: A Survey of Physicians', *American Sociological Review*, vol. 25 (October 1960), pp. 704–713.
25. Robert K. Merton, *Social Theory and Social Structure*, (Glencoe, Ill.: Free Press, 1957).
26. Francesco N. Nicosia, 'Opinion Leadership and the Flow of Communications', *Proceedings*, Winter Conference, American Marketing Association (1964), pp. 324–340.
27. Thomas S. Robertson and James H. Myers, 'Personality Correlates of Opinion Leadership and Innovative Buying Behaviour', *Journal of Marketing Research*, vol. 6 (May 1969), pp. 164–178.

475

28. Everett M. Rogers, 'Characteristics of Agriculture Innovators and Other Adopter Categories', in Wilbur Schramm, (ed.), *Studies of Innovation and of Communication to the Public* (Stanford, Stanford University Press, 1962).
29. Id., *Diffusion of Innovations* (New York; Free Press, 1962).
30. Id., and David G. Cartano, 'Methods of Measuring Opinion Leadership', *Public Opinion Quarterly*, vol. 26 (Autumn 1962), pp. 435–441.
31. Frank A. Stewart, 'A Sociometric Study of Influence in Southtown', *Sociometry*, vol. 10 (February 1947), pp. 11–31.
32. Eugene A. Wilkening, 'Informal Leaders and Innovators in Farm Practices', *Rural Sociology*, vol. 17 (September 1952), pp. 272–275.

Chapter 30

COLOUR TRENDS AND CONSUMER PREFERENCE*
by E. P. Danger

The author has made an intensive study of colour in its many commercial applications. The source of colour trends and their prediction are carefully analysed and recent instances are cited.

The underlying principle behind the techniques of using colour to sell is the application of knowledge about trends of consumer preference to a specific marketing situation. Trends are a reflection of the wants of the majority of people, but no one trend is applicable in all circumstances—which is one reason why it is so important to analyse the market before trying to make use of trends in consumers' preferences.

Trends of consumer preference are primarily of interest in connection with colour for goods used in the home, but at any one time there is usually one colour which is the top seller for virtually all products. The example of lilac was mentioned in Chapter 1 [not reproduced here]. The manufacturer who can join a bandwagon of this kind in its early stages is in a highly advantageous position. However, such a situation does not arise every day, and it may be difficult to identify in the early stages. Generally, trends tend to vary according to type of product and type of market, and it may not be safe to restrict colour choice to a marked trend colour. Remember that colour trends reflect the preferences of the *average* consumer and there will always be some who 'buck' the trend. Their needs must be met as well as the needs of those who like to follow the majority.

It is important to be quite clear what is meant by the term 'colour trends' in the present context and the term can be defined more clearly by using an illustration. If one takes the colour range of an average decorative paint manufacturer it will be found that it usually includes about thirty different shades of the basic hues—that is, red, green, blue, etc. If the sales of these shades in terms of gallonage are fed into a computer it is possible to project demand ahead for any required period but—and this is the point—the process will only project the demand for the actual shades included in the range. It will not indicate whether sales would have been better if other shades had been included, nor will it indicate what new shades should be introduced in the future to secure maximum sales.

* From *Using Colour to Sell* (Gower Press, 1968).

In theory, and assuming sufficiently sophisticated computer techniques, it should be possible to programme the computer to produce this latter information, but the results would be of significance only to the paint manufacturer. They would be no help to the producer of, say, kitchen furniture wanting to know what shades to paint it. Furthermore, the results would not take into account the possible effect of extraneous colour movements on the demand for paint nor the influences that might affect the wants and desires of the public.

In terms of using colour to sell, the manufacturer needs to interpret future demand. While past sales are a useful guide and an essential part of the process, they are not the whole story. In other words, colour trends are an interpretation of the many factors that will influence demand for colours in a specific product area and this involves consideration of a variety of factors.

At any given time there is usually one colour which is a general favourite, but it will be wanted in a number of variations and shades which will differ according to market and product. The trend colour can quite easily be identified from sales records and observation; its popularity will gradually build up to a peak and then decline. The problem is to know how quickly it will decline and what will take its place. A clue to this important information may be found in the sales of shades and variations.

Suppose, for example, that the general favourite is green. It may be found that there is a demand for shades of green on the blue side, rather than on the yellow, and this will be an indication that the trend is moving towards blue. A manufacturer may not have sufficient shades in his own current range to provide this sort of information and therefore has to obtain data from other sources. He also has to obtain information about other movements of colour if he is to retain a competitive advantage by forecasting correctly.

Colour trends move quite slowly and if demand for colour is charted it will be found that the life cycle is about ten years. Thus, the green mentioned above will gradually decline over the next five years and then begin to pick up again, although the demand for green will never disappear entirely. It would be possible to chart a similar course for a specific variation of green, but this would be affected by other, related, trends in favour of bright, pastel or earthy shades. The demand for bright shades in general also has a trend course of its own.

There is usually a broad similarity between the major trends but this is not always the case. In recent times, for example, there has been a strong demand for muted greens in carpets and furnishings, but green of any kind has been virtually unsaleable in hard goods. The situation is different in the United States, where the same colour may be found in virtually all products. Even refrigerators follow suit, and a best-selling shade of recent years has been 'coppertone', which is also the leader in carpets and (literally) kitchen sinks. The American consumer is more conformist than his British counterpart— but this is not to say that the British consumer does not follow trends.

If one looks at demand over a sufficient number of years it would appear that economic and political conditions have some bearing on the demand for bright colours. In times of depression people are apt to choose 'earthy' or muted colours, perhaps because they then tend to buy for the longer term and want things to last. The Second World War was followed by a 'pastel era', probably because pastel shades are gentle and contrast with the severities and shortages of war time. Pastels were followed by a period of 'sludge' shades—a reaction, possibly, against the gentle pastels—and this in turn is being followed by a demand for bright colours. Economic conditions influence demand for colour in another way. When people have plenty of money to spend they go for colour in a big way, and the right colour becomes more important to sales than ever.

The principal feature of modern experience of colour has been the tendency towards brighter colours and to use more colours. This is chiefly due to the influence of the young who have more money to spend than past generations and who are, therefore, able to give rein to their inherent liking for colour and experimentation. A very recent development has been the influence of the teenager on many products which are not necessarily bought by teenagers. Psychedelic colours are a case in point and may be found in the most staid furniture as well as in clothes.

Another present-day tendency which has a good deal of influence on purchasing is the growing tendency to buy for the short term instead of for a lifetime's use. This is another example of rising standards of living and greater security. Young married people will pay more attention to fashion and to emphemeral colours because they know that they can change the product in a comparatively short time and buy something else.

We have not yet adopted planned obsolescence to the same extent as they have in the United States but there is certainly a move in this direction. We are unlikely to follow the United States in everything that they do because we are basically less conformist but it is of interest that colour trends in the United States and here have moved much closer together in recent times. The United States has turned over to bright colours in a big way just as we have and many of the best selling shades in both countries are the same.

Colour Trends

How Trends Start. The main reason why trends arise at all is that people want change. They seldom buy the same colour twice and, using the instance already quoted, every housewife catches a spring fever which drives her to turn the house upside down and buy new curtains or whatever else she can afford. There is another factor at work here: when the average consumer makes a purchase for the first time, price and utility are the main considerations. When a second or replacement purchase is made, appearance becomes the most important consideration and hence colour plays an important part. If the housewife decides to replace her curtains she may or may not have a clear idea what colour she wants for the new ones, but it will certainly be different to the old.

The average consumer is basically fearful of making a decision for herself (or himself) and she will seek guidance from what is going on around her; from what Mrs Jones up the road is doing; from what she sees advertised or recommended in the press; and from various other influences, all of which are cumulative. As Mrs Jones up the road is doing exactly the same thing, they both tend to follow the same path because they are both influenced by the same pressures.

479

This is not to say that every consumer will choose exactly the same thing. Life would be much simpler if they did—although, by the same token, the penalty of failure on the part of the manufacturer would be greater. Some people have a preference for one colour and others have a preference for another, but likes and dislikes tend to move in the same direction. A woman who liked red, for example, would tend to purchase an orange-red rather than a rose-red if the trend was moving that way, but she might not purchase an orange-yellow.

If the manufacturer is to make the maximum use of colour he has to be able to forecast trends in advance. How far in advance depends on his manufacturing time scale. The object is, of course, to ensure that when his products appear on the market they are offered in the colours that the majority of consumers want *at that time.*

There is no point in asking consumers what they are likely to want in six, twelve, or eighteen months' time because they just do not know what pressures are likely to influence them then. Fortunately, it is possible for the manufacturer to forecast with a reasonable degree of success if he takes enough trouble. As a corollary, it should be obvious that, because there *are* trends, the demand for colour will change and the same shades cannot be used for ever. The process is a fairly slow one but the movement is quite definite.

Where Colour Trends Start. Life would be very much easier if it were possible to define this point with accuracy. In practice it is impossible to say that trends start at any one point, and many factors influence public choice.

It is probably true to say that most colour trends start with women's fashions. In *haute couture* it is the practice to promote a number of new colours and shades each year in the hope of stimulating new business. Many of them fall by the wayside, but one or two will appeal to the populace at large and will gradually find their way down to mass markets and consumer products. The art of forecasting trends is to pick up these key colours as they gain momentum.

The reason *why* certain shades 'catch on' is more difficult to pin-point, but generally speaking it is a reflection of that desire for change which has been already mentioned. If a certain area of colour has had a long run, people will grow tired of it and begin to look for something different. There will be a move towards the opposite end of the spectrum, but in practice this will be modified by the fact that it is economically impossible to make an abrupt change.

To illustrate this point it may be useful to take orange as a typical example. At the time of writing (1968), orange has been a trend colour for a considerable period but as it reaches its peak of popularity and begins to decline there will be a tendency to look at its complement, green. However, an abrupt change from orange to green would be difficult for most households. In practice there will be a compromise, and the next trend colour will be somewhere between the two.

There are, of course, other factors which start trends. The discovery of a new or improved dyestuff, for example, may trigger off demand for a new shade which has been impossible to obtain satisfactorily before. There is also an element of 'follow my leader'. A market leader may decide to promote a new shade just for the sake of change, and if it is successful every other manufacturer will follow suit. However, it is unlikely that a new shade will have very much success unless it follows the general direction of public demand because people cannot, or will not, change everything overnight.

When a colour is promoted, in the fashion trade or anywhere else, it tends to be picked up by the women's press and by a few discerning individuals and gradually builds up authority. It will eventually appear in all types of product because the buyer is the same in all cases. If a women sees a colour that she likes in woollen sweaters she will be equally attracted to it in carpets, furnishings and, if the attraction is strong enough, in products that she buys on impulse. Hence demand builds up because the majority of people are conformist.

There is always a tendency to link colour trends and 'fashion' but this can be a little misleading. In one sense of the word, a colour trend *is* a fashion and there is a close connection with fashions in clothing but it would not be true to say that fashions in women's clothing and colour trends in the home are one and the same thing. The essence of women's fashions is a flow of new ideas, but by no means all the shades which appeal to the purchaser of a new dress will appeal to the purchaser of a new carpet for the home.

Should the Product Lead or Follow the Trend?

New trends very often show up first in sales of paint. The reason is that the walls of any room in the home are usually the first thing to be redecorated. A scheme of redecoration will usually start with the walls and be built up gradually from there. When householders decide to redecorate they will usually choose something as different as possible from what they had before. They will study the recommendations of the Press, consult informed opinion, see what the neighbours are doing, take heed of advice from the paint manufacturer, and in the end will probably reach the same conclusions as everyone else.

Having repainted the walls, it is unlikely that they will replace everything else in the room at the same time but eventually the curtains, the furnishings and possibly the carpet will be renewed. The new items will be chosen to match, or contrast with, the walls, and so the trend gathers momentum.

A good-quality carpet will very often be chosen as the basis for a colour scheme and there is a case, therefore, for suggesting that the colours in carpets should be well in advance of trends, particularly as good-quality carpets will be bought by the more sophisticated purchaser. The mass-market carpet will tend to follow along behind. Smaller articles, on the other hand, are not likely to be bought until the colour scheme is well established. Hence demand for colour will follow the trends instead of being in advance of them.

With every product, it is necessary to establish by research and observation whether it is likely to lead fashion or trail along behind it. This is not always an easy question to decide, and in some cases the answer depends on the level of market in which the product is being sold.

Forecasting Trends

Forecasting trends is an art, not a science; it requires experience and the collection of information on a continuing basis. The first essential is as much information as possible about the colour sales of consumer products generally— about the shades which are selling well and those which are not. Such data is not always easy to obtain because surprisingly few firms keep detailed records of colour sales, but any practical information available can be supplemented by the opinions of retailers and by conversation in the shops.

The second essential is a close watch on what is happening in women's fashions. What colours are being promoted, which colours are catching on, which colours are appearing in mass markets, and any clue which may indicate that a particular shade is the beginning of a trend.

A careful study of the more influential women's journals, and particularly those which use good colour illustrations, is very useful, because it indicates what is being recommended—and there is no doubt that women do follow the advice given to them in the Press. Advertisements are also useful pointers to the opinions of other manufacturers. They will usually illustrate their copy with colours which are, or are expected to be, good sellers.

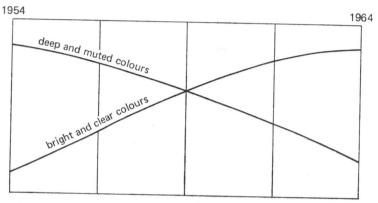

FIG. 1. The overall trend for colours (any and all) in general consumer goods. (Reproduced by courtesy of Faber Birren.)

Special study must be made of the products which are market leaders. Paint has already been mentioned and there are others which can be discovered by experience and from research. Rising sales of specific shades in these key products will be a reliable guide to future colour demand.

A watch must be kept for any other material which has a bearing on colour choice or on the way markets are moving. Surveys of particular markets are very often made by journals and other publications which contain valuable information on the way the ideas of the consumer are moving. A study of the market for travel goods, for instance, indicated that good luggage had become a status symbol among ordinary people going on coach trips overseas, and that purchasers had become very fashion conscious and frequently brought new luggage to match their clothes. This was an immediate indication to the travel goods manufacturer that more trouble with colour would pay dividends and it may have implications in other areas as well.

The more information that can be collected the better. It must be interpreted, analysed and applied to the market conditions of the product which is being considered. Much depends on the skill and experience of the analyst, but the task is made easier by remembering that whatever the product it is the same people who are buying it, and therefore what people do in one direction can also be applied in another direction. If sufficient sources of information are used, the data is self-checking and very reliable. When there is evidence from a number of different sources that a particular shade is becoming popular it is fairly safe to forecast that it will become widely acceptable. Unfortunately it is not easy to check the results in advance. The only really reliable check is a controlled sales test, and this may be justified where a great deal is at stake.

To demonstrate that it is possible to forecast trends with a reasonable degree of accuracy it may be useful to reproduce the charts shown in Figures 1 and 2 which were published in 1964. Readers with access to their own colour sales may care to check whether these prognostications coincide with actual results. They should bear in mind that the charts are in general terms and not related to a specific product.

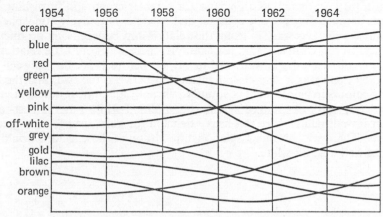

FIG. 2. Trend for twelve colours in home products and consumer goods. (Reproduced by courtesy of Faber Birren.)

Trends in Colours for the Home

In British markets it is possible to identify three major trends. One relates to soft goods such as furnishings, carpets, curtains, and so on, a second to 'hard' goods, and a third to kitchens. These are also minor variations according to the part of the home in which the product is used, and between the top and bottom ends of the market. These underline the necessity for identifying the market.

Colour trends in the home do not follow a straight line and each domestic product has its own peculiarities which must be discovered by careful study and research. There are marked differences between demand for colour in the kitchen, the living room and the bedroom, and between soft goods and hard goods, although there is usually a link between them. But it is not possible to say that there is one trend colour which will be applicable to everything.

In the kitchen, for example, there was a trend in favour of red for many years, followed by blue, and subsequently orange and yellow. The orange/yellow period coincided with a demand for orange in many other goods for the home and particularly in carpets—though no one would purchase an orange refrigerator. White is the accepted colour for refrigerators because people associate it with cleanliness. Yet there was a time when cream was the only acceptable colour, and the change to white coincided with the off-white era in interior decoration; thus there is a link which must be traced and identified.

A similar situation has occurred in household textiles. For years no housewife would consider anything but white pillow cases and sheets. Nowadays gaily coloured sheets and blankets have all but taken over. This has coincided with a demand for more colour generally, and with the trend towards brighter colours in the home. Once again there is a link between the different trends, but some products lead the way while others follow.

Marked colour trends in the home also exercise an influence of their own. For some years there has been a strong demand for off-white walls and sales of white and off-white have formed a very large proportion of total paint sales. This, in turn, triggered off a demand for brighter colours in furnishings and carpets because they provide contrast and create a more lively atmosphere.

Some care is necessary in using the relationship between one product and another. In the United States, for example, there was very little relationship between colour choice in walls and in carpets before 1950. But between then and 1960 there was a very close relationship between the two, and the best-selling colours in paint would be found in virtually all home products. Latterly the relationship has changed again, and while off-white was the best-selling colour in wall paints there was heavy demand for gold, orange, and green in carpets. There was no direct relationship, although these shades would harmonize well with off-white.

Chapter 31

PRODUCT STRATEGY AND MANAGEMENT IN BRITISH TEXTILE INDUSTRIES

by Saddik Saddik and Gordon Wills

This empirical examination of product management practice in three sectors of the British textile industry emphasizes the need for a more cogent approach to the problems. The general pattern of manufacturer reaction in the face of fashion changes is to avoid the problems rather than face up to them.

Marketing studies have continually manifest a tendency towards normative conceptual statements about areas of vital concern to business.[1] The price paid is a decreasing technological validity of much that is written in textbooks on the subject. Perhaps the most recidivistic area has been 'product strategy and management' which undeniably lies at the heart of marketing's claim to a major voice in corporate planning activity. The product is normally the company's sole revenue generator and attention to its health can readily be seen as fundamental to successful operations.[2]

Such recidivism is scarcely alleviated by the continual repetition of 'current best practice' in marketing which almost invariably means the way a few of the more public-relations conscious, untypically large businesses, in fast-moving consumer goods industries, set about developing product strategies and undertaking their management. Such firms undergo a process of continuous innovation, and have evolved techniques of venture analysis,[3] relying on new enterprise divisions or task forces to sidestep the present/future management dichotomy which is ever present in large/medium and small concerns. Bayesian decision theory, and even discounted cash flow, are unheard of and certainly unused in such organizations.[4] The product strategy and management problem is seldom faced because managements are absorbed with problems of their present operations.

Blakey and McGuire,[5] in a pilot study of innovation and organization structures in the wool textile industry found there a striking lack of innovation of any form, and new product introduction the exception rather than the rule. Most product changes introduced were classifiable as 'alterations to existing lines'. Rainie[6] has suggested that the pattern, or as he termed it 'the basic handicap', is an inability to shake off the attitudes of a craft-based family business, and to develop or acquire the management organization and technique of a progressive industrial organization'.

Within the engineering industries as whole (we shall be concerned there solely with textile engineering) Hammouda[7] has reported that 'in the application of the concept of product planning, the personalities of management (its philosophies and attitudes) and the environmental circumstances within which the firms operate, are the major factors which affect the evaluation and development of product planning. The former factor (the personalities of management) appears to be the more important of the two'. He continues: 'biased attention to the technical activity at the expense of marketing activities' is a common phenomenon. Liander[8] has reported in a similar vein concerning the dominance of technical consideration over marketing in the E.E.C. at large.

Only when we switch to big company evidence, as in Udell's examination[9] of key elements in competitive strategies amongst the leading 200 firms in the U.S.A., does 'product research and development' rise to anything like the normative status we give it textually. Udell found 79 per cent of his top 200 perceiving 'product research and development as one of the five most vital sectors for corporate marketing success'. (There can be little doubt that 'product research and development' is not synonymous with 'product strategy and management'. It seems a reasonable assumption to make, however, that most firms with the former will have the later even if only by implication in their R. and D. strategies.)

The challenge to normative thinking about the formalized way in which product strategy and management should be undertaken which this fragmentary medium and small firm evidence presented, led to an empirical examination of this area of marketing activity within three sectors of the textile industries. As we expected, and as we and other colleagues had found earlier in respect to the total marketing mix concept,[10] all was not normative. In this paper we report what does in fact take place in terms of product strategy and planning within the textile machinery, wool textile and clothing industries, together with their explanation as to why capable, competent, and in many cases apparently very successful organizations within their own industrial environments, deviate from textbook norms. We suggest that this is the unavoidable preliminary analysis which must be undertaken before we can presume to give advice to these industrial sectors on how to do things 'better' or in any 'optimal' manner. As such, our research study is intended to act as a modifying influence in the codification of marketing technology for all save the very large enterprise, and as a caution even to them when they become technique-bound and inflexible in their approach to product strategy and management.

The Sample and Research Method

This paper reports evidence from a wider ranging examination of all aspects of marketing practice within three selected sectors of the British textile industries —those covering textile engineering, wool textiles and clothing.[11,12] The investigation involved two stages; 36 in-depth company interviews ranging from one day to two weeks duration each, and 322 completed postal questionnaires constituting a 53 per cent response rate from the sample contacted. The postal universe was all companies in the three sectors listed in the current edition of Kompass Directory with over 25 employees. Questionnaires were answered by Chief Executives within the companies, and all responses were received during Summer 1968.

The 36 in-depth interviews were made with those companies who agreed to collaborate on the basis of a judgemental sample of 72 (a 50 per cent response rate). Judgement was used to select a cross-section of firm sizes and structures within each of the three sectors. The purpose of this initial stage was to generate worthwhile hypotheses for quantification and qualitative information to afford some explanations of the emerging statistics. The statistical significance of the qualitative data is hence of a lower order than the postal study.

TABLE 1 *Textile Sector Response Patterns for Quantification Study*

Industrial Sector	Positive Response		Negative Response		No Response		Total Approached	Universe
	N =	%	N =	%	N =	%	N =	N =
Textile machinery	73	65	4	4	33	30	110	110
Wool textiles	134	54	12	5	104	41	250	748
Clothing	101	40	10	4	139	56	250	763
	308	50	26	4	276	75	610	1621

Sector postal survey sample factors and response patterns are given in Table 1. The samples contacted within wool textile and clothing sectors were selected by an interval sampling procedure from an alphabetical listing within regional strata. A census was undertaken within the textile engineering sector.

Whilst response rates of 50 and 53 per cent in the two stages of this investigation are undoubtedly good by normal criteria for this type of study, we took special steps to check so far as possible on the representativeness of those who had replied. In stage 1, all non-respondent firms had been contacted by telephone initially to request permission for an interview following a letter announcing the conduct and nature of the study. Refusals were in four main groupings—lack of time to collaborate; engagement of late in similar studies; undergoing reorganization; felt the study to be irrelevant. The first category accounted for 60 per cent of all refusals.

A similar pattern of reasoning was given by the sample of 20 non-responding postal survey companies who were contacted by telephone. A new category appeared however—those who declined as a matter of corporate policy. On further discussion, 14 of these 20 companies completed the questionnaire and returned it. Analysis did not indicate any particularly unusual characteristic inherent in the non-respondent companies which would lead us to doubt that our sample of firms was representative of the universe in the study's key dimensions.

In this study company size was defined as: small, 24–200; medium, 199–500; large, over 499 employees.

Prevalent Product Policies

We have seen that the need for a product policy has been constantly emphasized in the literature; it specifies a company's product objectives, the types of product and/or services it should offer, and the market(s) at which the business should aim. Such a strategy can orient effort and set criteria for the selection of product avenues to corporate success. It should stem from the formalized, careful and skilful process of matching the capabilities of a company to the opportunities of the market it identifies as its bailiwick.

One of the most significant facts which emerged from our research was the lack of any acceptance or appreciation in most companies of any specific need to develop formal product policies. Only one of the 36 companies visited in depth had a written-down product policy, and fully one-quarter of them reported that they had no general view of a corporate product policy of any kind.

Such lack of formal clarity and attention manifests itself further in that most companies visited take their extant field of business for granted. The identification of 'which market a business is in' has normally been viewed as perhaps the most fundamental of all decisions. It must of necessity be made at least once, and the philosophy of a dynamic marketing concept requires that it be revised continually thereafter. This need for revision is dictated by constant change in the environment external to the company, and in germane technology, as well as by shifts in the pattern of internal weaknesses and strengths which can themselves be partially or wholly caused by external factors.

The absence of any pattern of review of the field decision is particularly demonstrated in the reluctance of managements to consider diversification seriously. Very few companies report any readiness to diversify even in face of potential profit opportunities. The majority reject diversification in principle without any attempt to support their attitudes in terms of the existence of sufficient opportunities in their existing product fields. Most advance explanations which usually amount to field inertia, an attitude of resistance to change. The postal survey revealed that one-third of companies had never given any consideration to the possibility of diversification. We do not wish to propose that diversification is necessarily the right answer to achieve business growth and health. What we do question is the validity of the attitude which refuses even to consider the possibility of change. It is epitomized by such comments as: 'It never occurred to us'; 'We have enough trouble on our hands'; or 'We'd better concentrate on what we know, which is always better than what we do not know'. All three comments were made by Chief Executives of companies which have been experiencing a decline in their turnover and profitability in recent years. Resistance to change also seems to account for the marked reluctance of most companies to search for opportunities in sub-sectors of their existing industries which they have not so far tackled. The focus of operations in particular sub-sectors seems to be a matter of heritage rather than deliberation.

All concepts of the product line seemed to rest on manufacturing rather than on market or marketing considerations. One company's Managing Director commented: 'Our policy is simply to produce goods that are suited to our machines'.

488

All companies did not reject normative concepts so vigorously. Textile machinery companies generally had a wider concept of product line than companies in the two other sectors. A number of wool textile companies had in fact developed appropriate strategies to enter new fields of business, strategies stemming from their conviction that old markets are either saturated, declining, or involve too much competition. Whilst many companies were unaware of market segmentation analysis and attempted to be all things to all people within their industrial sector, others were making effective use of segmentation, especially clothing companies. Inter-relationships of demand on the other hand received markedly less attention and that largely within the clothing industry.

Innovation Policy

Little effort was directed by the majority of companies toward the development and introduction of new products. Many companies reported that the only innovation they undertook was the improvement of their existing products. Several reasons were advanced to explain this behaviour. Some companies indicated that their small size limited their ability to invest in research and development. They behave as they do because they cannot do otherwise, and some argued that even if they did succeed in developing a new product at a cost which they could bear, they would not be in a position to take full advantage of it because of the strength of competitors who could produce substitutes in no time. Other companies followed this course because it was thought to be safer and easier. Still others postulated that there was nothing new under the sun, and hence very little room for innovation. One Managing Director observed: 'We are producing and selling virtually the same lines which we started with 40 years ago. What enabled us to survive for 40 years is able to carry us through for any period of time to come'.

Nevertheless, some companies reported that their innovation effort was directed both to improvements of existing products as well as development of new products and new processes. One wool textile company reported:

'Because we have got to keep our lines up to date in terms of fashion we have to fill any gaps in our line; we have to look for growth opportunities by introducing new cloths which we can profitably make and sell; we have to look for new applications for our products; and we have to investigate our processes continually to increase efficiency. We also watch for opportunities outside the clothing industry, outside the wool textile industry, and outside the textile industry as a whole.'

Generally, three patterns of orientation in the innovation process were identified:

(i) *Production-facilities orientation;* under which the company regards innovation as a process of developing improved versions of the same products or less frequently new products which are suited to its production facilities. 'You have got to take advantage of the facilities you have and confine yourself to what they can do. Then you have to convince customers that this is what they should buy. We do not think of something which our machines cannot do'.

(Managing Director, wool textiles.) Thus, the starting point is not what the market wants but what the existing machines can produce. Half the companies in these textile sectors conform to this pattern and not just the smaller enterprises.

(ii) *Product orientation;* under which the policy is to press for a technically superior product. Technical superiority is the main asset and hence research and development is a much more important function than under other patterns. Less than a quarter of the sample companies, mostly from textile machinery, adopt this approach. These companies tend more than others to introduce novel products.

(iii) *Marketing orientation;* under which the company endeavours to make products which are wanted by the market. The comment made by a clothing Managing Director illustrates this approach: 'Satisfaction of customers is what we are here for; they are the only road to success and the only guarantee against the future. Hence, our product policy is to introduce whatever styles, designs, weights or materials our customers want'.

Almost all textile machinery companies report, not surprisingly, that fashion considerations seldom affect their process of innovation. Companies in wool textiles and clothing pay considerable attention to the fashion element.[13] Their behaviour can be classified under three patterns:

(a) *Fashion creation;* very few companies in the study indicate that their policy is to set new trends in fashion. Where they do, however, their image is built around being leaders in fashion.

(b) *Fashion following;* the majority of companies report that they do not attempt to create fashion, or to influence a change in consumer tastes from a fashion point of view. They are content to follow it.

(c) *Fashion antagonism;* a very small number of companies pay no attention to fashion either because the users of their products are thought to be far from fashion-conscious, or because they believe that mass production of standard lines pays better dividends.

Differentiation and Variety Policy

Most companies in wool textiles and clothing report a policy of wide variety, which is considered to be most essential. In designing products to meet needs they attempt to achieve extensive rather than selective coverage. The product range is not designed to solve selected consumer problems but to embrace all or most needs which could exist. A basic reason for this behaviour is the uncertainty of the manufacturer as to what the customer wants, as this comment demonstrates:

'Since we are not sure about the market, we introduce 40–50 items and hope that three or four of them will hit the target. Other people can be more certain and shoot only one or two bullets which, they know, will hit the target. As for us, we cater for a big variety of tastes, qualities, etc., to cover all possibilities, and expect a few to achieve the object.' (Managing Director, wool textiles.)

This policy of wide ranges, it may be argued, is the extreme marketing orientation case, of attempting to satisfy all customers! However, trying to be all things to all people is normally reckoned as poor corporate strategy. Effective segmentation requires a company to concentrate on carefully selected groups of needs which it can serve best. The argument that companies are aiming at all groups of customer's needs, and can serve them all best, is superficial. The much more likely reason for adopting such a policy, far from the desire to satisfy known wants, is to hedge in the face of uncertainty. Large proportions of R. and D. can be wasted on the development of items that stand little chance of selling. The company knows it is a wasted effort, but does not know how to determine which part to cut. This situation focuses on a lack of knowledge about demand and an inability to improve that knowledge due to lack of resources. In such circumstances many companies feel they have no choice but to follow such a course. Whilst they feel they can afford to introduce products which never sell, the irony is that they feel they cannot afford to find out what will sell in advance.

Use of New Products as a Competitive Weapon

The majority of companies do not regard new products as a major element in their competitive strategies. Prevalent attitudes in wool textile companies suggest that development of new products is not their business; it is a task which should be accomplished by the machinery makers. Conversely, machinery and clothing manufacturers tend to criticize the wool textile industry for its lack of appreciation of the need for development and for its reluctance to undertake any notable innovative activity. For their part, clothing companies tend to assume that there is very little scope for innovation at their end and hence new products cannot be relied upon in their competitive strategies. In contrast, the majority of machinery companies indicate their use of new products as a major competitive weapon. We found significant patterns of company behaviour by sector in these textile industries with machinery companies most concerned with new products as a source of competitive advantage, and clothing companies least concerned. Large companies tend to be marginally more frequent users of new products as a competitive weapon than small or medium sized firms.

Use of New Products as a Growth Tool

Almost all companies report growth as a major objective. It can normally be expected to emerge by tackling the serious obstacles to growth that are encountered since they exert a significant influence on the choice of strategy. Managements emphasized the following obstacles, cited in order of frequency of mention:

(i) *Decline in total market demand;* this factor was widely and predominantly mentioned in wool textiles and textile machinery companies.
(ii) *Severe competition from home and foreign manufacturers;* this factor was mentioned across all industries.
(iii) *Shortage of labour;* only wool textiles and clothing companies mentioned this factor.

(iv) *Lack of finance;* in all sectors and most frequently in smaller companies.
(v) *Lack of managerial resources;* some companies find this the most insuperable obstacle of all.

The product/market combinations implicitly adopted as the basis for growth strategies in the 36 companies where in-depth interviews were made can be categorized in terms of the Ansoffian matrix[14] as follows:

Old products to old markets: 33 companies
Old products to new markets: 3 companies
New products to old markets: 12 companies
New products to new markets: 2 companies

Although some companies indicated more than one approach, nothing approaching a development portfolio was to be found along the classic lines we are led to anticipate in normative models.

The obstacles already reported scarcely indicate much chance of success through the first combination as a path to growth. Yet it predominates. Lack of virtually any propensity for the development of new markets is noteworthy; reliance on new products as a major growth tool is obviously very low.

In the postal study companies these indications of growth strategies were quantified. Companies were asked whether they relied *mainly* on existing products, *mainly* on new products, or on both equally. Their replies can be seen displayed in Table 2.

TABLE 2 *Strategies for Growth—Analysis by Sector*

Growth Attempted/Textiles Sector	Textile Machinery		Wool Textiles		Clothing	
	No.	%	No.	%	No.	%
Mainly through existing products	43	57	92	68	84	76
Mainly through new products	30	39	36	26	19	17
Through both courses equally	3	4	7	5	6	5
Not indicated	—	—	1	1	1	1
Total	76	100	136	100	110	99

The majority of companies do not regard new products as a major growth tool. More use is made of them in the growth strategies of textile machinery companies than among wool textile companies which are, in turn, more prone to use them than clothing companies. With such a low propensity to use new products as the basis for growth, it is perhaps not surprising that only a small minority report the use of test marketing. An oddly assorted set of reasons was advanced as follows:

(i) There is little production for stock, and many lines are merely dummies.
(ii) The cost/benefit of the situation rules out market testing.
(iii) Competition is feared or quick action is important.

(iv) The company does not believe in the efficacy of test marketing as an indicator of market performance, particularly in fashion sectors.

The majority of companies believe test marketing is useless, too costly, or unnecessary in the light of the product strategies, they deem appropriate for their sector of the textile industries.

There is a wide divergence between textile machinery companies and the other two sectors in the extent of test marketing; while 45 per cent of the former indicate use only 20 per cent of the latter do so. A similar gap exists between large and all other companies; while 46 per cent of large companies report its use, only 20 per cent medium and small companies do so. Use of test marketing was also significantly associated with whether the company had a formally trained Chief Marketing Executive and whether its Chief Executive had a favourable attitude toward the marketing concept. (This may, of course, be no more than a measure of the professional influence of a single function in the firm.)

Systems of Product Planning and Development

In order to gain further insight into the innovative behaviour of the textile sectors examined it was necessary to examine closely the process of product planning and development and the informational and philosophical environment of that process. Emphasis was placed on how decisions are made, by whom, and in what sequence. This type of examination does not lend itself to the format of a postal questionnaire, and it was consequently confined to the qualitative stage of the research with the 36 companies which were studied in depth.

As a result of this examination two basic systems of company product planning and development behaviour were identified. Although there is every possibility that these two patterns may overlap in practice, they are analysed separately because of the distinct characteristics of each

Present-Mix Oriented Model

The first pattern which we propose to describe as *Present-Mix Orientation* can be illustrated as the flow model shown as Figure 1. This empirical model analyses the process of product planning and development in wool textile and clothing companies. Some of these companies supplement this pattern with the second pattern which is discussed later.

The product planning and development activity is a continuing process from one year to another, or from one season to another. The company starts the process with a list of extant products and not with a list of new product ideas. Last year's sales performance of all items on the present product range is assessed to sort out the items which did succeed (in terms of sales volume) from the items which did not. The Product Planning Committee (P.P.C.) carries out this assessment. This is a process analogous to the popularly prescribed Product Range Audit.[2]

On the basis of this assessment a decision is taken on each item, either to continue or discontinue it, by the P.P.C./Chief Executive/Chief Marketing Executive, depending on who is assigned the authority to make such product

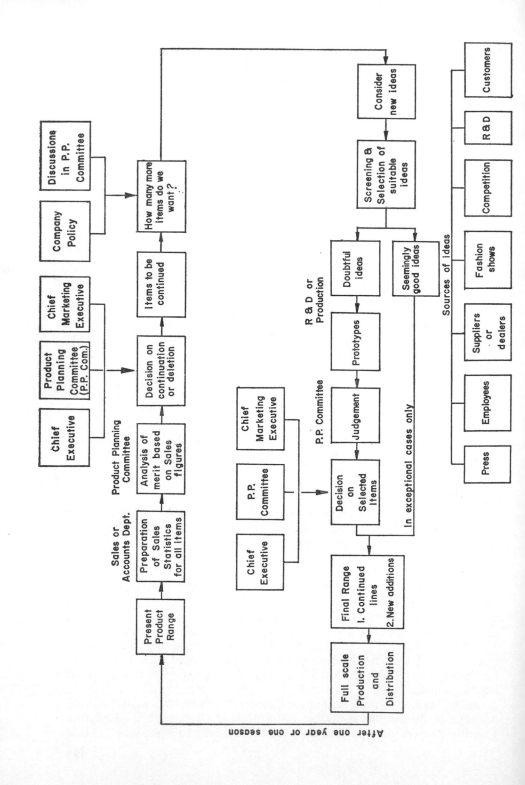

decisions. As a result of this decision a number of items are identified from the present range which will continue to appear on the range during the next period.

The next task of the P.P.C. is to decide how many more items should be added to the range to replace discontinued lines. This decision is an attempt to keep the breadth of the range in line with the company's variety and differentiation policy. At this stage there may be changes in policy stemming from discussions among P.P.C. members. When the decision is reached on *the approximate number of new items* to be added to the range, movement can be made to the next stage.

New-product ideas are assembled drawing on a number of sources which include press, employees, suppliers or dealers, fashion shows, competitors, research and development staff, and customers. The P.P.C. assesses the merits of these ideas and selects a number of them to go through the prototype stage. In exceptional cases, e.g. when a competitive product is being copied, the final go-ahead decision may be taken at this stage, and the research and development staff will be instructed to prepare the product for full-scale production. Even if a prototype is developed in these exceptional cases, it will be a matter of production requirements rather than for the purpose of revising the go-ahead decision which has already been given at the screening stage.

Apart from these exceptional cases, the normal course of events is to develop a prototype with R. and D. or the production department for all provisionally accepted ideas. Having developed these prototypes the P.P.C. meets again to evaluate all developed product alternatives. On the basis of these evaluations, a selection of new products gets the final go-ahead from the P.P.C./Chief Executive/Chief Marketing Executive, depending on who wields ultimate authority. This final selection of new products together with those products continuing from the previous range, constitutes the new product range which will be offered next cycle round. At the end of the following season or year this new range will itself constitute the next starting point for the product planning process.

Procedures. The present-mix oriented model of product planning behaviour does not attempt to garner the information which we would normally consider vital to make almost any decisions at almost any stage. Opinions of managers, albeit frequently successful, seem to be the most important basis for making choices. Only one piece of formally collated information is widely used, namely sales figures, but apart from this there are very few formalized sets of facts to guide product decisions.

Furthermore, the characteristic search for new products here is passive, rather than an active effort directed continuously towards the identification of new ideas. No procedures are employed to ensure a steady flow of new ideas in the model.

Giving the final 'go ahead' to some ideas at the screening stage is normally viewed as dangerous practice. Furthermore, the approval of the final selection on the opinions of managers with very little, if any, direct information from the marketplace is normally regarded askance. Test marketing is not employed by most such companies.

Philosophy. This model illustrates a *status quo* philosophy where management is so preoccupied with its present product mix that its product planning activity is in most cases a mere revision of that mix. The model does not provide a suitable environment for any constant effort to discover new ideas and to develop new products for old or completely new markets which are emerging to undermine present patterns of business. The model is therefore consistent with the attitude of management which is reluctant to change and is content to carry on as before. For example, if at the stage of evaluating the present range it was decided that all items were to be continued, the probability is very high that companies would skip all subsequent stages involving exploration for new ideas and new opportunities arising from new market needs, and continue to produce and distribute in the same way as for the previous period.

Despite these apparently fundamental weaknesses, the model provides a framework which successfully integrates most elements of product planning and development. With a refinement of some of its procedures, a reappraisal of the attitudes of those working it, and the addition of the elements of the product planning and development process which are missing from it, the model could perhaps be even more successful for such firms as employ it than it has already proved to be.

Innovation Oriented Model

Figure 2 presents a flow model which illustrates the second pattern of company behaviour with regard to product planning and development. It follows to a greater extent the normative text-book models of product planning and development.[15] Eight textile machinery companies follow this pattern exclusively, and four clothing and two wool textile companies adopt it to supplement their major product planning and development activity which takes place under the first pattern. The group of companies which adopts this pattern cuts across all size classifications.

The process of product planning and development starts with company objectives which will influence the choice or the revision of product fields. These product fields do not necessarily have to be within the limits of a present field of operations. Rather, management is preoccupied with the idea of exploiting *any* attractive opportunities which may lie within or outside the boundaries of present product/market mix. The setting of any constraints at this stage rests with top management.

Having decided on this, an active search for ideas within the defined product fields is carried out by technical and marketing personnel. This search cannot be regarded as being generally highly organized to ensure a steady flow of new ideas. There are wide variations from one company to another in this respect. Reliance on research and development, exhibitions, and competitors as sources for new ideas is heavier than reliance on customers. In that sense, the search is technically-oriented or imitation-oriented rather than customer-oriented. A few companies, however, report that their main source of new ideas is customers' problems.

Next comes evaluation of ideas. The tendency observed is to combine all steps of evaluation—screening, technical feasibility, and business analysis—in one process. Only a few companies conceive these steps as separate stages of

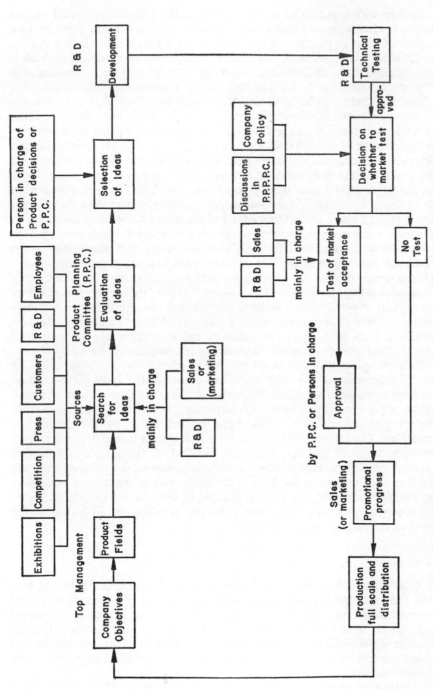

FIG. 2. The second pattern of product planning and development. Innovation-orientation.

evaluation with separate terms of reference. The information input in this process is more adequate than practices under the first pattern. Selection of a number of ideas to pass through to subsequent stages is made by the P.P.C., the Chief Executive, or the Chief Marketing Executive, depending on who is authorized to make the decision. Once approval for an idea is obtained, the development stage starts with the building of a prototype. Technical testing follows and there may be modifications as a result of technical tests. Market acceptance testing is the next task and here a variety of methods to conduct these tests was recorded. In textile machinery, for example, the company may invite a number of selected customers to attend demonstrations and to express their view on the merits of the new product regardless of whether they will buy it or not. Whenever well-founded, these views will result in modifications. These customers' reactions also largely constitute the basis for the decision to launch the new product. Three companies in clothing, all large, conduct market tests in the full sense of the term. Many companies do not carry out any tests of market acceptance. A number of reasons are reported which were synonymous with those described earlier. Company policy and discussions at the P.P.C. will indicate whether a test of market acceptance is advised.

If the results of the tests indicate a go-ahead, or if there is no market test, the launching stage is reached. Here we find that nearly all companies adopting this pattern undertake some form of impersonal promotion but with widely varying degrees of sophistication and intensity. Market reaction to the new product is then fed back to management and may effect new changes, new courses of action, or even a reconsideration of company objectives.

Whilst the present-mix oriented company approaches its product planning and development activity with a narrow outlook, the innovation-oriented company starts more appropriately with a statement of its objectives—profits, growth, etc. From there it defines those product fields it can legitimately enter whether they fall within or without the boundaries of the present field of operations. The focus in this second pattern is on making and/or identifying new opportunities and discovering new ideas which are capable of achieving company objectives. This is what we normally view as the more appropriate environment for innovation. This innovation-oriented pattern of behaviour conforms broadly with the pattern implied in the marketing concept. There are, however, wide variations among companies adopting this pattern in the extent of their customer-orientation.

Conclusions

There is no doubt that practices in the textile industries sectors examined diverge from the predominant normative approaches. New product strategy and management in these sectors is not what the textbooks lead us to suppose it ought to be. Are these firms just backward or are our models deficient? Ultimately, the answer will depend on a comparison of the assumed objectives behind the textbook models and the operationally effective objective of the business studied.

To take a prime example, almost all companies agreed that growth was a major objective, but few were manifestly prepared to pay the full price of securing the maximum theoretical potential available to them. Personality and environmental constraints hold business back from the total pursuit of the sort of goals which normative marketing models posit. The lesson should be salutary for our teaching efforts and for our research. It focuses attention on the need for a much closer examination of the true goals of business and the function of marketing in meeting them.

The marketing textbooks are making an arrogant value judgement, the sort economists are continually criticized for, when it is suggested that reluctance to change is a wrong attitude to adopt. Company goals are formulated through a process of trade-offs between such a legitimate reluctance and possible greater reward in terms of net cash flow.

Nonetheless, there seems to be ample evidence that sheer ignorance is at times leading to misallocation of effort and resource. Here, sensibly moderate views of the role of product strategy and management can surely be of considerable benefit to the firms engaged in these industries. The most obvious area is perhaps to be found in the proliferation of market offerings in the face of uncertainty rather than making a bold attempt to eliminate some of that uncertainty.

We have also, however, been made particularly aware of the constrained pattern of options available to a small resource business, to the business which is virtually unable to influence the general course of product development in its sector of operations. Much product policy is of necessity limited to applications engineering or direct imitation, rather than the grander alternatives of first-to-market and follow-the-leader so often mentioned in product strategy models.[16]

Finally, we have discussed an empirically viable pattern of product strategy and management for businesses operating in a seasonal market. This in itself is a facet of product planning which has not hitherto been examined in the literature to our knowledge.

References

1. Neil Borden's formulation of the marketing mix concept at Harvard in 1944 is the clearest instance of a normative statement of the marketing activity for a firm. See 'The Concept of the Marketing Mix', in G. Schwartz (ed.), *Science in Marketing* (John Wiley and Sons, 1965).
2. This theme and formal product range and audit procedures for large firms are fully developed in P. Drucker, *Managing for Results* (Heinemann, 1964).
3. The major contributions here include: M. Hanan, 'Corporate Growth Through Venture Management', *Harvard Business Review*, vol. 47, no. 1 (1969); J. T. O'Meara, 'Selecting Profitable Products for Development', *Harvard Business Review*, vol. 39, no.1 (1961); E. A. Pessemier, *New Product Decisions* (McGraw-Hill, 1966).
4. N.E.D.O., *Investment Appraisal* (H.M.S.O., 1963).
5. N. Blakey, and A. McGuire, *Innovation in the Woollen and Worsted Industry* (University of Bradford Management Centre Project Report, 1967).
6. G. F. Rainie, *The Woollen and Worsted Industry* (Clarendon Press, 1965), pp, 86–87.
7. M. A. A. Hammouda, *The Concept of Product Planning and the Contribution of Marketing to the Planning Activities in the Engineering Industry* (unpublished Ph.D. Thesis, University of Manchester, 1968), pp. 504–505.
8. B. Liander, *Marketing Development in the E.E.C.* (McGraw-Hill, 1964).

9. J. G. Udell, 'How Important is Pricing in Competitive Strategy?', *Journal of Marketing*, vol. 28, no. 1 (1964), pp. 44–48, reprinted in B. Taylor and G. S. C. Wills (eds.), *Pricing Strategy* (Staples Press, 1969), pp. 317–325.

10. See J. Mann, *The Nominal and Effective Status of Chief Marketing Executives in Yorkshire Industry*, Proceedings of 2nd Conference of Teachers of Marketing (University of Bradford Management Centre, 1967); also R. Hayhurst, J. Mann, S. M. A. Saddik, and G. S. C. Wills, *Organizational Design for Marketing Futures* (Nelson, 1970), Part 3.

11. The full results of the investigation are given in S. M. A. Saddik, *Marketing in the Wool Textile, Textile Machinery and Clothing Industries* (University of Bradford, Management Centre, April 1969).

12. S. M. A. Saddik, 'Marketing Orientation and Organizational Design', *British Journal of Marketing*, vol. 2, no. 4 (1968), describes in considerable detail the marketing organization structures currently in use.

13. G. S. C. Wills and M. G. Christopher review this facet more fully in, 'What do we know about Fashion Marketing?' *Marketing World*, vol. 1, no. 1 (1969), pp. 1–15.

14. H. I. Ansoff, *Corporate Strategy* (McGraw-Hill, 1965); (Penguin Books, 1969).

15. D. Ashton, P. Gotham and G. S. C. Wills, 'Conditions Favourable to Product Innovation', *Scientific Business*, vol. 3, no. 1 (1965), pp. 24–39, reprinted in B. Taylor and G. S. C. Wills (eds.), *Long Range Planning for Marketing and Diversification* (Crosby Lockwood for Bradford University Press, 1970).

16. H. I. Ansoff and J. M. Stewart, 'Strategies for a Technology-Based Business', *Harvard Business Review*, vol. 45, no. 6 (1967).